Warman's Country Antiques

2nd Edition

Mark F. Moran

Published by

700 East State Street • Iola, WI 54990-0001
715-445-2214 • 888-457-2873
www.krause.com

Library of Congress Catalog Number: 2001088101
ISBN: 0-87349-611-6

Printed in the United States of America

Please call or write for our free catalog of publications.
Our toll-free number to place an order or obtain a free catalog is
(800) 258-0929

Editor: Dennis Thornton
Designer: Donna Mummery

Contents

INTRODUCTION

When I began compiling the information for *Warman's Country Antiques*, I viewed it as a simple task. After all, for nearly three decades I've been buying and selling antiques in the Midwest, writing about antiques shows and auctions nationwide, and—most importantly—training my eye to spot the best of vintage Americana.

But when it came to summing up all that I've learned in the pages of this book, it was a much tougher project than I had imagined. Why do collectors in the 21st century still want to fill their homes with objects made over the last 300 years?

I'm convinced it has to do with the pervasive anonymity of the life we lead, and the relative ease with which we can acquire almost any creature comfort available.

Today, if we decide to buy a piece of furniture, or a kitchen utensil, or a toy or game, there are millions of options, all uniform in their respective designs. Do we stop to think about the men and women who made them? No, we just want to be certain that the price is right and the warranty card is handy in case anything goes wrong.

Two hundred years ago, a furniture purchase may have meant a trip to the cabinetmaker or wood smith, but more likely it was trip to the shed behind the house to see what wood was available, and whether the stain and paint on hand would fit the intended use.

Kitchen utensils often came from a blacksmith or tradesman who fabricated tin, and if the maker decided to incorporate a design element of his own choosing, that was usually all right, as long as it stood up to hard use every day.

Toys and games? Like as not, they were the creation of an inquisitive mind whose owner relaxed on the front porch with a whittling knife after a hard day's work, and the resulting plaything would first become an item of gentle amusement, and later, a treasured keepsake to be handed down.

Country antiques are valued, I believe, because after centuries of use (and even neglect), we can still see the mind and hand of the creator at work—the hand-planing on the back of a blanket chest, the close stitching on a quilt, the delicate grain painting on a dry sink, the tight weave on a gathering basket, the flourish of decoration on a stoneware jug.

The reasons for collecting country antiques are as varied as the thousands of items contained in this book, but I think it comes down to choosing craftsmanship over convenience, style or sterility, and quality over quantity.

If those are the values that spark your search for treasures, then *Warman's Country Antiques* will serve you well.

Mark Moran

Architectural Elements

Architectural fragments have become a popular decorative item, and prices have increased along with the demand. Wooden gingerbread trim has been turned into wall hangings, stained glass windows into room dividers, even old screened doors with unusual details (or simply a weathered look) have found their way into many homes. Whether from the country or city, select items with strong graphic appeal and interesting surfaces are popular. Pieces with faces (whether mythical, human, bird, or animal) usually bring a premium.

Because duplicating these items would be quite costly, preserving and recycling architectural elements has become quite popular, with whole salvage operations dedicated to retrieving and reselling these unique pieces.

References: A. Dureanne, *Ornamental Ironwork*, Dover Publications, 1998; Stanley Shuler, *Architectural Details from Old New England Homes*, Schiffer Publishing, 1997; H. Weber Wilson, *Antique Hardware Price Guide*, Krause Publications, 1999.

Collectors' Club: Antique Doorknob Collectors of America, PO Box 126, Eola, IL 60519.

Specialty Auction: Web Wilson Antique Hardware Auction, PO Box 506, Portsmouth, RI 02871, (800) 508-0022.

Bracket, cast iron, art nouveau style, delicate scrollwork and flowers with small flower bud drops at center, contemporary with black enameling and French signature, 12 3/4 in. tall by 60 in. wide. **$325/pair**

"Gingerbread" trim, circa 1900, painted pine, from a house dormer, with circular and scroll cutouts, spindle supports and a wheel motif, weathered surface, 108 in. by 62 in. **$500-$600**

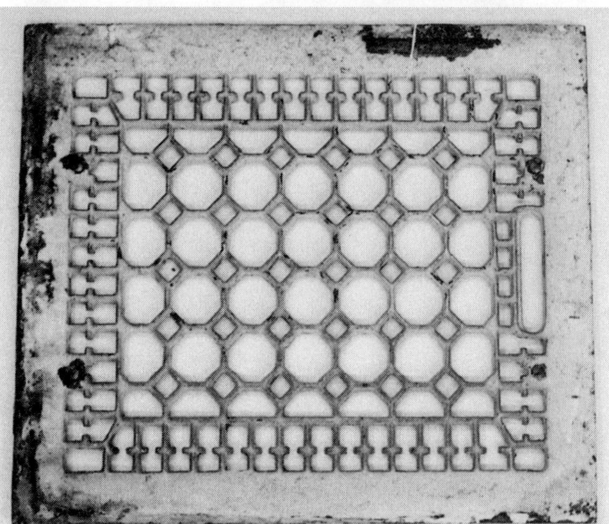

Floor grate, circa 1930s, cast iron with old worn paint, simple geometric pattern, 14 in. by 12 in. **$20-$30**

Carved eagle architectural element, pine, circa 1860, supposedly came off the exterior of a courthouse, one of several ornamental eagles that came off the building, three pieces of wood, 36 in. wide by 12 in. deep by 40 in. tall. **$10,000**

Hand-carved marble frieze with cherubs. **$2,800**

Floor grate, circa 1900, cast iron, marked "Design Patented Aug. 31, 1897, Manufactured by the Adams Co., Dubuque, Iowa," old black paint and significant rust, 15 1/2 in. diameter. **$50-$60**

Marble Gothic arch. **$1,250**

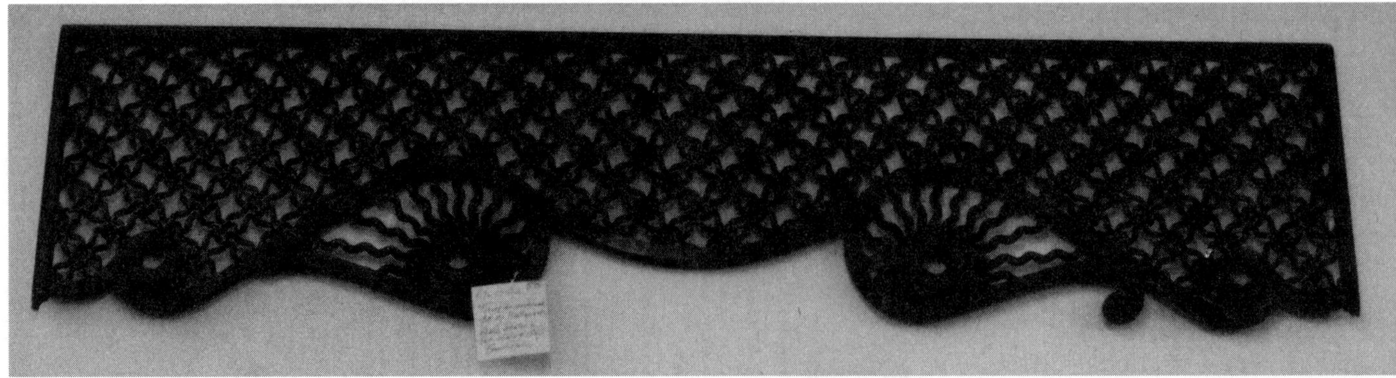

Ornate latticework valance made of hundreds of pieces of spiral-carved wood, probably maple, with walnut stain, dated 1885, minor age cracks, 16 in. by 8 feet. **$900**

Roof finial, tin, circa 1890, in the form of a tall conical spire topped by a ball and flanked by four tin flowers on metal stalks, above a round platform on a shaft joined to a formed tin sheet decorated with stylized leaves, weathered silver painted surface, 33 in. by 12 in. by 8 in. **$1,200-$1,500**

Lightning rod, circa 1860, wrought iron with round tapering central rod and four pigtail extensions alternating with four scroll extensions, original iron roof mounts, untouched original condition, 62 in. tall. **$1,400-$1,500**

Windmill tail, sheet steel, with stenciled brand name, "Little Giant" on one side and hand-painted name "Carl Trehns, Spring Grove, Minn." on the other side, riveted construction, excellent condition, 48 in. by 53 in. **$250-$300**

Capital, molded terracotta, circa 1890, in the form of scrolls with leafy motif, old paint and weathered surface, minor chipping, 17 in. square by 7 in. **$90**

Eagle, outstretched wings, on base with "1918" in raised numerals, old paint over gilt, formerly positioned at the entrance to the Boston Navy Yard, wear, 13 in. tall by 30 1/4 in. wide. **$2,100/pair**

Eagle head, cast iron, original from the West Point, N.Y., courthouse that burned in the 19th century, losses, rust, 16 in. tall by13 in. wide by 12 in. deep. **$2,500/pair**

Finial, eagle, spread wing on sphere, zinc, hollow body, old gold repaint, repairs, on stand, 16 in. tall.....**$350**

Finial, floriform, copper, American, 19th century, minor dents, 48 in. tall. **$2,200**

Finial, pineapple, cast iron, dark green repaint, 20 1/2 in. tall. ...**$250**

Finial, steeple form, square base, ball finial, copper, dents, 40 in. tall, 25 in. square. **$900**

Gothic arch, wooden, white enamel over earlier red, beaded tongue-and-groove boards, layered moldings, edge damage, minor cracks, 29 1/2 in. tall by 35 in. wide. **$125**

Hinges, door, wrought iron, double with hinged center, curved ends terminate in heart-shaped motifs, some rust, traces of later paint, 10 1/2 in. tall by 11 3/8 in. wide. **$200/pair**

Hinges, blanket chest, one large pair of shaped hinges, 19 1/2 in. long, one small pair with triangular ends (one broken off, the other damaged), 10 1/2 in. long. **$125/pair**

Panel, harp-shaped scrolls and flowers set within a bracket, central fleur-de-lis design, dark green repaint, pitting, small welded repair, 17 in. tall by 13 1/2 in. wide, set of three......................................**$425**

Post, cast iron, ball finial on baluster-form post with rosette, scroll, and

Frosted glass window with grid pattern, shield, and scroll motif, and shaped jewel at base of torch, 44 in. by 35 in. **$750**

Colorful window loaded with flowers, leaves, swags, jewels, and hand-painted scene with boats, 22 1/8 in. by 39 1/2 in. **$2,600**

swirl elements, red paint, wear, 421/2 in. tall. **$350/pair**

Roof ornament, owl, zinc, full-bodied, stands on hemispherical form, glass eyes, hinged head, painted brown, split on base, reinforcement, paint loss, dents, 27 3/4 in. tall. **$3,000**

Roof ornaments, star and crescent, tin and sheet iron, attributed to Crescent Mfg. Co., Rutland, Vt., molded five-point star above sphere above crescent with round

Three windows in unusual aesthetic movement style, each window approximately 24 in. square. **$1,600/set**

Large colorful window with hanging fruit clusters, with three arched panels, 84 in. by 29 1/2 in. **$1,650**

Classic urn and swag design in clear window, with beveled glass. **$975**

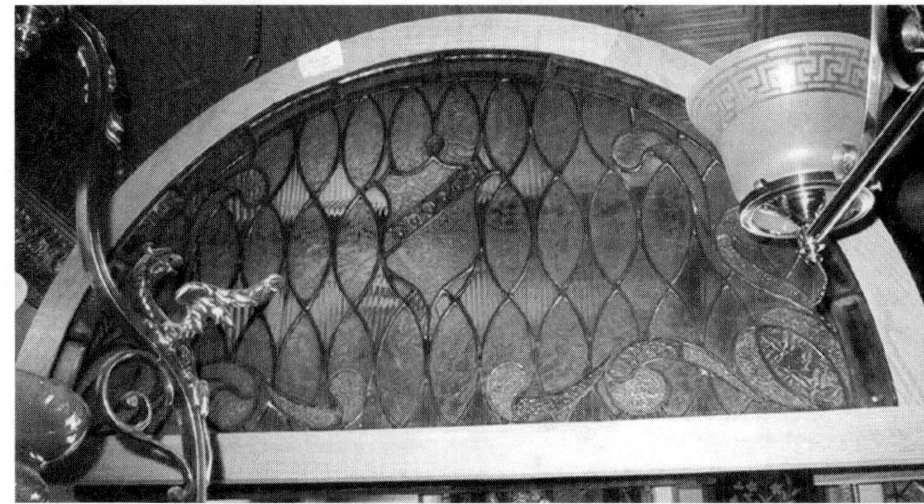

Arch-top window with shield motif, bevels, and jewels, new oak frame, 29 1/2 in. by 54 in. **$1,250**

Small arch-top window, 26 in. by 32 in. **$350**

Large double-hung landing window with arched top, shield, scroll, and fleur-de-lis motif, rectangular sash, 42 in. by 73 in. **$2,200**

Pebbled-glass window with simple Celtic-knot design, 18 in. by 36 in. **$400**

cutouts, resting on larger sphere, on hollow tapering shaft, corrosion, four bullet holes, 50 in. tall. **$1,100**

Valence, wooden, original old worn brownish-green paint over earlier pumpkin, scalloped aprons, applied pierced carved crests, edge chips, cracks, 39 3/4 in. wide.....**$450/pair**

Window insert, relief design, wooden, two-section framework in old white paint, geometric design inside in old red paint, weathered, a few chips missing, 39 1/2 in. tall by 63 in. wide....................................**$625**

Where can I find them?

Architectural Artifacts, Inc.
4325 N. Ravenswood
Chicago, IL 60613-1111
(773) 348-0622
www.architecturalartifacts.com
sales@architecturalartifacts.com

Architectural Artifacts, Inc. buys and sells architectural antiques and furnishings from North and South America, Europe, and Japan. The firm is housed in a facility that has 80,000 square feet of showroom space, with a 5,000-square-foot contemporary glass and steel atrium built to connect their two structures. The structures are being completely restored. The atrium will house owner Stuart Grannen's personal collection of architectural ornamentation from important Chicago buildings and their architects. Louis Sullivan and Frank Lloyd Wright will be featured, as well as many buildings significant to Chicago's past.

Architectural Emporium
207 Adams Ave.
Canonsburg, PA 15317
(724) 746-4301
http://www.architectural-emporium.com/
sales@architectural-emporium.com

❖ Lightning Rod Balls

Lightning rods used on homes and other structures in rural America were often embellished with decorative glass ornaments. Although some were odd shapes, most were round with embossed star or swirl designs. Dark blue and amber were fairly common, but rare colors such as red can also be found.

Reference: Rod Krupka, *The Complete Book of Lightning Rod Balls with Prices*, (Rod Krupka, 2615 Echo Ln., Ortonville, MI 48462).

Classic round shape, amethyst, copper caps, 3 1/2 in. diameter.**$60**

D&S, blue milk glass, 10-sided, with short rod and stand.................**$100**

D&S, white milk glass, 10-sided, copper caps, 4 in. diameter.......**$85**

Electra round, white milk glass, copper caps, 5 1/8 in. tall by 4 1/8 in. diameter...............................**$75**

Hawkeye, blue milk glass, rounded top with starbursts, tapering bottom, copper caps, 5 1/8 in. tall, 4 3/8 in. diameter. **$175**

Moon & Stars, white milk glass, copper caps, 5 1/8 in. tall, 4 3/8 in. diameter. **$75**

Ribbed grape, blue milk glass, copper caps, 5 1/8 in. tall, 4 3/8 in. diameter. **$100**

Ribbed grape, white milk glass, copper caps, 5 1/8 in. tall, 4 3/8 in. diameter. **$90**

Round pleat (Barnett Ball), cobalt, copper caps, 5 in. tall, 4 3/8 in. diameter. **$175**

Sharp pleated, sun-colored amethyst (original white milk glass), copper caps, 5 in. tall, 4 1/2 in. diameter. ... **$75**

Shinn System, white milk glass, copper caps, 4 1/2 in. diameter.**$32**

Smooth round, sun-colored lavender (original white milk glass), copper caps, 4 1/2 in. diameter............**$50**

❖ Snowbirds

Placed in rows on the roofs of 19th-century homes, snowbirds were small projections designed to keep the snow from sliding off the house (the blanket of snow added a layer of natural insulation). Generally made of cast iron, snowbirds were often in the shape of a bird or spade.

Snowbird, bird, standing with wings spread out to sides, cast iron, four with rods, 6 in. wingspan, set of five. **$225**

Snowbird, eagle, cast iron, brown paint, 5 in. tall, set of 16. **$450**

Snowbird, eagle, cast iron, dark brown paint, 4 3/4 in. tall by 5 3/4 in. long, set of 12. . . . . .**$500**

Artwork

❖ Paintings, Etchings, Drawings, Etc.

Works of art with a rural theme have long been the most prevalent in the marketplace and are the single most popular subject for both artists and collectors. Whether paintings, drawings, etchings, or mass-produced prints, the charms of a country scene (real or imagined) draw collectors at all price levels.

When assessing an oil or acrylic painting on canvas, don't be put off by holes, scratches, or stains. Most can be easily repaired by a good restorer, and the investment in restoration is almost always worth the expense, either from the standpoint of pure enjoyment of the work, or from a view towards resale. Keep this in mind: The better the quality of painting, the better the restorer required. Check with local museums and art centers to find the names of reputable art restoration specialists in your area.

Works on paper can also be restored, but the time and techniques required (and the expense) vary widely. A good restorer will tell you up-front if the cost of repairs is justified by the artwork.

As with any antique collecting area, buy the best example you can afford, get advice from established art and antiques dealers, and train your eye to distinguish between the average and the exciting. This process takes years to achieve, but the reward is an art collection that not only looks great, but will also appreciate in value.

Original artwork created circa 1930 by Hubert Morley (1888-1951) to illustrate a never-published edition of the most famous work of A.E. Housman (1859-1936), "A Shropshire Lad" (1896), a series of 63 verses set in a pastoral English setting, probably inspired by Housman's visits to the South Shropshire village of Clun and its environs. The artwork includes five small etchings, each approximately 3 1/2 in. by 2 3/4 in., all showing a solitary figure in a woodland landscape at different seasons, no titles or signatures, excellent condition.**$50 each**, plus:

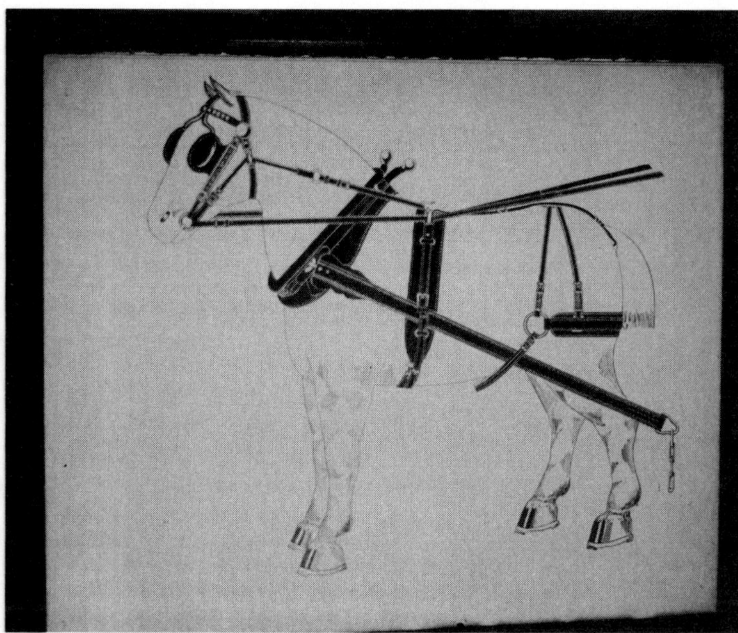

Drawing, ink, circa 1910, on artist board, illustrating parts of a horse harness, one of a series of dozens of images created for an Ohio harness manufacturer, minor handling wear, 18 in. by 22 in. **$100-$150**

Drawing, pen and ink, of a proposed book jacket for the edition, showing solitary figure in a wooded landscape, with penciled title and art credit line, excellent condition, image size 8 in. by 5 in. **$700**

Drawing, charcoal and white crayon on artist board, inscribed "Paris 1901," showing a French peasant woman in traditional attire, excellent condition, image size 22 1/2 in. by 17 1/2 in. **$350-$450**

Etching titled "Bloomer's Creek" by Hubert Morley (1888-1951), created as part of a series of Christmas cards over a 20-year period, signed on the front, undated, excellent condition, image size 3 in. by 2 3/4 in. **$50**

Etching by Hubert Morley (1888-1951), titled "Maple Syrup Time—Wisconsin," showing syrup-gathering using a horse-drawn sled, and a cabin in the background of a woodland landscape, circa 1930s, signed, titled, and numbered (4/100) in pencil, excellent condition, framed, image size 8 1/4 in. by 11 in. **$400-$500**

Etching titled "Christmas Weather in Wisconsin" by Hubert Morley (1888-1951), created as part of a series of Christmas cards over a 20-year period, signed on the front and dated 1938, with penciled greetings by Morley, excellent condition, image size 3 in. by 3 in. **$50**

Etching titled "January" by Hubert Morley (1888-1951), created as part of a series of Christmas cards over a 20-year period, dated 1943, signed on the front with penciled greetings by Morley, excellent condition, image size 4 in. by 3 in. **$50**

Etching titled "Christmas Weather" by Hubert Morley (1888-1951), created as part of a series of Christmas cards over a 20-year period, dated 1930, signed on the front with greetings in ink by Morley, excellent condition, image size 4 in. by 3 in. **$50**

Etching titled "Winter" by Hubert Morley (1888-1951), created as part of a series of Christmas cards over a 20-year period, dated 1945, signed on the front with greetings in ink by Morley, excellent condition, image size 4 in. by 2 3/4 in. **$50**

Etching titled "December" by Hubert Morley (1888-1951), created as part of a series of Christmas cards over a 20-year period, dated 1927, signed on the front with greetings in ink by Morley, excellent condition, image size 2 in. by 2 3/4 in. **$40**

Etching titled "After the Snowstorm" by Hubert Morley (1888-1951), created as part of a series of Christmas cards over a 20-year period, dated 1947, signed on the front with greetings in ink by Morley, excellent condition, image size 4 1/2 in. by 3 1/4 in. **$70**

Etching titled "White Christmas" by Hubert Morley (1888-1951), created as part of a series of Christmas cards over a 20-year period, dated 1936, signed on the front with greetings in ink by Morley, excellent condition, image size 3 in. by 3 3/8 in. **$50**

Etching titled "Edge of the Village," circa 1930s, by Hubert Morley (1888-1951), showing a boy walking a cow down a country lane, signed and titled in pencil, excellent condition, 4 3/4 in. by 5 3/4 in. **$60-$70**

Etching titled "End of Summer," circa 1930s, by Hubert Morley (1888-1951), showing a large tree next to a brook, and two figures gathering in the background, signed and titled in pencil, excellent condition, 7 7/8 in. by 8 in. **$100-$125**

Etching titled "Shore Work," circa 1930s, by Hubert Morley (1888-1951), showing fishermen repairing their nets, signed and titled in pencil, excellent condition, 6 in. by 6 in. **$60-$80**

Etching titled "January," circa 1920s, by Hubert Morley (1888-1951), showing a wintry woodland scene, signed and titled in pencil, excellent condition, 8 in. by 8 in. **$90-$100**

Etching titled "Storm Cloud," circa 1940s, by Hubert Morley (1888-1951), showing thunder clouds building over a rural landscape, done in "soft ground" technique, signed and titled in pencil, excellent condition, 9 in. by 7 1/2 in. **$90-$100**

Etching titled "Wind in the Willows," circa 1920s, by Hubert Morley (1888-1951), showing a woman in a long dress standing on a hill next to willow trees on a windy day, signed and titled in pencil, excellent condition, 6 in. by 6 in. **$70-$80**

Etching by John B. Murray, circa 1930s, a member of the Chicago Society of Etchers, showing a farmhouse flanked by tall trees, signed in pencil, excellent condition, 6 in. by 8 in. **$90-$100**

Etching titled "Rock Crusher," circa 1920s, by Hubert Morley (1888-1951), showing the site of a gravel-making operation, signed and titled in pencil, excellent condition, 3 3/4 in. by 4 1/2 in. **$50-$60**

Etching titled "January Thaw," circa 1930s, by Hubert Morley (1888-1951), showing a stream with open water in a wintry landscape, signed and titled in pencil, excellent condition, 6 in. by 6 in. **$70-$80**

Etching of three trees in a hilly landscape, circa 1930s, signed in pencil "B. Duncan," a member of the Chicago Society of Etchers, excellent condition, 7 in. by 8 in. **$70-$80**

Etching titled "Clammer's Shanty," circa 1920s, by Hubert Morley (1888-1951), showing a man tending a cooking fire near a dilapidated house on the shore of a quiet bay, signed and titled in pencil, excellent condition, 7 1/4 in. by 9 in. **$80-$90**

Etching titled "Springtime," circa 1930s, by Hubert Morley (1888-1951), showing a farmstead framed by a tall tree, signed and titled in pencil, excellent condition, 9 in. by 7 1/4 in. **$150-$200**

An etching done in "soft ground" technique of a hunter with rifle and dog walking near a woodland stream, mounted on a card, with penciled notation, "Shropshire Lad" by Morley, excellent condition, 5 in. by 4 1/8 in. **$150**

Etching showing a solitary figure sitting on a stone bridge in a woodland landscape, titled "In My Own Shire," signed in pencil by Morley, excellent condition, 5 in. by 3 3/8 in. **$125**

Large etching intended to face title page (?), showing solitary figure in a wooded landscape, excellent condition, image size 9 in. by 4 1/4 in. **$200**

An etching showing a solitary figure fishing by a woodland stream with a bridge in the background, titled "Watchful Waiting" and numbered "-/100," signed in pencil by Morley, excellent condition, 4 1/8 in. by 3 1/2 in. **$125**

Etching titled "In the Spring," circa 1920s, by Hubert Morley (1888-1951), showing a farm scene and budding trees, signed and titled in pencil, excellent condition, 4 in. by 3 3/4 in. **$70-$80**

An etching showing a man hanging on a gallows, no title or signature, excellent condition, 3 1/2 in. by 2 3/4 in. **$100**

Etching titled "Abandoned Farm," circa 1930s, by Hubert Morley (1888-1951), showing a lonely farmhouse against a cloudy sky, signed and titled in pencil, excellent condition, 7 in. by 8 in. **$70-$80**

Etching by Martin Petersen (1866-1956), showing three men raking hay, initialed in pencil "M.P.," excellent condition, framed, image size 10 in. by 9 1/2 in. **$500-$600**

Etching by Martin Petersen (1866-1956), showing a man plowing a field with a two-horse hitch, a farmstead in the background, initialed "M.P." and dated 1930, excellent condition, framed, image size 8 3/4 in. by 8 3/4 in. **$400-$500**

Painting, oil on board, circa 1930s, showing a snow-covered road running along the bluffs on the Mississippi River at sunset, indistinctly signed lower left, excellent condition, image size 26 in. by 48 in. **$900-$1,200**

Lithograph titled "November" by Charlotte Jeffery, circa 1950, showing horses standing dejectedly by a fence, signed and titled in pencil, excellent condition, 8 1/2 in. by 11 1/4 in. **$150-$200**

Painting, circa 1900, oil on board, showing two kittens walking along an oak branch, in original gilt frame, painting has been cleaned, excellent condition, image size 10 in. by 14 in. **$500-$600**

Linocut by Woldemar Neufeld (1909-2002), titled "Harvest," showing a woman carrying a bowl of apples while apple-picking is under way on a farm in the background, signed in pencil "W Neufeld," with note on reverse saying the print was issued by Collectors of American Art Inc. in 1946, excellent condition, framed, image size 9 1/2 in. by 5 1/4 in. **$500-$600**

Etching, circa 1920, showing a woman with a basket of twigs and branches on her back and a cutting implement in her hand, with other women working in a rural setting, title "The Wood Chopper," signed indistinctly, excellent condition, framed, image size 9 in. by 7 in. **$80-$100**

Painting, circa 1930s, Impressionist, oil on board, of a windy, mountainous landscape with a field of flowers, possibly California, signed lower left, "Eric W. Wittenberg," detail below, cleaned, in original frame, image size 12 in. by 16 in. **$1,000-$1,200**

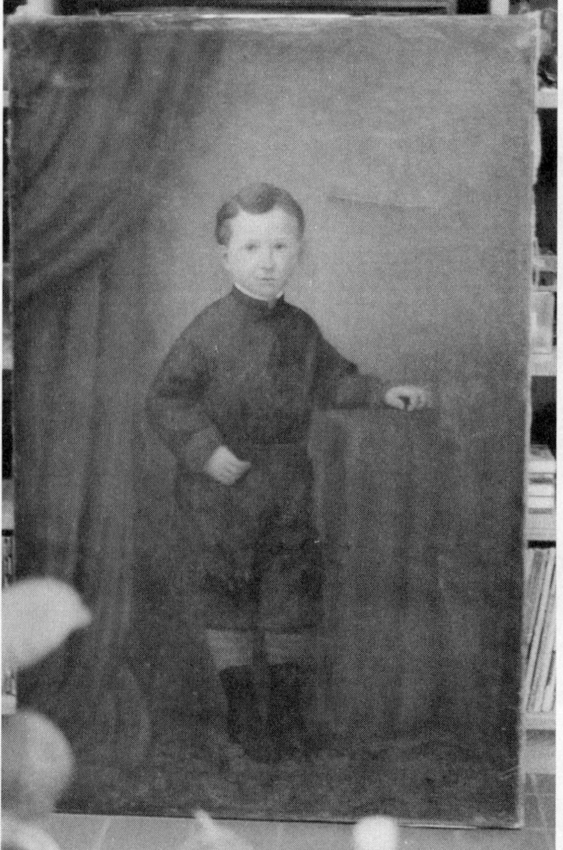

Painting, oil on canvas, showing a boy posing by a cloth-draped table, standing next to a red drape, circa 1860, found in rural Iowa, 60 in. by 44 in., restored and with new frame. Detail at right. **$2,000-$3,000**

Painting, oil on canvas, showing a swampy landscape at sunset, with tall trees and the profile of a bird by a stream, and a farmstead in the distance, signed and dated lower right, "G. Molnar 1920" (Geeza Molnar was a Hungarian immigrant who worked as a master woodcarver in Chicago at the turn of the 19th century, and later moved to rural Wisconsin), in finely carved frame also by Molnar, near mint, overall dimensions 50 1/2 in. by 70 in. (This painting is an interpretation—rather than a copy—of a work by George Inness [1825-1894] titled "The Home of the Heron," in the collection of the Art Institute of Chicago. This image has a slightly different perspective than Inness' work.) **$5,000-$6,000**

Painting, circa 1880, oil on wood panel, showing a soldier holding a rifle, with original gilt frame, moderate age staining, image size 9 in. by 6 1/2 in. **$1,000-$1,200**

Painting, oil on canvas, winter scene of a homestead on a Norwegian fjord, showing sod-roof dwelling, hunter with dog and game, man gathering wood with horse and sled on frozen fjord, village and hills in background, circa 1870, on stretcher made of scrap wood, minor restoration and cleaning, 16 in. by 22 in. **$700-$800**

Painting, circa 1920s, watercolor on artist's board, showing four children—two boys and two girls—posing in a rural setting, the two girls sitting on a gray donkey, unsigned and unfinished (the hands of the boy on the right and the hands and shoes of the boy on the left are not painted), image size 16 in. by 20 in. **$1,200-$1,500**

Painting, circa 1930s, watercolor, signed "JA Seaford" (John Seaford of Spiceland, Ind.), showing a country road in autumn, in large walnut frame, excellent condition, image size 15 in. by 20 in. **$700-$1,000**

Painting, circa 1930s, watercolor, signed "F Pearce" (Fred Pearce of Williamsburg, Ind.), showing bundles of corn stalks and pumpkins in a field, in large walnut frame, excellent condition, image size 15 in. by 20 in. **$700-$1,000**

Paintings, watercolor, circa 1930, by architect Harold Crawford, showing two hay-gathering scenes; in the first, hay is pitched into a pile, and in the second a loaded horse-drawn hay wagon is driven away, excellent condition, images sizes 15 in. by 22 in. **$1,500-$2,000/pair**

Painting, circa 1930, oil on plywood, showing a barn and silo next to bare trees and a pond, signed lower left, "Maley," with original gold-painted frame, rural Illinois origin, excellent condition, image size 32 1/2 in. by 22 1/2 in. **$400-$500**

Painting, circa 1890, by William Gozzard, oil on canvas, titled "The Gleaners," showing women gathering grain stubble from a field, signed and titled on the frame, and on the front and back of the canvas, excellent condition, old (probably original) frame shows significant wear, image size 19 1/2 in. by 29 1/2 in. **$3,000-$4,000**

Naïve painting, oil on canvas, showing an elderly bearded man in a black suit holding a cane, seated in a pressed-oak rocking chair, next to which rests a black dog, rural Minnesota origin, circa 1920s, unsigned, minor restoration and contemporary wood frame, image size 46 in. square. **$2,000-$2,500**

❖ Theorems

A theorem is a painting created with a stencil. Popular during the first half of the 19th century, theorems were most often done with watercolors on either velvet or paper; however, they have also been found on silk and wood.

Collecting Hint: Few theorem velvet paintings were signed.

Note: All listings are watercolor.

On paper

Bird, beside nest with eggs, foliage and cherries, shades of green, brown, red, and blue, signed in pencil "L. Lewis," old frame with red and yellow sponged repaint, 5 3/4 in. by 7 in. **$400**

Bird, on branch of small tree, brown, blue, black, yellow, red, and green, minor fly specks and stains, old red and black sponged frame, 9 in. by 7 in. **$350**

Flowers in blue bowl, framed, toning, creases, abrasions, 15 1/4 in. by 19 1/4 in. **$4,500**

Flowers in vase, blue, pink, green, yellow, and brown, old gilt frame, minor stains, 10 in. by 15 in. **$1,650**

Flowers in vase, pink and red roses, buds and carnations, also bird and bee, signed "Eliza A. Horan, May 1st, 1848," framed, fold lines, tears, top corners glued down, 15 3/8 in. by 12 3/8 in. **$325**

Flowers in vase, pink, yellow, and blue, green foliage, brown vase, oval format, framed, minor toning, stains, 12 1/2 in. by 10 in. **$500**

Floral, rose (pink) and blue columbine, stenciled and freehand painting, ink verse "...a token of friendship," signed "Miss Valentine," raised rose and morning glory border, worn gilt frame, stains, minor edge damage, 10 in. by 8 in. **$225**

Floral, roses, columbine, and bluebells, old faded colors, stains, old frame, 12 in. by 9 in. **$325**

Floral, tulips and other flowers, peacock feather, dragonflies, shells, and ladybug, in yellow, blue, green, white, brown, and tan, period frame with walnut veneer and gilt liner with touchup, light water stains, foxing in margins, minor damage at corners, 17 3/8 in. by 18 3/4 in. **$1,800**

Fruit, in basket, framed, stains, 10 in. by 14 in. **$1,100**

Fruit, in blue bowl, painted frame, toning, minor stain, crease, 7 1/2 in. by 9 1/4 in. **$8,000**

On velvet

Floral, bouquet, red, blue, green, and rust, framed, minor foxing, fabric abrasions, 18 3/4 in. by 14 1/4 in. **$500**

Floral, magnolia and lilies with foliage in blue, burgundy, teal, green, repainted frame, stains, 12 7/8 in. by 14 3/8 in. **$525**

Floral, rose in reds, pink, green, and white, damaged old gilt frame, 15 3/4 in. square. **$150**

Fruit, green, yellow, and dark blue, framed, foxing, fabric abrasions, 7 in. by 9 1/2 in. **$1,000**

Fruit, in bowls and a basket, framed, minor stains, toning, 24 1/2 in. by 21 in. **$12,000**

Fruit, peaches, pears, melon, grapes, cherries, and strawberries, basket with double handles, grass below, period gilt frame, background stained, 17 3/4 in. by 20 1/4 in. **$2,100**

Fruit, signed "Wm. Rank" (William Rank, 20th century Pennsylvania folk painter), red grained frame, 17 1/4 in. by 19 1/2 in. **$450**

Fruit, spilling from overturned Canton fruit bowl on marble table, red, blue, green, brown, and yellow, wear, minor age stains, old frame, 18 1/2 in. by 22 1/2 in. **$3,000**

Fruit, strawberry tree, signed "Wm. Rank" (William Rank, 20th century Pennsylvania folk painter), old molded frame, 14 in. by 11 1/2 in. **$325**

Fruit, with foliage, green, blue, yellow, and brown, with vintage note "Taken from frame by Carlton P. Crittenden at Fredonburg, 1862," unframed, wear, minor stains, damage to selvage, 16 in. by 20 1/4 in. **$3,750**

Fruit, with flowers and bird, signed "W. Rank" (William Rank, 20th century Pennsylvania folk painter), original grained frame, 20 1/2 in. by 21 1/2 in. **$525**

Currier & Ives: Attractive, available, affordable

By Wayne Mattox

On Jan. 13, 1840, the luxury steamboat *Lexington* burned and sank in Long Island Sound, killing 123 people. When the news reached editor Ben Day's office at the popular daily newspaper, *New York Sun*, an inspiration came to him that would revolutionize the newspaper industry and launch a young "lithographer" (printmaker) into one of the most influential careers in American history. "Why should newspapers consist of only words?" Day said to himself. "Would not a picture of the disaster sell papers?"

Day recalled that five years earlier, 23-year-old Nathaniel Currier made a reputation for himself by issuing the highly successful graphic print, "The Ruins of the Merchants' Exchange N.Y.," four days following the destructive Wall Street fire of Dec. 16-17, 1835. Currier was commissioned for the job.

In what was amazing speed at the time—three days—Nathaniel Currier produced for the *Sun* a violently realistic small print called "Awful Conflagration of the Steam Boat *LEXINGTON* In Long Island Sound on Monday Eve., Jan 13th 1840 by which melancholy occurrence 123 Persons Perished." (Currier was fond of long titles in his early years.) The venture was so successful, presses ran night and day to accommodate public demand. Ben Day's seven-column publication of *The Extra Sun*, complete with picture, would sell out five times and be distributed nationally, receiving glowing reviews. Other newspapers would follow Day's lead. The era of picture papers had begun.

Currier was not a man to ignore endeavors that proved successful. For years to come, not a blaze, shipwreck, or cataclysm would occur without finding its way to one of his lithograph printing stones. Great artists like George H. Durrie, Arthur Fitzwilliam Tait, James Buttersworth, Thomas Nast, and Louis Maurer were employed, each executing prints in their artistic element. For instance, Durrie turned out New England farm scenes, while Buttersworth focused on clipper ship prints. In 1852, Currier hired James Merrit Ives to keep his books. Ives proved so talented as an artist and businessman, he was made partner in the firm within five years. The firm would produce over 6,000 prints in the next 70 years—most selling well. Russel Crouse describes the partners in his 1930 book, *Mr. Currier and Mr. Ives*, as "sharing a keen and seldom-failing nose for news. They were the tabloid publishers of their day, seeking to catch the eye of the passing crowd with something strikingly graphic."

Currier and Ives recognized men's attraction toward danger and sport. They depicted scenes of whaling, bear hunts, baseball games, ship battles, and pioneers conquering the West. Horses in their numerous trotting prints would become models for almost all horse weathervanes.

The partners also recognized 19th century American women's fondness for sentiment. Their bustling company stamped out "God Bless Our Home" prints, and scenes depicting flowers, courtship, children, pets, buggy rides, and maple sugaring. For years, it was uncommon to enter an American home without at least one Currier & Ives print hanging prominently. Together, these prints constitute the most significant and influential pictorial record of 19th century America. Naturally, they are highly sought after as antiques today.

• • •

Nathaniel Currier was tall, thin, and fair. James M. Ives was short, plump, and dark. Standing side by side, the congenial partners probably looked like the number a discerning scoring judge would attach to their business—a perfect 10. In the second half of the 19th century, the Currier & Ives Company produced and sold over 10 million "Colored Engravings for the People" on nearly 10,000 subjects. They published over 700 different prints on horse racing alone.

Lithographs were priced according to size. A richly detailed "large folio," a print exceeding 14 in. by 20 in.,

retailed in 1870 from $3 to $5. "Small and medium folio" prints, approximately 9 in. by 14 in. to 14 in. by 20 in., were priced from $1 to $3. "Very small folio" prints, up to 7 in. by 9 in., usually sold for about 20 cents. I mention these size designations because they are still employed by collectors today. Other things being equal, the bigger-price for bigger-print principle still holds true as well.

Currier & Ives collecting is worthwhile as a hobby and investment because the prints are historical, attractive, available, and somewhat affordable—on a scale. I suggest working your way up the ladder. A 19th century framed small folio print of a toddler can still be found for under $200. A cat print will be a little more. A large still life of fruit generally is priced around $350. After you've bagged a few common Currier & Ives prints, you might set your sights on bigger game. Impressive large folio clipper ship engravings often exceed $3,000. Rare whaling and train prints can exceed $5,000. One of the most coveted examples over the last 50 years (now commanding $20,000+) is the large folio "Life of a Hunter–A Tight Fix." This winter scene print depicts a snarling grizzly bearing down on an unfortunate woodsman. In 1991, with big-spending baseball collectors entering into the competition, a whopping $44,000 was fetched at auction for the full folio "The American National Game of Base Ball."

Currier & Ives prints have been faked in great numbers. One such example is a small folio version of the famous baseball print. This rascal has battered many a dealer and collector over the years. The best way to insure you don't get stuck is to purchase Currier & Ives prints from a respected specialist in the field. If you stumble upon one at a tag sale, shop, or country auction and feel like gambling, here are a few tips. Inspect the print with a jeweler's loupe or powerful magnifying glass. If you see a series of tiny geometrically spaced dots, like putting your eyeball up to a TV screen, the print is a "photolithographic" reproduction. Currier and Ives produced all their prints in black and white and employed artisans to hand-color them before merchandising. Please note that some Currier & Ives reproductions are tricky—with no "dots" to alert you of their spurious nature.

Inspect for condition. Prints with brownish watermarks, foxing, or sun-bleaching should be avoided by novices unless they are purchased for a fraction of their "book price." Craig McClain wrote the best such guide called *An Illustrated Value Guide, Currier & Ives.* Prints with tears, rips, and clipped margins should likewise be avoided as they have little investment value in today's market.

(Wayne Mattox is the proprietor of Wayne Mattox Antiques, Woodbury, Conn., specializing in 18th and early 19th century furnishings, American folk art, and accessories.)

❖ Prints and Lithographs

References: Karen Choppa, *Bessie Pease Gutmann: Over Fifty Years of Published Art,* Schiffer Publishing, 1998; Karen Choppa and Paul Humphrey, *Maud Humphrey,* Schiffer Publishing, 1993; Max Allen Collins and Drake Elvgren, *Elvgren: His Life & Art,* Collectors Press, 1998; Erwin Flacks, *Maxfield Parrish Identification & Price Guide,* 3rd ed., Collectors Press, 1998; Martin Gordon, ed., *Gordon's Print Price Annual,* Gordon and Lawrence Art Reference, published annually; Tina Skinner, *Harrison Fisher: Defining the American Beauty,* Schiffer Publishing, 1999; Kent Steine and Frederick B. Taraba, *J.C. Leyendecker Collection,* Collectors Press, 1996.

Periodicals: *Illustrator Collector's News,* PO Box 1958, Sequim, WA 98382; *Journal of the Print World,* 1008 Winona Rd., Meredith, NH 03253; *On Paper,* 39 E. 78th St., #601, New York, NY 10021; *Print Collector's Newsletter,* 119 E. 79th St., New York, NY 10021.

Collectors' Clubs: American Antique Graphics Society, 5185 Windfall Rd., Medina, OH 44256; American Historical Print Collectors Society, PO Box 201, Fairfield, CT 06430; Gutmann Collectors' Club, PO Box 4743, Lancaster, PA 17604.

Museums: American Museum of Natural History, New York, N.Y.; John James Audubon State Park and Museum, Henderson, Ky.; Museum of the City of New York, N.Y.

Reproduction Alert

Reproductions of Maxfield Parrish prints are particularly common, but works by many other artists are also being copied. Shiny, crisp white paper is a sure indicator of newness. Early versions mellow with age and may even have acquired a light brown tone due to acids in the paper or from being framed against wood. Details that appear fuzzy and colors that separate into dots under magnification are both signs of later copies. But, since many early prints were copied soon after their introduction (particularly those attributed to Currier & Ives), reproductions can display the same aging characteristics as period pieces.

Note: Most descriptions include "sight" measurements—the size of that portion of the artwork that is visible within the frame. Sizes for the frames are not included.

Currier & Ives (hand-colored), "American Autumn Fruits," old gilt frame, margins slightly trimmed, minor stains, 27 1/4 in. by 33 1/2 in. **$4,000**

Currier & Ives (hand-colored), "American Express Train," margins trimmed slightly, minor soiling and stains, 25 in. by 33 in. **$9,000**

Currier & Ives (hand-colored), "American Field Sports–Flushed," 1857, framed, retouched, 20 3/4 in. by 27 1/2 in. **$2,725**

Currier & Ives (hand-colored), "American Hunting Scenes–An Early Start," 1863, framed, toning, margin stains, 20 1/2 in. by 28 in. **$5,000**

Currier & Ives (hand-colored), "The Champion Pacer Johnston," toning, stains, foxing, 23 1/4 in. by 30 1/4 in. **$2,000**

Currier & Ives (hand-colored), "The Deacon's Mare," framed, light water staining on bottom margin, 13 1/2 in. by 17 1/2 in. **$550**

Currier & Ives (hand-colored), "E. Pluribus Unum," reclining man steadying gun with bare foot, framed, 13 in. by 16 1/2 in. **$660**

Currier & Ives (hand-colored), "The First Bird of the Season," matted and framed, 13 in. by 16 3/4 in. **$500**

Currier & Ives (hand-colored), "The Fruit Piece," framed, 13 in. by 16 in. **$1,000**

Currier & Ives (hand-colored), "Hudson River–Crow Nest," matted/framed, trimmed, minor edge damage, stains, 10 1/8 in. by 13 3/4 in. **$300**

Currier & Ives (hand-colored), "Jay Eye See, Record 2:10," cherry frame, stains, minor damage, edge repair, 13 3/8 in. by 17 5/8 in. . **$400**

Currier & Ives (hand-colored), "Landscape, Fruit and Flowers," framed, minor crease/tear, few scattered fox marks, 21 1/2 in. by 28 1/2 in. **$10,000**

Currier & Ives (hand-colored), "Life in the Woods–Starting Out," 1860, framed, margin stains, pale foxing, 21 1/4 in. by 28 1/2 in. **$2,000**

Currier & Ives (hand-colored), "Little Snowbird," framed and matted, minor stains, 15 11/16 in. by 12 1/8 in. **$500**

Currier & Ives (hand-colored), "Longfellow," horse racing print, framed, stains, minor edge damage, 11 3/4 in. by 15 3/4 in. **$400**

Currier & Ives (hand-colored), "The Lovers Quarrel," period painted frame, foxing, 16 in. by 11 3/4 in. **$575**

Currier & Ives (hand-colored), "The Lovers Reconciliation," dated 1846, period veneered frame, 14 in. by 10 in. **$400**

Currier & Ives (hand-colored), "Lucy," period frame, foxing, tear, 14 in. by 10 in. **$300**

Currier & Ives (hand-colored), "A Mansion of the Olden Time," framed, minor stains, paint on top margin, 13 1/4 in. by 16 1/4 in.**$300**

Currier & Ives (hand-colored), "New England Winter Scene," framed, tears, toning, title trimmed from sheet and matted with image, 17 in. by 24 in. **$1,500**

Currier & Ives (hand-colored), "Newport Beach," matted/framed, damage, some repair, 11 in. by 15 1/2 in. **$200**

Currier & Ives (hand-colored), "The Old Mill-Dam," matted/framed, minor stains, edge damage, 11 in. by 14 in. **$300**

Currier & Ives (hand-colored), "On A Strong Scent," matted/framed, 16 in. by 10 in. **$500**

Currier & Ives (hand-colored), "Partridge Shooting," margins trimmed, old frame, 10 in. by 14 in. **$275**

Currier & Ives (hand-colored), "The Pride of the Garden," period decor frame, stains in upper right, 16 5/8 in. by 13 1/2 in. **$300**

Currier & Ives (hand-colored), "The Roadside Mill," framed, 10 in. by 14 in. **$400**

Currier & Ives (hand-colored), "The Star Spangled Banner," Lady Liberty with flag, period frame, foxing, two areas of touchup, 16 3/8 in. by 12 1/4 in. **$250**

Currier & Ives (hand-colored), "A Summer Landscape, Haymaking," margins slightly trimmed, minor stains, tape repair, old gilt frame, 13 in. by 17 1/4 in. **$400**

Currier & Ives (hand-colored), "View of Harpers Ferry, Va.," rosewood veneer frame with gilded liner, good margins, minor corner damage, 27 in. by 30 1/2 in. **$2,000**

Currier & Ives (hand-colored), "View on the Harlem River, N.Y.," framed, toning, 18 1/2 in. by 22 1/2 in. **$3,500**

Currier & Ives (hand-colored), "Washington's Reception by the Ladies," period walnut frame with ink graining, minor margin tears, 14 in. by 10 in. **$300**

Currier & Ives (hand-colored), "Winter Morning, Feeding the Chickens," framed, toning, unobtrusive stains, 17 in. by 21 1/2 in. **$10,000**

Currier & Ives (hand-colored), "The Wonderful Maud S., Record of 2:10," old beveled walnut frame, 12 in. by 15 7/8 in. **$500**

❖ Picture Frames

Picture frame, circa 1900, scrap wood decorated with acorn caps, saw-tooth profiles on crossed corners, original varnished surface, some caps missing, overall good condition, 20 in. by 16 in. **$300-$400**

Picture or mirror frame, circa 1900, pine with dark stain, painted with flowers, simple half-lap construction, some fading of flowers, excellent condition, 18 1/2 in. by 22 1/2 in. by 1 in. **$300-$400**

Picture frame, circa 1940s, elaborately carved from one piece of wood, probably walnut, containing a photograph of a child, the frame featuring an urn and what may be stylized angel's wings, and a cross, probably a mourning piece, original heavily varnished surface, 9 in. by 6 in. **$200-$250**

Picture frame, circa 1900, done in tramp art style with carved rosettes in the corners and a carved heart with a cross in the top center, the frame containing a chenille crucifix headstone (?) and rose mounted on black velvet, probably a mourning piece, moderate wear and some varnish loss along bottom edge, 17 in. by 21 in. by 2 in. **$350-$450**

Matched pair of picture frames, circa 1910, walnut and mixed woods, with applied carved decoration in scroll and geometric motifs, untouched original condition, 18 in. by 14 in. **$600-$700/pair**

Double picture frame, circa 1890, scrap wood done in tramp art style, nine levels of notch carving with regularly spaced carved rosettes, original crazed varnished surface, untouched condition, overall 18 in. by 32 in. Detail below. **$600-$700**

Picture frame, circa 1900, pine and mixed woods, done in tramp art style, with crossed corners decorated with carved butterflies, notch-carved overall with applied gilt vines and leaves, and sunbursts with tulips, back boards cut from painted house clapboards, found in Strawberry Point, Iowa, near mint condition, 40 in. by 28 in. by 4 in. **$1,500-$2,000**

Picture frame, circa 1900, walnut and mixed woods, elaborate tramp art creation with six-level corners done in fan motif, sides done in cutout "fence posts" with flower tops, and inner sections decorated with notched layers in arches, points, saw-tooth designs, near mint condition, 36 in. by 26 in. (Similar frames have been found in the Midwest, and all appear to be the work of the same maker. One frame was found with red, white and blue paint, which may have been a later addition.) **$4,000-$5,000**

Picture frame, circa 1890, done in tramp art style with complex corners and elaborate chip-carved decoration including round hex signs, the frame containing a photograph of a country wedding party, minor wear, original varnished surface, 20 in. by 18 in. **$425-$525**

Where can I find it?

Blondell Antiques
1406 2nd St. SW
Rochester, MN 55902
(507) 282-1872
Fax: (507) 282-8683
www.blondell.com/
antiques@blondell.com

Country Comfort Antiques
Third and Main Streets
Winona, MN 55987
(507) 452-7044

Freward & Alk Antiques
414 Lazarre Ave.
Green Bay, WI 54301
(800) 488-0321
(920) 435-7343
www.the-antique-shop.com
leesa@the-antique-shop.com

Wayne Mattox Antiques
82 Main St. N.
Woodbury, CT 06798
(203) 263-2431
www.antiquetalk.com
tiquetalk@aol.com

Mark F. Moran Antiques
5887 Meadow Dr. SE
Rochester, MN 55904
(507) 288-8006
mfmoran@charter.net

Bandboxes

The name bandbox is derived from the lightweight, utilitarian pasteboard boxes used by the English to hold neckbands and lace bands. Popular in America from 1820 to 1850, they were available in a variety of sizes and were generally covered with decorative wallpaper having floral or geometric patterns. Boxes covered with paper depicting historical scenes are especially prized, as are those with a maker's label and those that are part of a matched set.

Reference: Arene Burgess, *19th Century Wooden Boxes*, Schiffer Publishing, 1997.

Collecting Hint: A maker's label can double the value of a band box.

Hannah Davis, oval, 10 1/2 in. long, 5 1/2 in. tall, light yellow (darkened) wallpaper with white, pink, and brown floral designs, newspaper-lined interior, "Warranted Nailed Band Boxes, made by Hannah Davis, Jaffrey (N.H.)," wear. **$1,600**

Hannah Davis, oval, 14 3/4 in. long, worn original floral paper in green, white, and beige on wooden base, lined with old newspaper and labeled "Band Boxes made by Hannah Davis, Jaffrey, N.H." ...**$800**

Hannah Davis, oval, 19 in. long, Napoleon pattern paper in shades of green and white with touches of gilt, yellow ground, paper label, with booklet about Hannah Davis, imperfections. **$450**

Oblong, 7 in. long, 5 1/4 in. wide, 3 1/8 in. tall, colorful paper in green, yellow, white, and brown diamonds, lines and foliage scrolls, wear. **$475**

Oblong, 17 in. long, 10 in. wide, 10 in. tall, blue wallpaper, floral and landscape decor, wear, soiling. **$225**

Oval, 6 in. long, 3 1/2 in. wide, 3 in. tall, basket-weave pattern in blue, dark blue, and white, tan band with burgundy dots around lid, partial newspaper lining, minor edge wear, small flakes. **$750**

Oval, 7 1/8 in. long, 4 in. wide, 3 in. tall, mustard, green, and tan leaves around base, roses on lid, red and black band, pencil inscription, small hole in lid, minor flaking. **$650**

Oval, 8 in. long, 5 1/4 in. wide, 4 1/4 in. tall, base and lid covered with tan paper with green and brown scroll print, small edge flakes. **$550**

Oval, 9 1/4 in. long, 6 3/4 in. wide, 4 3/4 in. tall, poplar, brown, white, and cream design, lined with early advertisements for medicines, stains, edge wear to lid. **$175**

Oval, 12 1/4 in. long, 10 1/4 in. wide, 7 1/4 in. tall, blue with white lines and stars, pink and white flowers, green leaves, overall wear, insect damage on bottom. **$425**

Baskets

Early Basket Making

by Wayne Mattox

The foremost antique baskets in the world will be found in America. Native Americans and colonists discovered that basketry allowed them to take best advantage of the natural abundance available to them in the form of reeds, grass, straw, pine needles, roots, vines, corn shucks, and splints of willow, walnut, hickory, oak, and ash with a minimum of tools and hardware.

However, the most important determinant toward America's tradition of fine basketry will not be found in her citizen's environment and necessity, but in their collective perspective and taste. People here—be it New England Puritan carpenters, or seafaring craftsmen, or Quaker cabinetmakers, or Cherokee, Apache, and other American Indian artisans, or humble Shakers—all shared an eye and philosophy that beauty could be found in simplistic functional form, natural materials, geometric line, and strong attention to craftsmanship and detail. These elements, in addition to a nutty brown aged coloration and exemplary condition, are what you should seek toward collecting fine early baskets.

Baskets can be collected according to age, weave, materials, size, function, form, decoration, and community.

Early baskets will exhibit wear—as they were wrought to be used-and mellow patina. Hand-cut splints and handles will often appear thick and irregular. Rough tool marks will be evident, and the oldest examples will be held together with hand-wrought iron and copper tacks and animal sinew. Rattan (used in Nantucket baskets) was widely introduced to Americans by Cyrus Wakefield, founder of Wakefield Rattan and Wicker Furniture beginning around 1840. The first fully automatic basket-making machine was patented in 1894. Machine-made and later vintage hand-woven baskets are generally lacking in quality workmanship and inspired design.

Generally, basket construction falls within two broad categories, each with a plethora of methodology and pattern: plaited and coiled. Woven plaited baskets made by interlacing two or more elements—called the warp and weft—include willow, openweave, and wood splint. Sewing a spiral snakelike foundation together in a flat or ascending coil makes coil baskets. Pennsylvania Germans and American Indians are famous for their sweet-grass, figure of eight, "lazy squaw," and other varieties of laced coil baskets.

Unlike many other antique categories, size does not always determine value in baskets. In fact, miniatures are among the most sought after. The best of these will be indistinguishable from their larger brothers, except in size.

Interesting basket forms include superbly wrought examples that stand alone as art. Additionally, peach baskets of interest to basketball collectors, narrow-necked goose baskets that covered the bird's heads for feather plucking, buttocks-shaped baskets, picnic, sewing, creel, fish and eel trap, clothing, nesting set, cradle, cooking, gambling tray, bottle and egg, apple, and other types of gathering and holding baskets are much sought after by collectors.

Basket construction is one of the biggest determinants of value. Skilled basket makers took pride in the closeness and evenness of their sewing and weaving technique, and the overall balance and symmetry of their product. Be it round, square, or otherwise shaped, a basket should be strictly true to its form and harmonious in construction. The most valuable schools of basket include pictorial American Indian, cooper-influenced Nantucket lightship baskets, and tightly woven Shaker splint baskets. Still available at house sales, flea markets, estate auctions, and shops, antique American baskets embody our country's highest ideals toward form and craftsmanship.

(Wayne Mattox is the proprietor of Wayne Mattox Antiques, Woodbury, Conn., specializing in 18th and early 19th century furnishings, American folk art, and accessories.)

❖ Baskets

The appearance and construction of baskets has changed little in 5,000 years. Always utilitarian but sometimes with a decorative look, most are made of wood splint, willow rods, or various grasses. However, offbeat materials such as matchbook covers and bottle caps have also been used. Basket styles can vary widely, as can their values.

Reference: Don and Carol Raycraft, *Collector's Guide to Country Baskets*, Collector Books, 1985 (1994 value update).

Museums: Heard Museum, Phoenix, Ariz.; Old Salem, Inc., Winston-Salem, N.C.

Reproduction Alert

Modern reproductions and contemporary examples are plentiful.

Collecting Hint: Save your money for baskets that are in very good condition. Damaged examples tend to be poor investments, even at low prices.

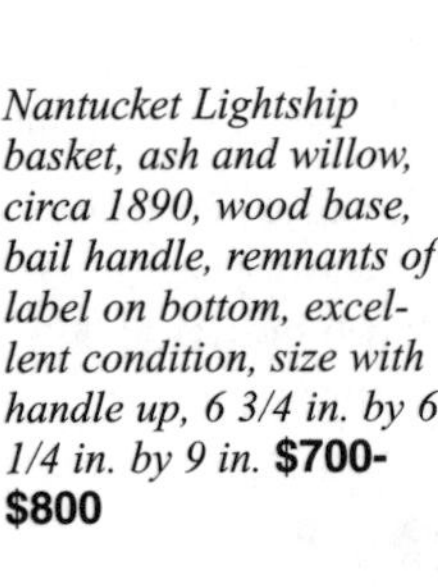

Nantucket Lightship basket, ash and willow, circa 1890, wood base, bail handle, remnants of label on bottom, excellent condition, size with handle up, 6 3/4 in. by 6 1/4 in. by 9 in. **$700-$800**

Birch bark covered basket with leather strap, woven top with loop handle, and woven top edge, with scratched floral decoration, Indian-made for tourists circa 1940s, minor handling wear, 6 1/2 in. by 6 in. square. **$50-$60**

Shaker-style utility or fancy work basket, poplar or ash, circa 1890, original dark blue paint with "kitten head" base (larger baskets have "cat-head" bases, named for the way the feet come to a point between arched sides, having the appearance of a cat's ears), minor wear, 10 in. by 10 in. by 4 1/4 in. **$80-$100**

Splint basket, ash, circa 1890, with carved handle, near mint, 9 in. by 14 in. by 12 1/2 in. **$125-$150**

Splint basket, ash, circa 1900, with carved handle, probably Winnebago, 8 in. by 12 in. by 9 1/2 in. **$90-$120**

Splint buttocks basket, hickory, circa 1870, with offset handle, excellent condition, 11 in. by 7 in. by 9 in. **$250-$300**

Splint basket, ash, circa 1890, with carved handle, minor wear, 7 1/2 in. by 8 in. by 7 3/4 in. **$50-$70**

Splint gathering basket, oak, circa 1920, moderate wear, very good condition, 19 in. by 11 1/2 in. by 9 1/4 in. **$150-$200**

Splint laundry basket, ash or poplar, circa 1900, with carved handles, traces of old red paint, moderate wear, 17 1/2 in. by 22 in. by 14 in. **$100-$125**

Splint bushel or apple basket, hickory, circa 1900, moderate wear, 13 1/4 in. by 13 1/4 in. by 8 1/2 in. **$125-$150**

Splint gathering basket, oak, circa 1910, with the name "Rose" written on the handle in ink, minor wear, 15 1/2 in. by 23 1/2 in. by 17 in. **$125-$150**

Splint flower basket, hickory, circa 1910, near mint, 13 in. by 10 in. by 7 3/4 in. **$70-$90**

Splint flower or garden basket, oak, circa 1890, with crimped sides, minor wear, 14 in. by 20 in. by 15 in. **$150-$175**

Splint garden or market basket, hickory, circa 1920, with slight buttocks profile, near mint, 8 3/4 in. by 7 1/2 in. by 7 in. **$200-$250**

Splint garden or market basket, hickory, circa 1920, with slight buttocks profile, significant wear, 10 1/2 in. by 10 1/2 in. by 10 in. **$70-$100**

Splint harvest basket, hickory, circa 1890, handle missing, moderate wear, 7 1/2 in. by 9 1/2 in. by 8 1/2 in. **$60-$80**

Splint basket, oak, circa 1900, ovoid with rounded handle and traces of old green paint, near mint, 12 3/4 in. by 13 in. **$200-$250**

Three views of miniature splint basket, 4 in. by 4 1/2 in. **$900-$1,100**

Splint "riddle" basket, oak, circa 1910, sometimes used to separate wheat from chaff, 13 1/2 in. by 15 1/2 in. by 4 in. **$150-$180**

Splint basket, circa 1930, with bail handles and stenciled on side "Smoked Pure Pork Sausage," possibly a manufacturer's promotional item, significant damage, 12 in. by 8 in. by 5 in. **$20**

Splint basket, oak, Norwegian, dated 1876, painted dark blue, red, and white with stylized floral motif, wood handle, hinged lid with tin hasp, minor handling wear, 10 1/2 in. by 11 1/4 in. by 15 in. **$550**

Splint basket, circa 1920, probably of Indian make, with carved wooden handle and brightly painted in yellow, blue, black, red, and orange, moderate handling wear, 10 in. by 9 in. **$30**

Woven canteen, grass or wicker, circa 1880, ring handles, minor wear, 10 in. by 8 1/2 in. by 4 1/2 in. **$200-$250**

Berry basket, woven splint, large "AP" on sides in black paint, square with flat bottom, sides flare to rounded rim, iron tacks, Shaker, 4 in. tall, 3 3/4 in. diameter..........**$110**

Buttocks basket, woven splint, 14 ribs, 2 1/2 in. tall (including handle), 3 in. long. **$450**

Buttocks basket, woven splint, 18 ribs, 3 1/2 in. tall (including handle). **$185**

Buttocks basket, woven splint, 20 ribs, 6 in. tall (excluding handle), 12 3/4 in. by 19 1/2 in. **$225**

Buttocks basket, woven splint, 23 ribs, 3 in. tall (excluding handle), 6 in. long....................................**$150**

Buttocks basket, woven splint, 24 ribs, 3 1/4 in. tall (excluding handle), 5 in. by 7 in., twisted handle with diamond at ends..**$175**

Buttocks basket, woven splint, 24 ribs, 8 in. tall (excluding handle), 14 in. by 16 in.............................**$250**

Buttocks basket, woven splint, 26 ribs, 4 1/2 in. tall (including handle). **$350**

Buttocks basket, woven splint, 26 ribs, splint breaks, 9 in. tall (excluding handle), 13 in. wide, 15 in. deep. $130

Buttocks basket, woven splint, 28 ribs, tightly woven, anchored handle, late stained finish, 8 1/4 in. tall. $250

Buttocks basket, woven splint, 34 ribs, minor damage, 7 in. tall (excluding handle), 14 in. wide, 12 in. deep. $225

Buttocks basket, woven splint, 36 ribs, minor breaks, 10 in. tall (excluding handle), 15 in. by 19 in. $250

Buttocks basket, woven splint, 54 ribs, minor damage at handle, 5 1/4 in. tall (including handle). ..$600

Cheese basket, 11 in. diameter, 4 in. tall, round top, six-sided bottom, woven splint. $150

Cheese basket, 22 1/2 in. diameter, 7 1/2 in. tall, round top, hexagonal base, woven splint, few breaks, one repair. $285

Cheese basket, 23 in. diameter, Shaker, woven splint. $275

Cheese basket, 24 in. diameter, woven splint. $450

Goose feather basket, rye straw, 18 in. tall. $150

Goose feather basket, woven splint, old red paint, domed lid, round, 18 in. tall, 15 in. diameter. $750

Half buttocks basket basket, woven splint, 8 ribs, bentwood handle, minor damage, 7 in. tall. $150

Half buttocks basket basket, woven splint, nine ribs, bentwood handle, dark finish, minor damage, 7 1/4 in. tall. $150

Half buttocks basket basket, woven splint, 16 ribs, bentwood handle, minor wear, 9 in. tall. $300

Half buttocks basket basket, woven splint, 28 ribs, minor breaks, 12 1/2 in. tall (excluding handle), 12 3/4 in. wide. $275

Indian basket, Mic Mac, hanging, 13 in. tall, 10 in. wide, 7 in. deep. .$250

Indian basket, Passamaquoddy, woven splint with lid, red and blue designs, ring handles, 19 in.

Winnebago splint hanging basket, circa 1920, with tiered back and arching handle in middle, moderate wear, 13 in. by 6 in. by 16 in. **$100-$125**

Interlocking wood basket, circa 1890, mixed woods, probably Norwegian-American, with woven splint panels and canted sides, mint condition, 10 1/2 in. by 10 1/2 in. by 11 1/2 in. **$250-$350**

diameter, 17 in. tall. **$90**

Indian basket, Woodland, woven splint, natural, red, blue, and green woven design, handles wrapped in splint, 14 1/2 in. wide. **$150**

Indian basket, Woodland, woven splint, buttocks, 28 ribs, two-tone brown and natural, 6 in. tall (excluding woven handle), 11 in. by 12 1/2 in. **$550**

Melon basket, woven splint, 18 ribs, flat base, bentwood handle, 7 1/4 in. tall. **$175**

Melon basket, woven splint, 28 ribs, five dark stained bands, 5 1/4 in. tall (excluding bentwood handle), 11 in. wide. **$550**

Nantucket basket, 4 1/8 in. diameter, 3 3/8 in. tall, woven, round, wooden bottom painted green, rounded bottom with straight sides, bentwood rim painted green, arched handle. **$2,100**

Nantucket basket, 9 in. diameter, 8 1/4 in. tall, woven, round wooden bottom, wrapped rim, swivel bentwood handle, minor rim break. **$750**

Nantucket basket, 9 1/2 in. diameter, 6 in. tall, round, woven, wooden bottom, bentwood swing handle, pieced repair at handle post. **$1,600**

Nantucket basket, 10 1/4 in. diameter, 9 in. tall, round, turned wooden base, carved wing handle. **$2,200**

Nantucket basket, 13 1/4 in. diameter, 5 in. tall, woven cane/splint, round, turned wooden base, swivel bentwood handle with brass ears, breaks on rim and edge of base, rim wrap incomplete. **$150**

Nantucket basket, basket purse, turned ivory fittings and two flying gulls on lid, marked "Wm. & J. Reis, 1973 Nantucket Island," swivel handle, 7 1/2 in. tall, oval 7 1/2 in. by 10 in. **$850**

Nantucket basket purse with cover, oval, cherry plaque and base, ivory seagull signed "C.F. Sayle," 20th century, 5 3/4 in. tall, 9 1/2 in. long, 6 1/2 in. deep. **$625**

Picnic basket, splint, hinged wood lid, oblong, metal reinforcement/straps, sheet-iron arched handle, open rectangular woven-in handles, 9 in. tall (excluding handle), 21 in. wide, 11 1/8 in. deep. **$140**

Rye straw basket, 3 3/4 in. tall, 8 7/8 in. diameter, coiled, round, flat bottom, single coil rye straw foot, rounded sides, bound with splint, some wear on foot, some loss of splint. **$80**

Rye straw basket, 4 5/8 in. tall, 12 in. diameter, coiled, round, bread basket, bound with splint, flat bottom. **$170**

Rye straw basket, 5 1/4 in. tall, 11 3/4 in. diameter, coiled, round, woven-in arched handles on top rim, round coiled foot. **$250**

Rye straw basket, gathering, coiled, bound with splint, round with flat bottom, coiled round foot, sides slightly rounded and are fitted with arched bentwood handles attached with woven splint, Centre County, Pa., 19th century, 8 3/4 in. tall (excluding handles), 13 3/4 in. diameter. **$3,100**

Rye straw basket, storage, swollen oval form, probably Pennsylvania origin, losses, 18 in. tall. **$325**

Splint basket, kettle shape, old black paint, 6 in. tall, 9 in. diameter. **$875**

Splint basket, kettle shape, worn yellow paint, minor damage, 8 in. tall, 13 1/2 in. diameter. **$570**

Splint basket, low, 4 in. square, 2 in. tall, potato-stamp decor. **$800**

Splint basket, low, 13 in. diameter, 5 in. tall, old dark green paint, round. **$570**

Splint basket, melon, 12 radiating ribs, coarsely woven, small breaks, 6 1/2 in. tall. **$90**

Splint basket, melon, 16 flat bentwood staves, arched handle, two short sections of splint missing, 13 1/2 in. tall. **$200**

Splint basket, melon, 20 flat ribs, tightly woven, two blue-green stained lines along the bottom, small breaks, 6 1/2 in. tall. **$90**

Splint basket, melon, 22 ribs, tightly woven, decorative stacked weaving where handle meets basket, minor breaks, 13 1/2 in. tall. **$90**

Splint basket, melon, 26 ribs, tightly woven, damaged bottom, 17 in. tall. **$240**

Splint basket, melon, tightly woven, designs beneath arched handle, 8 1/8 in. tall, 9 1/4 in. diameter. **$110**

Splint basket, miniature, 4 in. tall, 6 in. diameter, 2 handles. **$425**

Splint basket, oval, cross-weave design, bentwood top and bottom, natural finish, edge wear, 19 3/4 in. by 14 1/2 in., 9 in. tall. **$120**

Splint basket, oval, oval top, square base, oval rim, 7 in. long, 4 1/8 in. tall, old green paint over red, bentwood handle. **$525**

Splint basket, oval, oval top, square base, 20 in. wide, 20 in. deep, 16 in. tall, tightly woven, pierced handles, carved hickory feet, scrubbed. **$225**

Splint basket, rectangular, 11 1/2 in. wide, 12 1/4 in. deep, 4 1/2 in. tall, dark green paint, square design, narrow splints, minor breaks, paint wear. **$375**

Splint basket, rectangular, 12 3/4 in. wide, 11 1/4 in. deep, 6 1/4 in. tall, tightly woven wide splint base, loosely woven narrow splints on top, breaks. **$130**

Splint basket, rectangular, 13 in. long, watercolor designs in red, blue, and yellow. **$260**

Splint basket, round, 5 in. diameter, 4 in. tall, blue and red geometric potato stamp decor, square base, round top, few breaks on lid. **$1,100**

Splint basket, round, 10 in. diameter, 6 3/4 in. tall, swing handle. **$500**

Splint basket, round, 12 1/2 in. diameter, 7 1/2 in. tall, original blue paint, two wide splints at top, finely woven splints taper at bottom, minor breaks. **$275**

Splint basket, round, 14 1/2 in. diameter, double handles, minor edge chips on splints, one handle cracked. **$130**

Splint basket, round, 18 1/2 in. diameter, 14 3/4 in. tall, green paint around center band, other bands in reddish cast, damage. **$120**

Splint basket, round, round top, square base, 4 1/2 in. square, 4 1/4 in. tall (excluding handle), swing handle with looped and pierced ends. **$300**

Splint basket, round, round top, square base, 8 3/4 in. tall, bentwood handle....................**$300**

Splint basket, round, round top, square base, 9 in. tall, arched bentwood handle....................**$100**

Splint basket, round, round top, square base, canted sides, 13 3/4 in. tall, natural with stained salmon and black weaving, geometric loops around center, arched handle, few splint breaks. **$375**

Splint basket, square, handled, 12 1/2 in. tall, 11 in. square...........**$70**

Where can I find them?

Blondell Antiques
1406 2nd St. SW
Rochester, MN 55902
(507) 282-1872
Fax: (507) 282-8683
www.blondell.com/
antiques@blondell.com

Country Comfort Antiques
Third and Main Streets
Winona, MN 55987
(507) 452-7044

Country Side Antique Mall
31752 65th Ave.
Cannon Falls, MN 55009
(507) 263-0352
www.csamantiques.com

The Tinker
John W. and Mary Lou Hunziker
2828 Mayowood Common St. S.W.
Rochester, MN 55902
(507) 288-4898

John Kruesel's General Merchandise
22 Third St. SW
Rochester, MN 55902
(507) 289-8049
www.kruesel.com

Wayne Mattox Antiques
82 Main St. N.
Woodbury, CT 06798
(203) 263-2431
www.antiquetalk.com
tiquetalk@aol.com

Bellows

Bellows existed as early as the 15th century. Generally made of wood and leather with metal fittings, they are used to force a concentrated stream of air to assist in combustion of a fire. Turtleback bellows are those with a rounded surface.

Collecting Hint: Collectors look for decorated examples. Designs other than flowers and fruit are especially prized. Condition plays an important role in determining value.

Decorated, cornucopia of fruit, gilt, green, brown, and black, red ground, brass tip and tack decor, restored leather, 18 in. long. ...**$550**

Decorated, cornucopia, fruit and foliage design, original red paint, freehand and stenciled design in black, gold, green, and yellow, brass nozzle, old leather worn, 17 in. long.................................**$1,200**

Decorated, floral, original yellow paint, green and black striping and stenciling, freehand detail in red, green, gold, and black, brass nozzle, professionally releathered, minor wear, 16 1/2 in. long......**$325**

Decorated, floral, original rosewood graining (worn), worn leather, brass nozzle, 15 in. long. **$120**

Decorated, fruit and foliage in gold, bronze, and black, red ground, black striping, original paper label for "Eckstein and Richardson, No. 36 North Third Street, Philadelphia," extreme leather wear. **$300**

Decorated, fruit and foliage, original yellow paint, stenciled and freehand design in red, green, brown, and black, brass nozzle, old worn releathering, wear, 17 1/2 in. long. **$625**

Decorated, fruit and foliage, original yellow paint, stenciled and freehand design in red, green, brown, and black, brass nozzle, very worn old leather, wear.....**$300**

Decorated, fruit and foliage, yellow paint, green banding, 18 in. long. **$350**

Decorated, leaf and flourish, old dark red repaint, gold stencil, worn simulated leather, 18 3/4 in. long. **$75**

Decorated, turtleback, basket of flowers in gold and green stencil and freehand, red ground, stenciled gold borders, old releathering, brass nozzle, wear, flaking, 17 3/8 in. long............**$125**

Decorated, turtleback, bird and berries, old black paint, multicolor design, brass nozzle, worn old releathering, wear, 17 1/2 in. long. **$700**

Decorated, turtleback, fruit, mustard ground, brass nozzle, old repaint, wear, 16 1/2 in. long................**$250**

Decorated, turtleback, fruit in compote, original green paint, tan border, yellow stencil, brass nozzle, old releathering, minor wear, 17 in. long. **$1,000**

Blue & White Pottery and Stoneware

Although termed blue and white pottery and stoneware, this category also includes blue and gray pottery and stoneware. Widely produced from the late 19th century through the 1930s, these items were originally marketed as inexpensive wares for everyday household use. Butter crocks, pitchers, and saltboxes are among the most commonly found pieces. Many examples feature a white or gray body with an embossed geometric, floral, or fruit pattern. The piece was then highlighted with bands and splashes of blue to accentuate the molded pattern.

Reference: Kathryn McNerney, *Blue & White Stoneware*, Collector Books, 1995; Terry Taylor and Terry & Kay Lowrance, *Collector's Encyclopedia of Salt Glaze Stoneware*, Collector Books, 1997.

Collectors' Club: Blue & White Pottery Club, 224 12th St., N.W., Cedar Rapids, IA 52405.

Also See: Spongeware

Batter jar, Wildflower, glaze flaw, four chips on lid. **$400**

Bowl, Apricot pattern, milk bowl, 4 in. tall, 9 1/2 in. diameter. **$90**

Bowl, Blue Banded, 14 3/4 in. diameter. **$150**

Bowl, Colonial, base crack, 12 in. diameter. **$300**

Bowl, Diffused, 2 3/4 in. tall, 7 in. diameter. **$150**

Bowl, Diffused, chips, base cracked, 6 in. tall, 12 in. diameter. **$100**

Bowl, Flying Birds, berry bowl. **$150**

Bowl, Flying Birds, milk bowl, 2 chips, 3 3/4 in. tall, 9 1/2 in. diameter. **$525**

Butter crock, Basket Weave, base/rim/lid chips. **$150**

Butter crock, "Butter" in oval, blue sponging, 9 in. diameter. **$275**

Butter crock, Colonial, with lid, 4 1/4 in. tall. **$375**

Butter crock, Colonial, tall form, new lid. **$300**

Butter crock, Cows, minor base flakes, lid missing large piece. **$175**

Butter crock, Daisy, unusual scrollwork pattern, no lid. **$150**

Butter crock, Daisy & Trellis, with lid, minor glaze flake at bail. **$90**

Butter crock, Diffused, advertising "Rockwell City, Iowa," mint condition. **$175**

Butter crock, Eagle, with lid. **$1,100**

Butter crock, Indian & Deer, with lid. **$2,250**

Butter crock, Lovebird, with lid. **$550**

Butter crock, Peacock, chipped lid. **$320**

Canister, "Cake," blue bands, damaged lid. **$150**

Canister, "Cereal," Basket Weave, no lid. **$400**

Canister, "Coffee," Basket Weave, inner rim chips, mended lid. **$90**

Canister, "Cookies," two glaze flakes/chip, damaged lid. **$175**

Canister, "Raisins," Basket Weave, with lid, mint condition. **$400**

Canister, "Sugar," Basket Weave, hairline on jar, mismatched lid. **$75**

Canister, "Sugar," Wildflower, with lid, chipped. **$200**

Canister, "Tobacco," Basket Weave, with lid. **$900**

Chamber pot, Wildflower, hairline. **$175**

Coffeepot, Peacock, no lid. **$2,500**

Cooler, "Maxwell House Ice Tea," small lid chip, hairline. **$320**

Grease jar, Flying Birds, with lid. **$1,100**

Jardiniere, Tulip. **$600**

Lid, Apple Blossom, salt lid. **$150**

Lid, Apricot, salt lid. **$150**

Lid, Basket Weave "Tobacco" canister lid. **$325**

Lid, Flying Birds, 9 in. diameter. **$375**

Lid, Wildflower, salt lid. **$80**

Match holder, Flemish. **$110**

Meat tenderizer, Wildflower, crazed, replaced handle. **$400**

Meat tenderizer, Windmill. **$90**

Miniature, Canteen, G.A.R., Davenport, Iowa, 1914. **$325**

Mug, Basket Weave, gold trim. **$115**

Mug, Cattail, Western Stoneware, three flakes. **$170**

Mug, Dainty Fruit. **$600**

Mug, Wildflower. **$110**

Pie plate, rim chips. **$125**

Pitcher, American Beauty Rose. **$450**

Pitcher, Arches & Columns. **$575**

Pitcher, Avenue of Trees. **$300**

Pitcher, Basket Weave, water pitcher. **$150**

Pitcher, Beaded Swirl. **$1,200**

Pitcher, Cattail, small flake on base, 7 in. tall. **$150**

Pitcher, Cattails and Rushes, mint condition, 10 in. tall. **$220**

Pitcher, Cherry Band, plain, two hairlines, 6 in. tall. **$150**

Pitcher, Cherry Band, "A.E. Laidley, Pandora, Iowa," spider hairline in base, repaired chips on spout, 8 1/2 in. tall. **$425**

Pitcher, Cherry Band, "Merry Christmas, Andrew Westin & Co.," 8 1/2 in. tall. **$400**

Pitcher, Cherry Band, oval advertising "T.L. Jones & Co., 1916, Arnold, Neb.," 9 1/2 in. tall. **$3,000**

Pitcher, Cows, two inner rim chips, tight hairlines. **$175**

Pitcher, Dainty Fruit. **$400**

Pitcher, Daisy. **$850**

Pitcher, Dutch Boy & Girl. **$125**

Pitcher, Dutch Farm Scene, tall variation. **$175**

Pitcher, Eagle. **$400**

Pitcher, Flying Birds, two small lip flakes, hairline. **$350**

Pitcher, Garden Rose. **$325**

Pitcher, George & Martha Washington, White Hall, mint

condition. $375

Pitcher, Indian Boy & Girl, hairline, crazing. $250

Pitcher, Leaping Deer. $375

Pitcher, Old House & Trees (castle), chips, 8 in. tall. $220

Pitcher, Peacock, minor base flakes. $1,500

Pitcher, Rose & Fish Scale, repaired spout, hairline, 9 in. tall. $120

Pitcher, Swan. $525

Pitcher, Tulip. $375

Pitcher, Wildflower. $150

Pitcher, Windmill, tight hairline. ..$130

Rolling pin, Colonial. $1,200

Rolling pin, Wildflower. $275

Rolling pin, Wildflower, advertises "Compliments of C.N. Allen, Jr.," 8 in. long. $475

Salt crock, Apple Blossom, replaced lid, burst glaze bubble. $75

Salt crock, Butterfly, with lid. $300

Salt crock, Colonial, hanging, lid cracked/glued. $250

Salt crock, Eagle, with lid. $775

Salt crock, Good Luck, hanging, missing lid. $100

Salt crock, Peacock, missing lid, chips. $120

Slop jar, with lid. $900

Soap dish, Cat. $120

Soap dish, Scroll, back advertises "Capitol City Stoneware Co., Indianapolis," mint condition. ...$375

Soap dish, Wildflower. $175

Spittoon, Spongeware, blue bands, imperfections, 5 in. tall, 7 1/2 in. diameter. $120

Wash pitcher & bowl, Basket Weave, gold trim, mint condition. $350

Wash pitcher & bowl, Bowknot, spider hairline in bowl. $375

Wash pitcher & bowl, Bowknot & Rose, stenciled design. $175

Wash pitcher & bowl, Scroll, pitcher only, large size. $150

Water cooler, Apple Blossom, four-gallon, with lid, mint condition. $1,700

Water cooler, Cupid, four-gallon, replaced lid, interior repainted at spigot. $560

Water cooler, Cupid, five-gallon, lid damage, chips, glaze flaw on front. $320

Water cooler, Polar Bear & Elk, four-gallon, one large and one small chip on lid, manufacturer's flaw on base. $650

Water cooler, Rebecca at the Well, six-gallon, cracks. $375

Bottles

Some of the more highly collected types of bottles are listed here.

References: Ralph & Terry Kovel, *Kovels' Bottles Price List*, 11th ed., Three Rivers Press, 1999; John Odell, *Digger Odell's Official Antique Bottle and Glass Collector Magazine Price Guide Series*, Vols. 1 through 8, self-published (1910 Shawhan Rd., Morrow, OH 45152), 1995; Jeff Wichmann, *Antique Western Bitter Bottles*, Pacific Glass Books, 1999; —, *The Best of the West Antique Western Bitters Bottles*, Pacific Glass Books, 1999.

Periodicals: *Antique Bottle and Glass Collector*, PO Box 187, East Greenville, PA 18041; *Canadian Bottle and Stoneware Collector*, 179D Woodridge Crescent, Nepean, Ontario, Canada K2B 7T2.

Collectors' Clubs: Federation of Historical Bottle Collectors, 88 Sweetbriar Branch, Longwood, FL 32750; Midwest Antique Fruit Jar and Bottle Club, PO Box 38, Flat Rock, IN 47234.

Museum: The National Bottle Museum, Ballston Spa, N.Y.

Also See: Flasks

Amber, globular, 24 ribs swirled to the left, Zanesville, Ohio, minor scratches, tiny broken blister, 8 1/2 in. tall. $550

Bitters, Burdock Blood Bitters, Buffalo, N.Y., aqua, partial label, 8 1/2 in. tall. $40

Bitters, "Digestine Bitters, P.J. Bowlin & Son, Sole Proprietors, St. Paul, Minn.," amber, overall design, 8 1/4 in. tall. $300

Bitters, "S.B. Rothenburg, Sole Agent, U.S.," embossed horseshoe, milk glass, 9 1/8 in. tall. $140

Note: *All bride's bottles listings are polychrome enamel decor unless otherwise noted.*

Bride's bottle, clear, flowers on all sides, original pewter collar minus threads, 5 1/4 in. tall, 2 5/8 in. wide by 2 in. deep. $180

Bride's bottle, clear, flowers on all sides, original pewter collar, light residue, 6 1/2 in. tall, 3 1/2 in. wide by 2 1/2 in. deep. $375

Bride's bottle, clear, flowers on all sides, original pewter collar and screw cap, minor paint loss, minor light residue, 5 3/4 in. tall, 2 1/2 in. wide by 1 7/8 in. deep. $180

Bride's bottle, clear, flowers on all sides, original pewter collar with threads, 6 1/4 in. tall, 2 3/4 in. wide by 2 1/4 in. deep. $375

Bride's bottle, clear, flowers on all sides, original pewter collar with threads, minor paint loss, 5 3/4 in. tall, 2 1/2 in. wide by 1 7/8 in. deep. $180

Bride's bottle, clear, two green lovebirds on yellow heart on front, yellow urn and blue flowers on back, flowers and vines on sides and corners, original pewter collar with threads, minor paint loss, light residue, 5 3/4 in. tall, 2 7/8 in. wide by 2 1/4 in. deep. $475

Bride's bottle, clear, peddler on front, flowers on back, original pewter collar, some paint loss, 5 1/4 in. tall, 2 3/4 in. wide by 2 in. deep. **$375**

Bride's bottle, clear, standing lady in blue dress, "Love me as I love you" German inscription on back, flaring lip, 4 5/8 in. tall, 2 5/8 in. wide by 2 in. deep. **$475**

Bride's bottle, clear, standing man in red coat holding cup on front, flowers on sides and back, minor wear, light residue, 6 in. tall, 3 in. wide by 2 5/8 in. deep. **$650**

Bride's bottle, clear, white dove on branch, flowers on sides, original pewter collar with threads, heavy interior stain, minor paint loss, 5 in. tall, 2 5/8 in. wide by 2 1/4 in. deep. **$80**

Bride's bottle, clear, white hare in yellow oval on front, floral decor on sides and back, original pewter collar with threads, two minor paint flakes, 6 3/4 in. tall, 3 in. wide by 2 1/2 in. deep. **$525**

Bride's bottle, fiery opalescent, two blue lovebirds on red heart on front, floral decor on sides and back, flaring lip, minor paint loss, 5 in. tall, 2 5/8 in. wide by 2 1/2 in. deep. **$425**

Bride's bottle, opaque blue (pale), flowers on all sides, pewter collar with protruding threads, minor paint loss, 5 1/2 in. tall, 3 1/8 in. wide by 2 5/8 in. deep. **$475**

Bride's bottle, opaque white, flowers on all sides, original pewter collar and screw-on cap, paint loss to one bloom, 4 3/8 in. tall, 2 1/4 in. wide by 1 3/4 in. deep. **$375**

Bride's bottle, opaque white, standing lady on front, tulip decor on sides and back, original pewter collar and corked pewter stopper, lip flake, light wear to decor, 5 in. tall, 2 1/4 in. wide by 1 3/4 in. deep. **$525**

Bride's bottle, opaque white, tulips on all sides, flaring lip, 5 1/4 in. tall, 3 in. wide by 2 1/2 in. deep. **$275**

Bride's bottle, opaque white, yellow bird on branch above flowers on front, floral decor on sides and back, pewter collar, 5 in. tall, 2 3/4 in. wide by 2 in. deep. **$475**

Bride's bottle, opaque white, two yellow lovebirds on red heart on front, floral decor on sides and back, original pewter collar and screw-on cap, 4 7/8 in. tall, 2 5/8 in. wide by 2 1/4 in. deep. **$525**

Bride's bottle, sapphire blue, two white lovebirds on a green heart, floral decor, retains part of original pewter collar, 5 1/2 in. tall, 2 3/4 in. wide by 2 1/4 in. deep. **$1,100**

Bride's bottle, sapphire blue, flowers on all sides, plain lip, 6 1/2 in. tall, 3 1/4 in. wide by 2 5/8 in. deep. **$650**

Figural, acrobat, clear, probably Italian, female circus acrobat upside-down on ball, early 20th century, 16 1/2 in. tall. **$60**

Figural, black bear, deep olive green, European, late 19th century, 11 in. tall. **$150**

Figural, cabin, "St. Darkes 1860 Plantation X Bitters, Patented 1862," dark amber, circa 1870, 10 in. tall. **$175**

Figural, George Washington bust, yellow-green, bitters, mid/late 20th century, reproduction, 10 in. tall. **$35**

Figural, revolver, golden-amber to yellow-amber, 8 in. long. **$125**

Gin, olive, blown, American, late 18th or early 19th century, wear, 15 1/2 in. tall, 7 1/2 in. square. **$1,100**

Gin, olive-amber, American, early 19th century, flared rim, tapered body, 13 1/2 in. tall. **$325**

Ludlow, bottle green, blown, bubble-filled glass, applied lip, 5 1/8 in. and 5 3/4 in. tall. **$350/pair**

Ludlow, olive-amber, blown, applied lip, minor wear, 8 1/4 in. tall. ... **$250**

Medicine, "Dr. Liebig's German Invigorator, 400 Geary St., S.F.," light yellow-amber, lip flake, 8 1/2 in. tall. **$90**

Medicine, "Dr. Pierce Extract of Smart-Weed, R.V. Pierce, M.D., Buffalo, N.Y.," aqua, 5 in. tall. **$40**

Medicine, "The Great South American Nervine Tonic, Stomach & Liver Cure," clear, shaped like a Warner's Safe Cure bottle, weak embossing, 9 3/4 in. tall. **$120**

Medicine, "Hall's Pulmonary Balsam, J.R. Gates & Co., Proprietors S.F.," rectangular, aqua, 6 1/2 in. tall. **$75**

Medicine, "Indian Cough Syrup, Warm Springs, Oregon," rectangular, clear, 7 7/8 in. tall. . **$60**

Medicine, "Owl Drug Co.," rectangular, one-wing owl, amber, 4 1/2 in. tall. **$85**

Medicine, "Owl Drug Co.," square, one-wing owl, milk glass, 5 in. tall. **$75**

Medicine, "Wm. H. Gregg M.D., New York, Constitution, Life Syrup," plain back for label, gothic arches, aqua, 8 5/8 in. tall. **$75**

Medicine, "Wm. Radams Microbe Killer, Cures All Diseases," shows man hitting skeleton with bat, amber, 10 1/2 in. square. **$250**

Poison, "Melvin & Badger, Apothecaries, Boston, Mass.," irregular hexagon, cobalt, content stain, 5 in. tall. **$80**

Poison, "H.K. Mulford Co., Chemists, Philadelphia," skull/crossbones embossed above "Poison," rectangular with diamond ribbing on all four edges, cobalt, 3 1/4 in. tall. **$125**

Poison, "Owl Drug Co.," two-wing owl on pedestal embossed "T.O.D. Co.," "Poison" on left panel, light cobalt, 6 1/4 in. tall. **$350**

"Poison" on three panels, irregular hexagon shape, moss green, 5 1/2 in. tall. **$220**

Buckets

Buckets were a necessity in rural America, and many specialized bucket forms evolved over the years. Buckets were used to collect, store, and transport all manner of liquids, including milk, water, and sap. Many sugar buckets, the form most people are familiar with, found their way into homes where they were used as sewing baskets or storage containers.

Examples that retain their period paint or that have a manufacturer's mark command premium prices.

Bentwood staves and handle, dark patina, 10 1/4 in. tall, 12 in. diameter. **$275**

Bentwood staves completely cover exterior, swing handle, interior and base in worn red paint, exterior cleaned down to surface, 5 3/8 in. tall, 7 3/4 in. diameter..............**$250**

Miniature, tin, green with yellow stencil, "Linwood Park," bottom embossed with battleship and "Remember the Maine," wire bail, black wooden handle, wear, dents, three small rim splits, 4 in. tall, 6 in. diameter. **$150**

Miniature, wooden, painted, original orange-red, wear and fading, brass bands, turned lid, wire bail handle, minor age cracks, 4 in. tall. **$250**

Painted, blue, pinned handle, 17 in. tall. **$450**

Painted, blue-green, stave and lapped wooden bands, curved swing handle, pegged joinery, 14 1/4 in. tall.............................**$1,200**

Painted, mustard with black stencil "Armours Veribest Mince Meat," stave construction, metal bands, wire bail with wooden handle, top stuck, 11 in. tall, 11 3/8 in. diameter. **$250**

Painted, light gray, bentwood staves and handle, age crack in bottom, 7 1/2 in. tall, 11 in. diameter. **$575**

Painted, yellow, berry bucket......**$250**

Painted, yellow, metal bands, 11 1/2 in. tall..**$75**

Stave constructed, old black repaint, gold line borders, three wide bands with pegged bentwood handle, minor wear and chips, 13 3/4 in. tall, 11 1/4 in. diameter............**$600**

Candle Boxes & Molds

❖ Candle Boxes

A candle box is a hanging wall box in which candles were kept. Originally made of wood, the candle box was introduced in England during the 17th century. The form eventually evolved into tabletop examples, as well as boxes made of other material, such as tin.

Collecting Hint: Most examples were purely functional, and thus the form tends to be rather plain. Look for boxes with unusual designs, such as heart-shaped cutouts. Fancier woods, such as tiger maple, and original painted surfaces also boost value.

Hanging, one-drawer, mahogany, old dark finish, slant-lid top, scalloped crest with arched top, one dovetailed drawer with beaded-edge top, molded base, porcelain pull, brass hinges, one end of drawer repaired, 17 3/4 in. tall, 10 5/8 in. wide by 5 3/4 in. deep. .**$675**

Hanging, mahogany, old finish, slanted hinged lid, scalloped crest, dovetailed case, age cracks, base damaged, 8 1/2 in. tall, 9 1/2 in. wide by 6 3/8 in. deep. **$175**

Hanging, mahogany, old reddish-brown finish, dovetailed, arched back crest, 7 in. tall, 11 7/8 in. wide by 5 3/4 in. deep. **$165**

Hanging, pine, old red paint, three lollipop finials on crest, dovetailed case, chip-carved circle designs and trim across the front, molded base, rose head nails, split backboard, empty nail holes from missing brace, 15 in. tall, 15 3/4 in. wide by 7 in. deep. **$6,600**

Hanging, stenciled, silver and black roses on original dark green, yellow line detail, walnut, arched back with sides tapering down to the front panel, traces of red overpaint, chip on right side, square nails, 7 3/4 in. tall, 14 in. wide by 6 in. deep. **$350**

Candle box or wall shelf with mirror, Country Victorian, walnut turned rosettes applied to pierced scroll back with oval mirror, hinged-lid box, decal on front of box showing ship at sea, circa 1880, original finish, 14 in. wide by 7 in. deep by 26 in. tall. **$300**

Tabletop, pine, refinished, one-board sides, chamfered slide lid, square nails, slight damage along lid channels, 7 5/8 in. high, 20 in. wide by 10 1/2 in. deep. **$250**

Tabletop, tin, cylinder, scalloped crest, raised decorated lines, worn brown japanning, 5 1/2 in. tall, 11 1/4 in. long. **$175**

Tabletop, walnut, original dark finish, sliding lid, dovetailed, divided interior with 1 partition missing, chips, age cracks on lid, 6 in. tall, 18 in. wide by 6 3/4 in. deep. ..**$225**

Tabletop, wooden, decorated, original brown sponging and bands of green leaves, poplar, dovetailed, molded edge on rim, sliding lid with raised panel, found in Ohio, minor edge damage, 4 in. tall, 10 1/2 in. wide by 6 in. deep. **$6,200**

Tabletop, wooden, decorated, original brown ground with flowering tulip in red, white, and light blue with stars and buds beneath, freehand "Rarkus Anna 1869" in red on side, pine, dovetailed, minor edge wear, 6 in. tall, 13 in. wide by 9 in. deep. **$1,100**

Tabletop, wooden, decorated, original dark red paint, lid marked "ALAD 1843" in white relief-carved panel, dovetailed, sliding lid, molded edge around base, pegged, later interior pencil inscription, 4 1/2 in. tall, 14 in. wide by 6 1/2 in. deep. **$1,750**

Tabletop, wooden, decorated, "PMG" and "1874" painted on end, red

Candle box or wall shelf with mirror, country Victorian, walnut turned rosettes applied to pierced scroll back with oval mirror, hinged-lid box, decal on front of box showing ship at sea, circa 1880, original finish, 14 in. wide by 7 in. deep by 26 in. tall. **$300**

ground, softwood, nailed, slide lid with three carved finger notches, wear, 8 in. tall, 13 3/8 in. wide by 11 1/8 in. deep. **$275**

Tabletop, wooden, painted, old black worn paint over blue, hardwood, molded lid, replaced knob and end molding on lid, 4 in. tall, 10 1/4 in. wide by 6 in. deep. **$420**

Tabletop, wooden, painted green, slide lid, 3 in. tall, 12 in. wide by 4 in. deep. **$250**

Tabletop, wooden, painted old red, pine, sliding lid, tab handle, worn, 8 in. long (excluding handle). **$450**

❖ Candle Molds

During the 19th century, candle molds made it possible for families to make inexpensive candles at home. Tin molds were the most affordable, with examples having from one to 50 tubes. Candle molds were also made of iron, pewter, and redware. The latter are often found in wooden holders and tend to be more valuable.

Reproduction Alert

New tin candle molds have been made for years.

Tin, three-tube, round top and base, 6 1/4 in. tall............................**$250**

Tin, four-tube, two rows of two, 11 in. tall. **$100**

Tin, six-tube, two rows of three, oblong, rust, seam break, 10 1/8 in. tall.......................................**$75**

Tin, eight-tube, two rows of four, curved feet, ear handle, 11 in. tall. **$400**

Tin, 12-tube, unusual placement, four conical feet, 10 3/4 in. tall. **$375**

Tin, 12-tube, two rows of six, rectangular, significant rust, 10 3/4 in. tall....................................**$130**

Tin, 12-tube, round, two ear handles, some rust, 11 1/2 in. tall, 9 in. diameter. **$575**

Tin, 16-tube, four rows of four, rectangular, wear, dents, rust, 10 5/8 in. tall...............................**$170**

Tin, 24-tube, four rows of six, oblong, 10 3/4 in. tall..........................**$325**

Tin, 24-tube, four rows of six, rectangular, dents, significant rust, 10 3/4 in. tall..........................**$175**

Wooden frame, 12-tube, three rows of four, pine frame, pewter tubes, old refinish, high feet, scalloped ends, age cracks, 17 1/4 in. tall, 15 in. wide by 8 5/8 in. deep. **$750**

Wooden frame, 36-tube, four rows of nine, walnut frame, tin tubes, old finish, bootjack ends, square nails, 12 3/4 in. tall, 16 in. wide by 7 3/4 in. deep. **$900**

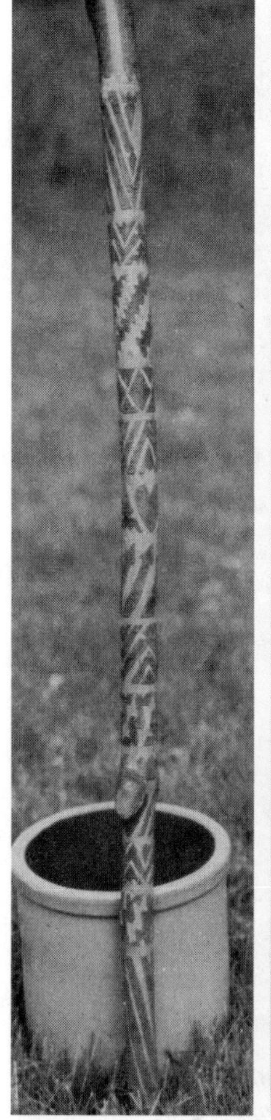

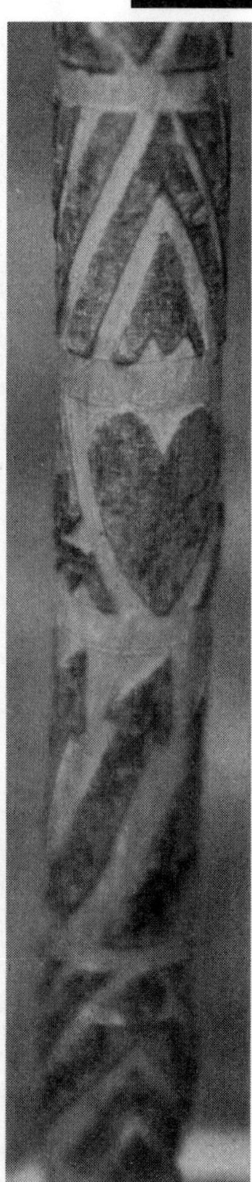

Adirondack cane with bark-carved decorations in geometric patterns, hearts, arrows, circa 1930s, minor handling wear, 37 in. long. **$300-$400**

❖ Canes/ Walking Sticks

Though many country-made canes and walking sticks (the terms can be used interchangeably) were simply props to help the infirm and elderly, their styles evolved from the purely functional to become personal expressions of the owner's imagination and skill.

Where the cane of the urbanite might have a large gold or silver knob, canes made by rural carvers usually had an element of whimsy, with the decoration following the growth of the branch or trunk.

Other canes incorporated horn, bone, leather, and even glass (the last made as an example of the maker's skill, not used for support).

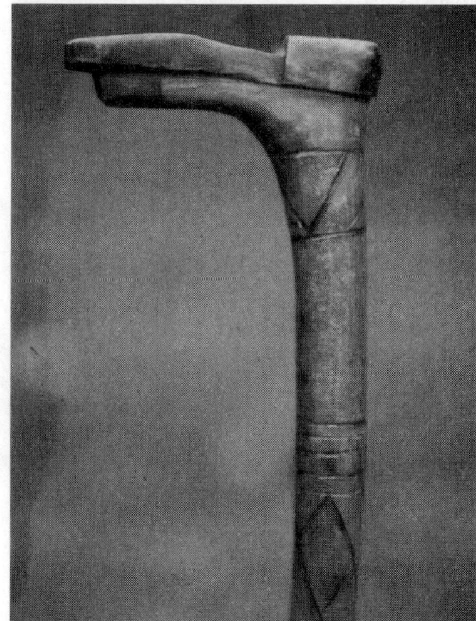

Carved cane with handle in the form of a thick-soled boot, black decoration on handle and geometric patterns on shaft, minor handling wear, circa 1930s, 34 in. long. **$150-$200**

Cane with carved and painted (red, white, and black) shaft in the form of an Indian face with feathered headdress, shaft decorated with shallow vine and geometric carvings, bark on handle, probably Penobscot origin, circa 1920s, minor handling wear, 37 in. long. Detail at right. **$300-$400**

Cane with carved shaft in the form of climbing lizards and crosshatched decoration, original light varnished surface, early to mid-20th century, 36 in. long. **$200-$300**

Two views of cane made of round and molded leather rings on a metal shaft, with bone inlay near handle, one side having initials "EJH" and a shamrock, the other dated "1919," possibly of prison make, with worn surface that has been treated with saddle soap, 38 in. long. **$300-$400**

Cane carved with entwined snakes and crosshatched decoration, burnt-wood details and faceted balls, possibly Mexican, early to mid-20th century, 38 in. long. **$200-$250**

Cane with round knob handle, large scoop carving along shaft and shallow line carving in geometric patterns, original varnished surface, ferrule is a thimble, circa 1940s, moderate handling wear, 36 in. long. **$70-$100**

Large cane with straight round shaft and applied carved handle, original varnished surface, minor handling wear, 41 in. by 7 in. **$40-$60**

Cane with crook handle, worn black painted surface, applied bone detail on handle on which is engraved, "D. Grover from B. Wilhelm ~ Sep. 12, '84," 35 in. long. Detail at right. **$100-$125**

Carved cane, diamond willow, with irregular carved pointed ovals at center of shaft and near tip, light varnished finish, minor handling wear, circa 1930s, 35 in. long, 6 in. at widest point. **$150-$250**

Cane made from a pool cue, applied T handle, remnants of ochre paint, circa 1930s, 34 in. long. **$60-$80**

Cane with round faceted shaft and handle made from the bakelite knob off a steering wheel attached with a length of copper pipe on which is hammered "WENCK," original varnished surface, minor wear, 36 in. long. **$100-$125**

Cane, circa 1910, carved in the form of a man with mustache, wearing a top hat, eyes made of tiny inset shells, shaft decorated with bands of brass tacks, light varnished surface with rich patina from handling, 37 in. long. **$500-$600**

Cane, circa 1920, the shaft carved in the form of regularly spaced curved oval disks of decreasing size from top to bottom, original painted surface in red, white, and blue, attached curving handle, significant handling wear and grime, overall excellent condition, 36 in. long. **$800-$1,200**

Three views of walking stick, with carved and painted decoration, including handle in the form of an open-mouth snake, shaft carved with coral snake, turtle, totem-like face and bare-breasted mermaid; metal tip, minor handling wear, circa 1940s, 37 in. long **$450-$550**

Walking stick with knob handle and three rings carved free of shaft, which tapers in a square notch-carved pattern, tip is a brass shell casing, rural Illinois origin, circa 1900, minor handling wear, 38 in. long. Detail at right. **$400-$500**

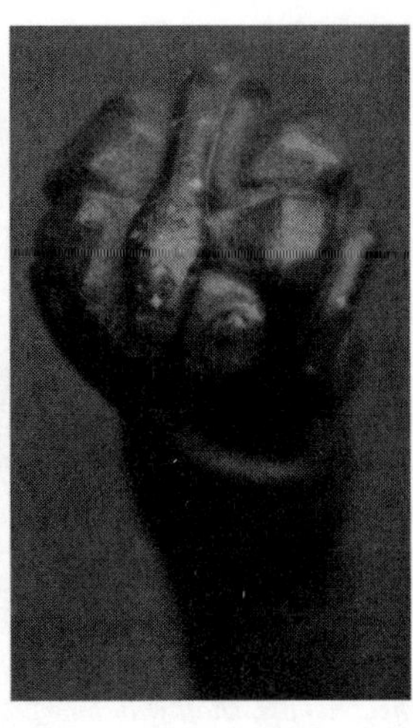

Walking stick with shaft carved in large spirals, attached knob handle carved in the form of a snake on a tree stump, circa 1900, light varnished surface, 34 in. long. Detail at right. **$175-$250**

Walking stick, carved from diamond willow, the shaft having raised pointed oval decorations, bulbous handle above brass collar, dark varnished surface, handling wear, 36 1/2 in. long. **$100-$150**

Two views of walking stick with handle carved in the form of a clenched fist, square tapering shaft with beveled corners, original black-painted surface, Southern origin, minor handling wear, 36 in. long, handle 3 in. across. **$350-$450**

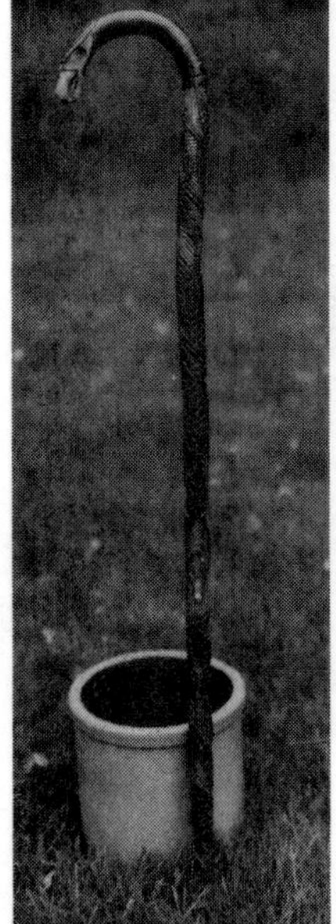

Walking stick with shaft carved in shallow floral and geometric patterns, handle carved in the form of an eagle's head with open beak, circa 1910, light varnished surface, 37 in. long. Detail above. **$400-$500**

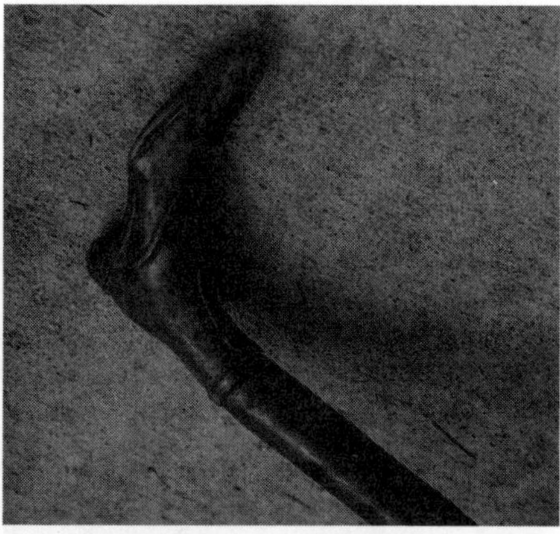
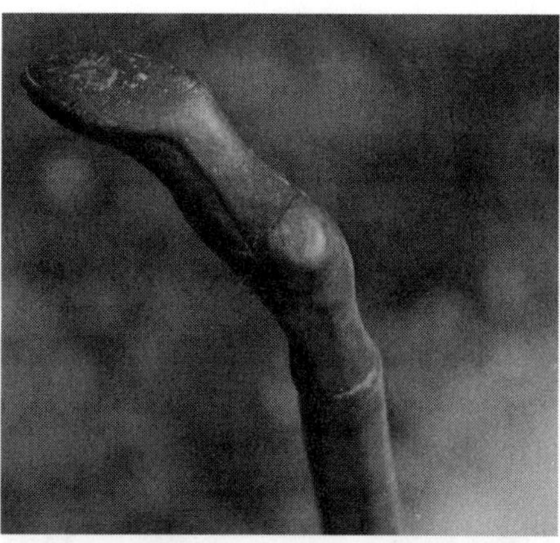

Two views of walking stick with handle carved in the form of a high-top woman's shoe with sole and heel details, shaft with burnt decoration, circa 1920, minor handling wear, 33 in. long. **$200-$300**

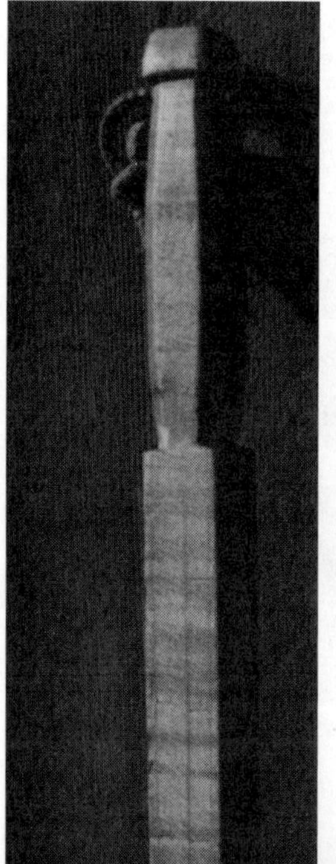

Walking stick made of curly or tiger maple, square tapering shaft with strong graining showing the full length, straight carved handle pierced for leather cord, minor handling wear, 37 in. long. **$100-$200**

Two views of walking stick with large, simplistically carved head of a man, shaft unadorned, minor handling wear, early 20th century, 36 in. long. **$100-$200**

Walking stick made of round tapering disks of walnut on a metal rod, rounded L-shaped handle, significant handling wear, circa 1920, 36 in. long. **$150-$200**

Walking stick carved from diamond willow, with carved pointed ovals painted gold on a black-painted shaft, knob handle, circa 1920, minor handling wear, 37 in. long. **$125-$175**

Walking stick with tapering faceted shaft made of maple and cherry segments on a metal rod, bulbous handle, original crazed varnished surface, metal ferrule, circa 1930s, 34 in. long. **$150-$200**

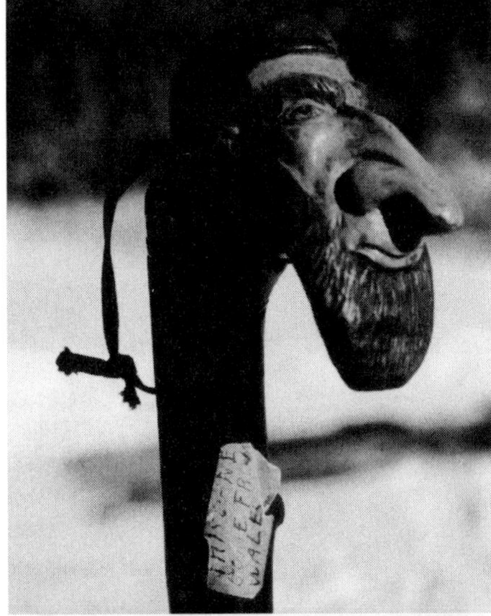

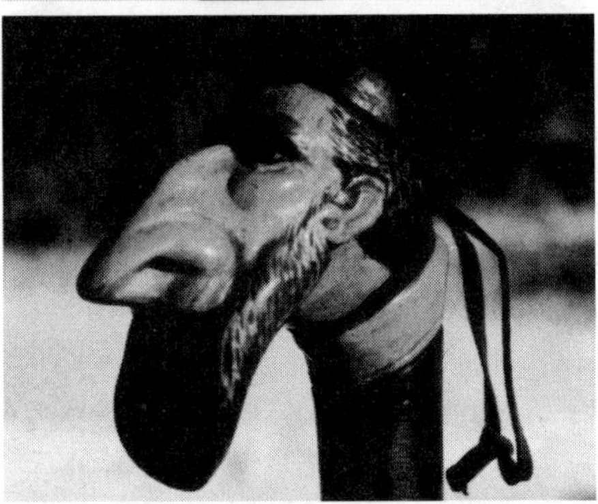

Two views of walking stick with carved and painted face of a bearded man with a large nose, probably an anti-Semitic cane since the man is wearing a close-fitting round cap (yarmulke), varnished shaft bears a label reading, "This cane came from Wales," black ribbon tied around handle probably for display, circa 1900, 35 in. long, minor wear to shaft and handle. **$1,500-$2,000**

Walking stick, originally a piece of lath, carved in the form of a pierced abstract figure painted gold on top, spiral carved shaft above pierced circle and diamond with X hole, remnants of white paint on bottom, circa 1950, 38 in. long. **$80-$120**

Walking stick, circa 1900, walnut with tight spiral-carved shaft and deer antler handle, original varnish surface, minor handling wear, 36 in. long. **$300-$400**

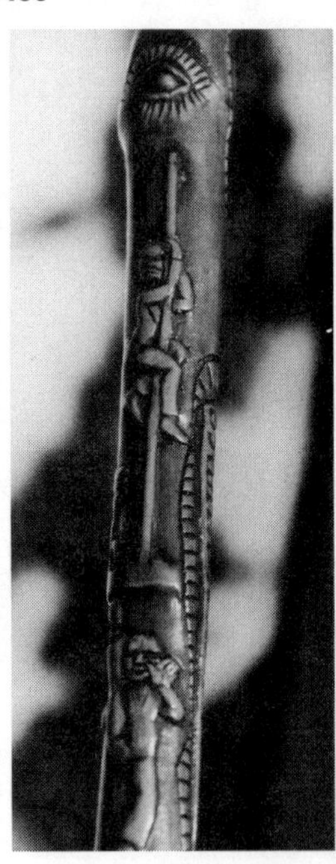

Four views of presentation walking stick carved by George W.B. McKnight (1839-1906) of Columbus, Ga., and given to James Anderson, Grand Master of the Columbus Oddfellows Lodge, dated Aug. 19, 1891; handle finely carved in the form of a hand holding the three links of Oddfellowship, and shaft carved with scenes from lodge initiation rites, and Anderson's name and title; original varnished surface, minor handling wear, overall excellent condition, 36 in. long. **$6,000-$7,000**

Masonic walking stick, circa 1880, with handle carved in the form of a two-headed eagle and the name "Hottinger," shaft carved with detailed Masonic emblems, including Mason in apron holding a hammer and staff, with a trowel at his feet, original varnished surface, near mint, 37 in. long, with several views of details. **$8,000-$10,000**

Walking stick, circa 1930, probably maple, with top of shaft finely carved in the form of a grasshopper sitting on a trumpet vine, light varnished surface, minor handling wear, 37 in. long. **$400-$500**

❖ Cast Iron

Cast iron was first made in the 18th century. As a result of its high carbon content, it is more apt to break under stress than is wrought iron. Articles formed from cast iron are made in molds and don't require the laborious, time-intensive effort that goes into producing wrought iron.

Collectors' Clubs: Cast Iron Seat Collectors Association, RR 2, Box 38, Le Center, MN 56057; Cast Iron Collectors, Southern Chapter, PO Box 355, Swainsboro, GA 30401; Cast Iron Toy Collectors of America, 1340 Market St., Long Beach, CA 90805; Griswold & Cast Iron Cookware Association, PO Drawer B, Perrysburg, NY 14129-0301.

Architectural ornament, clasped hands, bird and banner with "LOTM," flat relief casting, weathered red, black, and silver paint, worn, 6 in. tall. **$350**

Eagle, cast in two sections with hollow body, detailed feathers with wings spread and perched on a rock, late green paint, two mounting brackets on base, 13 1/2 in. tall by 30 1/4 in. wide by 10 in. deep. **$375**

Eagle finial, spread wings, gold repaint, 9 in. tall by 15 1/4 in. wide. **$175**

Grill, Horace Greeley, Campbell Foundry Co., Harrison, N.J., 19th century, fan-shaped grill with grease reservoir, three legs, 3 1/4 in. tall by 25 in. wide by 16 3/4 in. long. **$250**

Gate, rectangular openwork form centering a War of 1812 cap surrounded by military trophies including crossed rifles, swords, bugle, and shot bag marked "U.S.," and acorn leaves, flanked on each side by crossed darts and above and below by a band of circles, the top set with stars flanked by spear points, repainted in green, red, black, and white, American, late 19th century, 77 in. long, 45 1/4 in. tall. **$5,875**
Courtesy Christie's, New York, N.Y.

Far left and right: Andirons in the form of an African-American man standing with hands on bent knees, early paint with white shirt, red pants, black skin and painted facial features, paint imperfections, minor corrosions, circa 1870, 12 1/2 in. by 16 1/2 in., 19 1/2 in. tall, **$1,380/pair;** *center: Hitching post finial in the form of a stylized head of an African-American man holding a ring and chain in his mouth, 19th century, later stand, 5 1/2 in. by 6 in., 9 1/2 in. tall,* ***$2,300***
Courtesy Skinner Inc., Bolton, Mass.

Where can I find them?

Country Comfort Antiques
Third and Main Streets
Winona, MN 55987
(507) 452-7044

Mark F. Moran Antiques
5887 Meadow Dr. SE
Rochester, MN 55904
(507) 288-8006
mfmoran@charter.net

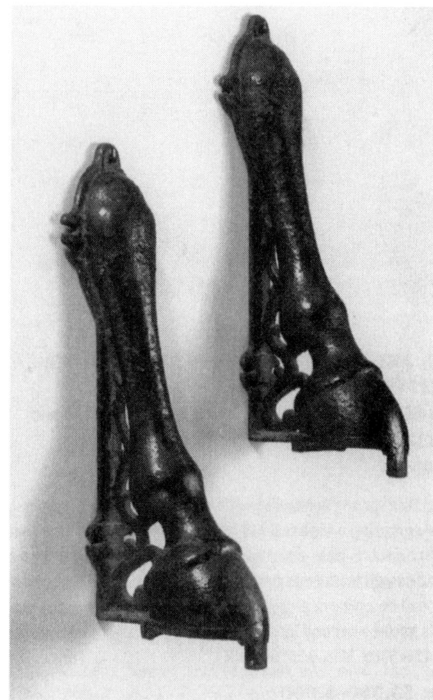

Carriage fenders, articulated horse hoof and ankle cast in the full round and backed by an L-shaped bracket and scrollwork, marked on sides with maker's name and address, painted black, William Adams & Co., Philadelphia, late 19th century, 6 in. by 10 in., 25 in. tall. **$2,585/pair**
Courtesy Christie's, New York, N.Y.

Gate weight, modeled as a full sun face, loop handle at top, Massachusetts, late 18th century, with stand, 9 in. deep. **$10,925**
Courtesy Skinner Inc., Bolton, Mass.

Top row, left to right: Model of a cat head, large stylized head with long whiskers, mounting holes in ears and nose, patinated, late 19th century, with stand, 8 in. by 8 in., **$1,495***; wrought iron model of a standing horse, silhouetted sheet on a rectangular stand, old pitted surface, possibly New York state, 19th century, 9 1/2 in. long, 8 3/4 in. tall, $978; architectural fragment, large, slightly curved plaque cast in bold relief with a lion head, old weathered surface, American, late 19th century, with stand, 1 in. by 11 in., 15 in. tall, $1,725. Front row, left to right: Model of a spread-winged eagle perched on a rock-work base, old black paint with white spots, American, late 19th century, 5 1/2 in. by 11 in., 3 1/2 in. tall, $242; doorstop in the form of a fat seated bear, open legs, painted brown, American, late 19th/early 20th century, 2 1/2 in. by 5 1/4 in., 4 1/2 in. tall,* **$1,150**
Courtesy Skinner Inc., Bolton, Mass.

Mirror, table model, the oval mirror swiveling on a frame cast with flags beneath a crown, oak leaves and acorns, set on two suits of armor raised on a base pierced with a military trophy and shield form feet, cold-painted, mid-19th century, 19 3/4 in. tall. **$800-$900**
Courtesy Sotheby's, New York, N.Y.

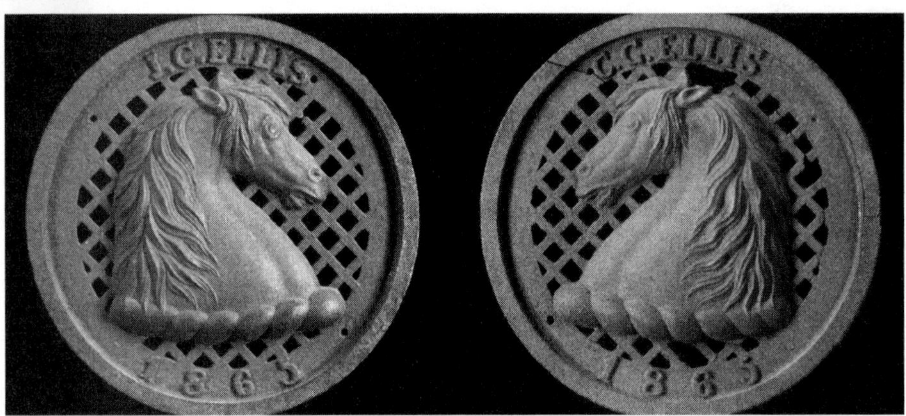

Stable vents, circular pierced form centering a relief-molded profile horse head above a torso on lattice ground enclosed by a roundel, one cast with "C.G. Ellis-1865," the other "J.C. Ellis-1865," probably J.W. Fiske & Co., New York, New York, circa 1865, 18 in. deep. **$1,998/pair**
Courtesy Christie's, New York, N.Y.

Wall plaques, half-round model of a fruit-filled cornucopia, the horn painted bright red with yellow trim, the fruits in red, green, and black, American, early 20th century, 15 in. long. **$225/pair**
Courtesy Christie's, New York, N.Y.

Stove plate, rectangular form, the top with two arched reserves separated with spiral columns, one side with a man on horseback, the other with an urn of vining flowers, embossed wording "Shfarwell Furnace in Oly-Dieter Weiker," Friedensburg, Bucks County, Pa., 19 in. by 22 in. **$605**
Courtesy Alderfer Auction Co., Hatfield, Pa.

Trade signs, a standing figure of a Native American princess cast in the full round, articulated hair, facial features, fringed clothing and shoes, applied green-painted hair ornament and tobacco leaf held in right hand, on a rocky base, remnants of brown paint, American, late 19th century, 7 1/2 in. by 7 1/2 in., 25 in. tall. **$11,163/pair**
Courtesy Christie's, New York, N.Y.

Umbrella stand, figural, a standing sailor holding a coiling rope support and resting atop crossed oars, anchor and various other nautical items, oblong low shallow drip pan base with acanthus leaf cast border, removable pan, marked "1927 Marcy Foundry Co.," repainted, 27 1/2 in. tall. **$2,750-$3,000**
Courtesy Skinner Inc., Bolton, Mass.

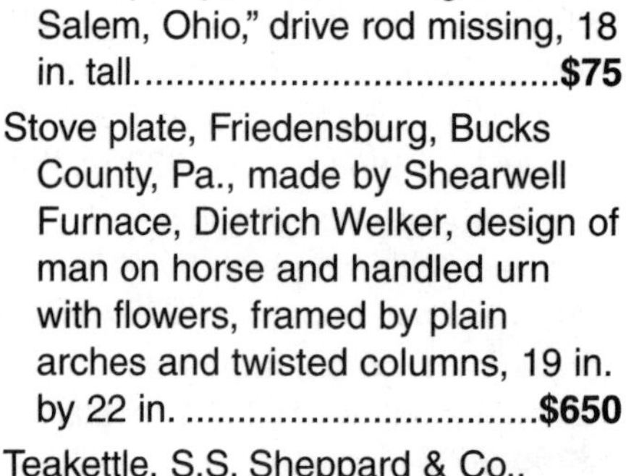

Muffin tin, hearts motif (eight). ...**$120**

Pitcher pump, "The Deming Co., Salem, Ohio," drive rod missing, 18 in. tall.......................................**$75**

Stove plate, Friedensburg, Bucks County, Pa., made by Shearwell Furnace, Dietrich Welker, design of man on horse and handled urn with flowers, framed by plain arches and twisted columns, 19 in. by 22 in. **$650**

Teakettle, S.S. Sheppard & Co., Philadelphia, flared sides, rounded shoulder curved spout, arched handle, late 19th century, marked "6 Qt," wear, rust, 7 1/4 in. tall, 8 in. diameter. **$150**

Umbrella holder, platform base, removable pan, ornate back plate with openwork columns and scrolling, relief squirrel on center medallion, dark green repaint, 33 1/2 in. tall by 18 1/2 in. wide. ..**$475**

Vegetable dish, open, oval, slightly flared sides, minor rust, 2 3/8 in. tall by 11 in. wide by 8 1/4 in. deep. **$120**

Left to right: Watch hutch, an upright scroll-cast frame with a round opening resting on a base cast with further leafy scrolling surrounding a spread-winged eagle, traces of black paint, light rust, 19th century, 10 1/4 in. tall, ***$800-$1,000****; card tray, a standing figure of a blackamoor holding a shallow basket-form tray, atop a stepped rectangular base, base with advertising for The Hoefinchoff & Lane Foundry Co., Cincinnati, Ohio, 1875-1903, old black, gold, silver, and red paint, 9 in. tall,* **$550-$600**

Courtesy Garth's Auctions, Delaware, Ohio.

Water trough, rectangular, a high arched back splash plate with the maker's name along the base and a small cast lion mask spout over a grilled overflow drain in the base, the main drain stopped with an iron plug, the whole set on a bracket base, J.W. Fiske & Co., New York, N.Y., late 19th century, 24 in. by 35 1/2 in., 38 in. tall. **$1,293**

Courtesy Christie's, New York, N.Y.

❖ Chalkware

Chalkware, a substance used by sculptors to imitate marble and also to harden plaster of Paris, was developed by English inventor William Hutchinson in 1848. Vendors sold early chalkware items, which were inexpensive and colorful and which were often copies of popular Staffordshire pieces.

Reproduction Alert

Don't confuse 19th century examples with 20th century chalkware that often served as carnival prizes.

Bank, roly-poly form, man with hands behind his back, nose chip, 8 in. tall. ....**$150-$175**

Bird on plinth, worn original black and goldenrod paint, 6 1/2 in. tall. ....**$800-$900**

Canary on square pedestal base with ball top, yellow with red, black, and brown accenting, worn paint, broken/glued, 6 1/8 in. tall. ....**$150-$200**

Cat, seated, worn original red, black, and yellow paint, wear and edge damage, 5 1/8 in. tall. ....**$350-$400**

Cat bank, reclining, with mouse in mouth, green polychrome body, red bow, brown highlights, base chips, 6 in. by 7 3/4 in. ....$200-$250

Deer, reclining, red, ochre, brown, and black paint, 19th century, repair, paint wear, 5 3/4 in. by 10 in. ....$450-$500/pair

Dog, painted collar, mouth, nose, and accents, 10 in. tall.........**$500-$550**

Dog, seated, molded detail, worn original red, black, and yellow paint, wear and base chips, hole between the legs, 5 3/4 in. tall. ....**$350-$400**

Dog, standing pug, painted collar and details, 10 in. long.........**$350-$400**

Dog, standing setter (?), traces of original paint, hollow examples are usually earlier than the solid ones, some wear to the features. **$350**

Doves, traces of paint on eyes, cast pewter feet, one with beak worn down, one with two toes broken off, 5 3/4 in. by 8 1/4 in.**$250-$300/pair**

Flowers and fruit in vase, and fruit arrangement in an urn, yellow, red, green, and tan paint, minor paint loss, 12 in. tall. .**$1,800-$2,000/pair**

Fruit, in footed urn, mantle ornament, red, yellow, green, and tan paint, repair, 16 in. tall. ......**$2,000-$2,200**

Fruit in urn, mantle ornament, orange, green, red, black, and yellow, minor touch-ups, chips, 8 in. and 11 1/4 in. tall. ....**$1,400-$1,500/pair**

Girl, white pantaloons, yellow dress with red stripes, matching hat, 9 1/2 in. tall. ....**$1,100-$1,200**

Lovebirds, kissing pair on pedestal, yellow bodies, red breasts, green wings, wear, one wing repaired, 5 1/4 in. tall. ....**$150-$200**

Parrot on plinth, very worn yellow, green, black, and red paint, stains on base, 7 1/8 in. tall. ....**$50-$60**

Poodle, old black repaint, red base and tail, roughness around base, 7 5/8 in. by 5 3/4 in. ....**$300-$350**

Rabbit, seated, worn original red, yellow, and black paint, 5 1/4 in. tall. ....**$500-$600**

Rooster, red, green, and black original paint, worn, 5 1/2 in. tall..... **$350-$400**

Rooster, red, mustard, black, and green paint, worn........**$900-$1,000**

Squirrel, chewing on nut in front paws, gray wash, tail with red details, 7 1/8 in. tall........**$400-$450**

Calendar shelf or mantel, Ithaca (New York) Calendar Clock Co., "No. 10 Farmer's Model," rectangular walnut case with stepped pediment and base, white dials, Roman numerals on clock face, Arabic on calendar face; top may be later addition, circa 1880, 24 in. tall. **$600-$700**

Clocks

The earliest domestic clocks were driven by weights and were of the hanging variety in order to provide enough room beneath the mechanism for the fall of the weights. Clocks driven by springs were perfected around 1525 and resulted in a much more compact piece. With the introduction of the pendulum as a regulator in the mid-17th century, the tall case clock was created. Originally, the tall-case clock was designed to protect the weights from outside interference, but it quickly gained importance as a decorative piece of furniture as well. Ultimately, shelf and mantel clocks became popular because they were less expensive and more convenient to display.

Reference: Kyle Husfloen/Mark Moran, *Antique Trader Clocks Price Guide*, Krause Publications, 2003.

Banjo, mahogany case, brass trim and façade, old gold repaint, brass works, painted steel face marked "A. Willard Jr., Boston," old replacement reverse-painted glass panels, bottom pan shows ship with American flag, eagle finial, with weight and pendulum, case has damage and loose seams, 33 in. tall...........**$1,200**

Banjo, by John Sawin, Boston, with a gilt metal eagle finial above the round bezel enclosing the signed dial with Roman numerals, tapering waist section with reverse-painted glass having patriotic motifs; bottom section with reverse-painted glass showing warships, eagle, and shield; eight-day time only, circa 1820, 31 in. tall. ....**$2,400-$2,600**

Grandfather, Federal style, cherry case, scroll-carved crest, glazed door flanked by free-standing

Grandfather, Federal style, mahogany, with molded pediment and pierced crest, three cast brass ball finials, arched glass door, painted face with rose decoration, Roman numerals for house, Arabic numerals at increments of 5 minutes, subsidiary seconds dial, straight case with quarter-round colonettes flanking long door, base section on bracket feet, eight-day time and strike, original pendulum and tin can weights, probably New Hampshire, circa 1820, 90 in. tall. **$8,000-$9,000**

Grandfather, by Krause (John J.), Northampton, Pa., Federal style, cherry case, swan's neck broken pediment with carved rosettes, glazed tombstone door over white enamel dial, Arabic numerals, signed on the face, "John Krause–Northampton," with flowers and fruit in painted spandrels, racetrack inlay on long door, short French feet, 30-day movement, old possibly original surface, circa 1810, 83 1/2 in. tall. **$4,500-$5,500**

colonettes, white painted dial with Roman numerals and moon phase, quarter-round columns flanking long door, step-out base with banded inlay and shaped apron, circa 1810, 86 in. tall. ***$3,000-$3,500***

Grandfather, cherry with figured mahogany veneer cross-banding, mellow finish, cutout feet, scrolled apron, chamfered corners, cove molding between sections, bonnet with freestanding columns, arched pediment with goose necks, turned finials, brass works stamped "J.E. Stretcher" (John Stretcher, worked 1828-1829, Cincinnati and Hillsboro, Ohio), second hand, calendar movement, painted metal face with polychrome flowers in crest, shells in spandrels, with pendulum, weights and keys, touchups to face, 94 in. tall. .**$6,500**

Grandfather, cherry, old finish, signed "Read & Watson," scalloped base, high feet, molded waist, tombstone door with beaded trim, dovetailed hood with freestanding pillars and broken arch top, wooden works, original painted Masonic decor on face, with weights and pendulum, restorations to works and bonnet, 90 1/2 in. tall........................**$2,750**

Grandfather, decor, pine, original reddish-brown vinegar grained paint, face in original painted decor with gilded spandrels and crest with red swag in the arch, signed "L. Watson, Cincinnati," cutout feet, scalloped apron, molded waist, reeded quarter columns with brass trim, bonnet with freestanding reeded columns, molded and curved cornice with fretwork, three brass finials, few areas of touchup, one finial replaced, Ohio, 91 in. tall. **$27,500**

Grandfather, decor, walnut, old dark transparent graining, ebonized moldings, gilded detail and date "1781," period case, painted detail probably Centennial, engraved "Adam Brant, New Hanover" (Montgomery County, Pa., died 1804), ogee feet, fluted quarter columns, moldings between sections, tombstone detail on door, dovetailed bonnet with freestanding columns and arched door, molded cornice with high goosenecks and turned gilded ornaments in crest and spandrels, calendar movement, second hand, phases of the moon dial, minor repairs, old replaced feet, finial missing, 94 1/2 in. tall................................**$17,000**

Grandfather, hardwood with some figure, country style, bracket feet, overlapping door with tombstone arch, bonnet with freestanding front columns, arched cornice, brass works, engraved face with old repaint, marked "Edward Spalding, Providence" (R.I.), face mismatched with works, replaced feet, replaced finials, refinished, 84 in. tall..................................**$3,500**

Grandfather, walnut, dark original finish, "Wilson" engraved signature on the back of works (possibly William Wilson, Newton, Pa.), ogee feet, inset panel in base, cove moldings between sections, overlapping door with scalloped top corners, dovetailed bonnet, freestanding turned columns, arched door and molded cornice with gooseneck pediment with brass rosettes and turned flame finial, brass works with second hand and calendar movement, painted iron face with pheasant crest and rose spandrels, with weights and pendulum, minor restorations, 97 in. tall..........**$7,500**

Pillar and scroll, Ephraim Downes, mahogany veneer, old finish, wooden works, painted wooden face, paper label "Ephraim Downes for George Mitchell, Bristol, Conn.," reverse painting on bottom glass, probably an old replacement with some flaking and old touchup repair, with weights and pendulum, minor repairs, replaced finials, 31 1/4 in. tall............................**$2,500**

Pillar and scroll, Mark Leavenworth, mahogany veneer, old finish, wooden works, painted wooden face, paper label "Improved Clocks Made and Sold by Mark Leavenworth, Waterbury, Connecticut," with weights and pendulum, repairs to case, replaced feet, very worn reverse painting, mismatched finials, 30 1/2 in. tall..................................**$1,000**

Pillar and scroll, Eli Terry & Sons, mahogany veneer, refinished, high bracket feet, scalloped apron, original paper label, worn reverse painting on lower part of door, freestanding pillars, arched crest,

Shelf or mantel, Atkins & Downs for George Mitchell, Bristol, Conn., double deck mahogany case with carved eagle crest and ring-knob finials, two-pane door with white painted dial, Arabic numerals and gold-painted spandrels and center ring, lower section with replaced mirror, door flanked by stenciled columns, carved paw feet, eight-day time and strike movement, eagle repaired, label possibly a replacement, stenciling touched up, replacement hands, circa 1830, 39 1/2 in. tall. **$1,300-$1,400**

Shelf or mantel, Birge & Fuller, Bristol, Conn., double steeple model, mahogany veneer, three-quarter round columns with conical peaks, two-pane door, the upper pane over repainted dial with Roman numerals and open escapement, lower pane reverse painted with stylized leaves, bottom door pane reverse painted with wreath, eight-day wagon spring time and strike, signed movement, some veneer loss, label not legible, circa 1850, 27 1/2 in. tall. **$3,000-$4,000**

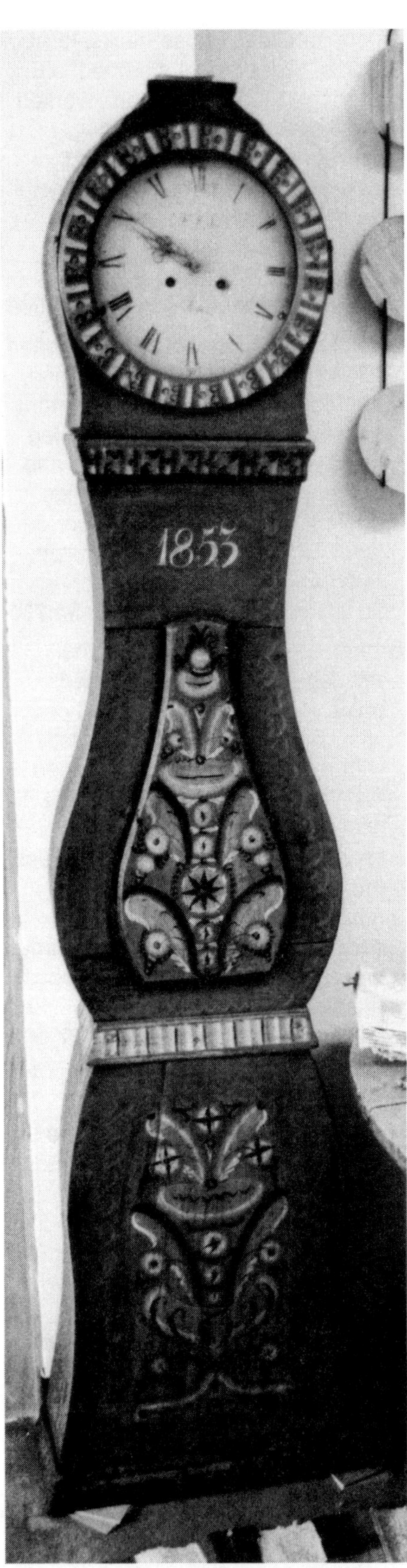

Tall case, pine, known as a Mora clock for the primary clock-making region of Sweden and distinguished by the rounded center section, dated 1853 and vividly painted in deep salmon red, black, green, and beige in stylized floral motif, 78 in. by 21 1/2 in. by 8 in. **$3,800**

Tall case, Scandinavian, pine, dated 1780 but possibly earlier, vividly grain painted in black and dark green, with roses painted on the door, 84 in. by 16 1/2 in. by 12 in. **$2,800**

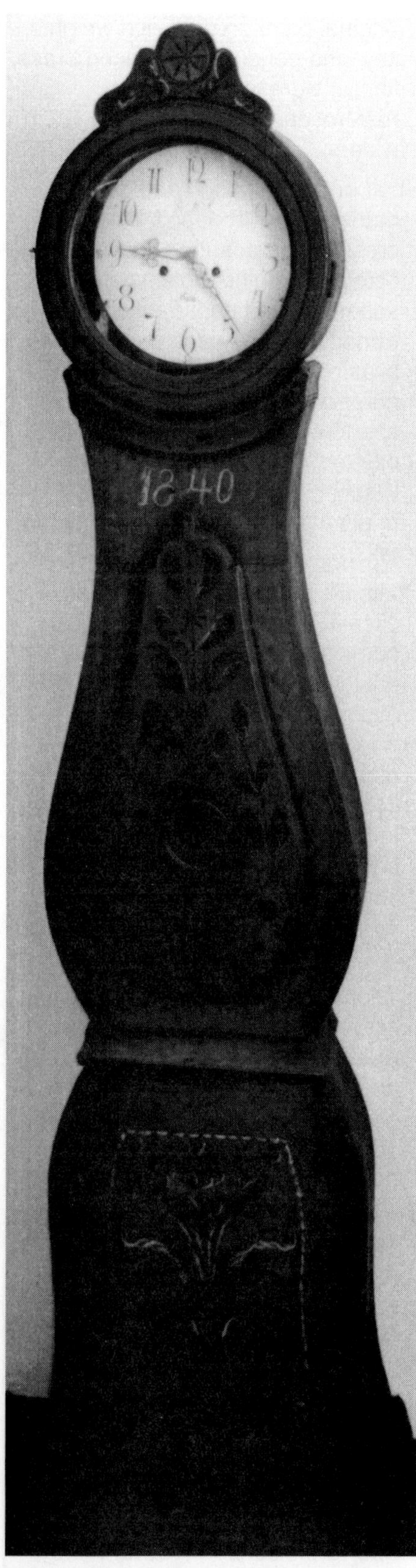

Tall case, pine, known as a Mora clock for the primary clock-making region of Sweden and distinguished by the rounded center section, dated 1840, with carved crest and painted in dark rusty red, green, and beige in stylized floral motif, 79 in. by 22 3/4 in. by 8 1/2 in. **$2,500-$3,000**

Tall case, pine, from Halsingland, Sweden, circa 1800, exuberantly sponge-painted in blue, rust, and yellow, with hooded top and carved panel in the base, 91 in. by 23 in. by 10 in. **$4,500**

Tall case, pine, known as a Mora clock for the primary clock-making region of Sweden and distinguished by the rounded center section, dated 1854, with carved crest and door, and grain painted in dark rusty red, green, and yellow, 84 in. by 20 1/2 in. by 8 1/2 in. **$5,800**

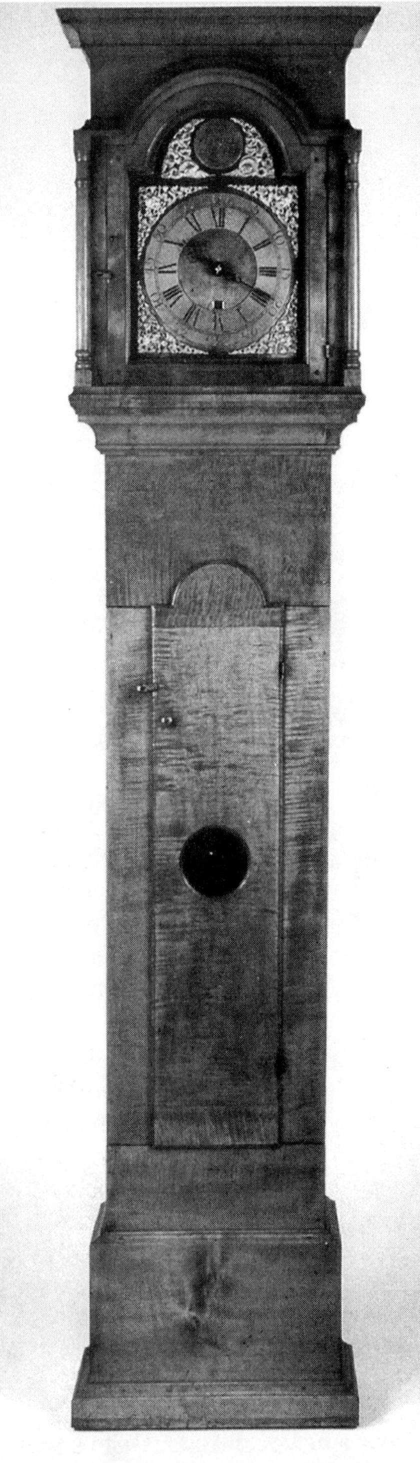

Tall case, Isaac Blasdel, Chester, N.H. (1738-1791), curly maple, hood with flat molded cornice above tombstone arch and glazed door flanked by full standing columns, brass dial, engraved "Isaac Blasdel, Chester," cast pewter spandrels framing the engraved chapter ring and calendar aperture, pull-up posted frame single-weight movement, waist with thumb-molded tombstone door with glazed opening, on molded stepped base, refinished, minor imperfections, 85 in. tall. **$25,000**
Photo courtesy Skinner Auctioneers & Appraisers of Antiques & Fine Arts, Boston and Bolton, Mass.

Tall case, cherry and curly maple, refinished, high bracket feet, scalloped apron, chamfered case corners, inset panels on base and door with applied burl band inlay, dovetailed hood with turned pilasters, bonnet top, wag-on-the-wall works with key and pendulum, repair to one gooseneck, 96 in. tall, (pen-and-ink note inside door: clock purchased from Frank Boutelle near Goshen, Ohio, in 1889, signed by Frank G. Fisher, Milford, Ohio, 1925).
$6,200
Photo courtesy Skinner Auctioneers & Appraisers of Antiques & Fine Arts, Boston and Bolton, Mass.

original paint on dial, with weights, key, and pendulum, replaced brass finials, worn, professional restorations, 32 in. tall by 16 1/2 in. wide.................................... **$1,500**

Shelf or mantel, double deck style, mahogany, with deeply carved crest having acanthus leaves, S-scrolls, and pineapple finials, square glazed door flanked by turned reeded and leaf-carved pilasters, white dial with Roman numerals and gilt-painted spandrels, lower door with reverse-painted image of George Washington, carved paw feet, original finish, circa 1830-40, 36 in. tall. .... **$1,000-$1,200**

Shelf, Eli Terry, Plymouth, Conn., circa 1817-1819, mahogany, flat cornice above glazed door enclosing painted and gilt wooden dial and 30-hour wooden weight-driven movement with outside escapement, flanking freestanding columns, lower section with farmstead painting, flat molded base, engraved label, old finish, imperfections, 20 3/4 in. tall by 16 in. wide. **$4,750**

Shelf, Empire, triple-decker, Seth Thomas, bottom door with eagle in scroll surround, top door with reverse-painted flowers, rosewood and walnut veneer case, applied gilt pilasters, stepped cornice, 32 1/2 in. tall by18 in. wide by 6 in. deep. **$575**

Tall case, William Cummens (1768-1834), Boston or Roxbury, Mass., Federal, mahogany, inlaid, the hood with pierced fretwork joined by three inlaid plinths and brass finials above the arched cornice molding, inlaid tombstone glazed door with brass beaded liner framing the white-painted iron dial with polychrome and gilt floral decor, second and calendar aperture inscribed "Warranted by Wm. Cummens," all flanked by reeded brass stop-fluted columns, the waist with inlaid molded rectangular door flanked by reeded brass stop-fluted quarter columns on the string-inlaid base, ogee bracket feet, original finials, old refinish, minor imperfections, 96 1/2 in. tall............................**$36,000**

Tall case, Daniel Dole, Hallowell, mahogany case, painted wooden dial, brass works, 86 in. tall. **$12,000**

Tall case, John Field, Cumberland, R.I., (worked 1760-1780), cherry, molded hood with carved rosettes and spiral-carved finials mounted on fluted plinths above glazed door with arched top opening to engraved brass dial with silvered engraved arch inscribed "Soon Man's Hour is Up and We Are Gone" over a Father Time figure moving against a painted landscape above a silvered chapter ring with numbers for date, hour, and seconds, silvered plate engraved "John Field Cumberland No. 2," eight-day brass weight-driven movement, flanked by fluted freestanding columns above thumb-molded shell-carved blocked waist door on blocked and shell-carved base, ogee bracket feet, old surface, imperfections, 95 in. tall. **$63,000**

Tall case, Jacob Gorgas, Ephrate, Pa., circa 1790, Chippendale, eight-day works, calendar and second dial, floral-painted face, gilt ornamentation, walnut case, broken arch pediment, flame finials, arched door with heart-shaped escutcheon, reeded quarter columns, side lights, over a conforming case, base with applied turtle, ogee feet, minor loss, 96 in. tall. **$17,500**

Tall case, John Gorgas, inlaid, circa 1810-1815, veneered case front, beehive scrolled top, shield-shaped side lights, hand-painted face with Arabic and Roman chapter rings, sweep second hand, fruit-decor spandrels, ship dial, colonettes, waisted case with chamfered corners, paneled base, finials missing, 93 in. tall. **$5,750**

Tall case, Emanuel Meily, Lebanon, Pa., Federal, cherry, inlaid, eight-day key-wound brass movement, hour strike with moon dial, calendar, sweep second hand, iron plate behind face stamped "Osborne," face and moon dial, steel and brass hands, roses in face corners, Arabic numerals, bonnet with broken arch top, plain scrolls flank center plinth surmounted by urn-shaped finial, small square plinths on top corners with urn-shaped finials, tombstone-shaped door, stringing and diamond inlay, waist with carved shell drawer, inlaid stringing and fans, front of base with eight-point inlaid star in oval and fans in corners, French feet, 93 in. tall by 18 in. wide.........................**$15,000**

Tall case, Michael Striby, walnut case, flat top, flat fluted columns, face with Arabic and Roman numerals, second hand, date, floral spandrels, moon-phase dial, over waisted case with fluted quarter columns, on base with conforming columns, ogee bracket feet, 87 in. tall. **$6,500**

Tall case, country style, pine, refinished, "E. Edwards, Ashby" painted face added, moldings between sections, one-board door, bonnet with freestanding columns, broken arch pediment, turned center finial, replaced spring-wind works from a shelf clock, restorations, 81 1/4 in. tall.......**$800**

Tall case, country style, poplar, old red finish, bracket feet, scalloped aprons, molded waist, narrow door, early embossed lion pull, flat hood, cove-molded cornice, brass works, original painted face including gilt, scrollwork spandrels and urn top with areas of repaint, two painted paper coverings for empty holes, signed "Turner," hood restorations, base board replaced, 82 1/2 in. tall, 15 in. wide by 9 in. deep. **$2,750**

Tall case, Federal, mahogany, inlaid, New York or New Jersey, circa 1800, scrolled pediment with brass rosettes above frieze with central inlaid keystone and edge inlays over polychrome painted iron dial with second hand and calendar aperture, eight-day movement, hood flanked by freestanding inlaid columns, over shaped waist door flanked by inlaid quarter columns, above base with cyma-curved skirt and bracket feet, case with neoclassical stringing and banding, also patterned and pictorial inlays, inlaid carved circles and rectangles, old refinish, veneer loss, glass cracked, 93 1/2 in. tall. **$14,200**

Tall case, Federal, mahogany, inlaid, New York or New Jersey, circa 1800-1810, hood with scrolling crest, cast-brass rosettes, plinth of contrasting stringing on keystone, frieze with inlaid fluting at the corners above the freestanding fluted columns flanking the glazed door, floral-painted arched dial, calendar aperture, second hand, eight-day brass weight-driven movement, waist with three bands of inlaid fluting at the top, fluted quarter columns at the corners, door with elliptical inlay within a rectangle at the bottom, base with cove molding at the top, circular inlay in the front and bracket feet, old refinish, replaced feet, 92 in. tall. **$8,500**

Tall case, mahogany and mahogany veneer, possibly New York or New Jersey, circa 1815-1820, hood with molded swan's neck cresting, glazed tombstone door flanked by reeded columns, painted iron dial with polychrome and gilt designs of an urn in the arch and shield spandrels, second hand, calendar aperture, eight-day brass weight-driven movement, waist with shaped door flanked by reeded quarter columns, base with cutout feet, old finish, minor imperfections.....**$6,500**

Tall case, transitional, Chippendale to Hepplewhite, figured mahogany and mahogany veneer, cut bracket feet, molded waist, chamfered corners, door with shaped top, hood with freestanding columns, broken arch top, refinished, pieced repairs on goosenecks and feet, replaced finials, wag-on-the-wall works cut to fit, repainted decor, with weight and pendulum, 91 in. tall. **$2,750**

Tall case, L. Watson, Cincinnati, signed face, cherry and burl veneer, bracket feet, band inlay around base, inset panel on front, cove-molded waist with chamfered corners, door fitted with light burl band of inlay on edge and dark burl oval at center with scalloped top, dovetailed hood, broken arch top, freestanding columns, brass finials, original painted floral detail on face, wooden works, with pendulum and weights, refinished, replaced hands, 92 1/2 in. tall. **$9,250**

Tall case, walnut, old dark varnish finish, bracket feet, line inlay on case with oval on door and circle on base, flower inlay at center, chamfered corners, cove-molded waist, broken arch top with arched door, freestanding columns, original painted face includes birds and flowers, calendar dial removed, plate added, 91 in. tall..........**$4,200**

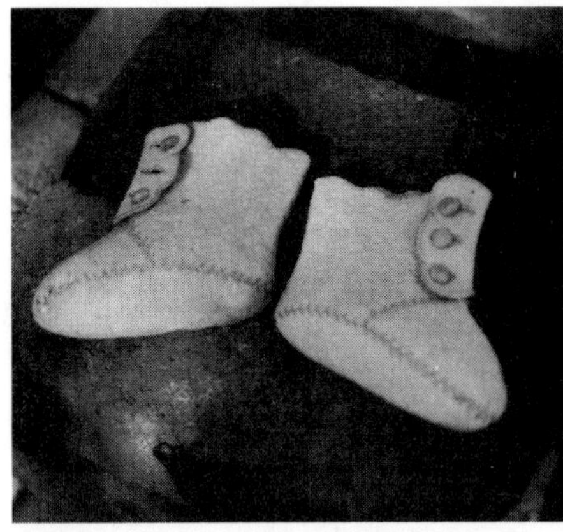

Baby booties, circa 1910, wool felt with vine stitching and turquoise glass buttons (one missing), moderate wear, overall very good condition, each measures 4 in. by 4 in. **$30-$40/pair**

Clothing

Authentic examples of country clothing simply are not in great supply. Shirts, pants, and coats could only be mended and darned for so long before they were discarded, while items that were used sparingly—like christening gowns—were locked away in trunks to charm—or puzzle—future generations. High-style Victorian clothing for both men and women seldom has a country connotation, and was usually store-bought.

Christening dress, circa 1900, white cotton, with embroidered lace on the long sleeves, bodice, collar, and bottom, rows of pintucks on bodice and at bottom of skirt, tie and button closure, buttons missing, the bottom of the bodice measures about 20 in. around, the neck is 11 in., the length is 30 in., excellent condition. **$85**

Baby bib, circa 1900, hand-quilted ecru silk trimmed with lace, with one fabric-covered button showing wear, and another that is not worn, excellent condition. **$15**

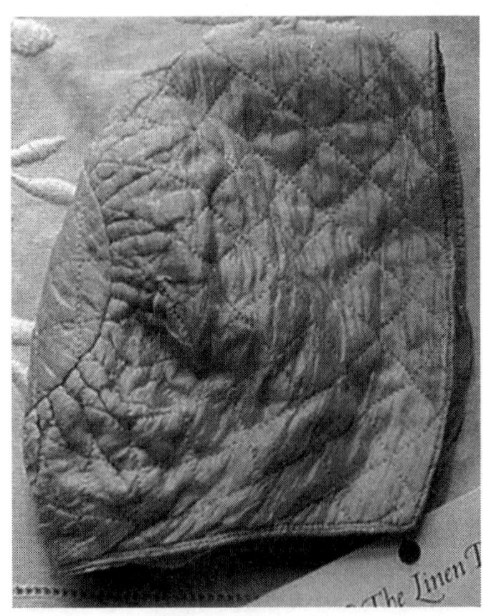

Baby bonnet, early 20th century, made of pale pink quilted silk. **$15**

Christening dress, early 20th century, white cotton, with embroidered lace on the long sleeves, bodice, and neck, vertical pintucks on back, 2 button close, the bodice is 2 in. high; and the length with the bodice is 30 1/2 in., it is 22 in. around the bottom of the bodice (under arm to under arm) and it is 60 in. around the bottom hem, with few wear holes on the sleeves and skirt. **$70**

Christening dress, early 20th century, white cotton, embroidery on the long sleeves, bodice, and neck, long ties close at the waist, and it ties at neck, front waistband also has embroidered panel, the front of the bodice has tiny gathers at the waistband, small tear on the ruffle of one sleeve, and a tiny hole near it, and a tiny pinhole on the back above the hem, the neck measures 10 in.; it is 11 in. wide armpit-to-armpit; it is 27 in. long and 54 in. around the bottom of the hem. **$70**

Ayrshire embroidered christening gown, circa 1800-1840, V-shaped bodice, short cap sleeves (long sleeves were not in fashion until later in the century), whitework embroidery (called Ayrshire), robe front (which has two embroidered ruffles that start at the bottom of the bodice), long, straight skirt and tie closure, near perfect condition, some small tears, old repairs, 43 in. long. **$300**

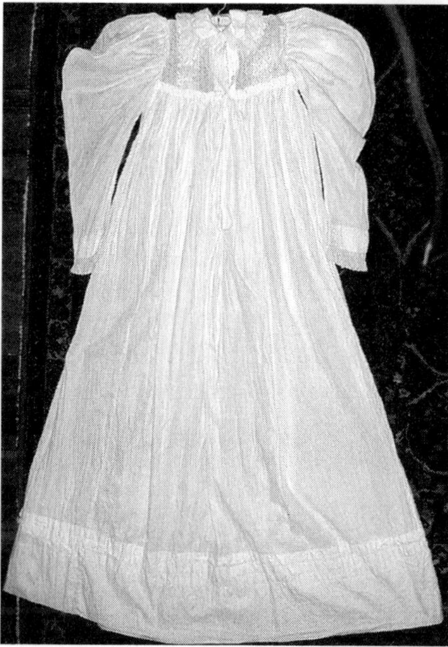

Victorian nightdress, fine white cotton, leg-of-mutton sleeves and frothy lace, the back and front of the bodice is made of embroidered white work bands alternating with lace, sleeves feature lace and embroidery, empire waist, 12 1/2 in. wide across back of shoulders, the bodice is 6 in. high and the dress is 52 in. long, one small rust spot inside the back of the collar, one small area of stain on the hem and one small hole, one sleeve has pale grayish stains. **$75**

Christening dress, late 19th century, off-white cotton, with tiny bobbin baby lace on the long sleeves and at the neck, diagonal pintucks on bodice and back and rows of pintuck on the sleeves, it closes with six tiny shell buttons plus ties at neck, the bottom of the skirt features an embroidered border above a series of nine pintucks, above another border, above an embroidered, scalloped ruffle, the fabric between the pintucks on the bodice is torn in six places because of the weight of the 44 in. long dress; there are holes on the front of the skirt, along with an old repair, embroidered lace has detached from a place on the front and on the back of the bodice and there are a few points of rust, there is a 2 1/2 in. by 5 in. area on the side seam that is dark gray, worth restoring. **$70**

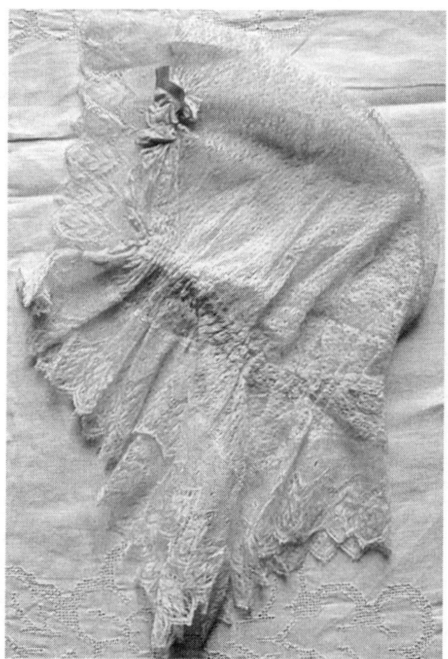

Lady's nightcap, circa 1890, all lace with pink ribbons and bows, satin ribbon is slightly ragged, when flat, it measures 9 in. by 15 in., excellent condition. **$36**

Short petticoat, early 20th century, fine white cotton with an eyelet ruffled bottom, waist 34 in., length 28 in., with worn area and old repairs, wearable, good condition. **$40**

Plain petticoat, early 20th century, in fine white cotton, waist 20 in., 40 in. length in front, gathered back with a slight 43 in. train, excellent wearable condition. **$50**

Victorian cotton slip, circa 1900-1920, features insets and straps of Mechlin lace, 44 in. long, 25 in. wide at narrowest point, bust is about 30 in., with a few holes in the lace and one small hole in the skirt, 84 in. around hem, button back. **$75**

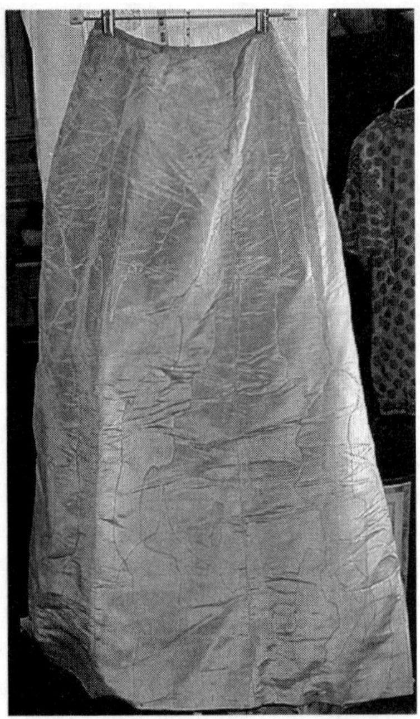

Moire silk skirt with train, late 19th century, pale golden mustard color, around the inside of the hem is a feathery shaped attachment that was meant to peek out beneath the skirt, 24 in. at the waist and 42 in. long in the front and 52 in. long in the back, minor wear and tear, overall very good condition. **$90**

Hat/beanie, circa 1940s, blue felt with saw-tooth edge turned up, decorated with beads, buttons, barrettes, a 1939 chauffeur's license, 7 1/2 in. by 4 in. **$110**

Where can I find it?

Cynthia's Antique & Vintage Linens
PO Box 586
Farmington, CT 06034-0586
(860) 677-5423
www.antique-linens.com/index.html
cynthia@antique-linens.com

Linen petticoat, circa 1880, made and trimmed with handmade knit lace, with some needle holes where the length was taken up and then let down, 24 in. waist, 43 in. long, and 105 in. around the bottom of the skirt. **$90**

Country Store Items

The country store of late 19th century America was both a retail outlet and a hub of social activity. Merchants who wanted to attract customers often used gimmicks, dispensers, and storage units that were gaudy, imposing, or ingenious. Those terms cover much of what is featured in this section, including coffee grinders, spool cabinets, and trade stimulators.

Cash register, model 421, circa 1910, cast brass with ornate "Amount Purchased" crest, highly polished, all original. .... **$1,500-$2,000**

Display case, "double tower" style with curved glass front and two tall display towers at each end, nickel plated, made by H.K. Ruse & Co. of Cincinnati, Ohio, 9 feet long, excellent condition. .... **$3,500-$4,500**

Enterprise #2 1/2 size cast iron coffee mill, made in Philadelphia, original paint, this style with nickel-plated tops (that are designated with the 1/2 after the number) are very rare, lid resoldered at one point, and there is one stress split in the body, base and drawer are original, decals are good, but somewhat faded, very good condition. **$2,450-$2,600**

Lander, Frary & Clark #20 cast iron coffee mill, with nearly 100% of its original green and gold finish; Lander, Frary & Clark put out a well finished and highly detailed series of coffee mills, and in their quest for market share with Enterprise and other makers of quality cast iron products near the turn of the 19th century, added details like ball bearing wheels and varying paint schemes to entice the buyer to purchase their version; excellent condition. **$1,700-$1,900**

Koffee Krusher #12 size double-wheel coffee mill by Simmons Hardware—Keen Kutter Brand, in blue (rare color), made by Simmons Hardware in St Louis, which distributed the products of other manufacturers under their name; the wheel layout and design are by Enterprise, but the ball bearing feature on the main shaft are typical of Lander, Frary & Clark, another producer of cast iron products during the 19th century; the paint is faded somewhat and the front knob is missing, but otherwise complete and free of damage. **$2,700-$3,200**

Riverside #7 size double-wheel coffee mill, very rare; from the construction details it appears that Enterprise may have made it, but the wheels, which measure about 17 in. in diameter, are a completely different casting; it is marked "Riverside Manufacturing Co. New York Trojan" in bold letters, it retains 90% or more of the deep red finish, and the paint on the wheels is dirty but still near perfect, excellent condition. **$3,500-$3,800**

White and blue enamelware Borden's Buttermilk "Churn"; supposedly a dispenser that sat on the countertop, it originally had a spigot and would have been filled with ice to cool the interchangeable jug of buttermilk that sat on top, much like a water cooler works today; thick white enamelware over metal, and fashioned to resemble a 16-sided wooden stave churn, 24 in. by 12 in. **$1,200-$1,400**

Apothecary, 40-drawer cabinet, oak, some Eastlake-style carving down each side, cast metal pulls, circa 1880, original finish, 76 in. wide by 22 in. deep by 36 in. tall. **$2,400**

Egg crate, circa 1910, painted pine with "PRIME PATENT EGG BOX" stenciled on side, turned wood handle, hook and eye clasp, original orange-red paint, cardboard egg holders still inside (held five dozen), paper label inside lid reads, "Prime's Patent Egg Case, Winchendon, Mass.," 11 1/2 in. by 9 in. by 8 1/2 in. **$200-$300**

Cast-iron trade souvenir for Cash's Woven Names (clothing labels), on the front is an image of a man dressed in a barrel and the words, "Mark 'em—I didn't," and the company name on the back, traces of original paint, 4 3/4 in. by 2 1/4 in. **$250**

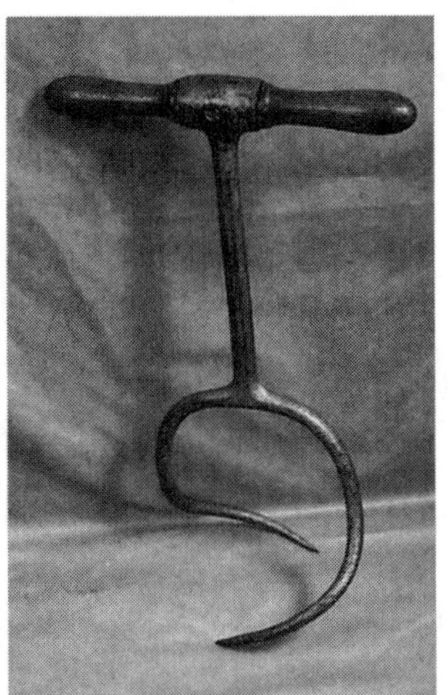

Unusual two-prong sugar devil, circa 1880, brass with wood handle, typical models also have a center guide screw, excellent condition. These were meant to be twisted down into a barrel of sugar (or dried fruit or whatever was stored in barrels and got stuck together) to break it up. **$225-$275**

Enterprise #2 size cast iron coffee mill, made in Philadelphia, with the color and paint being original and a deep rich red, rarely found in this condition. **$1,900-$2,100**

Ten-drawer spool cabinet, walnut, glass front on top of seven drawers with center metal pulls over three blind drawers with wood button pulls, circa 1880, original finish with traces of original advertising detail on front, sides and back, 20 in. wide by 16 in. deep by 24 in. tall. **$950**

Flour bin, circa 1900, sheet steel with fitted lid and hasp, bail handles, "Flour" with leaves and flowers and a hilt Greek-key border top and bottom hand-painted on the front, significant handling wear with numerous dents, 22 in. by 12 in. **$60-$70**

Grocer's scoop, circa 1910, maple, for grain or flour, minor wear, 15 in. long. **$200-$300**

Six-drawer Clark's spool cabinet, walnut, Eastlake details, fluted columns flanking drawers with inset painted glass panels in black and gold, cast brass hinged pulls, circa 1880, refinished, 22 in. wide by 18 in. deep by 22 in. tall. **$1,200**

Clark's spool cabinet, six drawers with teardrop pulls, red etched glass panels, refinished, circa 1870-1880, 22 in. wide by 16 in. deep by 20 in. tall. **$2,200**

Dispenser, Orange Crush, refrigerated, glass ball top and chrome-plated base, circa 1940s, near mint, 28 in. by 15 in. ....**$3,300-$3,600**

Ice box, commercial size, circa 1920, oak with two blind doors above two glass doors, and two more blind doors, zinc lined with wire shelves, heavy brass hardware, all original, 78 in. by 46 in. ....**$2,200-$2,800**

Sign, Coca-Cola, double sided "button" style, porcelain enamel over molded sheet steel, circa 1940s, near mint, 48 in. diameter. ....**$2,200-$2,600**

Where can I find them?

Mary Lou Beidler
Early American Antiques
2736 Pecan Rd.
Tallahassee, FL 32303
850-385-2981
www.antiquearts.com/stores/beidler/
beidler@AntiqueArts.com

Country Comfort Antiques
Third and Main Streets
Winona, MN 55987
(507) 452-7044

Country Side Antique Mall
31752 65th Ave.
Cannon Falls, MN 55009
(507) 263-0352
www.csamantiques.com

Freward & Alk Antiques
414 Lazarre Ave.
Green Bay, WI 54301
800 488-0321
(920) 435-7343
www.the-antique-shop.com
leesa@the-antique-shop.com

John Kruesel's General Merchandise
22 Third St. SW
Rochester, MN 55902
(507) 289-8049
www.kruesel.com

Larry and Carole Meeker
Purveyors of American Patented & Mechanical Antiques
5702 Vacation Blvd.
Somerset, CA 95684
(530) 620-7019
Sales: (888) 607-6090
Fax: (530) 620-7020

Coverlets

Antique Coverlets: An American Heirloom

By Wayne Mattox

www.patented-antiques.com
clm@patented-antiques.com

A coverlet is a type of bedspread fashioned by weaving on a loom. In Colonial days the master bed often accommodated not only mom and dad but several other family members as well. As the prominent article of furniture in most homes, the bedstead was beautifully arrayed. Although few of our foremothers could afford silk and damask, America's large variety of early woven blankets represents a sophisticated, decorative, and much sought-after remembrance of the past.

Coverlets were made in single woven and double woven layers. Germanic immigrants were prone to the former while Scottish and English weavers seemed drawn to the latter. Most commonly, a foundation of bleached cotton or linen, the warp, was interlaced with wool, the weft, that readily accepted coloring agents of blue indigo (by far the most popular dye), dogwood and bloodroot or madder root (red), goldenrod (green), butternut bark (brown), and bittersweet (orange). Synthetic dyes were introduced just prior to the Civil War. More than age or rarity, good condition, graphic color and design, and historical significance are the major determinants of coverlet value. Measurements range from about 70 inches to 100 inches. Collectors and dealers categorize their heirlooms as follows:

Overshot Coverlets: Also known as the float weave, 18th and rural 19th century examples made by home and itinerant weavers on four-harness looms that were once as common a household appliance as dishwashers are today. Because they were fashioned on crude weaving machines, overshot coverlets are necessarily geometric in design, incorporating a wide variety of stripe, square, diamond, medallion, and other patterns. Made in two parts, they are always seamed in the middle. These readily available coverlets are often undervalued and complement 18th century and high country design.

Double Weave Geometric, Summer Winter, and Star Work Coverlets: Forerunners of sophisticated jacquard bedspreads, these professionally woven second-stage examples feature strong, clear geometric design, flat to the surface tight weaving, and double-facing, in that the weaving on the back is the precise decorative reverse of that on the front.

Jacquard Coverlets: The Jacquard loom was first introduced by its inventor, Joseph Marie Jacquard (1752-1834), at the National Exposition in Paris in 1801. It is a player-piano-like device that facilitates reproducible complex woven designs using multiple sets of perforated cards that orchestrate a weaving machine like an ancestral computer. Jacquard's initial inspiration for his invention was an extract from an English newspaper offering a premium to "any man who should weave a fishing net by machinery." Accomplishing his goal, Jacquard was soon arrested by Napoleon Bonaparte's magistrate.

"Are you the man who pretends to do that which God Almighty cannot do, to tie a knot in a stretched string?" the magistrate named Carnot inquired. Jacquard was granted three weeks to reproduce his feat or spend his days knitting in prison.

The refined loom landed on American shores in the 1820s. Professionally woven jacquard coverlets are distinguished by bold colors, tight weave, double-facing, pictorial centerfield designs, and wide, often striking borders incorporating designs like American eagles, railroads, lions, buildings, trees, ships, and other elements. Most were produced full size without a middle seam. In the corner block of his coverlet, the weaver often included his name, the name of the owner/contractor, the owner's town, county, state, and date of weaving.

Even when they were loomed, great coverlets have always been considered a household treasure. Frequently mentioned in wills and safely stored for future generations in dower chests, they truly are American heirlooms.

(Wayne Mattox is the proprietor of Wayne Mattox Antiques, Woodbury, Conn., specializing in 18th and early 19th century furnishings, American folk art, and accessories.)

Pennsylvania jacquard wool woven coverlet, dated 1855, woven by B. Yordy of Lancaster County, Connestoga Township, Pa. (See "A Checklist of American Coverlet Weavers" compiled by John W. Heisey and published by the Colonial Williamsburg foundation in 1978, now out of print). The coverlet is signed and dated on two corners, the bird border alternates with trees and flowers; the "Biederman" weave as seen on this coverlet is a typical weave performed by the Pennsylvania German weavers, the colors are red, indigo, and green, colorful fringe is self-hemmed on the two sides and the fringe at the foot of the coverlet is attached, coverlet shows some wear but there are no holes or stains, 80 in. by 96 in.**$525**

Blue and white coverlet, circa 1850, signed by L.W. Steele, American, some minor wear. **$750**

Coverlet, circa 1860, graphic pattern in blues, reds, and greens, eagles along the border, excellent condition. **$650**

Pennsylvania German dated coverlet in red, brown, and cobalt natural dyed wool, dated 1843, signed "Manufactured by Jos. Klar, Reading, Pa." on two corners of the coverlet, wool fringe on three sides, horizontal rows of repetitive designs in floral and swirls, soft and light weight, very good condition, 82 in. by 98 in. **$850**

Coverlet, circa 1870, western Ontario, greens and burgundy woven in overshot pattern, colors still vibrant, excellent condition. **$450**

Pennsylvania jacquard coverlet, circa 1860-1880, in red, green, and brown wool woven on a cream background, the coverlet has an unusual border with a church in the center and floral scrolls; center scene: circular medallion surrounded by pointed stars; four angels at center corners, machine made, excellent condition, 78 in. by 85 in. **$475**

Pennsylvania jacquard coverlet in tricolors, dated 1854, signed by the weaver, "B. Yordy in Connestoga Township (Penn.) for Barbara Schoff," striking bird border on three sides, fringe on three sides. **$800**

Coverlet, circa 1850, Waterloo County, Ontario, woven in overshot pattern, striking colors and condition. **$650**

Pennsylvania jacquard wool red and white coverlet, circa 1840-1850, with eagles in four corners, red fringe on three sides, natural dyes (for red color, madder root), in very good condition, 82 in. by 85 in. **$600**

Jacquard woven wool coverlet, mid-19th century, Pennsylvania or Ohio origin, natural dyes in red, blue, and black, fringe on three sides, unusual overall pattern of circles, ovals and fans, wonderful color combination, excellent condition, 72 in. by 90 in. **$450**

Graphic wool blanket, circa 1930, made by the Pendleton Mills in Oregon, excellent condition except for the silk binding on the top and bottom of the blanket. **$400**

Pennsylvania jacquard wool coverlet, circa 1840-1850, in single weave with the spread eagle in four corners, rich natural colors in madder red, green, and indigo, floral border and a center swag medallion, fringe on three sides, very good condition, 74 in. by 82 in. **$450**

Jacquard woven coverlet, single weave, Pennsylvania, circa 1840-1850, geometric background design with a center medallion of flowers and leaves, red, dark blue, and green wool, fringe on three sides, very good condition. **$425**

Pennsylvania German Victorian woven coverlet, circa 1840-1850, designed with swags and flowers, with fringe on three sides, wool design with tricolors of indigo, red, and gold, Victorian design with a border of swags, floral design encompasses the center with a basket medallion, very good condition, 80 in. by 95 in. **$465**

New York State indigo blue woven wool coverlet, with an eagle border, signed and dated in two corners: "E.S. Roger N.Y. 1833," the border has a series of spread eagles separated by a standing tree, and this border is repeated on each side of the coverlet and the foot; the center is composed of repetitive floral medallions; New York State coverlets are usually not finished with fringe but are self hemmed; there is a center seam indicating that this coverlet was made on a small loom (36 in.), overall good condition with three very small holes on the top cover and the "head" edge is thin with wear (no stains), 79 in. by 98 in. **$525**

Where can I find them?

Mary Lou Beidler
Early American Antiques
2736 Pecan Rd.
Tallahassee, FL 32303
(850) 385-2981
http://www.antiquearts.com/stores/beidler/
beidler@AntiqueArts.com

Country Comfort Antiques
Third and Main Streets
Winona, MN 55987
(507) 452-7044

Cynthia's Antique & Vintage Linens
PO Box 586
Farmington, CT 06034-0586
(860) 677-5423
www.antique-linens.com/index.html
cynthia@antique-linens.com

Wayne Mattox Antiques
82 Main St. N.
Woodbury, CT 06798
(203) 263-2431
www.antiquetalk.com
tiquetalk@aol.com

Document Boxes

Eighteenth century desks typically had a small vertical drawer for storing important papers. This storage drawer evolved into the small document box used for the same purpose. These document boxes were made primarily of wood or tin, and both styles were often decorated.

Collecting Hint: The market for decorated boxes has exploded in recent years, with painted wood examples in elaborate decorations bringing high prices.

Basswood, mustard and red decor on finger-swirled vinegar background, original brass bail on lid, age crack on lid, minor wear, 6 in. tall by 15 in. wide by 17 1/2 in. deep. ..**$1,100**

Decorated, original black over red to simulate rosewood, gold and black line details on borders, pine, dovetailed, brass hinges, internal lock, minor wear, 7 in. tall by 11 5/8 in. wide by 6 1/2 in. deep. **$325**

Decorated, original floral decor on a green ground, yellow and black striping, poplar, dovetailed with molded base and lid, till, lock with key, wear and fading, age cracks in till, 6 3/4 in. tall by 16 in. wide by 8 1/4 in. deep. **$750**

Decorated, floral panels on front and lid, sponge-decor ends, original red, blue, yellow, and black, pine, minor hairlines, 6 1/2 in. tall by 13 in. wide by 7 1/4 in. deep. **$375**

Decorated, flowers hand-painted on sides, urn of flowers, bees, and swags across domed lid, mustard ground and old repaint, red interior with lock, key missing, 4 5/8 in. tall by 10 1/2 in. wide by 7 1/2 in. deep. **$250**

Decorated, foliage in red and green on top and front, old dark green over lighter green ground, basswood, dovetailed, original brass bail handle on top, iron hasp lock, wire hinges, 6 1/2 in. tall by 18 in. wide by 8 1/2 in. deep.**$1,500**

Decorated, geometric design in original orange and black, red ground, poplar, minor edge wear, 6 1/2 in. tall by 10 7/8 in. wide by 6 1/2 in. deep. **$175**

Decorated, leaves and fruit in gold stencil, original red paint, black border, pine, dovetailed, original brass bail on lid, wrought iron hasp lock, pencil signature "L.B. Lawrence 2-19-08" inside, 5 1/2 in. tall by 12 in. wide by 6 in. deep. **$4,000**

Grain decorated, old reddish-brown flame-grained repaint, poplar, dovetailed, brass lock with swinging keyhole cover having embossed eagle, pencil signature for "Geo. Quinby 1853," hasp missing, 7 in. tall by 20 1/2 in. wide by 10 in. deep.........................**$275**

Grain decorated, original graining imitates rosewood, stenciled gold decor on lid, yellow striping, poplar, brass lock, original brass bail on lid, 1910 pencil inscription in lid, 7 in. tall by 19 in. wide by 8 1/2 in. deep. **$950**

Mahogany and mahogany veneer, old finish, ebony line and trim inlay, beaded drawer front with ivory pulls, brass lion ring pulls on sides, diamond-shaped escutcheon inlay missing, edge chips, old replaced brass ball feet, English, 8 1/8 in. tall by 11 1/2 in. wide by 8 in. deep. **$250**

Mahogany veneer, string inlay, variegated diamonds, boxes, and large star, inlay lifting in spots, 3 1/2 in. tall by 12 in. wide by 8 in. deep. **$475**

Pine, old refinishing, six-board, dovetailed, incised molding around top/bottom, interior lock missing its catch, wear, restorations, 10 1/2 in. tall by 15 1/2 in. wide by 10 in. deep. **$125**

Poplar, molded base and trim around lid, nail construction, brass hinges, refinished, minor damage to interior lock, 6 1/2 in. tall by 14 in. wide by 7 5/8 in. deep.............**$275**

Rosewood veneer, ebonized edges, brass escutcheon and lid medallion, edge damage, 8 in. long. **$125**

Early Glass

Understanding Early Glass

by Wayne Mattox

Early molten glass was blown, as one would blow a balloon, then shaped with tools or molds by a gaffer. This is the first step toward identifying valuable antique glass in your own backyard. And it does show up frequently.

A friend bought a miniature blown glass bottle with an applied handle at a local tag sale. Despite a small heat-check crack (a crack that happened in the making when the red, hot gooey handle was applied to the cooler bottle), the insignificant-appearing, two-inch tall amber demijohn (a narrow-necked bottle usually enclosed in wickerwork) was later sold for $400, a pretty fair profit on a nickel investment!

Here are a few tips that may rouse your interest if you happen to cross paths with an old piece of glass.

Inspect the base for a pontil mark. Gaffers held the red-hot glass gobs that they fashioned with an iron pontil rod, which was snapped off when the article was finished. This handcrafted glass-making technique leaves a trail for antique detectives: a round jagged scar in the middle of the base. Sometimes, especially in finer pieces made after 1790, this pontil scar was removed by polishing, resulting in a smooth bowl-like indentation called a polished pontil. A pontil mark identifies blown glass, and opens the door to the possibility of age and value.

Inspect the base for wear. Remember: Unless wear is where it belongs, it does not belong. Old glass objects will have tiny flat spots on those small areas of the base where the object would come into contact with a table, counter, etc. Note that an uneven gaffer-fashioned base seldom presents a flat surface, and that a base that has been worn in non-contact areas is quite probably a fake.

Examine molded glass. Figural flasks, decanters, embossed bottles, decorative lacy glass, pattern glass, and many other old glassware items were shaped in molds. Unfortunately, fakes and reproductions of early molded glass far exceed original items today. Authentic pieces are weighty and sharply edged compared to contemporary examples. Identifying irregularities like spillover, where too much glass was poured into the mold, and annealing lines, hair-like inconsistencies on the surface, can also be of aid in ferreting out old glass.

Look for a few—and only a few—bubbles in the glass. Air bubbles were evidence of poor quality to older-day glassmakers, nevertheless, some did appear. Bubbly glass should be purchased by only those intent on building a collection of Mexican souvenirs.

Listen for a ping. When tapped, early flint glass emits a bell-like tone. Not all old glass rings, however. Lime or soda glass and closed-neck pieces like bottles and decanters seldom ping.

Extrinsic decoration, decoration introduced to glass after it was fashioned and allowed to cool, like cutting, engraving, etching, enameling, and gilding, can add considerable value to glass. This is especially true if the work is well executed and gives an indication as to its history. A bottle with "Amelung"-style engraving could bring in excess of $20,000 at auction. (Amelung glass includes bowls, bottles, and goblets that were made by John Frederick Amelung at his New Bremen Glass Manufactory in Frederick County, Md., from 1784 to 1795. His glassware was engraved with mottoes, monograms, crests, and flower wreaths. An engraved dark glass flask by Amelung, measuring less than 5 in. tall, can sell for more than $12,000; a stemmed wine glass by Amelung, standing under 6 in. tall, can bring $1,200 to $1,300.)

Early glass in color can be quite valuable. Authentic glass can often be recognized by the vibrancy of its color. Recognition can only be learned by experience. Visit a museum, like the Corning Glass Museum in Corning, N.Y., to study old glass. It's a beautiful window into yesterday.

(Wayne Mattox is the proprietor of Wayne Mattox Antiques, Woodbury, Conn., specializing in 18th and early 19th century furnishings, American folk art, and accessories.)

❖ Early Glass

This category focuses primarily on early American glass, a term that covers glass made in America from the colonial period through the mid-19th century. Early pressed glass and lacy glass made between 1827 and 1840 are included.

Prior to 1850, major glass-producing centers were located in Massachusetts (New England Glass Company and the Boston and Sandwich Glass Co.), South Jersey, Pennsylvania (Stiegel's Manheim factory and many Pittsburgh-area firms), and Ohio (several different companies in Kent, Mantua, and Zanesville).

References: George and Helen McKearin, *American Glass*, Crown, 1975; — *Two Hundred Years of American Blown Glass*, Doubleday, 1950; Kenneth Wilson, *American Glass 1760-1939*, 2 volumes, Hudson Hills Press, 1994.

Periodical: *Antique Bottle & Glass Collector*, PO Box 187, East Greenville, PA 18041.

Collectors' Clubs: Early American Glass Traders, RD 5, Box 638, Milford, DE 19963; Early American Pattern Glass Society, PO Box 266, Colesburg, IA 52035; Glass Research Society of New Jersey, Wheaton Village, Millville, NJ 08332; National Early American Glass Club, PO Box 8489, Silver Spring, MD 20907.

Museums: Bennington Museum, Bennington, Vt.; Chrysler Museum, Norfolk, Va.; Corning Museum of Glass, Corning, N.Y.; Glass Museum, Dunkirk, Ind.; Sandwich Glass Museum, Sandwich, Mass.; Wheaton Historical Village Association Museum of Glass, Millville, N.J.

Ale glass, clear, bull's-eye with fleur-de-lis, 6 1/4 in. tall. **$650**

Bell, cranberry, folded rim, clear handle with white looping, clear clapper, blown, 15 1/2 in. tall. .**$220**

Bowl, amethyst, blown, folded rim, wear, 3 7/8 in. tall, 6 1/4 in. diameter. **$550**

Bowl, clear, blown, three-mold, GIII-4, 3 1/8 in. tall, 5 1/2 in. diameter. **$990**

Bowl, clear, blown, three-mold, GII-22, wide rim, turned-over lip, 1 3/8 in. tall, 6 1/4 in. diameter. **$250**

Bowl, cobalt, blown, flared sides, rolled rim, kicked-up pontil base, 11 1/8 in. diameter. **$900**

Cake stand, clear, blown, 6 1/4 in. diameter to 8 3/4 in. diameter, domed base, open air stem, applied collar around center, round top, graduated set of four. **$1,700**

Cake stand, clear, blown, 9 in. diameter, 6 1/2 in. tall, solid stem, plain circular foot, pontil. **$150**

Cake stand, clear, blown, 9 3/4 in. diameter, 4 1/2 in. tall, applied reverse baluster teardrop stem, domed circular foot with folded rim, pontil, mid-19th century. **$450**

Candlesticks, Boston and Sandwich Glass Co., columnar, petal socket, canary, half of one petal missing, other chips, 9 1/4 in. tall. .**$180/pair**

Candlestick, Boston and Sandwich Glass Co., columnar, petal socket, clambroth with sand finish, circa 1850-1865, chips, 9 in. tall. **$60**

Candlesticks, Boston and Sandwich Glass Co., dolphin, clambroth, petal socket, single-step base, circa 1845-1870, 10 in. and 10 3/8 in. tall. **$900/pair**

Candlestick, Boston and Sandwich Glass Co., hexagonal socket and base, clambroth, circa 1840-1860, chip, roughness, 7 1/4 in. tall. ...**$90**

Candlesticks, Boston and Sandwich Glass Co., petal-and-loop design, clambroth, circa 1840-1860, flake, crack, 7 in. tall. **$110/pair**

Candlestick, Boston and Sandwich Glass Co., petal-and-loop design, yellow-tinged green, circa 1840-1860, flake, chips, 6 3/4 in. tall. **$140**

Canister, covered, 8 3/4 in. tall, Pittsburgh glass, two applied rings on base, wafer finial, small interior broken blister. **$220**

Canister, covered, 10 in. tall, Pittsburgh glass, two pale-blue applied rings on base, one on lid rim, pale-blue wafer finial. **$220**

Canister, covered, 10 1/4 in. tall, 5 1/2 in. diameter, blown, two applied rings on base, pressed finial, lid fits but slightly undersized. **$55**

Canister, covered, 11 3/8 in. tall, Pittsburgh glass, two applied cobalt rings on base, one on lid rim, cobalt wafer finial. **$660**

Canister, covered, 11 5/8 in. tall, Pittsburgh glass, two applied rings on base, wafer finial, slight amethyst tint, lid undersized. ..**$110**

Compote, covered, early Thumbprint pattern, clear, covered, ball form, 14 1/2 in. tall........................**$4,200**

Compote, covered, baluster pedestal, folded rim, clear, blown, finial with regrinding and roughness, 12 in. tall, 9 1/4 in. diameter. ...**$450-$500**

Compote, open, loop (Leaf) pattern, clambroth, attributed to Boston and Sandwich Glass Co., foot chip, bruise, small flakes, 7 1/2 in. tall, 9 in. diameter..........................**$1,700**

Compote, open, clear, blown, pillar-molded, eight-rib bowl flaring at rim, applied tapering high stem and circular foot, probably Pittsburgh, mid-19th century, 10 in. tall, 12 in. diameter. **$1,500**

Brazen Shield cobalt blue Tumbler, Indiana Tumbler & Goblet (Greentown), 1898

Compote, open, cobalt base, clear bowl, round foot and hexagonal stem with matching six panels on base of bowl, attributed to Central Glass Co., Wheeling W. Va., minor roughness on underside of foot, interior of bowl worn and scratched, 7 1/2 in. tall, 9 1/4 in. diameter. **$300**

Creamer, blown, clear diamond pattern, applied cobalt threading around rim, applied handle, crimped end, 4 3/8 in. tall. **$550**

Cruet, blown pillar-molded, applied handle, pewter jigger top, 16 ribs, bulbous body, circular foot, probably Pittsburgh, mid-19th century, 7 1/2 in. tall. **$150**

Cup plate, Lee/Rose #68, basket of flowers, clear with light touch of cloudiness, 3 11/16 in. diameter. **$2,400**

Decanter, clear, blown, baroque, scrolled leaf design, three rings on neck, three-mold, straw mark imperfections, mismatched flat stopper chipped, 9 1/2 in. tall..**$110**

Decanter, clear, blown, Greek Key design, matching stopper, three-mold, minor sickness, 14 in. tall. ....**$50-$70**

Fire grenade, Harden's Hand Fire Extinguisher Grenade, violet blue, some residue, 6 in. tall. **$825**

Fire grenade, Imperial Fire Grenade, green, Prince of Wales feathers at top, sealed contents. **$535**

Fire grenade, Nutting, embossed "HSN," four diamond panels, amber, 7 1/2 in. tall. **$200**

Fire grenade, marked "PSN," diamond shape, yellow, 7 in. tall. **$430**

Fire grenade, Sinclair, cobalt, raised diamond pattern on back, space for label on front, no contents, crack at neck. **$170**

Goblet, pressed glass, clear, Argus, rim flake, 6 1/4 in. tall. **$200**

Goblet, pressed glass, clear, Arched Leaf. **$160**

Goblet, pressed glass, clear, Bull's-Eye and Diamond Point. **$180**

Goblet, pressed glass, clear, Comet. **$150**

Goblet, pressed glass, clear, Excelsior Plus. **$30**

Goblet, pressed glass, clear, Hawaiian Pineapple. **$160**

Goblet, pressed glass, clear, Lincoln Drape. **$190**

Goblet, pressed glass, clear, Magnet and Grape with Frosted Leaf and American Shield. **$350**

Goblet, pressed glass, clear, Scarab. **$130**

Jars, storage, covered, 4 in. tall, and 5 1/4 in. tall, clear, blown, pontil on bases, tin lids, 1 lid replaced. **$1,000/pair**

Jars, storage, covered, 6 1/4 in. tall, clear, blown, pontil on bases, tin lids, hole in 1 lid. **$650/pair**

Jars, storage, covered, 7 1/2 in. tall and 8 in. tall, clear, blown, pontil on bases, tin lids..................**$500/pair**

Jars, storage, covered, 7 3/4 in. tall, and 8 in. tall, clear, blown, tin lids. **$400/pair**

Jars, storage, covered, 10 1/4 in. tall, and 11 1/2 in. tall, clear, blown, tin lids, small area of residue. **$275/pair**

Jar, storage, covered, 11 1/4 in. tall, etched foliage bands, scrollwork and medallions with flowers, bands and buildings, applied etched ball finial. **$550**

Jars, storage, covered, 12 in. tall, clear, blown molded glass, tin lid, rim chip. **$200**

Lamp, clear, Horn of Plenty, fluid lamp, Boston & Sandwich Glass Co., circa 1845-1870, 10 in. tall. **$275**

Lamp, clear, tulip font, hexagonal stem, round foot, pewter collar, minor chips, 9 in. tall. **$150**

Mug, etched bird and tulip in sun medallion, clear, blown, applied handle, 6 in. tall. **$275**

Mug, etched flower, clear, blown, 4 3/8 in. tall. **$250**

Mug, etched flower and foliage, clear, blown, applied handle, 5 5/8 in. tall. **$220**

Mug, white enamel floral decor, cobalt, blown, gilt rim, pontil, 4 in. tall. **$90**

Pitcher, aqua, lily pad type foot, applied handle with crimped ends, blown, broken blisters, 5 3/4 in. tall. **$1,900**

Pitcher, cleat pattern, clear, 8 1/2 in. tall. **$190**

Pitcher, New England Pineapple, clear, 8 in. tall. **$1,100**

Pitcher, New York Honeycomb, clear, 8 1/4 in. tall. **$230**

Pitcher, pillar molded, clear, blown, solid applied handle, polished pontil, probably Pittsburgh, mid-19th century, 8 1/2 in. tall. **$160**

Pitcher, ribbed Palm, clear, 9 in. tall. **$275**

Pitcher, South Jersey, deep amber, applied and tooled foot, bowl with four drawn fingers, applied handle, threaded neck, flared lip, base of handle chipped, stain, 7 in. tall. **$110**

Punch bowl, early Thumbprint pattern, clear, 12 in. tall, 14 in. diameter. **$5,250**

Rolling pin, free-blown, dark olive green with white spattering, rough pontil, 14 in. long, 1 3/4 in. greatest diameter. **$100**

Salt, octagonal, alternating panels of diamonds and vertical ribs, blown-molded, chips, flakes, 1 3/4 in. tall, 2 1/2 in. diameter. **$30**

Store jar, 6 1/4 in. tall, 3 in. diameter, clear, pushup pontil, tin lid. **$375**

Store jars, 6 1/4 in. tall, 4 3/4 in. diameter and 7 1/4 in. tall, 5 5/8 in. diameter, clear, pushup pontils, tin lids. **$325/pair**

Sugar and creamer, clear, balloon pattern, flakes, sugar 5 1/4 in. tall. **$325**

Target ball, Man Shooting in Circle, pink amethyst, circa 1880s, 2 5/8 in. diameter............................**$700**

Target ball, ribbed design, amber, marked "G2." **$185**

Tumbler, two red hearts flanked by

floral sprigs in enamel polychrome, inscribed, "We two will be true," clear, blown, American or German, late 18th or early 19th century, 3 in. tall. **$550**

Tumbler, copper wheel engraving of foliage and "I.F. Miller marr'd at Rudby Church Novr 16, 1784," probably Centennial, clear, blown, small interior broken blister, 4 3/4 in. tall.............................. **$150-$200**

Tumbler, floral decor in enamel polychrome, opaque white, blown, American or German, late 18th or early 19th century, 3 1/2 in. tall. **$300**

Tumbler, parrot in green and red enamel polychrome, additional floral decor, clear, blown, American or German, late 18th or early 19th century, 3 3/4 in. tall. **$700**

Vase, clear, flint, Pittsburgh, wide applied foot, flared bowl with cut panels and sheaves, wear, scratches, 8 1/2 in. tall. **$330**

Where can I find it?

Wayne Mattox Antiques
82 Main St. N.
Woodbury, CT 06798
(203) 263-2431
www.antiquetalk.com
tiquetalk@aol.com

Phyllis Petcoff Antique Glassware
http://www.petcoff.com/index.html
petcoff@earthlink.net

PatternGlass.com
Bill and Elaine Henderson
P.O. Box 36195
Albuquerque, NM 87176-6195
Elaine@PatternGlass.com

Early American Pattern Glass Society
http://www.eapgs.org/

http://eapg.com/
A site with auctions, specializing in Early American Pattern Glass.
feedback@eapg.com

Feed Sacks

Farmers have been using cloth bags for grain, seed, and feed ever since cloth was available. In the early days, homespun linen was hand sewn into bags for the grain that was kept for use in the home, and for next year's planting.

After the invention of the sewing machine in the mid-19th century, feed sacks became a commercially viable product and began to be mass-produced by the late 1800s. As the economy shifted from a rural, agrarian economy to a more urban, industrialized one, more and more of these sacks were used to ship and store grain, feed, and flour products. At first, the farmers would bring back the emptied sack to their feed supplier to be refilled, but it was easier for the miller to pre-fill the sacks, so the empty sacks found other uses in the home as towels, linens, or clothing.

Sometime in the 1920s, an enterprising manufacturer of cloth bags hit upon an interesting idea: Maybe he could sell more sacks if they were decorated to be more desirable for the farmer's wife. The era of the printed feed sack began. No longer just beige muslin with advertising for the feed company, now sacks began to appear in a wide variety of popular colors and prints. And paper labels were applied so that the fabric could be reused without the advertising.

Feed sacks like these hanging on an old drying rack, mostly made of burlap, can be found at most flea markets for just a few dollars. The better the graphics and materials used to make the sacks, the higher the price.

Due to shortages of money during the Great Depression and shortages of cloth during the war years, feed sacks filled the needs of thousands of women for fabric to create the things they could not otherwise buy. This was recycling at its best, with farmers' wives fighting over the prettiest patterns. Unfortunately, nothing lasts forever, and at the end of the 1950s, increasing costs led manufacturers to begin to use heavy paper and other materials for feeds, and the cloth bag fell out of use. The ones found today are almost all remnants of these 3 1/2 decades of production, carefully washed, folded, and stored away for use by thrifty farm wives.

American Beauty Wheat Gray Shorts, 100-pound bag, showing a large red rose, 36 in. by 21 in. **$32**

Big "C" Chick Starter, 25-pound bag, showing a bathing beauty, 26 in. by 13 in. **$60**

Buffalo Corn Gluten Seed, 100-pound bag, showing a buffalo on a red and black striped panel, 37 in. by 23 in. **$45**

Maysco Pennsylvania Dutch Brand Farm Seeds, showing a settler and an Indian, 31 in. by 15 in. **$35**

Snow Flake Flour, made by Farmer's Exchange Mills, 98-pound bag, 35 in. by 22 in. **$55**

Diamond High Patent Flour, 49-pound bag. **$22**

Red Rose Swine Feed, 100-pound bag, showing a pig in profile, 38 in. by 22 in. **$40**

A standard 100-pound feed sack averages about 37 in. by 43 in. when unstitched and laid flat. Most sell for between $25 and $50.

Lyons Best Blended Patent Flour, 25-pound bag, showing male and female lions, 26 in. by 12 in. **$40**

Snow Bird Winter Wheat Paten Flour, 49-pound bag, showing a bird on a snowy branch, two sizes: 29 in. by 16 in., **$26**; *25 in. by 12 in.,* **$22**

Where can I find them?

Sharon's Antiques and Vintage Quilts
(610) 756-6048
http://www.rickrack.com
quilts@rickrack.com

Firearms & Related

The 15th century Matchlock Arquebus was the forerunner of the modern firearm. The Germans refined the wheelock firing mechanism during the 16th and 17th centuries. English settlers arrived in America with the smooth-bore musket; German settlers had rifled arms. Both used the new flintlock firing mechanism.

A major advance was achieved when Whitney introduced interchangeable parts into the manufacturing of rifles. Refinements in firearms continued in the 19th century. The percussion ignition system was developed by the 1840s. Minie, a French military officer, produced a viable projectile. By the end of the 19th century cartridge weapons dominated the field.

References: Robert W.D. Ball, *Springfield Armory Shoulder Weapons 1795-1968,* Antique Trader Books, 1997; Ralf Coykendall Jr., *Coykendall's Complete Guide to Sporting Collectibles,* Wallace-Homestead, 1996; Jim Dresslar, *Folk Art of Early America: The Engraved Powder Horn,* Dresslar Publishing, 1996; Norman Flayderman, *Flayderman's Guide to Antique American Firearms and Their Values,* 7th ed., Krause Publications, 1998; Herbert G. Houze, *Colt Rifles and Muskets From 1847-1870,* Krause Publications, 1996; John Ogle, *Colt Memorabilia Price Guide,* Krause Publications, 1998; Nick Stroebel, *Old Gunsights 1850-1965,* Krause Publications, 1999.

Periodicals: *Gun List*, 700 E. State St., Iola, WI 54990; *Historic Weapons & Relics*, 2650 Palmyra Rd., Palmyra, TN 37142; *Military Trader*, PO Box 1050, Dubuque, IA 52004.

Collectors' Clubs: American Society of Military History, Los Angeles Patriotic Hall, 1816 S. Figuerora, Los Angeles, CA 90015; Winchester Arms Collectors Association, PO Box 6754, Great Falls, MT 59406.

Museums: Battlefield Military Museum, Gettysburg, Pennsylvania; Fort Ticonderoga Museum, Ticonderoga, New York; Museum of Weapons & Early American History, Saint Augustine, FL 32084; National Firearms Museum, Washington, D.C.; Remington Gun Museum, Ilion, New York; Springfield Armory National Historic Site, Springfield, Massachusetts.

Reproduction Alert

Reproduction and fake powder horns are plentiful.

Specialty Auctions: Sanford Alderfer Auction Co., 501 Fairgrounds Rd., Hatfield, PA 19440, phone (215) 393-3000, www.alderfercompany.com; James D. Julia, Inc., PO Box 830, Fairfield, ME 04937, phone (207) 453-7125.

Advertising, DuPont Black Sporting Powders poster, paper, 1909, winter scene with two children hunting, 20 1/4 in. tall by 14 1/2 in. wide. **$750**

Advertising, DuPont Sporting Powders poster, paper, 1919, winter scene with old man and boy on log by guns, dog listening, metal strips intact, 25 3/8 in. tall by 17 in. wide.....................................**$1,100**

Flask, brass, pear-shape, American eagle with wings partially spread on both sides, brass and steel spring mechanism at top, 4 3/8 in. long by 2 in. wide. **$150**

Long rifle, flintlock, "M. Fordney" (Melchior Fordney, Lancaster, Pennsylvania), Kentucky rifle, raise-carved walnut stock in old refinish, nine silver and brass inlays, carvings include C scrolls on butt stock and around cheek piece and tang, checkered wrist and relief scrolling ahead of lock and side plate, reconversion to flint, patch box and trigger guard replaced, shortened slightly, 55 1/2 in. long. **$6,250**

Long rifle, flintlock, "A. Schweitzer" (Abraham Schweitzer, Lancaster and Chambersburg, Pennsylvania), curly maple in old dark finish, raise carvings include C scrolls behind the cheek piece and detailing around the tang, engraved horsehead patch box with silver star and thumb piece inlay, Dreppert lock and old replacement, stock professionally ended out, 47 3/4 in. octagon to round smooth bore barrel, 63 in. long.........**$8,750**

Long rifle, flintlock, "D. Sheets," mark uncertain, curly maple in varnished-over old dark finish, simple raise carving around cheek piece and comb, brass hardware with bird's-head patch box, engraved eagle cheek piece inlay, old repair at tang, lock is reconverted, 62 3/4 in. long. **$3,250**

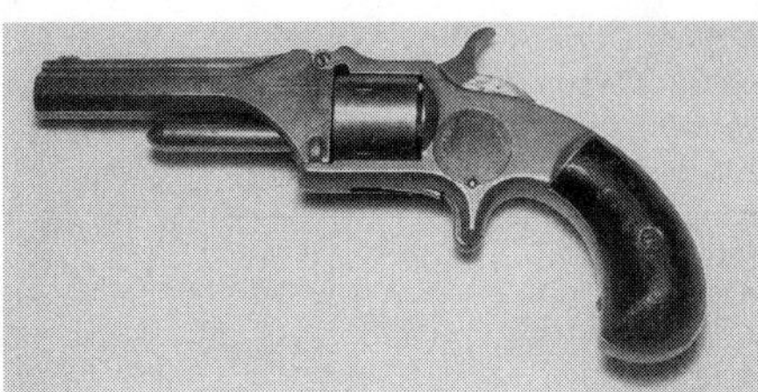
Revolver, Marlin XX Standard 1873, .22 caliber, brass frame, 6 3/4 in. long. **$120**

Pistol, pepperbox, Remington-Elliot, .32 caliber, rubber grips, 5 in. long. **$225**

Pistol, percussion, Aston model 1842, 8 1/2 in. long barrel. **$1,100**

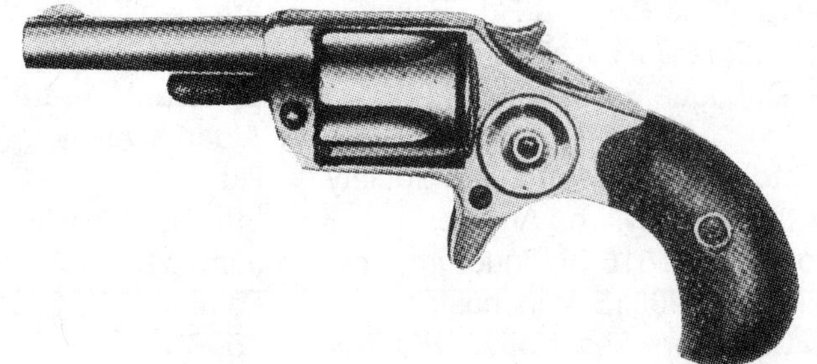
Revolver, Colt New Line 32, serial #13010, 6 in. long. **$175**

Long rifle, flintlock, unsigned, curly maple in old dark finish and over-varnish, full stock, brass hardware including four-piece patch box, Golcher lock with double-throated hammer, some characteristics similar to William or Peter Young, 39 1/4 in. octagon barrel, 54 1/2 in. long. **$2,750**

Long rifle, flintlock, unsigned, curly maple with good figure, brass hardware, engraved and pierced patch box, engraved silver cheek piece inlay and oval thumb piece, expertly restocked using old parts, brass repair near lock, with a few accessories, 56 1/2 in. long. **$1,500**

Long rifle, percussion, "J. Yeager" in block stamping, curly maple with good figure and patina, brass hardware including engraved patch box and toe plate signed "S. McClain," eagle inlay over cheek piece, some wear ahead of lock, 51 1/4 in. long. **$1,500**

Pistol, flintlock, Johnson, model of 1836, 8 1/2 in. long barrel....**$2,500**

Pistol, percussion, lock with abbreviated stamp for Middletown, Connecticut, dated 1847, walnut stock with age cracks, brass hardware, 8 1/2 in. round barrel, probably by Aston or Johnson, missing ramrod attachment, 14 in. long. **$475**

Powder flask, cow horn, incised "Lancaster" and with landscape scene, 17 1/2 in. long.............**$325**

Powder flask, deer head, fox, and

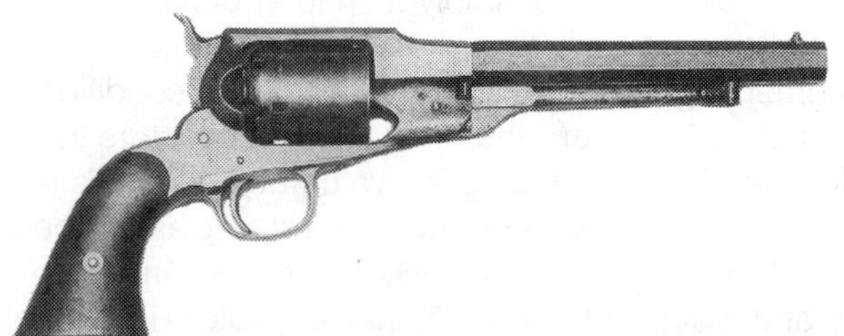

Revolver, Remington-Beals Navy, .36 caliber, hairline on grip, 13 1/2 in. long. **$725**

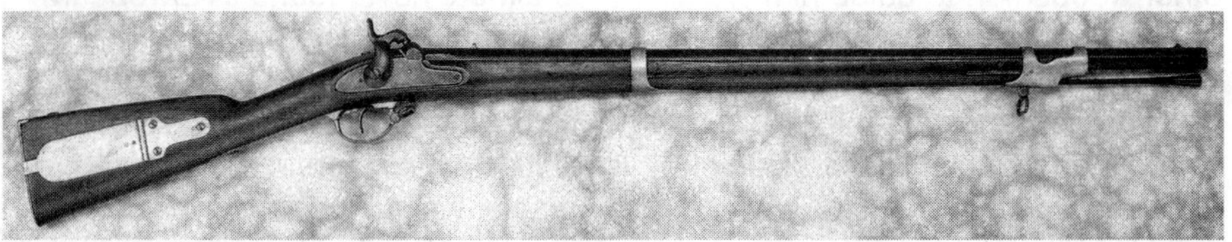

Rifle, Remington Model 1841, .58 caliber, 33 in. long barrel. **$2,200**

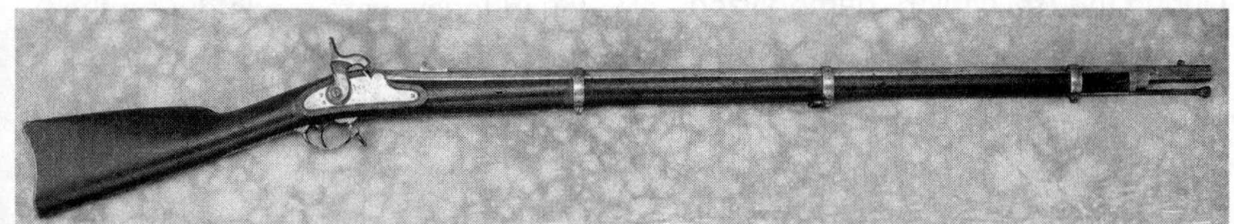

Rifle, Remington Zouve, Model of 1863, .58 caliber, with bayonet/sheath, 33 in. long barrel. **$3,500**

oak leaf pattern, Hawksley, brass top, three-slot charger, spring not working, 7 3/4 in. tall. **$150**

Powder flask, eagle, embossed, copper, 3 1/2 in. tall................**$125**

Powder flask, fluted pattern, American Flask & Cap Co., brass, two plugs on bottom, 4 1/2 in. tall. **$400**

Powder flask, hanging game pattern, copper. **$450**

Powder flask, ivy pattern, J.M. Hawksley, minor corrosion, dent, 9 in. tall, 4 1/2 in. wide. **$150**

Powder flask, lyre pattern, French, copper and brass, 5 1/2 in. tall by 2 1/2 in. wide. **$450**

Powder horn, cow horn, screw tip, curved, wooden butt, stopper missing, crack, 11 in. long.......**$375**

Powder horn, horn, wooden butt, cast brass knob, stopper and U-shaped piece of horn missing, 11 in. long. **$120**

Rifle, Springfield Model 1861, .58 caliber, with bayonet, 40 in. long barrel..................................**$3,750**

Gauging Kentucky Rifles

by Wayne Mattox

Just as a cherry tops a sundae, few household collections of American antiques can be called complete until a handsome "Kentucky rifle" (sometimes called a "Pennsylvania" rifle) is found to hang on a favorite wall.

Evolved from mass-produced, short, heavy, large-bore Jaeger rifles brought to North America by German colonists, the improved arm was designed to meet the challenges of a wild-game-filled and often dangerous new world. Around the mid-18th century, the rifle developed a long octagonal barrel and smaller bore for taking better aim. The slender slope of the beautiful native-wood stock (primarily tiger maple) was carved with shoulder pads and a deep crescent butt plate so that it would be comfortable to shoot, lighter to carry, and pleasing to the eye.

The right side of the rifle's rear-end handle was fitted with a clever new feature: a long narrow box cut into the wood for carrying greased wad patches necessary for shooting. The brass-hinged covers on these "patchboxes" were plain in the beginning, but soon this distinctive feature on Kentucky rifles was fashioned in elaborate rococo designs with fancy engraving. Often, the left side of the stock was carved with a "C," "S," and foliate scrollwork. Many were inlaid with silver and brass decals like moons, hearts, and fish.

The Kentucky rifle was not mass-produced. Thousands of variations were made in small shops by master gunsmiths. Each is a highly individualistic work of art.

History's greatest collector of the rifle and one of America's most preeminent antique dealers, the late Joe Kindig Jr. considered the long-barreled guns an expression of American folk art.

Norm Flayderman, the famous military and gun dealer, beautifully sums up the important position Kentucky rifles hold in Flayderman's Guide to American Firearms and their values. "There is likely more lore and romance surrounding the Kentucky rifle than any other American gun—or for that matter any style of firearm in the world. Quite a few qualities give Kentucky rifles their unique appeal. First, distinctive American flavor—they are truly one of the few indigenous American weapons. Secondly, sheer beauty—they are all attractive and pleasing to the eye. Aesthetically, Kentuckies represent the most handsome of all early American weapons, ranking with the finest products of Europe. Lastly, their unparalleled role in the develop-

ment of American history, from use prior to and during the American Revolution and the War of 1812 to the integral part in forging and expanding the western frontiers."

A beginning student of Kentucky rifles should know that collectors generally assign a gun to one of three major classifications:

1) A Transition Period Piece (1715-1775) —German design was still undergoing its transformation. Features: Flintlock hammer, 40-plus in. long barrel, approximately 60 caliber, early examples will have sliding wood patchbox covers, little embellishment. Rare and highly collected. $10,000+

2) A Golden Age Rifle (1775-1825) —Highest development of American rococo design and gunsmith art. Features: Flintlock hammer, 42 in. to 46 in. barrel, approximately 50 caliber, sophisticated relief carving, fancy brass and silver patchboxes, stocks are made from the finest grains of wood, usually tiger maple. Highly coveted. $3,000+

3) Percussion Phase (1825-1860) — Quality weapons made with less artistry. Features: Percussion ignition system hammer, 34 in. to 36 in. barrel, approximately 40 caliber, relief carving is rare but inlay work is often exceptional, plain brass patchboxes, good quality wood. Like all Kentuckies, still highly desirable. $1,000+

Surprisingly, one of America's earliest triumphs in artistic and functional design, the Kentucky rifle was not invented or generally fashioned in Kentucky. The name was coined from a hearty stock of Americans who used it.

Native Americans called Kentucky the "dark and bloody ground" because of the unending wars between Iroquois and Cherokees for its possession. Europeans thought of the first "wild west" as a hunter's paradise. In 1752, a stalwart American Indian trader named John Findley traveled the Ohio River documenting the valley's beauty and abundance. In 1769, a bold young explorer and skilled marksman, who was given an American-made flintlock rifle at the age of twelve, hired Findley and four other woodsmen to guide him through a wilderness country road between Kentucky and Tennessee, which is now know as the Cumberland Gap. In 1775, (Daniel) Boonesborough, Kentucky, was established.

During the Revolution, demoralized English officers wrote home about a new type of American-made long-barreled "rifle" that backwoodsmen used with astonishing skill. When the war was won, the new government paid debts to its officers by offering land grants in untamed land. Claiming their acreage, these adventurers brought their rifles to Kentucky with them.

Near the end of the War of 1812, American spirits were raised when 5,000 Americans, including 2,000 frontiersmen with long-barreled guns, under the command of Gen. Andrew Jackson, defeated the British in the Battle of New Orleans. A popular song called "The Hunters of Kentucky or The Battle of New Orleans" (no doubt written by a proud Kentuckian) forever named America's rifle: "But Jackson he was wide awake, and wasn't scar'd at trifles, for well he knew what aim we take, with our Kentucky rifles."

The Kentucky rifle was invented and predominantly made in Pennsylvania. A good gun cost half a man's yearly wage. Most were used for hunting on a daily basis. They were handed down from generation to generation, and are often found in worn condition. Antique dealers call this *patina* and charge additional fare for it. Many of the early flintlock rifles were converted to the improved percussion system in the 1830s. This does not ruin the value of a Kentucky rifle. It is simply a chapter of its life.

Age, artistic beauty, and condition are the most important factors in gauging the value of the world's most sought-after firearm. A classic specimen is stocked in native American tiger stripe maple. (Note: Tiger maple is almost never found in European furniture and thus is evidence of valuable American origin.) A rare colonial "transition era (1715-1775)" flintlock specimen in a plain grain of maple, walnut, cherry, or birch can command a huge sum. Keep in mind, most plain-wood Kentucky rifles found today were made during the third generation "percussion era (1825-1860)." These are generally $1,000 rifles, not five-figure antiques.

A hinge-door patchbox cut into the stock is the distinguishing feature of a Kentucky rifle. Most were made of brass and their decorative elements can often identify a gun's maker or geographic origin. Valuable "Golden age (1775-1825)" Kentucky rifles often have elaborate patchboxes and carved stocks.

Like paintings, a rare signed work (the maker's name or initials on the barrel or elsewhere) of a great gunsmith artist is an important document of history. Most Kentucky rifle makers, being humble Quakers, signed their work with their workmanship, not their name.

Seldom do I suggest that a line of antiques is a staple in an honorable collection. A good Kentucky rifle is one place where I make my stand. It is part of America itself.

(Wayne Mattox is the proprietor of Wayne Mattox Antiques, Woodbury, Connecticut, specializing in 18th and early 19th century furnishings, American folk art, and accessories.)

Fireplace Equipment

Andirons were used in pairs to support the logs in a fireplace. Consisting of a vertical standard with a horizontal bar attached in the rear, they were made of brass, bronze, iron, steel, or silver. Although their use has always been utilitarian, some andirons are quite decorative. Andirons relegated to kitchen duty were generally made of iron without decoration. Firedogs and brand dogs are other terms used for andirons.

Reproduction Alert

Among the more common reproductions and fakes are cast iron figurals, including those with an African-American motif.

❖ Andirons

Brass, baluster-like column with large turned finial, arched scrolled legs with spurs, ball feet, late 18th or early 19th century, polished, 18 3/4 in. tall. **$650/pair**

Brass, beaded belted ball and steeple top, faceted plinths, ball feet, American, early 19th century, repair to one leg at log support, 20 in. tall. **$3,500/pair**

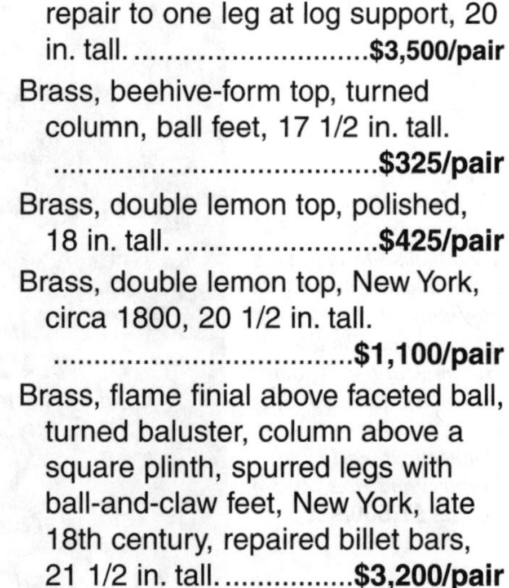

Brass, beehive-form top, turned column, ball feet, 17 1/2 in. tall. **$325/pair**

Brass, double lemon top, polished, 18 in. tall. **$425/pair**

Brass, double lemon top, New York, circa 1800, 20 1/2 in. tall. **$1,100/pair**

Brass, flame finial above faceted ball, turned baluster, column above a square plinth, spurred legs with ball-and-claw feet, New York, late 18th century, repaired billet bars, 21 1/2 in. tall. **$3,200/pair**

Brass, urn finials, turned column, ball feet with spurs, 21 in. tall. **$425/pair**

Brass, ball finial, belted ball, attributed to R. Wittingham, N.Y., early 19th century, square plinths engraved with flowers and bow-knotted wreath surrounding "B," flower on two sides, arched spurred legs, ball feet, scratches, 10 1/2 in. tall. **$4,500/pair**

Brass, ball finial, belted ball, turned baluster shaft, arched spurred legs, pad feet, early 19th century, wear, damage to log stops, 17 in. tall. **$700/pair**

Brass, ball finial, marked "Hunneman, Boston," legs possibly replaced, 16 in. tall. **$650/pair**

Brass, ball finial, marked "John Molineux, Boston," 19 in. tall. **$2,900/pair**

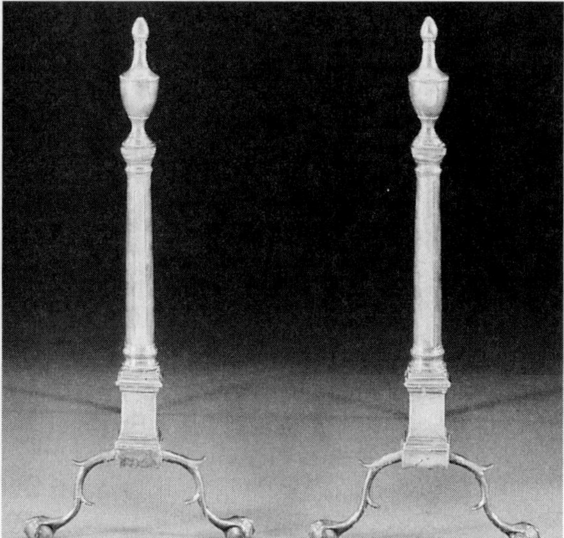

Brass, Federal style, an acorn on urn finial above a tapering columnar shaft over a box plinth, on spurred cabriole front legs with ball-and-claw feet, American, circa 1800-10, 25 1/2 in. tall. **$2,300/pair**

Fireplace insert, cast iron, a bow-front flat base with a small raised lip, scalloped side panels with relief-cast fans and faces, biscuit corners on the top with circular and oval fans, original seamed brass finials, signed "Wyer & Noble," early 19th century, originally had feet, back plate cracked, base 22 3/4 in. wide, 28 in. tall. **$350**

Brass, ball finial, matching ball log stops, 12 5/8 in. tall. **$500/pair**

Cast iron, bulldog, 16 in. tall. **$1,000/pair**

Cast iron, dogs sitting on tulips, scrolled base, ring top, 14 3/4 in. tall. **$250/pair**

Cast iron, George Washington, traces of old paint, 14 1/2 in. tall. **$250/pair**

Cast iron, woman motif, 14 in. tall. **$200/pair**

Wrought iron, penny feet, brass urn finials, one finial damaged, 14 1/2 in. tall. **$450/pair**

Wrought iron, primitive, straight shaft with gooseneck topped by faceted finial, bowed legs, 19 1/2 in. tall. **$600/pair**

Wrought iron, knife blade form, arched legs, penny feet, brass urn and acorn finial, 24 in. tall. **$850/pair**

Wrought iron, knife blade form, brass urn finial, early 19th century, seam separation, minor loss, 16 in. tall. **$450/pair**

Wrought iron, knife blade form, penny feet, urn finial, brass trim, 23 1/2 in. tall. **$775/pair**

❖ General Equipment

In the Colonial home, the fireplace was the gathering point for heat, meals, and social interaction. It maintained its dominant position until the introduction of central heating in the mid 19th century. In rural areas, however, farmhouses retained their working fireplaces as sources of heat well into the 20th century.

Reference: John Campbell, *Fire & Light in the Home Pre 1820*, Antique Collectors' Club, 1999.

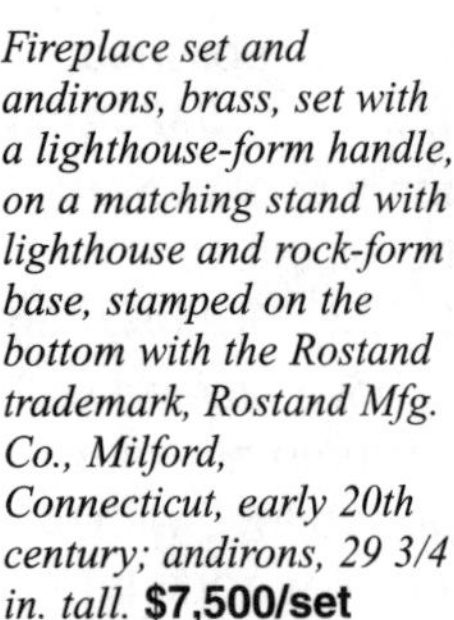

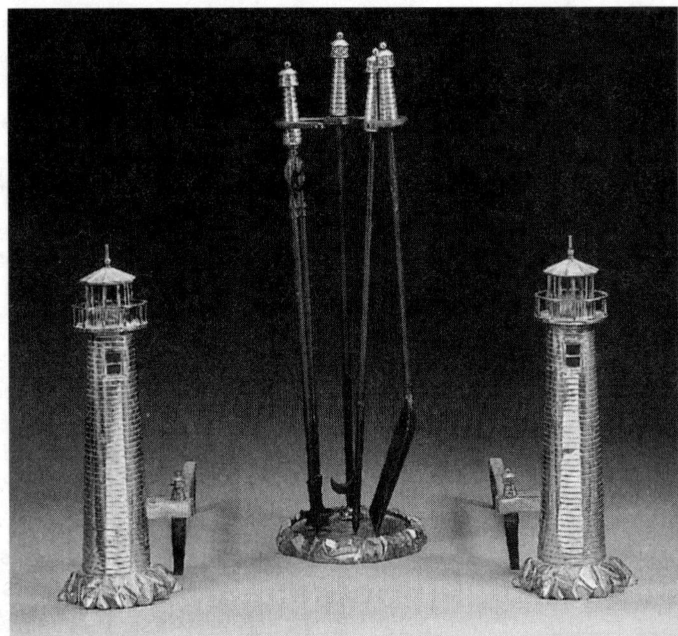

Fireplace set and andirons, brass, set with a lighthouse-form handle, on a matching stand with lighthouse and rock-form base, stamped on the bottom with the Rostand trademark, Rostand Mfg. Co., Milford, Connecticut, early 20th century; andirons, 29 3/4 in. tall. **$7,500/set**

Fireplace tools and stand, circa 1930, wrought iron and incorporating an old horseshoe, with poker, shovel, and tongs, rope-twist handles and splay legs, old black painted finish, 32 in. by 20 in. by 20 in. ***$50***

Reproduction Alert

Because fireplaces have retained their appeal and often serve as decorative focal points, modern blacksmiths have begun reproducing many of the old implements.

Broiler, rotating, wrought iron, round, seven parallel flattened bars across top, three squared legs, rectangular feet, tapered/flattened handle extends from one leg and has loop end, 19th century, rust, 3 3/8 in. tall, 15 5/8 in. diameter, 24 1/2 in. long. **$225**

Broiler, rotating, wrought iron, round, nine parallel flattened bars across top, Y-shaped base, three rectangular legs, bottom of Y curved up to form tapered flattened handle with pod end, 19th century, rust, 2 5/8 in. tall, 12 in. diameter. **$225**

Broiler, rotating, wrought iron, round, pinwheel design, Y-shaped base, three rectangular legs, square feet, tail of Y forms long flattened handle, loop end with scrolled tip, rust, 4 1/2 in. tall, 12 1/2 in. diameter, 30 5/8 in. long. **$420**

Broom, original red paint, black, yellow and gold striping, stenciled freehand floral decor in bronze powder and black, horsehair bristles, wear, flaking, 28 in. long. **$275**

Broom, wooden handle, 49 1/4 in. long. **$40**

Crane, wrought iron, 12 1/4 in. tall, 36 in. long, vertical bar, horizontal arm with large scrolled hook, substantial rusting. **$150**

Crane, wrought iron, 19 1/2 in. tall, 39 1/2 in. long, vertical bar, horizontal arm, both with square pegs on back for fitting into wall brackets, small hook end, some pitting. **$90**

Crane, wrought iron, 46 in. tall, 50 1/2 in. long, vertical bar, horizontal arm with small hook, slightly curved diagonal brace, bottom of vertical post with wall mount attached, substantial rust........ **$200**

Crane, wrought iron, 57 1/4 in. tall, 45 3/4 in. long, vertical bar, horizontal arm, diagonal brace, substantial rust......................... **$70**

Fender, brass top rim, scroll decor in vertical wirework, American or English, late 18th or early 19th century, 10 in. tall, 59 1/2 in. wide, 15 in. deep. **$3,100**

Fender, brass and wire, flattened base rim, American or English, early 19th century, wire breaks, dents, 27 in. tall, 40 in. long, 15 1/2 in. deep. **$250**

Fender, wire, curved sides, spiral design, brass trim, 12 in. tall, 44 in. long. **$675**

Fireback, cast iron, figures in relief, floral garland border, floral basket cartouche flanked by sphinx, dated 1663, cracked, 26 in. by 16 1/2 in... **$150**

Fireplace inset, Federal, cast iron, marked "Wyer & Noble," bowfront base, scalloped side panels with relief fans and faces, biscuit corners on top with circular and oval fans, original seamed brass finials, feet missing, back plate cracked, 28 in. tall, 32 1/4 in. wide, 22 3/4 in. deep. **$370**

Fire screen, mahogany with old finish, tripod base, snake feet, urn-turned column and pole, urn finial, oval frame with figured mahogany veneer, watercolor on silk scene of bird and flowers, 19th century, stains on silk, repairs to base of column, 54 in. tall. **$1,900**

Frying pan, sheet iron, round with long flattened wrought-iron handle, flared sides, 19th century, 10 in. brace attached to side of pan, pitting, black paint. **$60**

Gridiron, wrought iron, seven round parallel rods for square top, arched legs, slightly curved feet, flattened diagonal handle extends up from front leg and has round end, rust, 2 1/4 in. tall, 8 7/8 in. wide, 14 in. long. **$150**

Gridiron, wrought iron, nine flattened rods form square top, square legs, slightly curved tapering/flattened handle extends from front set of legs, pod-shaped end, 19th century, bottom of both front feet broken off, 4 in. tall, 9 1/2 in. wide, 20 3/4 in. deep. **$150**

Gridiron, wrought iron, nine iron rods form top, squared legs, scrolled feet, handle extends from front legs and bends up, 19th century, significant rust, 2 5/8 in. tall, 17 1/2 in. long, top 9 3/4 in. by 11 in....**$85**

Kettle tilter, wrought iron, flattened bar with two large scrolled hooks to hold kettle, curves upward forming handle that is round and ends in mushroom-like finial, small iron bracket on top of bar with swiveling loop for hanging on trammel, minor rust, 10 3/8 in. tall, 19 1/2 in. long... **$430**

Kick toaster, wrought iron, T-shaped tripod base, rectangular frame having two rods on either side, one above the other, forming rack for holding toast, handle extends outward and curves up slightly, ends in pod with hole for hanging, minor rust, 5 in. tall, 13 1/8 in. wide, 17 5/8 in. long. **$240**

Log fork, wrought iron, long round handle, cast brass ovoid finial, some rust, 44 in. long. **$35**

Set, four pieces, brass andirons with turned column, urn finial and ball feet, matching tongs and shovel, early 19th century. **$600**

Set, four pieces, brass ball-top andirons with ring-turned and faceted plinths on scrolled legs with ball feet, shovel and tongs with brass ring-turned and ribbed finials, minor dents, wear. **$775**

Set, five pieces, ribbed ring-turned andirons, similar tongs and shovel, jamb hook with urn finials, 19th century, minor wear................ **$775**

Shovel and tongs, wrought iron, brass finials, 30 in. long..... **$75/pair**

Trammel, wrought iron, top, slide bar, and catch with scalloped finials, engraved detail with cross and "1809," adjusts from 43 in. to 60 in. **$550**

Trammel, wrought iron, bar with eight holes and swivel loop at top, separate rod hooks into holes of bar and has large hook with scrolled tip at its base, 19th century, substantial rust, 25 1/2 in. long. **$180**

Trammel, wrought iron, round bar with loop having 3 3/4 in. diameter ring, flattened bar with ratchet device, rust, 46 1/2 in. long..... **$120**

Trammel, wrought iron, round bar with plain hook, wide flattened sawtooth bar with ratchet device, large hook at bottom of flat bar, substantial rust, 42 1/4 in. long. **$75**

Trivet, rotating, wrought iron, round top with straight center bar flanked by double-arched bars, mounted to tripod base with two cabriole-style legs and one round vertical, tapered flattened handle with large loop end, minor damage on top, 18 1/2 in. long, 9 1/2 in. diameter. **$450**

Waffle iron, cast iron, four rectangular compartments with geometric designs, long round double handles, 19th century, significant pitting, some rust, 8 1/4 in. by 6 1/4 in., 27 1/2 in. long... **$85**

Waffle iron, cast iron, double, rectangular with star-like designs, 4 1/4 in. by 7 1/8 in. by 26 in. long. **$85**

Waffle iron, cast iron, round, heart design, rod handles with ring ends, 8 1/2 in. diameter, 22 3/4 in. long.... **$175**

Waffle iron, cast iron, round, interior with graduated rows of rectangles, tapered handle, late 19th century, rust, 8 3/4 in. diameter by 23 in. long. **$40**

American, 13-star, mid-19th century, hand-sewn wool, double appliquéd cotton stars, from the family of a Massachusetts Civil War veteran, soiled, fabric loss, 60 in. by 100 in. **$2,300**
Photo courtesy Skinner Auctioneers & Appraisers of Antiques & Fine Arts, Boston and Bolton, Mass.

Flags

The Americana aspect of flags makes them a natural with collectors, and age and rarity play major roles in determining value. Condition is especially important when considering flags that are more readily available.

Collectors' Club: North American Vexillological Association, 1977 N. Olden Ave., Ste. 225, Trenton, NJ 08618.

American, 15-star, wool, soiled, fading, fabric loss, three rows of five stars, 30 in. by 66 in. **$3,100**

American, 16-star, homespun cotton, hand-sewn, circa 1800, four rows of four stars, fading, 37 in. by 66 in. **$4,800**

American, 20-star, cotton, hand-sewn, early 19th century, minor stains, small tears, 38 1/2 in. by 53 1/2 in. **$4,500**

American, 25-star, muslin, machine and hand-sewn, five rows of five stars, probably a naval ensign, probably pre-Civil War, scattered browning, 80 in. by 142 in.... **$1,100**

American, 35-star, Great Star flag, printed muslin, center star larger and bordered with blue then white border, two outer rings of stars and one star in each corner, circa 1863, slight discolor and wear, 19 1/4 in. by 28 in. **$1,700**

American, 39-star, silk, six rows of stars in a 6-7-7-6-7-6 pattern, 11 1/2 in. by 17 3/4 in. **$175**

American, 48-star, lopsided stars, circa 1920, attributed to Marie Miller.................................. **$1,300**

Confederate, United Veterans of the Confederacy (U.V.C.) battle flag, Army of Northern Virginia pattern, pieced silk, 1 in. hoist, three brass grommets, red ground, purple bars, white stars, machine- and hand-sewn, gold fringe border, uppercase "A" at top, probably for Company A, 34 in. square. **$375**

Confederate, U.V.C. battle flag, Army of Northern Virginia pattern, printed cotton, on wood staff with spear-point finial, toning, repaired tear, 12 in. square. **$300**

Confederate, U.V.C. flag, hand-sewn wool, red over white over red stripes, faded blue canton with circular pattern of five stars, mounted on wood staff, late 19th century, short tear, 10 in. by 18 in. **$975**

Nullification flag, 16-star Northern Abolitionist "exclusion" flag, circa 1851-1858, hand-sewn cotton, 23 red/white stripes, blue canton with four rows of four stars, moderate stains, small holes, minor edge tears, 45 in. by 47 in. **$4,100**

Folk Art

The term "folk art" is really one of perspective. The pieces that we now value as folk art often were not considered works of art by their makers, but rather had a form and function that were determined by the necessities of their day, or by the emotional investment in their creation.

It's still difficult to find a broad consensus on what exactly constitutes folk art. Should mass-produced, factory items like windmill weights and weathervanes be included? Such pieces have become icons of late 19th century and early 20th century America, but some collectors do not consider them folk art because of how and where they were made. Most agree, however, that folk art comes from a tradition outside of academic circles, and includes items both whimsical and utilitarian, whether elaborate or starkly simple.

This section deals with folksy art, antiques, and oddities that are not covered in other areas of the book (quilts, rugs, and samplers, for instance, are found in other sections, while canes and walking sticks, windmill weights, weathervanes, and tramp art have their own categories).

Two views of bottle whimsy, pale green glass, very thick, old bottle with turned wood stopper, containing a yarn winder with green thread that is placed between four whittled posts, on top of each post is a cloth flag, similar to but not American flags: red and white stripes, and a circular pattern of white stars on a blue field; it is signed "D. CARR" on one side of a cross piece below the winder, and dated 1879 on the other side, 13 5/8 in. tall including stopper, 4 1/2 in. **$1,500-$2,000**

Two views of bottle whimsy, made by Carl Worner, with puzzle stopper and showing interior of saloon with bartender, two men in suits, and woman seated at table, minor damage to interior base, circa 1910, 10 1/2 in. by 4 1/4 in. by 2 1/2 in. **$1,500-$2,000**

Bowling pin trophy, dated 1946, painted with names of bowlers from a rural Wisconsin league, maple, considerable wear, 15 in. tall. **$90**

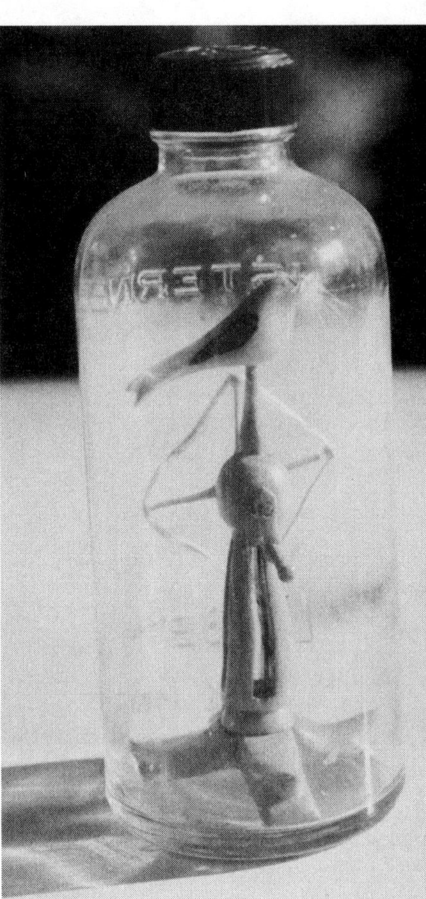

Two views of bottle whimsy, in a screw-cap Listerine bottle, containing a finely carved, painted, and polished single four-spoke spinning wheel on a turned shaft that stands on a carved pedestal; the wheel has a crank, and on a thin spike sticking out of the top of the shaft is a yellow and black bird. This is not the only bottle by this maker, who is anonymous and probably from the Midwest, 7 in. by 2 1/4 in. **$400-$500**

Stone carving, circa 1900, sandstone, showing the Last Supper with the apostles huddled around Christ in a medieval-style tableau, probably European but salvaged from a rural Wisconsin church, minor flaking and chipping, 14 in. by 8 in. by 2 in. **$800-$1,000**

Bowl, painted wood, circa 1880, showing horses pulling sleighs through a snowy village with house and church, mounted on a stained butternut board, from Goodhue County, Minn., excellent condition, bowl 14 in. diameter, board 18 1/2 in. square. **$800-$1,000**

Diorama, circa 1930s, showing a three-masted ship under full sail, flying both American and Norwegian flags, complete with miniature rigging, lifeboats, and tiny figures of sailors on deck; set in a box with simulated sky and water, and having a hole in the bottom into which a small electric bulb can be placed to make it appear the portholes are lighted; frame also decorated with flags and anchors, overall dimensions 40 in. by 24 in. by 8 in. **$1,000-$1,200**

Ship model, circa 1880, carved and painted wood hull with furled cloth sails and rigging made of string, plus handmade stand, made as a present for the captain of the ship, which brought Scandinavian immigrants to America, some rigging broken, overall very good condition, with stand, 22 in. by 15 in. by 5 in. **$1,200-$1,500**

Miniature bark canoe, circa 1910, probably of Indian make, with woven edges and seams, overall very good condition, 26 in. by 6 in. by 6 in. **$200-$300**

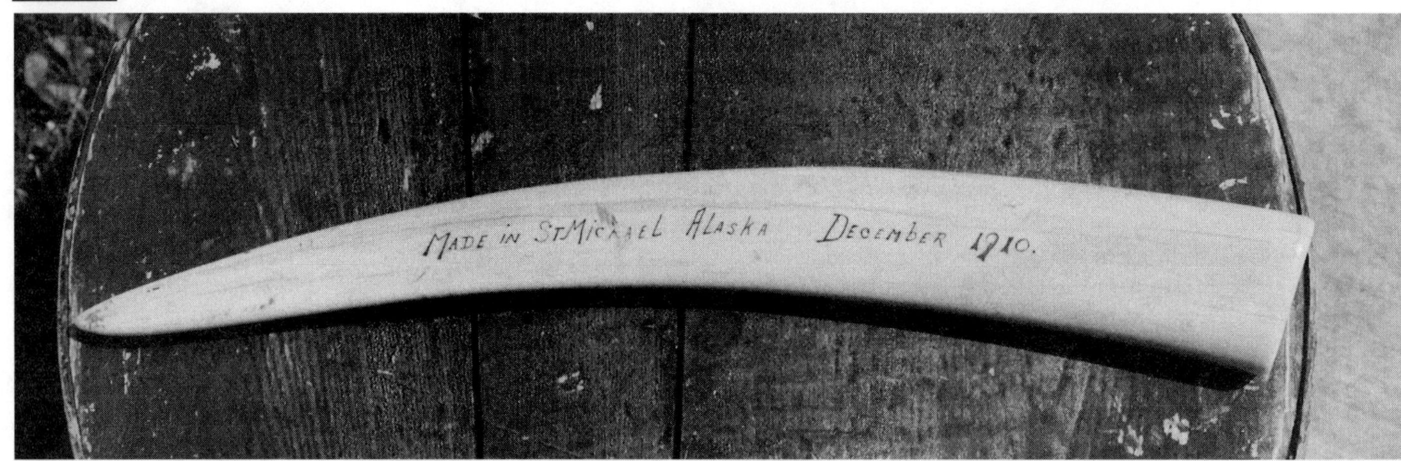

Walrus tusk with carved inscription: "Made in St. Michael Alaska December 1910," 14 in. long, perfect condition. **$300-$400**

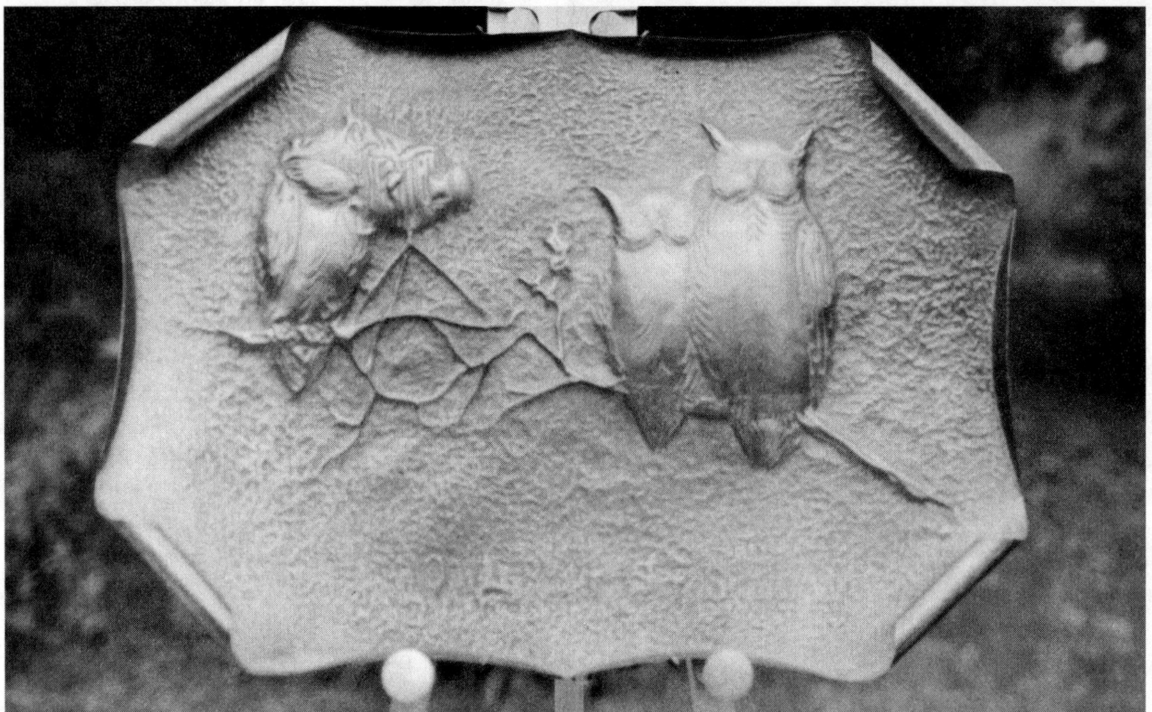

Wall plaque, brass, with curled corners and hand-hammered image of three owls sitting on a branch, one owl looking through a box camera on stand, barely visible below owls are the words, "Owl Right, Sit Still!"; possibly a student project, circa 1910, mint condition, 20 in. by 13 in. **$300-$400**

Two views of miniature Norwegian trunk, pine, American made, circa 1910, painted inside and out with flowers and gilt trim simulating ironwork, with open till inside, original lock and key, bracket feet, nailed construction, mint condition, 8 3/4 in. by 5 1/4 in. by 5 in. **$1,200-$1,500**

❖ Ingvald Skorgen Folk Art

Ingvald Skorgen (1876-1951) was born on his family's farm at Skorgedalen on the Isfjord across from Andalsnes, Norway. The name Skorgen was derived from the location of the farm at the bend in the fjord. "Skorg" means the wearing away of a bank by water.

At the age of seven, Ingvald traveled to America with his parents Peder and Gjertrude Rottum Skorgen. Settling in the South Fork Valley in Fillmore County, southeastern Minnesota, they built a log cabin, which still stands by the river.

Ingvald started collecting arrowheads, relics, rock, broken mirrors, and glass beads to decorate the concrete sculptures he began making in the 1930s. He eventually built an entire sculpture garden, which included towering figures of a black man and woman, an Indian with war paint, an alligator and turtle, a kubbestol (a Norwegian carved chair usually made from a single log, though Ingvald's was made of concrete), and decorative markers. He even made the marker for his mother's grave.

Many of Skorgen's creations were exhibited at the Cornucopia Art Center in Lanesboro, Minn., in 1996.

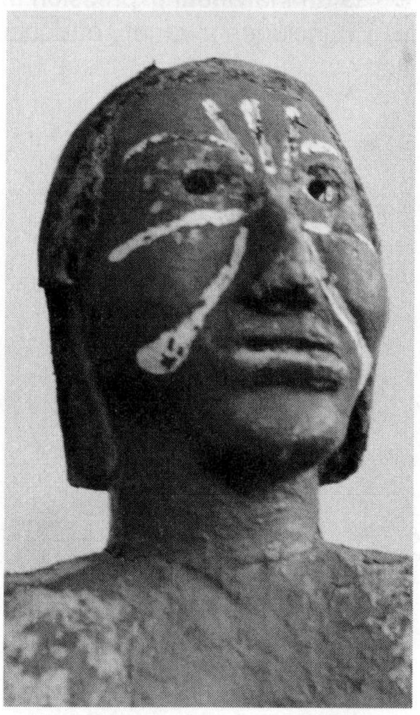

❖ Memoryware

Memoryware is the name used to describe a kind of folk art popular around the turn of the 19th century in which various vessels—bottles, jars, cups, vases, urns, etc.—are coated with a resin or clay-like substance and then small articles are pressed into the still-soft surface to create a collage of colors and textures. There is no limit to the kinds of trinkets that decorate memoryware: buttons, beads, coins, medals, tiny toys and novelties (like those found in boxes of Cracker Jack), keys, rings, barrettes, shells, glass and ceramic shards, etc. Because of the nature of the coating, it is normal to find chips, cracks, and missing trinkets. These flaws will affect value, but do not generally detract from the desirability of the pieces unless the damage amounts to more than 5 percent of the surface. Of course, pieces having little or no damage, or those whose decoration is especially imaginative or incorporates unusual trinkets (rare pinback buttons or fraternal emblems, for instance) command a higher price. Pieces decorated entirely with shells, which were often made as souvenirs, are not part of this collecting area and do not bring as high a price as memoryware that was created as an individual expression and which includes a variety of decoration.

Two views of memoryware mug, circa 1900, with hand-formed handle on a ceramic body, decorated with buttons, coins, tokens, shards, a crucifix, and a human tooth; it may have had a top, some loss to base, overall good condition, 9 in. by 7 in. by 5 in. **$150-$200**

Two views of memoryware planter made of molded paper pulp, circa 1920, decorated with buttons, beaded trim, metal brooches, plastic fragments, shells and glass shards, moderate loss of coating to upper edge, overall very good condition, 12 in. by 7 in. **$200-$300**

❖ Scherenschnitte

Scherenschnitte is the art of decorative paper cutting. Unlike silhouettes, this form involves more elaborate full-sized scenes, including landscapes. In addition to pictures, the term also includes decorative elements that may be part of a larger work.

Birth record, latticework border with leaves and tulips on top and bottom, "Jannes Stratingh, Ge Boren Den 4 October, 1812," two other names, leaf dividers, early mahogany veneer frame, margin stains, 16 5/8 in. by 21 in. **$1,400**

Decorative tree and four birds, lined school paper on green backing, old carved frame with note "Pa. Dutch Cutout, Lancaster County," 4 3/4 in. by 2 3/4 in. **$475**

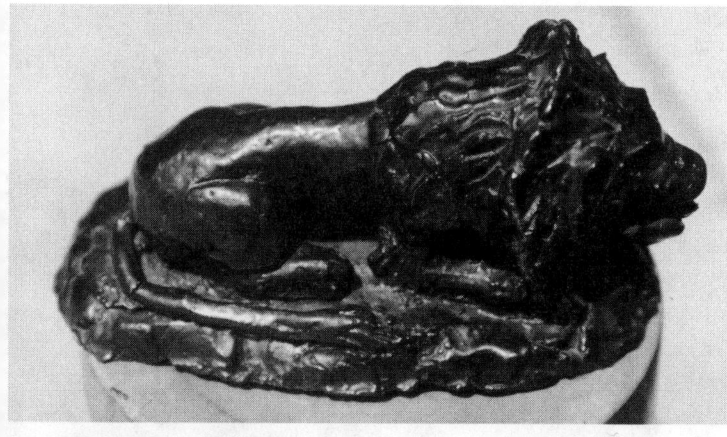

Lion, resting, with Albany slip glazed surface, probably Ohio origin, circa 1890, minor chipping, 9 in. by 5 in. by 4 1/2 in. **$350-$450**

❖ Sewer Tile

Also called sewer pipe, sewer tile was produced from about 1880 through the early 20th century. Sewer tile clay is heavy, red clay that was molded and glazed for making sewer or drain pipe. Draining tiles and sewer tiles were produced at the factories, but the workers often spent their spare time creating other items of utilitarian or whimsical nature from this material. Although some molded pieces were made, much of the production was one-of-a-kind items. Pieces that are signed and/or dated are especially prized.

Ohio is recognized as the leading producer of sewer tile, but other states, including Minnesota, New York, Pennsylvania, and Indiana, all had a strong presence in the sewer tile market.

Alligator, Ohio, 15 in. long. **$450**

Bank, dog, seated spaniel, slot in back of head, round opening on bottom, minor glaze flakes, probably Tuscarawas County, Ohio, 10 1/2 in. tall.......................... **$250**

Bust, Abraham Lincoln, shiny glaze, flowing black on jacket, incised eyes, minor edge damage, 7 1/8 in. tall. **$150**

Cat, seated, glaze with copper speckles, small chips, one front foot missing, 7 in. tall. **$350**

Chicken feeder, cylindrical, incised tree trunk decor, applied handle over top, opening on one side of base, 10 1/2 in. tall................. **$250**

Crow on stump, initialed "E.J.E" on base, shallow chip on tail feathers, 9 in. tall, 14 in. long. **$1,100**

Dog, seated, spaniel, 5 1/2 in. tall, minor edge chips. **$225**

Dog, seated, spaniel, 7 in. tall, bottom incised "Chas. Domino, C.D.," molded, tooled, foot repair. **$225**

Dog, seated, spaniel, 7 1/2 in. tall, base incised "E.J.E." (Tuscarawas County, Ohio). **$350**

Dog, seated, spaniel, 8 1/4 in. tall, incised detail up the back, over the head, and down the front leg, incised collar and chain, deep brownish-red glaze, oval base, minor base chips.................. **$325**

Dog, seated, spaniel, 10 in. tall, light brown glaze, black eyes and collar, incised detail on open front legs, made by George Bagnell, Newcomerstown, Ohio, glued crack on front, base chips. **$1,700**

Dog, seated, spaniel, 10 1/4 in. tall, bottom incised "Superior, 10-15-70" (Superior Clay Corp, Tuscarawas County, Ohio), few firing separations, shallow chip on back of base. **$275**

Dog, seated, spaniel, 10 1/2 in. tall, light brown glaze. **$350**

Dog, seated, spaniel, 11 1/2 in. tall, minor wear, few flakes. **$200**

Fish plaque, probably Ohio, 10 1/2 in. long. **$375**

Lion, reclining, rectangular base, base initialed "EJE" (Tuscarawas County, Ohio, maker), 6 in. tall by 8 3/4 in. long. **$570**

Lion, reclining, rectangular base with reeded edges, unglazed red clay, incised "4-22 34, W E, Wadsworth, O." 5 1/4 in. tall by 8 3/8 in. wide by 4 1/8 in. deep. **$300**

Owl, perched on log, 20th century, 8 1/2 in. tall.............................. **$175**

Owl, perched on tree stump, 12 3/4 in. tall...................................... **$570**

Planter, mortar shape, incised "Made by Donald Milby, June 16, 1958 at Perrless Clay," 9 1/2 in. tall, 10 in. diameter. **$120**

Planters, rectangular, raised feet and corners, marked "Cambria Clay Products, Plackfork, Ohio," one foot restored, 12 in. tall by 14 1/2 in. wide by 10 1/4 in. deep. ..**$225/pair**

Planter, triangular base, cast lion's heads and leaves, edge chips, cracks, 23 in. tall. **$225**

Planter, stump, 17 in. tall, four stumps rising from one base, chips, glued restoration........... **$180**

Planter, stump, 17 in. tall, 10 in. diameter, four branches. **$350**

Planter, stump, 17 1/2 in. tall, 10 in. diameter, two branches with Minerva heads, edge damage, cement patch. **$120**

Planter, stump, 19 in. tall, 9 3/4 in. diameter, hand-tooled bark, five molded and applied ducks (one resembles woodpecker), marked "Milburn Larson Clay," damaged branches. **$475**

Planter, stump, 24 1/2 in. tall, 14 1/2 in. diameter, molded and hand-tooled bark, incised "Margaret H.

Dryden, Born Aug. 22, 1890, Died Nov. 23, 1942," minor edge damage. $275

Planter, stump, 26 in. tall, 9 in. diameter, hand-tooled bark, three branches. $240

Planter, stump, 28 3/4 in. tall, 18 in. diameter, hand-tooled bark, three branches, one damaged. $425

Umbrella stand, tree trunk design, applied roses, chips on flowers, 25 1/2 in. tall................................$350

Wall pocket, tree trunk design, small cut limbs, 9 in. tall by 6 1/4 in. wide. $160

Tri-motor airplane, circa 1930s, wood covered with tin, carved wooden propellers, metal wheels and struts, with bicycle reflector mounted on one wing (second reflector missing), weathered surface with traces or original paint, overall very good condition, 20 in. by 18 in. by 9 in. **$500-$600**

❖ Whirligigs

A variation of the weathervane, whirligigs indicate wind direction and velocity. Often constructed by the unskilled, they were generally made of wood and metal and exhibited a rather primitive appearance. Flat, paddle-like arms are characteristic of single-figure whirligigs, but multi-figure examples are usually driven by a propeller that moves a series of gears or rods. Three-dimensional figures are commonly found on 19th century whirligigs, but silhouette figures are generally indicative of 20th century construction.

Reference: Robert Bishop and Patricia Coblentz, *Gallery of American Weathervanes and Whirligigs*, E.P. Dutton, 1981.

Indian in canoe, wooden, carved and painted, paddle arms, 14 in. tall by 18 in. long. $475

Man, light blue outfit, blue hat, rubber arms, composition, looks like weathered wood, contemporary, 24 1/2 in. tall................................$450

Man sawing logs, cut tin, wooden base, old worn gold, red, green, and black paint, directional in green and black, propeller in green and orange, 32 3/4 in. long. $150

Man, wooden, carved and painted, red jacket, blue pants, black boots, brown hat, painted paddle arms, 22 in. tall..................................$7,500

Patriotic motif, black man with hat pumping water for woman in polka-dot bandana with washboard, wooden, propellers in red, white, and blue with stars on the ends, white stars along the base, compass stars on the directional, glued age cracks in directional, other minor age cracks, wear, weathering, 26 1/2 in. long...$1,200

Pipe-smoking bass fiddle player, painted wood and metal with large fan blades and directional attachment topped by carved figure of a man who saws at varnished bass fiddle when blades spin, circa 1930s, old repaint, displayed on period stand, overall dimensions 62 in. by 37 in. by 24 in.$1,200-$1,500

Pot-bellied man, large hooked nose and pointed chin, black top hat and shoes with curled toes, face painted red and white, tin, wind-activated arm baffles, mounted on rod on wooden base, white and red paint shows under black on body, wear, age cracks, arms damaged and one replaced, 11 3/4 in. tall (excluding base)..................$3,500

Roosters, two facing each other on tower made resembling an oil derrick, wooden, red, green, and black paint, 62 in. tall. $140

Fat policeman (Keystone Kop?) directing traffic, painted wood with applied silver buttons and hand-cut metal badge, arms mounted on a metal rod, iron and wood base, mid- to late 20th century, weathered surface with some repaint, 29 in. by 16 in. **$150-$200**

Sawmill motif, wooden, two men running boards through saw under wooden roof, tail marked "Old Tiamciw (?)1860 Saw Mill," said to be from Vermont, circa 1939, 13 in. tall by 32 in. long....................$750

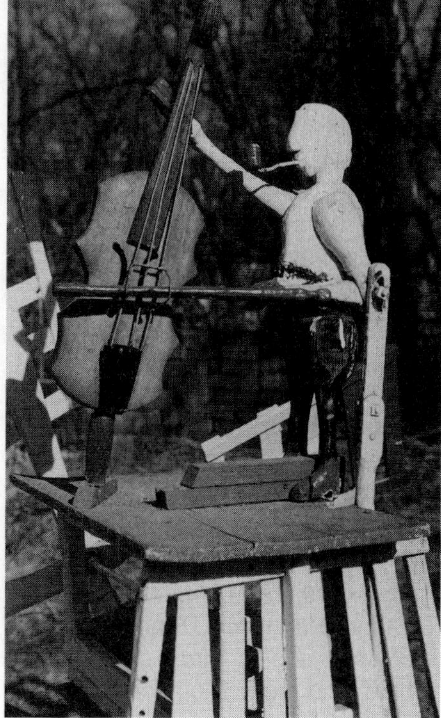

Three views of pipe-smoking bass fiddle player, painted wood and metal with large fan blades and directional attachment topped by carved figure of a man who saws at varnished bass fiddle when blades spin, circa 1930s, old repaint, displayed on period stand, overall dimensions 62 in. by 37 in. by 24 in. **$1,200-$1,500**

Where can I find it?

Adamstown Antique Gallery
2000 North Reading Rd.
Denver, PA 17517
(717) 335-3435
http://www.aagal.com/Antiquetobacciana.htm
adamsgal@dejazzd.com

Blondell Antiques
1406 2nd St. SW
Rochester, MN 55902
(507) 282-1872
Fax: (507) 282-8683
www.blondell.com/
antiques@blondell.com

Country Comfort Antiques
Third and Main Streets
Winona, MN 55987
(507) 452-7044

Country Side Antique Mall
31752 65th Ave.
Cannon Falls, MN 55009
(507) 263-0352
www.csamantiques.com

Freward & Alk Antiques
414 Lazarre Ave.
Green Bay, WI 54301
(800) 488-0321
(920) 435-7343
www.the-antique-shop.com
leesa@the-antique-shop.com

John Kruesel's General Merchandise
22 Third St. SW
Rochester, MN 55902
(507) 289-8049
www.kruesel.com

Wayne Mattox Antiques
82 Main St. N.
Woodbury, CT 06798
(203) 263-2431
www.antiquetalk.com
tiquetalk@aol.com

Mark F. Moran Antiques
5887 Meadow Dr. SE
Rochester, MN 55904
(507) 288-8006
mfmoran@charter.net

Frakturs

Mainly of Pennsylvania Dutch origin, certain illuminated birth and baptismal certificates, marriage certificates, awards of merit, family registers, and other family documents are called fraktur because of their similarity to a 16th century German typeface of the same name. These hand-lettered folk art records generally incorporated bright watercolor borders, stylized birds, and heart motifs.

Museum: The Free Library of Philadelphia, Pennsylvania

Note: All listings are Pennsylvania German unless otherwise noted. Dates refer to the event commemorated by the fraktur.

Birth record, 1818, Union County, Pa., by Francis Portzline, text in center, large circular design with bands of small hearts flanked by facing birds with small double entwined heart designs above and below text, sides flanked by large urns with tulips, brown and green, framed and matted, minor foxing, slight stains, minor border tears, 11 3/4 in. by 18 in. **$10,000-$12,000**
Courtesy Horst Auctioneers, Ephrata, Pa.

Birth record, 1772, pen and ink and watercolor on woven paper, orange, black, and brown, beveled frame with worn red graining, stains, fading, 7 5/8 in. by 12 1/2 in. ....**$800-$900**

Birth record, 1804, Berks County, Pennsylvania, by Martin Brechall, watercolor on laid paper, red border topped with stylized tulips and other flowers in red, blue, brown, and black, text in red and black, stains, paper damage, modern painted frame, 6 in. by 8 in. ....**$700-$800**

Birth record, 1808, Northumberland County, Pennsylvania, circular sunburst in center with text surrounded by four circular sunbursts in each corner, floral designs, tulips in center of all four sides, orange, yellow, blue, and brown, framed and matted, foxing, tears, minor paper loss, 13 1/8 in. by 16 1/2 in. ....**$7,000-$8,000**

Birth record, 1812, Berks County, Pennsylvania, by Martin Brechall, printed text, verse and eagle, hand-done decor in pen and ink on laid paper, red, blue, and yellowish-gray watercolor, framed, stains, damage and color bleeding, 13 1/2 in. by 9 1/4 in. ....**$400-$500**

Birth record, 1813, Noah Hampton County, labeled "F. Krebs," pen and ink and watercolor, printed format, heart motif, parrots, tulips, and stars, orange, brown, green, and yellow, framed, some damage, glue stains, 13 in. by 15 1/2 in. ....**$1,100-$1,200**

Birth record, 1820, Berks County, Pennsylvania, printed by "Rotter, Reading," printed and hand-colored, angels with cherub and birds, yellow, blue, orange, red, and purple, unframed, stains, margin tears, 16 in. by 13 in. ....**$200-$300**

Birth record, 1831, Schuylkill County, Pennsylvania, printed by "Ruth, Rube and Young, Allentown," hand-colored angels, birds, etc., in red, green, yellow, and blue, framed, wear, fading, 19 1/2 in. by 17 1/2 in. ....**$300-$400**

Birth record, 1833, printed by "D.P. Lange, Hannover, 1833," hand-colored, angels, birds, etc., in red, blue, and green, no information filled in, framed, paper damage, 14 3/4 in. by 18 1/2 in. ....**$200-$300**

Birth record, 1838, Lebanon County, Pennsylvania, by Jacob Stiver, Lebanon, printed and hand-colored, woodblock-printed flowers and leaves and eagle in black, red, yellow, blue, and green, framed, stains, wear, 12 1/2 in. by 15 1/4 in. ....**$500-$600**

Birth record, 1840, Centre County, Pennsylvania, signed "Daniel Diefenbach," printed and hand-colored, red, yellow, green, and blue, stains, worn edges, geometric inlaid frame, 8 1/4 in. by 13 in. ....**$700-$800**

Birth record, 1849, Schuylkill County, Pennsylvania, printed by "J.T. Werner, Pottsville, Pa.," printed and hand-colored, red and green, old reeded frame, stains, some damage, fold lines, 19 in. by 16 1/4 in. ....**$300-$400**

Birth record, 1852, Berks County, Pennsylvania, printed in Reading, Pennsylvania, printed and hand-colored, angels, cherub, and birds in yellow, red, green, and light green, minor stains, bird's-eye veneer frame with damage, 19 3/4 in. by 17 1/4 in. ....**$250-$350**

Birth record, 1859, attributed to

Wayne County, Ohio, watercolor and pencil, angel wearing pink and light orange dress, pink and green rose with hummingbird, blue lined paper, light stains, glued between mat, 16 3/4 in. by 13 3/4 in. ....**$350-$450**

Birth and baptism record, 1833, Mill Creek, Ohio, by Peter Kaufmann, printed and hand-colored, "Certificate of Birth and Baptism," angels, cherubs, and flowers, modern painted frame, fold lines, minor stains, 19 in. by 15 in. ....**$600-$700**

Birth and baptism record, 1852, Center County, Pennsylvania, by Henry Young, small multi-point stars in orange, yellow, and blue, two hand-drawn and colored figures of a man dressed in a black swallow-tailed coat with green pants and white/orange striped vest, handing a bouquet of flowers to a woman in a white dress having a floral print and lace collar; between the figures is a yellow tripod stand holding a vase with scrolled handles, green ground, minor tears and foxing, matted and framed, 11 3/4 in. by 7 3/8 in. ....**$8,500-$10,000**

Bookmark, heart design at bottom with alternating red and green sawtooth border, top corners with hearts and small red and green floral rosettes with black leaves, border of two black lines containing a sawtooth red line in the center flanked by green dots, framed, foxing, water stains, 5 in. by 3 in. ....**$5,000-$6,000**

Bookplate, 1829, pen and ink with red and yellow watercolor, bird on flower, verse, dark yellow frame with smoke decor and black corner blocks, stains, edge damage, 6 1/2 in. by 3 3/4 in. ....**$300-$400**

Bookplate, 1884, Amish folk artist Barbara Ebersol, small heart in center outlined with yellow and orange scallops and containing small floral rosettes, dots, and leaf motif in yellow, green, and orange, "Dieses Buchein Gehoret Mir Lea Speicher" in black letters above heart, "Geschriben den 30 ten May 1884" below, all surrounded by blue and purple stripes with small diagonal corner brackets, 5 3/4 in. by 3 5/8 in. ....**$425-$500**

Bookplate, pen and ink and watercolor on wove paper, tulips and urn in red, green, and brown, contemporary frame, glued down at corners, light stains, short tear, 5 1/8 in. by 3 1/8 in. ....**$700-$800**

Certificate, watercolor and pen and ink, "For a Good Boy" in red, yellow eagle with branch, two stars, old curly maple frame, stains, tears, 6 1/2 in. by 9 1/2 in. ....**$300-$400**

Birth record, 1827, Lycoming County, Pa., by Henry Young, soldier on horseback, horse with red, yellow, and blue saddle, blanket and bed roll, soldier dressed in red and brown striped pants, red coat with light blue front and yellow epaulets, wearing helmet with large blue plume and blowing a yellow trumpet, below the figures are three lines of text, "Northumberland Troop. In Hepburn Township. Lycoming County, State of Pennsylvania," eight-point star in red, yellow, and blue in each corner, period salmon-colored grain-painted frame, fold mark with some separation, foxing, water stains, frame damage, 10 in. by 8 in. **$18,000-$20,000**
Courtesy Horst Auctioneers, Ephrata, Pa.

Fruit Jars

Fruit jars are canning jars used to preserve food. Thomas W. Dyott, one of Philadelphia's earliest and most innovative glassmakers, was promoting his glass canning jars in 1829. John Landis Mason patented his screw-type canning jar on Nov. 30, 1858. There are thousands of different jars and a variety of colors, types of closure, sizes, and embossings.

Reference: Bill Schroeder, *1000 Fruit Jars Priced and Illustrated*, 5th ed., Collector Books, 1987 (1996 value update).

Periodical: *Fruit Jar Newsletter*, 364 Gregory Ave., West Orange, NJ 07052.

Collectors' Clubs: Ball Collectors Club, 22203 Doncaster, Riverview, MI 48192; Midwest Antique Fruit Jar & Bottle Club, PO Box 38, Flat Rock, IN 47234; Northwest Fruit Jar Collectors' Club, 12713 142nd Ave., Puyallup, WA 98374.

Note: In most cases, the date found on a jar refers to the patent date, not the age of the jar.

Upside down Ball Mason; only about a dozen of these jars are known to exist. Not an error, they appear to be a dispenser. **$300**

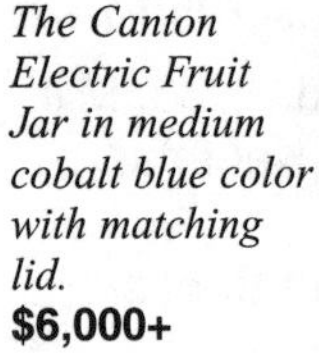

The Canton Electric Fruit Jar in medium cobalt blue color with matching lid.
$6,000+

Swirled honey amber Ball plain 3-L quart (no "Mason"). These are much scarcer than the jars with "Mason" embossed under Ball, with disconnected underscore, a variation long recognized as the "sperm jar," a term coined by the collector that first noted it. **$500+**

The Dandy in yellow with original closure.
$600

Acme Seal (script), clear, regular mouth, quart..............................$50

Atlas E-Z Seal, green, pint...........$15

Atlas Mason's Patent, apple green, pint. $25

Atlas Mason's Patent, apple green, quart. $35

Atlas Mason's Patent, light olive green, pint...............................$35

Atlas Mason's Patent, light olive green, quart. $25

Atlas Strong Shoulder Mason, apple green, quart. $20

Atlas Strong Shoulder Mason, light cornflower blue, pint.................$25

Atlas Strong Shoulder Mason, light

Canton Domestic Fruit Jar in rare cobalt blue.
$9,000+

Bright emerald green Flaccus Steer's Head jar, original metal band and a rare, unlisted domed milk glass insert, the insert has a starburst in the center surrounded by a circular wreath; no damage or stains, a few normal flakes on the sheared mouth, the insert is perfect. **$1,650**

Three views of teal Hemingray ribbed quart jar, sparkling glass and no damage or stains, with an old zinc band and glass insert for a closure. **$2,500**

Quart size Crowleytown jar in strong teal color. **$10,000+**

Three views of Calypso half-gallon jar, extremely rare, only a couple examples have ever been found, all original including the metal band and the straddle-lip sealing glass insert, the bottom surface of the insert was ground and polished in the original making, and has some minimal usage flaking on the polished surface, essentially perfect, with no damage or stains, slight rocker-base effect due to the heavily raised lettering in the middle of the base, size is equal to a standard U.S. half-gallon, possibly French Canadian. **$475**

E.C. Flaccus pint jar in bright emerald green with stag's head design and original closure. **$2,000**

olive green, pint........................**$40**

Atlas Strong Shoulder Mason, light olive green, quart.....................**$25**

The Ball, Patent Appl'd For, aqua, quart. **$180**

Ball Mason, apple green, quart....**$25**

Ball Mason, apple green, half-gallon. **$30**

Ball Perfection, blue, no closure, pint. **$100**

Bosco Double Seal, clear, quart. .**$43**

Boston Trade Mark Dagger Brand, with dagger, green, quart........**$250**

Brackett's Perfection Jar, aqua, lip chip, no closure, quart. **$325**

A.E. Bray Fruit Jar, Pat Pend'g, with four-leaf clover, amber, no closure, quart. **$750**

Brighton, clear, half-gallon. **$145**

The Canton Domestic Fruit Jar, clear, original wire, quart. **$120**

Commonwealth Fruit Jar, aqua, half-gallon. **$150**

Commonwealth Fruit Jar, clear, quart. **$100**

Quart size Crowleytown jar in strong teal color. ....**$10,000+**

Erie Fruit Jar, with E in hexagon, light green, plain lid, quart. **$225**

Everlasting Jar, light green, quart.**$30**

F A & Co. (on base), iron pontil, aqua, no stopper, pint. **$350**

The Family Fruit Jar, clear, pint......... **$1,000**

Flaccus Bros Fruit Jar, with steer's head, milk glass, original label, rayed insert, pint. **$725**

E.C. Flaccus pint jar in bright emerald green with stag's head design and original closure..**$2,000**

Fruit Keeper, GCC Co. monogram, aqua, quart...............................**$50**

The Gem on front, HGW monogram on reverse, whittled aqua, half-gallon. **$50**

Fridley & Cornman's/ Patent/Oct. 25th 1859/Ladies Choice pint in aqua with original cast iron lid that has star-shaped cutout. **$2,500**

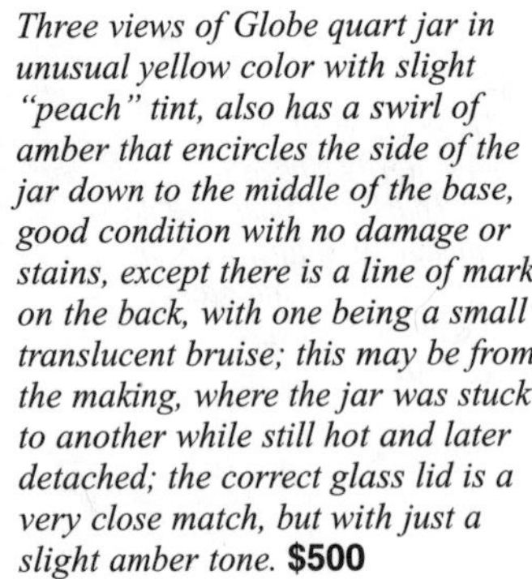

Three views of Globe quart jar in unusual yellow color with slight "peach" tint, also has a swirl of amber that encircles the side of the jar down to the middle of the base, good condition with no damage or stains, except there is a line of marks on the back, with one being a small translucent bruise; this may be from the making, where the jar was stuck to another while still hot and later detached; the correct glass lid is a very close match, but with just a slight amber tone. **$500**

Wm L. Haller, Carlisle, Pa., quart jar in aqua with original cast iron stopple. **$600**

The Hero quart in medium orange-amber color. **$5,000+**

E.C. Flaccus pint jar in pale yellow with stag's head design and original closure. **$1,500+**

H&S in script quart jar, with strong embossing and bubbly glass character, no damage or stains, replica metal closure. **$2,200**

Hemingray Jar, heavily "whittled" surface, extremely rare half-gallon size, sparkling glass with no damage or stains, except for one chip off the rim in back, very heavy and sharp embossing, no closure. Detail in right photo. **$1,500**

Two views of Hero 1876 four-gallon advertising jar, used in the Philadelphia Centennial Exposition of 1876; this jar promotes the Hero Glass Works of Philadelphia; no damage and retains the original shoulder-sealing lid with original milk glass liner in perfect shape. **$3,850**

Lightning jar in yellow with olive tone. **$300+**

Lightning jar, strong yellow-olive with matching colored lid and original hardware, pint. **$400-$800, depending on color**

The Magic (star logo) Fruit Jar, quart size in root beer amber with original matching lid and three-piece iron clamp. **$1,800**

Mason's, cobalt blue, embossed "Mason's CFJ Co. Improved" on front and "Clyde, N.Y." on back, with a matching cobalt colored unmarked insert, zinc band, quart. **$20,000+**

Lightning jar, shiny clean glass with no damage or stains, has a crude streak of slag embedded in the shoulder, yellow-olive, half-gallon. Details at right. **$700**

Mason's Patent Nov. 30th 1858, in rare forest green. **$100+**

Mason's Patent, Nov. 30th 1858, with ring for glass lid, in rare citron/amber with a touch of green. **$500+**

Three views of Mason's, deep amber, Cross-over-Mason's 1858, a deep reddish amber quart size with strong embossing and shiny glass, no damage or stains, good ground rim with minimal flaking, with an original stamped Hero Cross zinc lid. **$575**

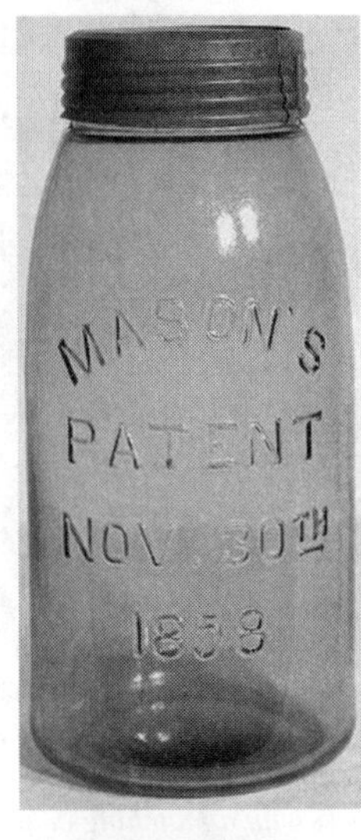

Mason, bright yellow-amber colored 1858 half-gallon with very bold embossing, improved style mouth finish with a plain amber glass insert and Bett's band, extremely heavy and sharp embossing. **$600**

Mason, circa 1920s, with screw caps, two jars marked "Mason's Patent Nov. 30, 1858," and the third marked "Swayzee's Improved Mason," 9 in. by 4 1/4 in. **$20-$25 each**

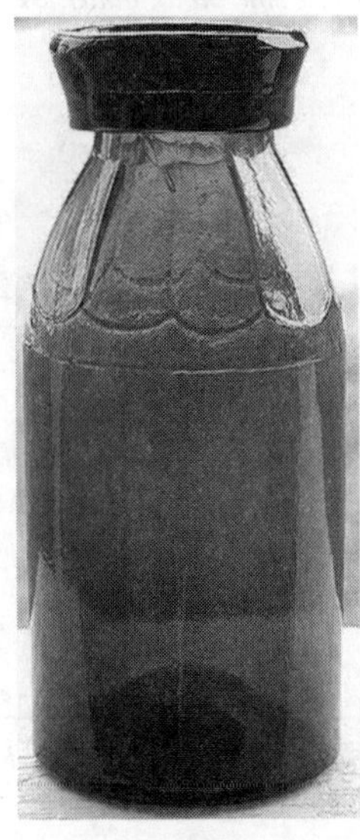

"Petal Jar" in dark green with iron pontil and crude top, quart. **$1,500**

Gimball's Brothers Pure Food Store Philadelphia, clear, pint............**$50**

Globe, amber, two lid chips, pint. **$100**

Globe, aqua, wide mouth, lip chip. **$155**

Hamilton, clear, half-gallon...........**$90**

Hamilton No. 3 Glass Works, cornflower blue, 58 oz..........**$1,000**

Hero over a cross, aqua, quart. ...**$40**

The Hero, aqua, original lid, half-gallon. **$80**

The Ideal Imperial, aqua, quart....**$35**

Lafayette (script), aqua, pint.......**$300**

Lafayette (script), clear, quart. ...**$200**

Trademark Lightning Putnam (on base), amber, 24 oz. **$135**

Trademark Lightning Putnam (on base), aqua, tall quart............**$100**

Trademark Lightning on front, HWP on reverse, Putnam on base, aqua, quart.......................................**$325**

Trademark Lightning Registered U.S. Patent Office, cornflower blue, pint. **$125**

Pontilled (and bell-shaped) wax sealer in sapphire blue, rare. **$3,500+**

Millville Atmospheric Fruit Jar/Whitalls Patent June 18th 1861, deep cobalt blue quart size jar, original cast iron yoke clamp and thumbscrew, with matching cobalt blue lid, extremely rare, only four examples known. **$25,000+**

The Scranton Jar in apple green color with odd closure that has wooden components. **$2,500**

Millville Atmospheric Fruit Jar (and on reverse) Whitall's Patent June 18th 1861, half-gallon in perfect condition. **$8,000+**

Potter & Bodine Philadelphia quart jar in brilliant yellow color with matching lid. **$6,000+**

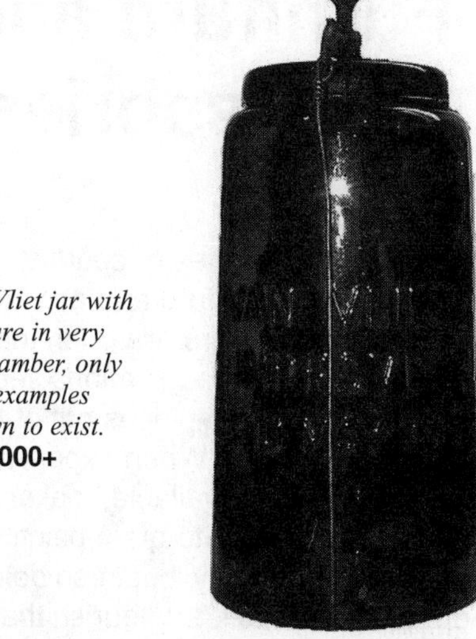

Van Vliet jar with closure in very rare amber, only two examples known to exist. **$15,000+**

Lightning jar, shiny clean glass with no damage or stains, has a crude streak of slag embedded in the shoulder, yellow-olive, half-gallon. **$700**

Manufactured for J.T. Kinney, Trenton, N.J., aqua, lip flake, quart....... **$250**

Mason, green, quart.................... **$50**

Mason, teal green, quart............. **$45**

Mason Fruit Jar (two lines), amber, pint. **$125**

Mason Improved, two dots below Mason, apple green, quart........ **$30**

Mason's Improved, with CFJCo. logo, amber, half-gallon. **$250**

Mason's Improved Butter Jar, with CFJCo. logo, aqua, quart........ **$250**

Mason's Patent, teal, half-gallon. . **$25**

Mason's Patent, Nov. 30th 1858, amber, quart. **$325**

Mason's Patent, Nov. 30th 1858, apple green, quart. **$70**

Mason's Patent,, Nov. 30th 1858, apple green, half-gallon. **$50**

Mason's Patent, Nov. 30th 1858, aquamarine, quart.................. **$520**

Mason's Patent, Nov. 30th 1858, aquamarine, half-gallon. **$450**

Mason's Patent, Nov. 30th 1858, sun, moon and star on front, Ball on back, aqua, half-gallon. **$175**

Mason's Patent, Nov. 30th 1858, CFJ Co logo, apple green, quart. **$60**

Mason's Patent, Nov. 30th 1858, CFJ Co logo, light olive green, half-gallon. **$100**

Mason's Patent, Nov. 30th 1858, with cross, aqua, lid unembossed, one gallon. **$2,000**

Mason's Patent, Nov. 30th 1858, with cross, light apple green, quart. . **$75**

Mason's II Patent, Nov. 30th 1858, aqua, quart............................... **$35**

Mason's III Patent, Nov. 30th 1858, aqua, quart, **$125**

Mason's 13 Patent, Nov. 30th 1858, aqua, half-gallon. **$65**

Mason's 18 Patent, Nov. 30th 1858, aqua, quart.............................. **$25**

Mason's 20 Patent, Nov. 30th 1858, aqua, quart.............................. **$30**

Mason's 24 Patent, Nov. 30th 1858, aqua, quart.............................. **$30**

Mason's 401 Patent, Nov. 30th 1858,

aqua, quart..............................**$275**

Mason's Union, with shield, aqua, quart.......................................**$135**

MGMCo monogram, clear, light embossing, half-gallon...........**$200**

Michigan Mason, beaded neck seal, clear, pint. **$30**

Peerless, aqua, quart................**$225**

Port Mason's, Patent Nov. 30th 1858, aqua, quart.............................**$250**

San Francisco Glass Works, aqua, two lip chips, half-gallon..........**$750**

Sidney Trade Mark Dingo Fruit Jar, with dingo, light green, quart. .**$525**

C.F. Spencers Pat. 1868 Improved Jar, aqua, repro closure, quart. **$425**

Where can I find them?

Greg Spurgeon Antiques
10644 US 41 N
Rosedale, IN 47874
(812) 466-6521
http://www.hoosierjar.com/
xx78@msn.com
www.antiquebottles.com

Two views of ashtray stand, circa 1930s, wood, in the form of a black butler wearing a red coat, white shirt, black tie, and black pants with red trim, on a square wood base, moderate wear, ashtray missing, 34 in. by 12 in. by 9 in. **$150-$200**

Furniture and Accessories

Like other categories of country antiques, the furniture and accessories included here are often the product of fertile imaginations seeking to make stylish pieces out of the materials at hand. When expensive woods were not available, makers might have turned to grain painting to simulate mahogany, but in so doing, often added a folk art flourish that would not be found on classical forms. Beds, chairs, chests, and tables made in this way may also have odd structural elements, or seem out of proportion when compared to more formal examples, but these peculiarities only serve to enhance their appeal in the broad market than we call country.

❖ Ashtray Stands

Ashtray stand or card holder, circa 1930s, pine, painted in the form of a butler, significant paint flaking, 14 in. by 31 in. by 9 in. **$85**

❖ Beds

Country Victorian rope bed, cherry and mahogany, hook-in headboard with cutout profile and heavy shell-carved and C-scroll applied decoration and arched recessed panels flanked by turned posts with trumpet finials, original finish, circa 1850, 56 in. wide by 76 in. long by 72 in. tall. **$1,000**

Early country Empire four-poster bed, poplar, turned and faceted tapering bed posts with mushroom tops, shaped head- and footboard, built to accommodate rope support, circa 1830, original finish, 58 in. wide by 90 in. tall. **$1,600**

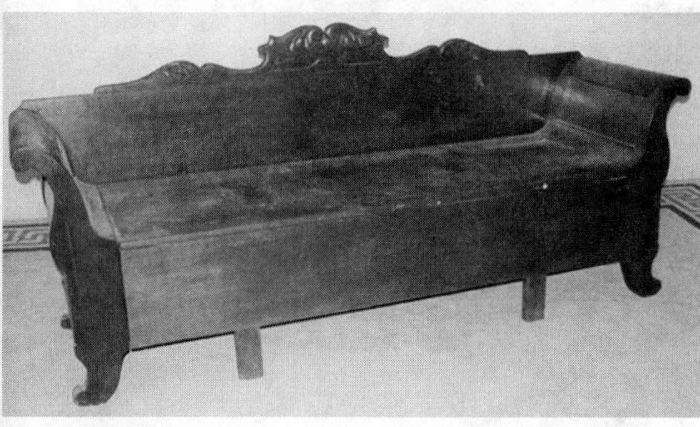

New England country daybed, walnut, Empire scroll arm with carved back crest, lift seat for storage, front panel pulls forward to double width as bed, circa 1860, original finish, 80 in. long by 28 in. deep by 33 in. tall. **$1,100**

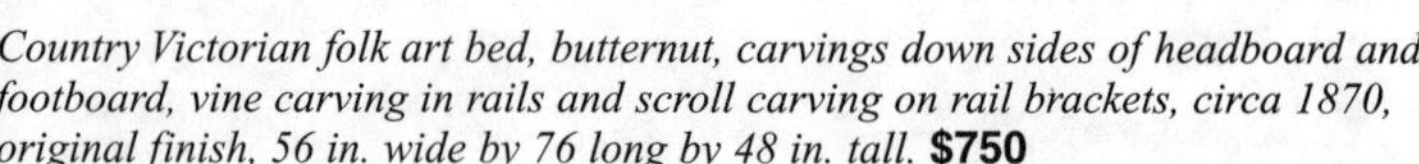

Country Victorian folk art bed, butternut, carvings down sides of headboard and footboard, vine carving in rails and scroll carving on rail brackets, circa 1870, original finish, 56 in. wide by 76 long by 48 in. tall. **$750**

Country daybed, Norwegian/American, walnut, original finish, circa 1860, some Empire influence, rolled side supports with horizontal shaped splats, would have had long cushion, 80 in. long by 28 in. deep by 30 in. tall. **$450**

❖ Benches

Windsor bench, pine and maple, straight crestrail with delicate spindles, curved arm, plank seat with eight legs and a pair of flat stretchers, circa 1820, old repaint, 72 in. wide by 22 in. deep by 36 in. tall. **$600**

Bench, circa 1820, maple, Windsor influence with arrow-back spindles, turned arms and legs, stretchers with faux bamboo turnings, excellent condition, 69 in. by 35 in. by 16 in. **$900-$1,200**

Bench, circa 1850, Sheraton style with grain painting on maple, straight back rails, scroll arms, turned legs with turned and flat stretchers, cane seat replaced, excellent condition, 80 in. by 38 in. by 16 in. **$1,200-$1,500**

❖ Bookcases

Country Victorian bookcase, walnut, arched top with applied carved crest, beveled front corners with carved details, glass door with carved molding at bottom and shelved interior, single wide drawer in base with brass bin pulls, may have had a base at one time, original finish, circa 1880, 36 in. wide by 18 in. deep by 80 in. tall. **$700**

❖ Bride's Box

Bride's box, bent or steamed pine or fur, original floral rosemaled decoration in rose motif with painted inscription in German around top, woven lap construction on sides, circa 1850-1860, 18 in. long by 10 in. deep by 8 in. tall. **$950**

❖ Candle Stands

Federal candle stand, cherry, vase form pedestal supported by arched legs, round fixed top, circa 1820, old refinish, 31 in. tall, top 14 in. diameter. ***$350***

Tilt-top candle stand, mahogany, rectangular top with rounded corners, turned pedestal with three outstretched legs and ball feet, circa 1830, original finish, 24 in. wide by 18 in. deep by 28 in. tall. **$350**

Pennsylvania tilt-top candle stand, Queen Anne style, one-board round top with raised lip, vase-shaped pedestal with three outstretched legs and snake feet, old refinish, circa 1790, 16 in. diameter, 30 in. tall. **$8,000**

Windsor Chairs

by Wayne Mattox

A good Windsor chair has sculpture. Understand this, and your chances of ferreting out a valuable specimen are immediately improved. The next time you're at an auction preview or busy antique shop where a handsome example is displayed, observe how people look at Windsors. The ritual is distinct from all other categories of antiques.

You'll see interested couples nestle the chair back and forth on the floor, touching it only with their thumbs and one finger for each hand, until they've positioned it just right. Next, they'll take a step backwards and give it a long, appreciative gaze. Then, they'll begin to circle. Walking slowly around the chair, taking it in from every angle because, like all good sculpture, a Windsor must please the eye from every vantage. This is when commentary ensues.

"Great form, the chair has great form!" the man will say.

An alert sales assistant will assert, "You have a good eye, sir!"

"I love how the legs splay outward. It's beautiful," the wife will reply.

"Gutsy turnings," the gentleman will add, commenting on the bold design of leg and arm supports achieved by the old-day wood "turner" on his lathe. Finally, just as the vendor thinks she has found a deserving home for the chair, all spirits are squashed by a single question: "Can you sit in this thing?"

Windsors, sometimes crudely referred to as stick chairs, have a light, airy appearance. They are distinct from other seating in that their rear legs and back brace are attached on separate lines to the seat rather than as a continuous element. Although many of the chairs and benches look like they would collapse under a man's weight, they are stout due to employment of multiple woods, and well braced by sturdy construction. Legs, usually turned from maple or oak, are forced through drilled holes in a carved plank seat that is made of a softer wood like poplar or pine. Fox wedges and wood-shrinkage from the drying of the carefully selected green stock secures this marriage. For the thin back spindles, hoops, or rails present in most Windsors, the turner selected even stronger lumber—hickory or ash. Finally, a coat of paint was usually applied by the joiner to mask the varying woods.

Windsors originate from the first part of the 18th century when they were said to be born in Windsor, England. One story is that King George I, while taking refuge from a storm in a peasant's cottage, was forced to sit down on a crude chair with upright spindles. It was not the throne he was used to in Windsor Castle, however, the king was so impressed with the chair's simplicity and comfort, he had it copied by his cabinetmakers. News spread, and soon the "Windsor" chair was the vogue.

A 1730 London newspaper ad by chair maker John Brown offering "All Sorts of Windsor Garden Chairs painted green or in the wood" adds weight to the argument that the first Windsors were made as outdoor chairs. This explains the airy design and green pigment that is often found in the cracks of old scraped-to-the-wood Windsors. By 1740, the line would come to America where it would reach its zenith in design. Shortly after the signers of the Declaration of Independence signed their names while seated in "sack back" Windsors, the line would outsell all other forms of seating combined. Thus, old Windsors do appear in great numbers today and a few of these have now attained a throne-like value.

• • •

Ax-chopped, burned, dog chewed, thrown in the dumpster—many great Windsor chairs have suffered horrible deaths over the years. Others have simply been abused—scraped naked or sold at yard sales for the price of a velvet Elvis painting. This is because, except in appraisal of line, everyday standards of value are not relevant to Windsors. Choice, undisturbed examples with crusty peeling layers of paint and considerable wear are often mistaken for beat up kitchen chairs.

Stylistic features must be considered when dating Windsors. Mid-18th century examples will often have bold ring-and-baluster turned legs ending in feet shaped like turnips, "blunt arrow feet," or colt's hooves. A worn or broken foot would require splicing a fancy lathe-fashioned replicate back on. A few years later, Windsor makers found that by grounding their chairs in just a slight conical taper, worn feet could be shaved flat again. This added to the economy of ownership and enhanced sales. In the Federal Period (1790-1825), bold baluster legs and arm supports were supplanted by lighter features including bamboo-like turnings, influenced by our fascination with new Oriental trade.

Less valuable Windsors of the Victorian (1860-1900) and later periods can often be distinguished by examining the seat. Early chairs will have a single thick plank that is scooped out like a saddle on the upside for downside comfort. Generally, the top of the legs can be seen protruding through this seat. Underneath, one may feel wavy undulations from hand planing and see a darkly oxidized surface with traces of unstripped paint near where the legs are socketed. Novices should not gamble on a Windsor with legs that do not protrude through the plank. Multiple board seats are the neon beacon of a contemporary chair. Other things being equal, armchairs are more valuable than sidechairs. A Windsor that has been stripped of its paint exposing the beautiful wood underneath can still have substantial value. However, five-figure Windsors retain their original paint. Form is essential. Gutsy bulbous turnings, balanced proportion, verticality, splay to the legs, rake to the back, a saddle shaped seat, carving (if present) to the knuckles and comb, lightness, strength, quaintness, durability, grace—the sum of these qualities can transform functional seating furniture into a work of art.

The spindled back can take on a number shapes: low back, fan back, comb back, brace back, loop back, continuous arm, sack back, rod back, and birdcage. Sometimes the chairs were designed with writing arms and storage drawers. Tiny chairs were turned and joined for wealthy tots. Windsor design also shows up in the form of highchairs, cradles, candle stands, tables, stools, settees, and racks. Writing arm, child-size, and Windsors of unusual form are competitively sought by collectors.

Fortunately, unlike most other forms of antique furniture, many Windsors were signed. The maker's name can often be found stamped, branded, or on a pasted label on the bottom of the seat. Obviously, a signed chair has additional merit. Antique English Windsors do show up in the United States. They are normally heavier than their American counterparts. Some retain curving "cabriole" legs in the front. Valuable English Windsors can sometimes be purchased cheaply at country auctions if the dealers are wearing their American-only horse blinders.

One of the most successful furniture forms of all time, Windsors lend themselves to any decorating style. Joiner David Lawrence got it right in his July 19, 1787, advertisement printed in the Providence, R.I., *U.S. Chronicle*, "Windsor Chairs. Neat elegant strong. Warranted of good seasoned materials. So firmly put together as not to deceive the Purchaser by an untimely coming to Pieces."

(Wayne Mattox is the proprietor of Wayne Mattox Antiques, Woodbury, Conn., specializing in 18th and early 19th century furnishings, American folk art, and accessories.)

❖ Chairs

Windsor captain's chair, knuckle arm grips, spindle supports, saddle seat, turned legs and medial stretcher, circa 1810, old repaint, 26 in. wide by 17 in. deep by 32 in. tall. **$500**

Country Queen Anne side chair, probably maple, urn back splat creating "perched bird" silhouette, scroll crestrail with ears, replaced woven seat, significant wear on turned front stretcher, circa 1750, old finish, possibly original black paint, 20 in. wide by 16 in. deep by 40 in. tall. **$175**

Country arrow-back side chair, pine and maple, original painted and stenciled decoration, plank seat, turned legs, and carved stretcher, circa 1820, 15 in. wide by 16 in. deep by 32 in. tall. **$200**

Chair, circa 1920, maple and mixed woods, barrel back with curved spindles and applied bosses on arms, bow legs set at right angles (as for a corner chair) and curved stretchers forming a circle, pegged construction, original dark varnished surface, minor wear, 32 in. by 22 in. by 16 in. **$200-$300**

Side chair, circa 1850, tiger maple, with scalloped crestrail and back stretcher, serpentine front on seat, saber legs, and bowed stretcher in front, cane seat missing, minor restoration and refinishing, 32 in. by 17 in. by 19 in. **$300-$350**

Child's high chair, circa 1810, maple, with turned legs, arms, and stretchers, ball finials, woven splint seat (replaced), and footrest, old blue paint, excellent condition, 40 in. by 16 in. by 19 in. **$800-$900**

Child's stenciled Hitchcock side chair, original paint-decorated surface on crestrail and back brace, also gold detail on seat front, legs, and stretcher, original woven rush seat, circa 1820s, 14 in. wide by 15 in. deep by 26 in. tall. **$200**

Child's ladder-back high chair, maple, turned arms, legs, and stretchers, original finish and woven rush seat, circa 1820, 18 in. wide by 16 in. deep by 40 in. tall. **$300**

Comb-back Windsor rocker, pine and maple, delicate comb back, rolled arms, original painted and stenciled surface with floral motif, scoop saddle seat, carpet-cutter rockers, circa 1830-1840, 24 in. wide by 30 in. deep by 46 in. tall. **$450**

Chair, rocker, circa 1880, Hitchcock influence with stenciled headrest in floral motif, gilt banding around spindles, stretchers, legs, and on seat, carpet-cutter rockers, natural wear on arm rests, overall excellent condition, 50 in. by 26 in. by 22 in. **$350-$450**

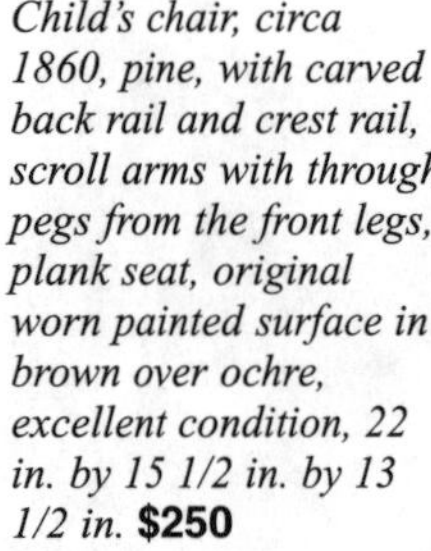

Child's chair, circa 1860, pine, with carved back rail and crest rail, scroll arms with through pegs from the front legs, plank seat, original worn painted surface in brown over ochre, excellent condition, 22 in. by 15 1/2 in. by 13 1/2 in. **$250**

Child's continuous-arm Windsor rocker, circa 1810, original painted surface, spindle back and sides, turned legs with carpet-cutter rockers, medial stretcher, 18 in. wide by 18 in. deep by 32 in. tall. $500

Child's Windsor side chair, circa 1810, old refinish, bamboo turnings to back spindles, 12 in. wide by 13 in. deep by 24 in. tall. $300

Unusual country Victorian wing chair commode, oak and walnut, pierced carved classical back splat, fan head rest, flat arm, back is adjustable, turned front legs with original wooden casters, cane seat lifts out to reveal hole for chamber pot, circa 1870s, original finish, 22 in. wide by 22 in. deep by 40 in. tall. $250

Child's country rocking chair, original red paint with black striping, original splint seat, straight spindles, supports, and stretchers, carpet-cutter rockers, circa 1850, 15 in. wide by 16 in. deep by 27 in. tall. **$200**

Painted country rocker, maple and pine, remnants of original stenciled and painted decoration, arrow supports in back and under arms, turned legs and stretchers, carpet-cutter rockers, circa 1820s, 24 in. wide by 32 in. deep by 46 in. tall. **$300**

Unusual country rocker, pine and maple, simple crestrail with serpentine stiles and straight spindles, turned arms, legs and stretchers, rolled Boston-style seat, carpet-cutter rockers, circa 1840, old refinish, 24 in. wide by 28 in. deep by 44 in. tall. **$300**

Chair, wicker, circa 1930s, from an order of the Eastern Star chapter, painted white with inverted star in back painted white, green, red, blue, and yellow, excellent condition, 36 in. by 16 in. by 14 in. **$150-$200**

Blanket Chests

by Wayne Mattox

Today, old blanket chests can serve two practical decorating purposes: They can be used as coffee tables (antique coffee tables don't exist), and they can be put at the foot of a bed to store your sleeping quilt during the day and your decorative bedcover, an antique quilt or coverlet, at nighttime.

An old blanket chest is usually fashioned out of a small number of wide boards, sometimes as few as six. Chests fashioned of multiple planks should be avoided. Fat virgin trees, and accordingly wide boards, were available to early American craftsmen and they used them. The wood is normally a soft wood, like pine or poplar, compared to a hard wood like maple, cherry, or mahogany. There are two exceptions: The hardwood oak was often used in pilgrim-period blanket chests (these are seldom encountered today), and walnut was often employed in Dutch communities like Lancaster, Pa., where they fashioned fancy blanket chests called dower chests.

The wood on a blanket chest should have few knots in it. Old-time cabinetmakers in Europe and America were proud and highly skilled, just as our craftsmen are today. They would not choose lumber with large knots that would fall out. A few small knots are acceptable, especially on the unfinished backboard of the chest that would normally be hidden against the bed. However, any antique furniture item made of knotty pine is most likely a fake.

The hinges connecting the lift-up top to the backboard of a blanket chest may be of several varieties: snipe or cotter-pin hinges (interlocking wormlike wrought-iron hinges that were driven through the wood and peened over); long, wrought-iron flat face hinges often hammered out in the shape of a strap; butterfly hinges; or, more common to 19th century chests, today's square-angled butt hinge.

Study hinges as a clue to integrity. When iron rests on wood for hundreds of years it often leaves a rust shadow. The backboard of an old blanket chest will commonly have a long dark line running vertically down from the hinges where rusty moisture has been leaking for many years. Inside an old blanket chest you may encounter a small box compartment called a till that was used to store candles and other small items. Remember to feel the wood with your hands to check for wavelike undulations that were left by old-time hand planing.

An old blanket chest should be purchased in one of two conditions: retaining its beautiful old paint, which is most desirable, or stripped down to the handsome bare wood. In addition to integrity and handsome surface, a blanket chest should be selected for its form. I know what you're thinking: "Wait a minute, it's just a box!" It is not. Is the blanket chest handsomely proportioned? Does it have a beautiful base?

One of nature's most beautiful forms is one of its simplest—the egg.

(Wayne Mattox is the proprietor of Wayne Mattox Antiques, Woodbury, Conn., specializing in 18th and early 19th century furnishings, American folk art, and accessories.)

New England blanket chest, pine, two working drawers in lower section, lift lid, Sheraton style legs, replaced bin handles, circa 1830, modern blue repaint, 44 in. wide by 18 in. deep by 40 in. tall. **$600**

Country blanket chest, pine, circa 1840, original grain-painted surface, open interior, brass escutcheon, original lock, bun feet, 38 in. long by 18 in. deep by 22 in. tall. **$400**

Blanket chest, circa 1880, pine grain-painted to simulate curly maple, four recessed panels, turned feet, locking lid, open interior, minor wear, 42 in. by 28 in. by 22 in. **$500-$600**

Chippendale blanket chest, pine, dove-tail construction, locking lift lid with till inside, cut-out bracket feet, two drawers in base, old refinish, original brass pulls, circa 1775, 46 in. wide by 21 in. deep by 24 in. tall. **$1,500**

Miniature three-drawer child's chest, oak, rope twist molding along top edge, scalloped base, brass button pulls, recessed panels on side, original finish, circa 1910, 22 in. wide by 8 in. deep by 20 in. tall. **$250**

❖ Chests

Bucks County, Pa., four-drawer chest, walnut, Hepplewhite influence with splayed foot, scalloped skirt, and chamfered corners, original bail-handle hardware and keyplates, circa 1810, original finish, 36 in. wide by 20 in. deep by 40 in. tall. **$1,800-$2,000**

Country Empire four-drawer chest, tiger maple and mahogany, stepout top section with mahogany banding on top drawer, full carved columns in acanthus motif, classic paw feet in front and turned feet in back, circa 1835, refinished, replaced hardware, 44 in. wide by 22 in. deep by 48 in. tall. **$900**

Country Empire chest of drawers, cherry and bird's-eye maple, circa 1850, old refinish, straight backsplash with scalloped ends above two shallow side-by-side drawers above two deep side-by-side drawers that step out slightly (and have small bracket supports) above three wide drawers, wooden mushroom pulls, brass escutcheons, bracket feet, and wooden casters, 40 in. wide by 20 in. deep by 48 in. tall. **$600**

Unusual country Empire/Sheraton chest, pine with faux-grain painted surface, cutout back board with the profile of two love birds at top, small two-drawer chest on top with turned columns and legs, which were attached to back, four-drawer base with turned and rope-twist carved columns, original brass hardware, circa 1850, 42 in. wide by 20 in. deep by 64 in. tall. **$1,200**

Chest of drawers, butternut, circa 1870, with painted bull's-eye decoration added circa 1920s, stepback top with two side-by-side drawers over three stacked drawers, the center drawer unusually deep, probably for blankets, wood mushroom pulls, all drawers hand dovetailed, moderate signs of wear but overall very good condition, 41 in. by 38 in. by 18 in. **$1,200-$1,500**

Chest of drawers, circa 1900, done in the "tramp art" style, varnished pine and mahogany, with raised geometric notch-carved designs on the four drawers (two side-by-side over two stacking) and on the sides; top drawers have turned wood mushroom pulls, bottom drawers have cast brass bail handles with birds, insects, leaves, and flowers, front feet carved in primitive foot shape, moderate wear with some carving replaced on front, overall very good condition, 46 in. by 30 in. by 21 in. **$4,000-$5,000**

Chest of drawers, circa 1850, pine, with brown grain painting, two handkerchief drawers over four stacked drawers, all with turned wood pulls, 38 in. by 40 1/2 in. by 17 1/2 in. **$800-$1,000**

Country Empire four-drawer chest, cherry and mahogany, carcass and veneers are mahogany, drawer fronts are cherry, top drawer steps out and is supported by turned and rope-twist carved columns, mushroom pulls are probably walnut, turned feet and paneled sides, original finish, circa 1840, 40 in. wide by 18 in. deep by 48 in. tall. **$750**

New England lift-top mule chest, pine and poplar, country Queen Anne style, two false drawers over two working drawers, strap-hinge lid for blanket storage area, bracket foot, circa 1820, old mustard paint over original red, replaced pulls, 38 in. wide by 18 in. deep by 42 in. tall. **$650**

Chippendale mule chest, pine and poplar, hinged cotter-pinned lid that drops open in front, top stationary, two wide drawers with original brasses and keyplates, bracket foot, old refinish, late 18th century, 48 in. wide by 18 in. deep by 42 in. tall. **$650**

Five-drawer country Empire chest, figured walnut and maple, scalloped backsplash, Bennington porcelain knobs, scalloped return brackets on skirt, circa 1840-1850, refinished, 38 in. wide by 18 in. deep by 45 in. tall. **$450**

Primitive country chest, pine, two wide drawers top and bottom with two pairs of stacked drawers in middle, scalloped valance, square nailed and dovetailed, refinished, circa 1870s, original cast iron pulls, 34 in. wide by 18 in. deep by 46 in. tall. **$500**

Country paint-decorated storage chest, pine, original sponge and dappled paint simulating inlay, bail handles on front and sides, circa 1850-1860, 40 in. wide by 18 in. tall by 20 in. deep. **$400**

Chippendale chest-on-chest, overhanging cornice above three side-by-side drawers over two side-by-side drawers above three stacked drawers in upper section, three stacked drawers in base, replaced brasses, inlaid keyhole escutcheons, chamfered corners, ogee bracket feet, turn-of-the-century refinish, circa 1780, mahogany, 42 in. wide by 23 in. deep by 80 in. tall. **$3,000**

Connecticut bonnet-top highboy, cherry, fan-carved upper and lower drawers, broken arched pediment with urn and cattail finials, scalloped skirt and pad feet, some original, some replaced brasses, old refinish, circa 1770, has had reconstruction, 40 in. wide by 22 in. deep by 84 in. tall. **$9,500**

Country Empire chest, walnut, cutout backboard, step-out upper section with two side-by-side drawers over a single wide drawer, lower section has three wide graduated drawers flanked by turned and carved columns, turned feet and original wooden casters, replaced hardware, circa 1850, old refinish, 40 in. wide by 20 in. deep by 52 in. tall. **$750**

❖ Cabinets

Unusual country pantry cabinet with cylinder-roll bin, pine, square-nailed, upper section has cabinet with blind door next to five drawers with button pulls, cylinder cover on potato or flour bin has cast iron bin handle, wide drawer in base with button pulls, scalloped apron, circa 1860, refinished, 24 in. wide by 18 in. deep by 54 in. tall. **$1,000**

Hanging cabinet with tambour cover, tiger maple and walnut, dovetailed construction, cutout backboard, roll-up tambour with two brass knobs, shelved interior, single stepout drawer with tiny brass bail pulls, brass escutcheon, circa 1820s, 14 in. wide by 9 in. deep by 22 in. tall. **$1,200**

Kitchen cabinet, fir, two pieces, would have been attached to wall though back is finished, molded cornice, five-door top, pull-out cutting board, three doors in base flanked by potato bin and a bank of four stacked drawers, circa 1920s, original paint, 110 in. long by 20 in. deep by 84 in. tall. **$800**

❖ Cupboards

Two-door corner cupboard, pine, one piece, top door has two raised chamfered panels, bottom door has single raised panel, beveled corners, interior has four shelves with old repaint, old refinish, circa 1780, 30 in. wide by 20 in. deep by 80 in. tall. **$2,000**

❖ Cradle

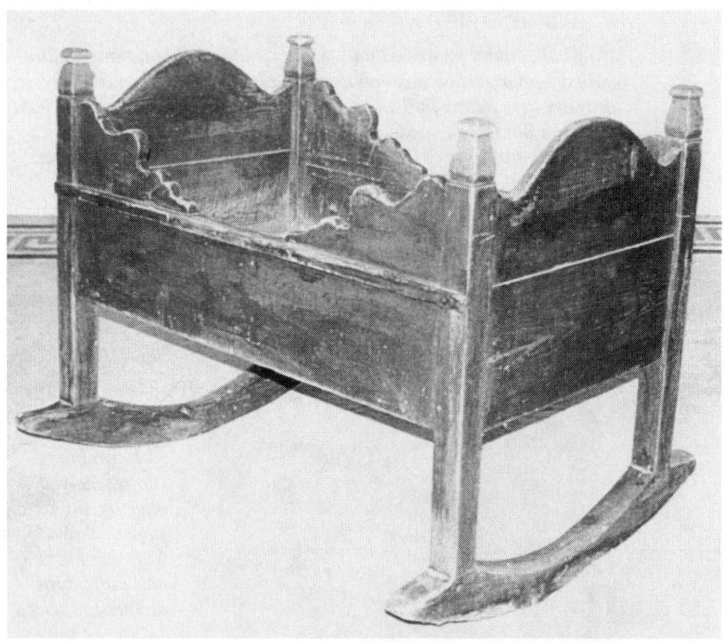

Primitive country cradle, butternut, found in Wisconsin, arched headboard and footboard with scalloped sides, original finish, circa 1850s, 36 in. long by 20 in. deep by 26 in. tall. **$300**

Folk art hanging corner cupboard, walnut, pierced-carved brackets on top with birds and grape vines, scalloped side boards, floral-carved and painted side panels with line carving and recessed star in door, turned pull, single shelf inside, circa 1880, original cleaned finish, 20 in. wide by 15 in. deep by 36 in. tall. **$850**

Cupboard, pine, from Halsingland, Sweden, dated 1801, vividly painted in blue, rusty red, and beige in stylized floral motif, stepback upper section and base with canted corners, 81 in. by 44 in. by 23 in. **$6,200**

Corner cupboard, circa 1890, pine, with three scalloped shelves in upper section, blind paneled doors in lower section, original light varnished surface, very good condition, 74 in. by 30 in. by 20 in. **$1,200-$1,500**

Country jelly cupboard in butternut and walnut, pegged construction, two dovetailed drawers and button pulls over blind recessed-panel doors, scalloped skirt and backsplash, circa 1860, refinished, 42 in. wide by 18 in. deep by 54 in. tall. **$750**

Two views of English pine corner cupboard, dentil molding, arched doors on top with raised panels on both upper and lower doors, scalloped shelves with old green repaint on interior, one piece, scrubbed pine with waxed finish, circa 1850, 40 in. wide by 24 in. deep by 84 in. tall. **$2,000**

Two-piece stepback country kitchen cupboard, stained maple, simple molding over two glass doors, with adjustable shelves, two drawers over two blind doors with recessed panels, cleaned down to original stain, circa 1890, 42 in. wide by 20 in. deep by 82 in. tall.
$1,000

Country jelly cupboard, pine, pair of side-by-side drawers with porcelain pulls over two blind doors with raised beveled panels, square nailed, circa 1870, refinished, 42 in. wide by 18 in. deep by 54 in. tall. **$450**

Hanging cupboard, pine, scalloped bi-level crest and bracket supports, tall narrow doors with crude walnut panels applied, single drawer with walnut mushroom pulls, square-nailed and dovetailed construction, circa 1880, refinished, 19 in. wide by 12 in. deep by 28 in. tall..... **$500**

Hanging cupboard, pine, traces of old green paint, overhanging cornice, one-board door with carved diamond over shallow drawer with wooden mushroom pull, circa 1920, refinished, 20 in. wide by 10 in. deep by 24 in. tall..... ....**$200**

Grain-painted jelly cupboard in the cottage style, pine, original faux oak and walnut graining, arched and scalloped backsplash with shallow shelf and bracket supports, pair of side-by-side drawers with porcelain knobs above recessed-panel blind doors with wood pulls, shelved interior, circa 1870, 42 in. wide by 18 in. deep by 64 in. tall. **$1,000**

Cupboard/pie safe (?) of unusual form, circa 1900, pine, with a single tall door into which has been placed a punched-tin panel with a pinwheel motif, not original, cornice with severely beveled profile, cutout bracket feet, boot-jack ends, shelved interior, refinished with a dark pine stain, 68 in. by 30 in. by 14 in. **$500-$600**

Cupboard/linen press, circa 1870, pine with grain painting to simulate flame mahogany, molded cornice with dark brown trim, raised panel doors with tombstone profile on stepback upper section and base, also trimmed in dark brown, shelved interior with secret compartment, bracket feet, untouched original condition, 84 in. by 50 in. by 22 in. **$3,000-$4,000**

Country jelly cupboard, poplar, turned wood knobs on two drawers over two blind doors with metal latch, simple backsplash and scalloped skirt, square nailed, original finish, circa 1870, 42 in. wide by 20 in. deep by 58 in. tall. **$600**

Two-piece stepback cupboard, pine, large cornice molding above arrowhead molding, beveled corners with applied decoration, two doors in top, each with eight divided lights over two drawers with raised panels and porcelain knobs, fixed shelving, lower blind doors have black iron hardware and recessed panels, circa 1860, refinished, 58 in. wide by 23 in. deep by 85 in. tall. **$4,500**

Norwegian/American country stepback cupboard, pine, mortise and tenon construction, two blind doors on top with scalloped framing, two side-by-side drawers above one wide drawer and three stacked drawers next to potato bin, all wood pulls except on bin, refinished, circa 1870, 42 in. wide by 21 in. deep by 84 in. tall. **$950**

Pennsylvania Dutch stepback cupboard in old repaint, poplar, two pieces, dentil molding below cornice, two glazed doors with unusual glazed central section, recessed pie shelf, three side-by-side drawers over two blind cabinet doors with contemporary paint decoration, bracket feet, circa 1790, repaint from the 1920s, 56 in. wide by 22 in. deep by 86 in. tall. **$4,400**

Ohio River valley stepback cupboard, walnut, two pieces, ogee molded cornice, two glass doors, shelved interior with traces of original paint, pair of side-by-side drawers with wooden mushroom pulls over two blind cabinet doors with shaped recessed panels, scalloped valance, refinished, circa 1850s, 46 in. wide by 19 in. deep by 87 in. tall. **$2,500**

Primitive country stepback cupboard, one piece, poplar, completely pegged construction—no nails, molded cornice, glass doors above recessed serving area flanked by arched supports, lower section has pair of side-by-side drawers over two blind cabinet doors, bone keyhole escutcheons, circa 1850s, refinished, 48 in. wide by 23 in. deep by 84 in. tall. **$1,500**

Pewter cupboard, pine, single-board scalloped sides, two-board back, two blind doors with replaced hardware, circa 1830, refinished, 42 in. wide by 21 in. deep by 80 in. tall. **$1,200**

Country cupboard, walnut, pair of six-pane glass doors above a pair of side-by-side drawers over a pair of blind cabinet doors, scalloped base, original wood pulls and metal hardware, original finish, circa 1880, 38 in. wide by 18 in. deep by 78 in. tall. **$1,000**

Pennsylvania open pewter cupboard, aesthetic influence, pine, diamond-cutout frieze, sides slant back, mortise-and-tenon shelf system with wedge blocks, two drawers over two doors, original Chippendale-style hardware, circa 1870, original finish, 58 in. wide by 22 in. deep by 90 in. tall. **$2,000**

Continental Welsh-style open cupboard, pine and poplar, scalloped sides and top, three shelves with plate grooves, fold-out work surface, five drawers and hinged door below, turned foot, waxed finish, circa 1910, 60 in. wide by 24 in. deep by 82 in. tall. **$1,400**

❖ Desks

Plantation or Wells Fargo desk, chestnut and walnut, two pieces, upper section has molded cornice and blind doors, interior has series of pigeon holes and scalloped dividers, two side-by-side drawers, one wide drawer with wooden pulls below work surface, turned legs, refinished, circa 1875, 38 in. wide by 24 in. deep by 76 in. tall. **$850**

Country S-curve roll-top desk, butternut, sliding tambour cover, four stacking drawers flanking kneehole area, paneled sides, refinished, circa 1890, 54 in. wide by 32 in. deep by 42 in. tall. **$1,200**

Norwegian/American country drop-front desk and chest, butternut, with front lowered, access is gained to interior with 14 drawers and a one-door compartment, three wide drawers—one above and two below desk area—with carved wood pulls, drawers flanked by boldly carved rope-twist columns that extend into cookie corners on top and rounded feet on bottom, bone keyhole escutcheons, original finish, circa 1860, 44 in. wide by 22 in. deep by 60 in. tall. **$2,500**

Desk/bookcase, circa 1880, walnut, with Sheraton influence in the tall slender turned legs, molded cornice, two four-pane glass doors above two bi-fold blind paneled doors that hide slots and storage compartments, hinged locking desk/lid with bone escutcheon, original varnished surface, excellent condition, 84 in. by 38 in. by 22 in. **$2,500-$3,000**

Country drop-front butler's desk on chest, varnished grain-painted pine to simulate crotch-grain rosewood, three drawers, false top drawer drops to reveal writing and storage area, original hardware and ivory pulls on interior drawers and doors, carved brackets on front corners, circa 1860, 38 in. wide by 16 in. deep by 42 in. tall. **$1,000**

Country work desk (also called plantation or Wells Fargo desk), butternut, large cornice, racetrack molding on sides, open pigeon holes and scalloped dividers with two drawers, lower section has single drawer, carved pulls, turned legs, c.1860-1870, 38 in. wide by 26 in. deep by 80 in. tall. **$1,750**

Norwegian/American two-piece drop-front bookcase/secretary, open and closed, cherry and mixed woods, pierced and cutout crestboard above complex molded cornice with cutout finials in front corners, two blind doors with inlaid pinwheel design and raised molding (this is repeated on front of drop lid and lower doors) shelves in upper and lower sections with a series of drawers and pigeon holes in middle section, single wide drawer with ogee profile below writing surface, recessed panels on sides, platform feet, circa 1870, original finish, 40 in. wide by 22 in. deep (closed) by 90 in. tall. **$5,000**

Unusual two-piece desk/cupboard, circa 1890, pine, refinished, six stacked drawers in base with porcelain pulls (three on either side of kneehole opening), open shelves in upper section topped by molded cornice, turned wooden legs, minor restoration, 51 in. by 25 in. by 77 in. (Displayed on the shelves are a variety of blue and white stoneware and Red Wing Collectors Society annual commemoratives.) **$1,200-$1,500**

Transitional Chippendale-Hepplewhite slant-front desk, walnut, lid drops open to reveal drawers, cubbies, etc., old replaced brasses on four graduated drawers, pullout supports, circa 1790, old refinish, 40 in. wide by 19 in. deep by 40 in. tall. **$1,800**

Norwegian/American bookcase/ secretary, butternut, gothic-influence canopy top with drop pendants, arched grillwork on tops of glass doors flanked by serpentine applied decoration, adjustable shelves, carved flowers on front of lid, three graduated drawers with carved pulls, scalloped skirt, original finish, circa 1870, 42 in. wide by 26 in. deep by 84 in. tall. **$3,000**

Country Victorian cylinder-roll secretary/secretary, cherry and burl walnut, angular scalloped crestboard above dentil molding border, arched glass doors with raised panels and iron latch, adjustable shelves, cylinder has pair of brass bail handles, lower section has blind cabinet doors with raised panels that are repeated on the sides, old refinish, circa 1875, 42 in. wide by 22 in. deep by 90 in. tall. **$2,000**

Country Empire drop-front secretary, mahogany, two pieces, ogee crown molding, glass doors above desk area with small drawers and pigeon holes, three graduated drawers in base with original glass pulls, scalloped apron, original finish, circa 1850, 42 in. wide by 20 in. deep (with lid up) by 84 in. tall. **$2,000**

Country slant-lid desk on chest, walnut, pair of side-by-side drawers above slant lid with recessed octagonal panels, three-drawer base with wooden mushroom pulls, scalloped apron, dovetailed, circa 1875, refinished, 38 in. wide by 22 in. deep by 44 in. tall. **$500**

Country Victorian bookcase/secretary, feather-grain walnut, two pieces, pierced-carved crest board above ogee molded cornice, pair of glass doors with double gothic arches and applied grillwork, scalloped valance above open area, fold-out writing surface above scalloped decoration and carved star, two wide drawers with carved pulls, turned half-column decorations on front beveled corners, cutout base, circa 1870, old refinish, 44 in. wide by 24 in. deep by 90 in. tall. **$2,000**

❖ Dressers

Country dresser with Eastlake influence, pine, rectangular mirror with shallow-carved frame flanked by pierced and carved scroll supports above two hanky drawers with porcelain knobs, dentil molding around underside of top, four graduated stacked drawers with carved wooden pulls, raised diamond panels on sides, cutout valance, circa 1880, refinished, 40 in. wide by 18 in. deep by 72 in. tall. **$650**

Country Sheraton dresser, probably poplar or maple, four drawers with wooden mushroom pulls, cutout apron and turned legs, circa 1830, scraped down to original blue, 40 in. wide by 20 in. deep by 44 in. tall. **$900**

❖ Dough Box

Country Sheraton dough box, pine and maple, removable work surface top above tapered trough, dovetailed construction, splay-leg base with pegged construction, turned legs, circa 1820, refinished, 44 in. wide by 22 in. deep by 28 in. tall. **$700**

❖ Dry Sinks

Dry sink, maple and tiger maple, deep well above two side-by-side drawers with mushroom pulls, two blind doors with original butt hinges and cast iron latch, bracket base, old refinish, circa 1860, 52 in. wide by 19 in. deep by 33 in. tall. **$800**

Country dry sink, poplar, three side-by-side drawers with porcelain knobs set into backsplash, two blind doors with original iron latches below sink, square nailed, circa 1870s, refinished, 48 in. wide by 19 in. deep by 45 in. tall. **$900**

❖ Music Stands/Cabinets

Victorian folk art music stand, walnut and maple, two-door cabinet on top with gingerbread edge, doors decorated with inlaid lyre and entwined horns, supported by five ornate fret-carved panels that echo the motif on the doors, base on raised legs with single drawer and brass ring pulls decorated in closed fret-carved basket weave design, original wood casters, circa 1890, original finish, 22 in. wide by 14 in. deep by 40 in. tall. ***$750***

Whimsical folk art Victorian music cabinet, walnut and rosewood, broken arch backboard above shallow shelf with pierced brackets, curio shelves down left side are supported with brackets shaped like a lyre, harp, and violin, right side has drawer with recessed panel and brass pull above recessed-panel door with the word "Musica" carved into it, circa 1870s, original finish, 24 in. wide by 16 in. deep by 42 in. tall. **$1,400**

❖ Hat Racks

Two views of hanging hat rack, circa 1900, varnished wood in the shape of a shield with seven hangers cut from the tops of old canes, original dry surface, minor wear, 24 in. by 16 in. by 6 in. **$350-$450**

Hanging hat rack (gun rack?), circa 1920, pine, in the shape of a shield with ink line decoration, four large carved pine pegs, minor wear, 22 in. by 18 in. by 9 in. **$200-$300**

❖ Hutch

Country Victorian stepback hutch, walnut, two pieces, heavy molded cornice above two glass doors, two shallow side-by-side drawers, front corners with applied half-turned decorations, four-drawer base with raised race-track panels and carved pulls, circa 1870, refinished, 40 in. wide by 22 in. deep by 84 in. tall. **$1,800**

Oak ice box, two doors, paneled doors and sides, original hardware, tin- or zinc-lined with wire shelving, circa 1910, refinished, 24 in. wide by 20 in. deep by 40 in. tall. **$400**

❖ Ice Boxes

Oak ice box, two doors, applied decoration to doors and front of base, hardware original, tin-lined, circa 1910, refinished, 24 in. wide by 18 in. deep by 40 in. tall. **$650**

Ice box, oak, applied carved decoration to frieze and doors, original heavy brass hardware, interior zinc-lined with wire shelves, recessed panel sides, circa 1900, old worn finish, 28 in. wide by 20 in. deep by 40 in. tall. **$450 as shown**

❖ Match Holder

Match holder, circa 1880, turned-wood cup with sawtooth bands, original varnished surface, 5 1/4 in. by 3 1/4 in. **$80**

❖ Pie Safes

Punched-tin pie safe, pine, 16 original tins, three shelves, replaced wooden casters, circa 1875, refinished, 42 in. wide by 17 in. deep by 64 in. tall. **$1,100**

Punched-tin pie safe, pine, pair of side-by-side drawers with carved pulls over two doors with three punched tins each, three punched tins on each side, raised feet, circa 1880, refinished, 42 in. wide by 17 in. deep by 60 in. tall. **$750**

Punched-tin pie safe, circa 1880, painted walnut with molded trim around top, scalloped skirt, six punched-tin panels in doors with star motif, two shelves inside, excellent condition, 56 in. by 42 in. by 14 in. **$1,800-$2,200**

Punched-tin pie safe, walnut, mortise and tenon construction, 16 hand-punched tins with pinwheel pattern, wide drawer in base with cutout legs, refinished, circa 1860s, 48 in. wide by 16 in. deep by 75 in. tall. **$1,500**

❖ Plant Stands

Plant stand, circa 1910, pine with square top that has molding on three sides, faceted tapering legs and round stretchers, 13 1/2 in. by 12 1/2 in. by 32 1/2 in. **$125-$150**

Country painted plant stand in the Empire style, pine, original grain painted surface, molded edge, octagonal top and base, faceted column, circa 1860, 10 in. across, 32 in. tall. **$300**

❖ Settle

Scandinavian-American country lift-lid settle, pine, mortise and tenon construction, scalloped back with spindles, turned arms with horizontal slats, seat hinged, circa 1870, original gray paint, 80 in. wide by 21 in. deep by 36 in. tall. ***$1,200***

❖ Shelves

Clock shelf, circa 1880, elaborate form done in tramp art and made from dynamite crates, in the form of a castle or cathedral painted gold with spires, balconies, and carved windows, clock sits behind central circular opening, all dormers and triangular trim can be removed, excellent condition, 44 in. by 24 in. by 10 in. ***$3,000-$4,000***

Corner shelf, circa 1870, turned and carved wood with four shelves trimmed in pierced and carved borders, spindles, and brackets, topped by 10 turned spires, central shelf having a drawer with rounded corners and decorated with applied round bosses and a carved disk with wings, original heavy dark varnished surface, minor damage to some trim pieces, overall very good condition, 85 1/2 in. by 33 in. by 19 in. **$5,000-$6,000**

Corner shelf, circa 1860, nailed construction with varnished pine or basswood with seven graduated shelves with serpentine profile, notch-carved shelf supports and front feet, corner of bottom shelf cut off (old alteration), overall very good condition, 73 in. tall by 18 in. by 16 in. ***$300-$400***

Display shelf, circa 1920, pine painted gold and decorated with spools on the shelf edges and with spool supports and legs on metal rods, with an elaborate tiered gallery made of spools and lath, cutout stylized decoration on the backs of lower shelves, excellent condition, 64 in. by 40 in. by 12 in. **$400-$500**

Display shelf, circa 1900, pine and wooden spools, four shelves of graduated size with supports and feet made of spools on metal rods, painted black with red trim, moderate wear, 32 in. by 22 in. by 8 in. **$150-$200**

Hanging display shelf, circa 1940s, plywood and mixed woods, with cutout tulip crest, notch-carved edging, hinged door with cutout center, scalloped and circular bracket supports with sawtooth braces, applied floral decals, minor wear, 20 in. by 6 in. by 3 in. **$80-$90**

Display shelf, two pieces, mixed woods, possibly a music stand, circa 1900, with cutout scroll decoration on back and bracket supports, applied spindles with gold trim, turned spindle supports on central shelves, separate base with large scroll legs and scroll brackets, round scalloped shelf, splay feet and original wooden casters, minor wear, overall dimensions 71 in. by 28 in. by 18 in. **$1,000-$1,200**

Hanging shelf, circa 1890, walnut with original varnished surface, four shelves with molded edges and turned spindle supports, scalloped top with two cutout stars, bracket supports and cutout skirt on bottom, excellent condition, 44 in. by 26 in. by 9 in. **$400-$500**

Top and bottom of footstool, circa 1940s, maple with inlaid designs including cross, crown, heart, star, anchor, and fans, plus "JOHN ["N" is backwards] 3-16," cutout legs held in place with braces and screws, beveled skirt, probably a school shop project, minor wear, 14 in. by 7 in. by 6 in. **$70-$90**

Victorian footstool with folk art influence, walnut, pierced-carved bracket ends and sides with acorn-shaped finials and drop pendants, and S-scrolls carved to simulate an interlocking design, tiny brass button feet, original needlepoint upholstery, circa 1870, original finish, 20 in. wide by 10 in. deep by 15 in. tall. **$350**

Footstool, circa 1910, pine with three dowel legs in original black painted surface, and the top covered in a hooked mat done in a floral motif, moderate wear and fading, 12 in. by 6 in. **$180**

Footstool, circa 1910, pine with three dowel legs in original black painted surface, and the top covered in a hooked mat done in a floral motif, moderate wear and fading, 12 in. by 6 in. **$180**

Footstool, circa 1920, pine decorated with spools in geometric and rayed designs, octagonal with original fabric-covered top and ring handle, original varnished surface with minor handling wear, 11 1/2 in. by 6 1/2 in. **$185**

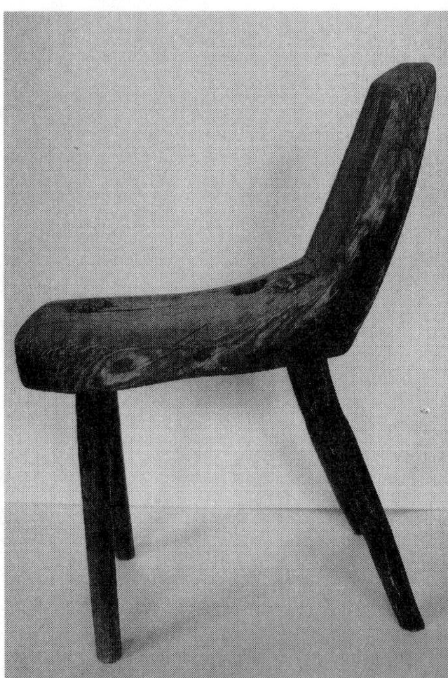

Primitive milking stool or saddle stool, Norwegian, pine, circa 1850, with four legs doweled into seat and unusual stomach rest in front, remnants of old rusty red paint or stain, 7 1/2 in. by 19 in. by 13 1/2 in. **$325**

❖ Tables

Rare country Victorian banquet table with folk art influences, Pennsylvania origin, walnut, floral and vine-carved pedestal and legs with carved flying buttress supports, circa 1860, original rack of five leaves and case, original finish, 30 in. tall, 60 in. diameter top. **$7,000**

County hutch table, pine, top pivots up on a pair of wooden dowels to create bench with back, circa 1900, original finish, 56 in. wide by 48 in. deep by 29 in. tall. **$650**

Unusual folksy end table with fold-out top, walnut, carved designs on hinged top that splits in the middle and two sides fold out, all four sides of table naively carved with stylized floral designs and the profile of a woman, one door on wide side, square carved legs sit on lower shelf that is supported by crude paw feet, circa 1900, original finish, 20 in. wide by 15 in. deep (leaves closed) by 31 in. tall. **$650**

Unusual folksy end table with fold-out top, walnut, carved designs on hinged top that splits in the middle and two sides fold out, all four sides of table naively carved with stylized floral designs and the profile of a woman, one door on wide side, square carved legs sit on lower shelf that is supported by crude paw feet, circa 1900, original finish, 20 in. wide by 15 in. deep (leaves closed) by 31 in. tall. $650

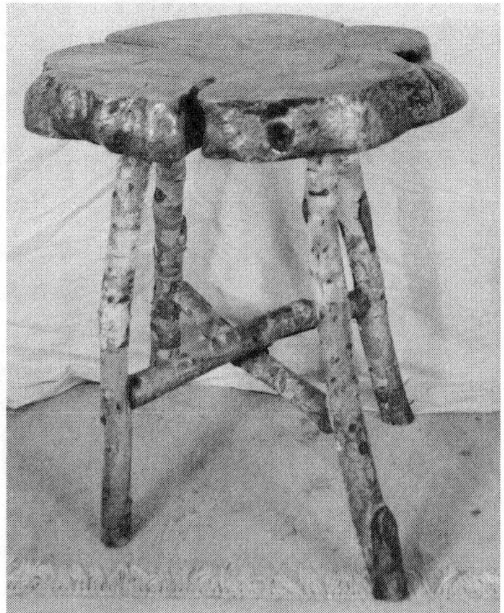

Rustic table, circa 1890, birch, with irregular tree trunk seat made of tiger maple, legs and X stretchers with bark, moderate wear, 22 in. by 14 in. **$300-$400**

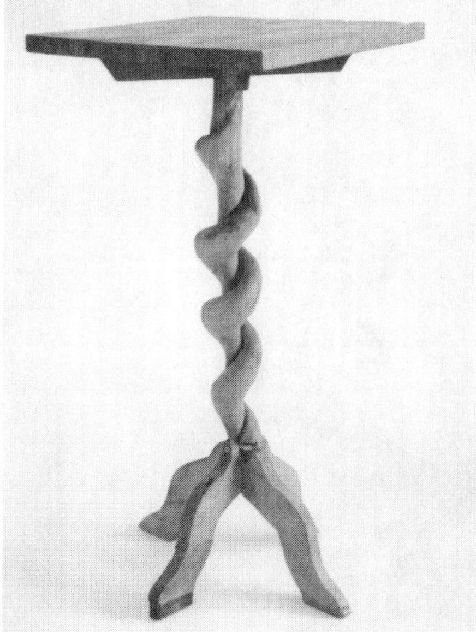

Table or candle stand, circa 1900, mixed woods, square top and spiral sassafras root column on splay legs, old green paint, 30 in. by 14 in. by 14 in. **$150-$200**

Country Sheraton two-drawer worktable, maple, lathe-turned legs with spiral twists, original sandwich glass pulls on two locking drawers with brass keyhole escutcheons, circa 1840, old refinish, 18 in. wide and deep by 30 in. tall. **$450**

Country taper-leg worktable, pine with original paint, oval top, small drawer in skirt with wooden pull, circa 1900, 28 in. wide by 18 in. deep by 30 in. tall. **$175**

Two views of table, circa 1920s, rustic style probably from a cabin, with burled tree-trunk legs, simulated half-timber skirt and lower shelf stretcher, original varnished surface, old cutout repair in top, overall excellent condition, 66 in. by 31 in. by 20 in. **$600-$700**

❖ Terrarium

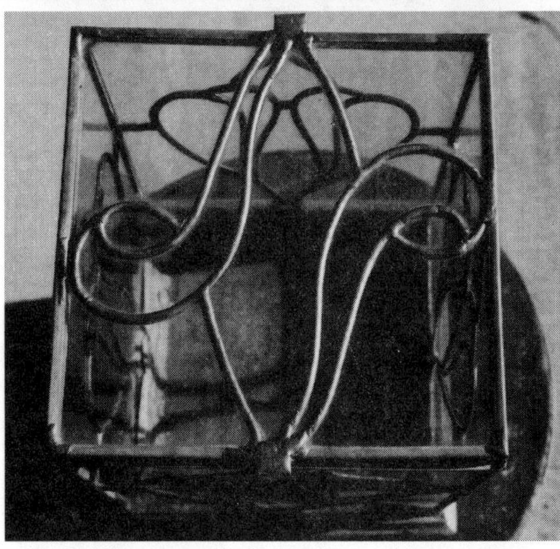

Three views of terrarium, homemade with leaded glass panels in a stylized floral motif, molded wood base, top hinged, bottom lined with zinc, circa 1930s, 12 in. by 8 in. square, moderate wear. **$150-$200**

❖ Trunks

Immigrant trunks and boxes—some as small as a Bible, others as large as a coffin—were brought to America by the hundreds of thousands between 1850 and the 1920s. The most desirable examples have vividly painted exteriors and interiors, dates and script that can be traced back to specific regions, and in some cases, the exact villages of origin. Bigger trunks do not always bring the biggest prices. Smaller examples with good paint and hardware, and those whose motifs include people and animals, bring a premium, ranging from **$2,000-$6,000**, depending on condition.

Immigrant's trunk, dome top, circa 1880, northern Europe, probably Scandinavia, pine with wrought iron fittings, painted green with yellow script lettering, significant handling wear, 28 in. by 14 in. by 10 in. **$500-$600**

Carpenter's tool trunk, pine, ornate copper brackets nailed to corners and raised panels on top, cast iron handles, hasp missing from lock, interior has shelves and recessed areas for holding tools, circa 1890, refinished, 36 in. wide by 20 in. tall by 20 in. deep. **$450**

Massive immigrant's trunk, oak, northern Europe, ornate wrought iron strap hinges, corner braces, handles and key plate, wooden pegged and dovetailed, carved design in top showing a cornucopia spilling fruit, base retains original wooden rollers, original lock and key, lidded till inside, circa 1840, original finish, 50 in. wide by 22 in. deep by 30 in. tall. **$1,500**

Immigrant's trunk, pine, northern European, traces of original paint decoration, name and inscription painted on front, dated 1856, till compartment inside, 36 in. long by 20 in. deep by 26 in. tall. **$400**

Immigrant's trunk, northern Europe, initialed and dated 1841, painted pine with dovetailed and pegged construction, dome lid, open interior with till on one end, original lock and key, wrought iron fittings and handles, 60 in. long by 24 in. deep by 24 in. tall. **$950**

Painted immigrant's trunk, pine, northern Europe, lid unpainted, applied carving and molding to front, iron hinges, handles, and hasp, roller base, open interior, 44 in. wide by 21 in. deep by 20 in. tall. ***$400***

Paint-decorated trunk, pine, stenciled ivy borders and floral decorations, hand-painted scroll banding on sides, original lock, circa 1850-1860, 20 in. long by 14 in. deep by 12 in. tall. **$400**

Immigrant's trunk, stained pine, northern Europe, dovetailed construction, carved floral motifs in lid and front, wrought iron hinges, handles, hasp, and keyplate, original lock and key, molded base, open interior, circa 1830s, 40 in. wide by 20 in. deep by 18 in. tall. **$650**

Small dome-top pine trunk, original sponge grain-painted surface, dovetailed, original hardware, circa 1860, 14 in. deep by 22 in. long by 12 in. tall. **$250**

Country grain-painted trunk, probably pine, circa 1840, original sponge-decorated surface, hinged lid, open interior, recessed panels on front and sides, turned legs, 44 in. wide by 22 in. deep by 28 in. tall. **$400**

Trunk, circa 1920s, pine with cutout applied panels and trim painted gray, white, black, and red, on tapered legs, hinged lid and open interior, possibly a circus piece, excellent condition, 28 in. by 28 in. by 22 in. **$800-$1,000**

Dome-top trunk, oak, pierced strap iron fitting and hinges, original lock and key, dovetailed and pegged construction, till inside, circa 1800, original finish, 40 in. long by 24 in. deep by 22 in. tall. **$950**

❖ Wall Pockets

Wall pocket, circa 1930s, fir or pine with original varnished surface, decorated with cutout profiles of dogs on the back and front panels, probably for mail or newspapers since the pocket is not open at the bottom, 14 1/2 in. by 6 1/4 in. by 3 in. ***$60***

Wall pocket, circa 1900, walnut, with cutout designs of stars in circles, tapering scalloped back, slanted front and sides, nailed construction, original unvarnished surface, mint condition, 18 in. by 10 in. by 4 in. **$200-$300**

Wall pocket, circa 1890, walnut, made of thick carved flat sticks connected with faceted and conical brass upholstery tacks, two pockets decorated with star motifs and lollipop cutouts, also constructed with faceted and conical brass upholstery tacks, inset mirror on upper pocket, original varnished surface, excellent condition (missing stick on upper right, later found), 36 in. by 20 in. by 8 in. (Wall pockets of similar design but made with thin strips of walnut, usually connected with porcelain-head tacks, are quite common. This example is unusual because of the weight of the wood used and the carved points.) **$500-$600**

Wall pocket, circa 1900, oak, with original dark stain, simple cutout back, visible circular saw cuts, excellent condition, 9 3/4 in. by 11 in. by 3 in. **$40-$50**

❖ Wardrobes & Armoires

Country armoire or wardrobe, possibly Norwegian/American, butternut, one piece, scalloped crest board with applied walnut fruit carving above molded cornice, two doors with tombstone-shaped applied walnut molding, two side-by-side drawers with wooden knob pulls and scalloped skirt, circa 1870, refinished, 50 in. wide by 20 in. deep by 88 in. tall. **$1,500**

Country gothic knockdown armoire, walnut, found in Missouri, heavy rounded crest with unusual horn-like protrusions, feather-grain walnut panels in doors that feature a gothic cutout, two drawers in base and cutout bracket feet, circa 1850, refinished, 52 in. wide by 20 in. deep by 86 in. tall. **$1,800**

Country Empire double-door armoire, walnut, massive crown molding, tombstone-shaped panels on doors with deeply carved ribbon molding, Chippendale-style ogee bracket foot, open interior, knockdown, circa 1840s, old refinish, 60 in. wide by 22 in. deep by 90 in. tall. ***$2,800***

Norwegian/American armoire, butternut, one piece, pegged and dovetailed construction, scalloped crest with drawer set in middle, molded cornice, open interior, recessed-panel doors with scalloped profile above two deep drawers with wooden mushroom pulls, unusual turned corner molding, scalloped skirt, refinished, circa 1875, 52 in. wide by 21 in. deep by 88 in. tall. **$1,800**

Victorian armoire, walnut and burl walnut, one piece, raised burl panels on arched blind doors, two-drawer base with carved pulls, circa 1870, refinished, 44 in. wide by 18 in. deep by 84 in. tall. **$1,500**

Country Victorian armoire with Eastlake influence, walnut, molded cornice above floral-carved frieze, recessed-panel doors with floral carving and raised medallions, pair of side-by-side drawers with line carving and iron bin pulls, cutout base, refinished, circa 1885, 48 in. wide by 18 in. deep by 86 in. tall. **$2,400**

Painted kas (wardrobe), pine with original salmon-red paint decoration and black trim, pegged construction, raised panels over false drawer fronts, wooden pegs inside, cutout bracket base, circa 1850-60, 46 in. wide by 19 1/2 in. deep by 76 in. tall. **$2,200**

❖ Washstands

Sheraton washstand, mahogany, straight backsplash with scalloped side returns, cabinet door above one drawer, turned legs, period hardware may not be original, circa 1820s, old refinish, 38 in. tall by 18 in. wide by 22 in. deep. **$450**

Country Sheraton washstand, pine, straight backsplash with cutout sideboards, hole cut in top shelf to hold bowl, lower shelf with skirt, turned legs, circa 1850, refinished, 18 in. wide by 18 in. deep by 38 in. tall. **$450**

Sheraton washstand, mahogany, shaped backsplash with side returns and scalloped valance below top shelf, turned rope-twist legs, single drawer below lower shelf with original hardware, brass-cap paw feet, refinished, circa 1820s, 20 in. wide by 16 in. deep by 34 in. tall. **$450**

Country washstand, pine, original painted surface simulating mahogany, exuberant cutout backsplash with yellow edging, pierced side returns, single drawer with rolled face, saber-like front legs and scalloped lower shelf, circa 1870, 25 in. wide by 18 in. deep by 42 in. tall. **$400**

Country Victorian washstand, walnut, shaped backsplash with turned towel bars and scroll supports, one drawer with carved pull over one blind door with applied wooden medallion, bracket feet, original finish, circa 1880, 22 in. wide by 15 in. deep by 35 in. tall. **$400**

Painted country three-drawer washstand, probably butternut or pine, scalloped backsplash, wooden mushroom pulls, dovetailed, circa 1870s, original paint, 24 in. wide by 15 in. deep by 36 in. tall. **$300**

Rare Sheraton double-basin washstand, mahogany, arched backsplash and cutout sides, two holes cut for bowls, bow front, scalloped side panels above open shelf and a pair of side-by-side drawers with original brasses, turned legs, original finish, circa 1820s, 48 in. wide by 20 in. deep by 38 in. tall. **$1,400**

Country Empire washstand or nightstand, cherry, single drawer with wooden mushroom pull supported by large S-scrolls, cutout platform base and scroll feet, refinished, circa 1860, 18 in. wide by 14 in. deep by 30 in. tall. **$275**

Gaudy Dutch

Gaudy Dutch is the name given to a particular type of English Staffordshire. Made specifically for the rural trade among the Pennsylvania Germans, most pieces featured flowers and bright splashes of red, green, and yellow. Gaudy Dutch was produced mainly between 1790 and 1825. Although the items had little appeal in England, they were enthusiastically accepted in Pennsylvania German communities because they were inexpensive and colorful.

References: Eleanor and Edward Fox, *Gaudy Dutch*, self-published, 1970; John A. Shuman III, *Collector's Encyclopedia of Gaudy Dutch & Welsh*, Collector Books, 1990 (1998 value update).

Collectors' Club: Gaudy Collector's Society, PO Box 274, Gates Mills, OH 44040.

Museums: Henry Ford Museum, Dearborn, Mich.; Philadelphia Museum of Art, Philadelphia, Pa.; Reading Art Museum, Reading, Pa.

Creamer, 4 in. tall. **$425**

Creamer, Double Rose pattern, 3 3/4 in. tall. **$525**

Cup and saucer, handleless, Carnation pattern, imperfections. **$475**

Cup and saucer, handleless, Dahlia pattern. **$8,100**

Cup and saucer, handleless, Double Rose pattern. **$600**

Cup and saucer, handleless, Dove pattern, imperfections. **$525**

Cup and saucer, handleless, Grape pattern, minor imperfections. **$525**

Cup and saucer, handleless, Oyster pattern. **$475**

Cup and saucer, handleless, Single Rose pattern, imperfections. **$450**

Cup and saucer, handleless, Sunflower pattern, imperfections. **$725**

Cup and saucer, handleless, Urn pattern. **$575**

Cup and saucer, handleless, War Bonnet pattern, cup with hairlines, professional repairs. **$375**

Plate, Carnation pattern, 8 1/4 in. diameter. **$975**

Plate, Carnation pattern, minor flakes, 10 in. diameter. **$3,200**

Plate, Double Rose pattern, 7 1/2 in. diameter. **$625**

Plate, Dove pattern, 7 1/2 in. diameter. **$550**

Plate, Grape pattern, 9 1/2 in. diameter. **$450**

Plate, Oyster pattern, 7 1/2 in. diameter. **$600**

Plate, Oyster pattern, 10 in. diameter. **$1,600**

Plate, 10 in. diameter. **$2,500**

Plate, Sunflower pattern, imperfections, 9 3/4 in. diameter. **$850**

Plate, Urn pattern, 10 in. diameter. **$975**

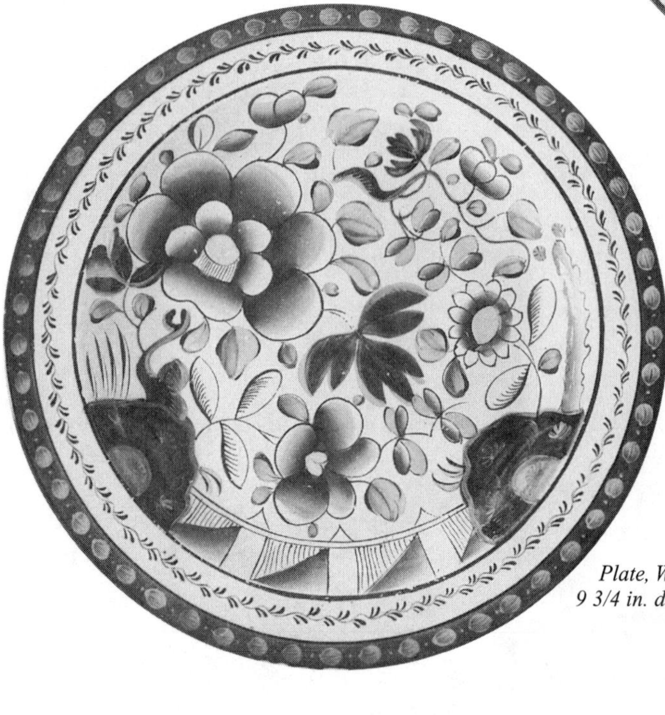

Teapot, War Bonnet pattern, with collar, spout chip, 7 in. tall. **$4,500**

Plate, War Bonnet pattern, 9 3/4 in. diameter. **$950**

Plate, Single Rose pattern, 3 1/4 in. diameter. **$575**

Plate, Single Rose pattern, 7 1/2 in. diameter. **$525**

Plate, Single Rose pattern, 8 in. diameter. **$450**

Plate, uknown pattern, 7 in. diameter. **$2,000**

Plate, Urn pattern, 8 3/8 in diameter. **$2,000**

Plate, War Bonnet pattern, 8 in. diameter. **$650**

Soup plate, Double Rose pattern, 10 in. diameter **$1,800**

Soup plate, Single Rose pattern, 10 in. diameter **$1,525**

Soup plate, Zinnia pattern, marked "Riley," 10 in. diameter **$4,700**

Sugar, covered, Single Rose pattern, shell handles, restored, 5 1/2 in. tall. **$575**

Sugar, covered, Sunflower pattern, shell handles, lid damage, 5 1/2 in. tall. **$800**

Teapot, Single Rose pattern, spout chip, 6 in. tall. **$1,300**

Teapot, Single Rose pattern, spout restored, 5 1/2 in. tall. **$1,100**

Teapot, Urn pattern, 6 1/4 in. tall. **$850**

Waste bowl, Sunflower pattern, 6 1/2 in. diameter **$525**

Graniteware

Like any group of avid collectors, the fans of graniteware have developed a system of descriptions based on color and/or maker that the uninitiated may find baffling. In addition to the ever-present gray, these descriptions include (but are not limited to):

Black and White Swirl
Plain Blue
Blue Mottled
Blue Relish
Blue and White Swirl
Brown Mottled
Brown and White Swirl
Chrysolite
Cobalt and White Swirl
Columbian
Confetti
End-of-Day
Emerald Swirl
Gray Mottled
Green Mottled
Green and White "Snow on the Mountain"
Green and White Swirl
Iris Swirl
Lava
Light Blue
Light Blue Mottled
Mulberry Swirl
Onyx
Red Shaded
Red and White
Red and White Swirl
Shamrock

And it should come as no surprise that the three factors driving prices are rarity, color, and condition.

Blue and white swirl chamber pot, circa 1920, significant chipping and rust to top of lid, 10 in. by 9 in. by 6 in. **$25**

Blue and white swirl coffeepot. **$150-$200**

Blue and white swirl coffee cups, two styles.

A red and white swirl tea steeper has sold at auction for $4,200, and a miniature (about 1 1/2 in. diameter) chamber pot reached $3,000.

Price ranges at auction for select graniteware items follow:

Black and white swirl: biscuit cutter, **$1,800-$2,000**; churn, **$1,000-$1,100**; salt and pepper shakers,

Blue and white swirl dairy pan.

Blue and white swirl gooseneck coffee pot.

Blue and white swirl Berlin-style pot.

Brown mottled: coffee pot with gooseneck, tin lid and wooden handle, excellent condition, 9 in. by 9 1/2 in. by 5 3/4 in. **$150**

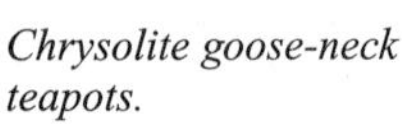

Chrysolite goose-neck teapots.

Chrysolite bucket.

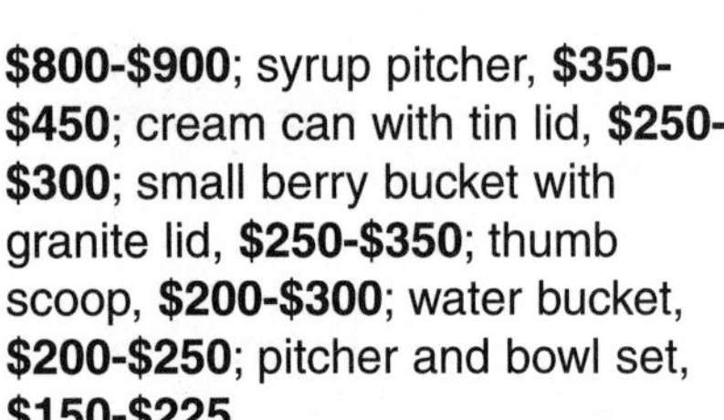

$800-$900; syrup pitcher, **$350-$450**; cream can with tin lid, **$250-$300**; small berry bucket with granite lid, **$250-$350**; thumb scoop, **$200-$300**; water bucket, **$200-$250**; pitcher and bowl set, **$150-$225**

Blue mottled: child's stove, **$650-$800**; gooseneck teapot, **$100-$150**; miniature dustpan, **$80-$120**

Blue relish: gooseneck teapot with tin lid, **$125-$150**; tilt coffeepot and tray with pewter trim, **$250-$300**

Blue and white swirl: pitcher and bowl set, **$600-$700**; cream can with granite lid, **$300-$400**; berry bucket with granite lid, **$250-$350**; round lunch box, **$250-$350**; berry bucket with tin lid, **$150-$225**; coffeepot, **$150-$200**; creamer, **$150-$200**; Windsor dipper, **$125-$150**; salesman's sample wash basin, **$100-$150**

Blue: child's miniature bottle holder. ....**$150-$225**

Bluebelle ware: water pitcher. ....**$150-$200**

Brown mottled: berry bucket with tin lid. ....**$70-$90**

Brown and white swirl: measure, **$1,200-$1,500**; berry bucket with granite lid, **$500-$600**; coffee boiler, **$400-$500**

Brown and white swirl oval lunch bucket, **$1,700-$1,900**; spooner, **$250-$350**; berry bucket with granite lid, **$250-$350**; funnel, 2 7/8 in. diameter, **$175-$225**; colander, **$125-$150**

Chrysolite: cream can with tin lid, **$1,000-$2,000**; syrup, **$600-$800**; water pitcher, **$550-$650**; colander, **$350-$400**; berry bucket with tin lid, **$350-$400**; tea steeper, **$250-$350**; coffeepot, **$250-$350**; coffee boiler, **$150-$225**; baking dish, **$125-$150**; sample washbasin, **$250-$350**

Cobalt and white swirl: miniature roaster, three pieces, **$1,500-$2,000**; syrup, **$1,200-$1,500**; small measure, **$1,200-$1,500**; bowl and pitcher set, **$750-$900**; one-cup biggin with strainer, **$800-$900**; cocoa dipper, **$700-$900**; three-piece oval lunch box, **$400-$600**; cream can with tin lid, **$400-$500**; eight-hole muffin pan, **$400-$500**; creamer and sugar, **$350-$425**; gooseneck teapot, **$400-$475**; round lunch bucket, **$400-$500**; gravy strainer, **$300-$425**; oval lunch bucket, **$300-$375**; spittoon, **$250-$350**; slop jar, **$150-$250**; miniature teapot, **$150-$200**; candlestick, **$125-$180**; sugar bowl with lid, **$350-$450**; colander, **$150-$200**

Cobalt relish: Windsor dipper. **$50-$70**

Columbian: gooseneck teakettle, **$900-$1,000**; cream can with tin lid, **$700-$800**; water pitcher, about 1 gallon, **$550-$650**; berry bucket with granite lid, **$500-$600**; gooseneck teapot, **$400-$500**; cream can with tin lid, **$400-$500**; roaster, embossed "Columbian," **$400-$500**; gooseneck teapot, about 8 in., **$350-$450**; oval tray, about 10 in. by 18 in., **$350-$450**; two-cup teapot, **$800-$900**; coffee

Cobalt and white swirl (left) and blue and white swirl berry buckets.

Cobalt and white swirl canning funnel.

Cobalt and white swirl gooseneck teapot.

Cobalt and white swirl coffeepot with wooden knob.

Columbian bean pot with tin lid.

Gray one-cup goose-neck coffee biggin with original paper label.

Gray frying pan.

Gray ladles.

Gray oval lunch or dinner bucket.

Gray scalloped mold.

Gray measures in three sizes.

Gray convex pitchers, each with a slightly different finish.

Gray milk pitchers, each with a slightly different finish.

An assortment of gray spoons.

Gray skimmers.

Teakettle, white with cobalt trim.

Gray small teakettles.

boiler, **$500-$600**; frying pan, **$400-$500**; Windsor dipper, **$300-$400**; eight-hole muffin pan, **$300-$350**; oval tray, **$200-$300**; berry bucket with tin lid, **$200-$250**

Confetti: miniature witch's hat funnel. ....**$275-$325**

Dutchessware: coffeepot, about 7 in., **$550-$650**; gooseneck teapot, about 7 in., **$550-$650**; berry bucket with tin lid, **$250-$350**

Emerald swirl: molasses or syrup pitcher, **$1,800-$2,500**; gooseneck teapot, about 10 in., **$1,750-$1,850**; small measure, **$1,150-$1,250**; creamer, **$800-$900**; cream can with granite lid, **$750-$850**; molasses pitcher, **$750-$850**; sugar bowl with granite lid, **$600-$700**; coffeepot, about 10 in., **$600-$700**; coffeepot, about 8 in., **$550-$650**; cream can with tin lid, **$600-$675**; "squatty" funnel, about 5 in. diameter, **$350-$450**; berry bucket with granite lid, **$300-$350**; cup, **$250-$350**; small kettle with tin lid, **$250-$300**; soap dish with granite insert, **$180-$225**; dishpan, **$180-$225**; berry bucket with tin lid, **$150-$200**; two-piece spittoon, **$150-$200**

End-of-Day: red soap dish with insert, **$180-$225**; red hanging shell soap dish, **$80-$100**; spoon in yellow, black, and red, **$80-$100**; Kerr Range Co. ashtray, **$30-$40**; gray dustpan, **$60-$70**

Gray: floor-model butter churn with gray drum, **$1,300-$1,400**; sugar shaker, **$1,000-$1,100**; hanging salt box, **$900-$1,000**; miniature straight-spout coffeepot, **$800-$850**; coffee carrier with tin lid, **$750-$850**; oval lunch bucket with canted sides and wooden lid, **$700-$800**; gooseneck teapot with granite biggin and lid, **$650-$750**; scoop with paper label, about 8 in. long, **$600-$675**; biscuit cutters, **$350-$550**; coffee carrier, **$450-$550**; cocoa dipper with a wooden handle, **$300-$375**; round lunch bucket, **$200-$250**; miniature colander, **$750-$850**; small coffee or canning jar, **$700-$750**; salt shaker, **$600-$700**; toddy strainer, **$400-$500**; straight-spout miniature teapot, **$400-$500**; stacking lunch set, **$300-$400**; biscuit cutter, **$300-$400**; hanging saltbox, **$300-$400**; coffee biggin, **$180-$225**; flat-bottomed scoop, **$150-$200**; strainer, **$150-$200**

Gray mottled: miniature cup and cup holder, **$300-$350**; round covered butter dish, **$180-$225**

Gray with pewter trim: three-piece set including tilt teapot, sugar, and creamer, **$2,800-$3,500**; fancy coffeepot, about 12 in. tall, **$2,500-$3,000**; square tray, **$800-$900**;

Gray and white spatter miniature graniteware pieces (six), including mold, handled pot, roaster, frying pan and plates, circa 1920s, minor wear, frying pan 4 in. long. **$350/set**

miniature teapot with gooseneck spout, about 5 in., **$650-$750**; waste jar, about 5 in. diameter, **$550-$650**; cup with footed base and canted sides, **$500-$575**; sugar bowl with lid, **$400-$475**; short candlestick, **$400-$457**; butter dish with insert, **$300-$375**; sugar bowl, **$250-$300**

Green and white "snow on the mountain": gooseneck teapot. ....**$90-$100**

Green and white swirl: funnel. ....**$90-$100**

Green mottled: sample pitcher. ....**$100-$125**

Iris swirl: cream can with granite lid, **$1,100-$1,200**; bulbous gooseneck teapot, **$700-$800**; salt shaker, **$450-$550**; water pitcher, **$200-$275**; roaster with insert, **$70-$85**, pitcher and bowl set, **$350-$450**

Lava: gooseneck teapot, about 7 in., **$250-$300**; tea steeper with granite lid, **$200-$250**; kettle with paper label, **$125-$150**; angel food cake pan, **$100-$125**; milk pan, **$65-$75**

Light blue: miniature hanging utensil rack with ladle and turner, **$600-$675**; miniature witch's hat funnel, **$90-$125**; miniature grater, **$55-$65**

Light blue mottled: cream can with granite lid. ....**$90-$100**

Mulberry swirl: coffeepot with tin lid, **$40-$50**; coffee boiler with tin lid, **$40-$50**

Onyx: coffee roaster, **$125-$150**; gooseneck teapot, about 5 in., **$100-$150**; biscuit tray, **$40-$50**

Red and white swirl: milk pan, **$650-$750**; bowl, **$300-$400**; coffee biggin, **$125-$175**; gooseneck teapot with tin lid, **$75-$90**; berry bucket with tin lid, **$1,800-$2,200**; dipper, **$450-$550**

Red shaded: ten-piece canister set, **$90-$125**; miniature bucket, **$12-$18**

Shaded blue: gooseneck teapot, **$150-$175**; straight-side teapot, **$90-$125**

Shamrock: kettle. ....**$60-$70**

Thistleware: berry bucket with granite lid. ....**$125-$175**

Where can I find it?

Graniteware is everywhere, but for specifics, contact:

National Graniteware Society
PO Box 9248
Cedar Rapids, IA 52409-9248
http://www.graniteware.org/
info@graniteware.org

Hitching Posts

Generally made of cast iron, hitching posts ranged from plain to fanciful. They typically had a looped ring to which reins could be attached in order to keep a horse in place.

Reproduction Alert

Various forms have been reproduced.

Black boy holding lantern with green and white slag glass panels, square base, cast iron, old green repaint, areas of rewelding at joints, 44 in. tall. **$950**

Horse heads, rings in mouth, round post, black paint, 57 1/4 in. tall. **$450/pair**

Standing black boy wearing a hat, scarf, vest, and long pants, his right arm extended with a closed fist, the left hand in his pocket, last half 19th century, repaired, 24 1/2 in. tall. **$800-$1,000**
Courtesy Garth's Auctions, Delaware, Ohio.

Left to right: Dog's head with a large ring in the mouth, traces of black paint, with stand, American, 19th century, minor surface rust, 11 in. wide, 12 in. tall, **$4,025**; *sand-gate latch, model of a duck's head, the head forming the articulated handle, possibly California, late 19th century, with stand, weathered surface, 3 3/4 in. by 7 in. by 3 1/2 in. tall,* **$230**; *diminutive horse head, long and small rings in the mouth, traces of black paint, Rochester, New York, c. 1850, on stand, 4 1/2 in. wide by 9 7/8 in. tall,* **$1,840**; *small horse head hinged on a post cap so it nods, traces of black paint, patented in 1889 by W.H. Vaughn, Quincy, Ill., no stand, losses, 7 in. wide by 5 in. tall,* **$316**; *hitching post top, model of a large horse head with loop and ring in the nose, old weathered surface, American, 19th century, with stand, 4 1/4 in. by 9 1/2 in. by 11 1/2 in. tall,* **$633**.
Courtesy Skinner Inc., Bolton, Mass.

Hitching post finial, a stylized head of Napoleon cast in the full round, detailed hair and facial features, fringed epaulets on shoulders, a ring on one side of shoulder, on a cylindrical attachment base, American, 19th century, 8 in. tall. **$4,465**
Courtesy Christie's, New York, N.Y.

Far left and right: Horse head with articulated ears, mane, eyes and nostrils, cast in the full round, pierced mouth with iron ring above a cylindrical post, on a later square base, American, 19th century, 20 1/2 in. tall, $621/pair; small hitching posts, a horse head with articulated ears, eyes, mane, and nostrils cast in the full round, mouth pierced and holding a bar with a ring at each end, on a cylindrical base, on a modern foot, American, 19th century, overall 9 1/2 in. tall, **$1,058/pair**
Courtesy Christie's, New York, N.Y.

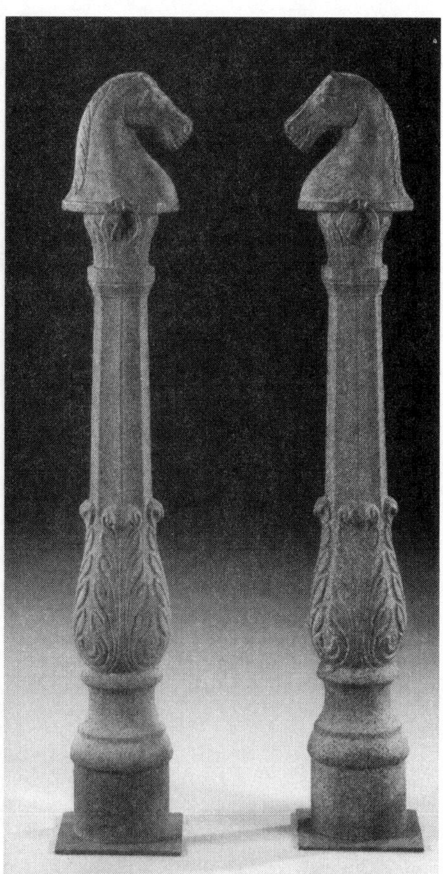

Horse head cast in the round with a detailed mane, eyes, nostrils, and mouth above a ring and oval leaf-cast capital above the faceted column with acanthus leaves around the bottom on a waisted cylindrical base, modern foot, attributed to J.W. Fiske & Co., New York, New York, late 19th century, 48 in. tall.
$4,465/pair
Courtesy Christie's, New York, N.Y.

*Left to right: Tall tree trunk with molded bark, cast in the round with stubby branches and a meandering berried vine above a grassy base, trunk painted brown, vine and grass painted green, American, 19th century, 35 3/4 in. tall, **$353**; hitching post with an open trefoil finial above a flattened flaring shaft pierced with quatrefoil and round openings, painted brown, American, late 19th century, modern base, 10 in. wide, 39 in. tall, **$705**; realistic horse head finial with detailed curly mane, ears, eyes, nostrils, and mouth with ring above a lobed capital flanked by rings, over a fluted column with lion heads and scrolls at the base, painted brown, modern square foot, American, late 19th century, 35 1/2 in. tall, **$2,233**; realistic horse head finial with finely cast details above a lobed capital over a tall fluted column footed by lion heads and scrolls above a faceted base, modern metal foot, American, late 19th century, 8 1/2 in. by 9 in., 48 3/4 in. tall, **$2,115**; stylized horse head finial with pronounced ears and delineated mane above a side ring and fluted column, new square, painted black, American, late 19th century, 27 1/2 in. tall, **$705**; hitching post with a ring finial above a tapering neck over a tall spiral-cast column with a stylized leaf base band and plinth, new square foot, painted yellow, American, late 19th century, 11 3/4 in. by 12 in., 49 in. tall,* **$1,058**
Courtesy Christie's, New York, N.Y.

Hitching post finial, modeled as a human hand with closed fingers above a ruffled cuff, cast in the full round, a chain attached from side to side, on a modern base, American, late 19th century, overall 9 1/4 in. tall.
$3,760
Courtesy Christie's, New York, N.Y.

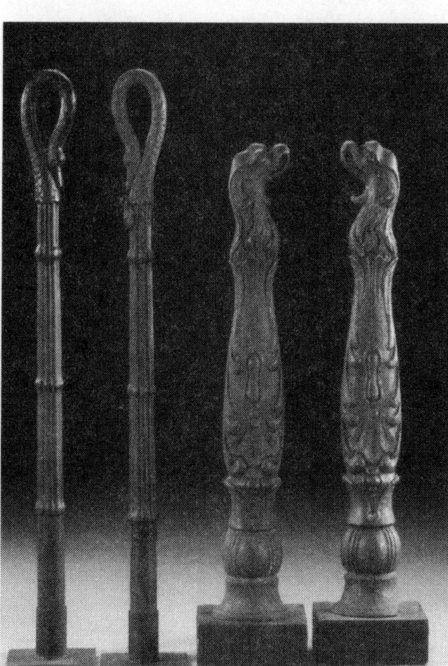

Left to right: Looped swan's head with a feathered and imbricated neck, above a slender three-part ribbed shaft, painted black, modern base, American, 19th century, 52 1/2 in. tall, $2,115/pair; hitching posts with the finial cast as eagle's head with detailed crown, eyes, and beak above a feathered neck over a baluster-form shaft with scrolled decorations above a ball and plinth base, traces of black paint, modern foot, American, mid-19th century, 46 1/2 in. tall, **$4,465/pair**
Courtesy Christie's, New York, N.Y.

Jockey, left arm extended, right hand on hip, cast iron, "Champion Iron Fence Co., Kenton, Ohio," red, white, and black repaint, 50 1/4 in. tall. **$500**

❖ Homespun

This 19th century cloth, which was made at home or made from yarn spun at home, was characteristically rough and loosely woven. Designs tended to be plain. Manufactured versions are also included in this term.

Bed Case

Check, blue and white, initialed, 60 in. by 73 in. **$475**

Check, blue and white, minor soiling, 64 in. by 72 in. **$325**

Check, blue and white, 58 in. by 67 in., with two matching bolster cases. **$275**

Check, red and white, five small sewn repairs, 58 in. by 62 in. **$150**

Check, yellow-brown and natural, 58 in. by 66 in., with matching bolster case. **$1,650**

Plaid, blue and white, 68 in. by 70 in., with matching bolster case with white fringe, initialed "WWK 1894," acquired at Lebanon County, Pa., farm auction. **$2,100**

Plaid, red and white, minor wear and soiling, 56 in. by 72 in. **$75**

Blanket, Wool

Check, black on natural, two-piece construction, wear, holes, 68 in. wide by 76 in. long. **$330**

Natural, black pinstripe, holes, 56 in. sq. **$93.50**

Navy blue and natural, two-piece construction, small holes, wear, 70 in. wide by 84 in. long. **$165**

Plaid, blue and tomato red, two-piece construction, small holes, repairs, 72 in. wide by 78 in. long. **$192.50**

Plaid, medium blue and tomato red, two-piece construction, fringe on one end, 80 in. by 88 in. **$522.50**

Plain, brown, woven, wear, soiling, seam separation, 72 in. by 82 in. **$120**

Bolster Cover

Blue and white, hand-sewn seams, some seams loose, 18 in. wide by 55 in. long. **$137.50**

Blue and white, 19-1/2 in. by 60 in **$99**

Linen Fabric, Piece

Check, brown and natural, 40 in. by 63 in. **$725**

Check, brown and natural, hemmed ends, 38 in. by 64 in. **$825**

Plaid, blue and white, minor soiling, 20 in. by 55 in. **$150**

Plaid, blue and white, minor soiling, 40 in. by 84 in. **$225**

Plaid, blue and white, minor stains, small sewn repair, 38 in. by 70 in. **$100**

Mattress cover, cotton, blue and white check, machine sewn, small holes, 68 in. by 73 in. **$165**

Show Towel

Dated 1806, embroidered diamonds, trees, urns of flowers, crowns, and hearts in pink and blue, six embroidered line dividers beneath with triple fringed bottom, small holes, minor stains, 17 5/8 in. wide by 61 in. long. **$192.50**

Dated "1848 with Seaver," hearts in stars, ladies in dresses, pots of flowers and birds, fringed bottom, stains, 15 in. wide by 72 in. long **$247.50**

❖ Other Household Items

Bed warmer, circa 1860, turned walnut handle and brass pan with hinged lid decorated with a hex sign, excellent condition, 12 in. by 3 in. by 4 in. **$200-$300**

Bed warmer, circa 1860, turned walnut handle and brass pan with hinged lid decorated with sunflowers, excellent condition, 10 1/4 in. by 3 in. by 42 in. **$300-$400**

Bed warmer, circa 1860, turned pine handle with original polychrome decoration and brass pan with hinged lid decorated with a snowflake motif, 10 1/2 in. by 3 in. by 42 in. **$200-$300**

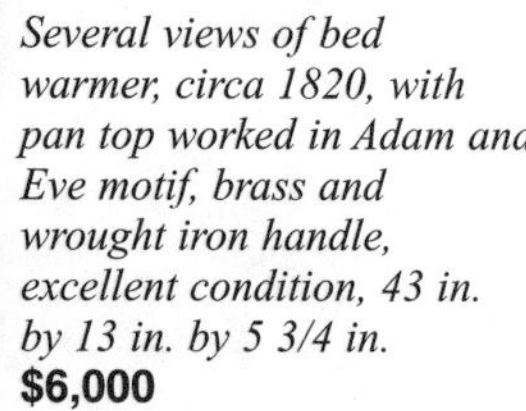

Several views of bed warmer, circa 1820, with pan top worked in Adam and Eve motif, brass and wrought iron handle, excellent condition, 43 in. by 13 in. by 5 3/4 in. **$6,000**

Birdcage, two compartments, with elaborately cut out and decorated wooden surface, arched tops with applied wooden rosettes and brass tacks, scalloped sides with four gold-painted balls in the corners, spring-loaded doors with notch carving, worn white painted surface, removable tin trays in bottom, carved wooden feet, 24 in. by 14 in. by 12 in. **$800-$1,200**

Hat boxes, molded leather with riveted seams on sides and tops, leather handles and straps and brass buckles, with applied railroad shipping labels, circa 1910, in sizes ranging from 18 in. to 26 in., moderate handling wear. **$150-$250 each**

Inkwell/pen rest, circa 1880, pine or fir, original dark varnished surface, delicately carved in a leaf shape, with carved holder for cobalt glass inkwell, moderate handling wear, overall excellent condition, 12 in. by 5 in. by 3 in. **$125-$150**

Bootjack, circa 1920, cast iron in the form of a lyre, original black painted surface, moderate wear, 11 in. by 4 1/2 in. by 2 1/2 in. (Beware of reproductions.)
$90-$100

Cigar box, circa 1910, hammered copper with wrought handle and riveted construction, on raised legs with curled feet, unsigned, probably of private make in emulation of pieces by Stickley and Roycroft, near mint condition, 10 in. by 8 in. by 7 in. Detail at right.
$300-$400

Four views of jewelry box in the form of a miniature chest of drawers, circa 1880, possibly converted from a child's toy or doll furniture, varnished walnut and mixed woods with applied scrollwork to drawer fronts, which have round brass pulls, arch-and-point decoration around top, which hides a spring-loaded door on a secret compartment; new velvet liners in drawers and top, otherwise original, 12 in. by 10 in. by 5 in.
$600-$700

Miniature commode in the form of a chest of drawers, circa 1880, done in tramp art style, cigar box mahogany and mixed woods, scalloped back with two small shelves and applied decoration in the form of a star, heart, and stylized leaves, hinged lid on top with porcelain knob, four drawers with scalloped and notch-carved profiles (two side by side, two stacked), the bottom two with porcelain pulls, bracket feet, original varnished surface, minor handling wear, 16 in. by 10 in. by 7 in. **$900-$1,200**

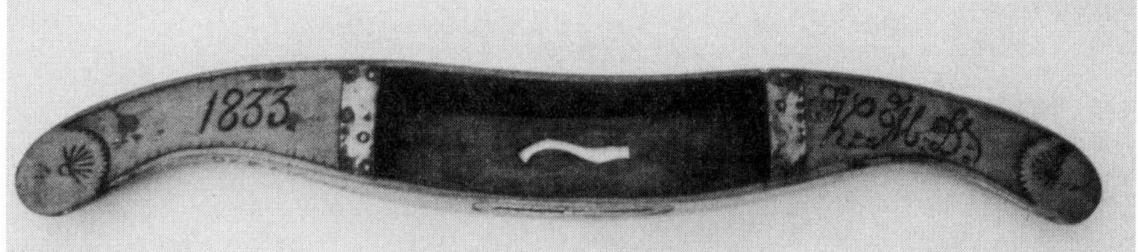

Loom shuttle, maple, Norwegian, with hollowed center section to hold weaving fiber, nailed brass fittings, carved with date of 1833 and the initials "KMD," original varnished finish, 13 in. by 2 in. by 1 1/4 in. **$300-$350**

Mangle board, circa 1780, oak, carved with hex signs, hearts, and geometric patterns, handle in the form of a primitive horse, moderate handling wear, 31 in. by 5 in. by 5 in. **$800-$900**

The Story of Mangles

Mangle boards, called *mangletre* or *mangletraer* in Norwegian, are highly decorated—carved and/or painted—boards with a single handle, often in the form of a horse or lion. They were used to smooth out the wrinkles from cloth that had been wound on a round stick after washing.

They were also used as betrothal gifts. Tradition says that a young man would make a mangle board for the woman he hoped to marry. He would then hang the carved mangle board on the door of the woman's house. If she accepted his proposal, she would bring the board into the house. If she refused, she would leave the board on the door. A man did not use the same mangle board for the next woman he proposed to, so some say the best woodcarvers in Norway were bachelors. There is a saying, "Beware a man with many mangles."

Three views of Mangle handle, pine, carved in the form of a crouching lion, with remnants of red paint, handling wear, bottom with carved name and date, "H Olin 1876," 7 3/4 in. by 6 1/4 in. by 2 1/2 in. **$500-$600**

Rustic carrier for vegetables or flowers, circa 1900, twig construction on oval wood base, entwined wood handle, with sides of interlaced branches, original white painted surface, some flaking, overall excellent condition, 18 in. by 14 in. by 10 in. (Most twig items, usually small tables or chairs, were exposed to the elements for many years and may become fragile or brittle. Look for pieces like this one, which was rigidly constructed and still has original paint.) **$200-$300**

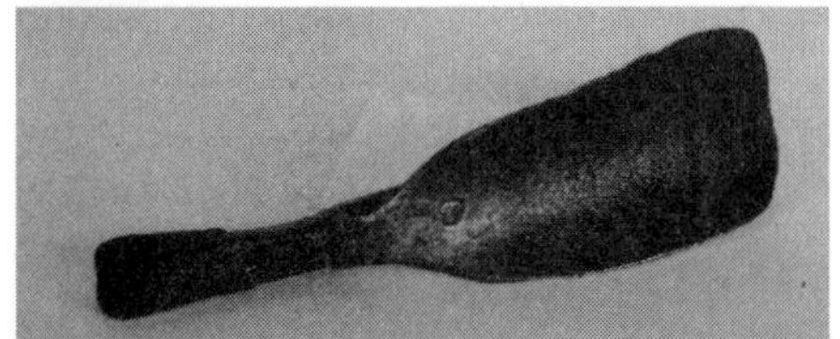

Shoe horn and boot puller, Norwegian, circa 1780, wrought iron with heart decoration, with handled clamp on reverse for pulling on boots, 6 1/4 in. by 1 3/4 in. **$250**

Snuff box, maple, Norwegian, circa 1880, carved in the form of a sleeping dog, with hinged door on bottom, original brown stain, moderate wear, 4 1/2 in. by 1 1/2 in. by 1 1/2 in. **$475**

Storage box, cast iron, in the shape of a dove, two pieces with top that detaches along line of dove's wing, circa 1840, 7 in. by 4 in. by 3 in. **$1,200**

Two views of storage box, circa 1890, made of varnished pine or fir and decorated on top and sides with hundreds of peach pits and varnished walnut shells and sections, Bennington stoneware knob on top, and a fragment of a piece of Schaefer & Vader pottery embedded in the front, brass handles on sides, lined with fabric, minor wear, overall excellent condition, 14 in. by 10 in. by 10 in. **$600-$800**

Storage box, circa 1910, cherry with mixed woods inlaid in bands on top and sides, and inlaid in panel on top the name "Mac," with original lock and varnished surface, minor handling wear and age cracks, 14 in. by 9 in. by 10 in. **$350**

Storage box, circa 1890, black-painted pine with beveled lid topped by a rounded walnut plaque on which is carved the initials "AR," hook and eye fastener, open interior, minor handling wear, 10 in. by 8 in. by 7 in. **$120-$150**

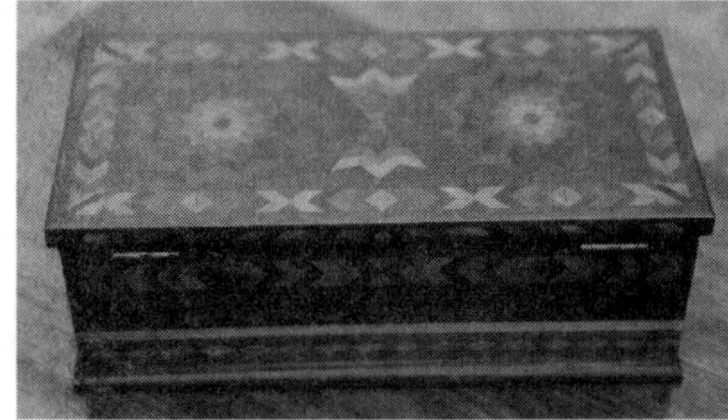

Two views of storage box, wood, circa 1910, with elaborate inlaid decoration of contrasting woods, including walnut, cherry, and maple, with pinwheel and fan motifs, and borders done in diamond and X shapes, inlaid with the name "ETTA," hinged lid, near mint condition, 10 in. by 6 in. by 4 1/2 in. **$200-$300**

Storage box, Norwegian, slant lid with molded trim, profusely painted with flowers and leaves, open interior with till, dated 1809 inside, moderate handling wear, 10 in. by 8 in. by 11 1/2 in. **$1,200-$1,500**

Tine (pronounced TEE-nuh), a Norwegian storage box, circa 1870, with carved lid in a stylized pineapple motif, applied handle with "thumb" braces on both ends, and rosemaled floral decoration, initials "HJ PD" carved in bottom, moderate handling wear, excellent condition, 6 3/4 in. by 4 in. by 3 1/4 in. **$400-$500**

Puzzle tine, Swedish, rare, pine, woven lap construction, with four carved knobs on top that must be turned in a certain order to open it, scratch-carved verse on sides and the date 1883, minor wear, 9 3/4 in. by 6 in. by 5 1/2 in. **$800-$900**

Tine, a Norwegian storage box, pine, lapped, pegged and woven construction with stylized burnt decoration, inked date inside lid of 1778 but may be later, moderate handling wear, 7 in. by 3 in. by 6 1/2 in. **$350-$450**

Vase, ceramic, made by George Ohr (1857-1918) with round footed base, bulbous body, tapering neck and dripping glaze in various shades of green, marked on the bottom with a stamp, "Geo. E. Ohr Biloxi," minor flaking to top rim, overall excellent condition, 7 in. by 3 1/2 in. (This is a simpler example of Ohr's work. Larger, more elaborate examples, which Ohr crimped and twisted, can sell for thousands—even tens of thousands—of dollars.) **$700-$1,000**

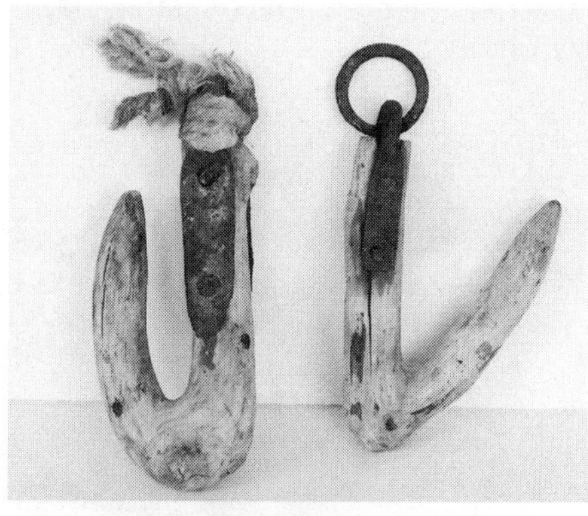

Primitive well hooks, maple, Norwegian, circa 1800, with wrought iron fittings, significant handling wear and remnants of old rope, hook on left is 7 in. by 3 in., hook on right is 7 1/2 in. by 4 in. **$30 each**

Tine, a Scandinavian storage box, circa 1850-1860, oval, bent pine, original dark blue background, rosemaled designs on lid and sides, lapped construction, 15 in. long by 7 in. tall by 8 in. deep. $800

Where can I find them?

Adamstown Antique Gallery
2000 N. Reading Rd.
Denver, PA 17517
(717) 335-3435
http://www.aagal.com/Antiquetobacciana.htm
adamsgal@dejazzd.com

Mary Lou Beidler
Early American Antiques
2736 Pecan Rd.
Tallahassee, FL 32303
(850) 385-2981
http://www.antiquearts.com/stores/beidler/
beidler@AntiqueArts.com

Blondell Antiques
1406 2nd St. SW
Rochester, MN 55902
(507) 282-1872
Fax: (507) 282-8683
www.blondell.com/
antiques@blondell.com

Country Comfort Antiques
Third and Main Streets
Winona, MN 55987
(507) 452-7044

Country Side Antique Mall
31752 65th Ave.
Cannon Falls, MN 55009
(507) 263-0352
www.csamantiques.com

Freward & Alk Antiques
414 Lazarre Ave.
Green Bay, WI 54301
(800) 488-0321
(920) 435-7343
www.the-antique-shop.com
leesa@the-antique-shop.com

John Kruesel's General Merchandise
22 Third St. SW
Rochester, MN 55902
(507) 289-8049
www.kruesel.com

Hunting/ Fishing

❖ Hunting

Calls

Duck call, carved rosewood, made by A.M. Bowles, Little Rock, Ark., circa 1900, with brass collar, 6 1/4 in. by 1 3/4 in. **$2,200**

Duck call, carved walnut, original leather thong handle with spring collar, brand of a duck in flight, 6 1/2 in. by 1 3/4 in. **$250**

Primitive duck call, carved walnut, marked "Aulus Lamb—E. Germantown, Ind.," circa 1910, 4 3/4 by 1 1/2 in. **$150**

Duck call made by Dan Crooks, Louisiana, circa 1950s, carved walnut in the form of two ducks in flight, each has nail eyes, 5 3/4 in. by 1 3/4 in. **$400**

❖ Decoys

Designed to coax waterfowl into target range, decoys have been made of wood, papier-mâché, canvas, and even metal. These hand-carved and even machine-made decoys have been recognized as an indigenous American art form.

References: Bob and Sharon Huxford, *The Collector's Guide to Decoys*, Vol. I (1990), Vol. II (1992), Collector Books; Carl F. Luckey and Russell Lewis, *Collecting Antique Bird Decoys and Duck Calls*, 3rd ed., Krause Publications, 2003; Loy S. Harrell Jr., *Decoys: North America's One Hundred Greatest*, Krause Publications, 2000; Donald J. Petersen, *Folk Art Fish Decoys*, Schiffer Publishing, 1996.

Collectors' Clubs: Midwest Decoy Collectors Association, PO Box 4110, St. Charles, IL 60174; Minnesota Decoy Collectors Association, PO Box 130084, St. Paul, MN 55113; Ohio Decoy Collectors and Carvers Association, PO Box 499, Richfield, OH 44286.

Museums: Havre de Grace Decoy Museum, Havre de Grace, Md.; Ward Museum of Wildfowl Art, Salisbury, Md.

Specialty Auctions: Decoys Unlimited, 2320 Main St., West Barnstable, MA 02668; Gary Guyette & Frank Schmidt, Inc., PO Box 522, West Farmington, ME 04992, (207) 778-6256.

The record price for a decoy sold at auction is $801,500 for a preening pintail, circa 1915, made by A. Elmer Crowell. It sold in January 2003 by Christie's New York and Guyette and Schmidt Inc., West Farmington, Maine.

Blue jay, original paint, carved wood, mounted on carved maple leaves, handwritten signature "A.E. Crowell Cape Cod," A. Elmer Crowell (1862-1952), East Harwich, Massachusetts, 5 1/2 in. tall by 7 1/2 in. long. **$2,800**

Brandt goose, wooden, old paint, glass eyes, wear, age crack in block, damage to bill, 17 1/2 in. long. **$275**

Canada goose, tin, painted, silhouette-type, 8 in. tall by 30 in. long. **$325**

Canada goose, waxed canvas-covered hollow body, carved neck and head, old paint, glass eyes, 15 1/2 in. tall................................ **$250**

Canada goose, wooden, preening, old gray, black and white paint, 8 in. tall by 20 1/2 in. wide.......... **$275**

Primitive coot (?) decoys, pine, circa 1900, painted black and white with tack eyes, minor handling wear, 10 in. by 5 in. by 4 in. **$700/pair**

Scaup or bluebill duck decoy, carved by R. Madison Mitchell, never used, 13 1/2 in. by 7 in. by 6 1/2 in. **$500**

Redhead duck decoy, carved by R. Madison Mitchell, never used, 13 1/2 in. by 7 in. by 6 1/2 in. **$500**

Bluebill decoy by Bill Cleveland, circa 1917-1920, Rhinelander, Wis., well worn paint, 12 in. by 6 in. by 5 1/2 in. **$225**

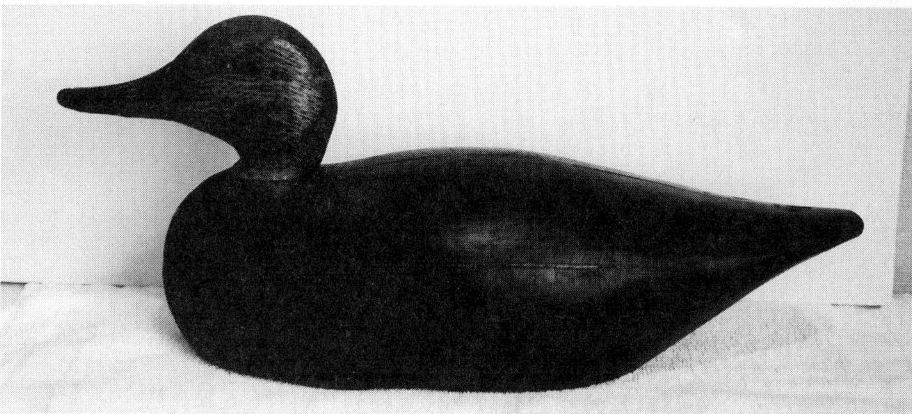

Oversize black duck decoy, circa 1915-1920, by A.E. "Elmer" Crowell (1862-1952), East Harwich, Massachusetts, oval brand, approximately 22 in. long. **$6,000-$8,000**

Pair of Percy Bicknell hollow mallard duck decoys, circa 1940, Vancouver, British Columbia, approximately 18 in. long. **$2,500-$3,500/pair**

Canada goose, wooden, preening, on large iron nail legs, painted with feather outlines, tack eyes, age cracks, 15 3/4 in. tall by 24 in. long. **$625**

Canada goose, wooden, preening, contemporary, original distressed finish, attributed to Walker family of Salisbury, 21 in. long..............**$950**

Canada goose, wooden, swimmer, dark brown and white paint, black head, unsigned, 11 1/2 in. tall by 31 in. wide.............................**$175**

Canada goose, wooden, swimmer, old brown, white and black paint, 26 1/2 in. long. **$150**

Canada goose, wooden, swimmer, original paint, oval Crowell brand, A. Elmer Crowell (1862-1952), East Harwich, Mass., repairs, age split, 11 in. tall by 23 1/2 in. long **$3,750**

Canada goose, wooden, extended neck, large iron nail legs, painted with feather outlines, tack eyes, hole drilled in base for stand, 25 1/2 in. tall by 24 in. long. **$700**

Canada goose, wooden, extended neck, old worn repaint, age cracks, square-nail repair, 21 1/2 in. tall by 29 in. wide.............................**$650**

Canada goose, wooden, unsigned, glass eyes, old worn and weathered black and white paint, 14 1/2 in. tall by 22 1/2 in. long. **$250**

Coot, Gus Wilson, carved wood, black, 17 in. long...................**$925**

Crow, balsa wood, worn black paint, wear, damage, 16 in. tall........**$225**

Duck, black duck, carved wood, original paint, oval Crowell brand, A. Elmer Crowell (1862-1952), East Harwich, Mass., minor paint loss, repairs, 6 1/2 in. tall by 17 1/2 in. long. **$1,500**

Duck, bluebill, wood/cork, worn repaint, glass eyes, old label attributes to Jim Foote, Pte Mouille, Mich., 14 in. long....................**$175**

Dodge County (Detroit) black duck decoy, circa 1885, approximately 18 in. long. **$1,200-$1,600**

Tuveson flying black duck decoy, made in Minnesota, circa 1920s, with applied canvas wings on wire frame, approximately 26 in. long, rare. **$1,000-$1,500**

Brant decoy by Percy Gant, Brickton, New Jersey, circa 1938, approximately 18 in. long. (A Gant decoy in the Shelburne (Vermont) Museum was used on a U.S. postage stamp.) **$1,500-$2,000**

Mason County (Detroit) blue wing teal drake decoy, circa 1910, approximately 12 in. long. **$2,000-$3,000**

Duck, Brandt, wooden, swimming position, hollow body, old repaint, 19 in. long. **$425**

Duck, canvasback, wooden, signed "R. Madison Mitchell, 1945," female with cracked neck, well done repaint, 16 in. and 16 1/2 in. long. **$900/pair**

Duck, canvasback, wooden, unsigned, original paint, replaced glass eyes, minor age cracks, 17 1/4 in. long. **$150**

Duck, canvasback drake, hollow body, old black, red and white paint, attributed to Clifford Moody Lind, Fremont, Wis., cracks in head, minor edge wear, 18 1/2 in. long. **$250**

Duck, mallard, wooden, painted feather details, glass eyes, two-part, early 20th century, 17 1/2 in. long. **$650**

Duck, mallard drake, wooden, old factory decoy, glass eyes, old repaint, edge damage, age cracks, 16 in. long. **$125**

Duck, mallard hen, wooden, sleeper, original paint, possibly a Maryland marker, chip on tail, 14 1/2 in. long. **$400**

Duck, Mason, black duck, glass eyes, 17 in. long. **$2,400/pair**

Duck, Mason, bluebill, original black, white, and gray paint, glass eyes, minor wear, professional repair to tip of tail, neck puttied, 13 3/4 in. long. **$275**

Duck, Mason, golden eye, 13 in. long. **$250**

Duck, Mason, mallard drake, early repainted finish, light and dark gray body with brown, green, black, and white, dark green head, glass eyes, orange bill, small chip on bill, thin piece of neck missing, 15 1/2 in. long. **$240**

Duck, Mason, mallard drake, wooden, worn repaint, tack eyes, some damage, 15 1/2 in. long.**$275**

Duck, Mason, teal, glass eyes. ..**$725**

Duck, merganser, painted, original plumes, wear, 17 in. long.**$950/pair**

Duck, merganser, worn old working repaint, glass eyes, age cracks, old puttied repair, 14 3/4 in. long. .**$250**

Duck, merganser drake, red-breasted, original paint, oval Crowell brand, A. Elmer Crowell (1862-1952), East Harwich, Mass., age split, minor paint loss, 5 1/2 in. tall by 19 1/2 in. long...........**$8,750**

Duck, pintail, wooden, painted, early 20th century, 20 1/2 in. long....**$250**

Duck, red head drake, wooden, old repaint, glass eyes, loose head, 14 1/2 in. long. **$325**

Goose decoy, Johnson's Folding Stake-out Decoy, a photographic replica of a goose printed on waxed cardboard, the head and neck fold down, the bottom of the decoy spreads open so that a triangular metal section with a metal rod can be inserted; this is then stuck into the ground, designed for use when shooting over shallow water and fields, 20 in. by 15 in., paper label inside from Wm. R. Johnson Co. Inc., Seattle, Wash., which includes instructions, very good condition. **$35**

Goldeneye drake decoy by Archie Bodette, Lake Champlain, Vt., circa 1940, approximately 11 in. long. (See "Decoys of Lake Champlain" by Loy Harrell Jr.) **$800-$1,200**

Wood duck drake decoy by Herter Decoy Co., Waseca, Minn., circa 1960s, approximately 15 in. long. **$400-$600**

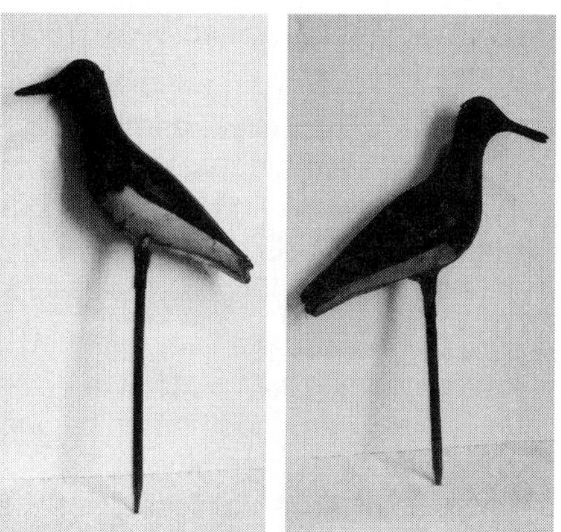

Yellowlegs, shorebird decoys, stamped metal, called "tinnies," made in 1874 in Boston, Mass., by Strater and Soher Co. **$275/pair**

Pair of "beetle head" golden plover shorebird decoys, circa 1900, Nantucket, Mass., each about 8 in. long. **$1,400-$1,600/pair**

Mallard drake decoy by John McLoughlin of Bordentown, N.J., Delaware River, circa 1936-1942, approximately 18 in. long. **$2,000-$3,000**

Black duck decoy by Charles Allen, Bordentown, N.J., Delaware River, circa 1930s, approximately 16 in. long. **$2,000-$3,000**

Mallard decoy, Minnesota, well worn paint, 15 in. by 7 1/2 in. by 6 in. **$250**

Mason Premier mallard drake decoy, 16 in. by 7 in. by 5 3/4 in. **$350**

Goose, wooden, old blue-green paint, black sponging, white head and tail, tack eyes, age cracks, chip on bill, 18 in. long. **$350**

Little blue heron, miniature, carved wood, original paint, mounted on carved wooden "rock," rectangular Crowell stamp, A. Elmer Crowell (1862-1952), East Harwich, Massachusetts, 7 in. tall by 6 1/2 in. long................................. **$4,250**

Pheasant, carved wood, painted, early 20th century, minor paint loss, 4 1/2 in. tall by 13 1/2 in. long. **$200**

Sandpiper, miniature, carved wood, original paint, mounted on carved clam shell, oval Crowell stamp, A. Elmer Crowell (1862-1952), East Harwich, Mass., 5 1/2 in. tall by 6 in. long................................. **$4,800**

Pair of spoonbill duck decoys by Bob White, Tullytown, Pa., Delaware River, 1984, approximately 12 in. long. **$2,000-$3,000/pair**

Pair of miniature mallard decoys, carved and painted by Joe Gigl, Fremont, Wis., circa 1930s, mint condition, each 5 1/4 in. by 2 1/2 in. by 2 1/2 in. **$1,000/pair**

Shore bird, curlew, old paint, bead eyes, on base, tip of beak damaged, 15 in. tall by 14 in. long. **$500**

Shore bird, plover, good age, old paint, wooden button eyes, inserted beak, some damage, beak split, 9 in. long. **$225**

Canvasback drake duck decoy, dated 1926, carved and painted by Joe Gigl, Fremont, Wis., cork body, board bottom, wood head with glass eyes, near mint, 16 1/2 in. by 9 in. by 7 1/2 in. **$500-$600**

Shore bird, yellow leg, old paint, tack eyes, on base, 11 3/4 in. tall by 15 1/4 in. long. **$175**

Shore bird, yellow leg, wooden, old paint, tack eyes, on base, 13 3/4 in. tall by 15 in. long. **$220**

Shore bird, unidentified, flying, some age with old paint, copper tack eyes, 15 1/4 in. tall, 15 in. wingspan. **$425**

Shore bird, unidentified, primitive, good age, old crusty paint, bead eyes, hole in tail, modern replacement for broken beak, 16 in. tall by 11 in. long. **$175**

Shore bird, unidentified, primitive, good age, old paint, tack eyes, shot scars, square-nail beak an old replacement, hole in tail, 10 3/4 in. tall by 10 3/4 in. long. **$175**

Swan, carved and painted, flattened full body, white with black and yellow features, mounted on carved oblong base painted blue and white, crackles, small losses on wings, American, 19th century, 13 in. tall by 16 3/4 in. wide. **$15,500**

Swan, carved and painted, two-piece hollow body, solid neck and head, late 19th century, wood loss, early repair, paint loss. **$5,250**

Wilson's snipe, carved wood, original paint, mounted on carved clam shell, rectangular Crowell stamp and paper label, A. Elmer Crowell (1862-1952), East Harwich, Massachusetts, 6 1/2 in. tall by 9 in. long.................................**$7,000**

Fishing

Collecting Fishing Items

By Jeff Savage
www.drexelantiques.com

Lures

Wooden lures, sometimes called plugs, are the mainstay of this category. The first wooden lures in general use were made in the late 1800s, but the golden age of wooden lures was from about 1915 to the 1950s.

For lure collectors, condition is very important. A "mint" lure with no damage will bring far more than the same plug in average or less condition. For some lures, certain colors of paint or paint designs are considered rarer than others and will bring a premium price. Lures that have been repainted or have lost most of their paint have little or no value unless they happen to be very rare. Many people collect lures made by particular companies such as Heddon, Creek Chub, Pflueger, South Bend, and Paw Paw, which were all major lure manufacturers.

The box in which a lure was packaged may be worth as much as the lure itself, and in some cases more. Some early boxes had sliding tops, boxed joints, and were made of wood. These boxes are rare and bring a premium price. Most boxes were made of cardboard, and many had beautiful graphics.

Some early metal spoons and spinners can be very expensive, but so far they have taken a backseat to the wooden plugs.

Reels

Reels are an area of collectible fishing tackle that has received less attention than lures. Reels by the better makers have been collectible for years, and most tackle collectors have acquired a few reels to add color to their lure collection.

Though the most collectible reels are expensive and hard to find, many of the more common reels are still inexpensive and relatively easy to find. Early fly and casting reels with names like Hardy, Vom Hofe, Conroy, Meek, and Milam are very collectible and can be expensive. Reels by Pflueger, Shakespeare, South Bend, Bronson, and others are much less expensive and are a welcome addition to many collections.

Single-action fly reels and multiplying fly reels are both eagerly sought; automatic fly reels are less so. Casting reels, both level wind and non-level wind, are collected. Spinning reels have received some attention, while spin-casting reels have received little notice. Ambassador casting reels made by ABU in Sweden have gained a loyal following from bass anglers and collectors. Early reels from England and Europe have sparked some interest, but with the majority being unmarked or in less-than-perfect condition, the top-of-the-line reels have received the lion's share of collector attention. Top-of-the-line American reels—the "Kentucky" reels, Vom Hofes, and the like—are quickly disappearing and escalating in price.

Rods

Collectible rods are dominated by split bamboo fly rods. Lately enthusiasts have also begun collecting some of the earlier fiberglass rods, split bamboo casting and spinning rods, and steel casting rods.

The earliest European fishing rods were made of different types of wood spliced together and were often very long, 18 feet being common. Tips were often made of greenheart (a tropical South American evergreen tree from the laurel family with a hard greenish wood), whale baleen, or bamboo cane on the later rods. These early rods are hard to find but aren't eagerly sought. It was only during the late 1800s that split bamboo was being used to make the entire rod.

Some of the names of bamboo rod makers to look for are Granger, Young, Dickerson, Phillipson, Devine, Edwards, Thomas, Payne, Leonard, and Hardy. Rods made for trademarks include Abercrombie and Fitch, Heddon, South Bend, and Abbey and Imbrie.

In split bamboo rods, shorter is better, and condition is everything. The shorter a bamboo rod, the more collectible it seems to be: 6-foot to 8 1/2-foot rods seem to be the most collectible. A 7-foot rod by a famous maker will usually be worth four to five times what a 12-foot salmon rod by the same maker will bring, despite the fact that the salmon rod is harder to find.

Condition is a tougher subject. A split bamboo rod, restored to near original condition by a professional restorer, seems to retain much of its value. The same rod poorly restored or used long and hard has little value. Beware of made-up rods, that is, poor quality cane rods to which an unscrupulous restorer has attached a handle from an expensive rod, and then will try to pass the whole conglomeration off as an expensive rod.

Of course, having a rod's original cloth bag and rod tube will add to its

value. Make sure any split bamboo rod is original length. Many tips will be short where they have been broken (many rods came with more than one tip). A good rule of thumb is to lay the rod on a table; each section should be approximately the same length. Not all rods were built this way but most were. Also, any split bamboo rod should be checked for a curve or a set. Again, a good way to check it is to lay the rod sections on a flat surface, roll them around, and watch for gaps formed by a bow in the rod.

Fly Fishing Tackle

There is an attraction to fishing with older fly tackle that isn't present with other types of fishing. Many old split bamboo fly rods, old fly reels, and old fly fishing accessories are purchased for fishing, even with a high price attached to them. It gives anglers a feeling of class, history, and being part of an earlier age to fool the wary trout with tackle from your grandfather's era.
Split bamboo rods are still being made to feed these urges, as well as handmade reels. A great deal of old fly tackle is purchased for decorative use: Creels, old landing nets, old bamboo rods, etc., look great hanging over the mantle.

There has always been a cachet of class and gentility associated with fly fishing. **Flies** are eagerly sought and are often beautifully framed as works of art. Fly rods, reels, creels, and the like are eagerly sought. Being part of the heritage of gentility, fly tackle leads the collectibles market in prices, and there seems no end in sight. Other more recent tackle that has received collector attention includes reels by Bogdan, Abel, Marryat, Walker, and other custom/hand-built modern makers.

Saltwater/Big Game Tackle

In many ways this area of the hobby is in its infancy, but there is just not that much big game tackle out there to feed growth.

In its early days, big game fishing was a hobby for the rich. Ernest Hemingway, Zane Grey, and other wealthy notables were big game fisherman. Early big game reels by Hardy, Vom Hofe, Kovalovsky, Coxe, and Zwarg are eagerly sought, as are rods by Tycoon, Edward Vom Hofe, and Hardy. Photographs, books, trophies, and medals are also collected. Recently a trend has begun in the collection of early saltwater fly tackle. Saltwater fly reels by Pate, Fin-nor, and others are being purchased and are expensive.

Accessories

Fishing accessories being sought include creels, fly vices, unusual tools and gadgets, split shot tins, hook containers, and fishing knives. There are collectors of just about anything to do with fishing—from photographs, postcards, sporting goods letterhead, and paper memorabilia to taxidermy fish, liquor bottles shaped like fish, and even fish plates from Europe. Some of the items that fit this category are still inexpensive and readily found, while others are expensive and quickly disappearing.

Books

Books dealing with fishing are very collectible. Popular trends tend toward fishing story books, rather than books on methods of fishing, unless they are very early. They range from extremely expensive books, such as early copies of Izaak Walton's *The Compleat Angler*, to more modern and inexpensive, like Ed Zern's *A Fine Kettle of Fish* stories. Book collectors, and we have to group angling book collectors here, are among the most sensitive to the condition of their collectibles. Any damage will significantly reduce the value of a book.

Hunting and Fishing Licenses

Many fishing collectors have a few hunting or fishing license badges to add variety to their collections. Dedicated license badge collectors are a small but growing group. Many states used small badges (typically under two inches) for anglers and hunters. Some used them as early as the teens, many in the 1920s and 1930s. With the exception of Pennsylvania, most states stopped using them in the 1940s. Some states issued license holders after the 1940s, into which paper licenses could be inserted.

The most eagerly sought badges are from the southern states: North Carolina, South Carolina, Georgia, Florida, and Mississippi. Badges are also sought from Hawaii, Michigan, and Connecticut. New York and Pennsylvania badges are collected, but are relatively common and inexpensive.

Canadian hunting and fishing license badges have started an upward trend. Demand for other foreign licenses may soon start growing. Non-resident (out of state) badges are typically harder to find, as are trapping and other specialty badges. Paper fishing and hunting licenses are also collected, particularly the very early ones from the turn of the century into the 1920s.

Trends in Tackle Collecting

A growing trend is the collecting of late 1950s, 1960s, and early 1970s bass fishing tackle, fed by the popularity of bass tournaments, interest in the early history of the tournaments, and enthusiasm from Japan. Categories include early fiberglass rods, early crank baits, UMCO tackle boxes, and Ambassador reels. There are many Japanese and American collectors who eagerly seek tackle from this era. So far prices have remained reasonable, especially

when compared to the prices of modern-day tackle. There are even tournaments that have been organized using fishing tackle from this era. Information, photographs, early tournament patches, and trophies are popular.

Collectors are narrowing their collecting field, buying top-of-the-line tackle in excellent condition. This happens as collecting fields mature. However, as these maturing collectors narrow their collecting interests, there are still scads of beginning collectors and dealers, buying just about anything to do with fishing.

Values

Values are a touchy subject. Fishing tackle prices seem to be continuing an upward trend. Some lure categories have made astounding leaps, while other areas seem to have stabilized. Pressure from the Internet selling/buying community seems to be bumping prices up slightly. Top-of-the-line tackle is still setting new records.

Value is sometimes driven by need as more and more collectors are paying just a slight bit more than they think something is worth just to fill holes in their collections. What once was a hobby for everyone is pricing itself beyond some folks' reach. Some of the more expensive tackle (that once was inexpensive) now takes consideration, commitment, and a little agonizing to purchase. As tackle gets harder to find, prices should continue to climb. Top-notch tackle should retain its value. Antiques dealers aren't always familiar with antique tackle and its prices. The best way to become more familiar with tackle is to find a helpful collector.

Fakes and Restoration

As with any antiques/collectibles area, as prices climb, unscrupulous individuals start seeing a profit to be made. So far this hasn't been a big problem with antique fishing tackle, but there are fakes out there.

First came the repainted lures. Wooden lures, with their enamel paint, are prone to flaking because of the environment in which they were used. Wood swells with moisture and shrinks as it dries. Bad paint can kill the value of a very good lure.

In recent years, some people have started buying these lures (called "beaters" in the hobby) and reproducing the factory paint job. Some are honest and tell their customers the lure has been repainted, but some are not. Even some very advanced collectors have been fooled. All repaints should be plainly and indelibly marked. A few outright fake lures have been found. Usually these are reproductions of very early lures that, because of their simplicity, are easy to fake. The Moonlight Dreadnaught is a good example, and I have seen several fakes. Once again, these reproduction lures should be permanently marked.

Reels haven't been a problem because the equipment needed to reproduce them has been just too expensive. The major problems that have arisen are fake markings stamped on unmarked reels with steel stamps. There has been some word of fake British brass reels, crudely made in India or Asia, but so far not many of these have surfaced.

Fake creels have shown up, typically hand-woven copies of what are called turtle creels.

Some bamboo rod restorers do such good work that their finished product rivals factory-new finishes, but again, rod restorations should be permanently marked. Some people find early rods by famous makers that are in poor condition, take the handles (where they are typically marked), and fit cheaper bamboo blanks to them with the intent to deceive novice buyers.

Finding Old Fishing Tackle

You can find old fishing tackle through conventional means such as flea markets, yard sales, antiques shops, fishing tackle shows, word of mouth, handing out business/collector cards, the Internet, and auctions, or you can go the extra mile. Advertise in papers, leave word with tackle shops, tell everyone about your hobby, create a Web site, get your friends who collect other things to watch for you, or take a nice display of old tackle to sports shows, county fairs, etc. Always follow up leads—nine out of ten times they won't be worth the trip, but that one-out-of-ten find makes it all worthwhile, and at the very least you will meet some interesting people. Also, what they don't have today, they may find in the future. Take along some books, pictures, or even actual lures, reels, etc., to show them what you are looking to acquire.

Finding Information on Antique Fishing Tackle

Information resources about antique fishing tackle are readily available on the Internet. There are also many excellent books available on antique tackle. I particularly recommend Karl White's *Fishing Tackle Antiques and Collectibles*, Dudley Murphy and Rick Edmisten's *Fishing Lure Collectibles*, and Carl F. Luckey's *Old Fishing Lures & Tackle*, all three of which are good general guides. There are also many books on specific companies or types of tackle.

Antique tackle clubs are good sources for information. Most publish either magazines or newsletters, including National Fishing Lure Collectors Club, Florida Antique Tackle Club, Carolina Antique Tackle Club, Old Reel Collectors Association, and the Michigan Lure Collectors Club.

❖ Creels, Spears, Etc.

Creel, center hole, made by the Micmac Indians, Adirondacks, with original leather and canvas shoulder strap, 9 in. by 8 in. by 10 in. **$225**

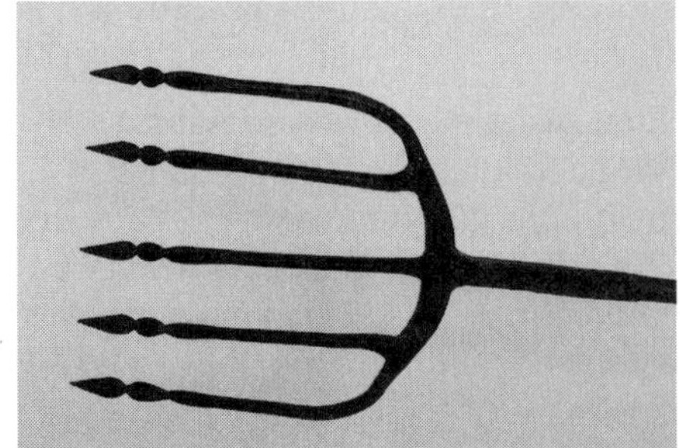

Fishing spear, circa 1920s, wrought iron, oak handle, overall length 47 1/1 in., tines are 7 1/2 in. by 4 in. **$75-$100**

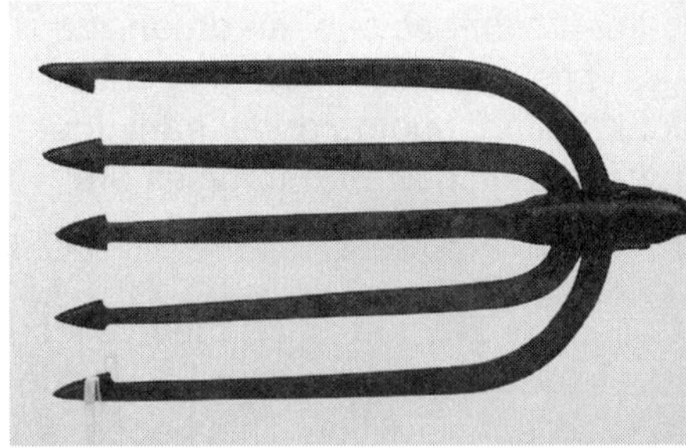

Fishing spear, early 20th century, wrought iron, tines with "pigtail" points, pine handle, overall length 70 in., tines are 6 3/4 in. by 6 in. **$200-$300**

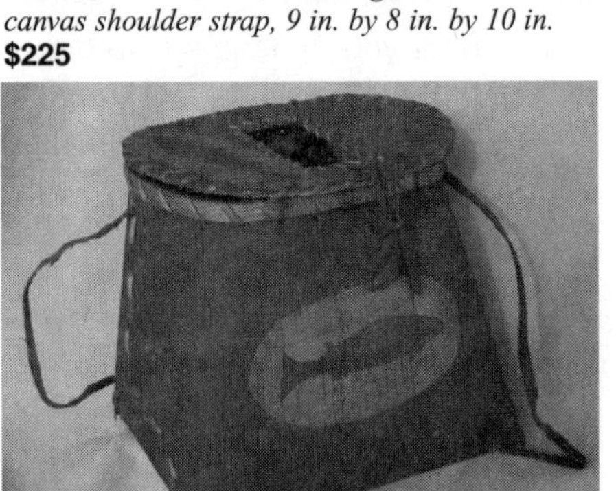

Fishing creel, Northeast Coast American Indian-made, center-hole, birch bark, mint condition. **$130**

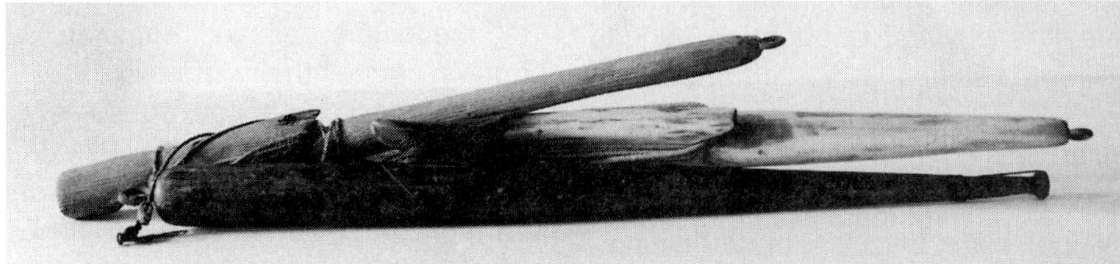

Ice fishing jigging sticks, circa 1920s, carved wood with eye screws and fishing line, moderate wear, from 9 in. to 12 in. long. **$40-$50**

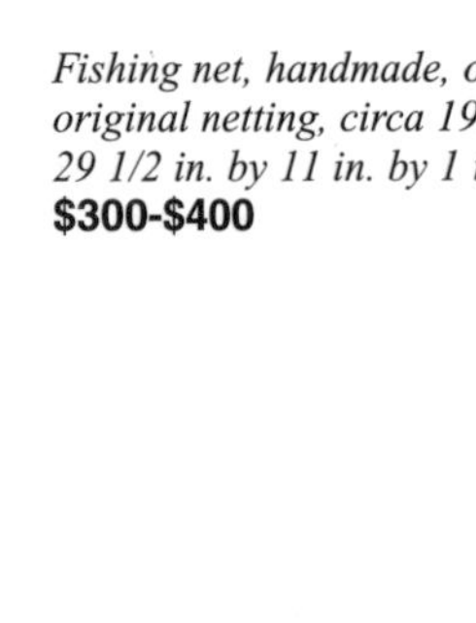

Fishing net, handmade, oak, original netting, circa 1930s, 29 1/2 in. by 11 in. by 1 in. **$300-$400**

Hall Fishing Line display, originally from the factory in Highland Mills, N.Y., made in 1939 with original cardboard mailing sleeve, more than 20 different spools, five cards of line, including the Hiawatha Indian brand, in detail two winders full of line, excellent condition. **$500-$600**

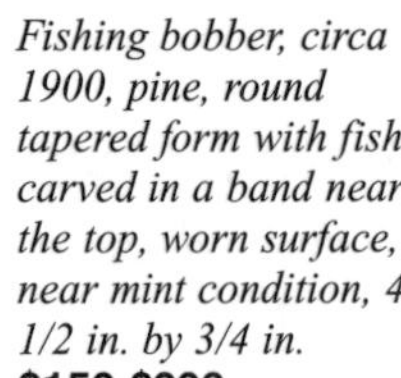

Fishing bobber, circa 1900, pine, round tapered form with fish carved in a band near the top, worn surface, near mint condition, 4 1/2 in. by 3/4 in. **$150-$200**

The Fish Decoy

By Tom Bachler
www.oldfishdecoys.com

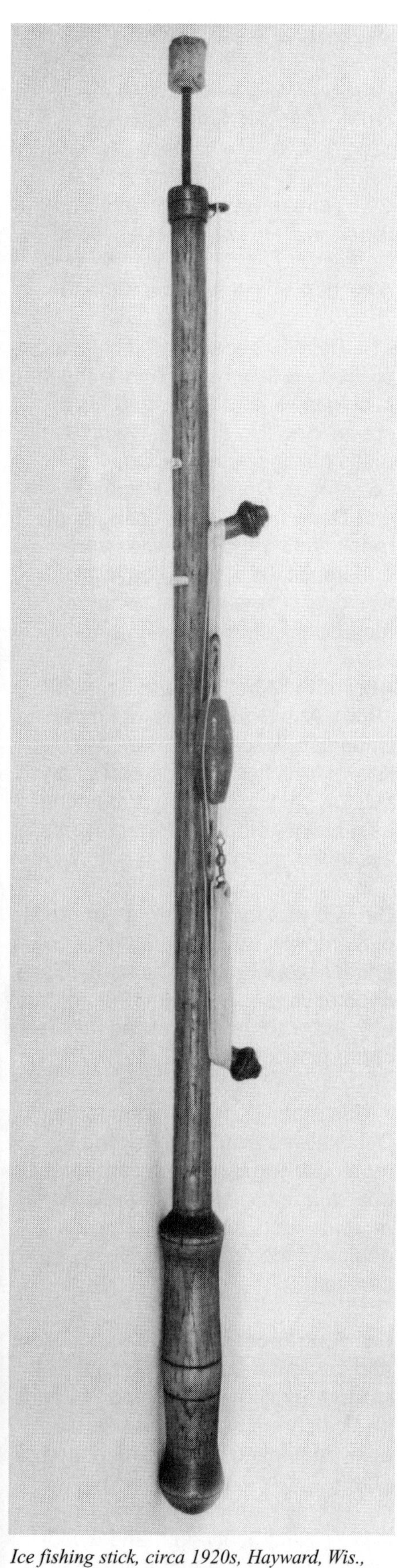

Ice fishing stick, circa 1920s, Hayward, Wis., turned oak with acorn knobs holding line and bobber, brass ferrule, 29 in. long. **$75-$100**

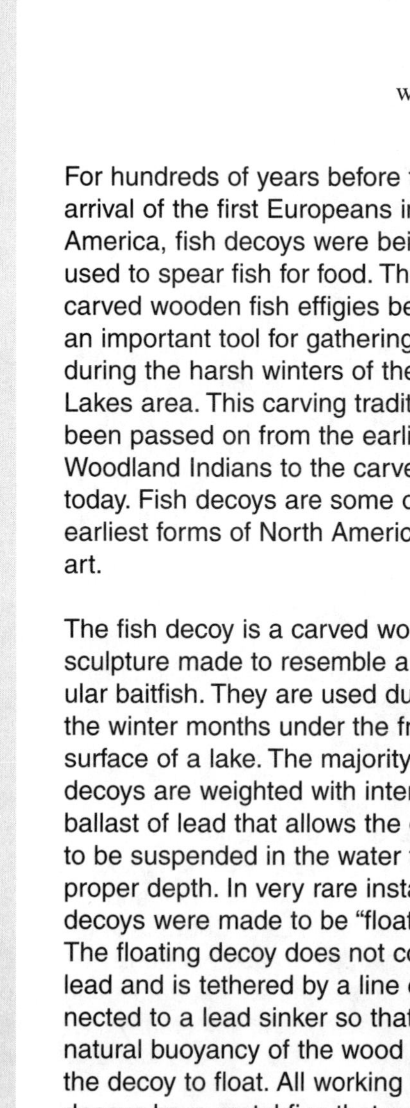

For hundreds of years before the arrival of the first Europeans in North America, fish decoys were being used to spear fish for food. These carved wooden fish effigies became an important tool for gathering food during the harsh winters of the Great Lakes area. This carving tradition has been passed on from the earliest Woodland Indians to the carvers of today. Fish decoys are some of the earliest forms of North American folk art.

The fish decoy is a carved wooden sculpture made to resemble a particular baitfish. They are used during the winter months under the frozen surface of a lake. The majority of fish decoys are weighted with internal ballast of lead that allows the decoy to be suspended in the water to the proper depth. In very rare instances, decoys were made to be "floaters." The floating decoy does not contain lead and is tethered by a line connected to a lead sinker so that the natural buoyancy of the wood allows the decoy to float. All working fish decoys have metal fins that protrude from the sides of the fish. Their purpose is to allow the decoy to glide through the water when jigged from a jigging stick. This is the same principal used by a glider when it flies through the air. Sinking decoys incorporate a style of line tie that is located on the top of the fish. Floating decoys have a tie located on the bottom of the decoy.

To swim a fish decoy properly, you need a jigging stick. The jigging stick allows the spear fisherman to present the fake fish to other larger game fish by means of a connected fishing line. When the tethered decoy is jigged properly, the decoy will dart and glide in the water as if it were a real fish. Larger game fish such as the northern pike and muskellunge can be fooled into thinking the decoy is a real fish. Typically, these larger fish will swim up to the decoy very slowly, which then affords the spear fisherman a chance to drop the weighted spear onto his quarry.

It is generally thought that the fish decoy originated in the Great Lakes area of Michigan. Woodland Indians inhabiting the Great Lakes area used decoys long before the arrival of the first European explorers in North America around the 16th century. The early French families around lakes St. Clair, Huron, and Superior were the first to use decoys as a necessary means for obtaining food during winter. These early settlers undoubtedly learned the art of decoy making from the Indians. Very few examples of the decoys made during this period survive today. Fish decoys documented as being made during the last half of the 19th century are also very few and should be studied closely. These decoys represent the keys to the regional carving patterns. Very few historical references, as far as documentation, survived on their uses.

• • •

An excerpt from the journal of fur trader Alexander Henry at Sault Ste. Marie, Ontario, in 1762:

"The Commandant and all the rest lived in one small house subsisting only by hunting and fishing. The woods afforded us some hares and partridges and we took large trout with the spear. In order to spear the trout under the ice, holes being first cut of two yards in circumference, cabins of about two feet in height built over them of small branches of trees and these further covered with skins so as to wholly exclude the light. The design and result of this contrivance is to render it practicable to discern objects in the water at a very considerable depth, for the reflection of the light from the water gives...(the ice) an opaque appearance and hides all objects from the eye at a small distance beneath its surface.

"A spearhead of iron is fastened on a pole of about ten feet in length. This instrument is lowered into the water and the fisherman, lying upon his belly with his head under the cabin. He then lets down a figure of a fish carved in wood and filled with lead. Round the middle of the fish-effigy is tied a small packthread; when at the depth of ten fathoms, where it is intended to be employed, it is made, by drawing the string and by the simultaneous pressure of the water, to move forward after the manner of a real fish.

"Trout and other large fish, deceived by its resemblance, spring forward to seize it: but by a dexterous jerking of the string, it is instantly taken from their reach. The decoy is now drawn near to the surface and the fish takes some time to renew the attack, during which time, the spear is raised and held conveniently for striking. On the return of the fish, the spear is plunged into its back and, the spear being barbed, is drawn out of the water."

• • •

Regional patterns vary widely. For example, fish from Minnesota typically have metal tails and are painted in bright colors. They are known to be great pike attractors. Vintage Minnesota fish decoys lack the realism of form and paint usually associated with vintage decoys found in Michigan. By contrast, Michigan fish decoys found around the Lake St. Clair area generally have wood tails. The decoys in this area range from 6 inches to 12 inches in length. They have a closer resemblance to the fish species than the decoys found in other regions.

In the Mt. Clemens and New Baltimore areas of Michigan, many decoys are found over 12 inches in length. These larger sculptures were used exclusively for spearing the muskellunge.

In contrast, fish found in the Saginaw Bay area of Michigan are usually small (4 inches to 6 inches in length). These decoys are painted in simpler colors such as silver and red/white. The Saginaw Bay had a very early spear-fishing culture centered around the town of Linwood, Michigan. From the 1870s to the early part of the 20th century, commercial spear fisherman would spend months out on the ice to spear walleyes. The fish companies would come out to these ice villages and pay the spearers cash for the fish.

Fish decoys found in New York State centered around the Lake Chautauqua area. These fish decoys are very old and are mostly found with leather tails. Lake Chautauqua fish decoys date to 1905 or earlier because this is the year spear fishing was abolished on the lake. Many beautiful and old decoys are found in this area.

With the coming of the Great Depression, spear fishing by use of decoys experienced somewhat of a rebirth. Many carvers made decoys out of necessity to put food on the table during these tough times.

• • •

The following is courtesy of fishdecoy.com:

The Great Lakes carvers are considered by most experts and collectors to represent the most influential and productive of the hundreds of artists who worked in the United States from about 1900 to 1940.

The list below represents the most influential of these artists.

Gordon Frances Charbeneau (1905-1966): A Mount Clemens, Michigan, native who worked for his father in the family fish market, Charbeneau was a sportsman and a fisherman. He was a skilled woodworker who made his own decoys, duck boats, and duck boat tenders.

Charbeneau became a highly accomplished ice fisherman, and in the long Michigan winters fabricated his own spears and fish decoys. He did most of his hunting with Abe De Hate, Louis Jock, Don Riley, Pecore Fox, and Dave Dreschel, a local group renowned for their prowess and endurance, frequently hunting for weeks at a time in remote parts of the Lower Peninsula.

Abraham "Abe" DeHate Sr. (1890-1966): Abe DeHate was of French Canadian descent and was widely known as a fine boat carpenter and builder, gaining an early reputation as a builder of the best duck boats available.

DeHate was the creator of hundreds of extraordinary duck and fish decoys and his work bridged the earlier, less decorative pieces of the 19th century with the elaborately finished mid-20th century decoys.

As his many fine ice spears attest, DeHate was also highly skilled in metal working, and as a carpenter, boatwright, sculptor, and metalworker, represents the multi-discipline genius of the greatest master carvers.

Gordon (Pecore) Fox: A boat builder and carpenter by trade, Pecore Fox started hunting at the age of 14 and was celebrated as a man who enjoyed hunting and fishing above all else.

An excellent boatwright and woodworker, Fox worked for Chris Craft, Hacker, and many of the most prominent Michigan boat marinas. He was

reputed to have crafted more duck boats than any other carver, well over 500 by his own count, besides his personal boats. He made bird decoys into the thousands and was well known for his fine fish decoys.

Augie Janner was the son of one of the finest of the Great Lakes fish decoy carvers, Hans Janner Sr.

Growing up in a Mt. Clemens household filled with artists/sportsmen, Janner was considered the most talented of the group and knew all the techniques and secrets of the masters.

As an artist, he was gifted as both a woodcarver and metalworker who created spears, decoys, shanties, and boats, which are widely collected today.

Hans Janner was possibly the finest of the Great Lakes fish decoy carvers and spear makers. A lifelong resident of Mt. Clemens, Janner's fish and duck decoys date from the 1930s.

In addition to his skill as a woodworker, Hans Janner was also a superb metal worker and spear maker. His ice-fishing spears are widely collected and considered the very finest examples of the art form.

Janner was the father-in-law of Andy Trombley, another prominent carver from the Mt. Clemens area.

Yock Meldrum was a woodcarver and boatwright who resided in Mt. Clemens, and produced a large body of work during the 1930s. Meldrum's style was realistic but highly stylized in both form and painting technique.

Like Hans Janner's fish, Meldrum's fish were fancifully carved, but with more austerely shaped fins and more realistic bodylines.

During his lifetime, Meldrum's creations were prized for their originality of design but even more coveted for their efficacy. Unlike many of the other master carvers' work, Meldrum's carvings were truly legendary in their ability to attract game fish.

Larry Joseph Peltier (1885-1965): A retired Detroit fireman, Peltier was an avid carpenter and woodworker who spent his spare time building boats, carving decoys, hunting, fishing, and generally living the life of an outdoor sportsman.

He resided in Harrison Township outside Mount Clemens and carved many fine examples of duck and fish decoys, which are collectible for both their distinctive style and Peltier's keen observation of the natural world.

Oscar Peterson: Born in Cadillac, Michigan, of Swedish parents in 1894, he was an outdoorsman who spent his youth hunting and fishing in the Lower Michigan Peninsula. He settled in the area permanently and was active as a wilderness guide all his life.

Peterson's involvement with decoys likewise began as a child and continued his entire life. He spent nearly 50 years carving and painting with a fluency, industry, and imagination unique to the craft.

Peterson's distinctive paint style and wonderfully whimsical approach to decoy carving have distinguished him as the pre-eminent creator of American ice-fishing decoys. Widely copied and counterfeited, his works have been among the most valuable and highly sought after of all American folk art objects.

A man of powerful imagination and equally well-developed technical gifts, his output ranged beyond decoys to include decorative objects and free-standing sculptures striking for their mix of folkloric naiveté and artistic refinement.

Peterson's prominence derives not only from the quality of his work, but also from its quantity. Unlike most of the other carvers, who worked when the spirit moved them or necessity demanded, Peterson approached decoy making as a profession, selling to the tourist trade and using the money to supplement his earnings as a landscaper. His exact output is impossible to calculate, but most estimates put it at between 10,000 and 15,000 decoys, of which perhaps ten percent still exist.

Although Peterson's work was prodigious, what endures is his sensitivity and his unerring eye for the truth of the natural forms he represented.

By the time of his death in 1951, a lifetime of carving had allowed him to create vivid sculptural forms with a kinetic energy that still captivates the viewer today.

Tom Schroeder (1885-1976): Schroeder was born in East Detroit, Michigan, and was an accomplished hunter and fisherman versed in the skills of the outdoorsman by the time he was in his early teens.

Schroeder's primary claim to fame was as a carver of outstanding duck decoys, and he carved them throughout his long life until he was in his late eighties.

A professional artist and later an advertising executive, he was one of the first Midwestern carvers to gain recognition in a field long dominated by East Coast craftsmen, winning many first-place awards at the International Sportsman's Shows in New York between the years 1949 and 1956.

After his death, an estate sale revealed a small number of unused fish decoys, which brought the total of his known production to only 15.

In the opinion of many collectors of American folk art, his fish decoys displayed a lifelike realism and were far superior to his many excellent and avidly collected duck and goose decoys.

Harry Seymour was one of the first master carvers from New York State. Born and reared in Bemus Point on the shores of Lake Chautauqua in the mid-19th century, Seymour earned his living as a general handyman.

Descended from English and Dutch roots, Seymour's decoys defined the output of the New York school; solid, utilitarian, blocky in form, and somewhat dull in coloration. Nonetheless, Seymour's work is memorable for its instinctive handling of shapes and his keen eye for painted texture. A hallmark of Seymour's that has been widely copied is the bright red paint he frequently applied to the gill slits of his decoys.

While perhaps not the equal of the lyrical masterpieces of the Great Lakes carvers, Seymour's work is highly sought after for its naive charm. Seymour decoys are extremely valuable, and one example sold at auction topped $11,000.

Andy Trombley (1919- 1975): The son-in-law of Hans Janner Sr., Trombley was an extraordinary woodcarver and an even better painter, often using a mesh hairnet in painting his decoys, to give the appearance of scales. He collaborated with other master carvers, his father-in-law among them.

Raised in a large family that fished and hunted locally, Trombley resided in Harrison Township with his wife and daughter. At the time of his death, he was the last surviving member of the "master" fish decoy carvers.

Theodore "Ted" Vandenbossche (1887-1958): Vandenbossche is renowned as a maker of fine duck decoys and duck boats. He was also well known for his highly detailed, extremely naturalistic fish decoys. Attention to detail earned him a substantial following as a carver.

His work was eagerly sought after even by his peers because his pieces also had the reputation of working better than almost anyone else's.

Like most of Michigan's master carvers, Vandenbossche was something of a rustic Renaissance man—carpenter, tool-and-die maker, a builder of homes, and as an occupation, was the owner of a fleet of barges and tugboats engaged in the dredging business.

He was well known in the Lower Michigan area as a market hunter and sportsman with a keen eye for both fishing and carving.

Minnesota

While the output of Minnesota can be described as diverse, certain similarities seem to apply to the state as a whole. Minnesota fish tend to be in the 4 inch to 10 inch range and are generally painted in brighter, more contrasting colors than fish decoys from surrounding states.

This is explained by the fact that the water in Minnesota's lakes tends to be darker, with a higher concentration of dissolved solids, than in other areas of the upper Midwest. Subsequently the decoys needed brighter colors and stronger patterning to attract fish below the ice.

Minnesota fish decoys appear in great numbers of size and types, and more factories for mass-producing them were located in Minnesota than other states.

Minnesota is also noteworthy for producing more "critter" fish decoys than any other state. These are usually small decoys resembling frogs, mice, tadpoles, beaver, and the like, and are very popular with collectors of both decoys and American folk art.

While the best decoys of Minnesota may not compare with the great works of Michigan, they are, as a rule, very appealing and may provide a good entry point for the new collector. Auction prices for the best of the pieces are setting new records and advancing the market at each successive sale and auction.

Wisconsin

The La Crosse area was a particularly good area for the production of decoys. Fish decoys carved in the area in the early 1900s are unique and highly sought after. Most of the local carvers made only a few decoys for their own personal use, so they were not produced in large quantities.

This, along with the high quality of the carving, contribute to their scarceness and desirability to collectors. La Crosse fish decoys are usually small in size, from 2 inches to 8 inches long, with the average size of 5 inches.

The bodies were usually straight, but some carvers curved the tail to give them a more natural action when being jigged. Lead weight was added to the base of the decoy. Eyes made of old hatpins or beads were added. They were painted with whatever was available, and sometimes house paint was used. Some of the carvers added such details as carved gills, mouth, and scales. Good examples of this detail work can be seen in the decoys carved by Clarence Zielke, Otto Peterson, and Art Wajahn.

Jigging sticks were used with most of the La Crosse area decoys. The fish decoys were worked around in a circle to give them a swimming action.

Short-handled spears were used because the fishing shanties were usually small so they could be easily moved and heated. Spear fishing was outlawed by 1940 in the La Crosse area, bringing fish carving to an end. Very few old-timers are left to reminisce and tell their stories of fish spearing on the Mississippi River, but

the old days will live on by the fishing artifacts that have been left behind.

New York

New York State fish decoys are among the first examples of the art known to be produced by non-indigenous people and generally date from the end of the 19th century, when spear fishing was a highly popular sport in New York State.

The sport became so popular that few examples date later than 1905, when ice fishing was outlawed throughout New York because of concern over declining fish populations.

New York State fish decoys from this period are among the most prized of collectibles.

Stylistically, the New York decoys are instantly recognizable and seem significantly related to Native American designs.

By the end of the 19th century, styles had solidified. New York State decoys were almost always made of wood and tended to be somewhat somber in color and impressionistic in terms of both design and detail. Generally, they are characterized by leather tails slotted into the bodies and single piece fins that pass through the body and protrude on either side.

The great master of the New York decoys is Harry Seymour. Seymour's elegant and sinuous carvings typify the New York style and have consistently set auction records.

❖ Decoys

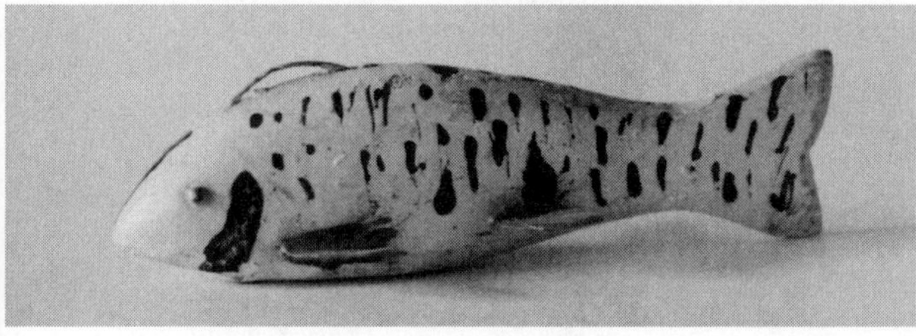

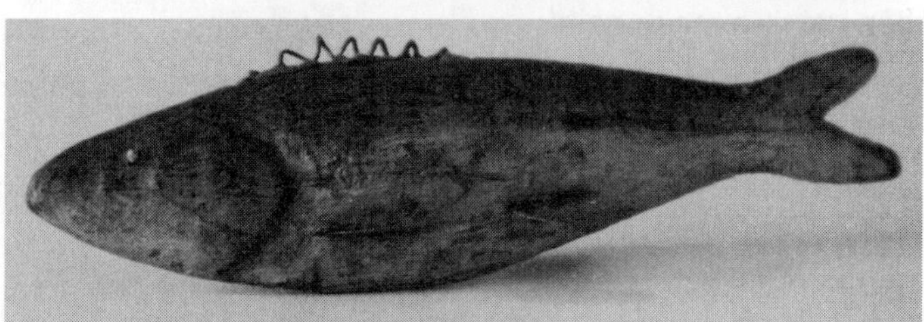

Five fish decoys, circa 1920s, from upper Mississippi River, Minnesota or Wisconsin, carved and painted wood with tin fins and tails, some with glass eyes, excellent condition with minor wear, measuring between 4 1/2 in and 6 in. **$300-$400 each**

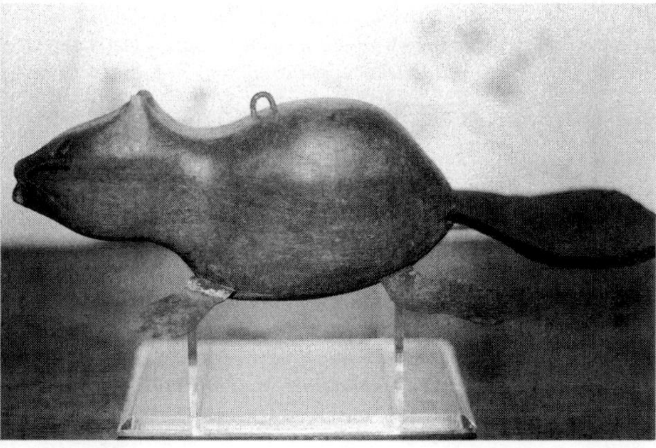

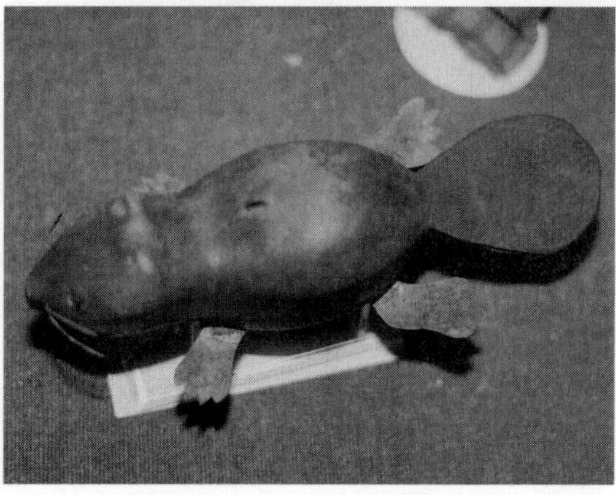

Two views of fish decoy, circa 1920s, carved wood in the form of a baby beaver, with leather tail, cutout tin legs, wire whiskers, and tack eyes, original painted surface in bluish/black, possibly of American Indian make, 8 in. by 4 in. by 3 1/2 in. **$1,000-$1,200**

Fish decoy, circa 1960s, carved wood with tin fins and five lead weights embedded in bottom, painted black with white spots, stripes and belly, eye screw in head, damage to tail, 17 in. by 4 in. by 1 1/2 in. **$200**

Fish decoy, circa 1980s, carved wood with metal fins and two weights embedded in bottom, dorsal fin drilled with four holes, tack eyes, painted green, white, black, and red, 9 in. by 4 7/8 in. by 1 1/2 in. **$200**

Fish decoy, circa 1930s, from Big Bay de Noc, Upper Peninsula, Michigan, painted orange with black spots, applied metal fins and tail, 7 in. long. **$1,200**

Fish decoy, sturgeon, circa 1930s, Lake Winnebago, Wisconsin, painted red and gold with yellow spots, applied fins, suspended on double eyehooks, excellent condition, 15 1/2 in. by 2 3/4 in., private collection.

Fish decoy, circa 1930s, carved by Otto or William Fau, Buffalo, Minnesota, with detailed painted surface in bass markings, applied metal fins and tail, excellent condition, 6 1/2 in. by 2 in. **$2,000**

Fish decoy, circa 1950s, carved wood with metal fins and one weight embedded in bottom, painted greenish-yellow and red with significant paint flaking, tack eyes, eye screw in head, 7 in. by 1 3/8 in. by 1 1/2 in. **$55**

Fish decoy, circa 1960s, carved wood with metal fins and two lead weights embedded in bottom, painted orange with black and white stripes, eye screw in head, 5 3/4 in. by 1 3/4 in. by 2 3/4 in. **$85**

Fish decoy, circa 1960s, carved wood with metal fins and four weights embedded in bottom, painted brown, white, and gold, eye screw in head, 7 1/4 in. by 2 1/4 in. by 2 in. **$125**

Fish decoy, circa 1960s, carved wood with metal fins and two weights embedded in bottom, painted green, white, red, and black, tack eyes, eye screw in head, 7 1/4 in. by 2 1/2 in. by 2 1/2 in. **$150**

Fish decoy, circa 1930s, carved by William "Slow" Batters, St. Cloud, Minnesota, painted green, red, and yellow with black spots, applied metal fins and tail, 5 3/4 in. by 1 1/2 in. **$500**

Fish decoy, circa 1920s, New York State, painted brown and orange with black and yellow spots, applied metal fins and tail, excellent condition, 7 in. by 2 in. **$350-$400**

Fish decoy, circa 1920s, New York State, painted orange with black stripes, applied metal fins and tail, excellent condition, 7 in. by 2 in. **$350-$400**

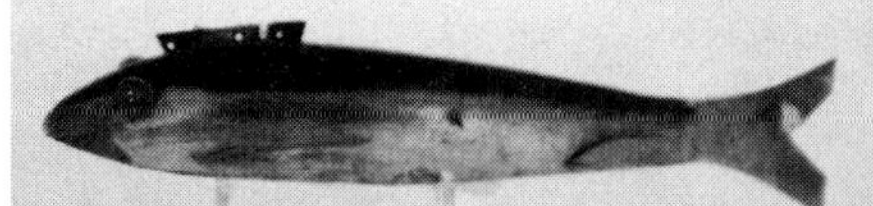

Fish decoy, circa 1920, carved by John Abraham Gottlieb (1892-1966), Le Sueur County, Minnesota, painted red, green, and yellow with large red glass bead eyes, applied metal fins and tail, excellent condition, 8 in. by 1 1/2 in. **$350-$400**

❖ Lures

Bleeder Bait fishing lure, very good condition. **$100**

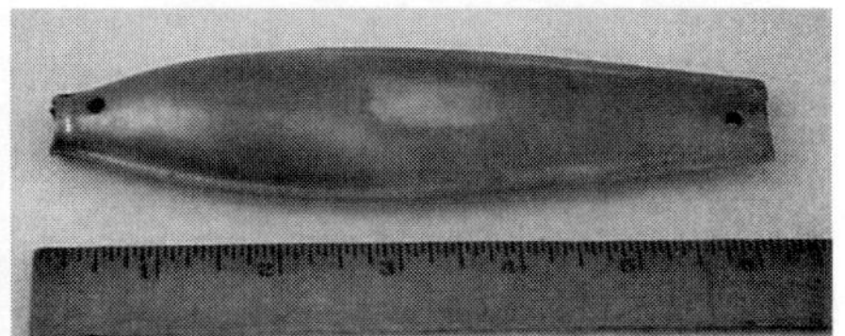

Carr #7 fishing lure, with instruction sheet that suggests filling it with salmon eggs or liver, very good condition. **$60-$70**

Creek Chub Baby Wiggler lure with box. **$125**

Creek Chub Bait Company Wiggler fishing lure, 3 3/4 in. long wood body with glass eyes, a few little spots of wear, circa 1920s. **$60**

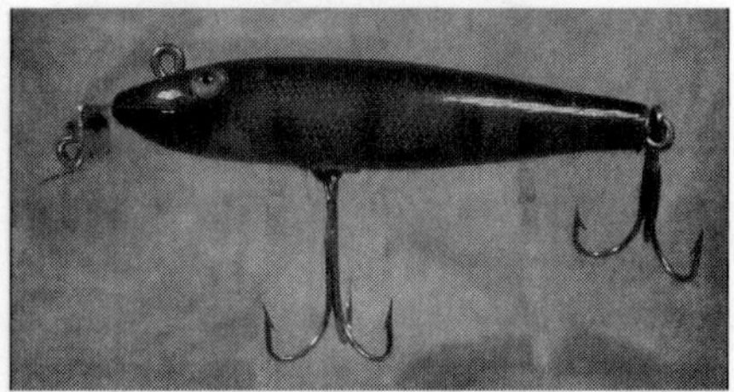

Creek Chub pike minnow, early first model, near mint. **$125**

Creek Chub Plunker lure with box and hang tag. **$125**

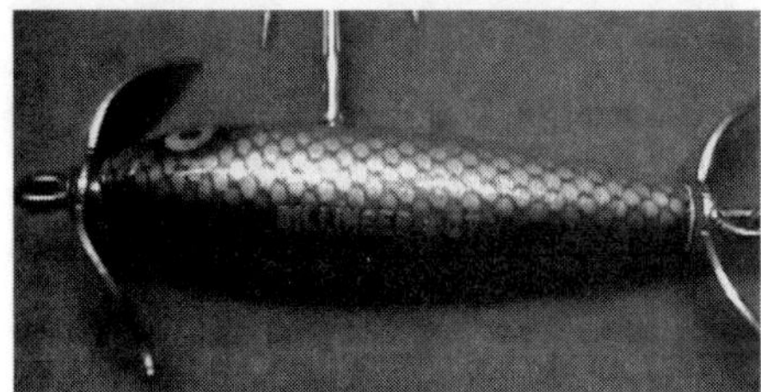

Eger #07 Baby Dillinger, Eger Bait Company, Florida, a few scratches, a bit of soiling, but very good condition, 2 1/4 in. long. **$35**

Heddon River Runt Spook Sinker, yellow perch, plastic, a few scratches on the back, surface hook rig, overall good, 2 1/2 in. long. **$11**

Heddon Stanley King fishing lure, both the lure and the box are in like-new condition, the body of the nickel-plated lure measures 2 3/4 in. long. **$65**

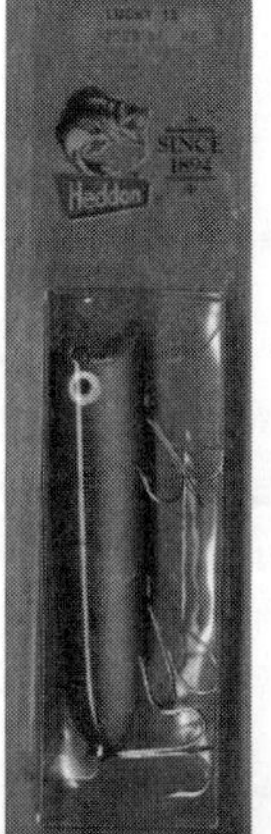

Heddon Lucky 13 fishing lure, frog scale color, in original bubble pack. **$20**

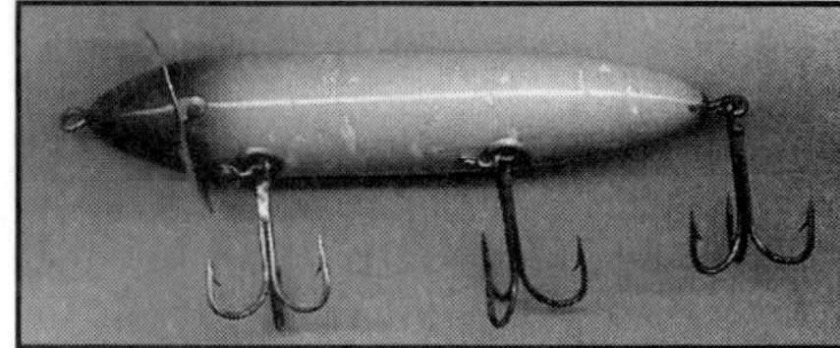

Heddon 200 L Rig, three-screw collar, 4 3/4 in. wood body. **$300**

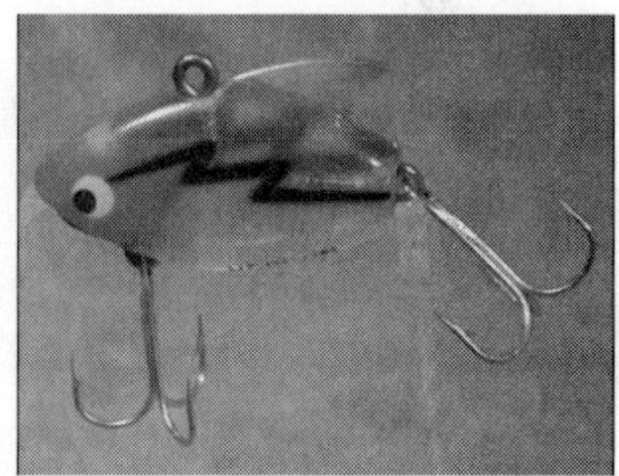

Heddon Sonic fishing lure, in the original box, box is marked "385 SF Sonic." **$25**

Heddon Tiny Tad Shiner Scale fishing lure, the body measures approx. 2 in. long, near mint condition. **$25**

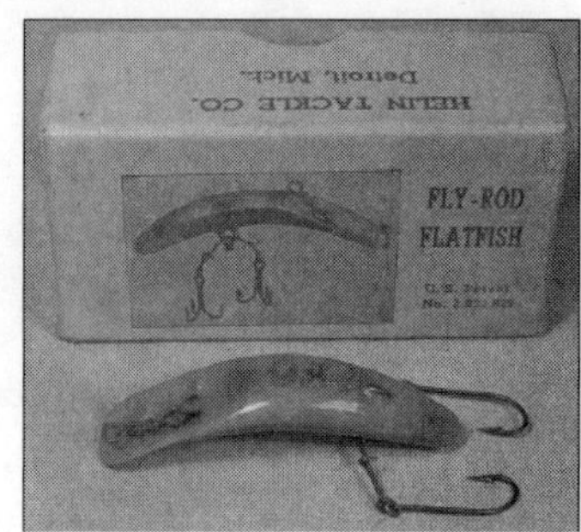

Helin F-6 fly rod flatfish lure in original box, wood body lure is approximately 2 1/4 in. long, both the lure and the box are stamped "F-6." **$35**

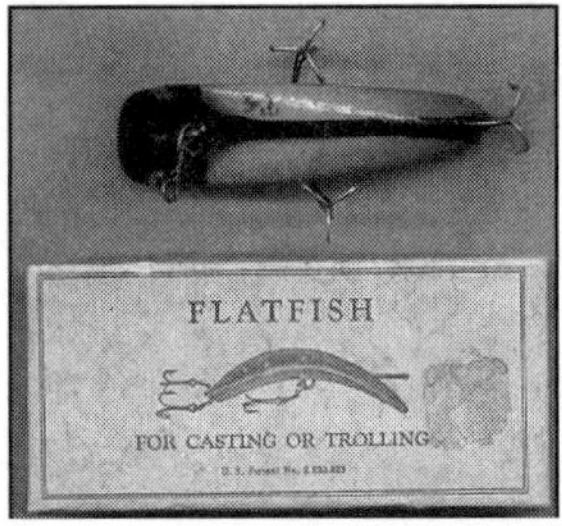

Helin Tackle Co., Detroit, Michigan, flatfish lure for casting or trolling, with original box. **$30**

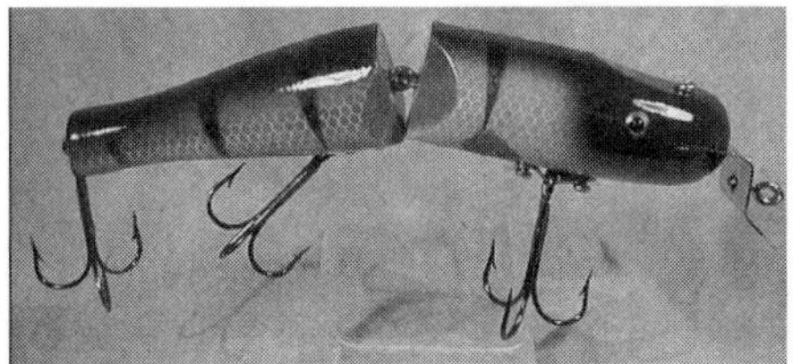

Lucky Strike jointed muskie minnow/perch, jointed wood body has painted tack eyes and measures 5 3/4 in. long, the lip is stamped with the words "Lucky Strike Canada," mint condition. **$40**

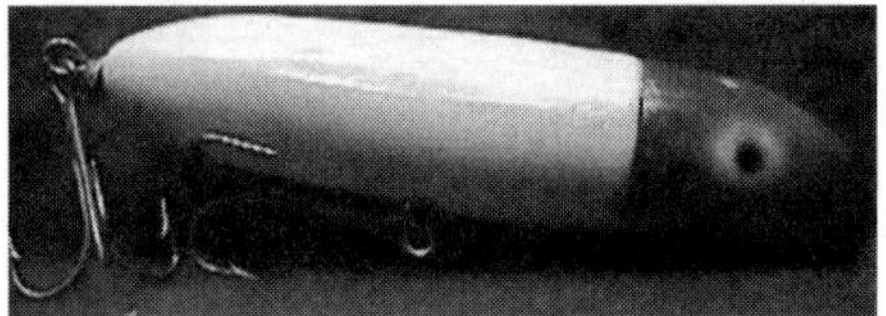

MOS combination casting plug, spring-loaded head turns to make it either a surface or diving lure, MOS Bait Company, Chicago, Illinois, with the box, unused, 3 1/2 in. long. **$33**

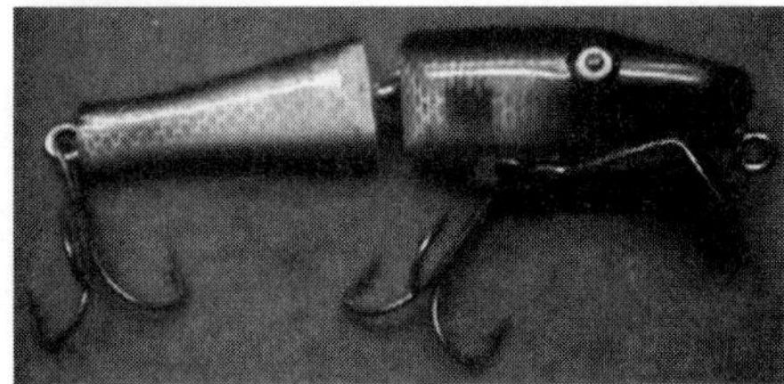

Paw Paw jointed pike lure, yellow perch color, painted metal eyes, some cracks in the paint, 3 1/2 in. long. **$27**

Pflueger metalized minnow fishing lure, 3 in. metal over wood body, glass eyes, "never fail" hardware, tight crack (typical) in metal on each side by hook hangers. **$450**

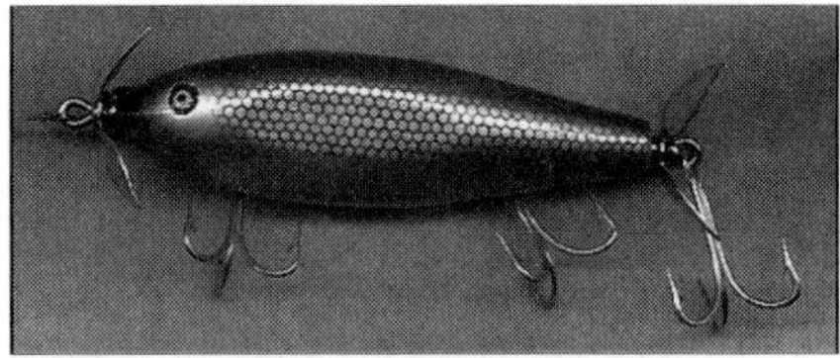

Pflueger Scoop with box, painted pressed eye, surface rig hardware, each of the three bladed props is marked, "PFLUEGER," "SCOOP," "MADE IN USA," box is mint condition cardboard with plastic lid and insert instruction sheet, box is marked, "3 5/8, #9302, Red Side Scale," mint. **$65**

Salmon (?) lure, wood, with indistinct name stamped on the belly, some wear to the paint, mainly on the edge of the face bottom of the diving lip, a few hook pointers, but overall good condition, pressed painted eyes, 5 1/2 in. long. **$33**

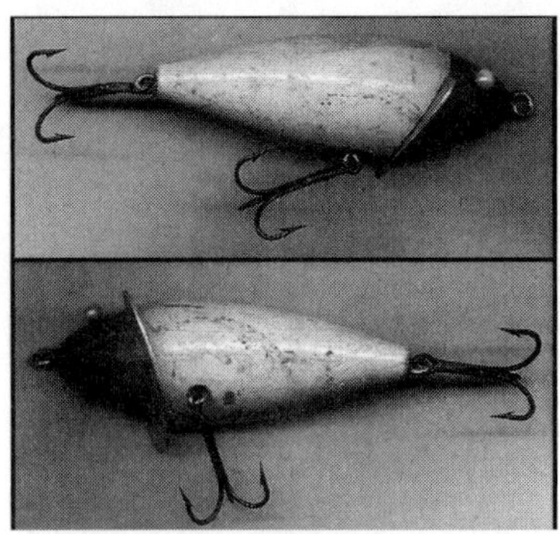

Two views of Swan Lake Wiggler, circa 1915, 3 1/2 in. wood body with pearl bead eyes. **$150**

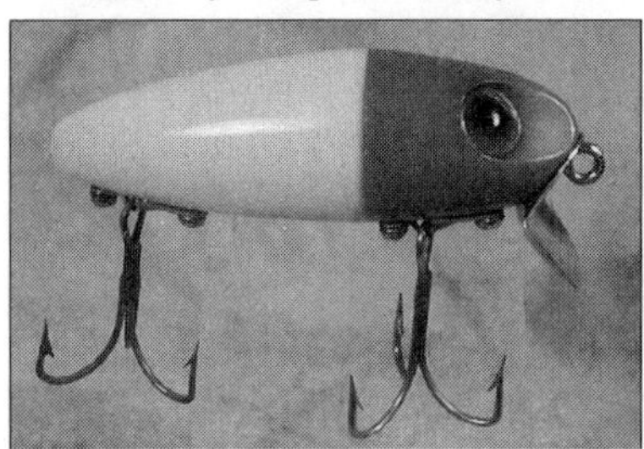

Wright & McGill Bug-A-Boo (?) lure, plastic body measures 2 3/4 in. long, tarnish on the hook hangers, otherwise excellent. **$25**

South Bend Min-Oreno lure, small worm burn on side, otherwise good. **$45**

❖ Rods & Reels

Reel, Shakespeare model No. 1924, nickel plate with celluloid handles, near mint, 3 3/4 in. by 3 in. by 2 1/4 in. **$30-$40**

Compac Golden fly rod, 105 in., three-piece, good condition with a bit of wear, guide wraps are dry, made in Japan, 1950s-1960s. ..**$90**

Kingfisher boat rod, 67 in. split bamboo with double guides and intermediate wraps, line-wrapped handle, fair condition only, some wear to metal parts, wraps are a bit dry, with some fraying, shows some wear and use. **$50**

Wright & McGill Granger Special split bamboo fly rod, professionally rewrapped and refinished, one tip is 5 1/2 in. short, the other 4 1/4 in. short (should be 102 in. long), with rod bag and aluminum tube....**$250**

❖ Trapping

Trap, iron, #13 Victor, size without chain, 8 1/4 in. by 5 1/2 in. by 4 in. **$40**

Trap, iron, #2 Newhouse, with standing bear-marked springs, circa 1910, 14 1/4 in. by 4 in. by 3 1/2 in. **$100**

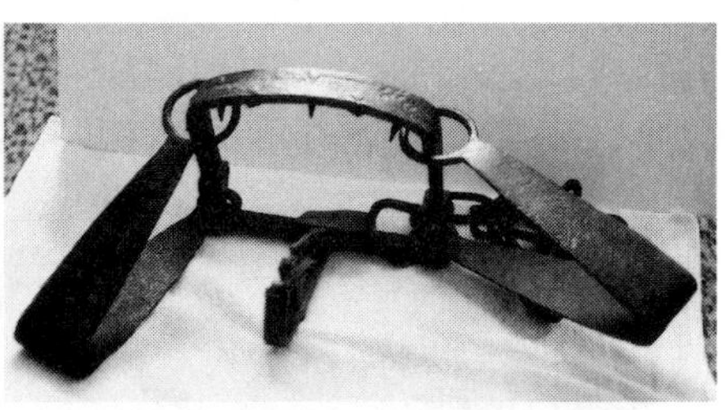

Trap, bear, made by Warren Peavey of Patten, Maine, wrought iron, circa 1850, 25 in. by 7 1/2 in., by 7 1/2 in. **$1,200**

Trap, bear, wrought iron, with hand-forged chain, circa 1840, 48 in. by 12 1/2 in. by 18 in. **$1,400**

Where can I find them?

Tom Bachler
www.oldfishdecoys.com

Drexel Grapevine Antiques
2784 US 70 E
Valdese, NC 28690
(828) 437-5938
www.drexelantiques.com
info@drexelantiques.com

Fritz Antiques
PO Box 575
Zephyr Hills, FL 33539
(813) 788-2312
www.fritzantiques.com
fritzantiques@earthlink.net

Dave Harmon
7445 Trailwood Dr.
Minocqua, WI 54548
(715) 358-3501
djharm@newnorth.net

Hawks Nest Antiques and Decoys
154 Mallard Pond Rd.
Hinesburg, VT 05461
(802) 482-2076
thegreatest35@gmavt.net

Michael R. Higgins
14485 117 St. S
Hastings, MN 55033
(651) 437-2980

Steven Michaan
www.fishdecoy.com
(914) 763-5022
smichaan@ix.netcom.com

W.L. "Ole" Olsen
15 Doe Lane, Antelope Acres
Townsend, MT 59644
wlmolsen@aol.com

Sportsman's Antiques
1967 Court
Memphis, TN 38104
(901) 726-5810
tbruehl@aol.com

❖ Miscellaneous

Snowshoes, circa 1940s, ash and rawhide supports, original leather toeholds, 13 in. by 48 in. **$200**

House sign, circa 1950, cast aluminum, decorated with the figure of a hunter with rifle and hunting dog pointing, original paint with later touch-ups, 16 in. by 17 in. **$175-$225**

Kitchen/ Dining Items

❖ General Kitchen Collectibles

In early America, the kitchen was often the focal point of a family's environment. Many early kitchen utensils were handmade and prized by their owners. These early examples, as well as later utilitarian kitchen items made of tin and other metals, are eagerly sought by many collectors of country.

References: E. Townsend Artman, *Toasters 1909-1960*, Schiffer Publishing, 1996; Kenneth L. Cope, *Kitchen Collectibles: An Identification Guide*, Astragal Press, 2000; Linda Fields, *Four & Twenty Blackbirds: A Pictorial Identification and Value Guide for Pie Birds*, self-published, 1998; Linda Campbell Franklin, *300 Years of Kitchen Collectibles*, 4th ed., Krause Publications, 1997; Helen Greguire, *Collector's Guide to Toasters and Accessories*, Collector Books, 1997; Frances Johnson, *Kitchen Antiques*, Schiffer Publishing, 1996; Barbara Mauzy, *The Complete Book of Kitchen Collecting*, Schiffer Publishing, 1997; David G. Smith and Chuck Wafford, *The Book of Griswold & Wagner*, Schiffer Publishing, 2000; Don Thornton, *Apple Parers*, Off Beat Books, 1997; —, *Beat This: The Eggbeater Chronicles*, Off Beat Books, 1994.

Periodicals: *Cast Iron Cookware News*, 28 Angela Ave., San Anselmo, CA 94960; *Kettles 'n Cookware*, Drawer B, Perrysburg, NY 14129; *Kitchen Antiques & Collectibles News*, 4645 Laurel Ridge Dr., Harrisburg, PA 17119; *Piebirds Unlimited*, 14 Harmony School Rd., Flemington, NJ 08822.

Collectors' Clubs: Griswold & Cast Iron Cookware Association, PO Drawer B, Perrysburg, NY 14129-0301; Kollectors of Old Kitchen Stuff (KOOKS), 501 Market St., Mifflinburg, PA 17844 (send long self-addressed envelope for information); The National Reamer Collectors Association, 47 Midline Ct., Gaithersburg, MD 20878.

Museums: Corning Glass Museum, Corning, New York; Kern County Museum, Bakersfield, California; Landis Valley Farm Museum, Lancaster, Pennsylvania.

Apple parer, Hudson Patent, 1882, made in Leominster, Massachusetts, with fragile kickoff, no rust or pitting, excellent condition. **$60-$70**

Apple parer, wooden tabletop, finely crafted, possibly from Zoar, Ohio, appears to be a tight-grained walnut. The parer arm and the fork operate on a direct drive with a forged iron crank, the uprights are through-mortised, and there are embellishment lines on the paring arm. The paring blade mount is attached to the paring arm with a delicate dovetail that is let in at an angle. The round wooden revolving disk that the end of the paring arm is attached to does not seem to aid in the functionality of the apple parer, although it allows for slightly more movement in the paring arm. There is a hairline crack across the wheel as would be expected from the forces exerted on this thin piece of wood, with the inscribed initials "A.F.H." as well as a pencil signature that appears to read "A. F. Hassler." Very good condition. **$750-$850**

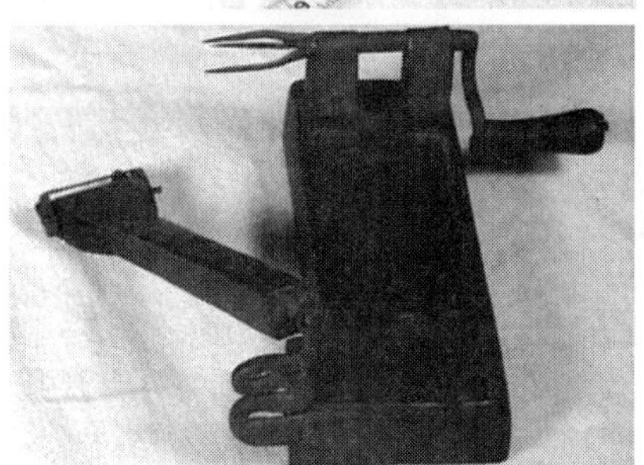

Two views of an apple peeler, diminutive tabletop wooden example, early 1800s, 6 in. long, mounts are through-mortised and pegged, cast iron direct-drive crank and "ribbon candy" design in the paring arm, excellent condition. **$650-$750**

Apple parer, Reading Hardware, manufactured by Harbister Bros., one of the first parers that was produced and distributed by the Reading Hardware Co., with double turntable, and return feature, no rust or pitting, excellent condition. When the crank is turned, table rotates, first in one direction, and then in reverse, all the while peeling the apple before the kickoff is finally activated and kicks the apple into the waiting bucket. **$300-$350**

Apple peeler, primitive, from New Hampshire, early 19th century, with hand-carved seat area, and heavy chamfering on both the base and upright, constructed with square head nails; clamp, hand crank, and paring arm holder are all hand-forged, very good condition. **$450-$550**

Apple slicer/corer, Shaker, first patented in 1858 by two brothers named Norton, the design comes from Farmington, Maine, an area once famous for its apples and devices to process them. These devices came in several different versions, with the main differences being in the design of the handle. The design of this slicer is different from most of the others, with some minor rust on the slicers, but seems to be fully operational in good condition. **$450-$550**

Two views of pour bowl with rounded handle and spout, circa 1800, made from one piece of pine, Norwegian, well used with remnants of original red stain, old repair to handle, 11 1/2 in. by 8 1/2 in. by 3 in. **$625**

Bowl, circa 1940s, press-wood with scalloped sides, center painted with floral display tied with ribbon, edge painted with white and brown border, minor handling wear, 10 in. square by 3 in. **$30-$40**

Bowl, circa 1870, turned wood with scribed decoration and flared foot, traces of old yellow paint, probably Norwegian-American, rich patina from handling and some tight age cracks, overall very good condition, 3 in. by 2 1/2 in. **$100-$120**

Ale dipper, circa 1820, carved from one piece of pine, Scandinavian, with hooked handle, moderate handling wear, 16 1/2 in. by 9 1/2 in. by 5 in. **$225**

Bowl, wood, circa 1910, maple, with shallow turned lip, significant wear stains on interior, excellent condition, 17 1/2 in. by 16 1/2 in. by 5 1/2 in. **$110**

Wood bowls, set of three, circa 1900, ranging in size from 4 in. to 8 in., moderate handling wear, if unpainted. **$100-$200/set; with original paint, $700-$900/set**

Butter mold, circa 1910, maple, factory-made, with stamp carved in acorn motif, 6 1/2 in. by 4 3/4 in. **$70-$80**

Buckets, sugar (also called firkins), painted, late 19th century, with wooden handles, finger-lap construction and original paint, in green, sky blue, rusty red, and golden yellow, sizes range from 13 1/2 in., 12 in., 11 1/2 in., and 9 in., ranging in price from **$200** *for the small green bucket to* **$500+** *for the sky blue bucket.*

Butter mold, circa 1880, pine, two pieces carved in the form of a fish, with detailed scales, mouth and eyes, possibly Norwegian-American, minor handling wear, 6 1/4 in. by 2 in. **$250-$300**

Butter paddle, circa 1890, pine with hand-painted flowers on one side, moderate handling wear, 8 in. by 4 in. **$80-$90**

Butter stamp, circa 1890, maple with carved rose, 4 in. diameter. **$350-$450**

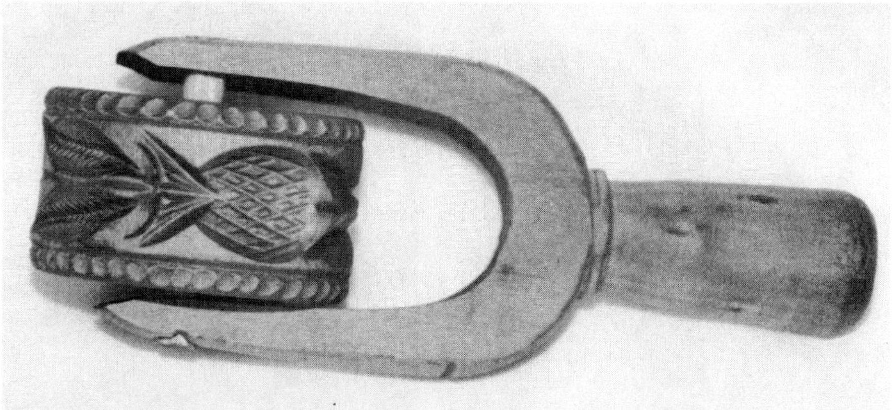

Butter stamp, rolling, circa 1880, maple with pineapple motif, 8 in. long. **$550-$650**

Butter stamp, lollipop, circa 1880, pine, probably European, with leaf motif, significant wear, 7 1/2 in. long. **$150-$200**

Butter stamp, circa 1880, maple with stylized floral and leaf motif, 4 in. diameter. **$250-$350**

Butter stamp, circa 1880, maple with carved eagle, 4 in. diameter. **$700-$800**

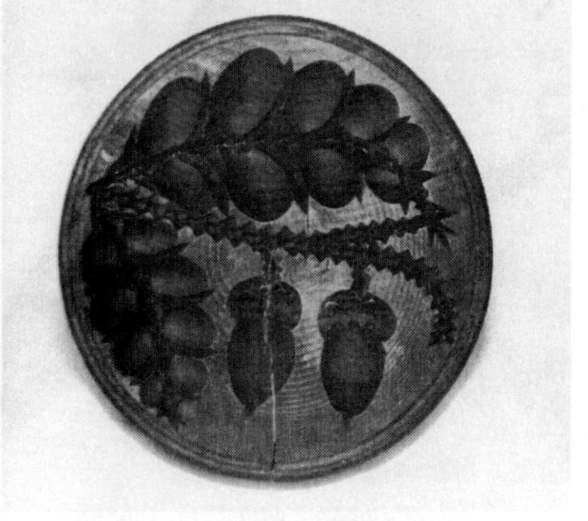

Butter stamp, circa 1870, maple with deeply carved oak leaves and acorns, 4 1/2 in. diameter. **$150-$200**

Butter stamp, square pineapple, 5 1/2 in. tall by 4 1/2 in. square, rich, warm even patina. **$225-$275**

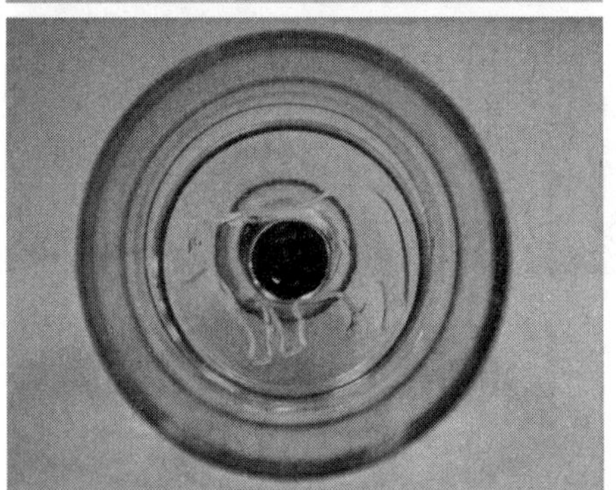

Two views of butter stamp/mold, glass, circa 1930, with wooden handle and stamp with the image of a cow, rare, 4 1/2 in. by 8 1/4 in. **$165**

Two views of candle box (?), circa 1900, decorated on two sides with cats and dogs, and on three sides with vividly painted red, yellow, and pink roses, may have originally held yeast or cheese, 9 in. by 7 in. by 7 in. **$1,200-$1,500**

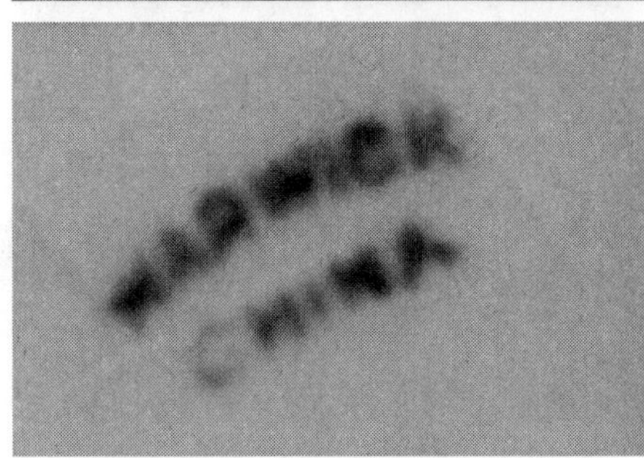

Chamber pot, white ironstone with wire handle and turned-wood grip, lid missing, bottom marked "Warwick China" in detail, circa 1920s, 10 in by 8 in. **$40-$50**

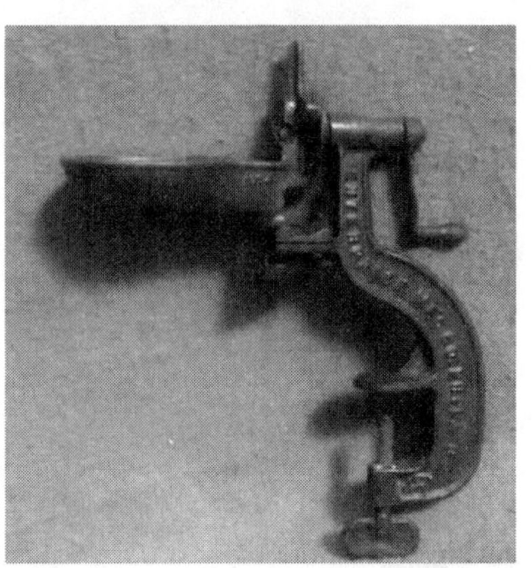

Cherry stoner or pitter, Enterprise #12; the sweeper arm sweeps the pitted cherry into a bowl, and the pit is forced through another hole into a waste bucket; very good condition. **$90-$100**

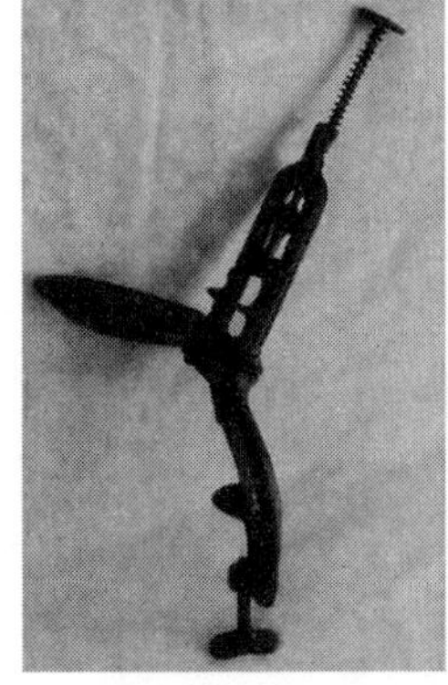

Cherry pitter, single, Rollman Mfg. Co. spring-loaded plunger-style made in Mt. Joy, Pa., by the most prolific manufacturer of cherry pitters or stoners and other kitchen gadgets, excellent condition. **$55-$65**

Cherry pitter, New Standard "Champion" four-station, clamp-on style made in Mt. Joy, Pa., With each turn of the crank the pitting fork lifts up, then back down through the cherry as the revolving four-station cherry holder moves the next cherry into place. The cherry is pierced, the pit falls into one trough, and the pitted piece of fruit then moves on to the next station where it falls into the second trough and down into a bowl or jar. As this was happening, the next cherry would have already been moved into position and would be in the process of getting pitted, and the other two holders were ready to be continuously filled with more cherries. Minor wear on the clamp wing nut, very good condition. **$100-$150**

Cherry pitter or stoner, New Standard "Duplex" No. 95, clamp-on mechanical pitter made by the N. S. Hardware Works of Mt. Joy, Pa., This machine handled two cherries at a time. The spring-loaded plunger activated the two forks, which simultaneously pierced two cherries that rolled down the holding tray. The two pits would then drop out the bottom. Excellent condition. **$90-$100**

Churn, square glass jar with screw-on crank top and wooden paddles, with paper label, "Dazey Churn," size No. 80, near mint, 16 in. by 7 1/2 in. square. **$200-$300**

Churn, square glass jar with screw-on crank top and wooden paddles, with raised letters on side in a circle, "Dazey Churn & Mfg. Co. St. Louis U.S.A.," size No. 20, near mint, 12 in. by 4 3/4 in. square. **$300-$400**

Cider jug, clear glass, in the shape of an apple with handles in the shape of stems and raised leaf details, paper label missing, 7 in. tall, no chips or cracks. (The price of these bottles has dropped dramatically in recent years due to their increased availability on the Internet.) **$20-$30**

*Cookie cutters, circa 1920, tinned steel, in the form of parsons, 6 1/4 in. (***$60***) and 3 3/4 in. tall (***$40***)*

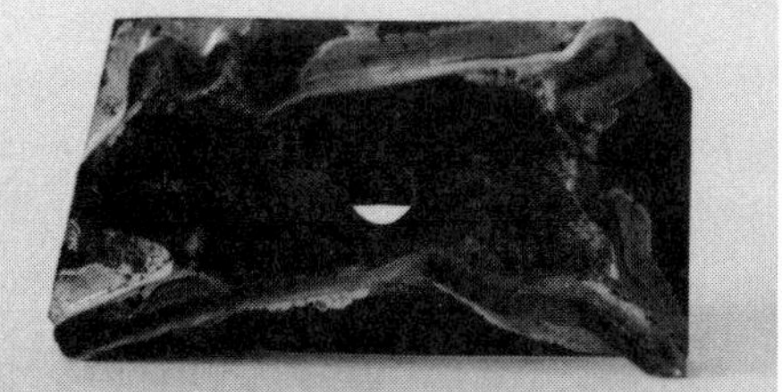

Cookie cutter, circa 1920, tinned steel, in the form of a running cat (?), 4 1/2 in. by 2 1/2 in. **$70**

Cookie cutter, circa 1920, tinned steel, in the form of a goose, 4 in. by 3 1/4 in. **$60**

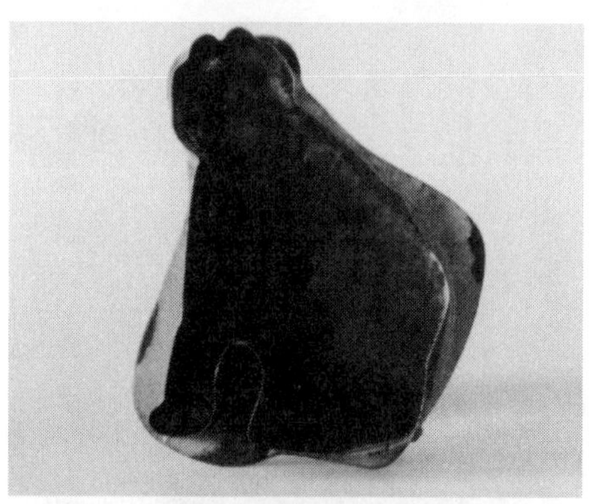

Cookie cutter, circa 1920, tinned steel, in the form of a seated cat, 4 in. by 3 1/2 in. **$75**

Cookie cutter, circa 1920, tinned steel, in the form of a heart, 5 in. by 3 1/2 in. **$45**

Cookie cutter, circa 1920, tinned steel, in the form of a lion, 4 1/4 in. by 3 in. **$80**

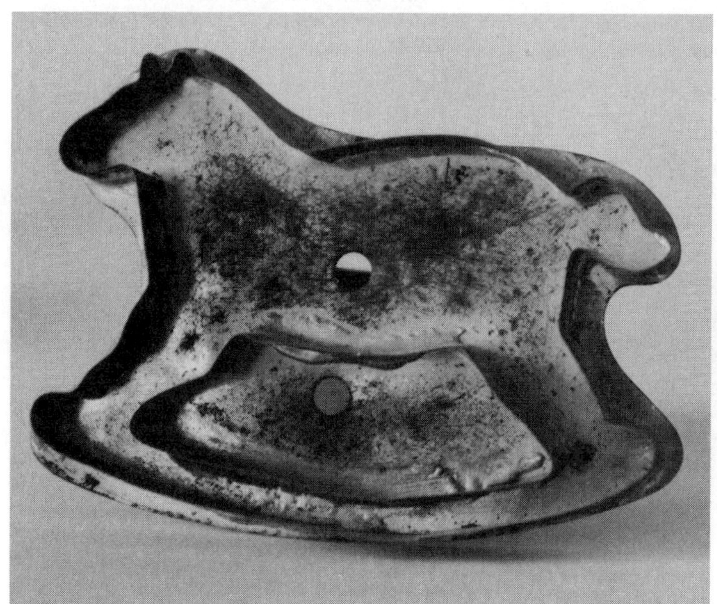

Cookie cutter, circa 1920, tinned steel, in the form of a rocking horse, 4 1/4 in. by 3 1/4 in. **$125-$150**

Cookie ... nned steel, in the *form of a fish, 5 in. by* ... *in.* **$50**

Cookie cutter, circa 1920, tinned steel, in the form of a swan, 4 in. by 5 in. **$80**

Cookie cutters, circa 1920, tinned steel, in the form of a man and woman, 5 in. by 2 1/2 in. **$200/pair**

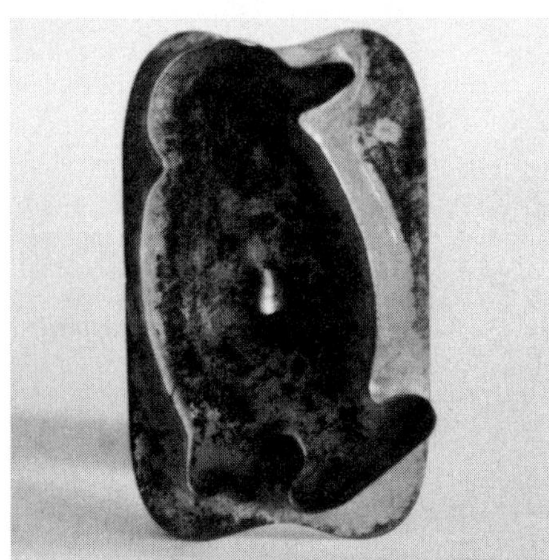

Cookie cutter, circa 1920, tinned steel, in the form of a penguin, 3 in. by 1 3/4 in. **$100**

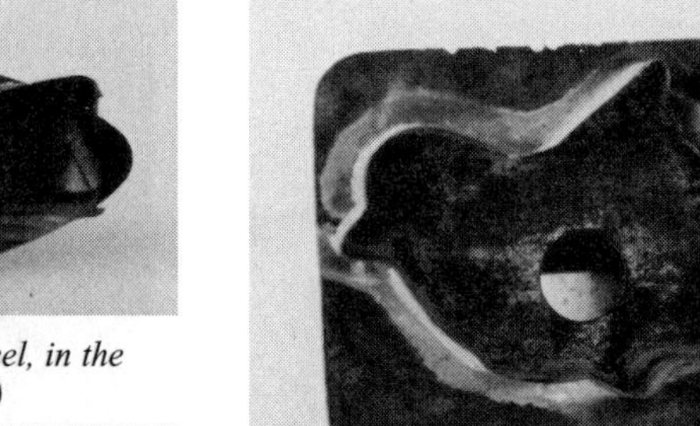

Cookie cutter, circa 1920, tinned steel, in the form of flying bird, 4 in. by 3 in. **$60**

Cookie cutter, circa 1920, tinned steel, in the form of a dog, 4 1/4 in. by 3 in. **$80**

Cutting board, circa 1880, pine, with carved border in the form of leaves, flowers and wheat stalks, worn surface, 11 3/4 in. by 1 in. **$150-$200**

Cutting board, circa 1880, pine, with worn carved border in the form of leaves, flowers and wheat stalks, and the words, "Our Daily Bread," 11 3/4 in. by 1 in. **$90-$120**

Cutting board, circa 1880, pine, with carved border in the form of flowers and wheat stalks, and the words, "Bread—Staff of Life," worn surface, 11 in. by 1 in. **$120-$150**

Cutting board, circa 1880, walnut, with deeply carved border in the form of leaves and flowers, and the words, "Give us our daily bread" in German, worn surface, 10 1/4 in. by 1 in. **$200-$250**

Cutting board, circa 1880, oak, with carved border in the form of wheat stalks, and the word "Brot" ("bread" in Norwegian), worn surface, 11 3/4 in. by 1 in. **$200-$250**

Cutting board, circa 1880, maple, with carved border in the form of leaves, flowers, and wheat stalks, and the word "Bread," worn surface, 11 3/4 in. by 1 in. **$150-$175**

Dipper, carved burl, Norwegian, dated 1601, with handle carved in the form of a primitive bird head, rich patina, 8 in. by 3 1/2 in. by 4 1/2 in. **$2,800**

Cutting board, circa 1880, maple, with carved border in the form of leaves, flowers, and wheat stalks, and the word "Bread," worn surface, 11 3/4 in. by 1 in. **$150-$175**

Dipper, miniature, carved in the form of a bird (also called an "ale hen"), Norwegian, pine, dated 1842, with stylized carved tail, original blue paint, minor wear, 5 1/4 in. by 2 3/8 in. by 2 1/2 in. **$1,800**

Dough scraper, circa 1880, shaped walnut handle and steel blade, hand painted circa 1900 on both sides with roses and pansies, near mint, 11 in. by 6 1/2 in. **$200-$250**

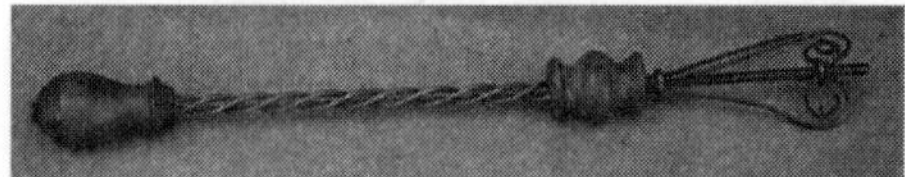

Eggbeater, Ashley, patented May 1, 1860, very rare, several sizes are known to exist, with this example being 11 1/2 in. long, patent info stamped in the wooden handle, with about 1/2 in. of wire broken off the end of one of the three scrolled dashers, very good condition. **$600-$650**

Eggbeater, Express "fly swatter," marked with an 1887 patent date, in near mint condition, very hard to find. **$1,900-$2,000**

Eggbeater, Improved Rapid Archimedes-style featuring a slide mechanism with a wooden knob running down the center shaft, rare, excellent condition. **$350-$450**

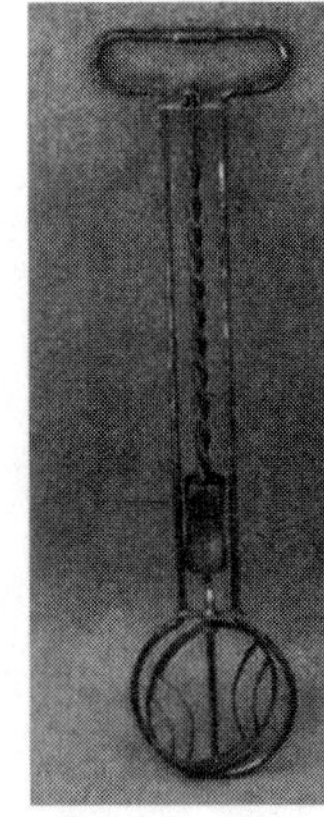

Eggbeater, Model Archimedean, marked "Model, Pat. Apld For," unusually long for this type of beater, 16 in., and the wide bands that comprise the dasher are a unique design, wooden handle has a red wash, very Good condition. **$90-$100**

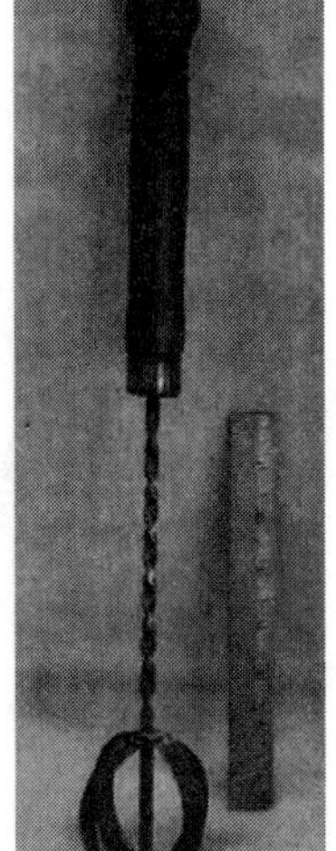

Eggbeater, Roberts Archimedean, patented in 1902, very good condition. **$60-$70**

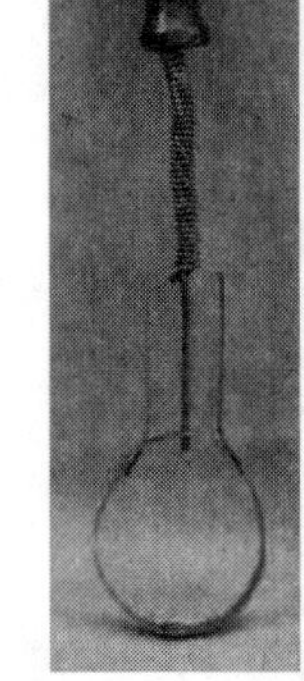

Eggbeater, Lyon double-propeller, early version of a double-prop beater, patented in 1897 in Albany, N.Y. Throughout the history of beater design, ingenious Americans were constantly coming up with ideas for the better eggbeater, and this often entailed the use of unusual—and inoperable—dasher configurations at the bottom. Excellent condition. **$150-$170**

Eggbeater, PD & Co., rare cutout wheel design, in like-new condition with just minor oxidation from storage on the dasher wires. **$1,400-$1,500**

Eggbeater, Standard, a "fold-flat" beater, made in Boston, marked with "Standard Egg Beater Pat. June 29 '80" on the gear wheel, excellent condition. **$400-$450**

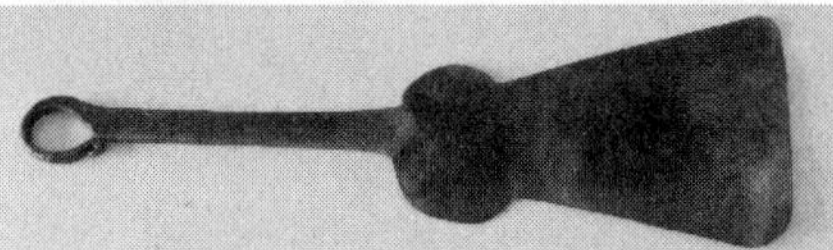

Food chopper or peeler, circa 1800, "thistle" shape, wrought iron with ring handle, 9 1/2 in. by 3 in. **$80-$100**

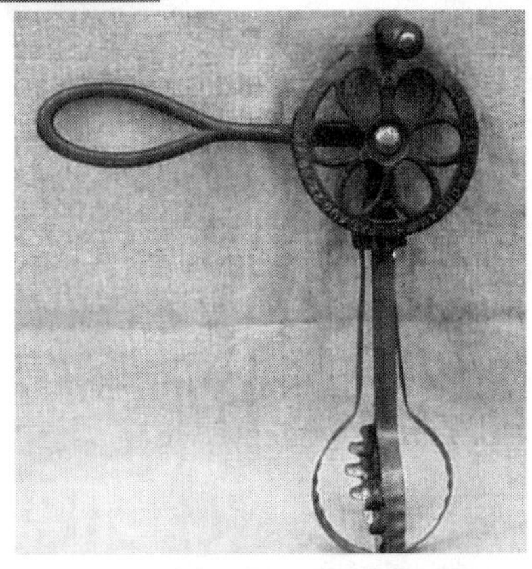

Eggbeater or cream whip, Holt right-angle. There are two patent dates in the wheel from 1899 and 1900, one likely for the unusual right-angle design and the other for the flared design of the dashers. These beaters were mainly produced in the 8 1/2 in. size, and in much fewer numbers in the next size up, which is about 11 in. tall. Very good condition. **$300-$350**

Funnel, circa 1910, copper with spring-loaded strainer, with applied silver metal plate that reads, "Compliments of Lash's Bitters Co.," 10 in. by 8 in. by 6 in. **$80-$120**

Eggbeater, Minute Maid, made in Seattle, Wash., and seldom found outside of the West Coast, with distinctive heart-shaped dashers, very good condition. **$350-$450**

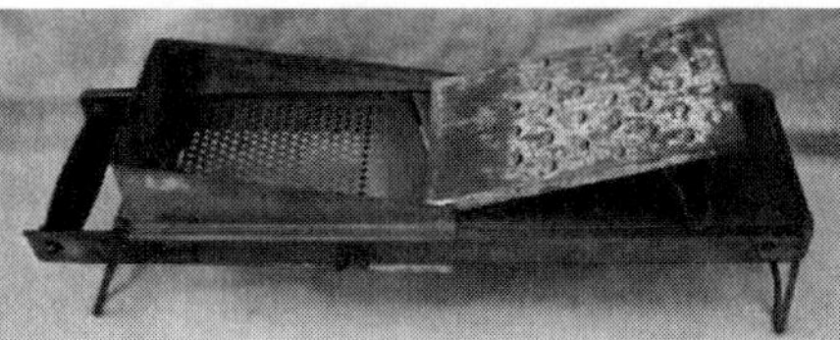

Grater/slicer, tin, marked "4-in-1 Food Slicer Patent Applied For—Four In One Co. Chicago, Ill.," 19 in. long, folding legs, very good condition. **$125-$175**

Patented and mechanical "Edgar" chocolate grater, similar to the more common "Edgar" nutmeg grater, with rectangular spring-loaded box to hold the chunk of chocolate to be shaved, which rides on two rods that run the length of the 7 1/2 in. pierced tin grating cylinder, marked with the two patent dates of 1891 and 1896, very good condition. **$300-$350**

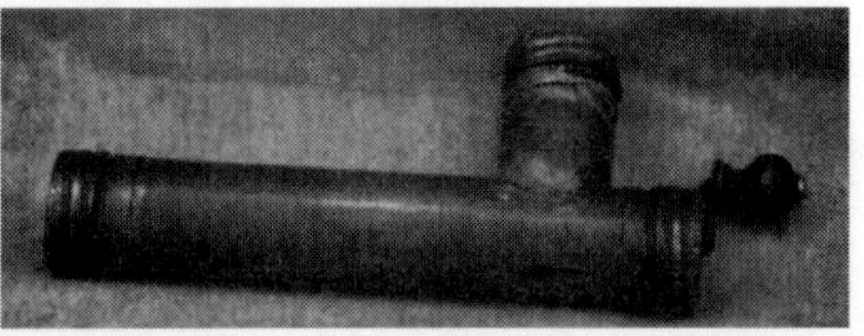

"Handy" nutmeg grater, made in Massillon, Ohio, often referred to as a "stovepipe" grater, several versions are known, with variations in length, the number of screw-cap ends, and designs of the wooden knobs. This example measures 5 1/2 in. in length, not including the crank, all three ends have threaded caps, one for the nutmeg storage compartment, one to allow removal of the crank and inner grating drum, and one to remove the spring-loaded mechanism that holds the nut against the drum, marked "Pat Apl'd For," in overall very good condition. **$400-$450**

Pocket nutmeg grater, toleware, designed so that one tube fits inside the other, thus protecting the grater surface and doubling as a storage unit at the same time, 3 3/8 in. long, 1 1/4 in. diameter, excellent condition. **$250-$350**

Kettle, large copper, circa 1860, handmade and riveted, heavy-gauge copper with goose-neck covered spout, fitted lid, swinging wrought-iron handle, Scandinavian, moderate handling wear, size with handle raised 15 in. by 13 in. by 9 1/2 in. **$325**

Kettle, small copper, circa 1850, with shaped swinging handle and three raised iron legs, riveted construction, goose-neck covered spout, dome lid with scroll finial, Scandinavian, moderate handling wear, size with handle raised 15 in. by 10 in. by 8 1/2 in. **$375**

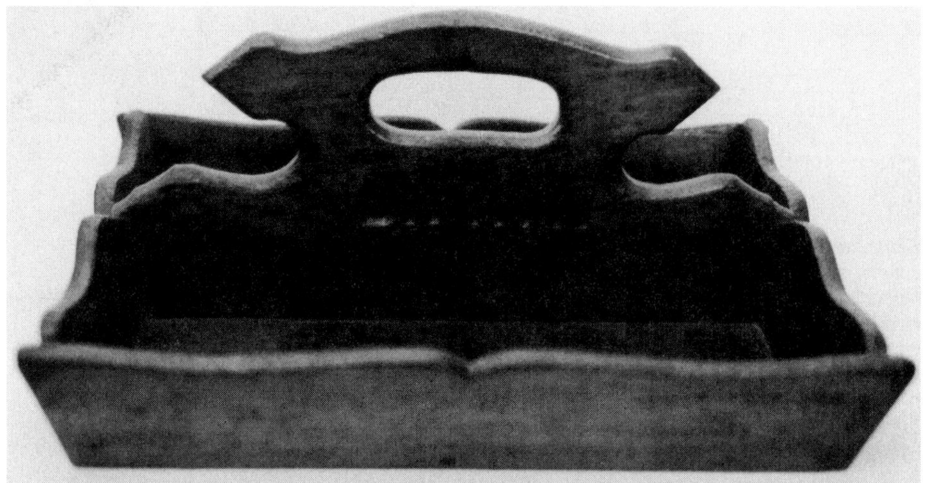

Knife or utensil tray, walnut, with cutout handle, scalloped and canted sides, with carved date, 1857, on one side of handle, and the initials "J.M.W." on the other side, near mint, 13 in. by 9 1/4 in. by 6 in. **$500-$600**

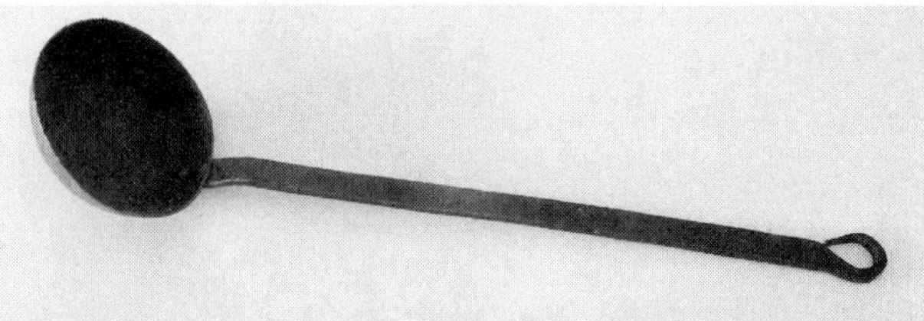

Ladle, circa 1830, wrought iron with ring handle, riveted construction, significant wear, 17 in. by 4 1/4 in. **$40-$50**

Milk bottles, assorted one-quart squared, from various dairies, minor to significant wear. (Milk bottle collectors generally prefer the rounded style or those with cream tops.) **$8-$10**

Nutcracker, cast iron, unusual and ornate Victorian-era model, with cut-out base design, either for table or wall mounting, excellent condition. **$400-$500**

Large brass pan or shallow pail, with wrought iron handle riveted in place, circa 1870, Scandinavian, with significant handling wear including dents, 13 1/2 in. by 12 1/2 in. **$185**

Three views of pantry box, circa 1900, wood with lapped construction held in place with heavy string and nails, fitted cover, painted a muddy green, moderate handling wear, 14 in. by 16 in. **$100-$150**

Pantry boxes, stacked, most in original paint, ranging in size from 2 1/2 in. to 14 in. diameter.

Three pie crimpers, cast brass, mid-19th century, crimper on left with wrought iron handle, 5 1/4 in. long; center crimper 4 3/4 in.; right crimper 6 1/2 in. **$80-$100 each**

Pitcher, circa 1930s, glazed terracotta in the form of a pineapple (?), green and orange, probably a Mexican tourist piece, decorative only, minor flaking, overall very good condition, 12 in. by 9 in. by 7 in. **$40-$50**

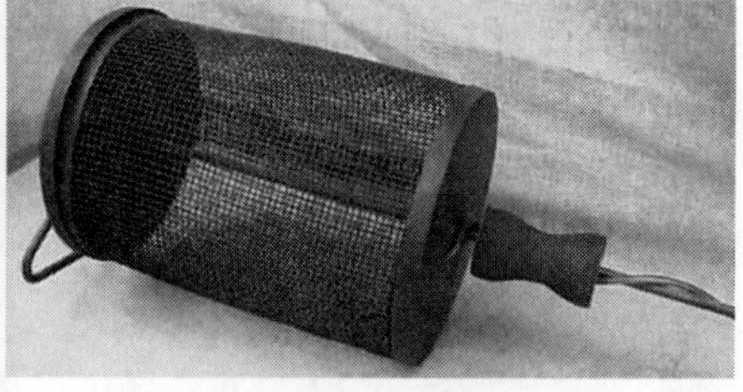

Revolving popcorn popper, Archimedean, patented April 18, 1887, designed to slowly turn the spinning basket over the fire to keep the corn moving, very good condition. **$350-$450**

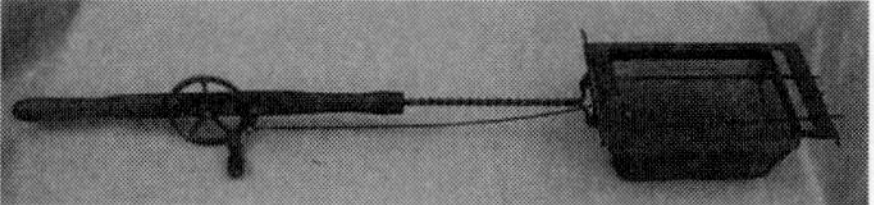

Mechanical popcorn popper, Quincy (Ill.) Hardware Mfg. Co., designed with an eggbeater-style geared wheel to keep the basket (7 in. by 10 in.) moving back and forth, patented on May 24, 1892, with two old small repairs to the wire basket, very good condition. This same company also manufactured a slightly larger model, sometimes referred to as a coffee bean roaster. **$550-$650**

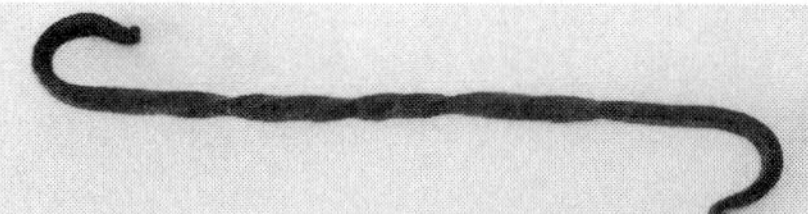

Pot hook, circa 1800, wrought iron with spiral twist shaft, 11 in. by 3 in. **$40-$50**

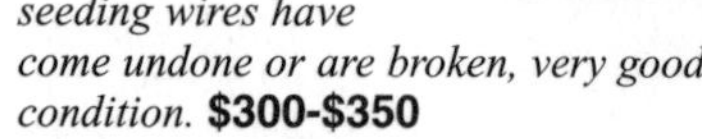

Raisin seeder, EZY, patented on July 21, 1895, the patent information and the words, "Scald The Raisins" are cast into the curvilinear lever arm, with nearly all of its original black japanning; also has the receiving cup, all original, three of the seeding wires have come undone or are broken, very good condition. **$300-$350**

Spice cabinet, circa 1890, walnut and maple, elaborate pierced fret-carved construction with scroll and vine motifs on all surfaces and gallery top and bracket supports on bottom, nine drawers with contrasting wood labels done in fret carving, central pierced door with round plaque, which features a woman in harvest setting, applied carved crest in gallery bears initials "WH," minor damage to gallery, overall excellent condition, 24 in. by 20 in. by 6 in. Detail below. **$1,200-$1,500**

Recipe box, circa 1930s, pine with white painted decoration, brass hasp, open interior, excellent condition, 8 in. by 6 in. by 6 in. **$80-$100**

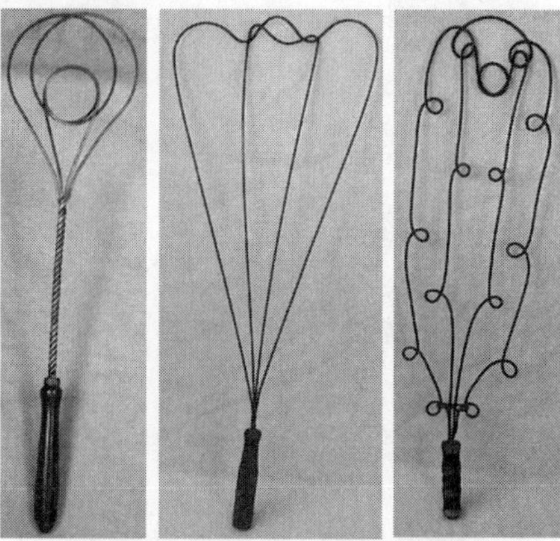

Rug beaters, early 20th century, shaped wire with wooden handles, measuring from 20 in. to 30 in. long. **$40-$125**

Spice cabinet, eight drawers, pine with heavy varnished surface, wood button pulls, scalloped trim on top, circa 1930, 14 in. by 10 in. by 3 1/2 in. **$200**

Spice cabinet of unusual design, early 20th century (?), mixed woods, with rectangular opening in center for mortar and pestle, 10 small drawers with small brass pulls over four drawers with sloped faces with small brass bail pulls, over two wide drawers with mismatched brass pulls, all drawers with half-lap joints, eye hooks for wall mounting, original honey-colored varnished surface, minor wear, 16 in. by 14 in. by 5 in. **$300-$400**

Stove, six-burner, dual-oven, gas, marked "Famous Good Luck," with broiler and roll-door warming oven, good original condition. **$6,800**

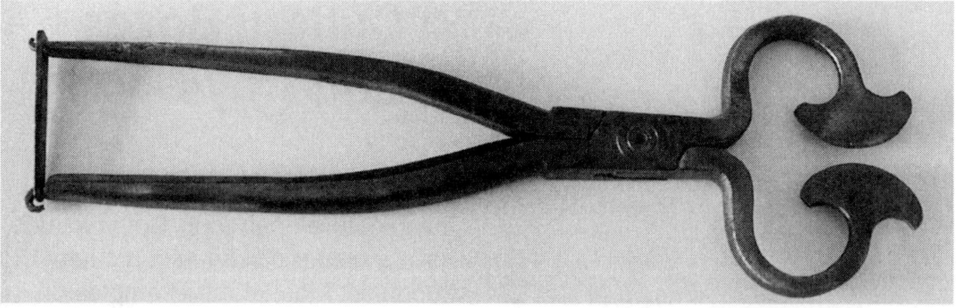

Sugar cutter or nipper, circa 1910, wrought iron with spring-loaded handle and catch, 9 in. by 3 in. **$60-$70**

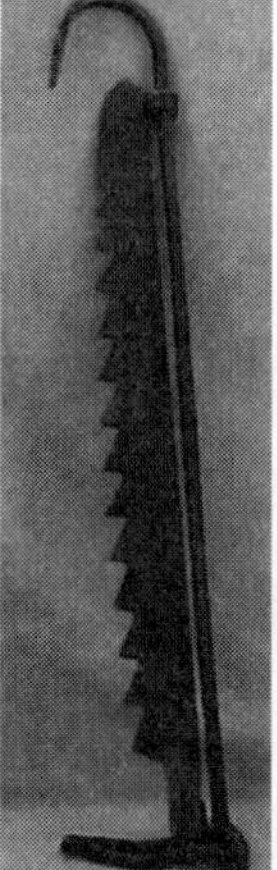

Primitive forged sawtooth pot trammel, circa 1850, with vine-like decoration, 29 in. long in the closed position, and about 50 in. when extended. These were hung in large fireplaces or over large open fires. **$200-$250**

Sugar cutter, Norwegian, circa 1840, wrought-iron blade mounted on a pine base, maple handle with brass collar, original pale green paint, minor wear, 13 3/4 in. by 7 in. by 10 in. **$165**

Washboard, primitive, circa 1880, pine with carved ridges and tapering profile, significant wear, 16 in. by 32 in. by 1 1/4 in. **$100**

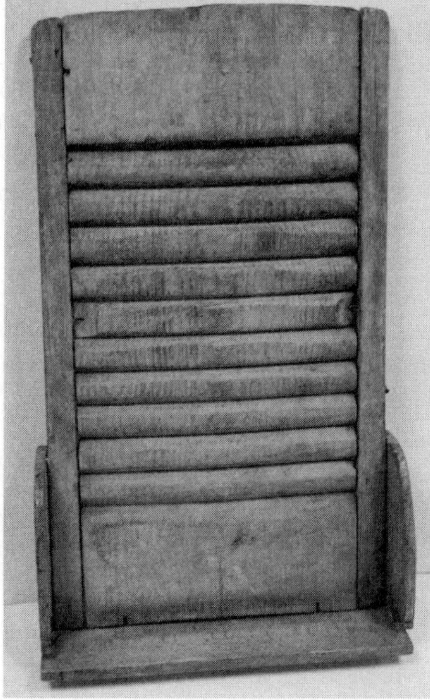

Washboard, primitive, circa 1880, pine with carved ridges and tapering profile, significant wear, 16 in. by 32 in. by 1 1/4 in. **$100**

Washboard, primitive, circa 1880, pine with carved ridges and "hooded" end made from maple, significant wear, 13 in. by 21 3/4 in. by 3 1/4 in. **$100**

Where can I find them?

There are many resources, but among the best we've found is:

Larry and Carole Meeker
Purveyors of American Patented & Mechanical Antiques
5702 Vacation Blvd.
Somerset, CA 95684
(530) 620-7019
Sales: (888) 607-6090
Fax: (530) 620-7020
www.patented-antiques.com
clm@patented-antiques.com

❖ Cookie Boards or Molds

Generally made of wood with a carved motif, cookie boards or molds were used to create cookies with a sculpted look by imprinting a design in the dough. Cake boards, marzipan boards, and springerle molds also fall into this category. Made in both Europe and the United States during the 19th century, they are often prized for the folk art nature of their designs.

Reference: Linda Campbell Franklin, *300 Years of Kitchen Collectibles*, 4th ed., Krause Publications, 1997.

Reproduction Alert

A variety of designs have been reproduced.

Cast iron, 12 segments, birds, animals, buildings, etc., rectangular, 7 3/4 in. by 5 1/4 in. .... **$200-$250**

Cast iron, acorn and oak leaves, oblong, 5 3/4 in. long. .... **$150-$250**

Cast iron, basket of flowers, oval, 5 1/2 in. long. .... **$125-$150**

Cast iron, bird on branch, almond shape, 5 1/4 in. .... **$150-$200**

Wooden, one-sided, animal, round, European, 12 1/2 in. diameter. .... **$80-$100**

Wooden, one-sided, dog sitting in basket, scrubbed finish, minor insect damage on back, 3 3/4 in. by 4 in. .... **$70-$80**

Wooden, one-sided, eagle with banner and "E. Pluribus Unum," Washington, Lady Liberty, harvest goddess, cornucopia, and stars, carved mahogany, very rare, 11 7/8 in. by 8 in. .... **$5,000-$6,000**

Wooden, one-sided, heart having three carved roses with vine border, dark refinish, age cracks, minor insect damage, putty filler, 7 3/4 in. by 6 3/4 in. .... **$400-$500**

Wooden, one-sided, man in kilt and woman in long dress (William of Orange and Mary Stewart), 18 in. by 6 1/2 in. .... **$400-$500**

Cookie mold, circa 1850, maple, carved with large heart decorated with flowers and a leafy border, mint condition, 8 3/4 in. by 9 3/4 in. by 1 1/2 in. **$600-$700**

Wooden, one-sided, round, pine, old patina, two boards with inset cleats and handle, 24 in. by 19 1/2 in. diameter. .... **$200-$250**

Wooden, one-sided, tree-like motif flanked by two elf figures, sailing ship at bottom, initialed "HM" on one side, 6 3/8 in. by 16 1/4 in. .... **$80-$100**

Wooden, two-sided, eagle and shield in almond on one side, basket of flowers in circle and cornucopia in an almond on other side, mahogany, old dark worn patina, unmarked, 7 3/8 in. by 15 in. .... **$4,500-$5,000**

Wooden, two-sided, man, woman in fancy dress, age cracks, worm holes, 13 3/4 in. by 5 1/8 in. .... **$100-$125**

Wooden, two-sided, man holding chicken by its feet on one side, woman with chicken in a basket on her back on other, age cracks in ends, iron staple hanger added, 15 in. by 7 1/2 in. .... **$150-$200**

Wooden, two-sided, various designs, six carved images per side, animals, windmills, fish, ship, etc., 25 in. by 3 1/2 in. .... **$200-$250**

❖ Cutlery Boxes and Trays

Cutlery boxes have lids while cutlery trays feature open tops. Both typically have a center divider with a cutout handhold. Most of the examples on today's market date to the 19th century.

Collecting Hint: Don't confuse cutlery boxes with knife boxes, which generally have a slanted top with slots for inserting knives, handle up.

Box, painted, black, elaborate scrolls and silhouette cutout, 7 in. tall by 11 in. wide by 7 in. deep. **$850**

Box, painted, worn green, yew or oak, arched divider with cutout handle, English, 7 in. tall by 12 1/2 in. wide by 8 3/4 in. deep. **$175**

Box, walnut, double lift lids, canted top, shaped crest with cutout handle, old finish, age cracks, 9 in. tall by 14 in. wide by 12 3/4 in. deep. **$450**

Box, walnut, double lids, dovetailed, beveled edge on base, canted sides, incised carved panels, raised divider at center, cutout handle, old dark finish, minor age cracks, 8 in. tall by 12 3/4 in. wide by 8 1/2 in. deep. **$325**

Box, walnut, double lids, oblong, straight sides, center divider with arched handle and oval cutout, iron locks, dovetailed, stained, wear, missing splinter of wood, 7 1/4 in. tall by 18 1/2 in. wide by 11 5/8 in. deep. **$350**

Tray, cherry, old mellow finish, canted sides, dovetailed, two compartments, arched center board, cutout for handle flanked with small scrolls, one scroll with old break on tip, 5 5/8 in. tall by 14 3/4 in. wide by 8 7/8 in. deep. .**$325**

Tray, curly maple, open, oblong, flared straight sides, center divider with arched top, oval cutout handle, dovetailed, small repairs, 5 1/2 in. tall by 15 1/4 in. wide by 8 1/4 in. deep. **$225**

Tray, grain-decor, original brown, pine, canted sides, pierced opening for handle, square nail construction, worn, 5 1/2 in. tall by 12 in. wide by 8 in. deep. **$275**

Tray, painted, green, canted sides, turned handle on center divider. **$150**

Tray, painted, putty, canted sides, shaped ends, divider with opening for handle, 5 in. tall by 14 in. wide by 8 in. deep...........................**$450**

Tray, painted, yellow, heart cutout handle in center divider...........**$150**

Tray, smoke-decor, canted sides, 9 in. long....................................**$850**

Tray, softwood, flared sides, center divider with oval cutout, refinished, 3 1/2 in. tall by 13 1/2 in. wide by 9 1/4 in. deep. **$75**

❖ Kraut Cutters

Also known as cabbage cutters, slaw cutters, and slaw boards, these common kitchen tools of the 19th and early 20th centuries were used to cut cabbage for use in making sauerkraut.

Small, commercial-made examples are common and are of minimal value. Industrial-size cutters are interesting because of their large size, but they generally have limited appeal. Instead, collectors look for homemade examples with interesting features, including shaped cutouts and hand-wrought hardware and blades.

Curly maple, 19 1/2 in. long, curved crest with heart cutout, old worn finish, nail hole, age crack. **$500**

Curly maple, 25 1/2 in. long, 8 in. wide, rounded top, old finish...**$350**

Softwood, 18 in. long, 6 3/4 in. wide, double arched top, single diagonal steel blade, applied molding at sides..**$60**

Walnut, 17 5/8 in. long, 4 7/8 in. wide, rounded top with heart cutout, double diagonal iron blades, applied molding......................**$525**

Walnut, 20 in. long, 8 in. wide, simple rectangular form.......................**$45**

Walnut, 20 1/2 in. long, well-shaped crest with heart cutout, molded and chip-carved detail, old finish, age crack in crest, worn from use..**$550**

Walnut, 22 in. long, 7 in. wide, well-shaped handle, chamfered edge, old patina. **$75**

Walnut, 22 7/8 in. long, 7 in. wide, large, rectangular pod-shaped top with large oval cutout handle. ...**$80**

Walnut, 23 in. long, 7 5/8 in. wide, arched top with heart cutout, single iron blade, applied strips at sides, some surface rust. **$130**

❖ Rolling Pins

Little has changed in the evolution of the rolling pin since it became a kitchen staple in the 19th century. Although they have been produced from a variety of materials over the years (including wood, glass, metal, and marble), the design has remained essentially the same. Collectors look for unusual variations and for examples with exceptional wood, such as tiger maple.

H-shaped handle, double-handled, two round turned dowels form handles, top dowel has simple tapered baluster turning with suppressed ball-shaped elements in center, bottom dowel slightly tapered with incised line designs, handles mortised into side brackets that extend down to hold rolling pin, 5 7/8 in. tall by 11 in. wide. **$185**

H-shaped handle, maple, round handle brackets at bottom with square tops, small squat ball-shaped finials, 6 in. tall by 12 in. wide.......................................**$140**

H-shaped handle, maple, ovoid-shaped handle brackets fitted with round horizontal dowel having tapered ring-turned handle, 5 in. tall by 12 5/8 in. wide. **$350**

H-shaped handle, wooden, shaped brackets on ends, turned and tapered handle with simple ring turnings, round dowel below handle with line banding in center, wear, 14 in. wide by 5 3/4 in. tall. **$250**

Traditional form, glass, free-blown, dark olive green with white spattering, rough pontil, 14 in. long, 1 3/4 in. greatest diameter. **$120**

Traditional form, glass, milk glass, maple handles, minor chips, 18 in. long. **$40**

Traditional form, stoneware, blue and white, Colonial pattern. **$1,300**

Traditional form, stoneware, blue and white, Wildflower pattern.........**$260**

Traditional form, stoneware, blue and white, Wildflower pattern, advertises "Compliments of C.N. Allen, Jr.," 8 in. long................**$450**

Traditional form, stoneware, "C.R. Kelly, General Merchandise, Floyd, Iowa," rust-color bands, minor flake,

Traditional form, circa 1870, tiger maple with strong graining, small turned knobs on both ends, minor handling wear, 15 in. by 2 in. **$200-$250**

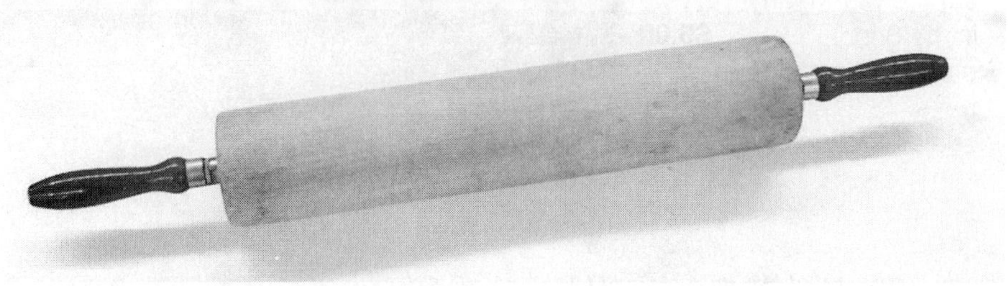

Traditional form, circa 1940s, red handles with nickel-plated fittings, 26 in. by 3 1/4 in. **$40**

15 in. long. $550

Traditional form, stoneware, Yellowware, turned maple handles, 15 in. long (excluding handles), 3 in. diameter............................$540

Traditional form, wood, attached mesh tin flour duster, 20 1/4 in. long. $240

Traditional form, wood, curly maple, pronounced curl, dark patina, 20 in. long...................................$240

Traditional form, wood, double, walnut and softwood, shaped brackets, simple ring turning, incised line designs 5 1/2 in. tall by 10 1/4 in. long. $375

Traditional form, wood, split handle and body. $40

Traditional form, wood, turned ivory handles on brass pins, one handle with scrimshaw inscription "Bark Lorietta out of Bath, Maine," one handle damaged, other missing pinhead, 19 1/2 in. long.

❖ Watt Pottery

Owned and operated by the Watt family, Watt Pottery was incorporated in 1922. Occupying the old Burley Pottery site in Crooksville, Ohio, the company's early years were devoted to manufacturing utilitarian stoneware. In 1935, the pottery dropped its crocks and churns in order to produce more modern ovenwares, and in 1949 the company began hand-decorating its products. The simple patterns and bright colors of the designs contrasted nicely with the creamy clay, resulting in a uniquely country look.

References: Sue and Dave Morris, *Watt Pottery*, Collector Books, 1998; Dennis Thompson and W. Bryce Watt, *Watt Pottery*, Schiffer Publishing, 1994.

Collectors' Clubs: Watt Collectors Association, PO Box 1995, Iowa City, IA 52244; Watt Pottery Collectors USA, PO Box 26067, Fairview Park, OH 44126.

Bowls, nesting, set of five, marked "Watt Oven Ware," tapering ribbed design with hand-painted apples and leaves, bowls measures from 9 in. to 5 in. diameter. **$450-$550/set**

Using clay that is close in color to that of the original pieces, Four Rivers Stoneware in Hazel, Kentucky, has reproduced Watt Pottery. These contemporary pieces are marked, but examples have been found with the marks ground off.

Reproduction Alert

Original Watt items have also been used to create molds that can then be used for producing reproductions that include the impressed marks found on the authentic pieces.

FYI: Most pieces of Watt ware are well marked, with large marks that often cover the bottom of the piece. The impressed phrases "Watt" and "Oven Ware U.S.A." are generally included with one or more concentric rings, although early marks consist of a script "Watt" without the rings. Additionally, most pieces have an impressed mold number for easy identification.

Bowl, Apple pattern, #7, two-leaf variation, wear..........................$75

Bowl, advertising, Apple pattern, #5, "Kinnards Dairy, Estherville, Iowa," wear. $55

Bowl, advertising, Apple pattern, #6, "1958 Becker Hardware, Janesville, Iowa."......................................$50

Bowl, advertising, Apple pattern, #6, "Bremer Oil Co." with Phillips 66 logo. $75

Bowl, advertising, Apple pattern, #63, "Anamosa Farmers Creamery," wear. $55

Bowl, advertising, Apple pattern, "Whittemore Co-op Elevator" with Phillips 66 logo, 9 in. diameter. .$75

Pie plate, advertising, Apple pattern, #33, "To A Good Cook, Frederika Co-op Creamery."....................$110

Pie plate, advertising, Autumn Foliage pattern, #33, "B&B Co-op Oil, Waverly, IA." $75

Pitcher, Apple pattern, #16, 6 1/2 in. tall. $110

Pitcher, Starflower pattern, #17, 8 in. tall. $150

Pitcher, advertising, Apple pattern, #15, "B&B Co-op Oil, Waverly, IA,"

5 1/2 in. tall................................**$75**

Pitcher, advertising, Apple pattern, #15, "Davison Hardware, Frederika, IA," 5 1/2 in. tall. **$75**

Pitcher, advertising, Apple pattern, #15, "Fecht's Service Station, Allison, Iowa," chip, 5 1/2 in. tall. **$55**

Pitcher, advertising, Apple pattern, #15, "Kalona Creamery, Arch Haberman, Old Fashioned Ice Cream," 5 1/2 in. tall. **$70**

Pitcher, advertising, Apple pattern, #15, "Lange's D-X Trucking, LaPorte City, IA," flakes, 5 1/2 in. tall. **$60**

Pitcher, advertising, Apple pattern, #15, "Fern Creamery Co.," 5 1/2 in. tall. **$150**

Pitcher, advertising, Apple pattern, #16, "Baker Lumber Co." **$90**

Spaghetti bowl, Apple pattern, #39, two-leaf variation, two cracks....**$90**

Lighting

Light sources of interest to collectors of country antiques range from 16th century rush lamps to 19th century whale oil lamps and even mid-20th century rustic chandeliers made of antlers. This section includes detailed information about a popular category for collectors, Aladdin lamps, and covers a wide variety of kerosene styles, with detailed descriptions and dates of production.

Large Arts & Crafts hanging fixture with powerful appearance, mica shades, 53 in. by 27 in. **$2,650**

Custom-made Arts & Crafts fixture, heavy cast top with all original bent slag glass, original patina. **$6,800**

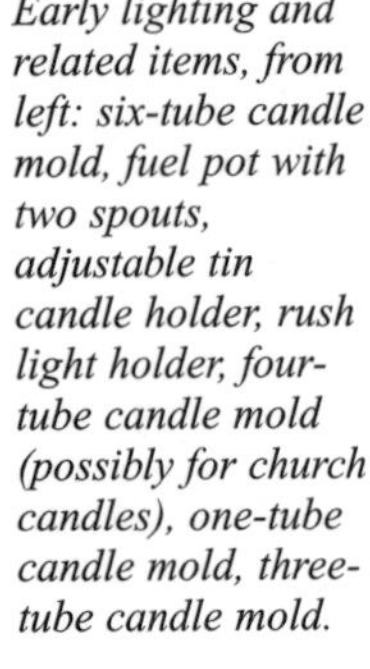

Early lighting and related items, from left: six-tube candle mold, fuel pot with two spouts, adjustable tin candle holder, rush light holder, four-tube candle mold (possibly for church candles), one-tube candle mold, three-tube candle mold.

Candleholder, circa 1780, wrought iron with scroll supports and feet, 14 in. by 6 in. **$800-$900**

Candlestick, brass, Norwegian, circa 1780, with spiral shaft, drip pan, and hand-hammered decoration in a fruit and floral motif, moderate handling wear, 9 in. by 6 in. **$950**

Carved wood candleholders made from small tree trunks, one carved and painted with the image of an eagle holding crossed flags (one the U.S. flag, the other a "Sons in Service" flag with a blue star on a red-bordered field), the second holder carved and painted with a "Sons in Service" flag and with a wood-burned inscription referring to the Army Corps of Engineers with the corps emblem, dated indistinctly, but probably during World War I, taker holder measures 9 3/4 in. by 4 in. With detail below. **$350/pair**

Candlestick, brass, Norwegian, circa 1780, with spiral shaft, no drip pan, and hand-hammered decoration in a fruit and floral motif, moderate handling wear with some cracks, 8 1/2 in. by 7 1/2 in. **$450**

Elaborate antler chandelier, circa 1940s, completely rewired, 42 in. diameter, 57 in. tall. **$6,800**

Early three-arm white metal fixture. **$2,650**

Gas "harp" style hanging lamp with deep etched crown shade, leopard on fixture body. **$1,500**

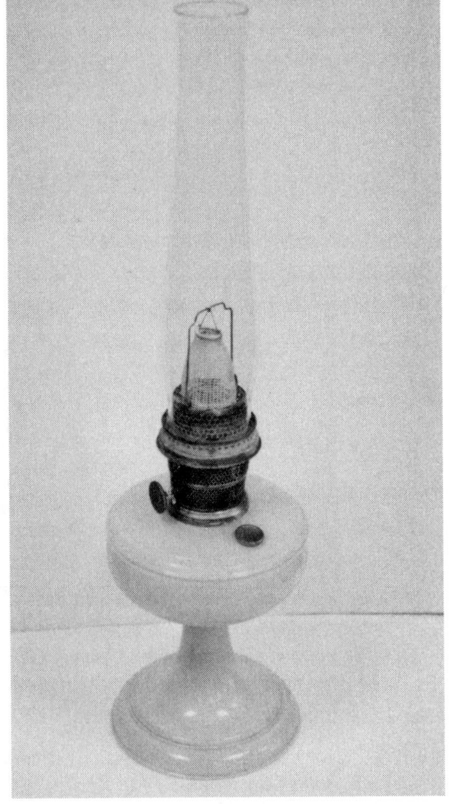

Lamp, kerosene, made by Aladdin, model 102, made circa 1932-'33, in the Venetian style, beige satin glass with new chimney, 23 1/2 in. by 6 1/2 in. **$150-$200**

Lamp, kerosene, made by Aladdin, model 23, nickel plated, old but probably not original chimney, 20 1/2 in. by 6 1/4 in. **$110-$130**

Lamp, kerosene, made by Aladdin, "Nu-Type" model B, clear glass base and fount with molded decoration, replaced burner, 12 1/2 in. by 6 1/2 in. **$100**

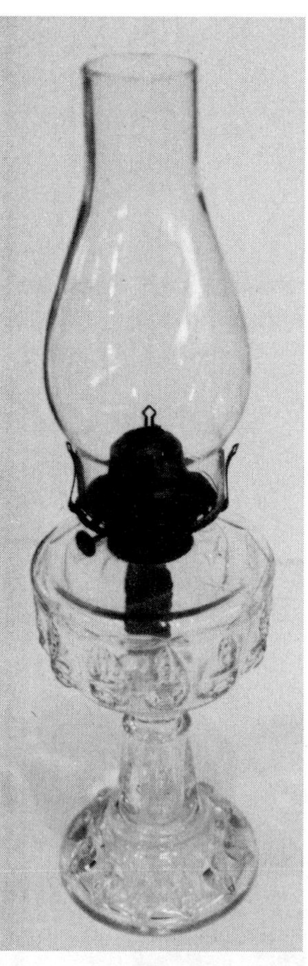

Lamp, kerosene, made by Thompson Glass Co. Ltd., Uniontown, Pa., model No. 2 (called "the torpedo"), circa 1890, clear glass base and fount with molded decoration, 18 1/2 in. by 5 1/4 in. **$160**

Lamp, kerosene, circa 1880, with elaborate amber molded-glass base with three arching columns, brass fitting connecting base with aquamarine molded-glass fount, chimney with acid-etched swans and fruit baskets, mint condition, 22 in. by 6 in. **$400**

Lamp, kerosene, circa 1880, ceramic column with hand-painted image of the actress Sarah Berhhardt (1844-1923), square spelter base, frosted glass fount with star pattern, near mint, 22 in. by 5 1/2 in. **$300**

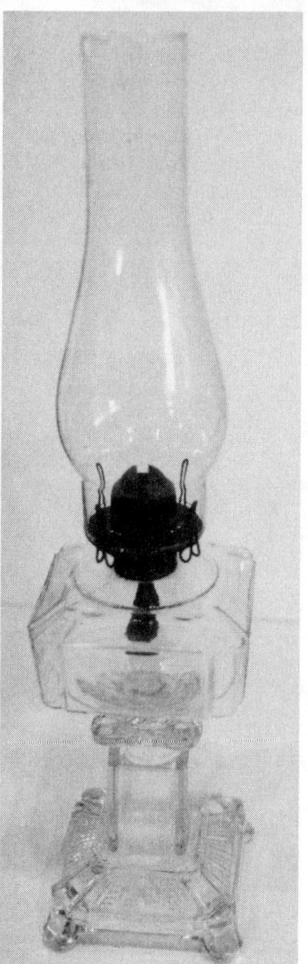

Lamp, kerosene, Ripley hollow-stem design, square clear glass base and fount with molded decoration inside, 20 in. by 4 3/4 in. **$225**

Lamp, kerosene, clear glass with simple finger ring base, 11 in. by 5 in. by 4 in. **$45**

Lamp, kerosene, with plain molded lead crystal fount and base, 13 in. by 6 1/4 in. **$50-$60**

Lamp, kerosene, with footed base and large finger ring, 13 in. by 6 in. by 4 1/2 in. **$75**

Lamp, kerosene modified for electric light, stoneware footed fount with raised scroll decoration, 18 in. by 6 1/2 in. ***$60***

Lamp base, kerosene, molded stoneware, urn form, with a brown glaze, with floral and scroll decoration, 11 in. by 6 in. **$65**

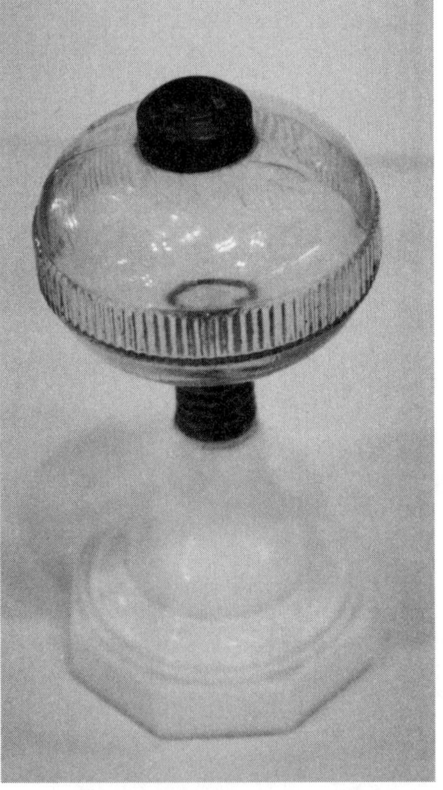
Lamp base, kerosene, circa 1850, molded milk glass base, brass screw collar and simple fount with reeded band, 8 1/2 in. by 4 1/4 in. **$225**

Parlor lamp, kerosene, circa 1880, with cast-brass base and glass column hand-painted with flowers, new replacement globe etched with wreaths and torches, 20 in. by 8 in. **$275**

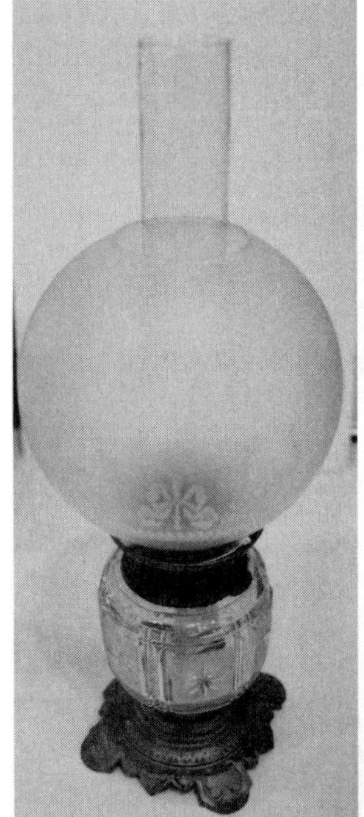
Parlor lamp, kerosene, circa 1890, with cast-brass base and clear and frosted molded glass fount with rayed stars, new replacement globe etched with wreaths and torches, 20 in by 8 in. **$225**

Parlor lamp, kerosene, circa 1880, with flared glass fount and original globe, both with transfer floral decoration and hand-painted highlights, 16 in. by 7 1/2 in. **$400**

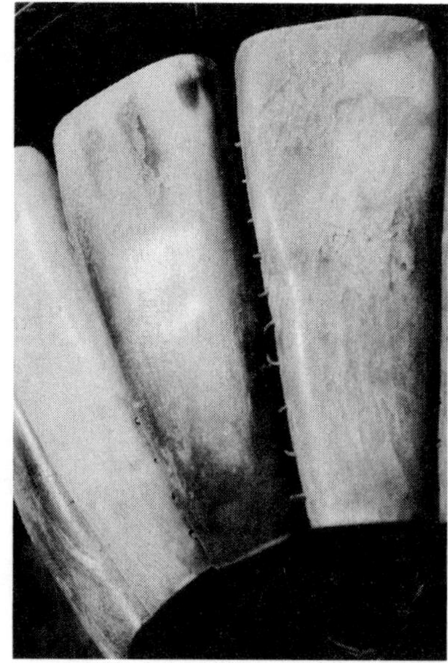

Lampshade made of molded sections of cow horn, mounted on a metal frame and held together with heavy wire, circa 1930, minor damage. 11 in. by 8 in. Details above and right. **$150-$200**

Hand-forged iron candle lantern with three glass panels, circular vents in conical top, ring holder, circa 1820, 13 in. by 6 3/4 in. by 6 in. **$300-$500**

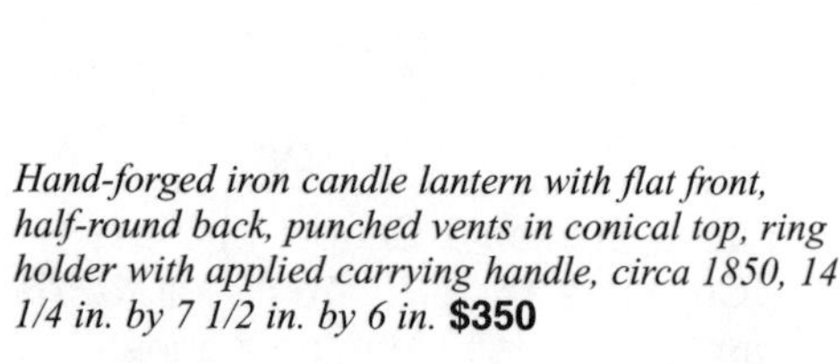

Hand-forged iron candle lantern with flat front, half-round back, punched vents in conical top, ring holder with applied carrying handle, circa 1850, 14 1/4 in. by 7 1/2 in. by 6 in. **$350**

Hand-forged iron candle lantern with shaved horn panes instead of glass, (originally called "lanthorne," hence the term lantern), with tapered vents in conical top, ring holder, French or English, circa 1750, 16 in. by 9 in. by 7 in. **$700**

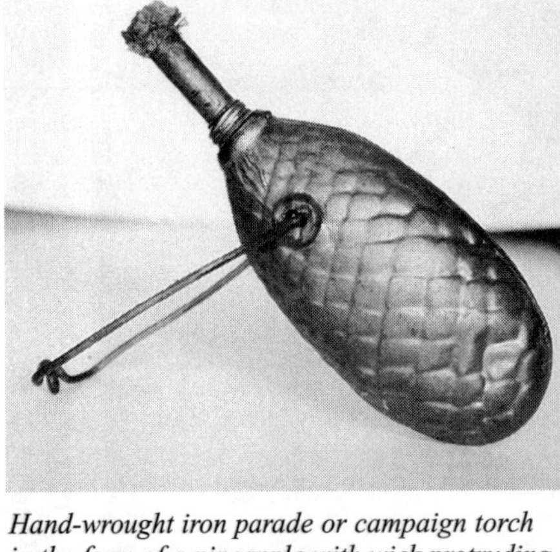

Hand-wrought iron parade or campaign torch in the form of a pineapple with wick protruding from tube in top, wire handle, often carried on poles at political rallies, old gold painted surface, burned either kerosene or whale oil, circa 1880, fully extended 9 3/4 in. by 3 in. by 3 1/4 in. **$350**

Hand-forged iron candle lantern with fluted reflector and pitcher handle, circa 1820, 9 1/4 in. by 7 in. by 5 in. **$250-$350**

*Hand-forged iron candle or whale oil lantern, French, circa 1750, with tapering vents and pierced top, wire ring holder, bull's-eye glass panes were both decorative and to diffuse light, 13 1/2 in. by 8 1/2 in by 8 1/2 in.***$500-600**

Hand-forged iron dark lantern, burned whale oil, red glass panes, 1835, supposedly carried at the age of 16 by James A. Garfield, later president of the United States, on an Erie Canal tow boat, 5 3/4 in. by 3 1/2 in. by 2 3/4 in. **$1,200**

Railroad lantern, kerosene, circa 1910, Rock Island Line, original globe and burner, well worn, size with handle down 9 1/2 in. by 7 1/2 in. **$200**

Hand-forged iron miner's candlestick called a "sticking tommy," used by miners as candle holder, could be fixed in cave wall, support timber or hung on cloth hat, circa 1840, 7 1/2 in. by 1 3/4 in. by 2 3/4 in. **$300**

Lamp, clear, Horn of Plenty, fluid lamp, Boston & Sandwich Glass Co., circa 1845-70, 10 in. tall. .**$275**

Lamp, clear, tulip font, hexagonal stem, round foot, pewter collar, minor chips, 9 in. tall. **$150**

Hand-forged iron lantern with punched decoration, early black paint, candle holder inside, early 19th century, 16 1/2 in. by 5 1/2 in. **$500**

Soldered sheet iron Christmas light in the shape of a star, with opaque white glass inserts (one missing), hole in hinged back for bulb, circa 1930, 12 1/4 in. by 12 1/2 in. by 4 1/2 in. **$150-$200**

Trench art lamp with shade made from a World War I helmet, base made from a large brass shell casing, embossed with a shield motif with thistles, and reading, "Verdun 1914," rewired, 16 in. by 12 in. **$200-$300**

Wall sconce, circa 1930s, hammered and cutout sheet steel with domed center that may have been silvered, surrounded by cutout and drilled decorations, three wrought-iron candle holders and drip pans at bottom, worn surface, overall very good condition, 20 in. by 20 in. by 6 in. **$180-$200**

Trench Art

The term "trench art" applies to items made by soldiers (and sometimes souvenirs sold to soldiers) who used primarily brass shell casings to create various items, including ashtrays, letter openers, lamps, bookends, and vases. The surfaces of the large shell casings were often worked into floral or figural decorations, and were often inscribed with the dates and places of battles. Pieces dating from America's involvement in World War I often include the initials "A.E.F.," which stands for American Expeditionary Force. Except for large and elaborate pieces, the prices for trench art have not risen as dramatically as for other forms of folk art.

Early Williamsburg-style fixture, believed to have originally been for candles, heavy brass with original finish and patina, 10 lights, overall 48 in. by 36 in. **$2,850**

Aladdin Lamps

By Darrell Kleckner
http://www.aladdincollector.com/

The 20th century had come to America, but it had yet to bring it from the age of darkness. People still lived by the flickering light of flat wick oil or kerosene lamps. The dawn of the century was about to change the lives of many people, and one company would be at the heart of bringing light into those lives. The Mantle Lamp Company of America (later to become Aladdin Industries Inc.) was about to bring America forth from its darkness with a unique product: the Aladdin mantle lamp.

Aladdin lamps were unique in the use of a round wick to provide an even, non-flickering flame, and a rare earth mantle that glowed to produce the light of a 60 watt lightbulb when heated by the flame from the kerosene lamp. The difference between the light of the Aladdin lamps and any other oil or kerosene lamp was so great that the company offered a $1,000 reward to any person who could show them an oil lamp that could equal its light. The reward was never collected, and by the early 1930s seven million Aladdins had been sold.

Aladdin was also one of the pioneers in modern sales techniques and would allow customers to trade in their old oil lamps on new Aladdin lamps. They were also one of the first companies to use radio as an advertising medium in the Midwest. They paid Henry Field, who owned the Henry Field Seed Company of Shenandoah, Iowa, along with a 1,000-watt station KFNF, $500 to talk about their lamp on his "Evening Letterbasket" program. Included in the program was a cash offer of $25 for the best 10-word slogan submitted. The response was 2,200 letters, and 800 of those didn't even submit a slogan—they just wanted more information on the lamp! As radio grew so did Aladdin's coverage until it covered the nation.

Aladdin lamps were manufactured in a wide variety of styles. The first were made of metal, either brass or nickel-plated brass. There were several models of the metal lamps including table lamps, bracket lamps, and some very unusual hanging lamps. The 1930s and '40s saw lamps made of colored glass, and included the now highly collected ruby crystal and cobalt blue tall Lincoln drape Aladdin lamps. Another that became the best-selling lamp in Aladdin's history was the Alacite tall Lincoln drape. Alacite was a unique trademark of Aladdin and resembled ivory in its color and texture. Moonstone glass was also unique to Aladdin lamps and was so named because the glass itself seemed to glow like the pale moon. The glowing quality of moonstone is as popular with collectors today as it was with customers in the 1930s.

Aladdin also manufactured many styles of electric lamps.

• • •

Victor Samuel Johnson (1882-1943) was born in Nebraska and grew up on a farm there. As a young schoolboy, he had to study by the flickering light of a flat-wick kerosene lamp. In spite of this, he learned his lessons well and became a bookkeeper and salesman for the Iowa Soap Company in Burlington.

In 1905 he saw a German lamp that made superior light with the use of a cone shaped "mantle" that was suspended above the lamp's flame. The flame heated the mantle, causing it to glow and produce a bright white light. The German lamp also made use of a round wick and a center draft tube that allowed an even-burning flame that did not flicker.

It did not take Victor long to realize the sales potential of such a lamp. In 1908 he incorporated The Mantle Lamp Company of America and in early 1909 the first Aladdin lamp was introduced to America.

The name Aladdin was actually derived from the story of Aladdin and his magic lamp in which old lamps were offered for new. One of the sales programs of the company provided a trade allowance for old lamps, and many Aladdin lamps were given away as part of their introduction to the public.

As The Mantle Lamp Company of America grew from the sales of the Aladdin lamps, it also diversified into many other products. In 1919 it formed a subdivision called Aladdin Industries Inc. to market its diverse product line. In 1949 The Mantle Lamp Company became known as Aladdin Industries Inc. This firm is still producing a variety of products, but is probably best known for the Aladdin thermos products it manufactures. It still produces and sells Aladdin kerosene lamps.

It is hard for us to think back to a time without television, VCRs, computers, and electrical appliances. Most of us, however, have experienced a power outage at one time or another and have been made keenly aware of our pampered lifestyles. In the dark of a power outage, what would the light of a 60-watt light bulb mean to you? Under those conditions you experienced just a small hint of what the Aladdin mantle lamp meant to those who bought them. The Aladdin lamp with its "rare earth oxide mantle" not only brought a light into the darkness, it changed the lives of millions of people.

Alacite, Developed in 1938

Alacite glass was the creation of Henry Hellmers, and he described it as "an ivory opal glass." It was described in Aladdin advertising material as "... a startlingly beautiful lamp base, and pedestal material, which resembles many of the semi-precious mineralites in texture, and has much of the softness and tone of tusk (genuine ivory)—the only color in which it is available."

Originally Alacite glass contained uranium oxide as a coloring agent, but the use of uranium oxide was banned by the government in 1942. You will often hear the terms "old formula" and "new formula" used in reference to lamps made of Alacite. The old formula contained the uranium oxide and will glow a yellow-green color under a black light, while the new formula without the uranium oxide will not. Uranium oxide was also a constituent of yellow moonstone and some green Washington Drape lamps. Both will glow brightly under black light.

Aladdin manufactured many other products from Alacite glass, including ashtrays, candy dishes, powder dishes, wall tiles, candleholders, egg plates, wall switch-plates, tissue box covers, vase bookends, wall vases, and figurines. Small quantities of dishware items were made from it as well, but a fault of Alacite is that it is quite brittle, making dishware items vulnerable to breakage.

All ivory glass is not Alacite, nor was it all made by Aladdin. Many other companies manufactured items in a glass that very closely resembled Alacite. Most, but not all, Alacite made by Aladdin was marked with the name Aladdin or with an A in the glass.

The most popular Aladdin lamp ever sold was the Alacite tall Lincoln drape, which speaks well of the appeal of Alacite glass! Several Aladdin lamps and founts were made of Alacite and are still favorites of many collectors.

Beehive, 1937 and 1938

The beehive lamp family is composed of six lamps. The white moonstone glass lamp is extremely rare. Probably the most sought-after lamp in this family is the ruby crystal beehive. The color of the ruby lamps can very from quite light with an amber cast to very dark red that almost appears black. The darker the red, the more it seems to appeal to collectors.

Bracket and Fount Lamps

Aladdin produced many different types of hanging and bracket lamps. Most of the metal table lamps were also available in hanging and bracket models. While the hanging and table lamps were most noted for style and elegance, the bracket lamps excelled in simplicity and practicality. Some were specialized in their use. One was called a "caboose" lamp. As the name implies it was used in the cabooses of trains to provide light. The bracket was designed to absorb the rocking and swaying of the train car, allowing both vertical and horizontal movement of the lamp to absorb sudden jolts. The shade was also a specialty item, having a heat shield attached to the inside surface that covered half its circumference. This helped to shield the wooden wall of the railroad car from the heat generated by the lamp. It is also believed that the "Lox-On" chimney was developed out of the need for a chimney on the caboose lamp that would not work loose from the motion of the train. The bracket also had a pair of clamps that were used to attach the fount securely into the bracket. The bracket also contained a spring clip that was used to retain a wick trimmer. While it may not have been very stylish, the caboose lamp was a marvel of ingenuity.

Cathedral, 1934

There are eight lamps in the Cathedral family. The crystal lamps are: green, amber, and clear, while the moonstone lamps include white, rose, "flesh," apple green, and jade green. The rose moonstone is pink, while the flesh moonstone is quite pale and has an amber cast to it. The jade green moonstone has a bluish tint, while the apple green moonstone has a yellow tint.

A fault shared with the Colonial lamps is the sensitivity of the fused glass joint between the bowl (fount) and the foot. This joint is susceptible to temperature changes, stress, and bumps. Care must be taken when handling these Aladdin lamps to avoid cracking them at the joint. It is also not advisable to set them in direct sunlight where they will heat up, or in areas that are too cool, such as basements or near air conditioning ducts.

Another problem with the Cathedral lamps is that the recessed oil-fill caps often become frozen with age and refuse to unscrew from the lamp. Too much force applied in trying to free the oil-fill cap can cause the glue holding the female threads to give and the assembly to separate from the fount, or worse, the glass fount itself will crack or break. Many of these lamps are found minus the oil cap and threads from this mistake.

Colonial, 1933

The Colonial Aladdin lamps have a hobnail design that runs through the glass of the oil reservoir (fount). For this reason they are often referred to as "hobnail" lamps rather than by their rightful Colonial name. The bowl and foot of these lamps were fused together when the glass was hot, and this joint is the weak spot of the lamp. Temperature changes caused by such things as cleaning the lamp in hot water, or bringing it from the cold into a warm house, can cause the joint to crack. Care must be taken with the Aladdin Colonial lamps not to bump or stress the joint.

Corinthian, 1935 and 1936

The Corinthian family of Aladdin lamps is the largest and most diverse group. It includes 16 different lamps. The solid colors include amber, green, and clear crystal along with white, apple green, jade green, and rose moonstone. The white moonstone and clear crystal founts were then used to create combinations consisting of: clear fount/green foot, clear fount/amber foot, white moonstone fount/rose moonstone foot, and white moonstone fount/jade green foot. A black crystal foot was also used to create clear fount/black foot and white moonstone fount/black foot combinations. This so-called "black crystal" base, when held up to a strong light source, may reveal a very dark shade of amethyst, cobalt, green, or red. To make the group even more diverse, there were three different styles of metal connectors used to join the founts to the feet. Two were "white metal" connectors of slightly different design, while the third was a smooth brass connector. The lamps were molded in two pieces and then glued together with the aid of the metal connectors between the fount and the foot. The glue used in the process is the inherent weakness in this family due to the fact that it is heat sensitive. If left in the sun and allowed to heat up, the glue will soften, which can allow the glass fount and foot to separate when moved, often with disastrous results to one or both parts.

Also, the foot often has a thin layer of glass running around the bottom edge. This glass "flash" should have been ground off in finishing at the factory but was often left on, creating an area that is very easily chipped. Some bases do appear to have been ground smooth and are the ones you will most often find without chips. You will recognize this problem area easily by running your finger along the edge of the base—if it feels sharp, it has not been ground. On close inspection you will see the thin jagged edge protruding from the base. If you should find a good lamp that has this troublesome area, be careful not to bump the edge when setting the lamp down, as this is what causes most chips.)

Diamond Quilt, 1937

The moonstone diamond quilt lamp gets its name from the pattern on the oil fount. It is made up of crisscross

lines that bisect the glass into a series of raised diamonds. The foot and oil fount are made in separate pieces and then glued together with the use of a brass connector.

Floor Lamps

The first Aladdin floor lamp was model 6, style 150 manufactured in 1915. It was fitted with a silk shade and sold for $60. Very few were sold and the remaining stock was eventually converted to electric and sold in cities to those who could afford the extravagant price. The Mantle Lamp Company (predecessor to "Aladdin"), tried marketing the kerosene floor lamp again in 1928 with a model number 12 in style 1250. Two big factors contributed to its success. One was the introduction of colorful paper shades. The other was a price that most people could afford!

Many new styles of floor lamps by Aladdin were created over the next 24 years, along with some striking paper shades to adorn them. Not all the styles were cataloged by Aladdin, so collectors can still find examples of kerosene floor lamps that are "unlisted." This came about due to the fact that Aladdin manufactured both kerosene and electric floor lamps at the same time, and parts were sometimes interchanged between the two. The last kerosene floor lamps to be manufactured by Aladdin left the factory in 1952.

While very few Aladdin collectors specialize in the floor lamps alone, it seems that most collectors of Aladdin table and hanging lamps do find room for examples of the floor lamps in their collections. The floor lamps can be quite hard to find in original condition due to the fact that many of them had painted finishes. Collectors often repaint the floor lamps in an attempt to restore their original color. You will also find that many of the restored lamps will also have reproduction shades as well.

Hanging Lamps

Hanging lamps were sold along with the table lamps. Many of the early metal lamp founts were used both on table lamps and in a hanging frame. The hanging Aladdin lamps often became the centerpiece of the rooms they occupied. While the kerosene lamp was simple in design and function, the hand-painted shades added beauty to that functionality. Oil lamps of this era were not just sources of light, but highlights of decor to many homes.

Aladdin manufactured a wide variety of kerosene lamps. This is a model No. 1214 hanging lamp with a 616s shade. The shade depicts a rural scene of a grain mill with waterwheel. Making it even more unusual is the fact that part of the scene is painted on the inside of the shade and part on the outside. These shades are quite fragile and finding one that is not cracked or chipped can be quite challenging.

This is another model 1214 hanging lamp with a 620s shade. The scene is of a windmill on a point of land surrounded by water. This shade also has part of the scene painted on the inside of the lamp and part on the outside.

This model No. 11 hanging lamp is complete with the 516 shade. This shade was also used on models 9 and 10 hanging lamps. The hardest item to find on hanging lamps is the smoke bell because it is easily detached and was often lost. Finding a hanging lamp with original shade, smoke bell, and correct flame spreader is a task that requires patience.

This model-B "tilt-frame" hanging lamp was unique in the fact that the metal ring that holds the fount was designed to tilt 90 degrees. This made filling or removing the oil fount easier. The lamp shown here is complete with an original 716 glass shade and smoke bell. The tilt-frame lamps were also sold with model 12 burners and parchment shades.

Majestic, 1935 and 1936

The moonstone Majestic lamps were offered in green, rose, and white moonstone, and although they appear quite grand, the finish on the metal base of these Aladdin lamps is fragile and easily worn. Very few of these lamps can be found with the original finish intact.

Metal Table Lamps

The Aladdin metal table lamps were the beginning of the great era of Aladdin. In 1908 sales began with the Practicus (also spelled Praktus) table lamp. This lamp was not manufactured in America but was imported from Germany. The Mantle Lamp Company sold the No. 2 and No.3 Practicus lamps. The No.3 Practicus is shown in sales literature and has a "snowflake" emblem on the wick-raiser knob.

Following the sales of the Practicus, lamps were marketed by model numbers, and between May 1909 and April 1935, 12 different models were sold. The brass lamps (lamp, bowl, and burner) for models 1 through 12, and the burners for Nu-Type A, Nu-Type B, and C, were made by Plume and Atwood Manufacturing Company (P&A) of Waterbury, Connecticut. Beginning with Model 5, the model number or letter was placed on the wick-raiser knob of Aladdin lamps. The model number also appears on the flame spreader for models 4 through 11.

Model 7 and 8 Table Lamps, 1919-1920

One question a new collector is apt to ask is, "What is the difference between the model No. 7 and model No. 8 Aladdin lamps?" The oil-fill caps on these lamps are not in the same location. The cap on the No. 7 is closer to the edge of the fount, while the cap on the No. 8 is closer to the burner.

Orientale, 1935 and 1936

The all-metal Aladdin Orientale lamps can be found in both painted and plated versions. There are five members of this group: Green Lacquer with Silver Plated trim, Ivory Lacquer with Rose Gold trim, Rose Gold plate (shown), Silver Plate, and Oxidized Bronze Plate.

The metal base on the lamp is threaded and screws onto the fount, and is then glued. The finishes on these lamps were not made to stand the test of time, and very few can be found with the original finish still intact. Many of the lamps have been repainted or plated by collectors.

Queen, 1937-1939

Like the Majestic lamps, the Aladdin Queen lamps also have a moonstone fount and metal base. The finish on their metal bases is quite delicate. Very few of these lamps can be found with the original finish intact.

There are four lamps in this group. The moonstone founts were offered in three colors: green, rose, and white. The green and rose moonstone lamps were offered only with a silver base, while the white moonstone fount was offered with both silver and bronze bases.

Short Lincoln Drape, 1939

The short and tall Lincoln drape lamps have been reproduced by other manufacturers. They have been reproduced in a variety of colors, but the new lamps are easily recognized by the presence of a metal collar where the burner screws into the lamp. Old lamps do not have this collar. Their burner threads are metal but are glued inside the lamp with no part of them visible from the outside.

There is also a clear crystal lamp in this series, however, it is extremely rare. Amber lamps can also be found with an opal quality that makes the amber color appear to be cloudy or milky. Some of the early lamps have an oversized foot, possibly modified from the "Solitaire" mold.

A Solitaire foot can be found on some of the early short Lincoln drape lamps. There is a definite stair step and the flat shoulder it creates in the glass foot. The foot found on most short Lincoln drape lamps is much more rounded from top to bottom. The stair step and flat shoulder are the things to look for when trying to identify if a short Lincoln drape has the Solitaire foot. While the Solitaire foot is also larger in diameter than the normal foot, this is not readily apparent without measuring the lamp or comparing it to another.

Simplicity, 1948 to 1953

The Aladdin Simplicity lamps, although colorful, have fragile finishes. The lamp known as a "Decalcomania" has a decal of flowers on the fount, and the top of the foot is accented with a gold band (paint). Other Simplicity lamps have painted finishes, which were applied to the outside of the glass lamps.

Care must be taken in cleaning these Aladdin lamps since the paint can be easily damaged with harsh cleansers. If the paint has absorbed too much dirt and grime over the years, the odds of restoring it by cleaning are very slim. The paint that Aladdin used on these lamps varied in shade, especially on the green and rose colored lamps. They can run from almost pastel to quite dark, with the darker lamps being the more desirable. Scratches can also be a problem with the painted finishes and detract from desirability. Luckily, due to the rounded surfaces on these lamps, they are not easily chipped, so while the paint may not be in the best of shape, the lamps themselves usually are.

Solitaire, 1938

While the white moonstone Solitaire is a handsome lamp, only 1,000 of them were ever produced. The bowl design is believed to be a predecessor of the Lincoln drape. The earlier lamps have flat panels in the design around the top edge (shoulder) of the foot. The mold was later modified by smoothing out these flat panels to create a smooth shoulder. No printed sales literature has ever been found on these Aladdin lamps, making their distribution a mystery.

Tall Lincoln Drape, 1940 to 1949

The tall Lincoln drape lamps are a favorite with collectors, and the Alacite tall Lincoln drape was the most popular kerosene lamp in Aladdin's history. Aladdin also produced a clear crystal tall Lincoln drape that is quite rare. It is believed that the clear crystal lamps were never sold to the public. The few that have been discovered have come from Iowa and Illinois, and their means of distribution remains a mystery.

Color is a big consideration in the red and blue lamps. The darker the ruby red or cobalt blue, the more sought after they become.

The old lamps were made in one piece, while the bowl and foot of the newer lamps were molded separately and then glued together. The joint is visible just above the filigree design on the pedestal. The angle of the oil fill cap and the pattern on the underside of the foot all provide ways of verifying their authenticity.

The Alacite lamps used two different formulas. Those produced prior to World War II contained uranium in the glass formula, which was removed due to regulations imposed by the government. The old formula Alacite glass will glow yellow or green when exposed to a black light while the new formula lamps show purple or blue.

Treasure, 1937 to 1953

In 1937 and 1938, the Aladdin Treasure lamps were the highest-priced lamps in the entire kerosene line! The metal Treasure had three finishes: chromium plate, nickel plate, and oxidized bronze plate. Many new collectors find it difficult to distinguish the chromium lamps from the nickel. The chromium lamp has a blue luster to the finish (the same as chrome on a car), while the nickel finish will exhibit a yellow luster that is not as bright as the chromium lamp.

One odd lamp that should belong to this family is the "Nashville Treasure." It has the characteristic oil fount of the Treasure lamp combined with the foot of a model 12 table lamp. A wide, heavy weight along with a felt pad was added to the 12's foot. It uses the "Nashville" model-b burner, and both burner and base were oxidized bronze.

Vase Lamps, 1930 to 1935

The Aladdin vase lamps consist of a hollow glass vase with a removable oil pot. The glass is quite fragile and is easily chipped or cracked. Removing and replacing the oil pot when filling or cleaning often leads to chipping at the vase's upper edge. These Aladdin lamps came in a wide variety of finishes and were most often sold with decorative parchment shades. There were three different heights: 12 inches, 10 inches, and 8 1/2 inches. The shorter "Florentine" lamps were made in 1935 and are highly sought by collectors. Although many vase lamps were sold in the 1930s era, very few can be found in perfect condition.

Venetian, 1932 and 1933

The Venetian is another two-piece glass lamp. The painted styles have hidden threaded metal connectors that join the fount and foot. The threads were covered with glue and then the two pieces were screwed together. As with the Aladdin Simplicity lamps, the paint was applied to the outside of the glass and is easily scratched or tarnished.

The threads for the oil-fill caps are also recessed on these Aladdin lamps, and the cap screws down into the fount. Like the Cathedral, force should not be used to try to free an oil-fill cap that is stuck in the lamp. The threads can give, causing the whole assembly to come out, or the glass fount itself may crack or break.

Another troublesome area is the edge of the base. It is very thin and easily chipped. When moving these lamps, be very careful not to bump this fragile area.

The clear crystal lamps were never sold in the United States, but were shipped to Canada. These lamps can be found both fused (referred to as one piece) and with a connector to join the fount and foot. The connector can be either metal or with the

threads molded into the glass. Again, care must be taken on those that are fused, to not to cause stress at the joint or it can easily crack.

Vertique, Moonstone, 1938

The moonstone name denotes the way the glass appears to glow like the light of the moon, and the name Vertique refers to the vertical ridges of the bowl.

There are a couple of unique characteristics to these Aladdin lamps. One is the intense glow the "yellow" Vertique displays under a black light. This is due to the use of uranium as a coloring agent in the glass.

Another characteristic of Aladdin Vertique lamps is that they can be found with what appears to be a foot from the Aladdin Quilt lamp. While quite similar in their design, there is a small difference. The Vertique foot has a smooth ring of glass running around the rim of the foot, just prior to the diamond design. On the Quilt foot the diamond pattern carries right to the edge of the foot. Vertique lamps found with the Quilt foot design were thought to be lamps that had been repaired and the feet exchanged. That idea was disproved when someone found a yellow Vertique lamp with a foot identical to the Quilt. Since the Aladdin Quilt lamps were never produced in yellow moonstone, this could only mean that a Quilt mold was used to make feet for some Vertique lamps.

Victoria, 1947

The Victoria is unique in being the only Aladdin kerosene lamp made of porcelain china. The flowers on the Victoria are a decal and may be found in two variations. Gold paint was used to accent the leaves on the side of the lamp as well as the three bands on the pedestal. The paint is quite fragile, causing portions of the gold bands to be worn through from handling.

Washington Drape, Plain Stem, 1941 to 1953

The Washington drape is probably the most recognized of Aladdin lamps. It was produced with four different bases and had two different designs in the glass on the base. One pattern is referred to as "crows foot," which resembles a three-toed bird footprint. The other is the "V" pattern being made up of two lines that seem to form a band around the foot.

Earlier variations include the round base, 1939; filigree pedestal, 1940; and the bell stem, 1941.

Where can I find it?

Architectural Emporium
207 Adams Ave.
Canonsburg, PA 15317
(724) 746-4301
http://www.architectural-emporium.com/
sales@architectural-emporium.com

Darrell Kleckner
http://www.aladdincollector.com/

Aladdin Knights
http://www.aladdinknights.org/

John Kruesel's General Merchandise
22 Third St. SW
Rochester, MN 55902
(507) 289-8049
www.kruesel.com

Mirrors

Practically unknown before the 17th century, mirrors are taken for granted today. The earliest American mirrors were in the Queen Anne style, made from about 1710 to 1765. Boston, New York, Philadelphia, Baltimore, and Charleston were important centers for mirror production during the 1700s. By the 19th century, however, production had spread widely.

❖ Architectural

Architectural, two-section, mahogany and mahogany veneer, old dark finish, reeded columns, corner blocks and molded cornice, worn glass, top glass with replaced reverse-painted scene of house, trees and fence, some molding replaced, repairs, 36 1/2 in. tall by 19 3/4 in. wide........................**$350**

Architectural, two-section, pine, old refinishing, country style, reeded pilasters, cove-molded cornice, original reverse-painted top section shows steamer "Ohio," pieced repairs at cornice...................**$625**

Architectural, two-section, pine, old refinishing, reeded columns, reverse-painted castle with landscape, minor edge damage, flaking to painting and silvering, restored moldings, 21 3/4 in. tall by 13 in. wide..............................**$225**

❖ Chippendale

Chippendale, scroll, hanging, 19 1/2 in. tall by 12 1/4 in. wide, cherry, old finish, mirror glass probably original, repairs and restoration to ears and scroll work, worn silvering.................................**$450**

Chippendale, scroll, hanging, 20 in. tall by 12 in. wide, mahogany, Chippendale style, molded frame, worn silvering on glass, 20th century. **$100**

Chippendale, scroll, hanging, 20 1/4 in. tall by 11 3/4 in. wide, mahogany, Chippendale style, old crazed varnish finish, 19th century. **$325**

Chippendale, scroll, hanging, 21 3/4 in. tall by 12 3/4 in. wide, mahogany and mahogany veneer, Chippendale style, refinished, silvering darkened, some age but not period..............................**$350**

Chippendale, scroll, hanging, 24 1/2 in. tall by 13 3/4 in. wide, walnut, gilded composition, Prince of Wales feather in crest, refinished, two ears ended out, glass replaced. **$400**

Chippendale, scroll, hanging, 24 5/8 in. tall by 14 3/4 in. wide, mahogany veneer on pine, glass with gilded liner, molded frame, ornate scrolled ears and crest, phoenix bird crest, veneer repairs, chips on inner liner, backboard replaced. **$400**

Chippendale, scroll, hanging, 26 in. tall by 14 in. wide, mahogany, applied eagle in old regilding, molded frame, refinished, age cracks, one ear reglued, silvering worn. **$1,100**

Chippendale, scroll, hanging, 36 1/2 in. tall by 20 in. wide, mahogany veneer on pine, scrolled framework, banded inlay, figured veneer on inner liner, refinished, restoration. **$425**

Chippendale, scroll, hanging, 42 in. tall by 23 1/4 in. wide, mahogany veneer on pine, eagle and molded liner regilded, refinished, restoration. **$900**

Chippendale, scroll, hanging, 45 in. tall by 21 in. wide, curly maple, good figure, Chippendale style, old finish, elaborate scrolls on crest, base and ears, one ear cracked and one small piece missing, worn silvering, early 20th century. ...**$675**

❖ Courting

Courting, hardwood veneer, old refinishing, reverse-painted rose on white ground in crest, minor edge damage, worn silvering, 12 3/8 in. tall by 7 3/4 in. wide. **$725**

Courting, molded rectangular frame, shaped crest enclosing reverse-painted glass panels, etched mirror glass with leaping stag, northern European, late 18th century, 18 1/2 in. tall by 11 1/4 in. wide.......**$3,800**

❖ Dressing

Dressing, cherry and curly maple, two drawers, turned posts, restoration, 27 1/2 in. tall by 30 in. wide, 11 3/4 in. deep..............**$375**

Dressing, Sheraton, three drawers, shield-shaped mirror, inlaid, 25 in. tall. **$350**

❖ Empire

Empire, hanging, two-section, 27 in. tall by 13 in. wide, half-turned pilaster frame in old black and gold paint, reverse-painted round scene of woman on stage, touchup repairs, old replaced mirror glass. **$200**

Empire, hanging, two-section, 31 3/4 in. tall by 15 3/4 in. wide, split columns and corner blocks, old black and gold repaint, old reverse painting on glass showing basket of fruit is probably original but with over-painting on edges, mirror replaced. **$120**

Empire, hanging, two-section, 38 1/2 in. tall by 22 3/4 in. wide, architectural, turned half columns on sides/bottom, worn original

Mirror, swivel, on elaborately carved stand whose motifs include stylized flowers, squares in circles, acorns and oak leaves, diamonds and stars; large turned and carved columns support mirror, which is held in place by brass thumb screws; rectangular base has recessed area in middle, and front of base has five small inset mirrors, three of which have scalloped frames; bun feet, overall red stain finish, signed and dated 1879 inside bottom of base, minor wear, 41 in. by 31 in. by 14 in. Detail at right. **$800-$1,000**

gilding, "James Todd, Looking Glasses, Portland (Maine)" paper label, top glass cracked. **$575**

❖ Federal

Federal, hanging, two-section, 22 1/2 in. tall by 12 in. wide, Federal style, black and gold half turnings, stamped tin rosettes, replacement reverse-painted ship "Constitution," flakes to silvering. **$525**

Federal, hanging, two-section, 34 in. tall by 17 1/2 in. wide, mahogany, carved, old dark finish, half-turned pilasters, leaf carvings, ring-turned dividers, reeding at base, applied carving and borders on crest, scalloped top, acorn drops......**$300**

Federal, hanging, two-section, 40 1/4 in. tall by 21 1/2 in. wide, two-tone gilding on half turnings, molded liner, gold painted rosettes in corners, reverse-painted glass of woman gathering flowers, gilt cornucopias in corners, paint in the border heavily crazed and flaking, few flakes in center, overall wear, mirror has worn silvering.........**$800**

Federal, hanging, two-section, 41 5/8 in. tall by 22 1/2 in. wide, mahogany and mahogany veneer, original dark finish, molded base, reeded stiles, cove-molded cornice, beveled mirror at bottom, original painted scene on top shows lady by anchor on the shore with ships in the distance, crack in top corner, touchups, small sections of base molding missing. **$225**

Federal, hanging, two-section, 42 1/2 in. tall by 19 in. wide, mahogany, Boston, circa 1820, molded cornice, frieze of applied scroll and flanking urns of flowers, tablet showing sailboat and cottages, flanked by half columns, old finish. **$1,200**

❖ Miscellaneous

Miscellaneous, hanging, two-part, mahogany flame veneer frame, old crazed finish, original reverse-painted top section shows basket of fruit in red, yellow, green, black and white, original mirror, back with partial label, flaking, 33 3/8 in. tall by 18 1/4 in. wide. **$250**

Mirror frame, circa 1930, pine, with large rounded corners and decorated along the edges with spools, minor handling wear, original varnished surface, mirror probably a later replacement, 17 in. by 15 1/2 in. by 1 1/2 in. **$150**

Miscellaneous, hanging, curly maple, frame and liner, 20th century, 17 1/2 in. tall by 27 1/2 in. wide. ..**$225**

Miscellaneous, hanging, curly maple, molded frame, good detail, old finish, 30 1/2 in. tall by 20 3/4 in. wide....................................**$1,750**

Miscellaneous, hanging, painted, original mustard with brown vinegar sponging, mirror glass and back replaced, 16 1/4 in. tall by 12 1/4 in. wide...................................**$325**

Miscellaneous, hanging, tramp art frame, dark finish over varnish, stepped saw-tooth border, stacked geometric designs, 15 in. tall by 17 1/2 in. wide.............................**$275**

Miscellaneous, hanging, walnut, scrolled crest, rectangular mirror within veneered molded surround, English or American, circa 1740, replaced glass, 21 1/2 in. tall by 12 in. wide................................**$1,300**

❖ Queen Anne

Queen Anne, hanging, mahogany, molded frame, old finish, replaced mirror glass, 11 1/4 in. tall by 10 in. wide..**$600**

Queen Anne, hanging, mahogany veneer on pine, old refinishing, scrolled crest, base and ears, molded frame, gilded liner, pierced and carved bird on crest, regilded, 34 in. tall by 19 in. wide.......**$1,350**

Queen Anne, hanging, pine, original black floral decor on red ground, molded frame, scalloped crest with original backboard, typewritten provenance of owners 1826-1941, minor age crack, silvering worn, 21 1/2 in. tall by 11 1/2 in. wide.**$3,250**

Queen Anne, hanging, pine, applied mahogany veneer, old refinish, two-section, lower section with beveled edge, applied veneer molded with a scalloped liner at top, top crest scalloped and scrolled, narrow piece of mirror glass missing, one corner glued,

Queen Anne, hanging, walnut, English, early 18th century, scrolled crest, shaped molded frame, scrolled bracket containing beveled mirror, minor imperfections, 33 1/2 in. tall by 14 1/2 in. wide. **$3,250**
Courtesy Skinner Auctioneers & Appraisers of Antiques & Fine Arts, Boston and Bolton, Massachusetts

found in Hartford, Connecticut, 44 in. tall by 17 1/2 in. wide.......**$2,250**

Queen Anne, hanging, pine with mahogany veneer, raised molded frame, gilded liner, ornate scalloped crest with pierce-carved and gilded leaf design, old worn finish, veneer restoration, small chips, 45 1/2 in. tall by 16 7/8 in. wide....................................**$5,100**

Queen Anne, hanging, rosewood veneer on pine, old finish, scalloped base, scrolled ears and crest, carved shell at center, molded liner with gilding, two ears replaced with veneer repairs, regilded, 25 1/4 in. tall by 16 3/8 in. wide..**$525**

Queen Anne, hanging, walnut veneer, English, circa 1740-1760, scrolled crest above rectangular molded frame, gilt liner, old refinish, minor imperfections, 39 in. tall by 16 1/2 in. wide. **$2,100**

❖ Shaving

Shaving, Federal bow-front, mahogany veneer on pine, turned feet, facade with banded inlay, one dovetailed drawer, beaded edge posts, adjustable mirror, veneer damage, replaced pulls, glass cracked, 16 in. tall by 14 1/4 in. wide, 6 3/4 in. deep................**$175**

Shaving, mahogany veneer on pine, line inlay, bow-front case, turned feet, two drawers, adjustable mirror with turned posts, country style, repairs, replacements, 23 1/2 in. tall by 18 1/2 in. wide, 7 1/2 in. deep......................................**$150**

Shaving, mustard paint, dark red trim, carved and pierced frame with open scrollwork, small shaped shelf at top, two half-barrel-shaped holders flank arched mirror, lower comb tray, cracks, wear, 21 1/2 in. tall by 10 1/2 in. wide. **$425**

❖ Transitional

Transitional, hanging, Chippendale to Hepplewhite, mahogany veneer over pine, well-detailed scroll framework, inner liner with band inlay, refinished, replaced glass, bottom altered, old restorations, 41 1/2 in. tall by 22 in. wide..........**$475**

Mocha

Named for the similar markings found on mocha quartz, mocha-decorated creamware and yellowware was made by numerous Staffordshire potteries for export to North America. Produced from the late 18th century to the late 19th century, the mocha decorations were the result of a simple chemical reaction. Tobacco or hops were added to colored pigment of brown, black, blue, or green in order to give it an acid nature. When this acidic colorant was then applied to an alkaline ground color, the ensuing capillary action of the slip resulted in delicate mocha designs. In addition to feathery Seaweed designs, mocha wares are also found with Cat's Eye and Earthworm patterns.

Collecting Hint: Marked pieces of mocha ware are extremely rare.

Bowl, Seaweed decor in blue, white band, blue stripes, footed, crazing, 6 1/2 in. tall by 14 in. diameter. **$550**

Bowl, Seaweed decor in black, brown band, white stripes, footed, 2 7/8 in. tall by 4 in. diameter. **$375**

Bowl, Seaweed decor in green, white band, brown stripes, spider in base, interior flaking, rim chip, 7 in. tall by 14 3/4 in. diameter........**$325**

Creamer, Cat's Eye decor in black and white, rust band, tooled zigzag line around the rim, rounded form, repaired handle, crazed interior, 2 1/8 in. tall.............................**$1,800**

Creamer, Marbleized decor in blue, brown and ochre, two blue stripes around neck, 4 1/4 in. tall.....**$1,700**

Creamer, Seaweed decor in black, ochre band, black stripes, green beaded and quilted bands, impressed leaf handle, rim chips, handle crack, crow's feet, 4 1/2 in. tall. **$1,500**

Cup, banded, white band between brown stripes, yellowware body. **$375**

Master salt, light blue band, dark brown stripes, footed, some discoloring, chip, 2 in. tall by 3 in. diameter. **$125**

Mug, Earthworm decor in brown, white, and light blue, light blue and gray bands, brown stripes, stains, crack, 3 1/8 in. tall. **$425**

Mug, Stripes, brown, blue and black on white ground, molded beaded band, handle with leaf ends, stains, crazing, crow's-foot hairline, 3 1/4 in. tall....................................**$225**

Mug, Stripes, green and brown, light blue and burnt-orange bands with machine-tooled lines, tooled foliage bands, impressed leaf handle, repaired, damage, 4 7/8 in. tall. **$750**

Mug, Stripes (blue) and geometric band, black and white ground, applied ribbed handle with leaf ends, stains, minor damage, 2 3/4 in. tall....................................**$475**

Mug, wide white slip band extends down from lip, 3 1/2 in. tall by 4 in. diameter. **$500**

Pepper pot, Earthworm decor in black and white, sand-colored band, brown stripes, chips, base damage, 4 3/8 in. tall. **$425**

Pepper pot, Stripes, blue and tan, brown-check tooled bands, small flakes on base, lid rim with wear on finial, 4 1/4 in. tall. **$1,300**

Pepper pot, Stripes, light blue and black, chips, 4 1/2 in. tall.........**$130**

Pepper pot, tooled brown lines (vertical), white ground, wear, 3 3/4 in. tall.................................**$1,300**

Pitcher, Banded decor in blue and black, white ground, hairlines, 4 1/2 in. tall....................................**$185**

Pitcher, Banded decor in light green, brown, and tan, yellowware, machine tooling, molded leaf handle, wear, chips, hairlines, 6 3/4 in. tall. **$2,200**

Pitcher, Cat's Eye decor in brown, blue and white, blue ground, green band, black stripes, badly cracked. **$1,100**

Pitcher, Cat's Eye (multiple) decor in blue and white, ivory ground, brown stripes, damage, stains, 7 1/4 in. tall. **$550**

Pitcher, Geometric and line decor in brown, pumpkin-color bands at top and bottom, pearlware, white ground, embossed leaf decor on handle and spout, minor chips and wear, interior glaze flakes, 7 7/8 in. tall. **$1,400**

Pitcher, Seaweed decor in black, tan stripes, embossed blue bands at top and bottom, impressed leaves on handle, stains, crow's foot in bottom, crack, 6 1/4 in. tall. **$575**

Pitcher, Seaweed decor in black, taupe ground, blue band, black stripes, minor hairline, 6 in. tall. **$450**

Pitcher, Earthworm decor, black and white, blue band, blue, tan, and black stripes, impressed leaves on handle, damage, 5 1/2 in. tall. **$350**

Pitcher, Earthworm decor, blue and black on brown band, black stripes, light blue and green bands, molded leaf handle, chips, stains, cracks, 7 1/8 in. tall. **$825**

Pitcher, Earthworm decor, blue, brown, and white, tan ground, white band, brown stripes, 5 in. tall. **$1,150**

Pitcher, Earthworm decor, brown, blue, and white (four designs), sage green bands, blue stripes, molded leaf handle, repaired base, rim and spout, 6 3/8 in. tall. **$475**

Pitcher, Earthworm decor, dark brown, tan, and white, light brown bands, dark brown stripes, damage, repairs, 6 in. tall. **$425**

Pitcher, Earthworm decor, white, pale blue, and brown, tan and dark brown stripes on tan band, molded leaf ends on handle, professional repair to handle, 5 in. tall. **$675**

Stein, Checkered decor, ochre stripes, green bands, brown machine-tooled lines, pewter lid with engraved laurel wreath, name and 1816, stapled repairs to handle, 7 3/4 in. tall. **$1,100**

Waste bowl, Earthworm decor in blue, white, and dark brown, blue stripes, tan band, impressed leaves on handle, wear, stains, hairlines, chip, 3 1/8 in. tall by 6 1/4 in. diameter. **$400**

Waste bowl, Marbleized band in blue, black, white, and umber, incised line with green at rim, stains, cracks, 3 in. tall by 5 5/8 in. diameter. **$550**

Mourning Items

During the 18th and 19th centuries, the death of infants and young children was very common, and many women died in childbirth. One way of coping with the loss was to channel the grief through artistic expression. This memorial art, or memento mori" (death keepsakes) included jewelry made of hair and jet, coffin photographs of the deceased, memorial cards with or without photographs of the deceased, and elaborate wreaths, which were often framed in shadow boxes.

Postmortem photography of the deceased, especially of children, was common. Some of these photos were given to family members and friends, or appeared on memorial cards announcing the child's death, or were sent to acknowledge the receipt of flowers.

Occasionally mourners were given mourning jewelry made from hair of the deceased.

Women whose husbands had died sometimes went into "deep mourning" for at least a year. This meant the widow would have to dress entirely in black at all times, and she was only to leave her house to go to church or to visit close relatives.

Some milliners specialized in black crepe mourning attire. In the second year after the death of her husband, the widow could include visiting close friends as well as relatives. Then, during the third year of mourning, she could start wearing the "half mourning" colors of gray, white, and purple.

The closer the relationship to the deceased, the more black was worn and the longer the time it was worn. In other words, a distant cousin might only require the wearing of black ribbons in the hair, or as a decoration on a white dress or parasol.

Wreaths in shadow boxes (sometimes made of feathers, wax, or fabric), funeral jewelry, and brooches were all made from the hair of the deceased.

Jewelry and hair ornaments made from jet were also popular. Jet is a fossilized coal that can be carved and polished to a high sheen. Other materials used were black onyx, black glass (called French jet), black enamel, and a hardened black rubber called vulcanite.

Besides black clothing and accessories, "mourning stationery" was used, and calling cards were also edged in black. The width of the border indicated how closely related one was to the deceased. Some black borders were as much as an inch thick.

Symbolism included butterflies, which were often printed onto memorial cards to symbolize passing into the next life. Roses were used to symbolize a "bloom cut early." Morning glories also symbolized a short life.

Postmortem photographs were often placed in the parlor along with a wreath of hair from the deceased, and other belongings as remembrances.

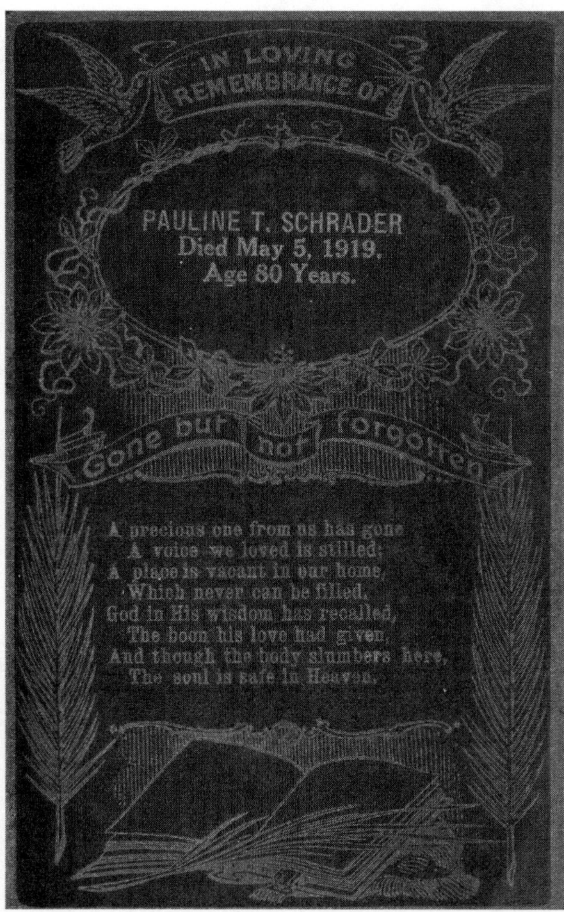

Mourning cards like this 1908 example (in a cabinet format) from a studio in Leipsic, Ohio, could be ordered from the funeral home, which would then add the name of the deceased. **$4-$6**

Mourning wreath, circa 1910, constructed of fabric and feathers and mounted on black velvet, with composition berries or buds in a floral display, with the words "At Rest" made of cardboard and painted blue, and a coffin plate that also says "At Rest," all mounted in a shadow box with original gilt and grain painted frame, excellent condition, 22 in. by 16 in. by 6 in. **$300-$400**

Large mourning photographs like this one, which feature floral tributes, often include an inset photograph of the deceased, 7 1/2 in. by 9 1/2 in. **$30-$35**

Mourning wreath, circa 1890, fabric flowers mounted on black velvet in a walnut shadow box of unusual form, arched back with inlaid star and frame with contrasting woods, untouched original condition, 18 in. by 14 in. by 4 in. **$400-$500**

❖ Memorial and Mourning

Pictures and special pieces of jewelry were two things 19th century Americans kept to remember the dearly departed. Mourning jewelry typically contained pieces of the deceased's hair. The most desirable artwork are pictures from the early 19th century, usually depicting a cenotaph (a monument honoring a dead person whose remains lie elsewhere), bearing an inscription to a deceased person, with one or more female figures under a tree.

Bracelets, gold-filled clasp with fine scroll engraving, woven light brown hair in intricate design, one damaged, each 7 3/8 in. long. **$300/pair**

Brooches, gold filled or plated, beveled glass with woven hair, two dated 1834 and 1883, four enameled and two with engraved borders, one damaged, one missing its pin, one lens cracked, group of six. .... **$600-$700**

Sampler, "To the Memory of W.H. Keely... This token was worked by Elizabeth Keely," strawberry border with willows and flowering trees above/below verse, two birds (one with a crest), circa 1844, minor edge damage, worn frame, 21 1/4 in. by 18 1/4 in. .... **$2,800-$3,000**

Sampler, "HM Rowe 1775 The Dying Infant to His Mother...," inspirational verse, geometric floral border, English or American, fabric loss, toning, fading, 12 1/2 in. by 16 3/4 in. .... **$700-$800**

Stickpin, lozenge-shape watercolor on ivory shows mourning figure at classical monument and urn, inscribed, "Be What Your Mother Was, and Claim The Skies," gold-plated mount, initialed, minor wear. **$275**

Watercolor, two women at memorial with urn and draped cloth, landscape ground with weeping willow, to "Mrs. Sarah S. Safford, 1810," framed, 17 in. by 20 in. .... **$6,000-$6,500**

Watercolor, Hammond-Bradley family, Massachusetts, unsigned, "Painted by Harriet M. Hammond about 1830, Miss Lois B. Batchelder, Teacher" in pencil on reverse, watercolor on paper, shows three classical memorials each inscribed with names and dates (1822-1829), landscape with trees, river, bridge, church and other buildings, minor foxing, stains, small tear, 17 1/2 in. by 24 3/4 in. ..**$3,000-$4,000**

Etching by Hubert Morley (1888-1951), titled "Maple Syrup Time—Wisconsin," showing syrup-gathering using a horse-drawn sled, and a cabin in the background of a woodland landscape, circa 1930s, signed, titled, and numbered (4/100) in pencil, excellent condition, framed, image size 8 1/4 in. by 11 in., **$400-$500**

Linocut by Woldemar Neufeld (1909-2002), titled "Harvest," showing a woman carrying a bowl of apples while apple-picking is under way on a farm in the background, signed in pencil "W Neufeld," with note on reverse saying the print was issued by Collectors of American Art Incirca in 1946, excellent condition, framed, image size 9 1/2 in. by 5 1/4 in., **$500-$600**

Etching by Martin Petersen (1866-1956), showing three men raking hay, initialed in pencil "M.P.," excellent condition, framed, image size 10 in. by 9 1/2 in., **$500-$600**

Painting, circa 1900, oil on board, showing two kittens walking along an oak branch, in original gilt frame; painting has been cleaned, excellent condition, image size 10 in. by 14 in., **$500-$600**

Painting, circa 1930s, impressionist, oil on board, windy, mountainous landscape with a field of flowers, possibly California, signed lower left, "Eric W. Wittenberg," cleaned, in original frame, image size 12 in. by 16 in., **$1,000-$1,200**

Nantucket Lightship basket, ash and willow, circa 1890, wood base, bail handle, remnants of label on bottom, excellent condition, size with handle up, 6 3/4 in. by 6 1/4 in. by 9 in., **$700-$800**

Picture frame, circa 1900, walnut and mixed woods, elaborate tramp art creation with six-level corners done in fan motif, sides done in cutout "fence posts" with flower tops, and inner sections decorated with notched layers in arches, points, sawtooth designs, near mint condition, 36 in by 26 in., **$4,000-$5,000** *(Similar frames have been found in the Midwest, and all appear to be the work of the same maker. One frame was found with red, white, and blue paint, which may have been a later addition.)*

Splint basket, oak, Norwegian, dated 1876, painted dark blue, red, and white with stylized floral motif, wood handle, hinged lid with tin hasp, minor handling wear, 10 1/2 in. by 11 1/4 in. by 15 in., $550

Interlocking wood basket, circa 1890, mixed woods, probably Norwegian-American, with woven splint panels and canted sides, mint condition, 10 1/2 in. by 10 1/2 in. by 11 1/2 in., **$250-$350**

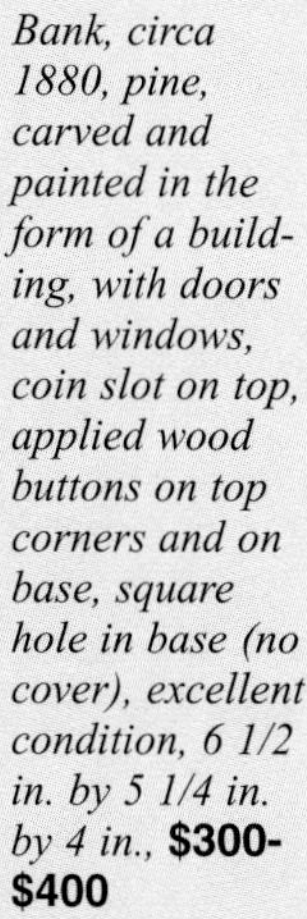

Bank, circa 1880, pine, carved and painted in the form of a building, with doors and windows, coin slot on top, applied wood buttons on top corners and on base, square hole in base (no cover), excellent condition, 6 1/2 in. by 5 1/4 in. by 4 in., **$300-$400**

Carving of a hen, circa 1920, pine with a walnut stain, marked on the bottom "Compliments of M.J. Porter," possibly a presentation piece or egg company trade stimulator, mint condition, 11 1/2 in. by 8 1/4 in. by 2 3/4 in., **$500-$600**

Stone carving, circa 1900, sandstone, showing the Last Supper with the apostles huddled around Christ in a medieval-style tableau, probably European but salvaged from a rural Wisconsin church, minor flaking and chipping, 14 in. by 8 in. by 2 in., **$800-$1,000**

A collection of miniature turned and painted cups, plus a chalice and round footed stand, Norwegian, pine, all with original paint; chalice decorated with red and black dots, 3 1/2 in. tall; cup second from the left dated 1851, 1 3/4 in. tall; center cup dated 1869, 2 in. tall; footed stand with original red and blue paint, 2 7/8 in. tall; cup on right with grain painting and dusty blue painted trim, 1/2 in. tall, from **$400** *for stand to* **$800** *for chalice and dated cups.*

Carved heads, circa 1930s, mostly walnut, made by an Iowa farmer, possibly for use as walking stick handles, ranging in length from 2 1/2 in. to 8 1/4 in., priced from **$50-$150**

Front and back of a bottle whimsy, pale green glass, very thick, old bottle, with turned wood stopper, containing a yarn winder with green thread that is placed between four whittled posts, on top of each post is a cloth flag, similar to but not American flags: red and white stripes, and a circular pattern of white stars on a blue field; it is signed "D. CARR" on one side of a cross piece below the winder, and dated 1879 on the other side, 13 5/8 in. tall including stopper by 4 1/2 in., **$1,500-$2,000**

Front and back of a bottle whimsy, made by Carl Worner, with puzzle stopper and showing interior of saloon, with bartender, two men in suits, and woman seated at table, minor damage to interior base, circa 1910, 10 1/2 in. by 4 1/4 in. by 2 1/2 in., **$1,500-$2,000**

Diorama, circa 1930s, showing a three-masted ship under full sail, flying both American and Norwegian flags, complete with miniature rigging, lifeboats, and tiny figures of sailors on deck; set in a box with simulated sky and water, and having a hole in the bottom into which a small electric bulb can be placed to make it appear as if the portholes are lighted; frame also decorated with flags and anchors, overall dimensions 40 in. by 24 in. by 8 in., **$1,000-$1,200**

Two views of a Memoryware mug, circa 1900, with hand-formed handle on a ceramic body, decorated with buttons, coins, tokens, shards, crucifix and human tooth; it may have had a top, some loss to base, overall good condition, 9 in. by 7 in. by 5 in., **$150-$200**

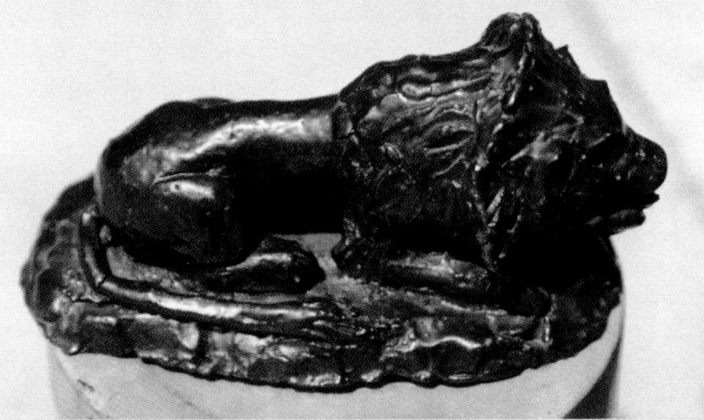

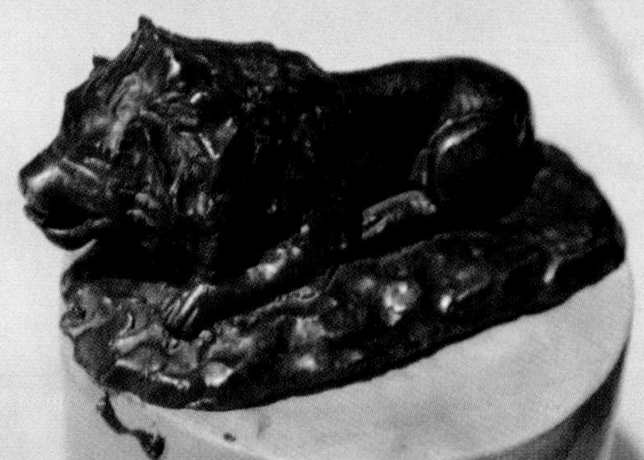

Two views of a sewer tile clay figure of a resting lion, with Albany slip glazed surface, probably Ohio origin, circa 1890, minor chipping, 9 in. by 5 in. by 4 1/2 in., **$350-$450**

Two views of a miniature Norwegian trunk, pine, American made, circa 1910, painted inside and out with flowers and gilt trim simulating ironwork, with open till inside, original lock and key, bracket feet, nailed construction, mint condition, 8 3/4 in. by 5 1/4 in. by 5 in., **$1,200-$1,500**

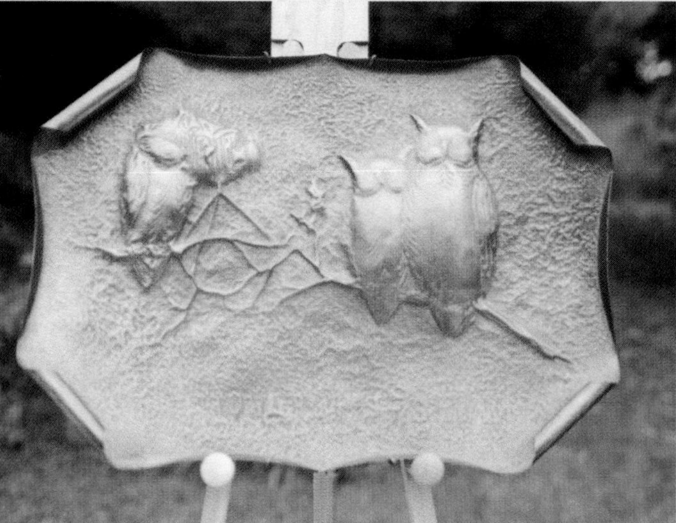

Wall plaque, brass, with curled corners and hand-hammered image of three owls sitting on a branch, one owl looking through a box camera on stand, barely visible below owls are the words, "Owl Right, Sit Still!"; possibly a student project, circa 1910, mint condition, 20 in. by 13 in., **$300-$400**

Cast iron trade souvenir for Cash's Woven Names (clothing labels), on the front is an image of a man dressed in a barrel and the words, "Mark 'em—I didn't," and the company name on the back, traces of original paint, 4 3/4 in. by 2 1/4 in., **$250**

Miniature castle, tin, circa 1900, possibly a 10th wedding anniversary gift, cutout windows and soldered turrets, battlements, and roofs, near mint condition, 10 in. by 10 in. by 8 in., **$350-$450**

Figures of an Amish boy and girl, signed "Ewertz," by Henry or Maxime Ewertz, circa 1949; terra cotta, made in Hatfield, Pennsylvania; the couple created a series of figures showing the Amish in various activities in the 1940s and 1950s; good condition with significant paint flaking, boy stands 19 in. tall, **$2,000-$3,000/pair**

Cast-plaster figure of a little girl seated on a wall, holding a bouquet, circa 1920s (?), with twigs embedded in back to act as reinforcement, moderate flaking to soft plaster, 8 1/4 in. by 5 1/2 in. by 1 3/4 in., **$85**

Handmade jack-in-the box, circa 1900, possibly German, paper-covered wooden box with hook-and-eye clasp, Jack with composition (papier-mache?) head, hand painted, and ruffled cloth collar, minor handling wear, size open 4 in. by 8 3/8 in. by 4 in., **$250**

Cast iron plaque commemorating the first radio broadcast (?) from a county fair in the United States, from Aug. 30 to Sept. 2, 1922, in Owatonna, Minnesota, original silver and black painted surface, 8 in. by 12 in., **$200-$300**

"Eat Short Orders" sign, circa 1930s, sheet iron with riveted iron border, yellow, and navy blue, minor weathering, 31 in. by 19 in., **$400-$500**

Egg crate, circa 1910, painted pine with "PRIME PATENT EGG BOX" stenciled on side, turned wood handle, hook and eye clasp, original orange-red paint, cardboard egg holders still inside (held five dozen), paper label inside lid reads, "Prime's Patent Egg Case, Winchendon, Mass., 11 1/2 in. by 9 in. by 8 1/2 in., **$200-$300**

Shooting gallery figures, circa 1910, painted sheet iron, in the form of Uncle Sam, Columbia ("Lady Liberty"), the Spirit of '76 fife and drum soldiers (three figures secured with screws), a Revolutionary War-era soldier blowing a trumpet, a spread-wing eagle, plus two clowns painted in a commedia del arte style, and a windmill with spinning blades; these were not targets, but were designed to become animated when certain targets were hit: Uncle Sam and Columbia each wave an arm (Sam also nods his head), the drummers have carved and painted wooden hands holding drumsticks to play drums (missing), and the bugler raised and lowered his instrument; some surface rust and bullet impact marks, with some paint loss, overall very good condition; Sam is 71 in. tall, Columbia is 64 in. tall, as is the tallest of the marchers; the eagle is 48 in. wide, and the clowns are 20 in. tall, **$75,000+/set**

Shoeshine box, scrap wood, sheet metal and wire, painted black and red, made in 1908 by James Horkau, Eau Claire, Wis. (?), with arching metal footrest (?), twisted wire handle and small upper compartment (lined with cut paper images) decorated with stylized horseshoes on sides, main section with applied wood panels on all four sides attached with pegs, each decorated with bent wire, also bent wire decoration on the corners, inside of main lid has a photograph of a public gathering and a label on which is written in ink, "James Horkau Maker Nov. 10, 1908," inside lined with cut paper images from popular magazines, original untouched surface, excellent condition, 13 1/2 in. by 13 3/4 in. by 11 3/4 in., **$1,500-$2,000**

Skorgen Folk Art

Ingvald Skorgen (1876-1951) was born on his family's farm at Skorgedalen on the Isfjord across from Andalsnes, Norway. The name Skorgen was derived from the location of the farm at the bend in the fjord. "Skorg" means the wearing away of a bank by water.

At the age of seven, Ingvald traveled to America with his parents Peder and Gjertrude Rottum Skorgen. Settling in the South Fork Valley in Fillmore County, southeastern Minnesota, they built a log cabin, which still stands by the river.

Ingvald started collecting arrowheads, relics, rock, broken mirrors, and glass beads to decorate the concrete sculptures he began making in the 1930s. He eventually built an entire sculpture garden, which included towering figures of a black man and woman, an American Indian with war paint, an alligator and turtle, a kubbestol (a Norwegian carved chair usually made from a single log, though Ingvald's was made of concrete), and decorative markers. He even made the marker for his mother's grave.

Many of Skorgen's creations were exhibited at the Cornucopia Art Center in Lanesboro, Minn., in 1996.

Whistle, circa 1930s, carved from a fir branch, with attached carved bird that adjusts whistle's pitch when tail is pressed, bark surface on whistle and burnt-carved decoration on bird, possibly a tourist item, mint condition, 8 in. by 3 in. by 2 in., **$150-$200**

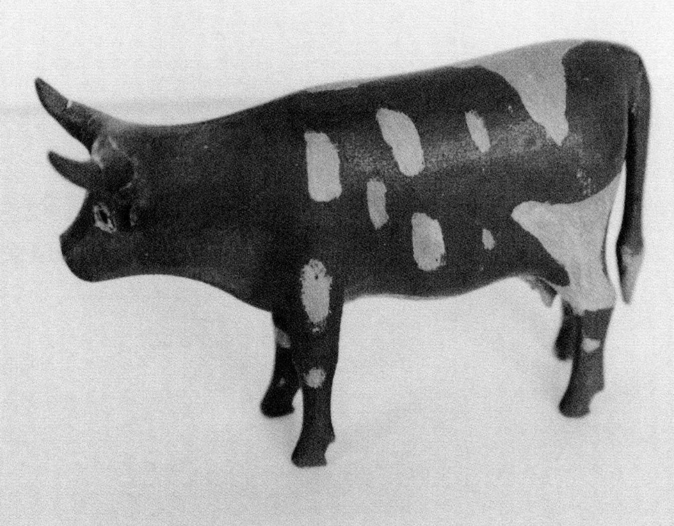

Toy cow, American made in Rhode Island, circa 1880, carved pine painted brown and white, near mint, 7 1/2 in. by 4 3/4 in. by 2 in., **$350**

Flour bin, circa 1900, sheet steel with fitted lid and hasp, bail handles, hand-painted on the front "Flour" with leaves and flowers and a gilt Greek-key border top and bottom, significant handling wear with numerous dents, 22 in. by 12 in., **$60-$70**

Skates, carved pine and wrought iron blades, Norwegian, circa 1830, with original leather fittings and green paint, significant wear, each skate 10 in. by 2 1/2 in. by 2 in., **$130/pair**

Rocking horse, circa 1890, horsehide over composition body, carved and painted mouth and nose, glass eyes, horse-hair tail, original saddle and harness, on painted rockers, excellent condition, 35 in. by 13 1/2 in. by 27 in., **$1,500-$1,800**

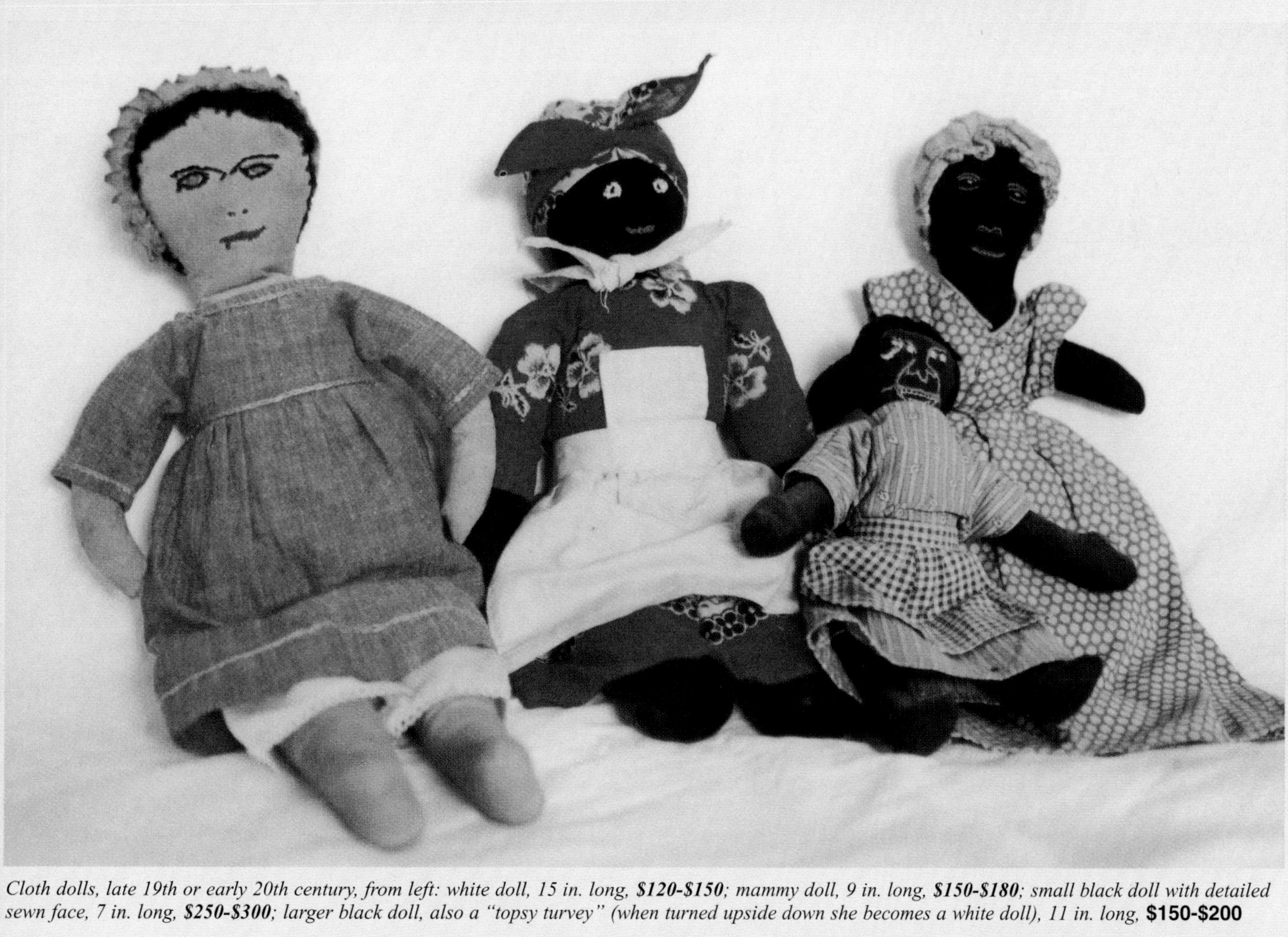

Cloth dolls, late 19th or early 20th century, from left: white doll, 15 in. long, ***$120-$150****; mammy doll, 9 in. long,* ***$150-$180****; small black doll with detailed sewn face, 7 in. long,* ***$250-$300****; larger black doll, also a "topsy turvey" (when turned upside down she becomes a white doll), 11 in. long,* **$150-$200**

Nesting bowls, set of five, marked "Watt Oven Ware," tapering ribbed design with hand-painted apples and leaves, bowls measures from 9 in. to 5 in. diameter, **$450-$550/set**

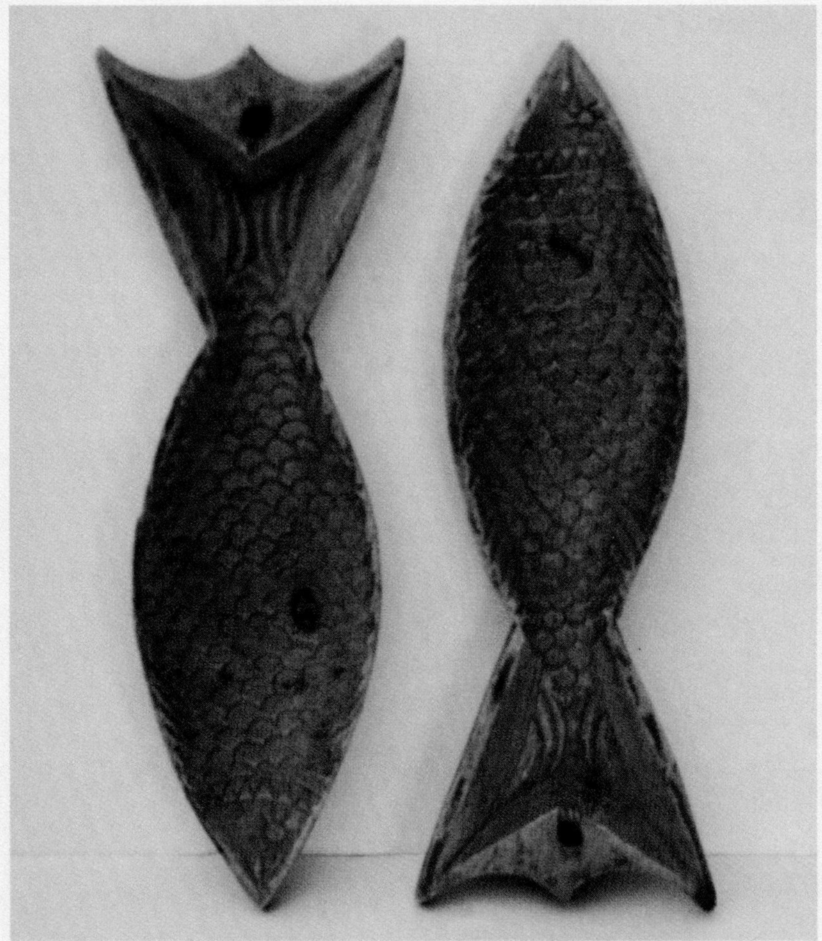

Butter mold, circa 1880, pine, two pieces carved in the form of a fish, with detailed scales, mouth and eyes, possibly Norwegian-American, minor handling wear, 6 1/4 in. by 2 in., **$250-$300**

Painted sugar buckets (also called firkins), late 19th century, with wooden handles, finger-lap construction and original paint, in green, sky blue, rusty red, and golden yellow, sizes range from 12 in., 13 1/2 in., 11 1/2 in. and 9 in., ranging in price from **$200** *for the small green bucket to* **$500+** *for the sky blue bucket.*

Fortune-telling game, circa 1920s, homemade wood box with applied paper to game board, glass cover and spring-loaded mechanism (not working), which made metal pointer spin to indicate good or bad luck, spell words, and answer "Yes" or No" (similar to a ouija board), with original fabric-lined carrying case, 8 in. by 8 in. by 3 in., **$200-$300**

Cookie mold, circa 1850, maple, carved with large heart decorated with flowers and a leafy border, mint condition, 8 3/4 in. by 9 3/4 in. by 1 1/2 in., **$600-$700**

Game board, pine, Norwegian, dated 1815, with cutout handle, black stain in scribed checkerboard pattern on front, reverse with black stain and diamond-shaped scribing and inscription in Norwegian, 9 1/2 in. by 15 in. by 1 in., **$600**

*Cookie cutter, circa 1920, tinned steel, in the form of a lion, 4 1/4 in. by 3 in., **$80***

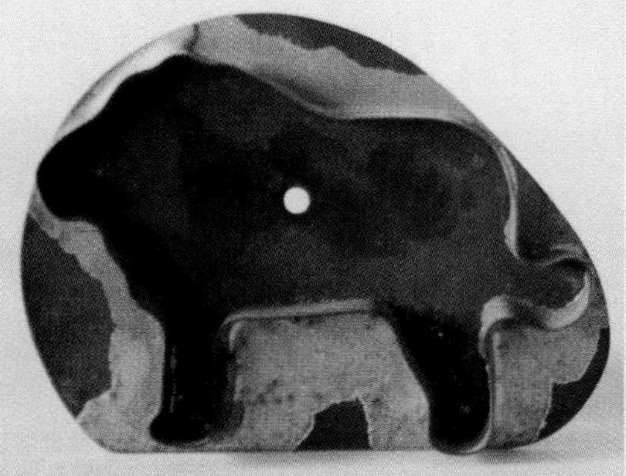

Butter paddle, circa 1890, pine with hand-painted flowers on one side, moderate handling wear, 8 in. by 4 in., **$80-$90**

Miniature carved dipper in the form of a bird (also called an "ale hen"), Norwegian, pine, dated 1842, with stylized carved tail, original blue paint, minor wear, 5 1/4 in. by 2 3/8 in. by 2 1/2 in., **$1,800**

Cookie cutter, circa 1920, tinned steel, in the form of a heart, 5 in. by 3 1/2 in., **$45**

Cookie cutter, circa 1920, tinned steel, in the form of a goose, 4 in. by 3 1/4 in., **$60**

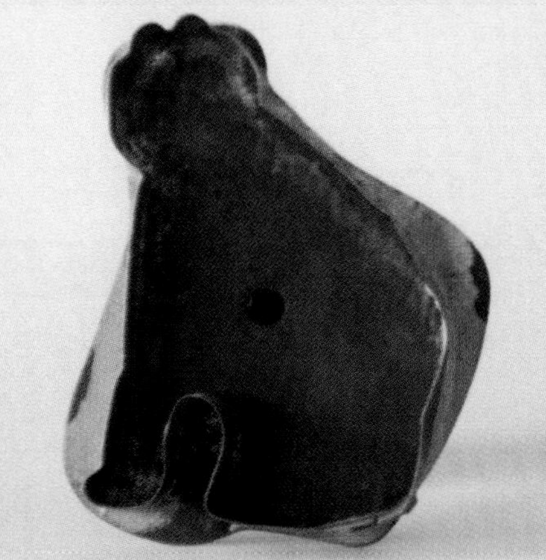

Cookie cutter, circa 1920, tinned steel, in the form of a seated cat, 4 in. by 3 1/2 in., **$75**

Carved burl dipper, Norwegian, dated 1601, with handle carved in the form of a primitive bird head, rich patina, 8 in. by 3 1/2 in. by 4 1/2 in., **$2,800**

Several views of a candle box (?), circa 1900, decorated on two sides with cats and dogs, and on three sides with vividly painted red, yellow, and pink roses, may have originally held yeast or cheese, 9 in. by 7 in. by 7 in., **$1,200-$1,500**

Front and back of a dough scraper, circa 1880, shaped walnut handle and steel blade, hand-painted circa 1900 on both sides with roses and pansies, near mint, 11 in. by 6 1/2 in., **$200-$250**

Two views of a knife or utensil tray, walnut, with cutout handle, scalloped and canted sides, with carved date, 1857, on one side of handle, and the initials "J.M.W." on the other side, near mint, 13 in. by 9 1/4 in. by 6 in., **$500-$600**

Rolling pin, circa 1870, tiger maple with strong graining, small turned knobs on both ends, minor handling wear, 15 in. by 2 in., **$200-$250**

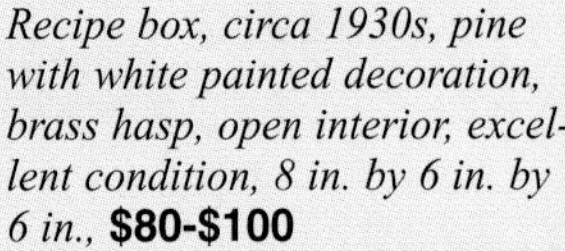

Recipe box, circa 1930s, pine with white painted decoration, brass hasp, open interior, excellent condition, 8 in. by 6 in. by 6 in., **$80-$100**

Primitive washboard, circa 1880, pine with carved ridges and tapering profile, significant wear, 16 in. by 32 in. by 1 1/4 in., **$100**

Storage box, cast iron, in the shape of a dove, two pieces with top that detaches along line of dove's wing, circa 1840, 7 in. by 4 in. by 3 in., **$1,200**

Birdcage, two compartments, with elaborately cut out and decorated wooden surface, arched tops with applied wooden rosettes and brass tacks, scalloped sides with four gold-painted balls in the corners, spring-loaded doors with notch carving, worn white painted surface, removable tin trays in bottom, carved wooden feet, 24 in. by 14 in. by 12 in., **$800-$1,200**

Spice cabinet, with details, circa 1890, walnut and maple, elaborate pierced fret-carved construction with scroll and vine motifs on all surfaces and gallery top and bracket supports on bottom, nine drawers with contrasting wood labels done in fret carving, central pierced door with round plaque that features a woman in harvest setting, applied carved crest in gallery bears initials "WH," minor damage to gallery, overall excellent condition, 24 in. by 20 in. by 6 in., **$1,200-$1,500**

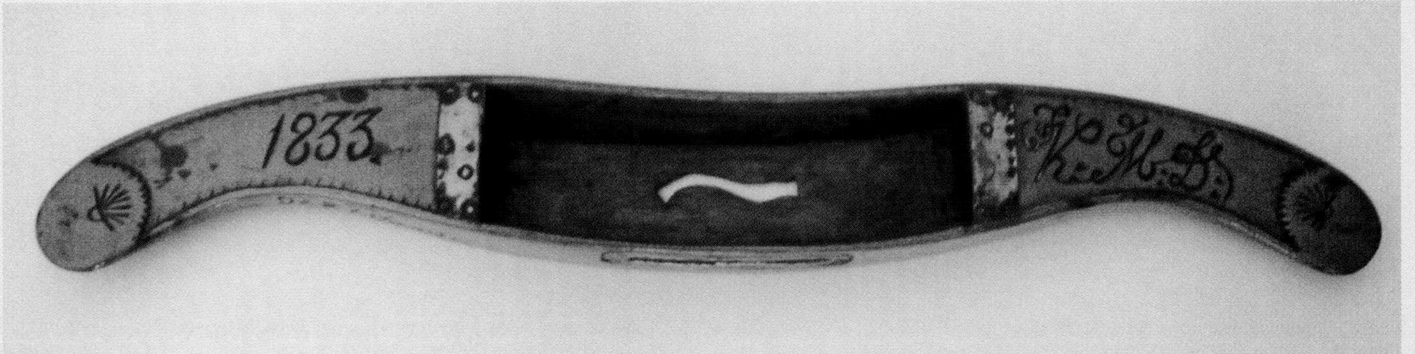

Loom shuttle, maple, Norwegian, with hollowed center section to hold weaving fiber, nailed brass fittings, carved with date of 1833 and the initials "KMD," original varnished finish, 13 in. by 2 in. by 1 1/4 in., ***$300-$350***

Three views of a storage box, circa 1890, made of varnished pine or fir and decorated on top and sides with hundreds of peach pits and varnished walnut shells and sections, Bennington stoneware knob on top, and a fragment of a piece of Schaefer & Vader pottery embedded in the front, brass handles on sides, lined with fabric, minor wear, overall excellent condition, 14 in. by 10 in. by 10 in., **$600-$800**

Rare Swedish puzzle "tine," pine, woven lap construction, with four carved knobs on top, which must be turned in a certain order to open it, scratch-carved verse on sides and the date 1883, minor wear, 9 3/4 in. by 6 in. by 5 1/2 in., **$800-$900**

Storage box, a Norwegian "tine," pine, lapped, pegged, and woven construction with stylized burnt decoration, inked date inside lid of 1778 but may be later, moderate handling wear, 7 in. by 3 in. by 6 1/2 in., **$350-$450**

Mangle board, circa 1780, oak, carved with hex signs, hearts, and geometric patterns, handle in the form of a primitive horse, moderate handling wear, 31 in. by 5 in. by 5 in., **$800-$900**

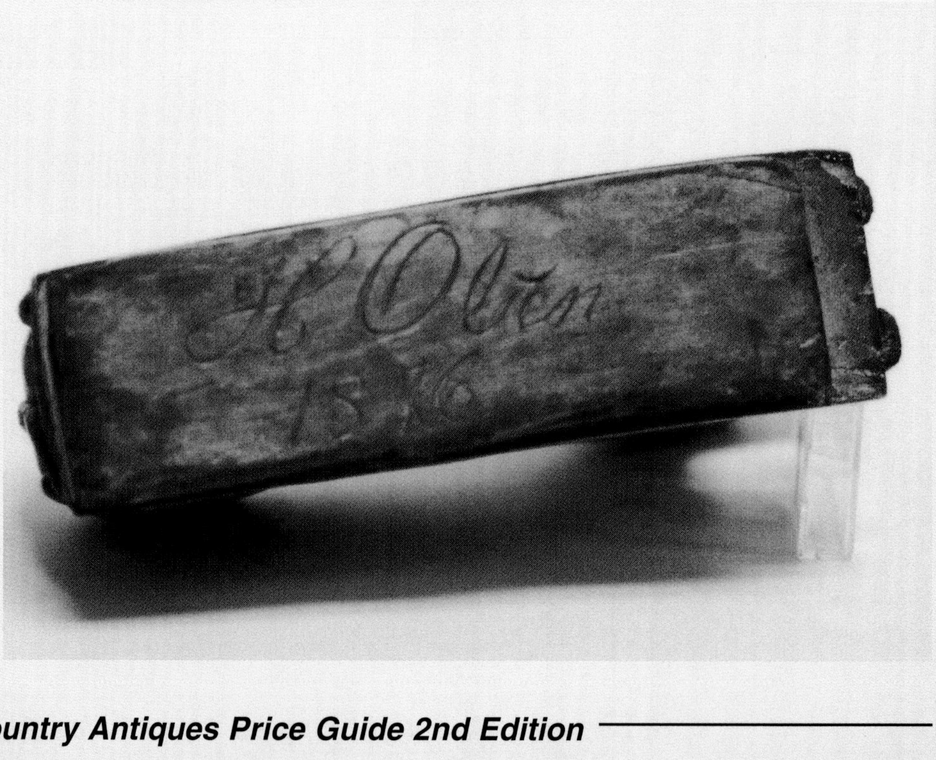

Three views of a Mangle handle, pine, carved in the form of a crouching lion, with remnants of red paint, handling wear, bottom with carved name and date, "H Olin 1876," 7 3/4 in. by 6 1/4 in. by 2 1/2 in., **$500-$600**

Vase, ceramic, made by George Ohr (1857-1918) with round footed base, bulbous body, tapering neck and dripping glaze in various shades of green, marked on the bottom with a stamp, "Geo. E. Ohr Biloxi," minor flaking to top rim, overall excellent condition, 7 in. by 3 1/2 in., **$700-$1,000** *(This is a simpler example of Ohr's work. Larger, more elaborate examples, which Ohr crimped and twisted, can sell for thousands—even tens of thousands—of dollars.)*

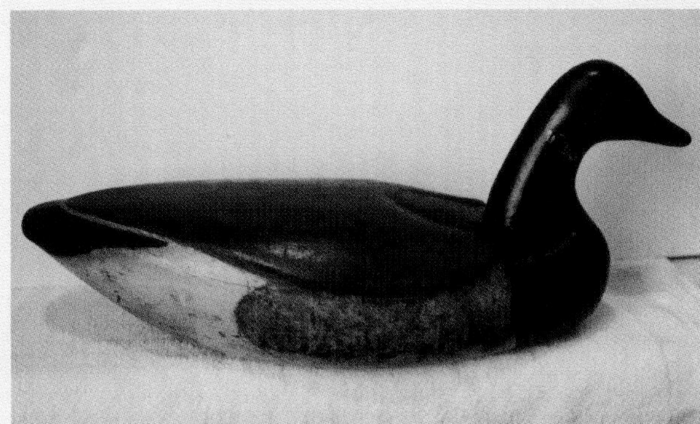

Brant decoy by Percy Gant, Brickton, New Jersey, circa 1938, approximately 18 in. long, ***$1,500-$2,000*** *(A Gant decoy in the Shelburne (Vermont) Museum was used on a U.S. postage stamp.)*

Wood duck drake decoy by Herter Decoy Co., Waseca, Minnesota, circa 1960s, approximately 15 in. long, **$400-$600**

Goldeneye drake decoy by Archie Bodette, Lake Champlain, Vermont, circa 1940, approximately 11 in. long, **$800-$1,200** *(See Decoys of Lake Champlain by Loy Harrell Jr.)*

Pair of Percy Bicknell hollow mallard duck decoys, circa 1940, Vancouver, British Columbia, approximately 18 in. long, **$2,500-$3,500/pair**

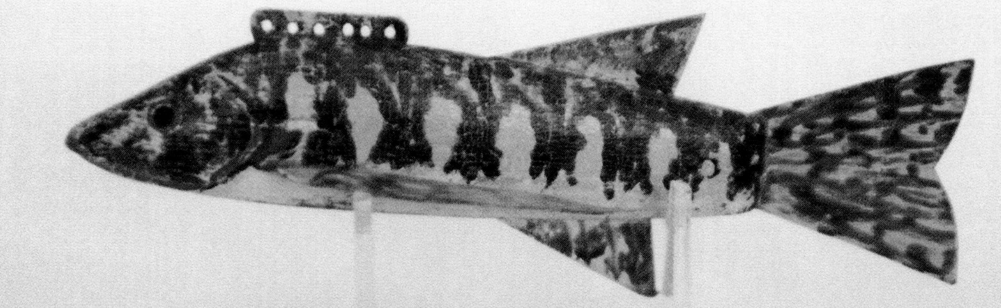

Fish decoy, circa 1930s, carved by Otto or William Fau, Buffalo, Minnesota, with detailed painted surface in bass markings, applied metal fins and tail, excellent condition, 6 1/2 in. by 2 in., **$2,000**

Fish decoy, circa 1930s, carved by William "Slow" Batters, St. Cloud, Minnesota, painted green, red, and yellow, with black spots, applied metal fins and tail, 5 3/4 in. by 1 1/2 in., **$500**

Fish decoy, sturgeon, circa 1930s, Lake Winnebago, Wisconsin, painted red and gold with yellow spots, applied fins, suspended on double eyehooks, excellent condition, 15 1/2 in. by 2 3/4 in., private collection. **No established value.**

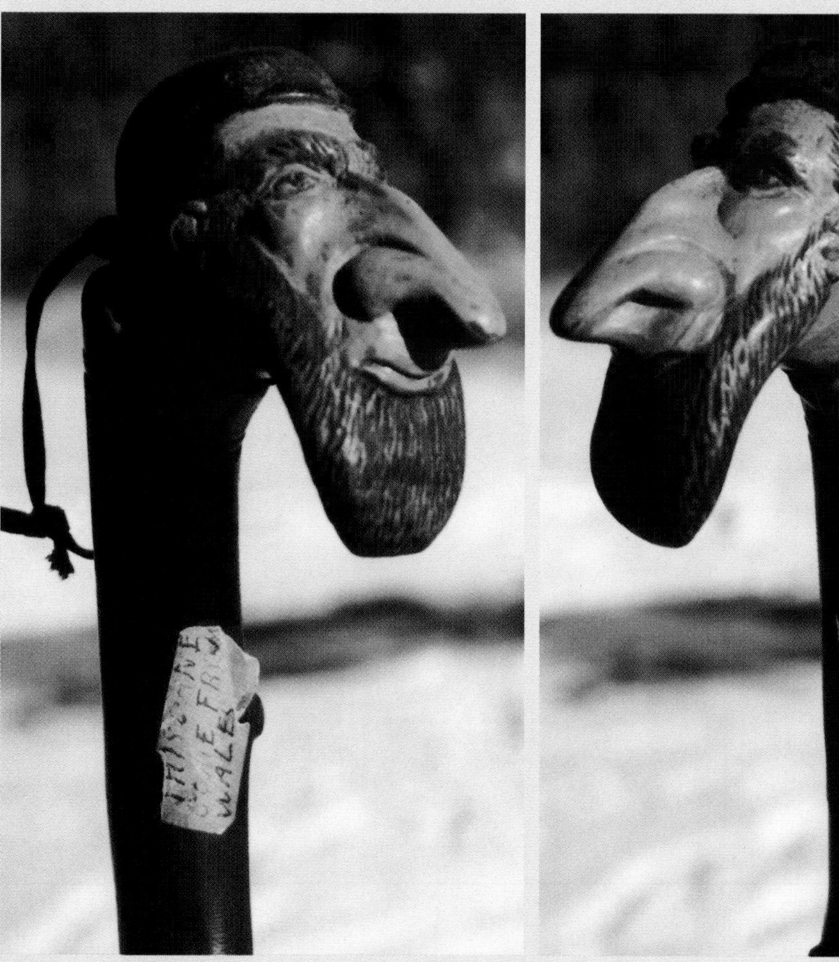

Two views of a walking stick with carved and painted face of a bearded man with a large nose, probably an anti-Semitic cane since the man is wearing a close-fitting round cap (yarmulke), varnished shaft bears a label reading, "This cane came from Wales," black ribbon tied around handle probably for display, circa 1900, 35 in. long, minor wear to shaft and handle, **$1,500-$2,000**

Several views of a Masonic walking stick, circa 1880, with handle carved in the form of a two-headed eagle and the name "Hottinger," shaft carved with detailed Masonic emblems, including Mason in apron holding a hammer and staff, with a trowel at his feet, original varnished surface, near mint, 37 in. long, **$8,000-$10,000**

Several views of a presentation walking stick carved by George W.B. McKnight (1839-1906) of Columbus, Georgia, and given to James Anderson, grand master of the Columbus Oddfellows Lodge, dated Aug. 19, 1891; handle finely carved in the form of a hand holding the three links of Oddfellowship, and shaft carved with scenes from lodge initiation rites, and Anderson's name and title; original varnished surface, minor handling wear, overall excellent condition, 36 in. long, **$6,000-$7,000**

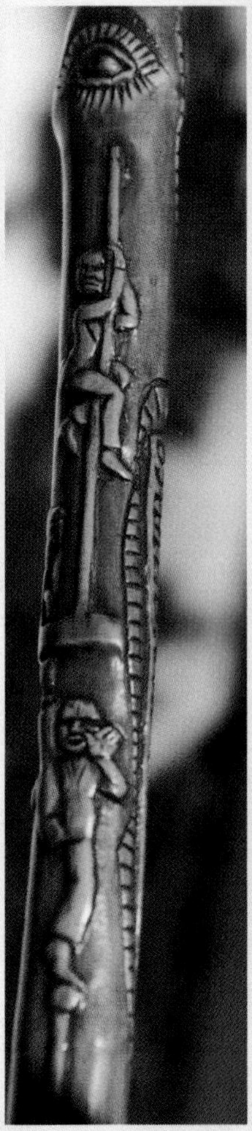

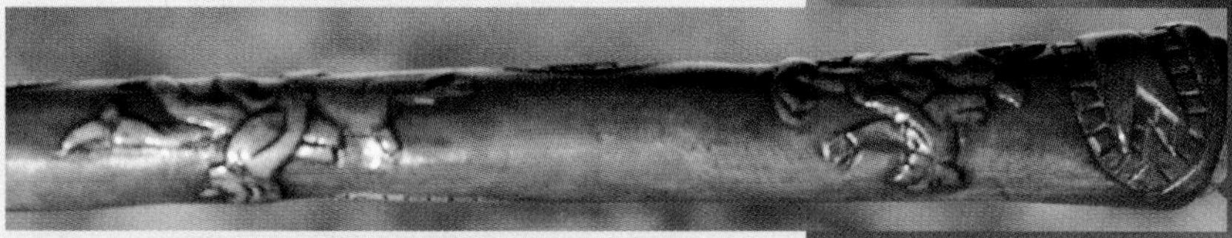

Bench, circa 1850, Sheraton style with grain painting on maple, straight back rails, scroll arms, turned legs with turned and flat stretchers, cane seat replaced, excellent condition, 80 in. by 38 in. by 16 in., **$1,200-$1,500**

Chest of drawers, butternut, circa 1870, with painted bull's-eye decoration added circa 1920s, step-back top with two side-by-side drawers over three stacked drawers, the center drawer unusually deep, probably for blankets, wood mushroom pulls, all drawers hand-dovetailed, moderate signs of wear but overall very good condition, 41 in. by 38 in. by 18 in., **$1,200-$1,500**

Chest of drawers, circa 1900, done in the "tramp art" style, varnished pine and mahogany, with raised geometric notch-carved designs on the four drawers (two side by side over two stacking) and on the sides; top drawers have turned wood mushroom pulls, bottom drawers have cast brass bail handles with birds, insects, leaves, and flowers, front feet carved in primitive foot shape, moderate wear with some carving replaced on front, overall very good condition, 46 in. by 30 in. by 21 in. Detail below. **$4,000-$5,000**

Footstool, circa 1910, pine with three dowel legs in original black painted surface, and the top covered in a hooked mat done in a floral motif, moderate wear and fading, 12 in. by 6 in., **$180**

Footstool, circa 1920, pine decorated with spools in geometric and rayed designs, octagonal with original fabric-covered top and ring handle, original varnished surface with minor handling wear, 11 1/2 in. by 6 1/2 in., **$185**

Child's chair, circa 1860, pine, with carved back rail and crest rail, scroll arms with through pegs from the front legs, plank seat, original worn painted surface in brown over ochre, excellent condition, 22 in. by 15 1/2 in. by 13 1/2 in., **$250**

Crazy quilt, circa 1930s, done in bold color blocks of red, rust, black, blue, and taupe, with at least eight different styles of decorative stitching, all hand-pieced, near mint condition, 74 in. by 84 in., **$400-$500**

Corner shelf, circa 1870, turned and carved wood, with four shelves trimmed in pierced and carved borders, spindles, and brackets, topped by 10 turned spires, central shelf having a drawer with rounded corners and decorated with applied round bosses and a carved disk with wings, original heavy dark varnished surface, minor damage to some trim pieces, overall very good condition, 85 1/2 in. by 33 in. by 19 in., **$5,000-$6,000**

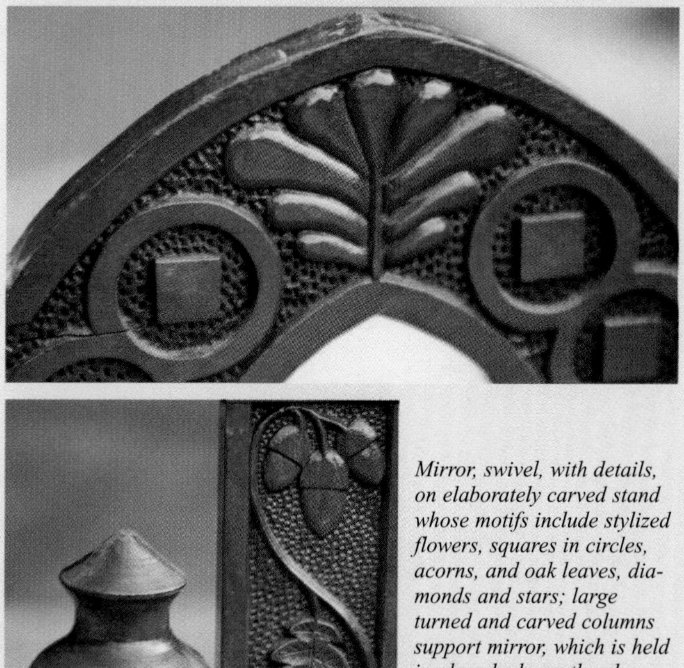

Mirror, swivel, with details, on elaborately carved stand whose motifs include stylized flowers, squares in circles, acorns, and oak leaves, diamonds and stars; large turned and carved columns support mirror, which is held in place by brass thumb screws; rectangular base has recessed area in middle, and front of base has five small inset mirrors, three of which have scalloped frames; bun feet, overall red stain finish, signed and dated 1879 inside bottom of base, minor wear, 41 in. by 31 in. by 14 in., **$800-$1,000**

Fanciful display shelf, two pieces, mixed woods, possibly a music stand, circa 1900, with cutout scroll decoration on back and bracket supports, applied spindles with gold trim, turned spindle supports on central shelves, separate base with large scroll legs and scroll brackets, round scalloped shelf, splay feet and original wooden casters, minor wear, overall dimensions 71 in. by 28 in. by 18 in., **$1,000-$1,200**

Windmill weight, early 20th century, cast iron in the form of a rooster (this one is called the "rainbow tail"), made by Elgin Wind Power and Pump Company, Elgin, Illinois, remains of original paint, on contemporary stand, size without stand 18 in. by 16 in. by 3 1/2 in., **$2,500-$3,500**

Gaudy Dutch creamer, Grape pattern, 4 in. tall, **$425**

Weathervane figure of a rooster, circa 1890, cut sheet iron riveted to an iron rod with cork ball, remnants of red paint, weathered surface with slight corrosion, on a custom-made wood base, overall dimensions 30 in. by 20 in. by 4 in., **$1,200-$1,500**

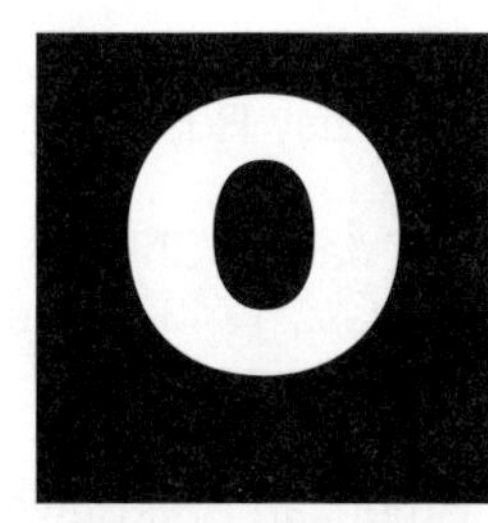

Old Sleepy Eye

A Sioux Indian chief inspired the name for Sleepy Eye, Minn., as well as its Sleepy Eye Milling Co. The mill was in business from 1883 to 1921, using the American Indian's bust as its trademark. From 1899 through 1905, the Weir Pottery Co. in Monmouth, Ill., produced the mill's first premiums—a Flemish butter crock, salt bowl, stein, and vase—which were given away in sacks of flour. After the merger of seven potteries in 1906, the resulting Western Stoneware Co. produced the Sleepy Eye premiums until 1937.

In addition to the original four premiums, Sleepy Eye pottery and stoneware included five sizes of pitchers, along with various mugs, steins, sugar bowls, and tea tiles. Most were blue and white, but pieces were also made in brown, gold, and green. Non-ceramic items, including bakers' caps, lithographed barrel covers, beanies, fans, pillow tops, postcards, and trade cards were also used to advertise the company.

In 1952, Western Stoneware Co. produced 22- and 40-ounce steins with a redesigned American Indian's head and a chestnut brown glaze.

Reference: Jim Martin and Bette Cooper, *Monmouth-Western Stoneware,* Collector Books, 1998; Elinor Meugnoit, *Old Sleepy Eye*, self-published, 1979.

Collectors' Club: Old Sleepy Eye Collectors Club of America, PO Box 12, Monmouth, IL 61462, http://maplecity.com/~oseclub/index.htm

Reproduction Alert

Old Sleepy Eye items manufactured during the Western Stoneware period are being reproduced. Toothpick holders and salt and pepper shakers are also being made, although these items were never originally produced. Most common are pitchers with a cobalt decoration.

Bowl, Flemish, rounded bottom, 4 in. tall, 6 1/2 in. diameter. **$375**

Butter crock, Flemish, straight-sided, 5 in. tall, 6 1/2 in. diameter....... **$425**

Mug, 4 1/4 in. tall. **$150**

Mug, 8 in. tall, mint condition. .. **$1,800**

Pillow top, Chief Sleepy Eye before the Great Father, known as the Monroe top, 1901..................... **$500**

Pitcher, blue and white, No.1, blue rim, 4 1/8 in. tall. $325

Pitcher, blue and white, No. 1, plain rim, 4 1/8 in. tall. $225

Pitcher, blue and white, No. 4, blue rim. $450

Salt crock, hanging, blue and white, 5 1/2 in. tall, 5 1/4 in. diameter. $1,750

Vase, Flemish, cylindrical, 8 1/2 in. tall. **$350**

Vase, cylindrical, with Indian profile, cattails and dragonfly, excellent condition, 8 1/2 in. tall...... **$400-$500**

Pitcher, blue and white, No. 2, 5 1/4 in. tall. **$325**

Paper Ephemera

When used by collectors, the term ephemera generally refers to paper objects such as letterheads and bookplates that were intended to be used for a short time and then thrown away.

References: Ron Barlow and Ray Reynolds, *Insider's Guide to Old Books, Magazines, Newspapers, and Trade Catalogs*, Windmill Publishing, 1995; Gerard S. Petrone, *Cigar Box Labels: Portraits of Life, Mirrors of History*, Schiffer Publishing, 1998; Robert Reed, *Advertising Postcards*, Schiffer Publishing, 2001; —, *Paper Collectibles*, Wallace-Homestead, 1995; Gene Utz, *Collecting Paper*, Books Americana, 1993.

Periodicals: *Paper & Advertising Collector*, PO Box 500, Mount Joy, PA 17552; *Paper Collectors' Marketplace*, PO Box 128, Scandinavia, WI 54977.

Collectors' Clubs: Calendar Collector Society, American Resources, 18222 Flower Hill Way #299, Gaithersburg, MD 20879; Cigar Label Collectors International, PO Box 66, Sharon Center, OH 44274; Citrus Label Society, 131 Miramonte Dr., Fullerton, CA 92365; Ephemera Society of America, PO Box 95, Cazenovia, NY 13035; The National Association of Paper & Advertising Collectors, PO Box 500, Mount Joy, PA 17552; Society of Antique Label Collectors, PO Box 24811, Tampa, FL 33623.

FYI: You can blame Benjamin Franklin for a portion of your junk mail. He issued the first mail-order catalog in 1744, starting the trickle that would ultimately become a deluge of paper-bound advertising material. Catalogs were particularly useful for spreading information about innovations, fashion, and health care to those who lived in rural America.

Account book, John Ross (first husband of Betsy Ross), 15 entries. **$125**

Account book, James Short, Newbury, Mass., 1743-'96, leather-bound, tears, stains, wear. **$250**

Almanac, "American Anti-Slavery Almanac for 1840," woodcut print of free man standing on a whip, a mother and children burying their chains, wear, soiling, back missing

Bag, "Genuine Case Parts," Racine, Wis., new old stock, 1950s, with Case eagle, 9 1/2 in. by 5 in. **$2**

corners. $150

Bookplate, watercolor on lined paper, red and green checked lettering, border and geometric flowers, "29 November 1863 Barbara Lapp," worn grain-decor frame, glued down, few stains, 7 1/4 in. by 5 1/4 in. $1,800

Exercise book, 88 pages, pen and ink math problems on both sides with calligraphic headings and some drawings, 11 in watercolor, name and dates 1831 to 1842, cardboard covers, wear, paper damage, 12 7/8 in. by 8 1/2 in. $325

Insurance policy, nautical, 1772, for sloop named "Molly" sailing from Philadelphia to Boston, 16 1/2 in. by 12 1/2 in. $150

Insurance policy, nautical, 1791, for sloop named "Parrot" sailing from Philadelphia to Newbury, 16 1/2 in. by 12 1/2 in. $125

Land indenture, Pennsylvania, 1763, Northern Liberties, splits, 23 in. by 24 in. $110

Land indenture, Pennsylvania, 1764, Bucks County, signed by John Penn, sale of 1,000 acres, seal with some chipping, 15 in. by 32 in. $250

Land indenture, Pennsylvania, 1772, Lancaster County, 24 1/4 in. by 29 5/8 in. $350

Letter, concerning release of George Washington's slaves, Jan. 4, 1800, from John Butcher to Sarah Horner, Alexandria, Va., one page.. .... $5,000

Sale bill, March 1893, printed in Bellefonte, Pennsylvania, framed, folds, 10 3/8 in. by 14 1/8 in...... $50

Stock note, Free Society of Traders in Pennsylvania, 1683, society seal, 21 1/2 in. by 7 1/2 in. $800

Stock note, Free Society of Traders in Pennsylvania, 1683, heavily damaged Society's seal, 21 1/2 in. by 7 1/2 in. $600

Stock notes, Salem Glass Works, never issued. $300/pair

Tax log, Newbury, Mass., 1755, contains order by assessors of Newbury to Ambros Berry (constable) to collect taxes due to the town and province, lists townspeople and amounts, tears, wear, 7 1/2 in. by 9 1/2 in........ $125

Tray, papier-mâché, shows maiden holding gray graniteware milk pail and standing next to a cow, "Souvenir" in the upper-right corner and "To the Patrons of Granite Ironware" below the image, back marked "Patent Granite Ironware, The Best Cooking Utensils Ever Made, Light, Wholesome, Durable, Easily Cleaned," tear, 10 in. by 7 in. $125

Peaseware

The Pease family worked in Ohio during the 19th century. They are known for their turned wooden containers, which were sometimes painted.

Covered jar, 3 1/4 in. tall, turnings on body, lid with urn finial, pencil inscription with name and 1863 date, age cracks..................... $300

Covered jar, 4 in. tall, squat form, turned rings, urn finial, uneven worn finish, age cracks in body. $475

Covered jar, 4 1/2 in. tall, turned rings, domed lid, tall urn finial. $275

Covered jar, 4 3/4 in. tall, turned rings, urn finial, worn finish, lid slightly warped. $250

Covered jar, 5 1/8 in. tall, turnings, flattened ball finial. $350

Covered jar, 5 1/4 in. tall, squat form, turnings, urn finial. $675

Covered jar, 6 1/4 in. tall, 5 1/4 in. diameter, turned rings, urn finial, worn finish, short age crack in foot, small stain on lid. $425

Covered jar, 6 1/4 in. tall, 5 3/4 in. diameter, turnings on body, lid with flattened ball finial, darker patina on lid. $525

Covered jar, 7 in. tall, 6 1/2 in. diameter, turnings on body, lid with sloping shoulders, urn finial, lightly worn patina, age cracks in bottom. $525

Covered jar, 7 1/4 in. tall, 8 in. diameter, footed base, stepped ring turnings on body, urn-shaped finial. $1,100

Covered jar, 8 1/2 in. tall, 8 in. diameter, maple, turned rings, tall urn finial, minor rim damage on body, glued chip on lid. $525

Covered jar, with bail and wooden handle, 3 3/8 in. tall, turnings on body, lid with flattened ball finial, age cracks, small stains.......... $260

Covered jar, with bail and wooden handle, 3 3/8 in. tall, turnings on body and lid, shiny varnish, ink inscription "From Oran...Sept. 29/89. Bought at the Detroit Exposition Sept. 25th 1889." ... $950

Covered jar, with bail and wooden handle, 4 in. tall, high foot, turned rings on body, lid with elongated finial....................................... $425

Covered jar, with bail and wooden handle, 4 1/2 in. tall, turnings on body, lid with flattened ball finial. $625

Covered jar, with bail and wooden handle, 4 1/2 in. tall, turnings on body, lid with high urn finial, age crack in lid. $425

Covered jar, with bail and wooden handle, 6 3/4 in. tall, 6 3/4 in. diameter, ring turnings on body, flattened knob finial, slightly out of round, age cracks in body....... $350

Covered jar, with bail and wooden handle, 7 3/8 in. tall, 6 1/2 in. diameter, turned rings on body, lid with urn finial, small chip and age crack in lid. $750

Covered jar, with bail and wooden handle, 8 in. tall, 6 1/2 in. diameter, ring turnings, urn finial, wire bail handle missing. $475

Covered jar, 6 1/2 in. tall, 5 in. diameter, turned rings, urn finial, lightly worn patina. **$625**

Covered jar, with bail and wooden handle, 9 in. tall, 10 1/2 in. diameter, turnings on body, flattened finial, light stains....**$1,800**

Covered jar, with bail and wooden handle, 9 1/2 in. tall, 9 in. diameter, turned rings, flattened urn finial, worn finish, areas of dark color, short age crack in foot, lid split and reglued....................................**$450**

Covered jar, with bail and wooden handle, 9 3/4 in. tall, 10 in. diameter, turned foot, raised rings at shoulder, turned finial, glued cracks....................................**$525**

Sewing caddy, three-part, metal rods for spools, paper label "D.M. Pease Manufacturer of American Hollow Ware, Spool Stands ... Address orders to D.M. Pease, Concord, Lake Co., O.," worn finish, lid chips, 5 3/4 in. tall.............................**$325**

This young man's name was Alexander and he was photographed in 1897, complete with lace-trimmed dress and broad hat (in his left hand). **$6-$10**

Photographs

Collectors of late 19th and early 20th century photography can quickly accumulate a wide array of images for less than the price of filling up the average gas tank.

Cabinet photos (averaging 6 1/2 in. by 4 1/4 in.) and carte-de-visites (4 in. by 2 1/2 in.) were produced by the millions from the 1860s to shortly after the turn of the century, when do-it-yourself photography became affordable. Many early photographs—including some tintypes (images on thin sheet steel)—are still available for prices starting at less than a dollar, depending on the subject matter. Daguerreotypes (images on coated copper plates) and ambrotypes (images on glass) usually cost considerably more, depending on subject and condition, as do their ornate molded cases made of gutta-percha or thermal plastic.

Here are a few areas that some collectors focus on when searching for vintage images of rural (or urban) origin.

Some collectors devote themselves solely to images showing boys in dresses, a common 19th century practice. Here's another young man, named Gilbert, in a plaid dress and perched on a wicker photographer's chair in Aberdeen, S.D. **$3-$5**

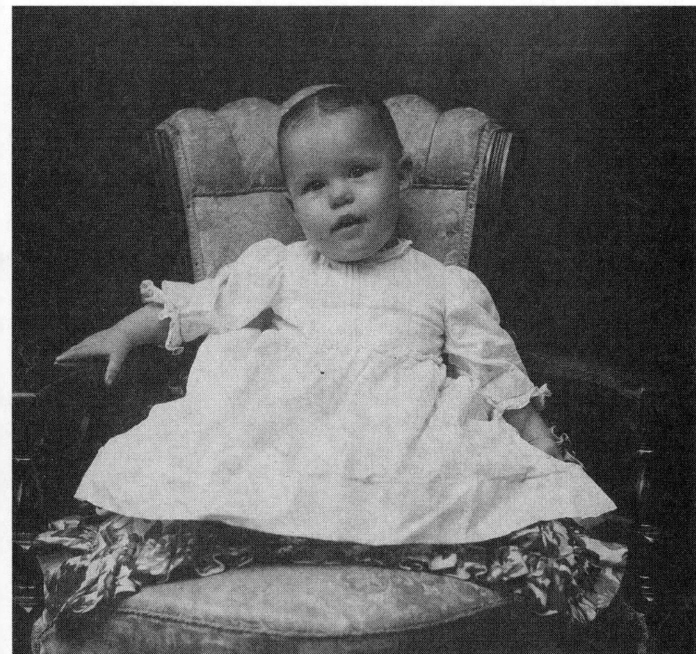

Notice the careful center part and closely cropped hair of the boy in the wide upholstered armchair. **$2-$4**

This young lady marked the occasion of her First Communion by posing for this photograph in Wausau, Wis., in about 1910. **$3-$5**

While the child in this cabinet photograph is cute enough, some collectors of wicker furniture are more attracted to the elaborate photographer's chair on which the baby is seated. This card came from Omro, Wis. **$8-$10**

Subjects for cabinet photographs whose heritage is not European (blacks or American Indians, for example) are also highly collectible. This young lady of Asian descent was photographed in Stacyville, Iowa, in about 1905. **$4-$6**

These five children were photographed about 1900 in a studio in Peterson, Minnesota. Note the matching outfits worn by the two older girls, and how four of the children are directing their attention to the left, while the girl on the right stares stoically at the photographer. **$5-$7**

This image, made using a single light source (probably a sitting room window) has a striking "American Gothic" quality, but collectors of early lighting may be able to date the photograph based on details noted in the hanging kerosene lamp. **$5-$8**

The image of these siblings, including a girl with a doll and a boy with a bicycle, makes this cabinet photograph cross over into other collecting areas, and also increases its value. **$12-$15**

The details of this young lady's large hat can only be guessed at, but she took care to show off a large nosegay (also called a "tussie mussie") and a distinctive brooch in the shape of a butterfly on her lace collar. **$2-$4**

The first thing one might notice about this young man is that he appears to be well over six feet tall, but a collector of rustic furniture would also spot the twig table in the right background in front of the faux hallway. Also, note the crazy-quilt cover on the footstool under his right foot. This image came from Dexter, Minn. **$3-$5**

The young man in this photograph wanted to feature his heavy watch chain and fob (and maybe a new hat), but other details of the photograph are recurring elements in studio shots of the day, including the rustic fence and the pedestal with deep-relief decoration to his right. **$3-$5**

Some collectors devote themselves to images showing men with distinctive facial hair. The elderly man with long white beard, far right, was photographed in Loup City, Neb. **$2-$4.** *The young man showing off his handlebar mustache, right, posed in Guttenberg, Iowa.* **$2-$4**

This cabinet photo has sustained damage from being stored in an album where the surface rubbed against another card. The card is virtually worthless, but the image can be saved, using a computer program like Photoshop.

Images of kids and dogs—even a rather static one like this—are popular with collectors. **$8-$10**

At first, one thinks, "What a lovely christening gown," but this is soon followed by, "Did the worried parent really think no one would notice that there are two arms holding this baby in place?" **$1-$3**

Tintypes like these typically have irregular borders that were masked by a cardboard frame. Each is 4 in. by 2 1/2 in. **$10-$15 each**

Group images, like this one of workers posing outside their plant (?), are valued as slices of late 19th century life, but the price of the image increases if it is accompanied by its place of origin and the names or occupations of the subjects, 7 1/2 in. by 9 1/2 in. **$40-$50**

Mystery shots like: Why is this young couple perched on the back of an old sleigh and wearing boxing gloves? Newlyweds mugging for the in-laws?, 4 in. by 2 in. **$1-$2**

The photograph of this boys' athletics team from Keewatin, Ontario, is posing at the U.S. border. Even with the inked notations, sports photos like this are highly collectible, 2 1/2 in. by 4 in. **$10-$15**

The border and design on this cabinet photo suggest that the subject has died. Many turn-of-the-century photographic studios kept images on file for years, and advertised the service as this Clarinda, Iowa, studio did on the back of the card. **$3-$5**

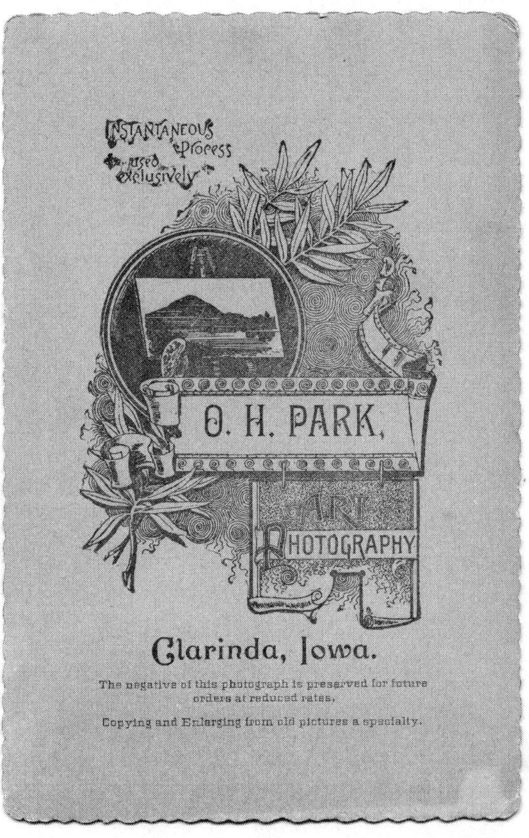

Ninety-nine out of a hundred cabinet photos and carte des visites show the subjects seemingly staring off in the distance. This woman's somber gaze directly at the camera is both striking and unusual. **$3-$5**

While photos of siblings are common, images showing mothers and daughters are not. **$5-$8**

Sometimes the backdrops used in early photo studios have an unintended effect. Though this woman seems to be posing in front of a large walnut pier mirror, both the mirror and its reflection are an illusion. **$4-$5**

The Vandike Bros. studio in Arcadia, Neb., used line art showing a box camera and photographic chemicals on the front of its cabinet cards. **$2-$4**

The expression on this girl's face is about as close to a smile as most subjects could muster. **$2-$4**

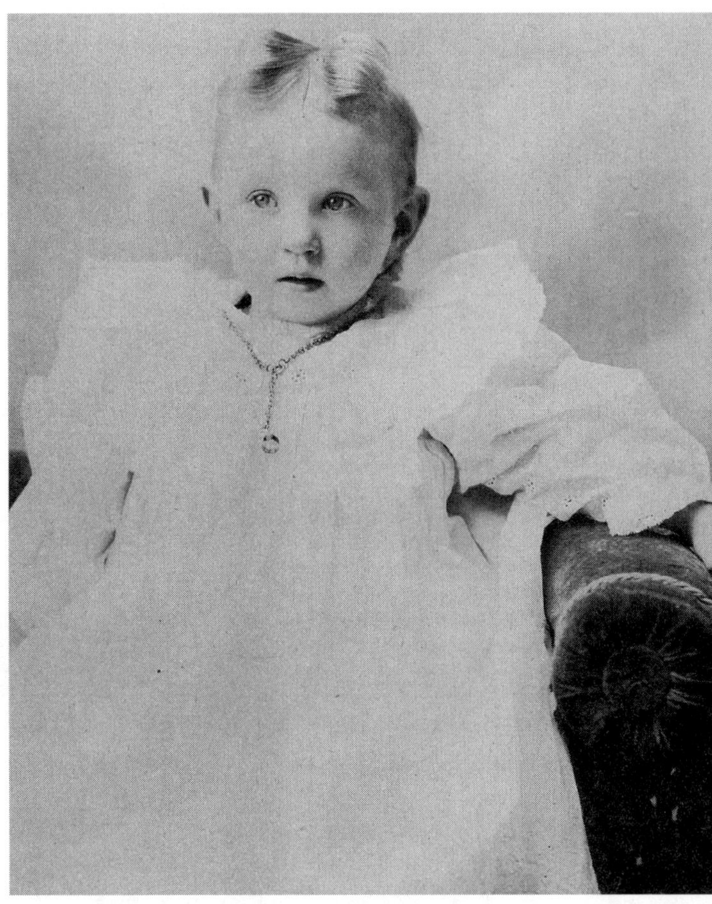

Baby rings were a popular ornament for Victorian children. This young boy wore his on a chain around his neck. **$5-$7**

The photographer, F.H. Burgess of Augusta, Maine, captured this young boy with his ball. **$5-$7**

Ambrotype of a young woman, lined with red velvet, stamped gilt frame and gutta-percha case, size closed 3 in. by 2 1/2 in. **$100**

Tintypes, 1/9th plate, of a man and woman, probably wedding or anniversary photos, in stamped gilt frames, gutta-percha case in the "three pears" pattern, made by Holmes, Booth and Hayden, mint, size closed, 3 in. by 2 1/2 in. (Israel Holmes, John Booth and Henry Hayden, of Waterbury, Connecticut, and New York City, operated one of the largest photographic supply houses in the United States. They began to produce daguerreotype plates in 1853.) **$110**

Where can I find them?

Old photos are available in every corner of the country, but some excellent resources include:

Country Comfort Antiques
Third and Main Streets
Winona, MN 55987
(507) 452-7044

John Kruesel's General Merchandise
22 Third St. SW
Rochester, MN 55902
(507) 289-8049
www.kruesel.com

Pyrography

Pyrography is the process of burning a picture or design into a wooden surface. Skilled artisans introduced the art form to America in the mid-1800s, but it became a hobby for the masses around the turn of the century, when several companies began offering items with designs stamped on them for burning. The Flemish Art Co. of New York was the largest producer of pyrographic products, and the term "Flemish art" has become synonymous with burnt wood pieces of that era. The hobby was most popular from about 1890 to 1920.

Pieces decorated freehand generally bring more than those created using a printed pattern.

Reference: Frank L. Hahn, *Collector's Guide to Burnt Wood Antiques*, Golden Era Publications, 1994.

Box, poinsettia and leaves on lid, basket weave design on sides, interior stained green with felt bottom, 4 in. by 14 3/8 in. by 10 1/2 in. **$45**

Chair-table, floral and other decor, sides with two large oval cutouts, 47 in. tall.......... **$550**

Game board, triangle-design surface, owl on reverse, 11 in. by 14 in. **$150**

Plate rack, fruit motif, 12 in. by 42 in. **$250**

Plate rack, water scene with stork, swans, cattails, etc., scalloped top, 52 in. long. **$375**

Table, pedestal, floral and geometric design, three scrolled legs, triangular base, 29 in. tall, top 29 in. square. **$350**

Wastebasket, woman's bust and grapes decor, square, scalloped top, 14 in. tall.......... **$85**

Quilts

Quilts represent the most basic form of recycling: Making something useful and beautiful out of scraps and tatters that would otherwise go to waste. At last count, there were about 4,000 documented quilt patterns. They range in price from less than $100 for a plain (and worn) covering for the hired man's bed, to many thousands of dollars for the most striking appliquéd examples with figural and patriotic themes.

"Album Quilt," circa 1860, with many of the blocks signed by their makers, some were signed by ink and some by threads, some are signed "Ligonier Valley Pa 1867"; designs include flowers, wreath, leaves, pinwheels, and crossed American flags; probably never used or washed as there are still pencil marks evident where the quilting was done; rope, diamond, and straight line quilting at seven stitches to the inch, 74 in. by 76 in. **$3,750**

"Amish Sunshine & Shadow" quilt, circa 1930-1940, Lancaster, Pa., made of a variety of fabrics including wool, cotton, crepe, and rayon; the border is teal blue cotton, and the corner blocks are purple rayon; quilted in a meandering rose vine and baskets in the border; rose wreath in the corner blocks, and in cross-hatch quilting through the squares; about 10 stitches per inch in black thread, very good condition; squares measure 1 1/2 in., 79 in. square. **$1,850**

Quilting in the Ditch

Quilting in the ditch means that stitches are made in the seam lines between the pieces. In this technique the stitches barely show, but create a puffiness emphasizing the design of the pieced top.

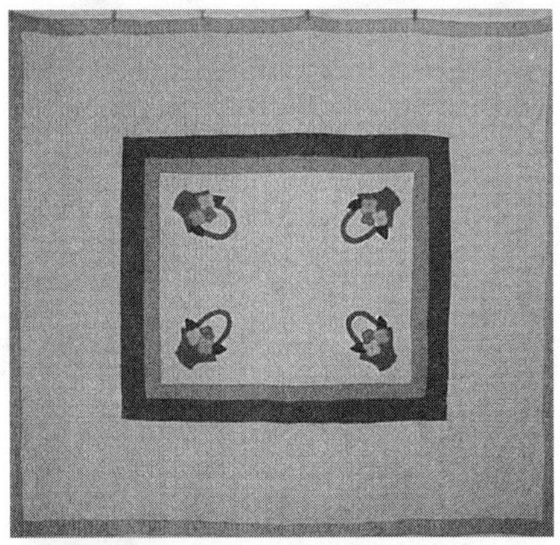

"Appliqué Baskets" quilt, and detail, circa 1930, cotton sateens in three shades of lavender, flowers have a little bit of embroidery, minimal design serves as a canvas for the quilting, designs include a feather wreath in the center, pumpkin seeds over most of the quilt, tiny diamond grids, and cables in the two inner borders, about nine to 10 stitches per inch, excellent condition, washed, clean, 75 in. by 85 in. **$450**

"Bars" quilt, circa 1880-1910, Pennsylvania, striking graphic, done in Lancaster blue, double pink, and yellow calicoes, quilted in multiple cables in the blue bars, and diamond grid in the pink and yellow bars, at six to seven stitches per inch; back is a mourning print, very thin batting, unused condition, 76 in. square. **$500**

"Brickwall Trip Around the World" Mennonite quilt, circa 1910, Pennsylvania, treadle-machine pieced "bricks" measure 1 3/4 in. by 3 3/4 in., repeating fabrics include blue calico, solid teal blue, yellow calico, cheddar, double pink, and solid turkey red; three borders in green calico and double pink, brown print back, separately applied double pink binding, six stitches per inch, thin batting, very good, unused, unwashed condition, 84 in. by 94 in. **$800**

"Barn Raising Log Cabin" quilt, circa 1850, chintz and other printed fabrics including a conversation print (one that has a design on it other than a floral or geometric pattern, i.e., a person or animal), center chimney is a four block, quilted "in the ditch" at eight stitches to the inch, 82 in. by 96 in. **$1,250**

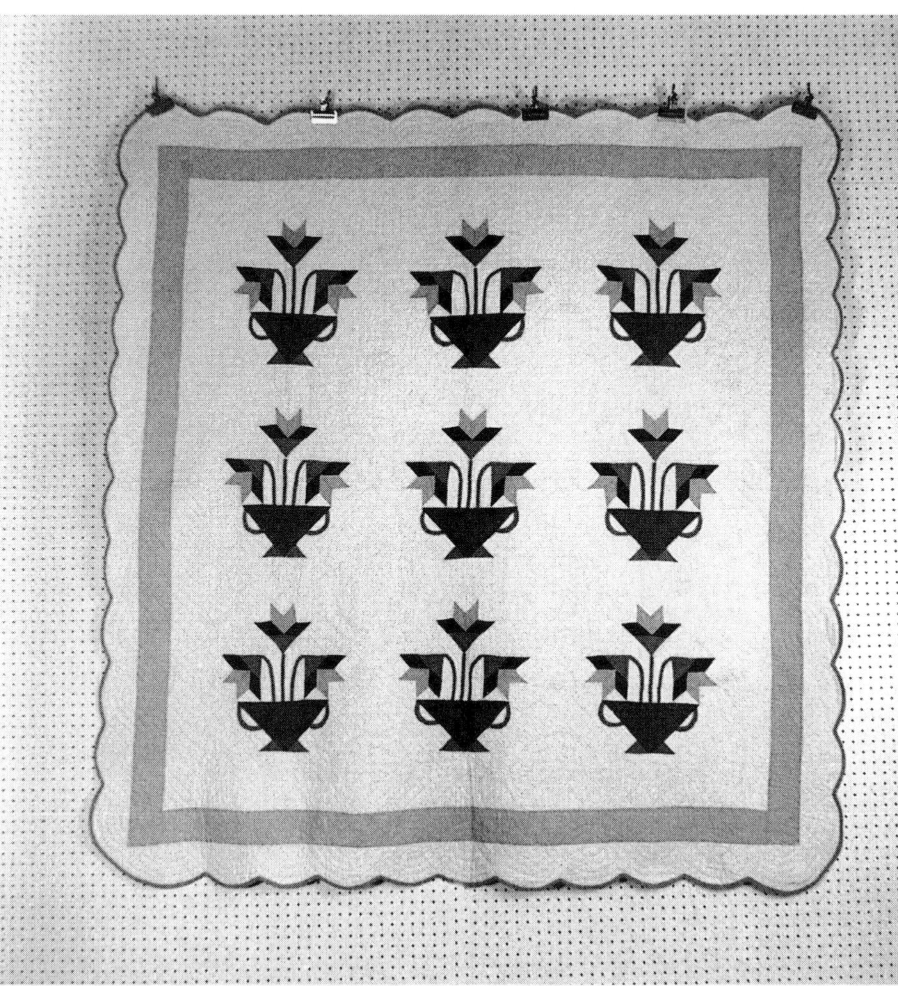

Basket of Tulips" quilt.

"Chimney Sweep" Mennonite quilt and detail, circa 1870, Pennsylvania, strong colors: saffron yellow calico, dark brown, and dark green solids, bordered with a rose calico, very thin, unwashed, unused, excellent condition, water stain on the chocolate brown back that doesn't show though to the front, quilted in straight lines and a one-inch grid with clam shells in the border at six to seven stitches per inch, 87 in. square. **$550**

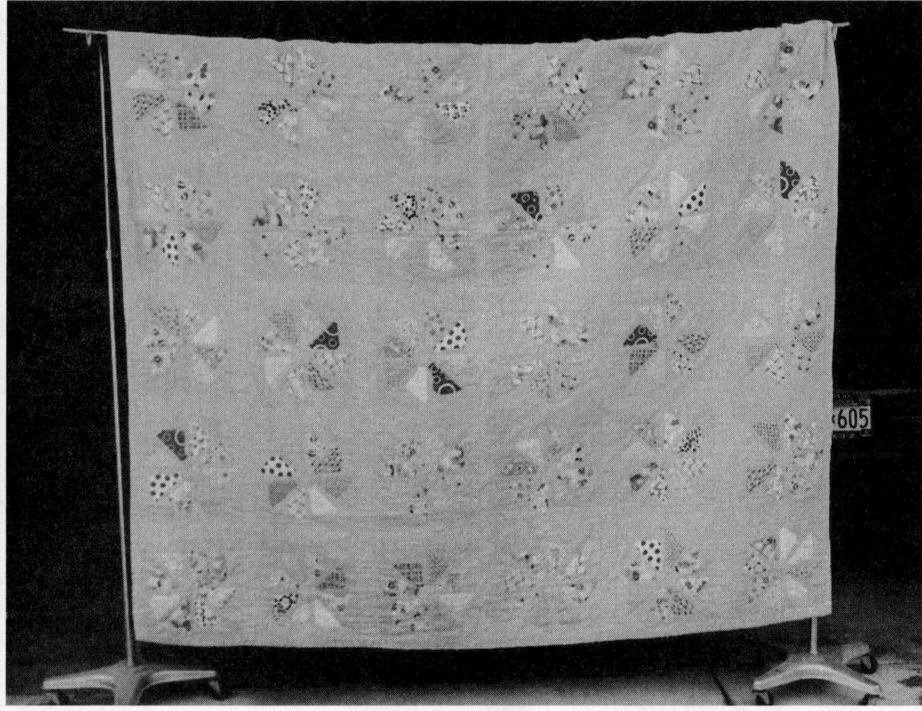

"Boxed Pinwheel" pattern, summer-weight quilt, in pale green and pink field with assorted fabrics in pinwheels, all hand-stitched, circa 1940s, minor wear, 84 in. by 80 in. **$200-$300**

"Chips and Whetstone" (variation of "Ocean Wave") quilt, circa 1840, New England (probably Massachusetts), 80 in. by 94 in. **$2,900**

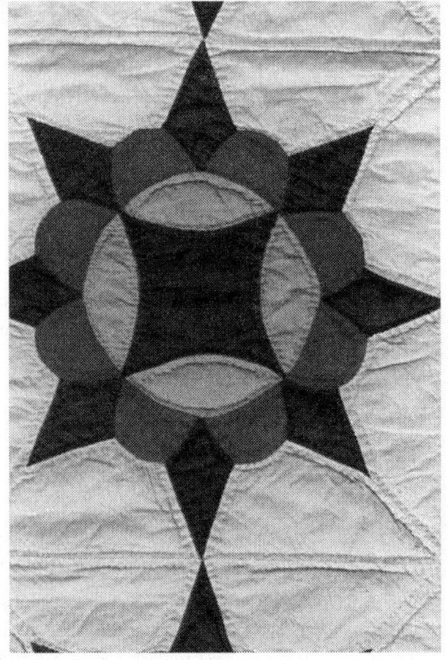

"Compass/Caesar's Crown" Mennonite quilt, circa 1850, York, Pa.; 81 in. by 80 in.; 36 12 in. off-white blocks have eight-point pieced compass in solid turkey red, mustard yellow, and vegetable-dyed green; compasses touch over field; 3 1/2 in. off-white border has alternating single green triangles with double triangles of solid red and green; expertly hand pieced; seven to eight stitches per inch quilting outlines pieces and blocks; excellent condition; several restored pieces. **$930**

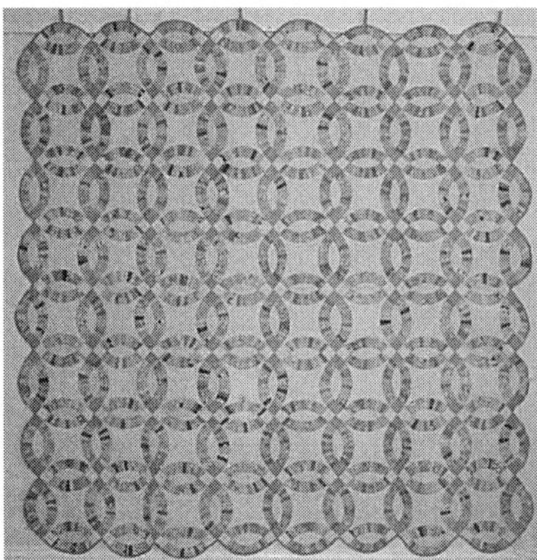

"Double Wedding Ring" quilt, and details at right, circa 1930, Missouri, well made with small pieces and many rings, great assortment of 1930s prints set with unbleached muslin, heavily quilted in floral straight-line designs at eight stitches per inch, excellent, unwashed condition, 80 in. square. **$450**

Crazy quilt, circa 1930s, done in bold color blocks of red, rust, black, blue, and taupe, with at least eight different styles of decorative stitching, all hand-pieced, near mint condition, 74 in. by 84 in. **$400-$500**

"Drunkards Path" quilt, circa 1880, blue and white, dark indigo blue color with wide white outer border, diamond quilting at eight stitches to the inch with a grid of 1/2 in., 74 in. square. This pattern originated with the Women's Christian Temperance Union's campaign for prohibition. **$1,100**

"Flock of Birds" quilt, circa 1930, red and white, striking graphics with blocks surrounded with stars in the sashing and on the four corners; feather and straight line quilting at eight stitches to the inch, 71 in. square. **$1,200**

"Floral and Bow" appliqued quilt, with detail, circa 1930, made with soft chambrays on an ecru ground and bordered in blue, heavily quilted in a small 3/4-inch diamond grid over the whole quilt, and around the appliqués, about nine to 10 stitches per inch; thin batting; off-white cotton back, corners are rounded and blue border is turned from front to back to make the binding; unwashed condition, 76 in. by 94 in. **$750**

"Extended Nine Patch" quilt, circa 1890, Pennsylvania, 44 in. by 52 in. **$1,200**

"Drunkard's Trail (or Path)" quilt, circa 1910, New Oxford, Pa.; 82 in. square; 3 in. blocks are neatly pieced; red (with tiny black print) paths cross off-white field; 2 in. inner and outer red print border, 2 in. middle off-white border; off-white binding; entirely hand pieced; seven to eight stitches per inch quilting, concentric circles over field, concentric waves on borders; excellent condition. **$800**

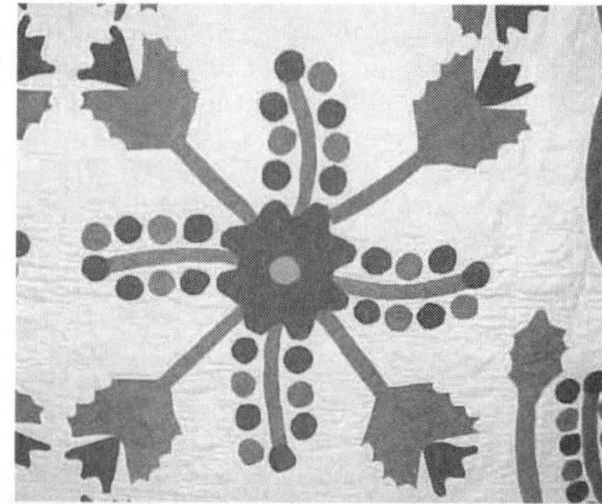

"Folk Art Appliqué" quilt, circa 1850, 90 in. square, dating to 1850, with many quilted hearts, possibly a wedding gift. **$2,900**

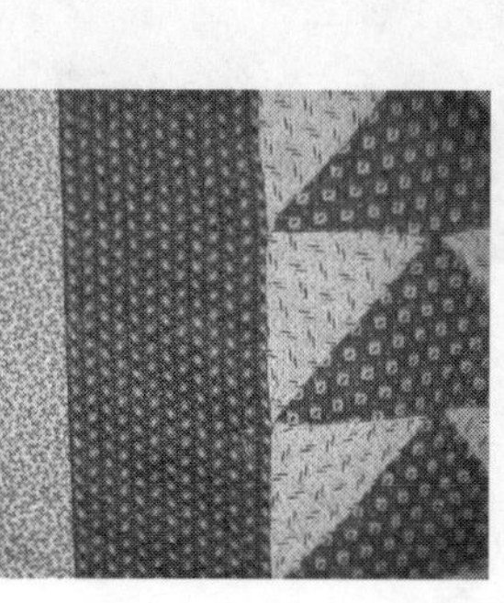

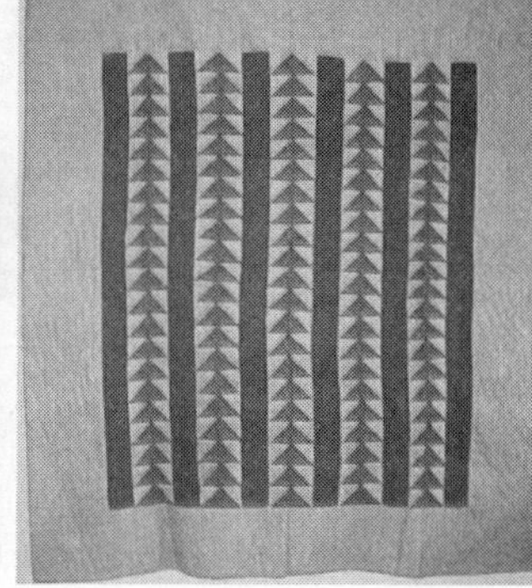

"Flying Geese" quilt, with detail, circa 1880, Pennsylvania, in rust, yellow, and green calicoes, bordered in Lancaster blue calico, brown, and "madder" (moderate to strong red) stripe print backing, quilted in cables, straight lines, and by the piece, at six to seven stitches per inch, very thin batting, unwashed, 72 in. by 82 in. **$475**

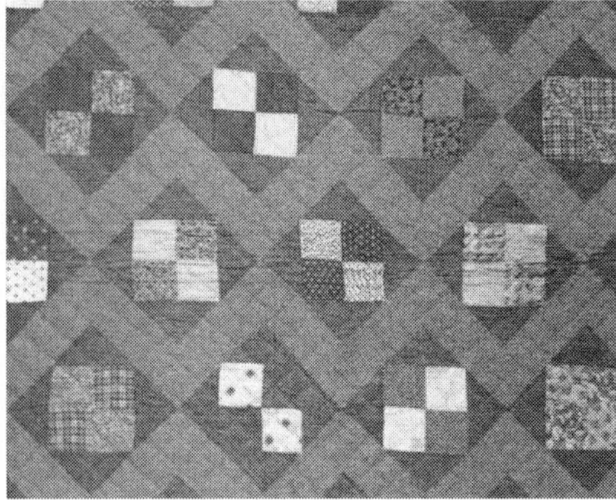

"Four-Patch Square-in-Square" quilt from the Oley Valley of Berks County, Pa., 98 in. by 85 in, circa 1890, in crisp, unused condition; double pink border on three sides and a green calico border on all four enclose an unusual setting of four-patch blocks in green squares set on point, sashed with a zigzag of double pink, a large dogtooth inner border of Lancaster blue also surrounds the central field of blocks; the fabrics in the four-patch blocks include practically every color available to the turn of the century quilter; quilting is done in a 1 1/2 in. grid overall, at six to seven stitches per inch; "Bars" pattern on back in red and brown calicos; the binding is a dark green calico. **$675**

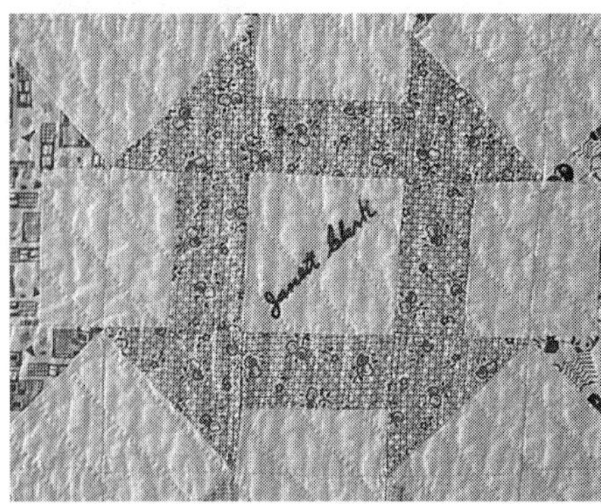

"Friendship Monkey Wrench" quilt, circa 1930, Logan, Ohio, with 56 blocks, hand-pieced with pastel fabrics; 28 of the blocks are signed with names; quilt has three borders, including a graphic inner zigzag border, thin batting, off-white cotton back; separately applied blue binding; well quilted in diagonal lines one inch apart, at eight to nine stitches per inch, excellent condition, 72 in. by 80 in **$500**

"Geese in Flight" quilt, circa 1850, New England, 88 in. by 98 in. **$2,900**

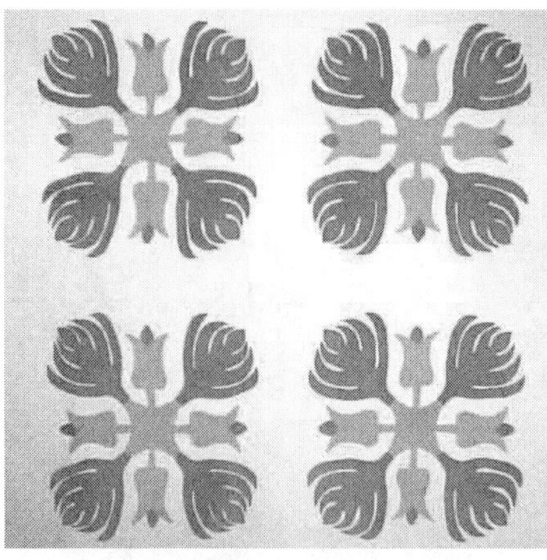

"Gothic Four Square" quilt, Pennsylvania or Ohio, 68 in by 82 in **$2,500**

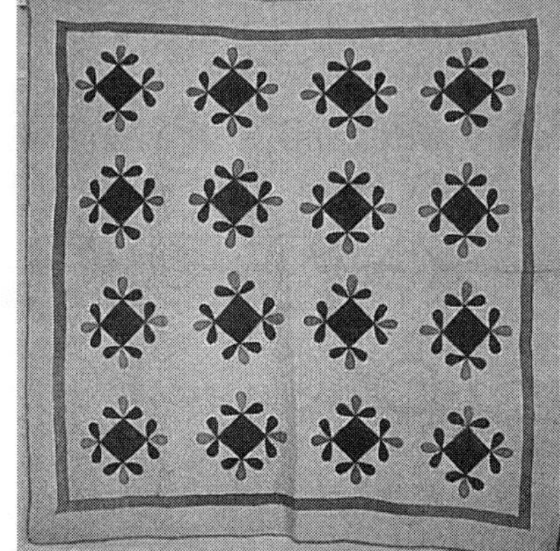

"Honeybee" or "Bayleaf" quilt, with details, circa 1890, Missouri, a pieced and appliquéd pattern that doesn't come up too often, made with green calico and solid cinnamon-tan (probably originally red that has faded), set with off-white cotton, same off-white cotton is used on back; quilted in large feather wreaths, grids, and straight lines at five to six stitches per inch, unwashed, overall excellent condition, 85 in. by 90 in. **$450**

"Honeybee/Checkerboard" quilt, circa 1900, Lancaster County, Pa.; 81 in. by 78 in.; 10 in. off-white blocks turned on point have hand-pieced solid turkey red diamond and appliquéd "teardrops" at each corner forming the honeybee pattern; alternating solid off-white blocks; 2 in. solid red inner border, 2 in. off-white outer border; red and white four-patch checkerboard corners; red binding; seven to eight stitches per inch quilting, double quilted horizontal lines on honeybee blocks, double feather leaves on white blocks; double quilted diagonal lines on borders, excellent condition. **$925**

"Indigo Double Nine Patch" quilt, circa 1880-1900, Ohio, dark indigo print background, set with small nine-patch blocks that measure just 3 1/4 in., thin batting, brown print back, quilted in diagonal lines 3/4 in. apart, at eight to nine stitches per inch, excellent condition, 74 in. by 76 in. **$500**

"Jack in the Pulpit" quilt, circa 1910-1920, New Harmony, Ind., scrap quilt set on a yellow and black print, using a variety of early 1900s prints; quilted in a grid at seven to eight stitches per inch, mint, unwashed condition, 74 in. by 86 in. **$550**

"Lady of the Lake" quilt, circa 1880, Ohio; 77 in. by 69 in.; 7 in. blocks have solid off-white and navy (with white dots) triangles; 2 1/2 in. sashing has smaller solid off-white and navy print triangles; off-white binding; entirely hand-pieced; seven to eight stitches per inch quilting; 3/4 in. diamonds on large triangles, diagonal lines on small triangles; excellent condition. ***$1,700***

"LeMoyne Star/Double Irish Chain" Mennonite quilt, circa 1910, 1930s back, Lancaster County, Pa.; 86 in. by 86 in.; 2 in. pieced squares of red (with black print) and yellow (with red and black print) form double chains diagonally across quilt; navy with off-white print field has appliquéd eight-point star with alternating red print and yellow print diamonds; 4 in. red (with black print) border; medium blue (with floral print) binding; entirely hand-pieced; five to six stitches per inch quilting in navy thread outlines stars, 2 in. squares over quilt, diamond cable on border; excellent condition. **$1,150**

"Nine Patch Plaid with Single Irish Chain" quilt, circa 1890, 78 in. by 80 in., Maine. **$2,900**

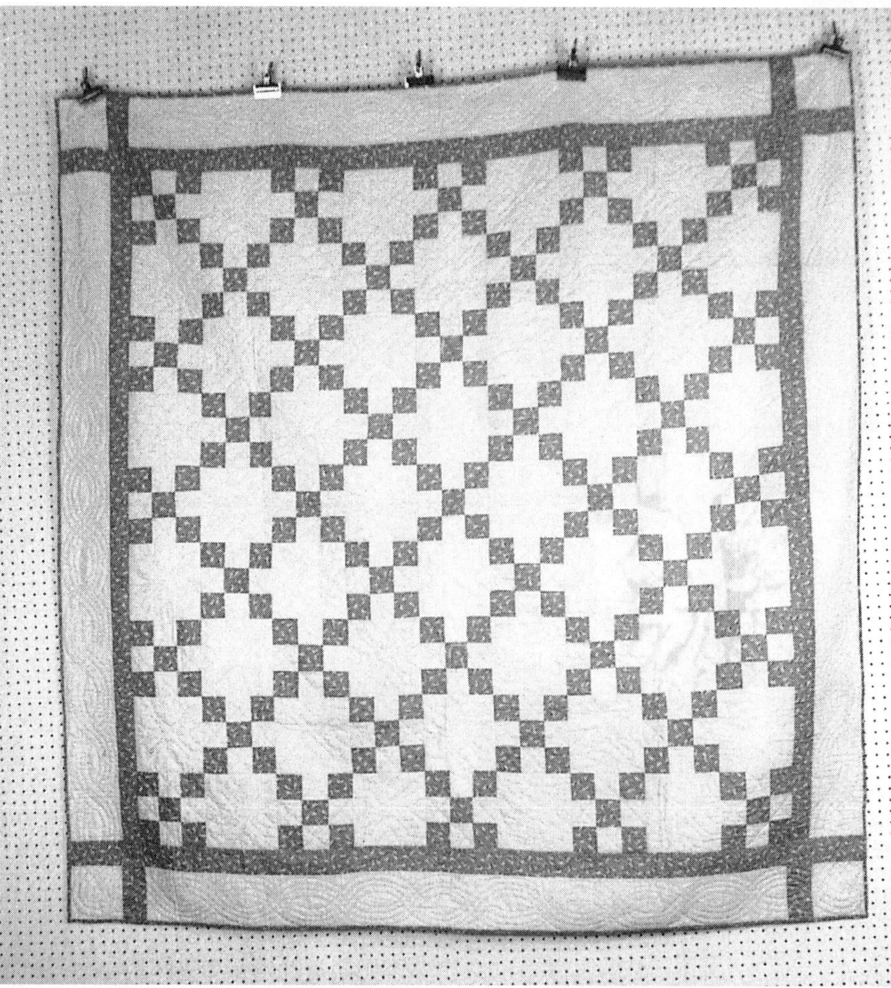

"Nine Patch" quilt, circa 1890-1910, Pennsylvania, unusual, striking color combination: primarily greens, blacks, maroon, and shirting prints, blocks measure just 4 in., border is a gray-green calico; back is a blue floral print, thin batting, quilted in a 1 1/2 in. grid in black thread, at six to seven stitches per inch, unwashed, excellent condition, slight fade in border in places, 72 in. by 74 in. **$450**

"Oak Leaf and Reel" quilt, circa 1835, New England, 78 in. by 86 in. **$2,800**

"Ohio Star" pattern variation quilt in orange and blue, with detail, 82 in. square, all original, in excellent condition, circa 1930s; a 7 in. wide border of solid orange surrounds the field of on-point star blocks pieced from orange, light yellow, and blue print fabrics; quilted in a grid pattern, with floral ornaments in the setting blocks, at eight stitches per inch. **$400**

"Pinwheels" quilt, with detail, circa 1930-1940, solid colored pinwheels set with off-white cotton, quilted squares on point with Xs, and by the piece at seven stitches per inch, thin cotton batting; off-white cotton backing same as on front; separately applied binding in same white fabric, excellent, unused condition, 82 in. by 86 in. **$350**

"Postage Stamp Checkerboard" quilt, circa 1865, New York, 70 in. by 82 in. **$1,400**

Pennsylvania appliqué quilt.

"Ohio Star" quilt, circa 1860, blue and white, striking graphics, borders, quilting, and large size, appliquéd outer swag border and inner sawtooth border, cotton seeds in the filling; wreath, triple straight line, and straight line quilting at 11 stitches to the inch, with varying blue print fabrics, 77 in. by 92 in. **$1,950**

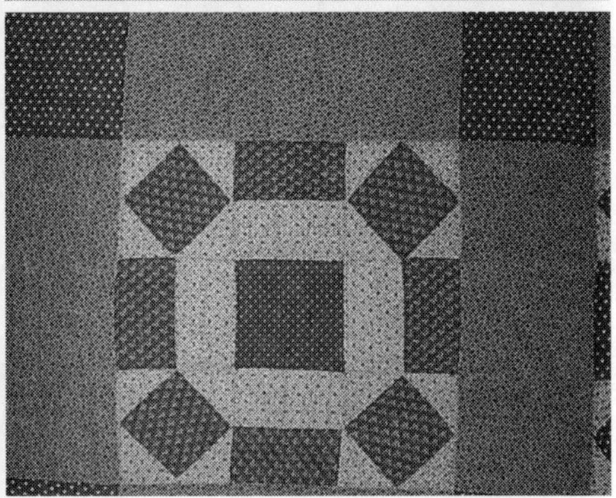

"Rolling Stone" quilt, with detail, circa 1870, Pennsylvania, mint condition; vibrant early prints in red, yellow, and Lancaster blue calicoes, all handmade; separate red calico binding, zigzag border in same red print; copper/brown print backing, thin batting, outline quilted with blue thread in blocks and grid in borders, at six stitches per inch; unwashed condition, 82 in. by 98 in. **$750**

"Rolling Stone" quilt, with detail, circa 1870-1880, probably Pennsylvania, graphic, early quilt with intense colors of dark green, yellow, dark brown, chrome orange, and double pink, all calicoes except for the orange and brown, brown print back, separately applied solid brown binding; thin cotton batting, quilted in large fans over the whole quilt at about six stitches per inch, excellent, unused condition, 75 in. by 91 in. **$500**

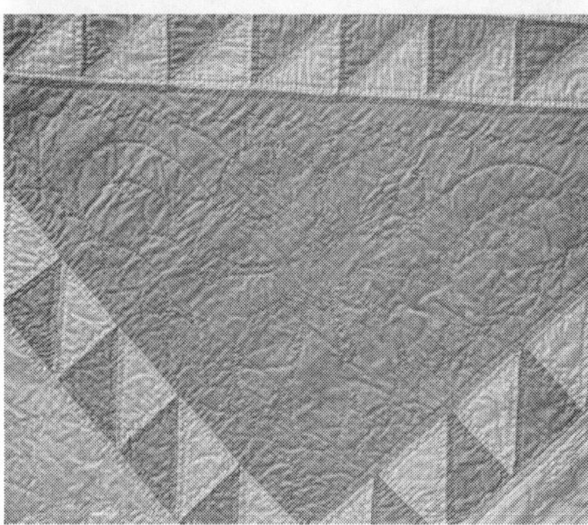

"Sawtooth Diamond" quilt, with detail, circa 1930, peach and true white cotton, thin batting, white cotton back; separately applied peach binding, quilted at eight to nine stitches per inch, designs include a large feather wreath surrounded by flowers in the center, stylistic butterflies in the large peach triangles, meandering feather chain in the white border, and cable quilting in the peach border, excellent condition, 74 in. square. **$750**

"Rose Wreath Appliqué" quilt, circa 1860, red and green, unusual basket of flowers in each of the four corners, the borders are slightly different on each of the two adjoining sides, reverse appliqué work of a yellow calico fabric in the center of the flowers; flower, leaf, diamond, conforming, and other quilting at 10 stitches to the inch, 96 in. square. **$2,500**

"Sawtooth Diamond" quilt, circa 1930, cotton sateens in creamy white and lemon yellow, well pieced with sharp points on the triangles, heavily quilted with a wreath in center, tiny diamond grid, cables, floral patterns, scrolls, and a running leaf pattern, at eight to nine stitches per inch, thin cotton batting, yellow binding, white cotton backing; excellent condition, may be unwashed, 78 in. by 88 in. **$650**

"Schoolhouse" quilt, circa 1900, Indiana; 80 in. by 64 in.; 20 11 in. white blocks have pieced turkey red schoolhouses; 4 in. white sashing separates schoolhouses; 4 in. white border and binding; seven to eight stitches per inch quilting; horizontal lines on houses, small clamshells on roof, 1/4 in. squares on chimney, double-quilted diagonal lines 1 in. apart on sashing and border; excellent condition. **$2,300**

"Shoo-Fly" quilt, from the Oley Valley of Berks County, Pennsylvania, circa 1890, 78 in. by 86 in., in crisp, unused condition; pieced from red, yellow, green, and pink calico fabrics, with a 1 1/2 in. inner border of yellow, and a 10 in. wide outer red border; an unusual feature is the added zigzag in solid turkey red fabric around the central field of blocks; the binding is a dark green calico, the quilting is done at seven to eight stitches per inch, in a 1 in. grid in the central field, with a cable design in the border; classic "Bars" pattern on back in dark green and double pink calicos. **$650**

"Snowflake" quilt.

"Steeple Chase" quilt, circa 1865, Vermont, 68 in. by 80 in. **$2,200**

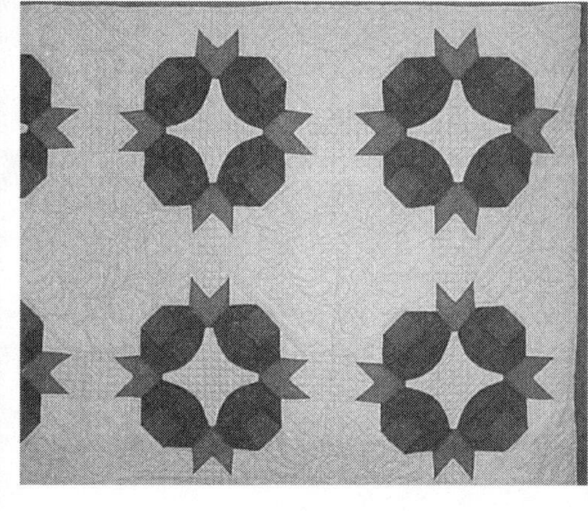

"Tulip Wreath" variation quilt, detail at right, circa 1930, unusual, pieced pattern made and quilted by an expert, solid pink, blue, and lavender on ivory-white ground, finely quilted with feather wreaths, small grids and cross-hatching, multiple borders, very thin batting, same white cotton used on back; separately applied blue binding; unused, unwashed condition, 78 in. by 95 in. **$650**

"World Without End" quilt, details above, circa 1930, a favorite graphic pattern of illusion, quilted in cables over the whole at six to eight stitches per inch, thin cotton batting, white cotton backing; separately applied white binding, tightly hand-pieced, very good condition, 63 in. by 78 in. **$425**

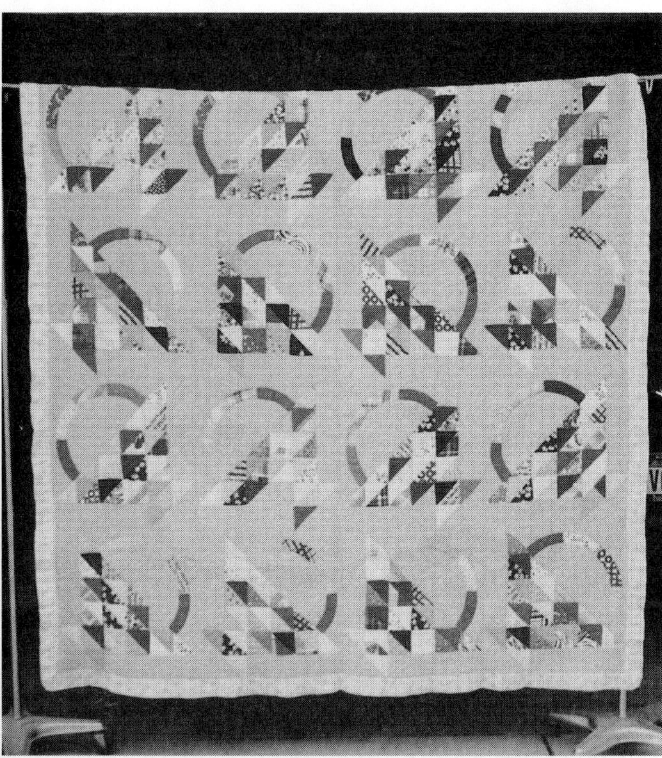

"Tumbling Basket" summer-weight quilt, in lavender field with white border, assorted fabrics in baskets, all hand-stitched, circa 1940s, 84 in. by 80 in. **$200-$300**

"Tumbling Stars" quilt, circa 1870, Maine, 83 in. by 83 in. **$2,400**

"Variable Rolling Star" quilt from New England, circa 1810, 76 in. by 78 in., hand-pieced and hand-quilted, the dark brown fabrics on this quilt are hand-painted block prints and the backing is a whole cloth block print. Most of the time, early fabrics were taken from clothes, beds, and other random articles and used in the background, but in this case, the background fabric on this quilt is comprised of many different shapes and pieces. **$2,900**

Where can I find them?

Some of the following resources also carry fine vintage rugs and samplers:

The Antique Quilt Source
3064 Bricker Rd.
Manheim, PA 17545-9644
(717) 492-9876
http://www.antiquequiltsource.com/
strongg@paonline.com

Marie Miller Antique Quilts
1489 Route 30
PO Box 983
Dorset VT 05251
(802) 867-5969
http://www.antiquequilts.com
larry@antiquequilts.com

Sharon's Antiques and Vintage Quilts
(610) 756-6048
http://www.rickrack.com
quilts@rickrack.com

Carol Telfer Antiques
312 Cobourg St.
Stratford, Ontario
Canada N5A 3G5
(519) 271-0941
http://www.caroltelferantiques.on.ca/index.php
ctelfer@caroltelferantiques.on.ca

Betsey Telford Antique Quilts
dba Rocky Mountain Quilts
130 York St.
York Village, ME 03909
(800) 762-5940
(207) 363-6800
http://www.rockymountainquilts.com/
quilts@rockymountainquilts.com

Mary Ann Walters
Log Cabin Antiques
4200 Peggy Ln.
Plano, TX 75074
(972) 881-2818
www.quiltsquilts.com
logcabin@flash.net

Redware

American colonists began making redware in the late 17th century, using the same clay used for bricks and roof tiles. Ready availability of the clay meant that items could be produced in large quantities to supplement the pewter and treenware already in use. The lead-glazed items retained their reddish color, hence the name redware, although various colors could be obtained by adding different metals to the glaze.

References: Susan and Al Bagdade, *Warman's American Pottery and Porcelain*, 2nd ed., Krause Publications, 2000; William C. Ketchum Jr., *American Redware*, Henry Holt and Company, 1991; Kevin McConnell, *Redware: America's Folk Art Pottery*, Schiffer Publishing, 1988.

Redware, Marked

Bank, jug-shaped, mottled brown and orange ground, ovoid, impressed "John Bell," 4 in. tall.............**$3,250**

Bowl, green-brown glaze, impressed "John Bell, Waynesboro" on bottom, 3 in. tall, 7 5/8 in. diameter. **$1,900**

Butter jar, Upton M. Bell, Waynesboro, Pa., dark greenish-brown glaze, molded bands, arched twisted handles, impressed "Upton M. Bell, Waynesboro, Pa." on bottom, crack, one handle restored, 3 1/2 in. tall, 5 1/2 in. diameter. **$1,100**

Canning jar, orange glaze, cylindrical shape, impressed "J. Bell" on bottom, side repairs, chips, 5 5/8 in. tall, 4 5/8 in. diameter.........**$425**

Crock, light greenish-brown glaze, slightly rounded sides, impressed "John Bell" below collar, cracks, 4 3/8 in. diameter. **$270**

Crock, "Thomas & Bro." (Huntingdon, Pa.), crock, one-gallon, ovoid, impressed mark. **$130**

Flowerpot with attached saucer, green glaze, impressed "John Bell, Waynesboro, Pa." on side of pot, poorly repaired crack, 5 in. tall, 5 5/8 in. diameter. **$1,000**

Food mold, turk's head, mottled brown glaze, impressed "John Bell," hairlines, base chip, 3 3/4 in. tall, 6 3/8 in. diameter. **$300**

Jar, dark-brown glaze, ovoid, impressed "J. Bell" on shoulder, glaze wear, flaking, crack, 6 5/8 in. tall, 6 in. diameter................**$1,200**

Jar, Christian Link, Berks County, Pa. (1870-1900), ovoid, dark-brown glaze, impressed "C. Link," lip chip, 3 5/8 in. tall...............................**$75**

Jug, "Samuel Mellvill, Always this full of good whiskey," folk-decorated, dark ivory glaze, red glaze underneath, scratch decoration of man in top hat, coat, and breeches carrying a shovel, beside a dog and farm, heart with banner and "SM, JM, 1816," glaze flakes, handle crack, 7 1/8 in. tall....**$4,000**

Lady's spittoon, mottled green and brown glaze, handled, impressed "John Bell" on bottom, 3 1/2 in. tall, 4 in. diameter. **$850**

Pitcher, Solomon Bell, Strasburg, Va., mottled green, brown, yellow, and orange ground, ovoid, stamped "S. Bell, Strasburg" on shoulder, chips, 6 1/8 in. tall..........................**$4,000**

Preserve jar, "A. Wilcox, West Bloomfield," with lid, brick red glaze, chips on finial of lid, pot stone near base, 9 3/4 in. tall. **$450**

Vase, Jacob Medinger, ovoid, two handles, mottled green and orange ground, coggled band around rim and shoulder, inscribed "Made By Jacob Medinger for Thomas L. Rhoads," 11 in. tall. **$5,500**

Redware, Vintage, Unmarked

Bank, black glaze, indented ring around the center and around the upper top, one small chip at the bottom of the base, glaze is smooth and unblemished, 3 1/2 in. tall, 3 in. diameter. **$250**

Bank, unglazed, with label: "J. K. Sharpless Sons, Druggists, corner of Maine & 4th St., Catawissa, Pa. To: Mildred from: Kersey Sharpless," good condition, 4 in. tall. **$275**

Bank, acorn form, painted brown, gold textured cap, 4 1/2 in. tall. **$264**

Bean pot with lid, one handle, orange-brown lead/manganese interior glaze, unglazed exterior, interior glaze flaking, chipped lid/finial, 5 1/8 in. tall, 5 1/2 in. diameter. **$375**

Birdhouse, globular shape, flat bottom, knob finial, impressed scroll and rosette design in wide band, arched hole, sloping rim-like perch, Schofield, Pa., late 19th

Bank , hand-painted yellow and green leaves, bottom marked with a hand-painted rooster that may be the logo of the potter, small chips on bottom rim, good condition, 6 1/2 in. tall. **$250**

Bowl, over-all black splashed decoration, one old light hairline on interior, 4 in. by 8 in. **$250**

century, chip on finial, 6 1/4 in. tall, 5 1/2 in. diameter. **$175**

Bottle, fish shape, Moravian (North Carolina), incised features, dark brown glaze, some wear and flaking, 5 in. long................. **$4,200**

Bowl, 7 in. diameter, 3 1/4 in. tall, dark brown sponging on deep orange ground, tooled band, rolled rim.. **$450**

Bowl, 8 in. diameter, cross and dots in yellow slip, wear, edge chip.**$325**

Bowl, 11 in. diameter, spit decoration. **$275**

Bowl, 11 1/2 in. diameter, three rows of squiggle decoration around rim in yellow slip, shallow, hairline, glaze flakes......................... **$2,750**

Bowl, 13 1/2 in. by 10 1/2 in., oval, mottled green and brown decoration, lipped, surface damage, chips........................ **$150**

Bowl, 15 1/2 in. by 12 1/4 in., serving, three-line yellow slip decoration in three sets of wavy lines, imperfections. **$625**

Canning jar, glazed with black splotches, tooled lines at shoulder, glaze flakes, edges rough, 10 5/8 in. tall...................................... **$400**

Chamber pot, Gonic glaze, incised line decoration, New Hampshire, 19th century, applied strap handle, glaze chips, 5 1/2 in. tall. **$700**

Charger, four-line yellow slip decoration in wavy lines with straight lines highlighted in green slip, coggled rim, old chips, wear, glued repair to rim, 11 3/4 in. diameter. **$375**

Chargers, plain glaze, imperfections, 12 1/4 in. and 12 3/4 in. diameter. **$450/pair**

Crock, bean, red glaze, well decorated, several chips on bottom edge and two small chips on upper edge, from New Berlin, Pa., 19th century, 6 1/2 in. by 4 1/2 in. **$250**

Charger, yellow slip decoration and green wavy lines, olive glaze, damage, glued repair, attributed to the Moravians, 14 1/2 in. diameter. **$150**

Dish, two-line decoration in yellow slip, minor wear, crazing, 7 1/2 in. diameter. **$475**

Dish, brown sponging on orange ground, minor chips, 4 3/8 in. diameter. **$350**

Dish, leaf decoration in brown slip on amber ground, coggled rim, old chips, 5 1/2 in. diameter......... **$425**

Dish, windmill stylized decoration in green glaze, ochre splotches, mustard ground, tapered, attributed to Bucks County, Pennsylvania, chips, 1 in. tall, 3 5/8 in. diameter. **$450**

Distlefink, molded, unglazed, old black patina, hanging hole, 6 1/4 in. long..................................... **$75**

Dog, reclining, dark brown glaze, forlorn expression, on base, flakes, 3 1/8 in. tall by 8 7/8 in. long...**$130**

Flowerpots, dark sponging, tooling, wear and chips, no saucer, 5 1/4 in. tall and 5 5/8 in. tall. ...**$150/pair**

Food mold, spiraled flutes, scalloped rim, brown sponging on pinkish-amber ground, wear, slight hairline, 8 in. diameter. **$150**

Food mold, straight flutes, dark sponged rim, deep orange ground, minor chips and wear, 4 3/8 in. diameter. **$1,250**

Food mold, turk's head, for pudding, with black deposits of material due to wear, no mottling but the red glaze is striking, the swirls are very well molded, 8 in. by 3 in. **$125**

Jar, dark brown running glaze, ovoid, applied shoulder handles, chips, 10 1/2 in. tall............................... **$500**

Jar, flower decoration in yellow slip with touches of green, reddish-brown ground, tapered oval body, textured band around neck, hairline, chips, 8 7/8 in. tall. .**$5,100**

Jar, orange spots, dark green and brown glaze, flared rim, embossed tin lid with shield and "Banner Jelly," glaze hairlines, 5 3/4 in. tall. **$150**

Jar, mottled brown glaze, tooled lines, flared rim, handle, 5 1/8 in. tall, 4 5/8 in. diameter............. **$350**

Jug, ovoid, brown splotches, Maine, chips, 7 1/2 in. tall. **$650**

Jug, ovoid, dark brown glaze, black running spots around shoulder and strap handle, tooled foot and neck, old edge chips, 8 in. tall. **$600**

Jug, ovoid, running green, tan and brown glaze, rim chips, flakes, 10 3/4 in. tall............................ **$1,350**

Loaf pan, three-line yellow slip decoration, coggled edge, chips, hairlines, flaking, 3 1/4 in. tall by 15 1/2 in. wide by 11 1/2 in. deep.**$250**

Loaf pan, tree decoration in yellow slip, also wavy lines, tapered sides, coggled rim, wear, glaze flakes, old restoration to rim, 2 1/2 in. tall by 14 in. wide by 10 1/4 deep...**$6,600**

Milk pan, unglazed exterior, flared rim, tapered sides, glazed interior with small brown running streaks, chips, found in Virginia, 9 1/2 in. tall, 18 in. diameter................ **$250**

Milk bowl, brown glazed interior, molded rim, wear and flaking to interior, 3 3/4 in. tall, 16 1/2 in. diameter. **$150**

Milk bowl, daubs of brown glaze on orange ground, tooled band, wear, 5 1/2 in. tall, 13 in. diameter....**$725**

Milk bowl, floral decoration in yellow, green, and brown slip, interior glaze, wear, chips, hairline, 2 3/4 in. tall, 8 1/2 in. diameter........ **$200**

Milk bowl, slip decoration, piecrust

Mug/cup, no handle, "black splash" decoration shows on the exterior as well as the interior, excellent condition, 3 in. tall. **$225**

Mug, with handle, few old chips around the rim, overall very good, 1/2 in. by 3 1/2 in. **$265**

edge, worn interior, hairline, 3 1/4 in. tall, 12 in. diameter. **$110**

Miniature jug, Schofield, Pennsylvania, dark brown lead and manganese glaze, globular shape, minor flake, 3 5/8 in. tall. **$175**

Mixing bowl, brown sponge decoration around rim and in lines down the side, raised rim with tooled band, hairlines, in base, rim flakes, 4 3/4 in. tall, 10 3/4 in. diameter. **$325**

Pie plate, two-line swag decoration, yellow slip, imperfections, 11 1/2 in. diameter. **$250**

Pie plate, two-line wavy decoration in yellow slip, shallow rim flakes, 7 1/2 in. diameter. **$467.50**

Pie plate, three-line decoration in green slip, coggled rim, shallow rim chips, interior glaze wear, 11 3/4 in. diameter. **$880**

Pie plate, three-line, yellow slip, coggled rim, minor chips, 7 in. diameter. **$250**

Pie plate, three-line, yellow slip, wavy decoration, wear, hairlines, 8 1/2 in. diameter.............................**$450**

Pie plate, three-line, yellow slip, coggled rim, wear, chips, some slip wear and flakes, 10 1/4 in. diameter. $450

Pie plate, three-line, yellow slip, coggled rim, glaze and edge chips, 11 in. diameter. **$725**

Pie plate, three-line, yellow slip, coggled rim, edge chips, interior ear, hairline, 11 3/8 in. diameter. **$425**

Pie plate, four-line, squiggled lines, yellow and green slip, imperfections, 8 in. diameter. ..**$350**

Pie plate, four-line, yellow slip, wear, hairline, 8 in. diameter............**$425**

Pie plate, other, "ABC" in script over flourish, tooled rim, old black on back, chips, 11 1/4 in. diameter. **$1,100**

Pie plate, other, "ABC" in script over wavy line and flourish, flaking, hairline, 10 1/8 in. diameter.....**$850**

Pie plate, other, bird's-claw decoration in three-line yellow slip, coggled rim, hairlines, rim chips, 9 1/2 in. diameter. **$250**

Pie plate, other, crossed double wavy lines in yellow slip, slightly scooped bottom, 1 7/8 in. deep, 9 in. diameter. **$500**

Pie plate, other, flower in yellow slip, coggled rim, wear, 11 in. diameter. **$400**

Pie plate, other, slip decoration (no distinct pattern) in yellow, edge wear, flakes, 9 in. diameter. **$350**

Pie plate, other, slip decoration (no distinct pattern) in yellow, wear, hairlines, old chips, 9 in. diameter. **$400**

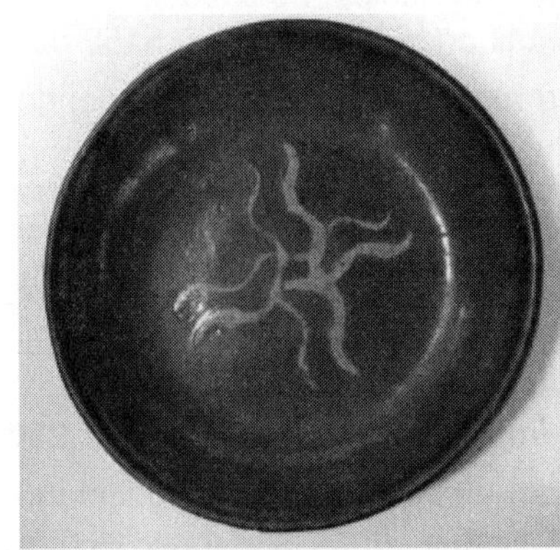

Pie plate, four squiggled lines in "X" pattern, early 19th century, no chips or cracks, 7 3/4 in. diameter. **$350**

Pie plate, probably Pennsylvania, two stylized chickens separated by three rows of dots, a few rough areas around the edge, overall excellent condition, the back shows use with black deposits, 7 in. diameter. **$200-$225**

Pie plate, other, undecorated, burnt orange glaze, coggled rim wear, 10 1/2 in. diameter. **$175**

Pie plate, other, "W" monogram in sweeping yellow slip decoration, coggled rim, chips, minor flaking, hairline, 9 in. diameter..........**$1,000**

Pie plate, other, wavy daubs in green, 7 1/8 in. diameter. **$625**

Pie plate, other, wavy lines in yellow slip, running brown, coggled edge, glaze wear, crazing, chips, 9 1/2 in. diameter. **$175**

Pie plate, other, wavy lines and flourishes in yellow slip, minor flakes, 10 3/4 in. diameter.......**$725**

Pitcher, tan brown running glaze, 7 1/8 in. tall................................**$400**

Pitcher, dark brown sponged vertical lines, with lid, rim flakes, 5 3/4 in. tall. **$675**

Pitcher, dark brown sponging, ovoid, diagonal decoration, slightly larger lid, edge chips at lip, 8 in. tall..**$400**

Pitcher, green and light brown, dark brown splotches, ovoid, flared rim, edge chips, firing separation, 9 1/4 in. tall.....................................**$900**

Pitcher, green and orange spotted decoration, 7 1/2 in. tall...........**$325**

Pitcher, green and red spotted decoration, 5 in. tall................**$120**

Pitcher, decorated well with black splotches all around the exterior, two small chips on the exterior lip of the crock, 6 in. tall. **$300**

Pitcher, green and yellow slip decoration, tooled lines, applied ribbed strap handle, chips, 4 1/4 in. tall. **$500**

Pitcher, mottled green, brown, and ivory glaze, illegible mark, possibly Shenandoah Valley, wear, flakes, 7 in. tall..................................**$2,100**

Pitcher, peach glaze with brown drip decoration, 4 1/2 in. tall..........**$550**

Pitcher, red glaze with brown spots, 6 1/2 in. tall...............................**$425**

Plate, three-line yellow slip decoration, coggled rim, three shallow rim chips, hairline, 8 1/4 in. diameter. **$500**

Plate, five wavy lines, yellow slip, wear, chips, 10 in. diameter. ...**$275**

Plate, Initials "S.B." in yellow slip decoration, glaze wear, chips, 9 1/4 in. diameter............................**$475**

Plate, swag decoration in faint yellow slip across two sides, coggled rim, medium brown glaze, chips, 9 in. diameter. **$225**

Plate, twist yellow slip decoration, red-brown ground, textured rim, 9 in. diameter............................**$825**

Preserve jar, dark brown splotches, minor edge damage, 10 1/2 in. tall. **$550**

Preserve jar, greenish-cream colored slip, reddish-tan mottled glaze, brown squiggles, applied handles, flared lip, gallery for lid, paper label from "George McKearin Collection of American Pottery," chips, 8 in. tall. **$3,000**

Roof tiles, Zoar, tulip design, edge chips, 15 3/4 in. long. **$75/pair**

Tray, three-line wavy yellow slip decoration, four sets of lines, wear, chips, 13 1/2 in. by 9 in. **$725**

Washboard, child-size, brown glaze, wooden frame, top of backboard replaced, 13 3/8 in. tall by 6 5/8 in. wide.......................................**$575**

Whistle, red clay, mottled black glaze with specks, 2 1/2 in. tall. **$400**

Rugs

When collectors started taking rugs off the floor and hanging them on the wall, prices also moved in an upward direction.

Large rag hooked rugs (around 3 feet by 5 feet) incorporating folksy images of animals seem to be the most popular, with late 19th and early 20th century examples in the best condition selling for between $1,000 and $3,000. But smaller, simpler rugs are still available for less than $200, sometimes much less, depending on the shop or show you are browsing.

Hooked rug, circa 1930s, made of rags in red, white, and green, and showing a goose surrounded by flowers in a black border, burlap backing, 31 in. by 27 in. **$150**

Hooked rug, circa 1930s, made of rags in green, black, white, beige, brown, and yellow, and showing geese flying toward the sun from a marsh with cattails, 21 in. by 16 in. **$80**

Hooked rugs made with yarn are not as sought-after as those that use shredded rags, but some yarn rugs are quite appealing and usually sell for a fraction of rag examples. Whether yarn or rag, repairs are usually not too expensive.

The prices for large oval braided rugs have dropped in recent years as reproductions (usually good quality) have flooded the market. Old braided rugs were often used in high-traffic areas like dining and living rooms, and most were faded and ragged within a few years of being laid down.

Large floral hooked rug, with detail at right, done in shades of red, blue, and green with beige fill-in, slight edge wear on two short ends, one side has been repaired, otherwise excellent condition, 32 in. by 73 in. **$200**

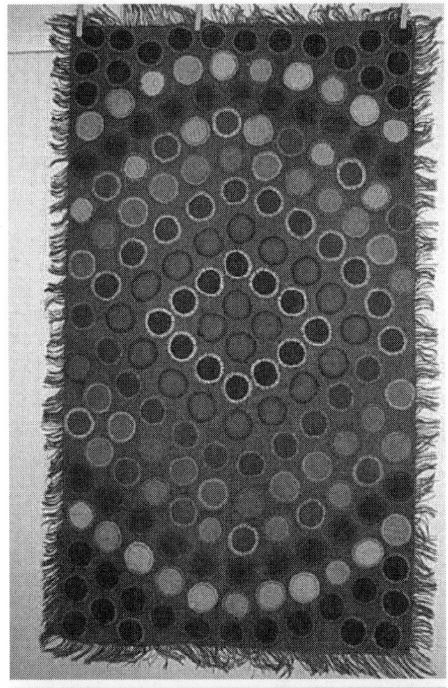

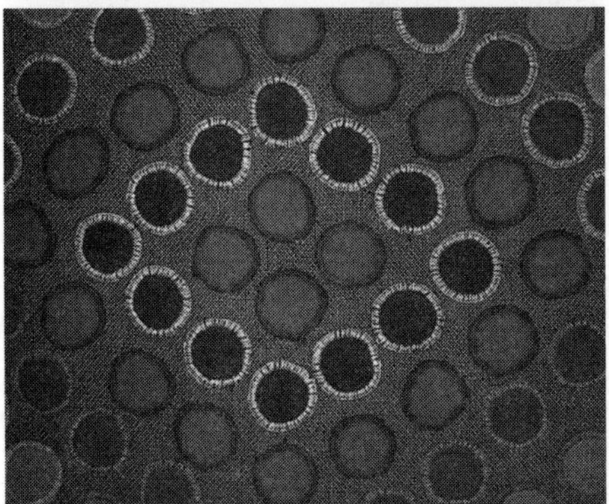

Penny rug, with detail, circa 1920-30, Pennsylvania, colorful wool circles set on dark green burlap, contrasting button-hole stitching around the circles, excellent condition, fringe is intact, 25 in. by 44 in. **$250**

Folksy hooked rug, with detail, circa 1930, showing a fireplace with cat on blue rug, excellent condition, light stain, 23 in. by 34 in. **$250**

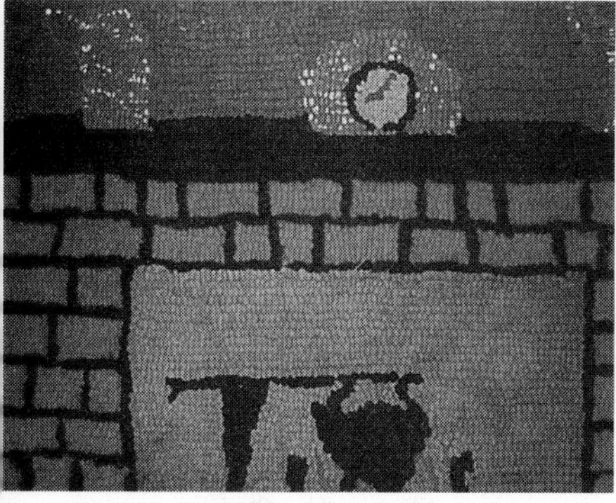

Oval hooked rug, with detail, yarn, in muted red, green, brown, and gray, excellent condition, 24 in. by 45 in. **$125**

Grenfell "House" hooked mat, circa 1930, colorful and detailed mat; there appears to be snow on the roof and lights in the windows; label reads "Grenfell Labrador Industries Hand-made in Newfoundland & Labrador," 6 1/2 in. diameter. **$225**

❖ Grenfell Rugs

The Grenfell mission in Labrador was known primarily for its production of hooked rugs, mostly depicting traditional Northern themes. Although rug hooking was a local art form prior to Dr. Wilfred Grenfell's arrival in 1892, he was responsible for promoting the work. Producing and selling the rugs filled the eight months each year that the fishing and fur-trapping society was locked in by ice.

Grenfell rugs have the tightest, finest hooking of any hooked rug. Their smooth surfaces give the rugs a needlepoint-like appearance.

Grenfell "Two Hunters" hooked rug, circa 1930, hunters appear to be fishing under the ice; label reads "Made in Labrador," 8 1/2 in. by 8 3/4 in. **$500**

Grenfell "Hunter with a Dog" hooked rug, circa 1930, detailed with a hunter holding a rifle running alongside his dog, the dog appears three-dimensional with the raised coat, banded borders on two sides; label reads "Grenfell Labrador Industries Hand-made in Newfoundland & Labrador," 11 in. by 15 in. **$900**

Grenfell "Sailboat" hooked rug, circa 1930, colorful ship under sail with icebergs all around, some wear to the edges and a little fabric pull; label reads "Grenfell Labrador Industries Hand-made in Newfoundland & Labrador," 11 1/2 in. diameter. **$400**

Grenfell "Ski Jumper" hooked rug, circa 1930, in a design that is not often seen; label reads "Grenfell Labrador Industries Hand-made in Newfoundland & Labrador," 8 1/2 in. diameter. **$475**

Grenfell "Sailboat" hooked mat, circa 1930, label reads "Grenfell Labrador Industries Hand-made in Newfoundland & Labrador," 7 in. by 9 in. **$400**

Grenfell "Geese" hooked rug, circa 1930, very large scene at 39 1/2 in. by 53 in., label reads "Grenfell Labrador Industries Hand-made in Newfoundland & Labrador." **$4,200**

Where can I find them?

Some of the following resources also carry fine vintage quilts and samplers:

The Antique Quilt Source
3064 Bricker Rd.
Manheim, PA 17545-9644
(717) 492-9876
http://www.antiquequiltsource.com/
strongg@paonline.com

Marie Miller Antique Quilts
1489 Route 30
PO Box 983
Dorset, VT 05251
(802) 867-5969
http://www.antiquequilts.com
larry@antiquequilts.com

Sharon's Antiques and Vintage Quilts
(610) 756-6048
http://www.rickrack.com
quilts@rickrack.com

Carol Telfer Antiques
312 Cobourg St.
Stratford, Ontario
Canada N5A 3G5
(519) 271-0941
http://www.caroltelferantiques.on.ca/index.php
ctelfer@caroltelferantiques.on.ca

Betsey Telford Antique Quilts
dba Rocky Mountain Quilts
130 York St.
York Village, ME 03909
(800) 762-5940
(207) 363-6800
http://www.rockymountainquilts.com/
quilts@rockymountainquilts.com

Mary Ann Walters
Log Cabin Antiques
4200 Peggy Ln.
Plano, TX 75074
(972) 881-2818
www.quiltsquilts.com
logcabin@flash.net

Samplers

The earliest samplers were often used as references by an embroiderer or seamstress to determine how certain stitches were done. These were often kept in a needlework basket or box to be referred to when needed and added to as new stitches and designs were learned. Random or spot samplers were most common, with motifs and newer stitches placed closely together to conserve space.

Girls as young as three years old attended "dame schools" or female schools and learned plain sewing, the basics of reading and writing, as well as moral instruction. These girls made simple samplers, consisting of darning patterns, stem and outline stitch, and frequently the alphabet and a "pious" verse.

More elaborate samplers could depict family events, such as births, deaths, weddings, etc., family histories, homes, maps, even math tables. Others feature landscapes, pets, ships, and political themes.

Elizabeth Benson, 1840, showing the alphabet, fruit baskets and flowers in handled urns, with floral border and verse, very good condition, in original bird's-eye maple veneer frame, sampler size 14 in. by 10 in **$400-$500**

Annie Elliott Jeffery, circa 1890, unfinished, unframed. The sampler is worked in wool on canvas ground, in cross-stitch throughout, simple embroidered border, colors of pink, red, black, orange, magenta, purple, and green. Alphabets A-Z in uppercase and lowercase. Signed "Annie Elliott Jeffery Aged 12 Years"; fair condition, two holes, a few small stains, stitch losses to the border, divider lines, letters of the alphabets and signature, colors are all good and strong with no noticeable fading, 16 1/2 in. by 11 in. **$60**

Annie Elliott Jeffery, circa 1890, unfinished, unframed. The sampler is worked in wool on canvas ground, in cross-stitch throughout, simple embroidered border, colors of pink, red, black, orange, magenta, purple, and green. Alphabets A-Z in uppercase and lowercase. Signed "Annie Elliott Jeffery Aged 12 Years"; fair condition, two holes, a few small stains, stitch losses to the border, divider lines, letters of the alphabets and signature, colors are all good and strong with no noticeable fading, 16 1/2 in. by 11 in. **$60**

Circa 1860 sampler, alphabet, framed in an old wood frame with rippled, old glass, loose mounted over a wood dust cover, wool on canvas ground, in cross-stitch throughout, no border, only simple divider lines to separate the rows of letters, colors of purple, royal blue, cream, olive green, pink, orange, and pale blue, alphabet A-Z in uppercase and lowercase, good to fair condition, no holes, one stain, stitch losses to the divider lines and letters of the alphabet, colors are all good and strong with no noticeable fading, no color run, stretching is slightly uneven, frame showing slight wear, 6 1/2 in. square. **$160**

1883 sampler by Annie L Calvert, in an old wood frame with glass, fixed to board with wood and brown paper dust cover. The sampler is worked in wool on canvas ground, in cross-stitch throughout, zigzag border, colors of red, blue, yellow, green, pale blue, pale green, black, pink, light green, orange, magenta, purple, and white, alphabet A-Z in uppercase and lowercase with numbers 1-18, aphorism's read "They who sow in tears shall reap in joy" and "A stitch in time saves nine" and "Jesus wept," signed and dated "Annie.L.Calvert.1883," motifs including stars, a cross, and birds; very good condition, no holes, a few pale stain specks, no stitch losses, colors are all good and strong with no noticeable fading, no color run, neatly and evenly stretched, frame in very good condition, 10 in. by 12 1/2 in. **$180**

Circa 1890 alphabet and numeral sampler, unframed, stitched to a material backing. The sampler is worked in cotton on canvas ground, in cross-stitch throughout, simple embroidered border with divider lines in various patterns, a great variety of colors including red, yellow, burgundy, gold, black, pink, purple, orange, magenta, and different shades of blue and green, alphabet A-Z in uppercase and lowercase with numbers 1-17, good condition, one small hole, a couple of pale stains, some stitch losses to letters of the alphabet, numbers, border and divider lines, colors are all good and strong with no noticeable fading, no color run, 10 1/4 in. by 11 3/4 in. **$180**

border, "By Anna Margaret Houghtaling aged 9 years 1835," American, unfinished, toning, fading, 16 1/2 in. square. .... **$2,800-$3,000**

Landscape, silk on silk, scene in shades of green, brown, yellow, white, and black, old label marked, "The handiwork of Miss Chloe, a school teacher...born in Abington, now Rockland, Mass. in 1786," wear, tear in sky, 18 1/4 in. tall by 20 1/4 in. wide. .... **$400-$450**

Panel, two figures in wooded setting, wool in needlepoint and petit point, ogee bird's-eye maple frame with gilded liner, wear and damage, 30 in. tall by 23 3/4 in. wide. .... **$700-$750**

Panel, shepherd with flock and pots of flowers in green, tan and red, sailboat and trees in background, portion of house shown in upper-right corner with red and salmon checked roof, areas of

❖ Needlework

Needlework is a general term for work produced by hand with a needle. In particular, it refers to all kinds of handmade embroidery.

Adam and Eve with snake in apple tree, green, yellow, red and browns, on homespun, framed, small stain, some bleeding of colors, 8 3/8 in. tall by 10 in. wide. .... **$80-$90**

Church and federal house flanked by trees, fenced garden, and duck pond, gentleman walking with dog, surrounded by floral meandering vine

Rachel Downs, including vintage wood frame, Scottish sampler is signed and dated "1811 Rachel Downs Aged 10," referred to as a "Scottish House Sampler," the central house is surrounded by a fence and a front yard worked in chenille, with trees, flowers peacocks, rabbits, and dogs, intricate and unusual bottom border, family initials and a delicate trefoil border surrounding the outside of the sampler, across the top of the sampler is stitched a garland of birds and flowers; five poorly repaired areas, also a small area of wear in the bottom right edge of the fabric, and another rough area just above the center of the house, very small holes and a uniform darkening of the fabric, 13 in. by 17 in. **$3,275**

Betsy Dowse, including period (probably original) wood frame with rippled old glass; Scottish sampler is stitched on a very tiny count fabric and filled with peacocks, crowns, floral motifs, rabbits, butterflies, and trees; there are also two sets of "ascending strawberries" that are worked in queen stitch; within a floral cartouche is the verse "Lamb of God I look to thee/thou shalt my example be/thou art gentle meek and mild/thou wast once a little child," below that, "Betsy Dowse 1844," with family initials below each of the crowns and a floral border around the outside of the piece; there are a few holes, mostly along the bottom and the right edges of the sampler; there is no thread loss and the colors are still quite vibrant,12 in. by 14 in. **$3,250**

Sarah Claridge, new frame, featuring the alphabet, numbers, a brick house, birds, trees, and flowers, signed, "Sarah Claridge A 11," circa 1850, no holes, no losses to the cotton-like fibers and the colors are bright, there is some bleeding in the blue areas, small stains, framed on acid-free board, 11 in. by 17 in. **$950**

restored moth damage, early reeded frame with wear, 22 in. tall by 24 1/4 in. wide.....................................**$200-$250**

Sailing ship with American flag, on canvas-covered stretcher, in brown, yellow, red, tan, and blue,

MJ Scottish sampler, including period (possibly original) burled maple frame, sampler with honeysuckle vine border; the first band has a series of crowns over crossed swords and initials, the next band of undulating pansies is typical to Scottish samplers; the verse reads "I'm not ashamd to own my lord or to defend his cause maintain the glory of his cross and honor all his laws"; this is surrounded by trees, birds, and rabbits; below the verse is another undulating band worked in double running stitch featuring acorns and flowers; the final band has a house, large satin stitch flowers, and two bare trees, dated 1821, the initials "MJ" appear above the house, small holes, 14 1/2 in. by 17 1/2 in. **$3,895**

contemporary frame, edge wear, some floss missing, 22 in. tall by 35 in. wide. ....**$900-$1,000**

Verse, Greek key line in oval, "June 9th 1798 Daily Word, Rejoice, O ye nations ...," black and ivory silk thread on homespun, framed, small holes, 6 1/2 in. square. ....**$650-$700**

Where can I find them?

Needlework Antiques
524 N. Oklahoma Ave.
Morton, IL 61550
(309) 263-7766
Fax: (309) 263-4304
www.needleworkantiques.com
Dawn@NeedleworkAntiques.com

www.madelenaantiques.com/

Sewing Items

Although sewing can hardly be considered exclusive to country folk, there is something about many of the items listed here that speaks to a certain self-reliance (and remoteness) often associated with rural seamstresses. We have included handmade crochet hooks, sock darners, sewing "birds" and clamps, and thread holders in this category.

Crochet hooks, circa 1890, set of six carved out of walnut, each handle slightly different with spiral, spoon, and notch carving, each about 7 in. long, mint condition. **$300-$400/set**

Chatelaine, sterling silver, marked with a double-headed eagle, clip decorated with scrolls, a hunter, cherubs, dogs, etc., overall length is 10 1/4 in., continental Victorian..........**$900-$1,000**

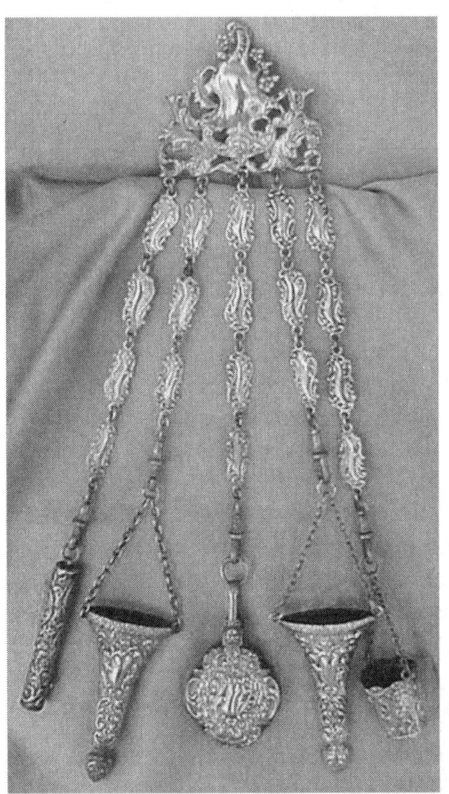

Chatelaine, silver-plated, English, circa 1880, with five ornate chains holding a retractable pencil, scissors sheath, pin safe, another matching scissors sheath and thimble holder, 11 1/2 in. long. **$1,400-$1,500**

Dress form, circa 1930s, possibly from a kit, layered paper on a composition form, mounted on a wood base, minor wear, 54 in. by 16 in. by 14 in. **$100-$125**

Griffin Rug Machine in original box, marked with two patent dates of Aug. 28, 1881 and April 19, 1888, complete with the original instruction sheet, moderate wear to box, excellent condition. **$125**

Pincushion, circa 1920s, blue silk in the form of a purse, with hand-stitched orange panel and the name "Flossie," minor wear, 4 1/2 in. by 2 1/2 in. by 1 1/2 in. **$35**

Knitting needle gauge, bell-shaped, marked "H. Walker London" with Archer trademark, knitting needle sizes from 1 to 24 are indicated, very good condition. **$35-$45**

Sewing bird, cast brass or bronze, crosshatched lines to simulate feathers, and two eyes, dark untouched patina, very good condition. **$150-$250**

Sewing bird, patented and dated on wings, April 1853, brass, with two pincushions, all original and complete, American. **$300-$350**

Pincushion, circa 1920s, black felt in the shape of a dog's head, with hand-stitched eye, nose, tongue, and teeth, and attached collar with brass button, near mint, 4 in. by 3 in. **$30**

Sewing box, circa 1900, mahogany with original varnished surface, done in tramp art style, two-tiered design with smaller single-drawer section on top of larger single-drawer section, pin cushion on top and drawer fronts covered in red velvet, wood button pulls, notch-carved feet, excellent condition, 12 in. by 10 in. by 8 in. **$400-$500**

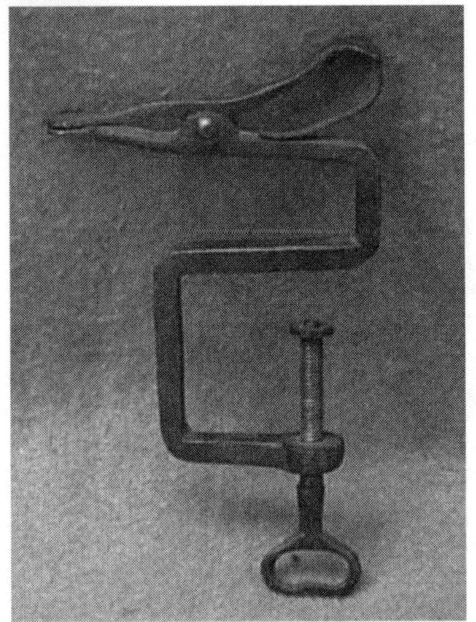

Sewing clamp, blacksmith-made iron, 9 1/2 in. long, with stylized and abstract bird form, excellent condition. **$450-$550**

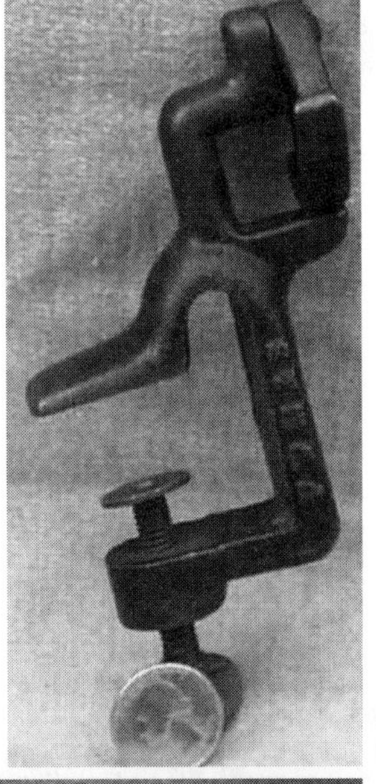

Sewing or leatherworking clamp, cast iron swing-arm style, possibly for use on canvas, wool, leather or a heavier weight fabric, marked "F W M & S," very good condition. **$150-$200**

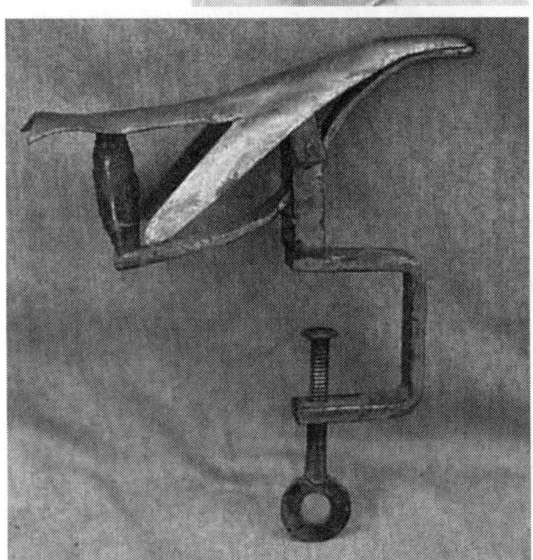

Sewing clamp, figural, meant to represent a dolphin or porpoise (?), 5 in. long, with most of its original gold paint, very good condition. **$250-$350**

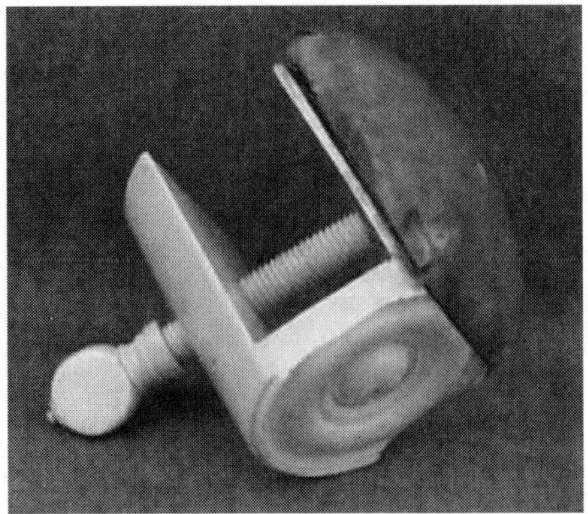

Sewing clamp or vise, ivory pincushion-style, 19th century, excellent condition, with no chips or cracks, symmetrical carving on both the screw portion and the end panel, 3 1/2 in. long, the pincushion is original and the silk fabric cover shows wear. **$100-$150**

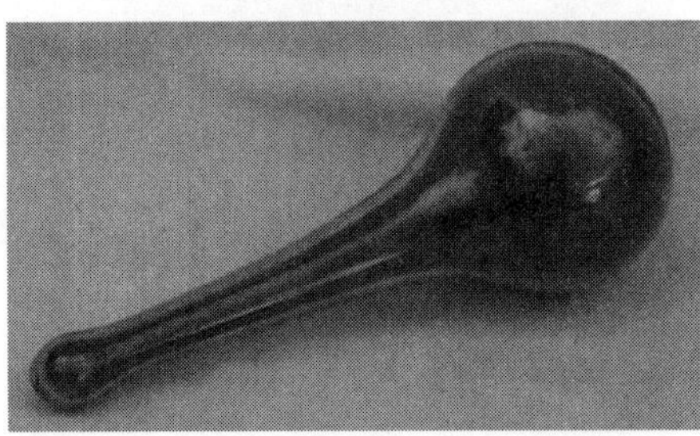

Sock, stocking, and glove darner, powdered glass, 5 in. long, with ball-shaped end and tapering handle, with closed and polished pontil, for gloves, excellent condition. **$150-$250**

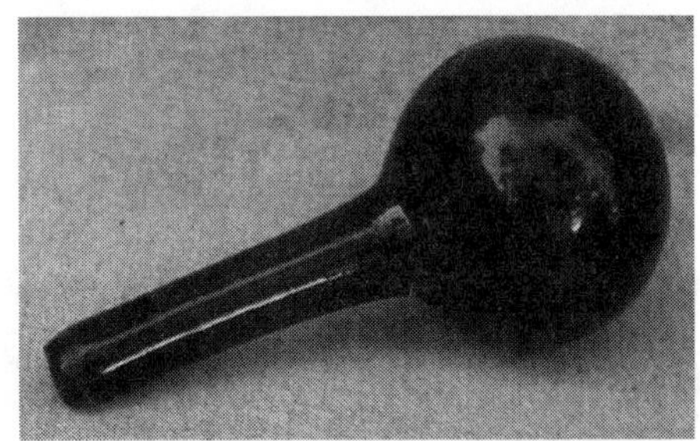

Sock/stocking darner, amber brown glass, traditional shape but the color is unusual, with orange highlights, 6 in. long with an open pontil, very good condition. **$80-$90**

Sock/stocking darner, cobalt blue glass, possibly made by the Dorflinger Glass Co., 7 1/2 in. long with an open pontil, excellent condition. **$225-$275**

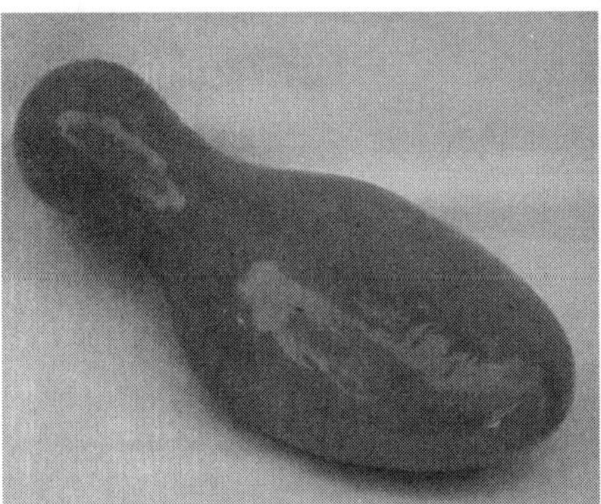

Sock/stocking darner, green glass foot-form, 5 in. long, the narrow end has a polished closed pontil, excellent condition. **$150-$200**

Thread stand, Victorian, cast iron, two-tier, with pins to hold 24 spools of thread, a bottom tray to hold thimbles or needlework tools, and a top piece that was most likely meant to be made into a pincushion, gold wash over red and black paint, 10 in. tall, excellent condition. **$400-$500**

Sewing vise, early 19th century, carved from cherry with a wood screw-shaft clamp for mounting on a table, original fabric on cushion top, 6 1/2 in. by 3 in. ....**$350-$400**

Thimble holder, sterling silver, with raised scroll and floral design, 1 in. by 7/8 in. ....**$300-$350**

Thimble holder, brass, egg-shaped, circa 1900, 1 1/2 in. long and 1 in. wide, snaps shut and has a push-button release. ....**$150-$175**

Yarn winder, circa 1880, carved butternut (?) with three prongs, spiral-carved center section and ovoid handle, original varnished surface, 13 1/2 in. by 1 1/2 in. **$50**

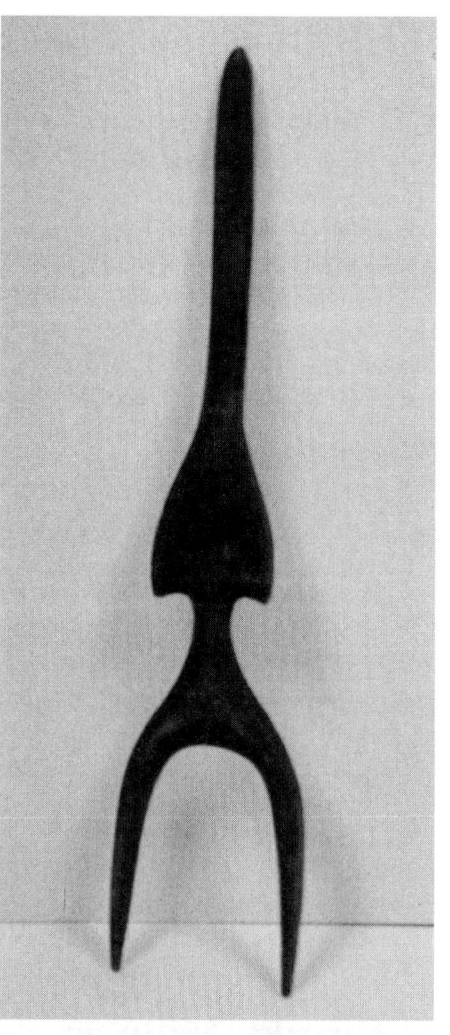

Yarn winder, circa 1890, pine with original red stain, with two prongs and shield-carved handle, minor handling wear, 8 in. by 2 in. by 1/4 in. **$30**

Where can I find them?

Larry and Carole Meeker
Purveyors of American Patented & Mechanical Antiques
5702 Vacation Blvd.
Somerset, CA 95684
(530) 620-7019
Sales: (888) 607-6090
Fax: (530) 620-7020
www.patented-antiques.com
clm@patented-antiques.com

Anne Powell Ltd.
PO Box 3060
Stuart, FL 34995-3060
(561) 287-3007
For Orders Only: (800) 622-2646
Fax: (561) 287-3007
www.annepowellltd.com/index.htm
info@annepowellltd.com

Silhouettes

A profile or shadow outline of an object is referred to as a silhouette. Early examples were made by projecting a shadow on a sheet of white paper by the light of a candle and then filling in the resulting outline with black. The term also refers to a profile cut from a piece of black paper with scissors.

An impressed stamp marked "Peale" or "Peale Museum" identifies pieces made by members of the Peale family, which was well known for its silhouettes.

Museums: Essex Institute, Salem, Massachusetts; National Portrait Gallery, Washington, D.C.

FYI: The name "silhouette" is taken from Etienne de Silhouette. As the French Minister of Finance, he enacted strict economic measures and proposed many unpopular forms of taxation. Driven out of office after only four months, his name became synonymous with anything extremely simple or plain.

❖ Double, Male and Female

Hollow cut, black lacquered frames, with edge damage, minor stains, 6 1/8 in. by 5 3/8 in.................................. **$300/pair**

Hollow cut, pen and ink details, eglomise glass with gilded frame, some damage, stains 5 1/2 in. by 8 5/8 in. **$350**

Hollow cut, woman with hair comb, penciled names of Sarah and Samuel Wilcox, woman possibly reversed in frame, some damage to man, stains, cracked frame, 5 in. by 3 7/8 in..... **$375**

Lady and gentleman, reverse-painted glass, attributed to Henry Williams,

Boston, embossed brass frames, oval, 6 3/4 in. by 5 1/2 in. **$900/pair**

Man in chair, bust of woman with bun, each 3/4 view, black paper, gilded detail, white ground, beveled maple frames with gilded liners, 7 1/4 in. by 6 in. **$500/pair**

❖ Single, Female

Black paper with gilded detail, white ground, red printed label "Cut with common scissors by Mr. Seville," pencil inscription with name and "1825," black lacquered frame with gilded liner, 4 5/8 in. by 3 7/8 in. **$675**

Black paper, stenciled label "Gallery of Cuttings, Cut by Master Hankes with Common Scissors," embossed brass on wood frame, 5 1/2 in. by 4 1/4 in. **$525**

Old paper label "Judith Sturn, First Wife of Phillip Tomy," black cloth backing over board, foxing, fold lines, fame with black foliage decor, 5 5/8 in. by 5 in. **$350**

Hollow cut, black ink hair and bodice, signed "Doyle," with 1808 newspaper ad for silhouettes by Wm. M.S. Doyle, worn gilt frame, creases, pinpoint holes, 5 3/8 in. by 4 in. **$475**

Hollow cut, full-length, hair up, wearing fancy dress and carrying bouquet, traces of green watercolor at flowers, worn gilt frame, stains, 6 1/4 in. by 4 3/8 in. **$275**

Hollow cut, hair in a bun, laid paper with minor stains, black frame with oval opening, 5 3/8 in. by 4 in. **$130**

Hollow cut, ribbon at top of bonnet, black cloth backing, period mahogany frame, stains, tears, 4 3/8 in. by 3 1/2 in. . **$300**

Hollow cut, wearing bonnet, black cloth backing, erased pencil inscription, old backing labeled "Mrs. Nichols Johnson," old black molded frame, 6 3/4 in. by 5 1/2 in. **$275**

Hollow cut, with book, backed with woven fabric, black watercolor costume and embellishments, framed, minor toning, 3 3/4 in. by 2 1/8 in. **$1,500**

Hollow cut, with hair comb, paper embossed with floral scrolls, curly maple frame, fold lines, minor stains, 6 in. by 4 3/4 in. **$1,200**

Hollow cut, with hair comb, puff sleeve dress in ink wash, old glue stains, glued to backing board, which is glued to underside of eglomise mat, flakes on mat, worn gilt frame, 7 1/4 in. by 5 7/8 in. **$475**

Hollow cut, young girl, cut and penciled detail, black cloth backing, minor damage, old pen and ink label on back, "Sally Tilton 5 years old, 1822," frame in black repaint, 5 1/4 in. by 4 1/4 in. **$400**

Hollow cut, young woman, black fabric backing, bodice is black printed, old molded walnut frame, stains, 6 in. by 4 3/4 in. **$225**

Hollow cut, young woman, possibly Peale Museum, black cloth backing, added oval mat, old black frame, 6 7/8 in. by 5 1/4 in. **$225**

Hollow cut, young woman wearing bonnet and blue dress with puffy sleeve and holding flower sprig, watercolor, American, c. 1830-'31, framed, minor creases, 3 5/8 in. by 2 in. **$5,200**

❖ Single, Male

Black paper, back with stenciled label "Cut with Scissors by Master Hubard...," old gilded frame, 6 1/4 in. by 5 1/4 in. **$325**

Black paper on heavy stock, worn gilt frame, 5 5/8 in. by 4 3/8 in. **$75**

Full-length, ink, man has coat, ruffled sleeves and walking stick, slight discoloration to ink, black frame, gilt liner, 12 in. by 9 5/8 in. **$130**

Ink, blue and white watercolor highlights including striped vest and cap, early frame in old crazed red, light stains, fold lines, edge damage, 4 5/8 in. by 3 3/4 in. **$120**

Ink on heavy paper, black on black-and-white detail, old black reeded frame with gilded liner, 6 in. by 5 1/8 in... **$325**

With hat, cut black paper, old but not original backing paper labeled "Nicholas Johnson Jr. born 1760," back of silhouette paper labeled "Gallery of Cuttings, Cut by Master Hankes with Scissors," with pencil inscription "Nicholas Johnson Jr. N.P. 1810," ink smudges, oval ebonized frame with age crack. **$350**

Young man with dark-blue kepi, pen and ink portrait, shiny white paper, penciled names "W. Becke, -- Dupre...11/4.56," framed, 5 5/8 in. by 4 3/4 in. **$250**

Young man with high collar, illegible penciled note on front, back note "By Mr. Chapman. This is the part from the hollow cut," oval frame, 4 in. by 3 3/8 in. **$325**

Hollow cut, black cloth backing, faint "Peale Museum" mark, framed, 6 1/4 in. by 5 in. **$400**

Hollow cut, boy, good detail, shows hair and bow at neck, identified in old brown ink on front as "Robt. Watson," partial Peale embossed mark at bottom, black cloth backing, mahogany veneer frame with corner chips, margin stains, 5 in. by 4 in. **$425**

Hollow cut, embossed stamp "Museum" (possibly Peale's Museum), ink note, backed with black cloth, walnut frame, 7 in. by 5 in. **$130**

Hollow cut, profile head of gentleman topped by large crown and flanked by flowers and an "S" (two other letters missing), later pencil inscription, found in Lancaster County, Pennsylvania, stains, matted and framed, 7 1/4 in. by 6 1/4 in. **$350**

Hollow cut, young man, black ink detail, sawtooth cut oval borders, tin frame, 3 7/8 in. by 3 in. **$475**

Hollow cut, young man, black paper backing, faint embossed "Peale Museum" label, old frame with gold repaint, 5 3/4 in. by 4 3/4 in. **$325**

Hollow cut, young man, framed, slight stains, 5 5/8 in. by 4 3/4 in. **$130**

Watercolor, lady in black dress sitting sidesaddle on gray horse, man standing in front of horse and wearing gold pants with black coat, faces in silhouette, some gold tinting, background fence with blue-gray flecks, period frame in old red paint, 7 7/8 in. by 10 in. **$1,200**

Stoneware

Before refrigeration, stoneware was the most common form of storage for perishable items and liquids. Crocks, jugs, and churns decorated with cobalt glaze using a slip cup have always attracted collectors, but the top prices in the market have gone from around $10,000 to closer to $30,000 for mid-19th century pieces with accomplished decoration.

In order of desirability (from common to rare), forms and decorations are: undecorated crocks, hastily brushed or stenciled numbers, simple swirls or geometric lines, hastily executed flower, flower in a pot, simple bird with no detail, detailed basket or floral bouquet, chicken pecking, simple house with no detail, double birds on a branch, chicken pecking with ground cover and fence, detailed house with landscape, deer in landscape, fraternal decoration, house with landscape and people, stag in landscape, man in the moon, American flags, exotic animal (lion, elephant, or zebra) with detail, human face in eight-pointed starburst, or genre scene (for example, baseball players).

Regional differences and demand for stoneware remain, especially for those pieces made by the potteries in Red Wing, Minnesota (see "Red Wing Stoneware" history, page 274). Early (1880 to 1910) salt-glaze examples with strong decoration and in mint condition are the most expensive ($2,000-$5,000), while the rare and one-of-kind forms can top $30,000. Simple salt-glaze pieces, or those in white stoneware with stenciled decoration, can still be purchased for prices ranging from $50-$200.

The following stoneware pieces represent some of the finest decorated examples available. In the mid-1980s, these could be purchased for prices ranging from $1,500 for the simple bird churn to around $8,000 for the Centennial crock.

Cane stand, no maker's mark, but slip decorated with lovebirds and flowers on reverse.

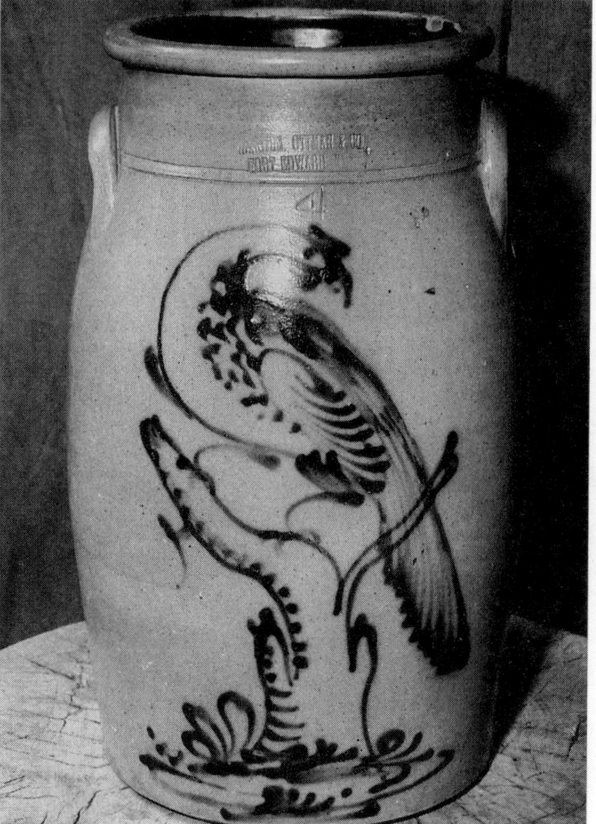

Churn, four-gallon, marked "Haxstun Ottman & Co. Fort Edward, N.Y.," slip decorated with a peacock (?).

Churn, five-gallon, marked "Ottman Bros. & Co. Fort Edward, N.Y.," slip decorated with a stag in detailed landscape with birds flying overhead.

Churn, five-gallon, marked "T. Harrington–Lyons (N.Y.)," slip decorated with elaborate eight-point starburst and face of a "jockey boy" with cap.

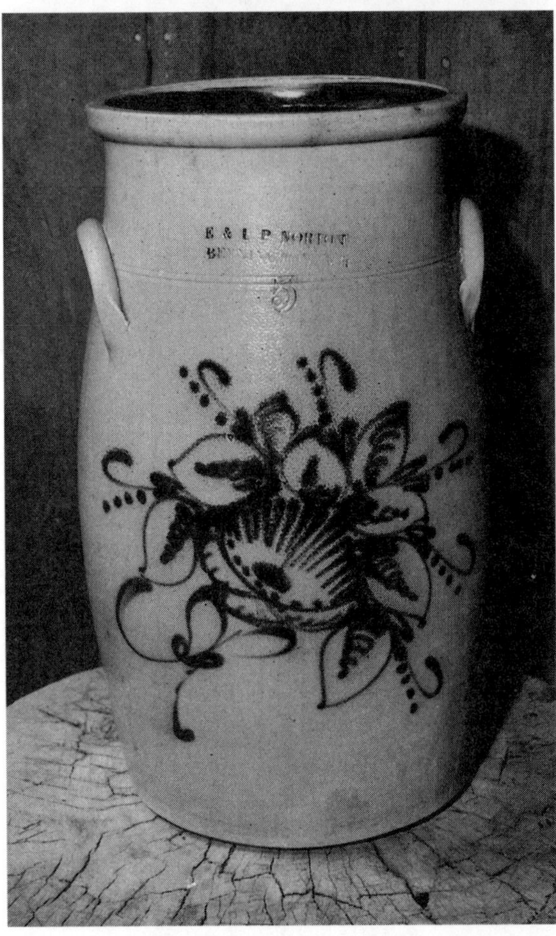

Churn, five-gallon, marked "E. & L.P. Norton Bennington, Vt.," slip decorated with elaborate leafy flower.

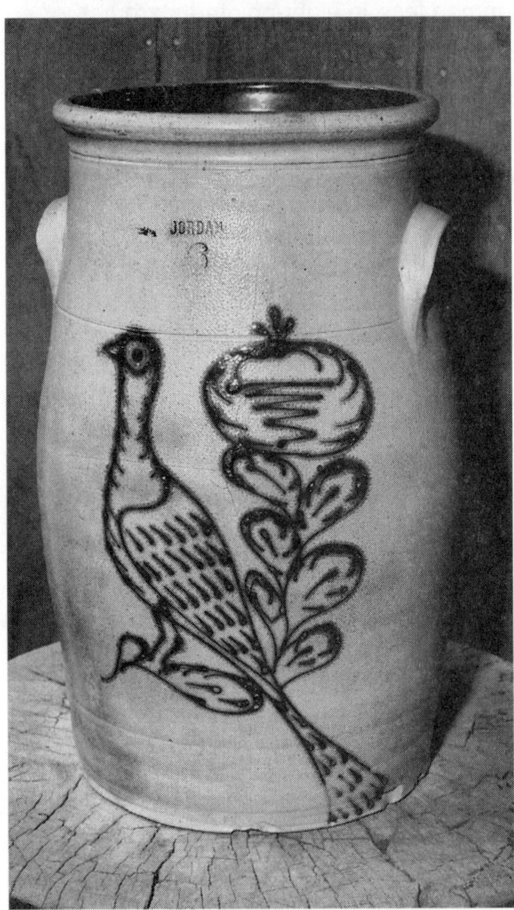

Churn, six-gallon, slip decorated bird on a branch, marked "Jordan."

Crock, two-gallon semi-ovoid, marked "A.O. Whittemore Havana, N.Y.," slip decorated with a trout.

Crock, three-gallon, marked "West Troy N.Y. Pottery," slip decorated with a tethered horse pawing the ground.

Crock, four-gallon, marked "C.W. Braun–Buffalo, N.Y.," slip decorated with a turkey.

Crock, three-gallon, marked "West Troy, N.Y. Pottery," slip decorated with a running elephant next to a stump on which is perched a bird.

Crock, four-gallon, unmarked but probably West Troy, New York. Pottery, slip decorated with a running elephant.

Crock, four-gallon, marked "C.W. Braun–Buffalo, N.Y.," slip decorated with a turkey.

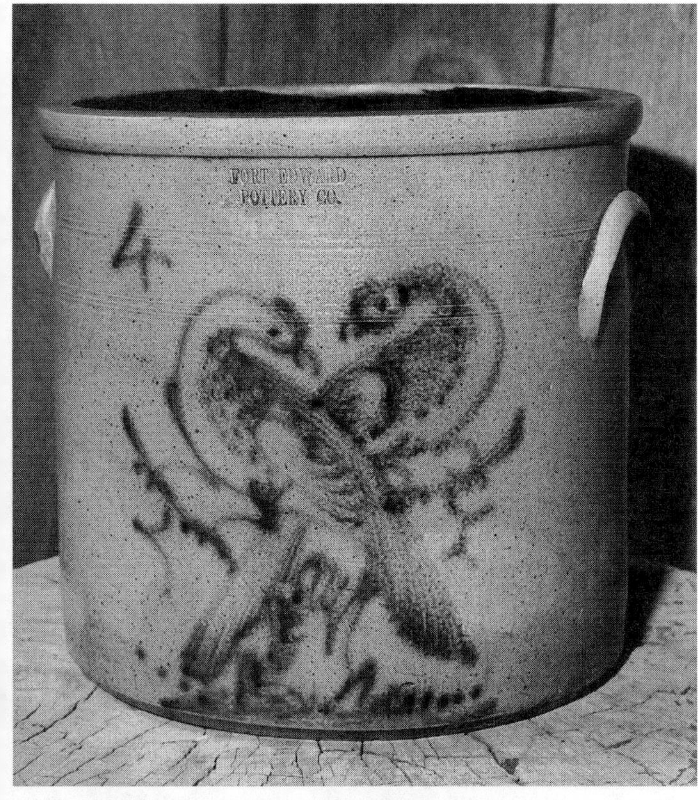

Crock, four-gallon, marked "Fort Edward Pottery Co.," slip decorated with lovebirds.

Jar, three-gallon, marked "F.A. Gale – Gales-Ville, N.Y.," slip decorated with two gamecocks.

Jug, one-gallon, marked "Ottman Bros. & Co. Fort Edward N.Y.," slip decorated with the word "Centennial" (1876) and a long-nosed man seated on a keg, holding a liquor bottle.

Jug, one-gallon, ovoid, marked "N. Clark & Co.," slip decorated with a battleship flying the American flag.

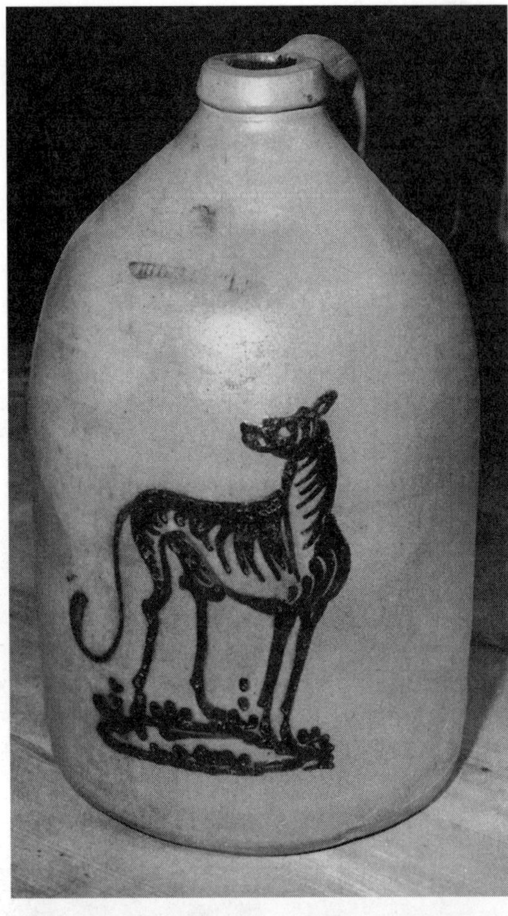

Jug, two-gallon, marked "Whites Utica," slip decorated with a Great Dane (?).

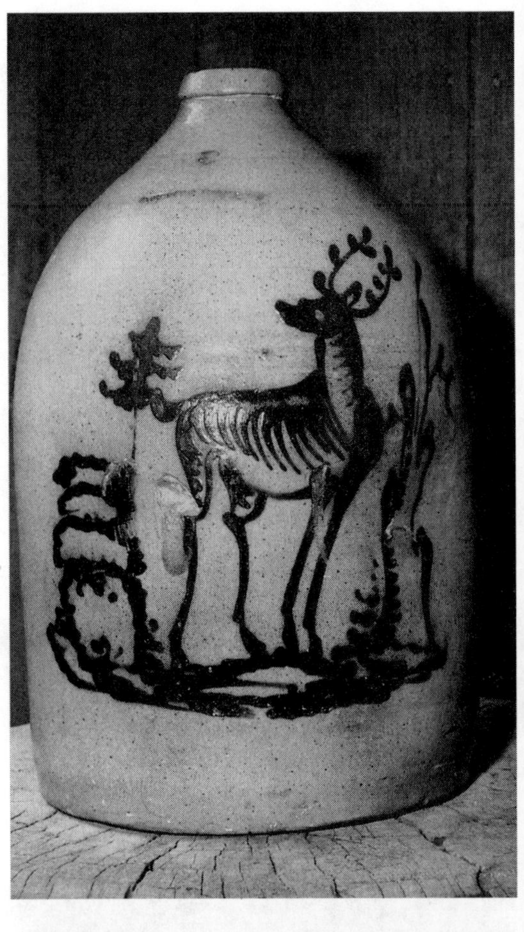

Jug, three-gallon, marked "Whites Utica," slip decorated with a stag in detailed landscape.

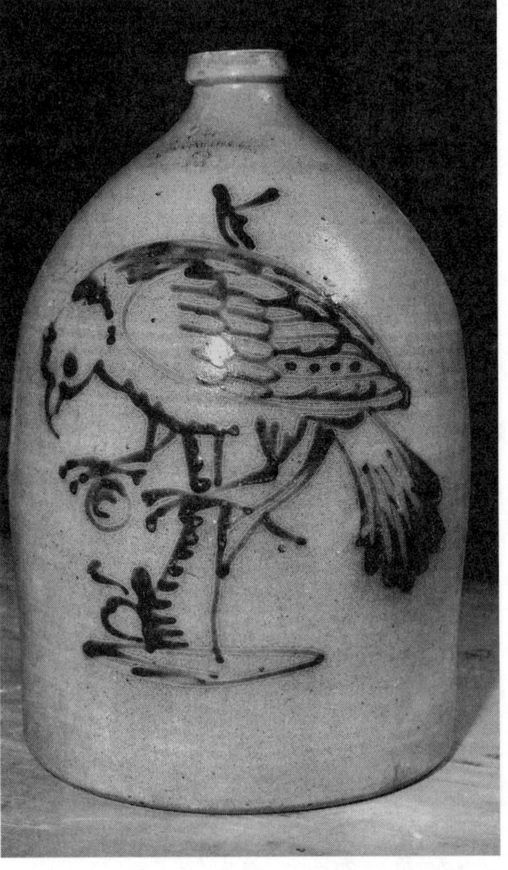

Jug, two-gallon, marked "J. & E. Norton–Bennington, Vt.," slip decorated with a hawk perched on a branch.

Jug, three-gallon, slip decorated with bird on a branch, marked "Bergan and Foy," but may be the product of Whites Pottery, Binghampton, New York.

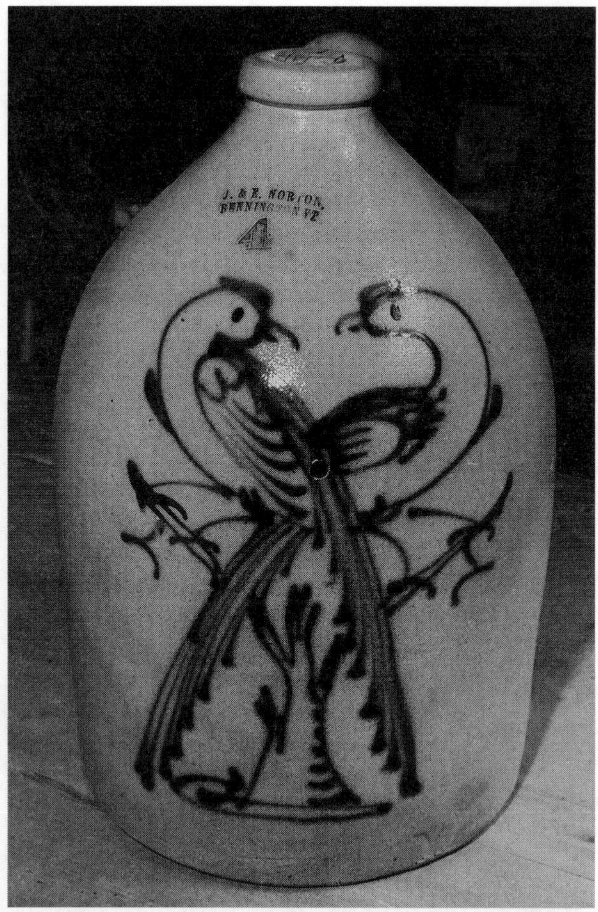

Jug, four-gallon, marked "J&E Norton, Bennington, Vt.," slip decorated with lovebirds.

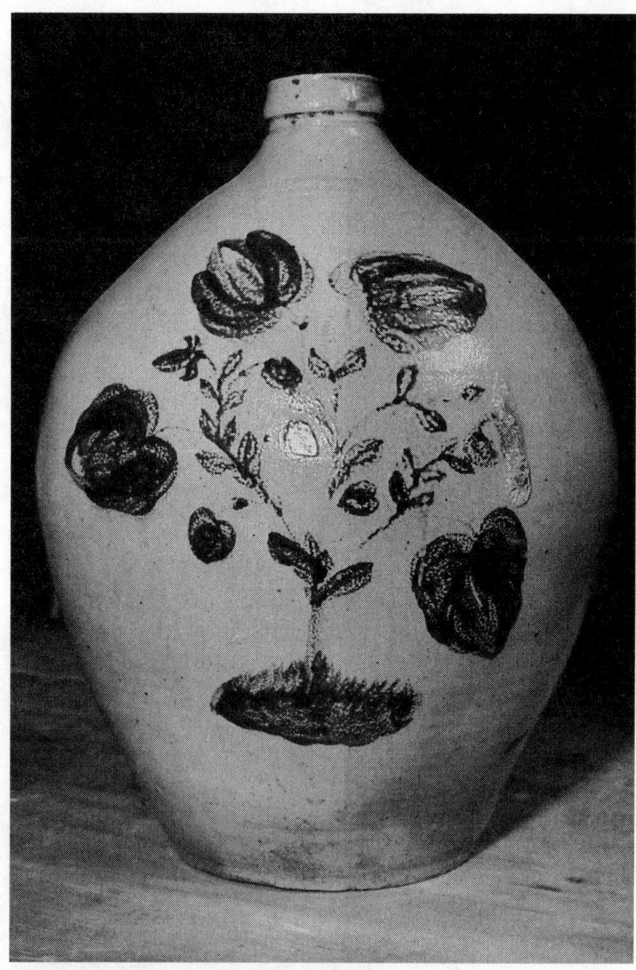

Jug, three-gallon ovoid, marked "Norton & Com. Bennington," slip decorated (brown) of a primitive flowering plant.

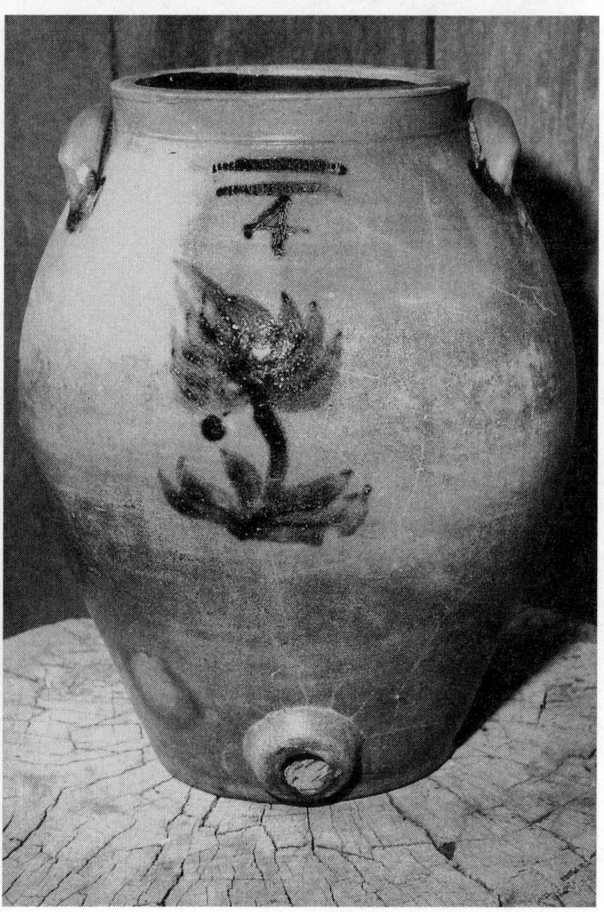

Water cooler, four-gallon, open-top, circa 1820, slip decorated with a primitive tree; rare and possibly unique example marked "Bennington Factory."

Water cooler, four-gallon, open-top on unusual footed base, marked "N. White & Co. Binghampton," slip decorated with elaborate flowers.

Mixing bowls, paneled, complete set, Red Wing, sponge-decorated, mixing bowls, circa 1930s, seven bowls ranging in size from 5 3/8 in. to 11 in. diameter, blue and red sponge decoration, all mint. **$1,500-$2,000/set**

Mixing bowl, paneled, with sponge decoration in blue and red, near mint, 10 in. by 6 in. **$100-$150**

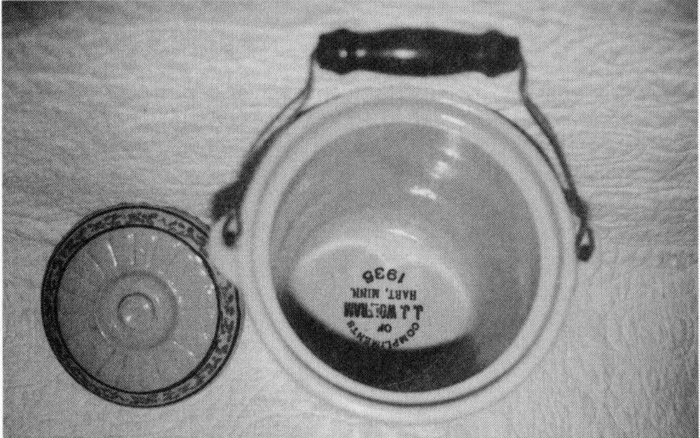

Butter pail, with detail, made in Red Wing, Minn., with red sponge band in blue-lined border, five-pound size with bail handle and turned wooden grip, marked in the bottom, "Compliments of J.J. Wolfram, Hart, Minn.," tight hairline cracks in base, 7 1/2 in. by 6 1/2 in. by 7 1/4 in. **$300-$400**

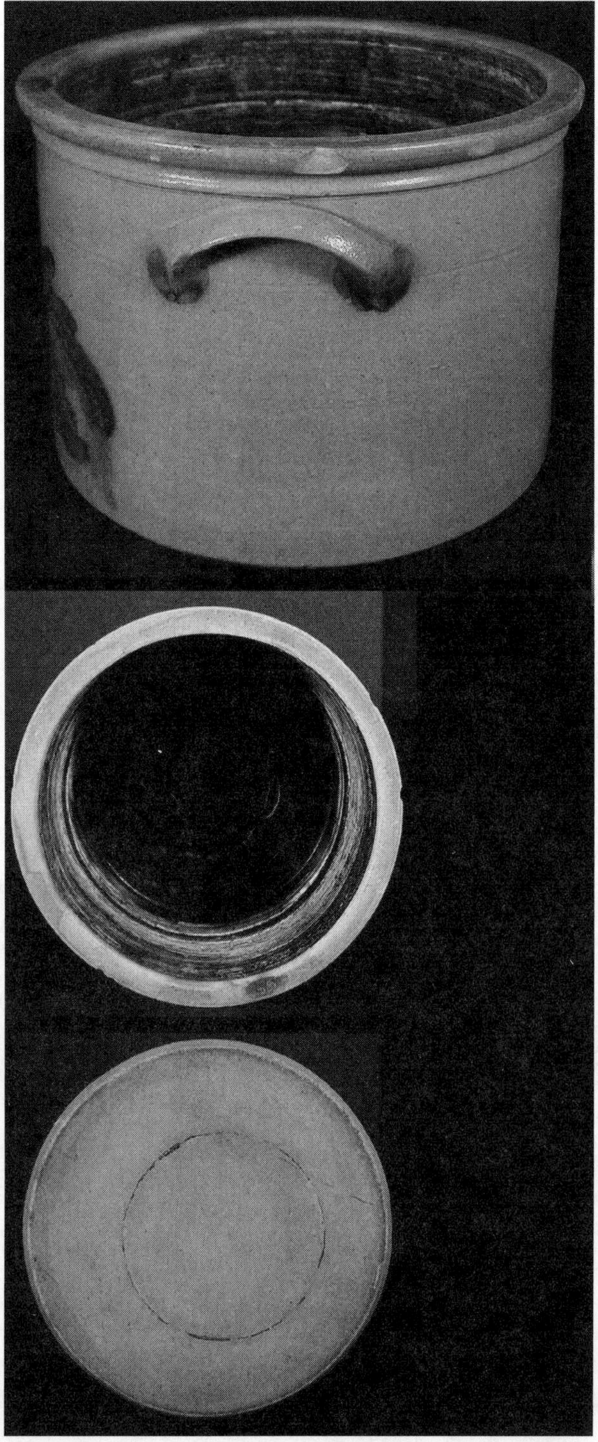

Several views of cake crock, Cowden and Wilcox with floral decoration, 9 in. by 12 in. **$700-$800**

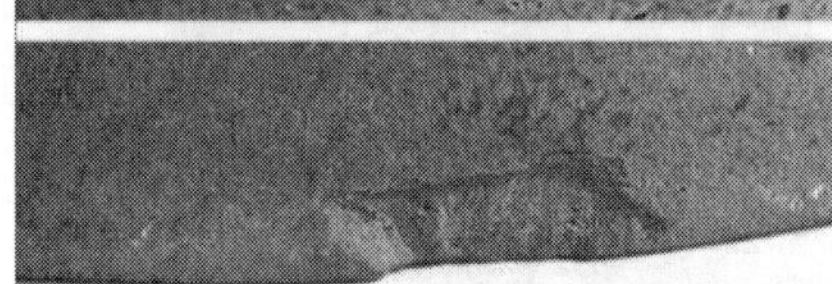

Two views and detail of canister, floral decorated, 1870s, Baltimore, with impressed "I" or Roman numeral 1, 3/4 in. chip on bottom, 6 1/4 in. diameter. **$250-$350**

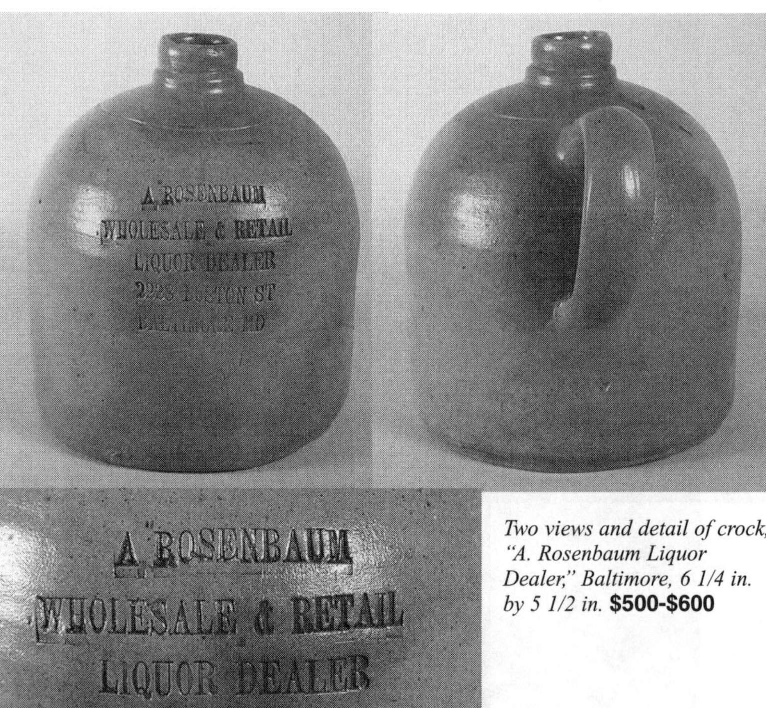

Two views and detail of crock, "A. Rosenbaum Liquor Dealer," Baltimore, 6 1/4 in. by 5 1/2 in. **$500-$600**

Two views of crock, tall, two-gallon, with feather-like cobalt decoration, 13 in. tall. **$100-$125**

Crocks and jugs, mid-to-late 19th century, mostly from New York and New England, all with cobalt decoration of flowers, leaves, vines, and birds, ranging in size from 8 in. to 14 in. tall. **$200-$600, depending on condition**

Jug, one-gallon, made in Red Wing, Minnesota, with brown top, advertising Griesel Bros. Wines, Whiskies, Cordials of Winona, Minnesota, shoulder and base chips, 11 in. tall. **$200-$300**

Several views of jug, White Rose Whiskey, circa 1898, 8 in. tall. **$550-$650**

Several views of jug, Cowden and Wilcox, three-gallon, with floral decoration, 15 in. tall. **$2,500-$3,000**

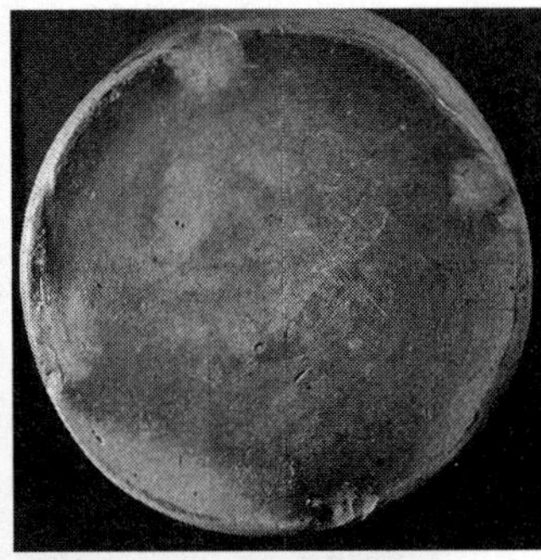

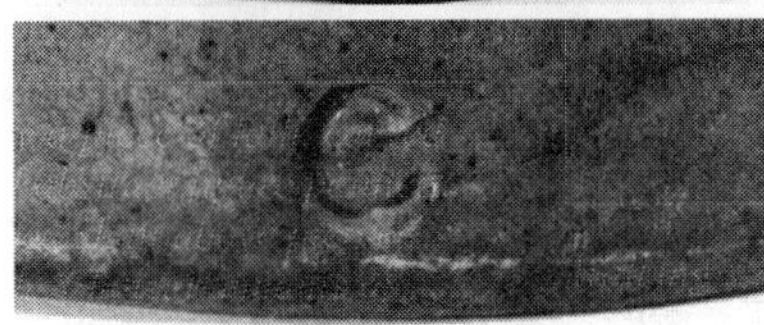

Several views of jug, "C" impressed, late 1880s, Philadelphia, 18 1/2 in. by 11 1/2 in. **$500-$600**

Pitcher, Remmey, one-pint, with floral decoration, 7 in. by 6 in. **$1,800-$2,000**

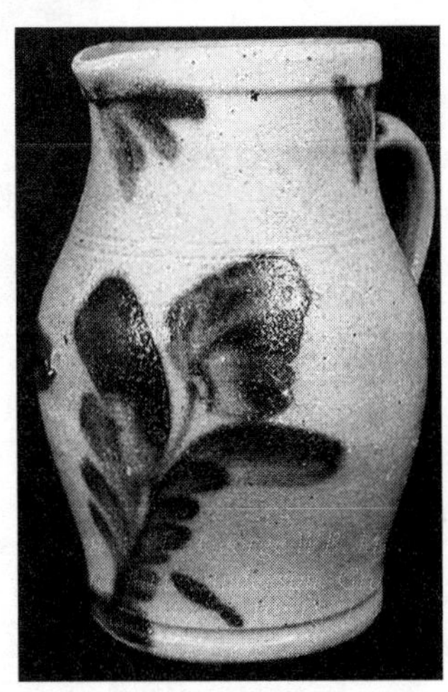

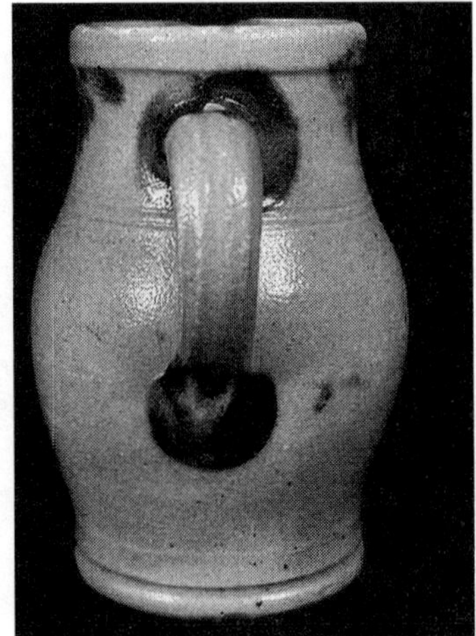

Pitcher, blue decorated with floral motif, high-gloss glaze, 1880s, 12 in. by 7 in., 3/4 in. chip in top rim, factory repair to spout's rim. **$450-$550**

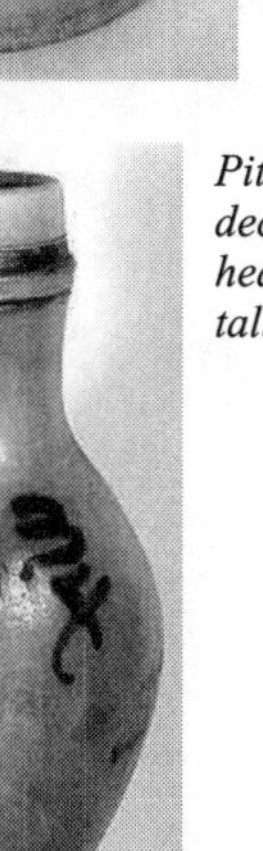

Pitcher, floral decorated, late 1870s, heavy cobalt, 15 in. tall. **$500-$600**

Pitcher, one-quart, floral decorated, 7 1/4 in. by 4 in. **$1,000-$1,100**

Pitcher, water, Remmy Philadelphia, inscribed with leafy motif and "Jos Kubek 1900," 10 1/2 in. tall. **$850-$950**

Pitcher, crude floral decoration, 7 1/4 in. tall. **$650-$750**

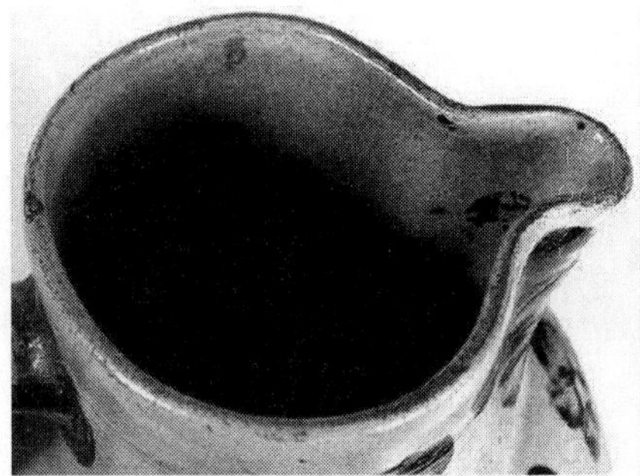

Pitcher, two-gallon, with floral decoration, 13 1/2 in. by 6 1/4 in. **$1,100-$1,200**

Jug, Utica, N.Y., four-gallon, with bird decoration, stamped "N.A. White & Son." . . . .**$1,400-$1,600**

Red Wing Stoneware

From the Red Wing Collectors Society Inc., www.redwingcollectors.org

An assortment of Red Wing stoneware pieces: top, 10-gallon water cooler with wing and oval stencil, without lid, 18 in. tall. **$950**; *12-gallon crock with birch-leaf and oval stencil, 17 in. tall.* **$165**; *and a 25-gallon crock with wing and oval stencil, 24 in. tall.* **$575**

Most accounts agree that the industry got its start when a German immigrant settled in Minnesota's Goodhue County in 1861. The spot that he chose is what would someday become the site of the clay pits. By some accounts, Joseph Pohl was the first; by others, John Paul was the man's name. In fact, one reference uses both names.

At any rate, the German immigrant settled as a farmer and began making pottery pieces for his own use. Before he knew it, he had a cottage industry. As might be imagined, the work was very labor intensive at that time with only a wheel and a wood-fired kiln. He made his ware for only a short period of time.

In 1866, Francis F. Philleo, a former mayor of Red Wing, Minn., announced that he would take advantage of the rich clay deposits that were in the area. He intended to open the first real pottery factory. He and his son William (who really owned the plant) manufactured pickle jars, crocks, and churns that were used by the nearby farmers. Unfortunately the factory was destroyed by fire in the summer of 1870. The plant was rebuilt the same year and was named Philleo and Williams.

In 1872, the Red Wing Terra Cotta Works was formed, and in 1874 David Hallum started the Minnesota Pottery (which is called by other names in some accounts).

The first really large endeavor began in 1877 or 1878, under the corporate name of Red Wing Stoneware Company. This company was innovative for its day and was soon well respected in the industry. Fire again plagued Red Wing when parts of the factory went up in flames in the mid-1880s. A bigger and better factory was soon built to replace it.

In 1883 the Minnesota Stoneware Company was formed. Though this company could have been said to be in direct competition with the other, the two often made pieces that were compatible with the other's stoneware. It seemed that both would be able to thrive.

In 1891, The Red Wing Sewer Pipe Company and the J.H. Rich Sewer Pipe Works began using the local clay that was deemed unsuitable for the products made by the Red Wing Stoneware Company and the Minnesota Stoneware Company. The fit was a good one for the community. The different products of the sewer pipe companies helped to secure the prominence of the clay industry in Red Wing.

The North Star Stoneware Company began in 1892, however, and this made three major stoneware manufacturers in one small town. This was one company too many and was a drain on the industry.

The solution came in 1894 when the three firms joined forces and formed the Union Stoneware Company. In 1896, the North Star division of the Union Stoneware was closed. In 1906 the merger of the two companies was complete, and the new name was Red Wing Union Stoneware Company.

As times changed so did the products manufactured by the company. The name "stoneware" ceased to be appropriate as the products began to be less geared toward the farm—and the "old fashioned ways" of storing food products—and more toward modern living and refrigeration. The name was changed to Red Wing Potteries Incirca in 1936. From the 1930s on, flower vases and pots, pitchers, ashtrays, and eventually dinnerware were the favored products.

In 1967 the labor force went on strike, and the factory shut down.

For more information about the history of Red Wing, visit http://www.goodhuehistory.mus.mn.us.

Crock, rare, two-gallon, with double stenciled markings, 10 in. tall. **$2,200**

Crock, rare two-gallon, with both stenciled marks in red, 10 in. tall. **$2,200**

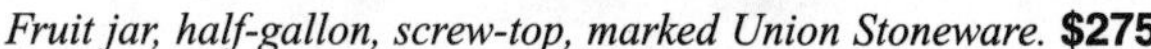
Fruit jar, half-gallon, screw-top, marked Union Stoneware. **$275**

Fruit jar, one-gallon, screw-top, marked Union Stoneware. **$750**

Where can I find it?

Adamstown Antique Gallery
2000 North Reading Rd.
Denver, PA 17517
(717) 335-3435
http://www.aagal.com/Antiquetobacciana.htm
adamsgal@dejazzd.com

Country Comfort Antiques
Third and Main Streets
Winona, MN 55987
(507) 452-7044

Country Side Antique Mall
31752 65th Ave.
Cannon Falls, MN 55009
(507) 263-0352
www.csamantiques.com

John Kruesel's General Merchandise
22 Third St. SW
Rochester, MN 55902
(507) 289-8049
www.kruesel.com

Wayne Mattox Antiques
82 Main Street N
Woodbury, CT 06798
(203) 263-2431
www.antiquetalk.com
tiquetalk@aol.com

20 21

9

18 14 13

17

19 15

▲16

An assortment of Red Wing stoneware pieces: (1) rare four-gallon salt-glaze beehive jug with cobalt leaf and glaze drippings (called "turkey droppings"), **$1,400**; *(2) eight-gallon salt-glaze crock with cobalt leaf, with hairline cracks,* **$600**; *(3) 30-gallon crock with wing and oval stencil,* **$325**; *(4) four-gallon birch-leaf jug,* **$400**; *(5) 12-gallon crock,* **$100**; *(6) two-gallon batter jug (not Red Wing),* **$140**; *(7) 25-gallon crock,* **$250**; *(8) four-gallon crock,* **$115**; *(9) 20-gallon crock,* **$185**; *(10) four-gallon jug from Red Wing Liquor Co. jug,* **$600**; *(11) one-gallon crock with single wing,* **$300**; *(12) one-gallon jug from William Steinmeyer Co.,* **$170**; *(13) three-gallon crock marked "J.F. Cairns Crockery Dept. Saskatoon,"* **$1,300**; *(14) Transitional water cooler,* **$600**; *(15) mug with blue bands,* **$32**; *(16) small bowl with blue bands,* **$100**; *(17) 32-pound Bishop's Peanut Butter crock (not Red Wing),* **$650**, *cover is Red Wing,* **$135**; *(18) four-gallon beehive jug,* **$475**; *(19) three-gallon beehive with glaze flaws,* **$300**; *(20) two-gallon brown-top wing jug,* **$525**; *(21) saffronware pitcher,* **$150**.

Toleware

Tole is sheet metal, especially tinplate, for use in domestic and ornamental wares. It is usually japanned (to apply a hard, dark coating containing varnish and ash or asphalt) or painted, and often elaborately decorated.

Chestnut urns, covered, deep rounded oblong body raised on a square slender pedestal on a stepped rectangular base, S-scroll shoulder handles, and a waisted flaring neck supporting a high domed and stepped cover with a paneled and pointed gilt finial, decorated overall with painted foliage in gold and sienna on a black ground, Europe, 19th century, 5 in. by 9 1/2 in., 12 in. tall. **$2,300-$2,500/pair**

Canister, covered, cylindrical with hinged flat cover with wire loop handle, red japanned ground, decorated around the top and cover with red cherries and green leaves on a white band, yellow stylized leaves and swag borders, leaf decoration on top of cover, minor scratches, 19th century, 6 1/2 in. deep by 6 in. tall. **$400-$600**

Coffeepot, covered, domed and hinged top above a flaring cylindrical body with applied strap handle and arched spout, on a flaring round base, black ground painted with red and green fruit and leaves and yellow trim, Pennsylvania, 19th century, 10 1/2 in. tall. **$4,500**

Left to right: Coffeepot with a tall tapering cylindrical body with flared foot, the domed cover with a small finial, angled long spout, C-form handle with hand grip, original black ground decorated with yellow birds, red pomegranates, and yellow stylized leaves, lid unattached, minor paint loss, repair to finial, 19th century, 10 1/2 in. tall, **$1,100-1,400***; deed box, deep rectangular sides with hinged domed cover with wire loop handle, old red japanned ground decorated with red, yellow, and green fruit and foliage and yellow stylized leaf borders, 19th century, minor scratches, 5 1/8 in. by 9 1/2 in., 6 1/2 in. tall.* **$5,500-$6,000**

Left to right: Tall coffeepot with a flared foot below the gently tapering body, angled gooseneck spout, strap handle with grip, domed cover with small finial, old polychrome floral decoration with bands on dark brown ground, in white, green, yellow, and red with some touch-up, early 19th century, 10 1/2 in. tall, **$523**; *mug, tall, cylindrical, with strap handle, original floral decoration in red and yellow on a worn dark ground, early 19th century, 5 3/4 in. tall. **$245***

Tin coffeepot, covered, the angled ovoid body decorated on each side with wrigglework flowers in two-handled pots and four spiral-twisted punchwork lower bands, the hinged domed cover with a turned finial, angled gooseneck spout, strap handle with grip impressed "J. Ketterer" for John B. Ketterer, Pennsylvania, mid-19th century, 11 1/2 in. tall. **$3,300**

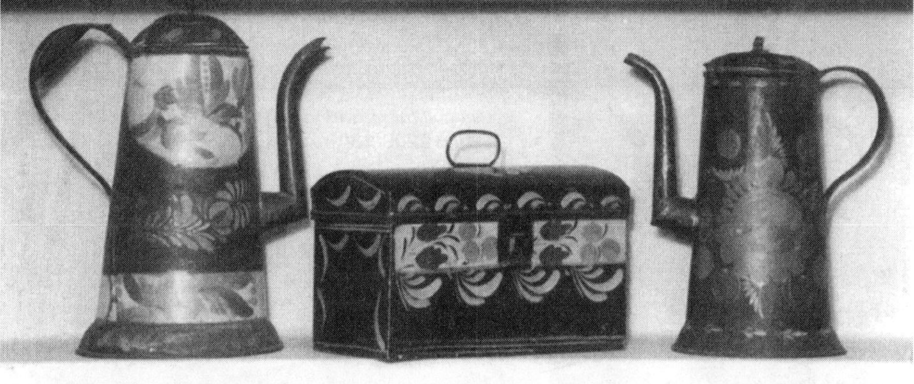

*Left to right: Tall coffeepot with tapering cylindrical body with flared base, hinged domed cover, large strap handle with grip, angled spout, dark brown japanning decorated with colorful florals in red, green, brown, blue, and yellow, wear, old paint touch-up, repairs, 19th century, 10 1/2 in. tall, **$500**; deed box, deep rectangular sides with hinged domed cover with small wire bail handle, dark brown japanned ground decorated with a band of colored scallops around the cover edge and further scallops around the sides, leafy sprigs on front below a white band painted with colorful florals in yellow, red, green, and black, painter's mark on band, bottom seams loose, minor wear, 19th century, 8 3/4 in. long,* **$850-$950**; *tall, slightly tapering, cylindrical coffeepot with flared foot, domed hinged cover, strap handle, angled spout, black ground decorated with colorful florals in red, green, yellow, and white, crusty surface with some touch-up repair, interior and bottom rust, some battering, 19th century, 9 1/2 in. tall.* **$900-$1,000**

Document box, covered, rectangular with a gently domed hinged cover with wire loop handle, the front decorated with two birds and leafy branches of fruit, the sides with a band of leaves in orange, green, yellow, and white on a black ground, attributed to Mercy North, Flycreek, New York, late 18th/early 19th century, wear, 6 1/2 in. by 9 5/8 in., 7 1/4 in. tall. **$1,150**

Deed box, covered, rectangular with domed top with applied wire bail handle, scrolled strap on front, the base decorated with red, yellow, and green painted floral decoration on a black ground with yellow trim, Pennsylvania, 19th century, 4 in. by 8 1/4 in. by 4 1/2 in. tall. **$2,000**

Figures of a man and woman, each in traditional peasant dress and carrying a cylindrical kindling basket on their back, polychrome decoration, stepped round base, Switzerland, 19th century, 14 in. tall. **$2,500-$3,500**

Left to right: Deed box, deep rectangular sides with low domed hinged cover with wire bail, hasp at front, original dark brown japanning decorated with stylized florals in red, yellow, white, and faded green, minor wear, 19th century, 10 in. long, **$950-$1,000;** *mug, tall, cylindrical, strap rim handle, worn original dark brown japanning with a large single stylized blossom on the front in red, yellow, and white, 5 3/4 in. tall.* **$975-$1,200**

Left to right: Document box, deep rectangular form with hinged, gently arched cover with loop bail handle, decorated with flowers and fruit in red, yellow, and green on a black ground, wear, small dents, early 19th century, 4 3/4 in. by 10 in., 6 1/2 in. tall, **$400**; *coffeepot, tall tapering cylindrical form with gooseneck spout and strap handle, hinged domed cover with scrolled finial, decorated with fruit and leaves in a diamond formation in shades of orange, yellow, and green on a black ground, wear, small hole, first half 19th century, 10 1/4 in. tall.* **$870**

Left to right: Mug, tall, cylindrical, with a strap handle, original dark brown japanning with a white rim band with floral decoration in red, green, and yellow, good color, 19th century, some wear, 4 1/2 in. tall, $675-775; deed box, deep rectangular sides with hinged flat cover with ring bail handle, worn original brown japanning with white band and stylized floral bands in red, green, and yellow, with hasp, good color, 19th century, 8 1/8 in. tall. **$600-700**

Pitcher, spouted, circa 1850, tin with painted decoration of a gold ribbon and remnants of blue paint and gold trim on base and handle, fitted cover with turned wood knob, originally part of a set that included tin basin, minor handling wear and surface rust, overall very good condition, with handle extended, 16 in. by 14 in. by 9 in. **$200-$300**

Spice box, rectangular, six tins, with original purplish japanning in excellent condition on the individual tins, 11 in. by 8 in. by 4 1/2 in., tins measure 3 1/2 in. square, each with the original name stenciled on the top, with grater mounted inside lid. **$200-$250**

Tray, rectangular with rounded corners and cut-out end handles, the rim in black and gold bronze bands, the center painted with a walking tiger framed by a border of stenciled flowers and leaves in red, green, and gold on a black ground, American, 19th century, 15 3/4 in. by 22 in. **$3,300**

Tea canisters, covered, cylindrical form with rounded shoulder and short cylindrical neck, dark green ground decorated in gilt with Chinese characters, applied label reading "Parnall & Sons Ltd. Manufacturer - Complete Shop Fitters for all Trades - Narrow Wine St. Bristol," England, 19th century, now mounted as lamps. **$1,600/pair**

Tray, rectangular with rounded corners and wide flanged rim with pierced end handles, the center decorated with a scene of the Annunciation in color, stylized flowers around border on a dark ground, losses, wear, Europe, 19th century, 24 in. long. **$400-$800**

Tray, rectangular with rounded flared ends, incurved sides, japanned ground with yellow stripe and red and green daubing, white edge on ends with red and green fruit decoration, some wear, 8 in. by 14 in. **$385**

Urn, Classical style, the tall body raised on a slender pedestal with a flared round foot, fitted with a tall slender pointed cover with acorn finial, high wide arched loop side handles, decorated with floral sprays and birds with scalloped floral and repeating gilt leaf borders, weighted base, paint loss, one lower handle detached, probably France, 19th century, one of a pair. **$600-$1,000/pair**

Tray, rectangular with rounded corners, angled edges with end hand holes, the center decorated with a garden landscape with classical ruins and figures, Europe, early 19th century, paint loss, 30 in. long. .... **$2,000-$2,200**

Tools

Required reading:

Encyclopedia of Antique Tools & Machinery, by C.H. Wendel, Krause Publications, www.krause.com

Encyclopedia of American Farm Implements and Antiques, by C.H. Wendel, Krause Publications, www.krause.com

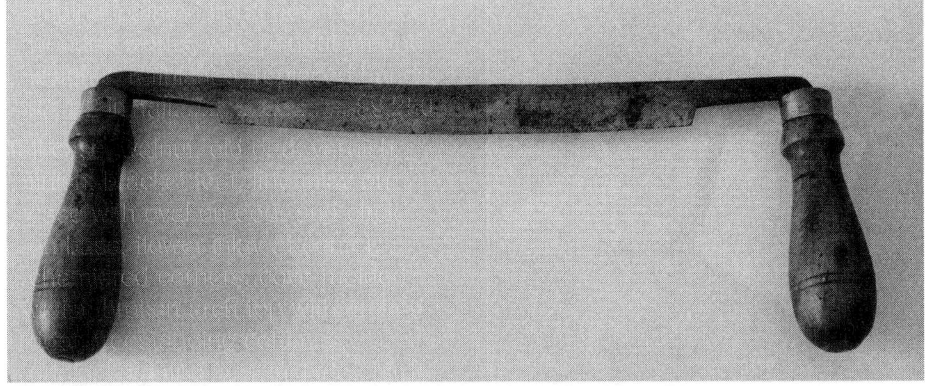

Draw knife, circa 1880, blade forged from an iron rasp, turned maple handles with brass collars, 12 in. by 4 1/4 in. **$100-$125**

Many of the tools featured here were not simply utilitarian, but were also an artistic statement about a craftsman's skill.

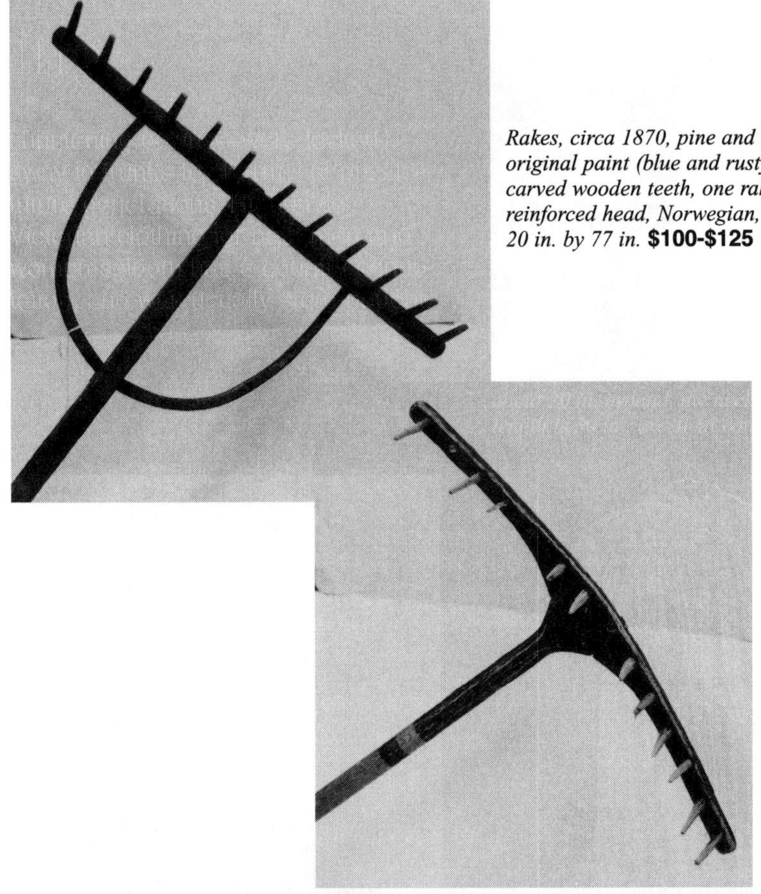

Rakes, circa 1870, pine and maple with original paint (blue and rusty red), with carved wooden teeth, one rake having a reinforced head, Norwegian, handling wear, 20 in. by 77 in. **$100-$125**

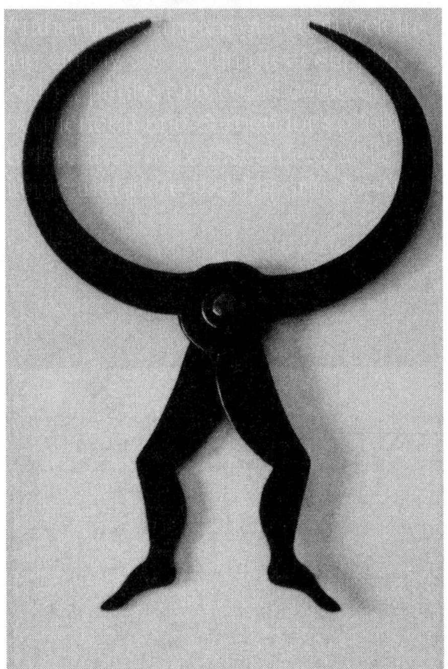

Inside-outside calipers, circa 1860, hand-cut sheet iron with "dancing legs," mint condition, 6 in. by 4 1/4 in. **$100-$125**

Compass, circa 1900, wrought iron with faceted points, hand-stamped "C.E. Chelgren," 16 1/2 in. by 4 1/4 in. **$100-$125**

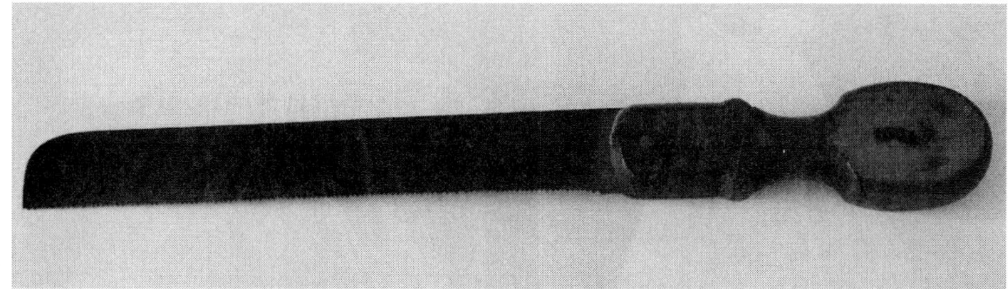

Small saw, circa 1890, steel with shaped tiger or curly maple handle, possibly for cutting dovetails, 10 1/2 in. by 1 1/2 in. by 1 in. **$50-$60**

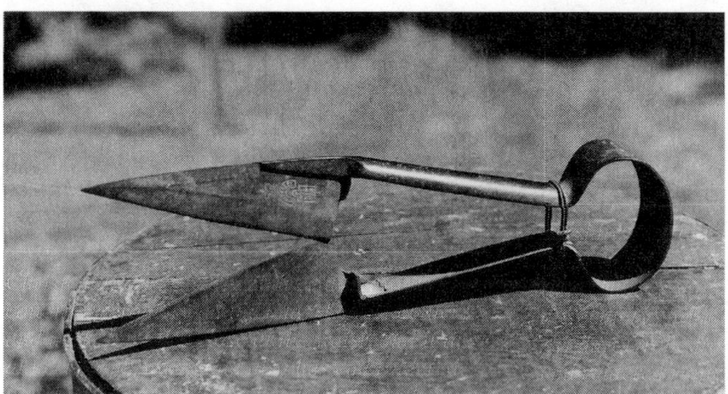

Sheep shears, molded steel handle with tempered steel blades, probably English, marked on one blade with a crown above an arch, with sliding wire loop to hold blades shut, circa 1900, 12 in. by 4 in. **$30-$40**

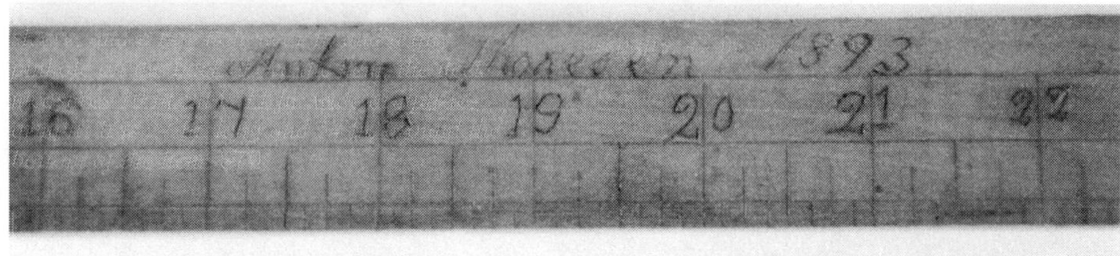

Detail of square, curly maple, handmade and scribed, signed and dated, "Anton Thoreson 1893," 24 3/4 in. by 16 in. **$125-$150**

Wood plane, primitive, Scandinavian, pine, circa 1800, with shallow carved decoration and applied carved head of a lion (?), wrought iron blade, 5 3/4 in. by 3 1/4 in. by 1 3/4 in. **$350**

Buggy wrench, #450, well marked, with one side flat and one round, good condition. **$15-$20**

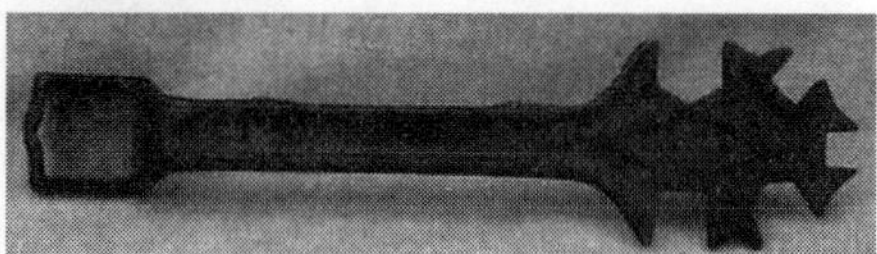

Buggy wrency, with most of its original finish, marked #1 on one side and #13 on the other inside the diamond on the head, excellent condition. **$50-$60**

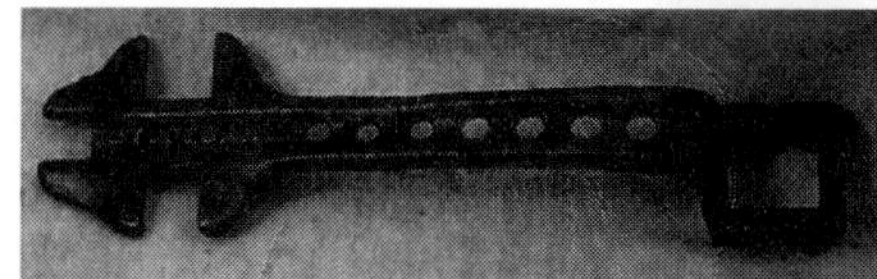

Buggy wrench, Studebaker, 7/8 in., good condition **$70-$80**

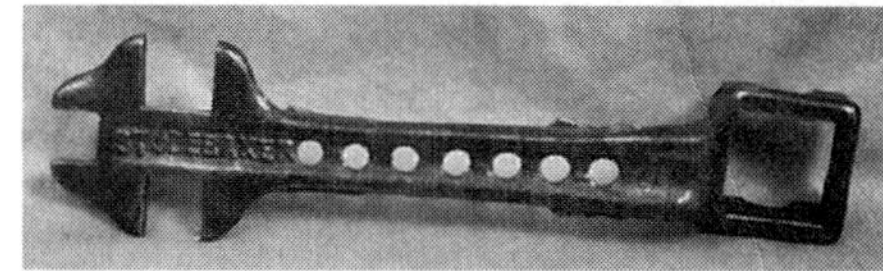

Buggy wrench, Studebaker, 1 1/8 in., good condition. **$90-$100**

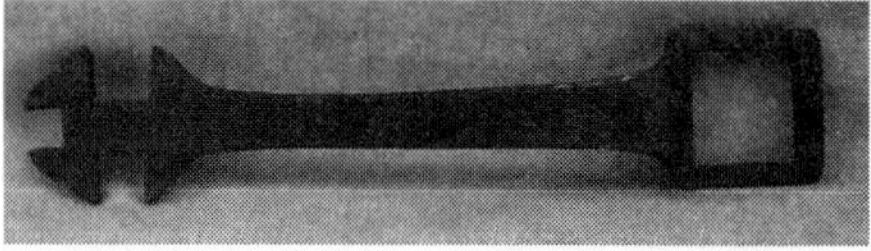

Buggy wrench, unusual and primitive, unmarked, the boxed end is 1 1/2 in., and the top is flat while the bottom of the grip is rounded, 10 7/8 in. long, good condition. **$25-$30**

Buggy wrench, unusual, marked "IV," strong casting gate mark on the side, 8 3/4 in. long, good condition. **$30-$40**

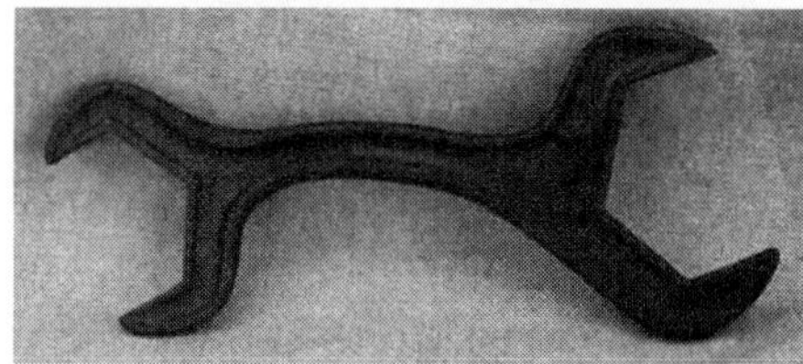

I-1 double wrench, well marked, little used, 7 in. long, good condition. **$20-$25**

Implement wrench, La Crosse Plow Co. #K29, good overall condition with small crack in one jaw, strong markings, and the ruler on the reverse side was used to measure the depth of furrows (?), good condition. **$25-$30**

Where can I find them?

Larry and Carole Meeker
Purveyors of American Patented & Mechanical Antiques
5702 Vacation Blvd.
Somerset, CA 95684
(530) 620-7019
Sales: (888) 07-6090
Fax: (530) 620-7020
www.patented-antiques.com
clm@patented-antiques.com

The Tinker
John W. and Mary Lou Hunziker
2828 Mayowood Common St. SW
Rohester, MN 55902
(507) 288-4898

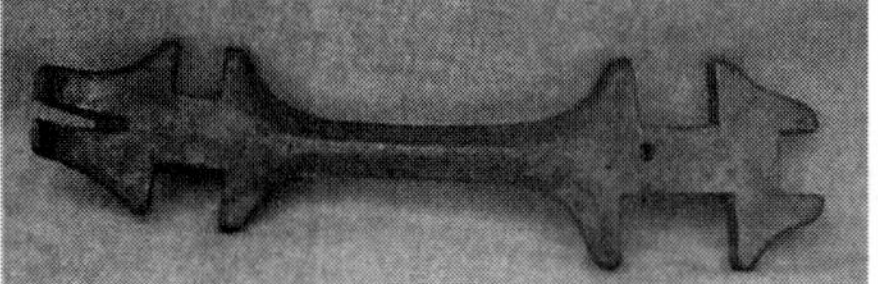

Implement wrench, unmarked, with nail puller, good condition. **$25-$30**

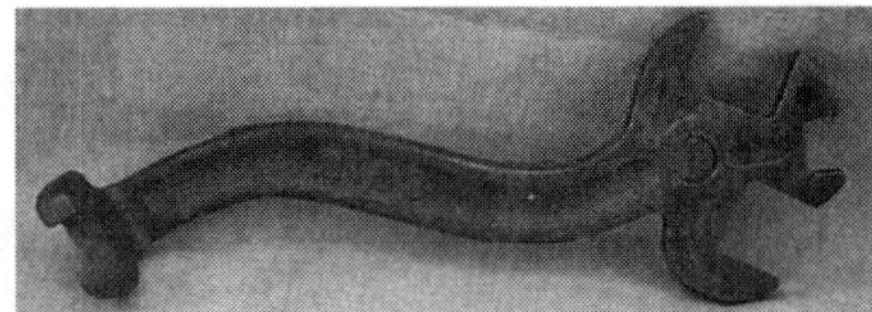

M183 implement wrench, with the single end being set at 90 degrees, good condition. **$15-$18**

"S" wrench, circa 1920, wrought iron made from a rasp, hammered surface with snake-scale appearance, 10 1/2 in. by 2 1/2 in. **$40-$50**

Toys/ Dolls/Games

Hardly any of the items in this chapter were mass-produced. Playthings made of tin and cast iron were enjoyed by children in big cities and tiny villages, but the examples here represent a creative energy that was not stamped out of a mold.

❖ Toys

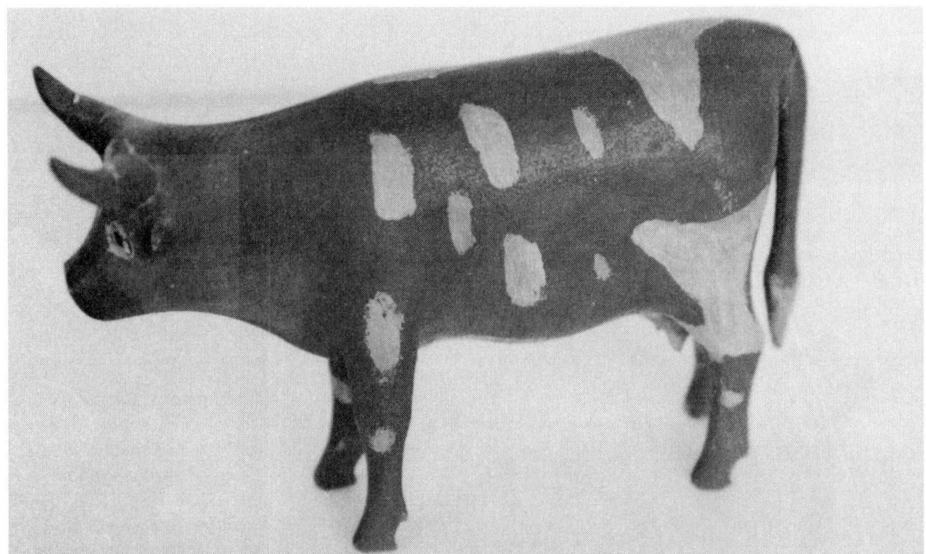

Toy cow, American made in Rhode Island, circa 1880, carved pine painted brown and white, near mint, 7 1/2 in. by 4 3/4 in. by 2 in. **$350**

Toy cow, Norwegian, circa 1880, carved pine painted brown and white with wire horns, applied leather ears, 6 in. by 4 1/2 in. by 2 in. **$300**

Toy dog, circa 1940, carved and painted pine, probably a husky or sled dog, excellent condition, 6 1/2 in. by 5 in. by 2 in. **$80-$100**

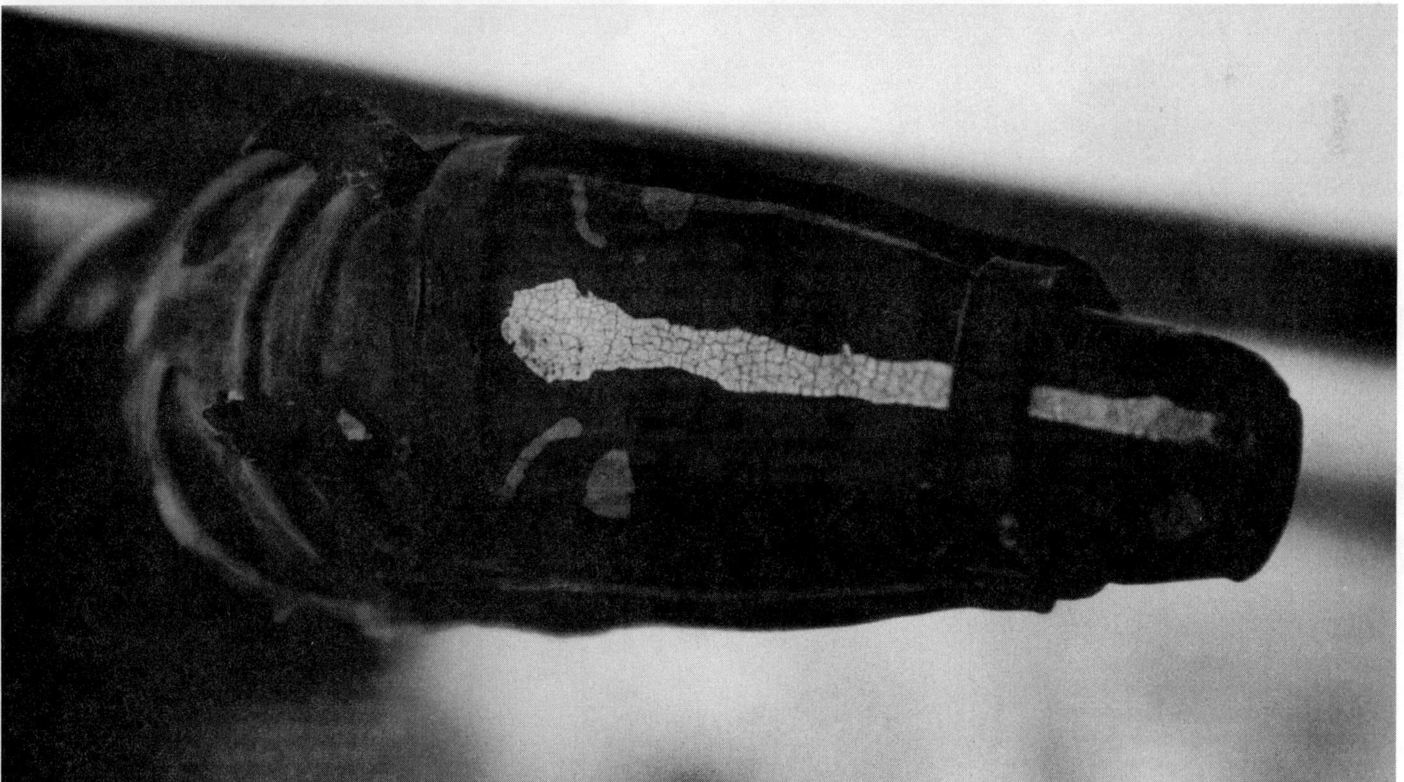

Three views of hobbyhorse, circa 1890, with carved and painted wooden head and handmade leather bridle, horse's head painted with white blaze on face, red eyes and nostrils, and applied leather ears; copper collar around horse's neck; head mounted on a varnished wood shaft with trailing end tipped with large brass hame off an actual horse collar, minor handling wear, 40 in. long overall, horse head 10 in. long. **$600-$800**

Primitive toy horse, pine, Norwegian, circa 1800, remnants of horsehair tail and traces of gray paint, broken legs replaced with hand-carved dowels, 7 1/4 in. by 5 1/2 in. by 2 in. **$300**

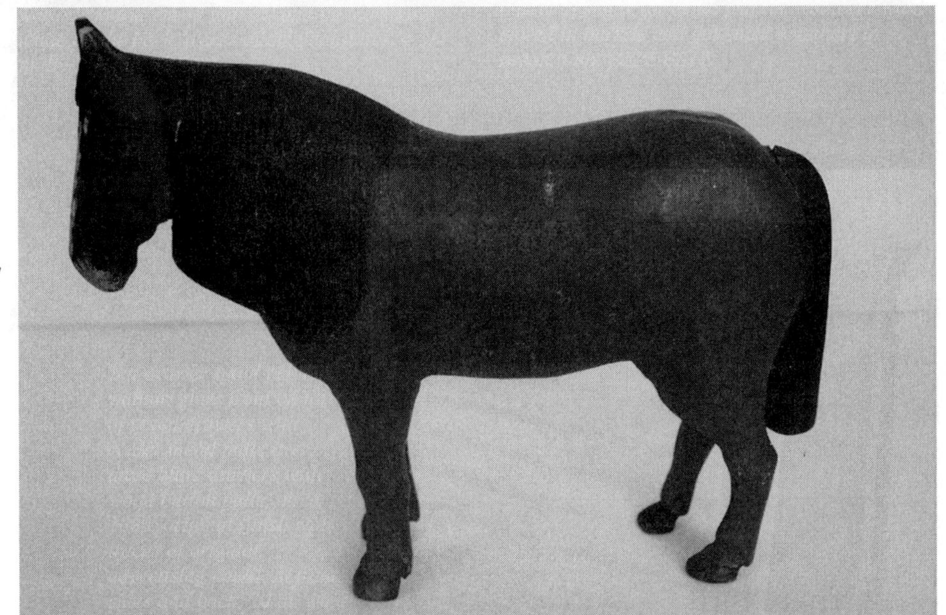

Toy horse, pine, Norwegian, circa 1850, carved and painted brown and black, with detailed carving in mane, minor wear, 11 1/2 in. by 9 1/2 in. by 3 in. **$475**

Toy horse, pine, Norwegian, circa 1830, carved and painted brown and white with horsehair tail, near mint, 11 1/2 in. by 9 1/4 in. by 3 in. **$625**

Toy horse, pine, Norwegian, mid-19th century, carved with original brown stain and old, possibly original fabric saddle blanket, applied leather bridle held in place by brass tacks, remnants of horsehair mane and tail, 19 in. by 18 1/2 in. by 6 in. **$450**

Toy horse, circa 1940, carved and unpainted basswood, lifelike details, 7 in. by 6 1/2 in. by 2 1/2 in. **$60-$70**

Toy horse, circa 1920, carved and painted pine, probably a Percheron, lifelike details, 8 1/2 in. by 6 in. by 3 in. **$120-$150**

Rocking horse, circa 1890, horsehide over composition body, carved and painted mouth and nose, glass eyes, horsehair tail, with original saddle and harness, on painted rockers, excellent condition, 35 in. by 13 1/2 in. by 27 in. **$1,500-$1,800**

Two views of miniature house, circa 1900, possibly part of a larger setting, scrap wood with nail construction, with three dormers, scribed windows and door, and fireplace, original worn red paint, rodent hole in roof, moderate handling wear, 16 in. by 12 in. by 10 in. **$300-$400**

Jack-in-the box, handmade, circa 1900, possibly German, paper-covered wooden box with hook-and-eye clasp, Jack with composition (papier mache?) head, hand painted, and ruffled cloth collar, minor handling wear, size open 4 in. by 8 3/8 in. by 4 in. **$250**

Skates, carved pine and wrought iron blades, Norwegian, circa 1830, with original leather fittings and green paint, significant wear, each skate 10 in. by 2 1/2 in. by 2 in. **$130/pair**

Sled, circa 1930s, stamped steel and wood with art deco influence in the form of a rocket, with worn red paint and old reinforcing repairs to bottom, steering mechanism worn, 51 in. by 26 in. by 8 in **$50-$80**

Miniature steam locomotive and coal car, wood and metal, painted black, made by Harold Ibach, Spring Valley, Minnesota, in 1946, mint condition, locomotive measures 4 in. long. **$200-$300/pair**

Several views of miniature steam locomotive and coal car, circa 1930s, wood and metal, painted black, red, and white, locomotive measures 20 in. by 9 in. by 4 1/2 in. **$700-$800/pair**

Turtle pull toy, circa 1930s, pine, painted red and black, with notched cylinder on bottom, which causes turtle's legs to move when pulled, minor wear, 10 in. by 8 in. by 5 in. **$300-$400**

Child's wagon, pine, Norwegian, circa 1890, dovetailed construction, cradle-like profile on sides, with wooden wheels and leather pull, original dark blue paint, moderate handling wear, 10 1/2 in. by 8 1/4 in. by 15 in. **$300**

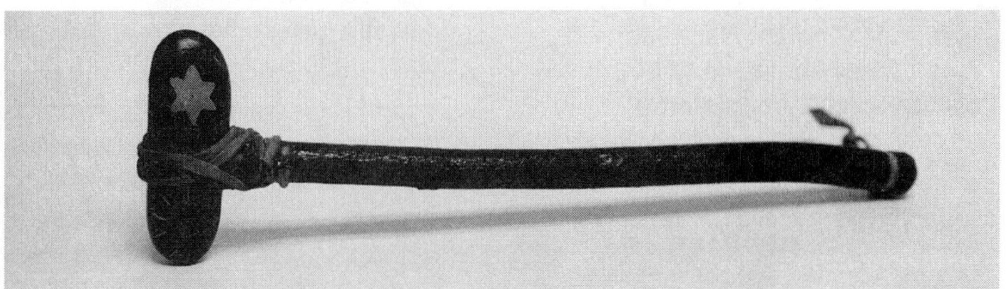

Miniature American Indian war axe, circa 1930s, wood shaft with varnished bark, stone head painted with star, sun, swastika, and stripes, attached with leather thong, probably a tourist souvenir, 11 in. by 3 in. by 1 in. **$60**

Whistle, circa 1930s, carved from a fir branch, with attached carved bird that adjusts whistle's pitch when tail is pressed, bark surface on whistle and burnt-carved decoration on bird, possibly a tourist item, mint condition, 8 in. by 3 in. by 2 in. **$110**

❖ Dolls and Accessories

Made from a wide variety of materials, dolls have always been favorite playthings of the young and the young at heart. Their enduring popularity convinced makers to design entire lines of miniature accessories, complete wardrobes, and a plethora of houses for them.

References: Maryanne Dolan, *The World of Dolls*, Krause Publications, 1998; Jan Foulke, *Insider's Guide to China Doll Collecting*, Hobby House Press, 1995; —, *14th Blue Book Dolls & Values*, Hobby House Press, 1999; Dawn Herlocher, *Doll Makers and Marks*, Antique Trader Books, 1999; R. Lane Herron, *Warman's Dolls*, Krause Publications, 1998; Constance King, *Collecting Dolls Reference and Price Guide*, Antique Collectors' Club, 1999; Patsy Moyer, *Doll Values, Antique to Modern*, 3rd ed., Collector Books, 1999; John Darcy Noble, *Rare & Lovely Dolls of Two Centuries*, Hobby House Press, 2000; Lydia Richter, *China, Parian, and Bisque German Dolls*, Hobby House Press, 1993.

Collectors' Clubs: Annalee Doll Society, P.O. Box 1137, Meredith, NH 03253, www.annalee.com; Delightful Doll Club, 4515 Rita St., La Mesa, CA 91941; Doll Collector International, P.O. Box 2761, Oshkosh, WI 54903; Doll Family Collectors' Club, 1301 Washington Blvd., Belpre, OH 45714; Madame Alexander Doll Club, P.O. Box 330, Mundelein, IL 60060.

Museums: Aunt Len's Doll House, New York, NY; Children's Museum, Detroit, MI; Doll Castle Doll Museum, Washington, NJ; Doll Museum, Newport, RI; Toy and Miniature Museum of Kansas City, MO; Gay Nineties Button and Doll Museum, Eureka Springs, AR; Margaret Woodbury Strong Museum,

Rochester, NY; Mary Merritt Doll Museum, Douglassville, PA; Mary Miller Doll Museum, Brunswick, GA; Washington Dolls' House and Toy Museum, Washington, DC.

Specialty Auctions: McMasters Doll Auctions, P.O. Box 1755, Cambridge, OH 43725, phone 614-432-4419; Skinner, Inc., Bolton Gallery, 357 Main St., Bolton, MA 01740, phone 508-779-6241; Theriault's Auction, P.O. Box 151, Annapolis, MD 21404.

Dolls

Advertising, Miss Flaked Rice, printed cloth, fitted with handmade cotton dress in blue print, wear, a few holes, 23 1/2 in. tall. **$275**

Amish doll, 8 3/4 in. tall, hand sewn, stuffed cotton body and head, light blue dress, light blue apron, black bonnet, clothing machine-sewn, early 20th century, replaced bonnet ties, soiling, stains..................**$100**

Amish doll, 11 1/2 in. tall, hand sewn, stuffed cotton body and head, medium-brown cotton dress, black bonnet, early 20th century, wear, soiling....................................**$150**

Amish doll, 13 3/4 in. tall, machine-sewn stuffed white oilcloth body, orange dress, white apron, black bonnet, light blue knit booties, early 20th century, wear, soiling. **$120**

Amish doll, 14 3/4 in. tall, hand sewn, stuffed cotton and denim body, purple machine-sewn dress, white cotton apron and bonnet, early 20th century, soiling, minor stains. **$90**

Amish doll, 16 in. tall, coarsely woven white cloth body, light blue long-sleeve dress and gray sleeveless dress, blue wool cape with buttons, black bonnet...........................**$225**

Amish doll, 17 1/2 in. tall, stuffed fabric, purple hand-sewn head and body, blue arms and legs, gray dress, white cap, Centre County, Pennsylvania, early 20th century. **$200**

Amish doll, 19 in. tall, stuffed fabric, blue body with white head, white arms and legs pinned with safety pins, blue dress, white apron and cap, Centre County, Pennsylvania, early to mid-20th century, soiling. **$110**

Bisque head, German, Ernest Heubach, jointed kid body, sleep eyes, open mouth, black wig, white cotton dress, straw hat, late 19th century, soiling, 21 1/2 in. tall..**$275**

Bisque head, German, Schoenau and Hoffmeister, ball-jointed composition body, stationary glass eyes, open mouth, black wig, red dress, black shoes, early 20th century, one finger restored, soiling, 26 1/2 in. tall. **$150**

Bisque head, German, Simon and Halbig, ball-jointed composition body, sleep eyes, open mouth, pierced ears, marked "SH-719-12," fair wig, white cotton dress, black leather shoes, mid/late 19th century, cracked head, restoration, 22 in. tall................................**$220**

Bisque head, German, Simon and Halbig, jointed composition body, sleep eyes, open mouth, pierced ears, marked "SH1079, 3, DEP," fair wig, white cotton dress, black shoes, late 19th century, legs restored, 11 1/4 in. tall. **$200**

Bisque head, German, Adolf Wislizenus, ball-jointed composition body, sleep eyes, open mouth, pierced ears, fair wig, white cotton dress, late 19th century, 23 in. long. **$350**

Bisque head, German, stuffed jointed kid leather body and legs, sleep eyes, open mouth, marked "dep 154, 8 1/2," brown wig, leather arms, white cotton dress, knit stockings, late vinyl tie shoes, late 19th century, 20 1/2 in. long....**$450**

Black, cloth, hand and machine stitched island lady, multi-color long dress, broad striped sash, embossed brass earrings, matching turban, flat woven hat beginning to unravel, 15 3/4 in. tall. **$225**

Cloth dolls, set of eight, circa 1930s, with bodies in the shape of fruits (orange, strawberry, apple, pear, plum, banana, and pineapple), with hand-stitched features and yarn hair, excellent condition, average size 7 in. by 5 in. **$80-$100/set**

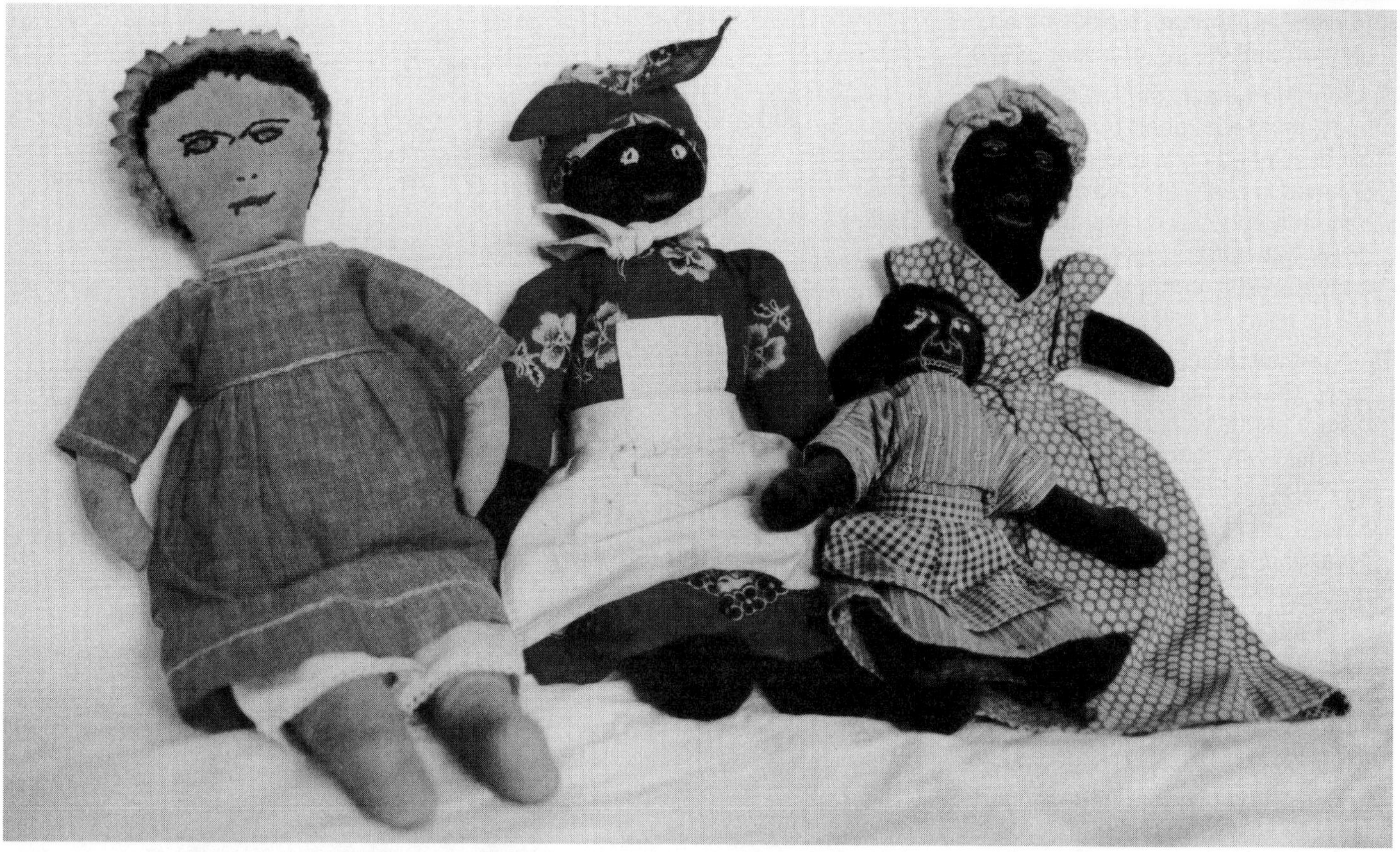

Cloth dolls, late 19th or early 20th century, from left: white doll, 15 in. long, ***$120-$150****; mammy doll, 9 in. long,* **$150-$180***; small black doll with detailed sewn face, 7 in. long,* **$250-$300***; larger black doll, also a "topsy turvey" (when turned upside down she becomes a white doll), 11 in. long,* **$150-$200**

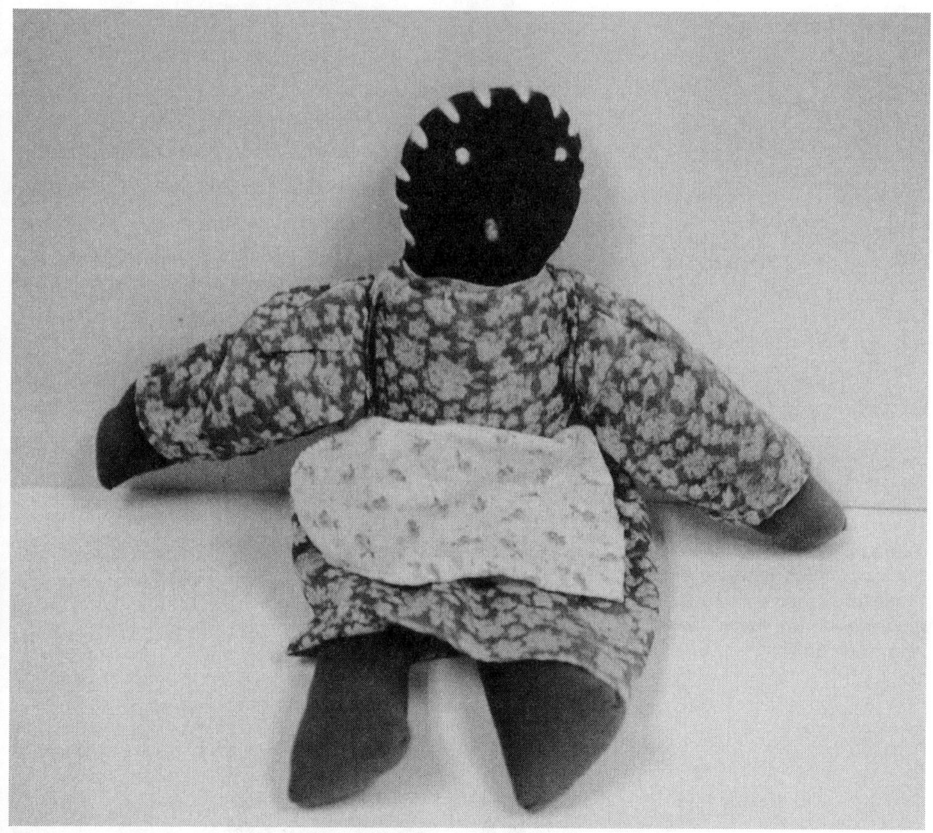

Cloth black doll, circa 1940s, yarn hair and face, in floral print dress and apron, some fading and minor handling wear, 12 in. by 12 in. **$50**

Mennonite doll, female, white and brown polyester body, green long sleeve dress, 16 in. tall. **$75**

Mennonite doll, male, white fabric body, yellow cotton shirt, green pants, black suspenders, Jefferson County, Pennsylvania, early 20th century. **$200**

Papier-mâché gentleman, original paint and clothes, 27 in. tall. **$3,300**

Papier-mâché head, excelsior-filled oilcloth-like body, stationary glass eyes, painted closed mouth, fair wig, composition arms, white cotton dress, leather button shoes, mid-19th century, hands damaged, lower legs partially detached, 31 in. tall. **$150**

Penny doll, molded composition head, carved wooden arms and legs, kid body, pained features, black hair, blue eyes, red shoes, white dress, neck and feet repaired, two loose limbs, 8 1/2 in. tall. **$275**

Shrunken apple head, black women, original clothes, set of three....**$120**

Stocking doll, black, stuffed cloth body, head with pearl buttons for eyes, stitched nose and mouth, dressed in red/white polka-dot bandana and green floral print dress with white shawl and apron, early/mid-20th century, soiling, 13 1/2 in. tall................................**$120**

Tin head, German, stuffed cloth body, painted fair hair, blue eyes, bisque hands with chips on fingers, original plaid cotton dress soiled, paint flakes, 14 in. tall. **$80**

Tin head, stuffed rag body, old worn repaint, one eye damaged, Amish-made dress, 19 in. tall.............**$225**

Wax head, stuffed cloth body, glass eyes, fair wig, jointed composition arms and legs, blue high-top shoes, dress in early fabric, 10 1/2 in. tall......................................**$220**

Wooden, carved and turned, pegged and articulated limbs, crudely carved body with stained finish, painted head and facial features, old hand-stitched dress, undergarments and cloak, 13 in. tall. **$425**

Wood-jointed, Mason and Taylor, composition head with crudely molded features, painted eyes, molded hair painted brown, bottom of legs painted white with blue shoes, redressed, 11 1/2 in. tall. **$550**

❖ Doll Accessories

Buggy, wood, red paint, mustard stencil, wood spoke wheels with white line details, turned handle, seat upholstery replaced, minor wear, touchups, 27 1/4 in. tall. **$275**

Buggy, wood and metal, original yellow and orange paint with blue, white, and red striping, folding sunscreen with worn leatherized cloth covering, wooden spoke wheels with metal rims, 26 in. tall by 34 in. long...........................**$350**

Primitive child's or doll's chair, Norwegian, pine, circa 1820, pegged construction with carved crest rail, splayed legs, remnants of white paint, moderate wear, 10 1/2 in. by 11 1/2 in. by 9 in. **$1,000**

Doll's chair, pine, Scandinavian, circa 1890, with original green and red paint, plank seat with hand-carved round back rail, spindles, legs and stretchers, moderate wear, 6 3/4 in. by 9 1/2 in. by 6 1/4 in. **$200**

Miniature cupboard, circa 1920, made as a child's toy or for a doll, pine or fir painted green and beige, with two shelves in upper step-back portion and hinged doors, lower section open with hinged doors, 9 in. by 13 in. by 4 in. **$85**

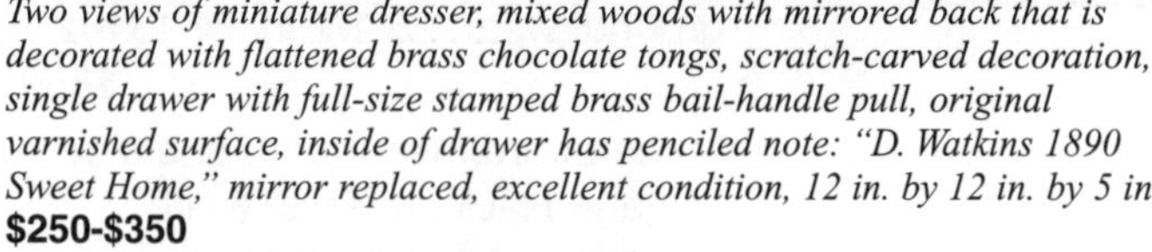

Two views of miniature dresser, mixed woods with mirrored back that is decorated with flattened brass chocolate tongs, scratch-carved decoration, single drawer with full-size stamped brass bail-handle pull, original varnished surface, inside of drawer has penciled note: "D. Watkins 1890 Sweet Home," mirror replaced, excellent condition, 12 in. by 12 in. by 5 in.
$250-$350

Shoes, high-top, black leather, black glass buttons, fringed tassels, 4 1/2 in. tall...................................**$150**

Sled, doll-size, poinsettia in red and yellow, dark green paint over earlier blue, yellow stripe, pine, curved metal runners, three small holes, minor paint wear, light rust, 17 in. long. **$600**

❖ Doll Furniture

Rufus Bliss, of R. Bliss Manufacturing Co. in Pawtucket, Rhode Island, was a well-known dolls' furniture maker. In addition to his painted tin furniture, he produced a popular line of "cottage furniture," which consisted of wooden bedroom furniture decorated with lithographed paper. Cast iron dolls' house furniture worthy of note was manufactured by J.&E. Stevens Co. of Cromwell, Connecticut.

References: Nora Earnshaw, *Collecting Dolls' Houses and Miniatures*, Pincushion Press, 1993; Dian Fillner with Patty Cooper, *Furnished Dollhouses 1880s-1980s*, Schiffer Publishing, 2001; Dian Fillner and Patty Cooper, *Antique and Collectible Dollhouses and Their Furnishings*, 1998; Herbert F. Schiffer and Peter B. Schiffer, *Miniature Antique Furniture: Doll House and Children's Furniture from the United States and Europe*, Schiffer Publishing, 1995; Margaret Towner, *Dollhouse Furniture*, Running Press, 1993.

Museums: Mineral Point Toy Museum, Mineral Point, Wisconsin; Washington Dolls' House and Toy Museum, Washington, D.C.

Bed, rope, cannonball, cherry, refinished, scalloped headboard, arched footboard, 22 in. long, 13 3/4 in. wide...........................**$225**

Bed, rope, pine, spool-turned posts, turned footboard, peaked headboard, 15 1/4 in. tall by 14 1/2 in. wide by 21 1/2 in. long. **$90**

Chair, four-spindle, plank seat, old green paint with strawberries and foliage on seat and crest, wear, some edge damage, 9 1/4 in. tall. **$650**

Chest of drawers with mirror top, cast iron, three drawers, overall pierced diamond and hearts design, painted yellow, red, and gray, one mirror bracket broken, 6 3/8 in. tall by 4 3/4 in. wide.....................**$375**

Cradle, birch, northern New England, circa 1820, two-panel hood, pieced scrolled dovetailed cradle with canted sides, cornice with inlaid oval panel, old finish, 11 1/2 in. tall by 21 in. long by 8 in. wide...**$2,300**

Cradle, painted orange, dark green trim and decor, curved sides and headboard, wear, 11 1/4 in. tall by 14 in. wide by 18 in. long. **$375**

Cradle, softwood, straight dovetailed sides, arched foot and headboard, broad curved rockers with tapered rounded ends, wear, one rocker tip broken off, 8 1/2 in. tall by 17 1/4 in. long....................................**$120**

Dresser, tramp art, three drawers, old white repaint, gold trim, worn, age cracks, 21 1/2 in. tall by 15 1/2 in. wide by 8 3/4 in. deep.............**$375**

Dry sink, old brown over tan comb-graining, pine, cut bracket feet, two doors in base, surface-mounted iron hinges, white porcelain pulls, small drawer at left below flat work surface, trim molding across backsplash, 13 1/4 in. tall by 13 1/2 in. wide by 8 in. deep. **$900**

❖ Doll Houses

Early doll houses were reserved for the wealthy and were designed primarily as display cabinets for collections of valuable miniatures rather than as playthings for children.

The first American doll houses were made in the late 18th century, but it wasn't until 1860, with the development of chromolithography, that they were mass-produced.

References: Nora Earnshaw, *Collecting Dolls' Houses and Miniatures*, Pincushion Press, 1993; Dian Fillner with Patty Cooper, *Furnished Dollhouses 1880s-1980s*, Schiffer Publishing, 2001; Dian Fillner and Patty Cooper, *Antique and Collectible Dollhouses and their Furnishings*, 1998; Constance Eileen King, *Dolls and Dolls' Houses*, Hamlyn, 1989.

Museums: Mineral Point Toy Museum, Mineral Point, Wisconsin; Washington Dolls' House and Toy Museum, Washington, D.C.

Colonial Revival style, white siding, porch with columns, mansard roof with wooden shingles in old black paint, two brick painted chimneys, windows trimmed in red, removable sides reveal rooms, roof removes to reveal attic with stairs, 40 in. tall by 40 in. wide by 30 in. deep. .**$350**

Wooden, two-story brick design, printed paper covering imitating red brick and gray slate, glass windows, rag curtains, gray interior, open at back and roof, two chimneys, paper worn, 25 1/4 in. tall by 26 in. wide by 14 in. deep. **$425**

❖ Game Boards

Before the advent of radio and television, entertainment took on a simpler form. Almost every house had at least a homemade checkerboard. Typically made of wood and often with a painted surface, checkerboards and other game boards have become highly popular with collectors.

Hints: Unusual color combinations and elaborate decorations bring the most interest. Look for examples that have gallery ends and/or compartments for storing the checkers.

Reproduction Alert

The simple construction and painted designs have been easily recreated.

Checkerboard, decorated, one side, grain-decorated, dark red swirl and sponge decorated, mustard ground, black checks, linear scroll decorated, molded border, wear, 16 1/2 in. square. **$2,100**

Checkerboard, decorated, one side, gray and brown squares, 10 in. by 13 in. **$325**

Checkerboard, decorated, one side, green and yellow squares, salmon red and black borders, 19 in. square. **$1,500**

Checkerboard, decorated, one side, red and mustard squares, back used as cutting board, 14 in. by 9 1/2 in. **$325**

Checkerboard, decorated, one side, red and black squares, 18 in. by 27 in. **$250**

Checkerboard, decorated, one side, red and black squares, rounded ends, chamfered edges, scribed checks painted black on red ground, wear, 25 1/2 in. by 13 1/2 in. **$850**

Checkerboard, decorated, one side, red and black squares, white pinstripes, 14 in. square.......**$1,100**

Checkerboard, decorated, one side, red and black squares, white border, 14 in. square..............**$850**

Checkerboard, decorated, one side, red, black and white, 9 in. square. **$425**

Checkerboard, decorated, one side, yellow and black squares, yellow ground, black border, wear, 16 in. by 19 in. **$750**

Checkerboard, circa 1900, black painted squares on an oak board with clear circular saw cuts front and back, minor handling wear, 20 in. by 16 in. by 1/2 in.
$100

Checkerboard, decorated, one side, yellow and black squares, red ends, 19 in. by 29 in. $525

Checkerboard, decorated, one side, pine, original black and red striping, stylized flowers in corners, yellow ground, lid slides off revealing pine board inlaid with walnut, with wooden checkers, found in Maine, 14 in. square. $7,300

Checkerboard, decorated, one side, pine, original black paint, red and black squares, yellow border, applied gallery, 14 1/4 in. square. $1,800

Checkerboard, decorated, one side, old pine cutting board, scribed checkerboard filled in with faded black marking ink, rounded ends, two wooden braces nailed to ends to stabilize age crack, worn, 18 1/8 in. by 19 3/4 in. $225

Checkerboard, decorated, one side, pine, old black paint, red and yellow squares, earlier paint beneath, wear, 16 1/2 in. by 20 in. $2,500

Checkerboard, decorated, one side, pine, old worn brown, white, and black paint, applied molded edge, hole for drawer, age cracks, edge damage, found in Maine, 15 in. square. $675

Checkerboard, decorated, one side, poplar, hardwood ends, old black, green, and yellow paint over gray, 18 1/4 in. by 13 1/2 in. $1,800

Checkerboard, decorated, one side, old dark brown paint with green and yellow, 13 in. by 13 3/4 in. $1,950

Checkerboard, decorated, one side, pine, original red and black paint, applied molded edge, 13 1/2 in. by 13 3/4 in. $1,850

Checkerboard, decorated, one side, softwood, original black paint, red ground, checkerboard on one side with edge striping, all red on other side with black edge striping, dated "1880," 18 1/2 in. by 24 3/4 in. $2,800

Checkerboard, decorated, two sides, black repaint (old), mustard and red checks, Parcheesi in green, red, and yellow, applied molding, age cracks, 19 1/4 in. by 28 1/4 in. $850

Checkerboard, decorated, two sides, folding, black and white squares, red and black borders, backgammon board in green, red, and white on other side. $250

Checkerboard, decorated, two sides, old red and black repaint, other side with geometric design in black, white, and red flourish, white line border around checkerboard, signed "H. Petty," 13 in. square. $750

Checkerboard, inlaid, mixed woods, herringbone trim, decorated borders include dog, pipe, and cards, 24 in. square. $2,200

Checkerboard, inlaid, mixed woods including ebony, mahogany, walnut, and birch, checkerboard at center surrounded by 16 miniature checkered panels, variegated band near edge, "Made by C.H. Klingberg" carved on back, moth damage to green wool backing, 22 in. square. $950

Checkerboard, inlaid, pine, walnut inlay, diamonds on the border, other side has painted backgammon game in original green, black, and red, original varnish, one small piece of inlay missing, 17 in. by 17 1/8 in. $725

Cribbage board, inlaid, mahogany and beech, inlaid geometric designs on case and top, dovetailed drawer, 5 in. wide by 15 in. long...................................$275

Folding game board, checkerboard pattern, red ground, interior with backgammon and star motifs in shades of red, green, orange, yellow, and black, white ground, paint wear, 14 1/2 in. by 17 1/4 in. (folds to 14 1/2 in. by 8 3/4 in.). $375

Game board, decorated, one side, pine, old red, yellow, and black decorated, slide-lid compartment, wooden checkers, minor edge wear, 21 in. by 31 3/8 in.......$4,400

Game board, decorated, one side, pine, original light green paint with black and dark green, cross-shaped design, two-board, molded edge, wear, 26 1/4 in. by 27 1/4 in. $600

Game board, decorated, one side, poplar, old black and green paint, maroon striping and borders, wear, white paint shows beneath, 17 in. by 17 1/2 in. $750

Game board, decorated, one side, poplar, old dark red and black paint, edge gallery with areas at both ends for checkers, relief-carved surface with raised squares, 13 in. wide by 23 1/4 in. long. .$650

Game board, decorated, one side, wooden, old black, green, and red in worn repaint, gallery edge worn and damaged, 15 1/2 in. by 18 1/2 in. $350

Game board, decorated, one side, old worn yellow and dark green, raised gallery edges, two-board, second game penciled on back, 18 1/4 in. by 28 in. $375

Game board, decorated, one side, dark mustard and white repaint over earlier salmon, gallery edges, two boards with nailed braces on back, age cracks, green paint splotches, 14 in. by 27 in. $275

Game board, decorated, one side, pine, one-board, original painted decorated, five circles in corners and center in salmon, blue, and red, cross-shaped grid in blue, red, and white, 16 in. square..........$350

Game board, decorated, one side, old red over green repaint, black on reverse, rectangular, molded trim, age cracks, chips on rim, 18 in. by 28 1/2 in. $350

Parcheesi game board, decorated, two sides, in shades of dark red, mustard, and black paint on one side, backgammon in red, green, and yellow on reverse, 19th century, minor wear, some edge roughness, 18 in. by 18 3/4 in. $2,200

Game board, pine, Norwegian, dated 1815, with cutout handle, black stain in scribed checkerboard pattern on front, reverse with black stain and diamond-shaped scribing and inscription on Norwegian, 9 1/2 in. by 15 in. by 1 in. **$600**

Fortune-telling game, circa 1920s, homemade wood box with applied paper to game board, glass cover and spring-loaded mechanism (not working), which made metal pointer spin to indicate good or bad luck, spell words, and answer "Yes" or No" (similar to a Ouija board), with original fabric-lined carrying case, 8 in. by 8 in. by 3 in. **$200-$300**

Parcheesi game board, decorated, two sides, multicolor with dark green border on one side, checkerboard on dark red ground on reverse, 19th century, paint wear, some rough edges. **$5,500**

Parcheesi game board, decorated, one side, red, yellow, blue, brown, and white, 19 in. by 27 in........**$950**

Where can I find them?

Adamstown Antique Gallery
2000 North Reading Rd.
Denver, PA 17517
(717) 335-3435
http://www.aagal.com/Antiquetobacciana.htm
adamsgal@dejazzd.com

Mary Lou Beidler
Early American Antiques
2736 Pecan Rd.
Tallahassee, FL 32303
(850) 385-2981
http://www.antiquearts.com/stores/beidler/
beidler@AntiqueArts.com

Blondell Antiques
1406 2nd St. SW
Rochester, MN 55902
(507) 282-1872
Fax: (507) 282-8683
www.blondell.com/
antiques@blondell.com

Country Comfort Antiques
Third and Main Streets
Winona, MN 55987
(507) 452-7044

Country Side Antique Mall
31752 65th Ave.
Cannon Falls, MN 55009
(507) 263-0352
www.csamantiques.com

Freward & Alk Antiques
414 Lazarre Ave.
Green Bay, WI 54301
(800) 488-0321
(920) 435-7343
www.the-antique-shop.com
leesa@the-antique-shop.com

John Kruesel's General Merchandise
22 Third St. SW
Rochester, MN 55902
(507) 289-8049
www.kruesel.com

Trade Signs

Trade signs served as a symbol of the services or goods offered by early American businesses. Typically made of wood or metal, they depicted the object handled by a particular establishment, such as a pair of eyeglasses for an optometrist. The figural representation was particularly important during the 18th and 19th centuries, when many people couldn't read.

Barber pole, circa 1910, porcelain and leaded glass with red and white stripes, all original, 36 in. tall. ....**$1,500-$2,000**

Barber pole, turned wood, painted, 34 in. tall, red, white and gold, ball-shaped ends. **$900**

Barber pole, turned wood, painted, 40 in. tall, blue and white stripes, acorn-shaped ends. **$4,000**

Barber pole, turned wood, painted, 76 in. tall, red and white repaint, filled age cracks and chips on base, tin cover on top.............**$600**

Barber pole, circa 1900, turned wood with ball top, with remnants of red, white, and blue paint, with two iron mounting brackets top and bottom, overall weathered surface, excellent condition, pole only measures 16 in. by 3 in. **$400-$500**

Barber pole, turned wood, painted, 7 ft. tall, red, white, and blue design, ball top, worn paint...............**$1,700**

Boot, cast zinc, wrought iron angle bracket, painted golden-brown, American, 19th century, paint loss, 22 1/2 in. tall.........................**$1,500**

Boot, pine, worn patina and repair in red, heel and back edge restored, 20th century, 34 in. tall. **$475**

Boot, white repaint, black detail over earlier gilding, contemporary steel stand, age cracks, 25 1/2 in. tall. **$400**

Cigar, turned wood, "Papa's Best" in red letters on brown ground, late 19th century, paint losses, 37 in. long. **$425**

Drugstore, painted wood, molded frame on rectangular sign, ochre colored raised lettering, dark blue ground, minor wear, 19 in. tall by 72 in. long. **$2,500**

Fish, copper, gilded, full-bodied fish painted "Tackle," original forged hinges, with provenance from original owners, 25 in. long.**$10,000**

Hand axe, painted zinc, 21 in. tall by 9 in. wide................................**$450**

Mortar and pestle, sheet zinc, three-dimensional, old worn gilt paint with traces of black, contemporary stand, dents, 36 in. tall. **$800**

Optometrist, cast iron and zinc, double-sided, polychrome decor with "Glass Fitted" arched above/below eye on one lens, "Eyes Tested" above/below eye on other lens, late 19th century, wear, old touchups to paint, 11 1/2 in. tall by 26 1/4 in. long. **$4,500**

Pawn broker, wrought iron bracket with scrolled decor and twisted flame atop, three copper balls approximately 14 in. diameter, brass fittings, worn black paint, 61 in. tall by 50 in. wide.............**$1,800**

Pocket watch, cast and sheet zinc, traces of gilt and Roman numerals, 19 1/2 in. tall...........................**$400**

Three-section wood sign from a carnival sideshow, hand-painted in pale green, black, and red, with the words, "Fool the Guesser—Age within 2 years—Weight within 3 pounds," wired for 15 electric lights, circa 1950s, minor wear, all light sockets work, overall 12 ft. by 3 ft. **$300-$400**

"Eat Short Orders" sign, circa 1930s, sheet iron with riveted iron border, yellow and navy blue, minor weathering, 31 in. by 19 in. **$400-$500**

County fair promotional poster, circa 1950s, for Uncle Heavy and the Pork Chop Revue featuring "Oink" the Singing Pig, printed on poster board, minor handling wear, 30 in. by 16 in. **$40-$50**

Cast iron plaque commemorating the first radio broadcast (?) from a county fair in the United States, from Aug. 30 to Sept. 2, 1922, in Owatonna, Minnesota, original silver and black painted surface, 8 in. by 12 in. **$200-$300**

Rifle, carved wood with gesso, old repaint, resembles Henry rifle, wrought iron hangers, old repair at trigger guard, 70 in. long......**$1,200**

Shoe, wooden, high heel with bow on front, laminated, yellow, blue, and salmon paint, worn and weathered, early 20th century, 25 in. long. **$2,500**

Shoe, wooden, similar to Dutch shoe, white paint, 8 in. tall by 22 1/2 in. long. **$350**

Straight razor, carved wood, blade painted "Razors Ground" in black on gray ground, black handle, wear, 14 1/2 in. tall by 31 in. long. **$1,000**

Pawn shop sign, wrought and cast iron, circa 1890, with old gold paint, three arms with chain supports hold three round balls on which is painted "MONEY–GUNS–LOANS," weathered surface but overall excellent condition, 44 in. by 40 in. by 18 in. **$1,200-$1,500**

Sign, circa 1930s, painted wood, advertising the 1812 House Restaurant near Clear Lake, Iowa, vertical braces on back, earlier paint underneath also indicates miles to restaurant, weathered surface with some flaking, overall very good condition, 28 in. by 16 in. **$200-$300**

County fair poster, circa 1950s, for Maggie and Scotty's Hi-Diving Donkeys, with blank section to fill in current dates, in bright red, yellow, and green, near mint, 14 in. by 22 in. **$25**

Straight razor, carved wood, painted black and white, wear, scratches, 43 1/4 in. long. **$950**

Poster, Winchester shells, "Shoot them and avoid trouble," shows skunk coming out of hollow log and spraying black man and dog, cropped, framed, 18 3/4 in. by 27 in. ....**$300-$350**

Sign, painted metal, "Tractors With Lugs Prohibited," embossed, black text, yellow ground, 8 in. by 12 in. ....**$60-$70**

Sign, painted wood, "Meat Market," brown letters and border, yellow highlights, white ground, 13 in. by 98 in. ....**$400-$450**

Sign, painted wood, "Wall Papers," old black crazed paint, gray lettering, applied molding, 7 3/4 in. by 40 1/4 in. ....**$300-$350**

Sign, painted wood, "We Do Razor Honeing & Concaveing," black letters, red-and-white diagonal stripes, 9 1/2 in. by 62 in. ....**$1,000-$1,200**

Sign, painted wood, "White Mt. Grange," arrow shape, white letters, black ground, 101 in. long. ....**$200-$250**

Sign, paper, "Corn King Manure Spreaders, International Harvester Company of America," oval images of brook and horse-drawn manure spreader in field, two panels show two different models, copyright 1908, archival backing, 25 1/2 in. by 20 in. ....**$500-$600**

Sign, paper, "Success, The Horse's Friend, E.L. McClain Mfg. Co., Greenfield, O.," shows horse writing testimonial letter, includes 1889 calendar, 24 in. by 19 in. ....**$1,200-$1,400**

Sign, porcelain, "5¢," oval, white text, red ground, edge nicks, 7 in. by 5 1/2 in. ....**$150-$200**

Sign, porcelain, "Barber Shop," flange sign, white on cobalt panel, red, white, and blue diagonals slant toward center, 12 in. by 24 in. ....**$225-$275**

Sign, porcelain, "Ice Cold Water," two-

Large and rare advertising stoneware two-handled jug, circa 1890, 15-gallon salt-glazed, promoting "Regnier & Shoup Crockery Co.—'We sell the Red Wing Stoneware Co.'s Stoneware and Flower Pots—Red Wing, Minn.," with glaze drips on body (called "turkey droppings"), cracks around mouth, overall excellent condition. (Private collection.) **$30,000-$35,000**

sided, black ice-capped text on white ground, circa 1950s-1960s, 20 in. by 10 in. ....**$125-$150**

Sign, porcelain, "Pony Express Trail, 1860 1861," silhouette of rider on horseback, minor chips to edges, minor water stain, 14 in. diameter. ....**$800-$900**

Sign, reverse-painting on glass, "Entrance," gold-colored tin backing, white text, rust spotting, paint running on some text, 3 3/4 in. by 18 in. ....**$20-$30**

Sign, reverse-painting on glass, "Spectacles, Eye Glasses & Artificial Eyes," chipping to gold, black ground, framed, restored, 8 in. by 20 in. ....**$400-$450**

Sign, reverse-painting on glass, "Spectacles Properly Fitted," two eyes over white text, black ground, framed, paint chips, 17 3/4 in. by 33 3/4 in. ....**$250-$300**

Sign, tin, "Dr. Hess Stock & Poultry Preparations Sold Here," flange sign, litho tin, banner shape, shows farm animals on yellow and blue ground, 11 in. by 18 1/4 in. ....**$850-$900**

Sign, tin, "Kreso Dip No. 1 For All Live Stock and Poultry, Parke Davis & Co.," round vignettes of sheep, cow, horse, and pig, also shows chickens, collie, and turkeys, nail holes, minor bend, scattered scratches, 18 in. by 28 in. ....**$1,400-$1,500**

Thermometer, painted wood, "Dr. A.C. Daniels' Famous Veterinary Medicines, Home Treatment For Horses and Cattle, Dog Remedies," with advertising for New York merchant, 20 3/4 in. by 5 in. ....**$350-$400**

Thermometer, painted wood, "Dr. A.C. Daniels' Warranted Horse Remedies/Horse Medicines," lists various horse cures, 21 in. by 4 7/8 in. ....**$350-$400**

Thermometer, painted wood, "International Stock Food and Veterinary Preparations, Guaranteed," shows harness horse, rounded top, 24 in. by 6 in. ....**$900-$950**

Tramp Art

Tramp art refers to a popular craft that reached its peak in the United States during the late 19th and early 20th centuries in which scrap wood—usually taken from crates or cigar boxes—is notch carved along the edges, and then pieces of decreasing size are layered to form a bristling, faceted surface effect. Common forms include picture frames, boxes, and crucifixes. Furniture and case pieces done in tramp art are the rarest, and consequently the most expensive. In all forms, the most desirable pieces involve rounded or complicated designs (hearts, flowers, or stars, for example) or those with signatures and dates.

There is also a second form of tramp art called "crown of thorns", in which squared sticks of wood are notched and interlocked to form an open grid work of bristling points. Because of the construction technique, this form is easily damaged, and though it is usually seen on picture frames, it has also been found on small pieces of furniture, like night and candle stands, and even walking sticks.

The name "tramp art" is a misnomer, given in the mistaken belief that it was the work of itinerants who would create pieces in exchange for a meal or place to sleep. Hardly any tramp art is the work of tramps; it was, in fact, a popular Victorian-era craft in the United States. The form originated in northern Europe, especially Germany, and pieces are still being imported today. European pieces generally have smaller, finer notch carving, while American pieces are often more robust and chunkier, though this is not a hard and fast rule.

Tramp art has also been erroneously used to describe pieces made with popsicle sticks, matches, and even stones, but this is more of a marketing ploy. Only those pieces constructed using layered and notch-carved wood can accurately be called tramp art.

Also see Furniture.

References: Michael Cornish and Clifford Wallach, *They Call It Tramp Art*, Columbia University Press, 1996; Helaine Fendelman and Jonathan Taylor, *Tramp Art: A Folk Art Phenomenon*, Stewart, Tabori & Chang, 1999; Clifford A. Wallach and Michael Cornish, *Tramp Art: One Notch at a Time*, Wallach-Irons Publishing, 1998.

Cabinet, hanging, mirrored door and fall-front compartment on shaped plaque with razor holder, comb box, and pincushion, carved marquetry, five-point stars, circles and hex signs, loss to comb holder, 45 in. tall by 23 in. wide........... **$900**

Cabinet, medicine, mirrored door and drawer over shelf and comb box, scalloped crest rail, step-down chip carving, 24 in. tall by 10 1/2 in. wide.. **$420**

Comb box, hanging, arched scalloped back with layered notch-carved rosette in center accented with small round white porcelain knobs, front of open box slopes forward and has scalloped top edge, double dart-shaped ornament on front, dark red paint, 10 1/8 in. tall by 8 3/4 in. wide. **$210**

Doll dresser, three drawers, old white repaint, gold trim, worn, age cracks, 21 1/2 in. tall by 15 1/2 in. wide by 8 3/4 in. deep............ **$375**

Dresser box, old finish, raised diamond designs, applied embossed decor, velvet-lined interior with lift-out divided tray, mirror in lid, brass paw feet, name on front, acorns and medallion on lid, lion pulls on ends, "1893" on back, edge chips, one small piece missing, 6 1/4 in. tall by 10 in. wide by 6 1/2 in. deep. **$375**

Frame, old varnish finish, X design in corners, one small piece missing, 10 1/2 in. tall by 8 in. wide. **$185**

Frame, applied notch-carved molding with hearts and Xs around sides, stained finish, 12 1/2 in. tall by 10 1/8 in. wide............................. **$250**

Frame, five layers of notch-carved strips of wood, two tiers with top tier having a single frame for a postcard-size picture with three frames below with equal openings, 14 3/4 in. tall by 14 1/2 in. wide. **$225**

Frame, projecting corners, two small pieces missing, 18 1/2 in. tall by 15 3/8 in. wide............................ **$150**

Frame, gold and silver repaint on inner liners and outer border, dark original finish in-between, graduated strips of wood stacked and chip-carved, minor wear, holds 8 in. by 10 in. picture, 23 in. tall, 21 in. wide. **$550**

Frame, tapered pine plinth with carved interlocking sections of wood, arched crest, applied relief stars on either side, finials, few broken points, one finial missing, 44 in. tall, 28 in. wide. **$350**

Jewelry box, hinged lid, four square layered notch-carved feet, one back foot missing, 6 in. tall, 14 in. wide by 8 1/4 in. deep............ **$150**

Jewelry box, hinged lid, layered sides, round ornament on front faced with mother-of-pearl, lid with four notch-carved hearts, 4 1/4 in. tall by 11 in. wide by 6 3/4 in. deep. **$320**

Jewelry box, paint-decor, four ball feet, sides and front with scalloped molding with floral decor in center of panel, one end with applied diamond design in corners, opposite end with applied hearts, front with applied clubs, top of lid with applied tapered ribbed molding to form a rayed motif surmounted by ball-shaped finial in center, brown ground accented in black, wear, 6 1/2 in. tall by 12 1/4 in. long................................... **$250**

Mirror, frame with dark finish over varnish, stepped sawtooth border, stacked geometric designs, 15 in. tall by 17 1/2 in. wide. **$325**

Sewing stand, dark original finish, four molded legs, applied sawtooth trim, shelf in base, well at top with handles on each side, large rectangular pincushions on front and back, lid missing, 27 in. tall by 18 1/4 in. wide by 13 1/4 in. deep. **$450**

Side table, projecting square top and medial shelf, square legs, applied multi-layer shape and chip-carved decoration, old varnish finish, 26 in. tall, top 16 in. by 15 1/2 in....... **$750**

Treenware

Small, utilitarian household items made from treen—another term for wood—are referred to as treenware. Although most examples were made of maple, other woods such as ash, oak, pine, pear, apple, and walnut were also used. A wide range of objects was made, including bowls, spoons, spice boxes, mortars and pestles, drinking vessels, snuff boxes, and even nutmeg graters.

Bowl, round tapered foot, rounded sides, dark brown paint, cracks, rim broken and glued, 4 in. diameter, 3 1/4 in. tall.................................**$40**

Bowl, covered, green paint, flat base, straight sides, rounded shoulder, slightly rounded lid, oblong finial, age cracks, 5 in. diameter, 2 3/8 in. tall. **$35**

Bowl, covered, flat base, rounded sides, squat shape, rounded lid with oblong finial, black over earlier red paint, crack, 7 in. diameter, 3 1/4 in. tall...............................**$170**

Bowl, 9 1/2 in. by 10 ? in. (excluding handles), 3 1/2 in. tall, oval, rounded bottom, flattened flared handle. **$150**

Canister, round, painted, reeded band, lid with knob-shaped finial, black and red ground, wide band of foliage motifs, top split in half with early repair, cracked body, chip, paint wear, 6 1/2 in. tall, 5 1/2 in. diameter. **$250**

Charger, turned with decor rings on both sides, slightly oval, 19 3/4 in. by 21 in. **$225**

Churn, red paint, 14 1/2 in. tall...**$425**

Cup, vinegar grained, 3 1/2 in. tall, 3 in. diameter..............................**$725**

Egg cup holder, fruitwood, sun-bleached finished, ebonized trim, turned base, three bun feet, incised rings, six-cup, turned column with turned spoon rack, ball finial, glued repair on spoon rack, with six coin silver spoons, 12 1/2 in. tall. ...**$260**

Ink sander, green paint, turned. **$250/pair**

Inkwell, sponge-decor, brown and yellow, gilt stenciling, glass insert, “Manufactured by S. Silliman & Co…Conn.,” wear to top, 2 1/2 in. tall, 4 1/4 in. diameter.............**$225**

Jar, decorated, sponge-decor, green and yellow, turned bands at top and bottom of base, age cracks, 3 1/4 in. tall, 3 1/2 in. diameter. **$1,850**

Jar, decorated, red tulips and green leaves, footed base, lid with conical finial, yellow over-varnish flaking, 5 in. tall, 4 5/8 in. diameter. **$130**

Jar, decorated, grain-decor, brown graining over yellow, yellow and black sponged tree or feather design, covered, wear, age cracks, 6 1/4 in. tall, 6 1/2 in. diameter. **$1,500**

Jar, decorated, sponge-decor, reddish brown with yellow sponging and dots, flared foot, conical finial, 7 1/2 in. tall, 6 5/8 in. diameter. **$1,150**

Jar, decorated, grain-decor, brown graining, yellow sponged tree or feather design, covered, wear, edge damage, age cracks, 8 in. tall, 6 in. diameter. **$425**

Jar, decorated, original reddish-brown vinegar sponge decor over yellow, poplar, footed base, raised ring around the top, domed lid with turned finial, minor grain separation on interior of lid, base cracks, 12 in. tall, 9 1/4 in. diameter......**$3,950**

Jar, decorated, red vinegar decor over yellow ground, raised rings around base and top, slightly domed lid, turned finial, 12 1/4 in. tall, 13 1/4 in. diameter.........**$5,400**

Match holder, barrel-form, brown and tan sponge-painted, 2 1/8 in. tall. **$125**

Noggin (a small mug or cup), scrubbed finish, possibly American Indian, 12 in. tall.....................**$375**

Pitcher, carved, salmon paint, 7 in. tall. **$290**

Plate, curly maple, old finish, incised rings around the top and under the rim, 9 1/8 in. diameter. **$500**

Sander, barrel-shape, top is bowl-shaped with pierced star design, sides with reeded bands, minor chips, 3 3/8 in. tall, 2 3/8 in. diameter. **$55**

Spice container, decorated, original reddish-brown vinegar decor over mustard, “Spice” in gold, turned foot and rim, raised ring around center, glued crack, rim chips, possibly missing its lid, 4 in. tall, 7 in. diameter.............................**$225**

Storage container, turned, with cover, bulbous form, brown stain, bail handle, 19th century, 8 in. tall, 9 in. diameter. **$1,100**

Wagons/ Buggies/ Cutters/ Tractors and Accessories

Recommended reading:

Encyclopedia of American Farm Implements and Antiques by C.H. Wendel, Krause Publications, www.krause.com

Farm Tractors, 1860 to 1960 by C.H. Wendel, Krause Publications, www.krause.com

Vintage wooden-wheel wagons, often dating from the late 19th century, are still readily available for those seeking either decorative or working examples. Prices range from about $700 for simple one- or two-seat buggies to around $3,000 for more elaborate buckboards or flare-side wagons with good paint and sound structure. Simple freight wagons can be had for as little as $500 in rough condition, while the large metal water wagons bring upwards of $2,000, depending on condition and age. Wood wagon wheels range in price from $40 to $150, depending on size and condition. Wagon restoration specialists, using traditional materials and manufacturing techniques, can be found on the Internet.

Branding iron, circa 1900, wrought iron, in the shape of a heart, minor rust and handling wear, heart measures 6 in. by 4 1/2 in., overall 42 in. **$100**

Doctor's buggy, 38 in. wheels in front and 42 in. in the rear, steel tires, road worthy, new box, shafts and seat. **$750**

Harness/yoke, Norwegian or Swedish, possibly of reindeer antler, dated 1728, with wrought-iron fittings and scratch-carved decoration in stylized floral motif and scrolls, excellent condition, 20 in. by 7 in. by 4 in. **$1,500**

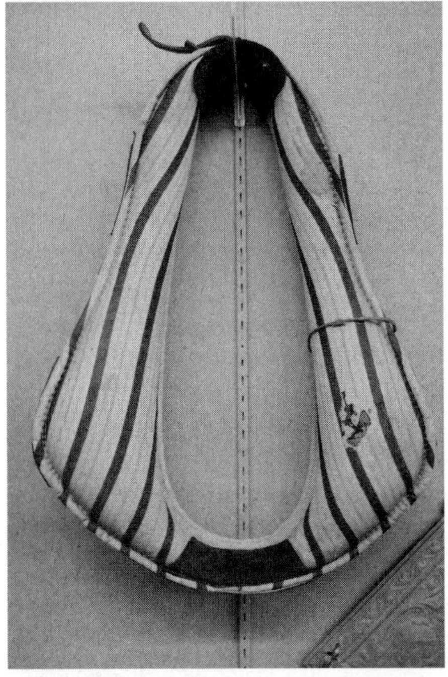

Horse collar, circa 1920s, Dandy Brand, striped canvas, leather trim, remnants of original paper labels, 20 in. by 27 in. by 6 in. **$90**

Saddle, Norwegian, late 18th century, pine with wrought iron fittings, intended for carrying goods rather than a rider, original blue paint, significant wear, 8 in. by 14 1/2 in. by 21 in. **$450**

Assorted sleigh bells, 11 cone-shaped bells on 34 in. collar, **$200***; three large bells on 10 in. leather collar fragment,* **$70***; 25 small bells on 64 in. collar,* **$140***; seven bells on 14 in. collar fragment,* **$70**

Tractor seat, cast iron, circa 1910, marked "Milwaukee" in the middle of the seat, with mount, excellent condition, 18 in. by 14 in. **$170-$200**

1954 Allis Chalmers WD 45 tractor, factory front, new paint, overall condition excellent. **$3,875**

1956 Allis-Chalmers WD45 tractor, factory wide front, new paint, tilt seat, 12 volt, includes AC #17 loader. **$3,450**

1960 Ford 861 tractor, five-speed with power steering, 2,400 hours, excellent condition. **$8,200**

1952 Ford 8n tractor, high/low transmission, front bumper, three-point hitch with rear draw bar, hour meter, very good condition. **$3,475**

Two-seat Handy Wagon, made by the Moline Plow Co., Fairbanks, Indiana, nine-foot bed with 40 in. wheels in front and 44 in. wheels in the rear, with brakes, seats are removable. **$1,500**

Depot wagon with enclosed carriage and new wheels, museum quality, approximately nine feet long. **$3,500**

Keystone farm truck freight wagon, 1935, triple box, original paint with orange gears and tongue, green box, double-tree hitch and yoke, heavy duty wooden wheels and steel rims, 12-foot bed, excellent shape. **$5,000**

1961 Farmall 560 62-hp tractor, new paint, 15 1/2 in. and 38 in. wheels, motor, transmission, and rear end excellent condition. **$4,850**

Two views of John Deere high-wheeled horse-drawn wagon, complete with John Deere box and gear, wooden wheels, all boards on the front, sides, and rear are present and in very good condition, the tongue is included. **$3,500**

Rare Ajax wagon, all original, standard 126 in. by 38 in. box, two boards high, tailgate complete, gear and box in excellent condition, short tongue, 14-spoke wooden rear and 12-spoke wooden front wheels. **$2,800**

Nashville wagon with a standard 126 in. by 38 in. three-board box, 14-spoke 52 in. wooden rear wheels, 12-spoke 45 in. wooden front wheels, with brakes and rare crank-up rear tailgate, horse tongue, gear, and box in excellent condition............................**$3,000**

Brown Lynch and Scott wagon in very good condition, two boards high, standard 126 in. by 38 in. box, 14-spoke 44 in. rear wooden wheels, 12-spoke 39 in. wooden front wheels, excellent gear and box with short tongue...........**$2,200**

❖ Sleighs

"Come on, it's lovely weather for a sleigh ride together with you..." Before the advent of motorized vehicles, horse-drawn sleighs were often the easiest way to get from one place to another over snowy roads. While few people today have room to display a full-size sleigh, smaller versions, such as children's sleighs and skating sleighs, attract considerable interest.

Albany cutter sleigh, mustard yellow, full-size.....................**$1,800-$2,000**

Child's, decorated, black ground, red and gold lines and flourishes, 34 in. long. ....**$1,000-$1,200**

Skating sleigh, old repainted decor in blue with black and red borders, runners in red, black, and yellow, gold finials, brown grained seat, scrolled and chamfered runners, iron and wood handle, composition eagle finial, carved lions' heads on front of sides, 30 in. by 54 in. by 26 in. ....**$1,100-$1,200**

Where can I find them?

Chats Tractors
Bob Chatterton
1550 Tower Rd.
Macomb, IL 61455
(309) 833-5697

Dick Chatterton
5117 E. Co. 17
Avon, IL 61415
(309) 465-3364
http://www.chatstractors.com/
ron@chatstractors.com

Colonial Carriage Works
N5109 Highway 151
Columbus, WI 53925
(920) 623-1998
http://www.colonialcarriage.com/
cw@powerweb.net

First Shot Carriage
PO Box 282
Gonzales, TX 78629
(830) 857-6521
www.firstshotphoto.com
Hugh@firstshotphoto.com

Weathervanes

by Wayne Mattox

Just as yesterday's ladies and gentlemen gowned themselves with hats, so too were their homes, sheds, and barns attired on top. In fact, towards the end of the 19th century, it was an exception to encounter a handsome building that was not adorned with a weathervane on its roof. Seafarers and farmers consulted their vanes regularly as an indicator of the wind and weather.

Today, these valuable old objects fashioned out of copper, zinc, iron, and wood are being removed from roofs where they are at risk from bandits with ladders (and even helicopters) and being sold for big prices. It is among the most coveted categories of folk art sculpture.

The first thing you should understand about weathervanes is that you don't have to deal in them, or collect them, to enjoy them. I am no birdwatcher. I am a weathervane spotter. Birds are small and fast and hard to spot, especially from a moving car. Old weathervanes, however, can make the most repetitious of country rides or city walks a fresh new journey.

Although weathervanes have been made and used throughout the world, probably for thousands of years, America is said to be the place where the form reached its sculptural zenith. Prior to 1850, weathervanes were fashioned by woodcarvers, blacksmiths, and other artisans from material at hand. Beginning around 1850, and especially in the years following the Civil War, when metalsmiths had to adapt to a peacetime economy, great weathervane industries sprouted around Boston and New York. Most of these mass-produced vanes were fashioned out of molded copper and zinc.

Thousands of forms were made: horses, cows, stags, pigs, cocks, fish, American Indians, patriotic symbols, banners, fire wagons, trains, etc. Weathervanes were available in stores and by illustrated mail-order catalog. Some of these catalogs containing dimensions, dates, and original prices, published by leading makers like J.W. Fiske, A.L. Jewel, Cushing & White, and J. Harris & Son, are available today at major libraries.

Authentic antique weathervanes can vary in price from several hundred to over $100,000, depending on condition, form, size, and rarity. Here are a few hints.

Weathervanes designed with drama, movement, and interesting subject matter are coveted by collectors. A horse is nice, a prancing stallion is better, a team of galloping stallions pulling a fire wagon is better still!

The most desirable pieces are those in good condition, with traces of original paint, gilding, or rich undisturbed patina (verdigris).

Few weathervanes were marked by the maker. Those found today can bring premium prices.

Other things being equal, the older and bigger the better.

Weathervanes were fashioned by individual craftsmen who shaped copper, iron, or wood. Sadly, few of these highly individualistic vanes survive today. Seek out authentic one-of-a-kind vanes because those old-day artists often introduced stunning drama to their sculpture.

Mass-produced vanes, made from 1850 until today, are most commonly fashioned from thin copper sheets formed by hand-hammering over finely detailed carved wooden molds, or pressure molding between female/male, iron/lead, and lead bead-filled bag press molds. After the mirrored copper sheet parts were formed, they were trimmed, matched, and soldered together. Quite often, zinc parts such as cast zinc heads were introduced during this stage. Finally, the vane was filed, buffed, and decorated in gilt, paint, or left to its natural color.

Authenticating any weathervane is tricky business, and your best bet as a collector is to rely on a dealer with seasoned judgment. However, here are a few tips:

Study new and faked vanes. Logical and simple as it sounds, this invaluable training exercise is practiced by almost no one. Next time you see a display of copper weathervanes you do not want to hang on your favorite wall, ask yourself why. You will find you don't like the chemically aged color and poor definition achieved from hydraulic press molding. And you will train your eye. Remember, to discern the difference between apples and pears, one must first be able to recognize a pear.

Study authentic vanes. One of the world's great collections of early weathervanes is housed in the Shelburne (Vermont) Museum.

Authentic vanes have a life to them. Fine old weathervanes have a striking appearance that reproductions don't capture. Just as a painting by a great artist stirs feelings the way no copy can, so too, does a good vane.

Copper weathervanes should be studied for patina. A green verdigris crust blankets vanes exposed to weather for 50-plus years, giving them a beautiful appearance that cannot be duplicated by painted-on chemical aging solutions. Study large bronze and copper statues in your local parks to learn about patina.

Authentic early wood vanes have a driftwood character to them. Edges are dry, shrunk, cracked, and rounded by the wind.

Old iron vanes should have a hard, dark-rusted, nonuniform, pitted surface. Extra weathering and darker color are found on all old vanes on top and near edges where bird droppings accumulated. Contact areas, where the hand-forged strapping and rivets give structure to old iron vanes, are areas where moisture accumulates and therefore should be extra rusty and decayed. Reproduction iron vanes will have a brown/orange hue that appears too uniform. This chemically produced rust may be rubbed off like a powder.

Authentic vanes may be recognized by inspecting to see if one side was more exposed to wind and sun, and accordingly, suffers greater wear and discoloration than the other. I call it the wind side. Detailed inspection with a loupe will often reveal that the edges on the wind side of a vane may be minutely more rounded than the backside edges.

Have fun weathervane watching.

(Wayne Mattox is the proprietor of Wayne Mattox Antiques, Woodbury, Connecticut, specializing in 18th and early 19th century furnishings, American folk art, and accessories.)

Weathervane, c. 1860, bannerette style, wrought iron with spiral and scroll decoration on shaft tip, bannerette with cutout of scrolls, heart, and the profile of a man pointing a sword on horseback, directionals with scroll arms and cutout letters, original mounting brackets, weathered black painted surface, 62 in. by 44 in. **$4,000-$5,000**

Weathervane figure, c. 1930s, hand-cut sheet iron of a German shepherd dog, riveted construction, old black painted surface, mounted on a contemporary wooden base, excellent condition, size without stand 20 in. by 9 in. **$300-$400**

Left to right: gilt-copper weathervane, running horse with a flattened body, no stand, couple of small dents, American, late 19th century, 26 1/4 in. long by 16 in. tall, ***$2,500;*** *gilt-copper weathervane, running horse, full-bodied animal with copper head and hollow body, no stand, American, late 19th century, gilt wear, minor dent, 41 1/2 in. long by 21 in. tall,* **$4,200**

Weathervane figure, c. 1920s, in the form of a horse, hand-cut sheet iron and riveted construction, painted white and black (not original) with applied iron repairs, mounted on iron rod, figure only measures 29 in. by 25 in. **$150**

Copper weathervane, molded and gilded model of a steeplechase horse, molded in two parts, the horse with hole-eyes, notched mouth, windswept, stamped, and serrated mane and tail, leaping with forelegs tucked under and rear legs extended over a stamped sheet metal fence on a vertical rod support, A.L. Jewell, Waltham, Massachusetts, mid-19th century, on modern base, 37 in. long by 34 in. tall. **$94,600**

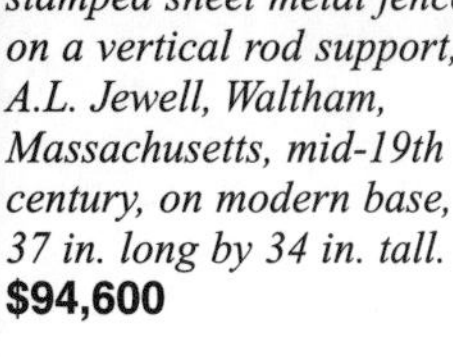

Sheet copper and zinc weathervane, silhouetted figure of a Native American with a zinc left arm drawing a bow and arrow, traces of yellow paint, attributed to A.L. Jewell, Waltham, Massachusetts, mid-19th century, 16 1/2 in. wide by 26 in. tall. **$11,750**

Weathervane, stamped sheet iron in the form of a rooster with fancy tail, scroll brackets on directional arrow, plastic mount and egg-shaped sleeve, direction indicators attached with screws, adjustable base, c. 1950, 26 3/4 in. by 22 3/4 in. by 12 3/4 in. **$400**

James weathervanes and lightning rods often feature a rooster, cow, pig or running horse; vanes with ruby glass panels bring a premium. **$200-$300**

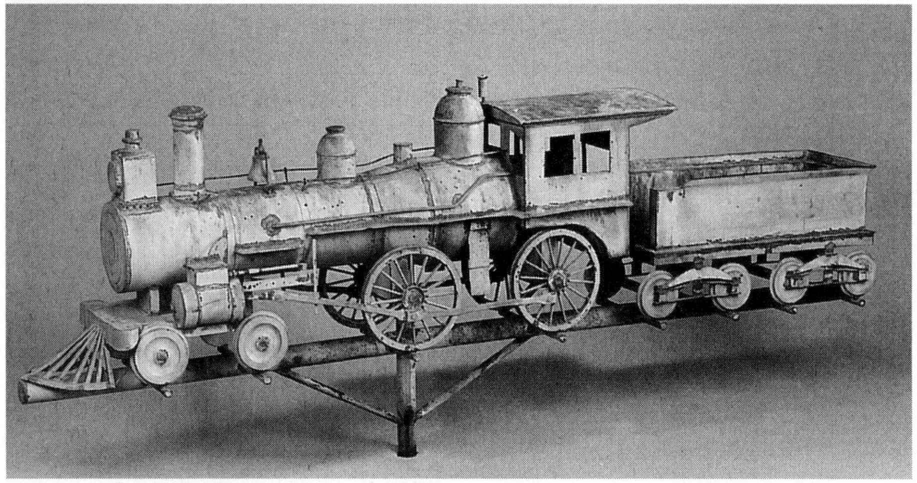

Copper weathervane, molded copper model of a steam-driven locomotive and tender car, overall verdigris patina, mounted on a hollow copper rod, no stand, American, late 19th century, minor dents, 75 in. long, 29 1/2 in. tall. **$237,000**

Copper weathervane, copper and iron, molded copper figure of the Statue of Liberty wearing a radiating crown and holding a torch in an extended hand, on a rectangular platform, the arrow below with a corrugated copper tail, mounted on iron directionals and two copper spheres, no stand, several dents, minor loss on tail, American, c. 1886, 56 1/2 in. tall. **$23,500**

Weathervane, early 20th century, wrought iron with hand-cut metal rooster and elaborate wrought scrolling from top to base, old red painted surface and minor weathering and corrosion, possibly French Canadian, 39 in. by 39 in. **$2,500-$3,500**

Weathervane figure of a rooster, c. 1890, cut sheet iron riveted to an iron rod with cork ball, remnants of red paint, weathered surface with slight corrosion, on a custom-made wood base, overall dimensions 30 in. by 20 in. by 4 in. **$1,200-$1,500**

Where can I find them?

Weathervanes are available in all price ranges and in all parts of the country. Consider these resources:

Country Comfort Antiques
Third and Main Streets
Winona, MN 55987
(507) 452-7044

Country Side Antique Mall
31752 65th Ave.
Cannon Falls, MN 55009
(507) 263-0352
www.csamantiques.com

Wayne Mattox Antiques
82 Main St. N.
Woodbury, CT 06798
(203) 263-2431
www.antiquetalk.com
tiquetalk@aol.com

Mark F. Moran Antiques
5887 Meadow Dr. SE
Rochester, MN 55904
(507) 288-8006
mfmoran@charter.net

Windmill Weights

There are several kinds of iron windmill weights, but the most common is the counter-balance or tail weight, which was larger and heavier, ranging from 30 to 150 pounds, and served to balance the windmill's flywheel; and the regulator weight, which was much smaller, usually no more than 15 to 20 pounds, and was used to maintain a consistent revolution speed no matter how fast the wind was blowing.

Prices range from about $200 for common (or damaged) examples, to more than $6,000 for the largest version of the "W" made by Althouse-Wheeler Co. of Waupun, Wis., which measures about 11 inches high, 19 1/2 inches wide, and 5 1/4 inches thick. A slightly smaller version of the "W" measures 17 inches by 9 1/4 inches by 3 inches.

These pieces are being reproduced using old molds, so be careful when buying, and look for good, weathered surface and paint. Repaints are common but less desirable.

Windmill weight, early 20th century, cast iron in the form of a rooster (this one is called the "rainbow tail"), made by Elgin Wind Power and Pump Company, Elgin, Ill., remains of original paint, on contemporary stand, size without stand 18 in. by 16 in. by 3 1/2 in. **$2,500-$3,500**

Windmill weight, cast iron, circa 1920, known as the Hummer E 184 short-stem, with ball base (which could be filled with rock or metal for additional weight), old but not original paint, 18 in. by 10 1/2 in. **$900-$1,100**

Windmill weight, cast iron, circa 1920, known as the Hummer E 184 short-stem, with old paint, on contemporary wood base, 9 1/2 in. by 9 3/4 in. **$700-$800**

Windmill weight, early 20th century, cast iron in the form of a rooster, made by Elgin Wind, Power and Pump Company, Elgin, Illinois, old but not original paint, 17 in. by 15 1/2 in. by 3 1/2 in., weight is 45 pounds. **$1,800-$2,000**

Windmill weight, cast iron, circa 1920, known as the bobtail horse, made by Dempster Mill Manufacturing Company, Beatrice, Nebraska, traces of old paint, the bridle is a later addition, 17 1/2 in. by 17 in. **$300-$400**

Dempster Mill Manufacturing Company long-tail horse windmill weight.

Fairbury bull windmill weight (no name).

Squirrel windmill weight, made by Elgin Wind, Power and Pump Company, Elgin, Illinois, 13 1/4 in. by 15 1/4 in. by 5 7/8 in.

Boss bull windmill weight.

A selection of Eclipse windmill weights, made by Fairbanks, Morse & Company, Chicago, Illinois, most are about 10 1/2 in. long.

Buffalo windmill weight (beware of reproductions).

"W" windmill weight made by Althouse-Wheeler Company of Waupun, Wis.

Windmill weight in the form of a seated squirrel, light brown paint, on original base, attributed to Elgin Wind Power & Pump Co., Elgin, Ill., early 20th century, new black metal stand, 13 1/2 in. by 17 1/4 in.
$3,220
Courtesy Skinner Inc., Bolton, Mass.

Star windmill weight, made by U.S. Wind Engine and Pump Company, Batavia, Ill., 15 in. wide.

Left to right: Windmill weight in the form of a stylized rooster with detailed sawtooth comb, eyes, beak, and wattle on an integral rectangular base, late 19th/early 20th century, 3 1/2 in. by 17 in., 15 1/2 in. tall, **$1,410***; windmill weight in the form of a stylized rooster head with detailed comb, eyes, beak, wattle, and saw-tooth tail, tail marked "10 FT No. 2," integral rectangular base, American, late 19th/early 20th century, 3 1/2 in. by 17 in., 15 1/2 in. tall,* **$940***; windmill weight in the form of a large rooster, full round in Mogul form with detailed orange-painted comb, eyes, and wattle, and white-painted beak, body, and molded tail, on a rectangular base fitting over a later stepped stand, American, early 20th century, 19 1/2 in. wide, 23 in. tall,* **$8,813***; windmill weight in the form of a small rooster with a detailed comb, eye, wattle, and notched tail above an integral rectangular base, on a later stand, tail marked "Hummer-E184," American, 19th century, 3 1/4 in. by 10 in., 9 1/4 in. tall,* **$1,998***; windmill weight in the form of a rooster with pointed comb, detailed eye, beak, and wattle with a rainbow-style arched tail above an integral rectangular base, on a later flaring cylindrical stand, painted red, American, 20th century, 16 in. wide, 24 3/4 in. tall,* **$5,640**
Courtesy Christie's, New York, N.Y.

Where can I find them?

Windmill weights are available in all parts of the country. Consider these resources:

Country Comfort Antiques
Third and Main Streets
Winona, MN 55987
(507) 452-7044

Country Side Antique Mall
31752 65th Ave.
Cannon Falls, MN 55009
(507) 263-0352
www.csamantiques.com

Wayne Mattox Antiques
82 Main St. N.
Woodbury, CT 06798
(203) 263-2431
www.antiquetalk.com
tiquetalk@aol.com

Mark F. Moran Antiques
5887 Meadow Dr. SE
Rochester, MN 55904
(507) 288-8006
mfmoran@charter.net

Wood Carvings

Largely recognized for their folk art characteristics, wood carvings range from well-executed items made by professional carvers to crudely crafted pieces by unskilled makers.

Among the noted American woodcarvers was John Bellamy (1836-1914). He was often commissioned by the U.S. government to carve figureheads, ship decorations, and patriotic symbols. He is especially noted for his eagle carvings, including numerous examples of the regal bird carrying an American flag in its beak or talons.

Wilhelm Schimmel (circa 1840-1890) was born in Germany and came to the Cumberland Valley near Carlisle, Pennsylvania, in the late 1860s. He was an itinerant handyman, doing occasional chores in exchange for food and (too frequently) drink. Schimmel also carved birds (including eagles) and animals, human figures, and even stylized poodles to use as barter. They were naive and crude, usually brightly painted. Most of Schimmel's animals were carved from pine, covered with gesso or plaster, and painted.

Angel, head and wings, white paint, glass eyes, 12 in. tall by 30 in. long. **$2,750**

Angel, on ball, spread wings, 28 in. tall. **$250**

Black Uncle Sam, red-and-white striped pants, red vest, dark jacket with white stars, stained hands and face, old crazed varnish has yellowed, missing cane, 11 in. tall. **$6,200**

Set of four carved animals, circa 1920, walnut, two horses (one of them a colt) and two dogs (one a boxer, one a pointer), original varnished surface, on walnut stands, each dog has one old repair to one leg, largest is 6 in. tall. **$400-$500/set**

Puzzle bank, circa 1910, six pieces of walnut with finger-carved ends that interlock to form bank, original varnished surface, moderate wear, 4 in. by 4 in. by 4 in. **$80**

Two views of carved and painted wood figure of a bird, circa 1920s, with detailed carving on wings and beak, glass eyes, original painted surface, wire legs, minor handling wear, 7 in. by 6 in. by 3 1/2 in. **$100-$120**

Bank, circa 1880, pine, carved and painted in the form of a building, with doors and windows, coin slot on top, applied wood buttons on top corners and on base, square hole in base (no cover), excellent condition, 6 1/2 in. by 5 1/4 in. by 4 in. **$300-$400**

Collection of carved and painted birds, Norwegian, the largest (the dove in the left foreground, 8 in. long, and the tall bird center left background, circa 1870), **$300-$400**; *the bluebird on the right,* **$150-$200**; *and the rest, circa 1920s to 30s,* **$125-$150**

Bookends, walnut, circa 1930s, striking faceted carving in art deco style of cats with arching backs, original heavy varnished surface, set into walnut burl bases, mint condition, 12 in. by 6 in. by 7 in. **$300-$400/pair**

Carved walnut head of a boxer dog, with carved collar and buckle, mounted on a walnut plaque with wooden hanger, circa 1930s, one ear damaged, 6 in. by 5 1/2 in. by 3 in. **$60-$75**

Miniature carved ale bowl, Norwegian, pine, circa 1800, with handles carved in the form of primitive horse heads, remnants of original blue paint, moderate wear, 5 in. by 2 1/2 in. by 2 3/4 in. **$2,500**

Miniature carved footed bowl (gravy boat?), Norwegian, circa 1820, pine, with tiny scroll handles, original blue, white, and black paint, minor handling wear, 5 1/4 in. by 2 1/2 in. by 2 7/8 in. **$1,200**

Bust, man, minor age cracks, 14 in. tall. **$225**

Cat, worn paint, detailed facial features, 15 in. tall................... **$750**

Cricket, rectangular shaped top, four turned legs, light blue paint, 19th century, wear, imperfections, 6 1/8 in. tall by 6 1/4 in. wide by 11 5/8 in. long.................................... **$200**

Eagle, spread-wing, clenching three arrows in talons, gold paint, gilt highlights, 19th century, wear, 12 1/2 in. tall by 19 1/4 in. wide.**$2,300**

Eagle, spread-wing, gilt, "E Pluribus Unum" banner in red, white, and blue in beak, 45 in. wide. **$550**

Eagle, spread-wing, on limb or perch, gilt, 38 in. long...................... **$2,100**

Eagle, spread-wing, pine, worn gilding, red beak, some age, 10 3/8 in. tall by 18 3/4 in. wide.......... **$550**

Eagle, spread-wing, sitting on rock, laminated, contemporary, attributed to Earnest Brumbergh, 11 in. tall by 32 1/2 in. long. **$350**

Two views of carved and painted wood figure of a cowboy on a bucking Appaloosa, with varnished string for reins, on an oval wood base, minor damage to cowboy, which can be removed from horse, circa 1930s, 10 in. by 7 in. by 3 in. **$150-$200**

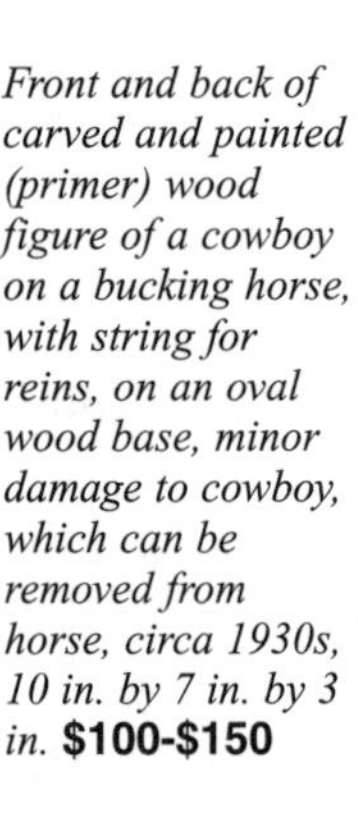

Front and back of carved and painted (primer) wood figure of a cowboy on a bucking horse, with string for reins, on an oval wood base, minor damage to cowboy, which can be removed from horse, circa 1930s, 10 in. by 7 in. by 3 in. **$100-$150**

A collection of miniature turned and painted cups, plus a chalice and round footed stand, Norwegian, pine, all with original paint; chalice decorated with red and black dots, 3 1/2 in. tall; cup, second from the left, dated 1851, 1 3/4 in. tall; center cup dated 1869, 2 in. tall; footed stand with original red and blue paint, 2 7/8 in. tall; cup on right with grain painting and dusty blue painted trim, 1/2 in. tall. **$400** *for stand to* **$800** *for chalice and dated cups.*

Carved head of a man, circa 1950s, walnut with light varnished surface, textured hair and finely carved features, 12 in. by 8 in. by 7 in. **$500-$600**

Carving of a hen, circa 1920, pine with a walnut stain, marked on the bottom "Compliments of M.J. Porter," possibly a presentation piece or egg company trade stimulator, mint condition, 11 1/2 in. by 8 1/4 in. by 2 3/4 in. **$500-$600**

Eagle, with banner, attributed to John Hales Bellamy (American, 1836-1914), carved and painted pine, banner motto "Dum Vivimus Vivamus," eagle with breast shield, 8 1/4 in. tall by 25 1/2 in. long. **$25,000**

Eagle, with banner, "Live and Let Live," talons hold shield of stars and stripes, late 18th or early 19th century, minor restoration, 23 in. tall by 74 in. wide. **$6,900**

Carved heads, circa 1930s, mostly walnut, made by an Iowa farmer, possibly for use as walking stick handles, ranging in length from 2 1/2 in. to 8 1/4 in. **$50-$150**

Primitive carving of a hen, pine, Norwegian, circa 1870, worn surface with nail eyes, round carved base, 6 in. by 4 in. by 1 1/2 in. **$375**

Carved figure of a horse, basswood, circa 1930s, unfinished and unpainted, with visible pencil marks around eyes and mouth, minor handling wear, 7 in. by 7 in. by 2 1/2 in. **$60-$80**

Farmer and wife loading hay wagon pulled by ox, impressed "Andre Dube, St. Jean-Port Joli," chip on woman's hat, 9 in. tall by 22 in. long. **$675**

Hobo with knapsack and patched clothes, incised "P. Arpin," stamped "Paul Arpin Inc., Phillipsburg, Que. Ch 8-3161, Made in Canada," 15 in. tall. **$250**

Horse heads, mahogany, old dark worn finish, chip-carved detail, possibly some sort of architectural element, 20th century, wear and damage, 32 in. long. **$350/pair**

Horse, prancing, bobbed tail, old black paint, newer base, 7 in. tall. **$850**

Horse, running stallion, original buckskin-colored paint, age cracks, ears and one leg missing, one leg repaired, driftwood base, 6 3/4 in. tall by 11 in. long. **$120**

Side and front of carved burl pipe bowl with the face of a king wearing a stylized crown, circa 1850, Scandinavian, with silver metal wind cap, minor handling wear, 6 1/4 in. by 4 1/2 in. by 2 1/4 in. **$450**

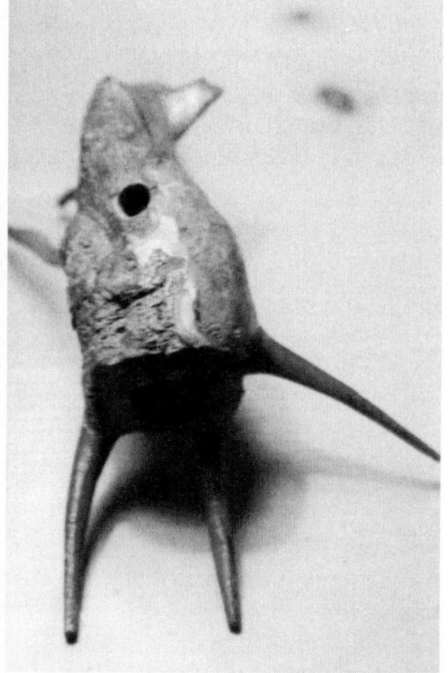

Two views of carved wood pipe bowl decorated with a leering face and spiky horns painted red, eyes made of shell beads, possibly a tourist item made by the Penobscot, Passamaquoddy, Maliseet, Micmac, or Abenaki people in Maine, circa 1940s, mint condition, 7 in. by 5 in. by 3 in. (Such tourist carvings, usually dating earlier than this piece, often take the form of clubs and have shallow vine carving on the handles.) **$80-$100**

Carved rabbit, circa 1920s, original white paint, excellent condition, 8 in. by 6 in. by 1 1/2 in. **$150-$200**

Carved plaque, circa 1930s, pine, showing a heavy athletic boot and soccer ball, possibly a student shop project, original varnished surface, 10 in. by 7 in. by 1 1/2 in. **$50-$80**

Carved souvenir plaque, redwood, cut from the Michigan Tree, which stood in General Grant National Park (now part of Sequoia & Kings Canyon National Park near Three Rivers, Calif.) until it fell in 1931; inscribed plaque created by a member of the Civilian Conservation Corps in 1933, moderate wear, 14 in. by 8 in. by 1 1/4 in. **$100-$150**

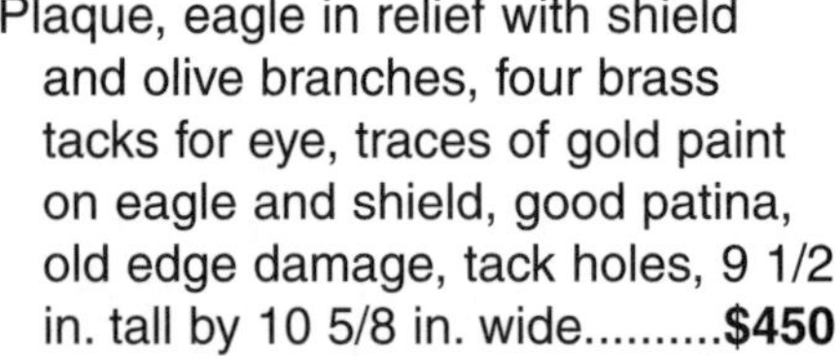

Plaque, eagle in relief with shield and olive branches, four brass tacks for eye, traces of gold paint on eagle and shield, good patina, old edge damage, tack holes, 9 1/2 in. tall by 10 5/8 in. wide.......... **$450**

Plaque, eagle, spread-wing, gold paint, 20th century, glued repairs, 19 1/2 in. tall by 17 1/2 in. wide. **$325**

Plaque, fruit on shield, walnut, 13 in. tall by 11 in. wide. **$110**

Plaque, patriotic shield and furled American flags, blue banner, “Our Country and Our Liberty,” motto “Let The Flag of Freedom Wave Over Our Country For Ever,” molded edge panels bordered by silver and gold stars on black ground, fading, paint and minor wood losses, 16 in. tall by 40 1/2 in. wide. **$7,500**

Rooster, antiqued polychrome paint, 20th century, 14 1/2 in. long.... **$120**

Rooster, old finish, good details, carved initials “C.S.” (Carl Snavely, 20th century Pennsylvania carver), 7 in. tall.................................. **$325**

Rooster, polychrome paint, minor loss to tail, 22 1/2 in. tall. **$1,500**

Rooster, red, brown, and yellow crazed paint, on twig stand, 5 1/2 in. tall..................................... **$325**

Carving of a squirrel holding a nut, pine, circa 1900, painted rusty red and brown, damage to one ear, 3 1/2 in. by 3 in. by 1 1/4 in.......... **$70**

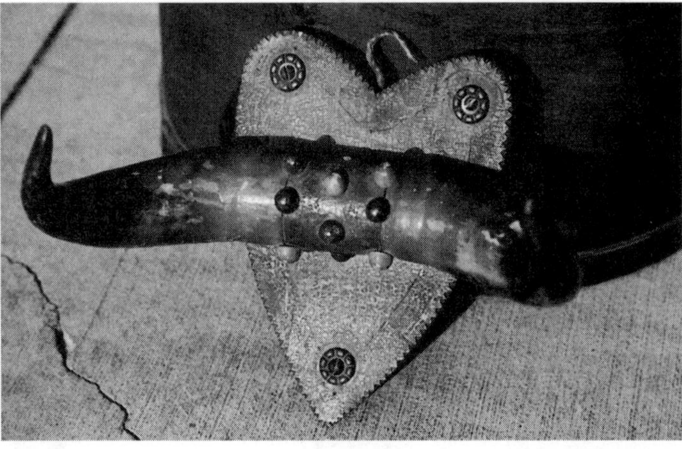

Carved plaque, wood cut in the shape of a heart, with notch-carved edge and small cow horns mounted on front, painted red and green, with three screws and decorative collars attached to front, circa 1920, 8 in. by 10 1/2 in. by 6 1/4 in. **$150**

Carved rooster, circa 1880, pine, with original crazed varnished surface, base carved with protruding sections as though it fit into a larger piece, minor damage to beak and tail, overall excellent condition, 6 1/4 in. by 5 in. by 2 in. **$500-$600**

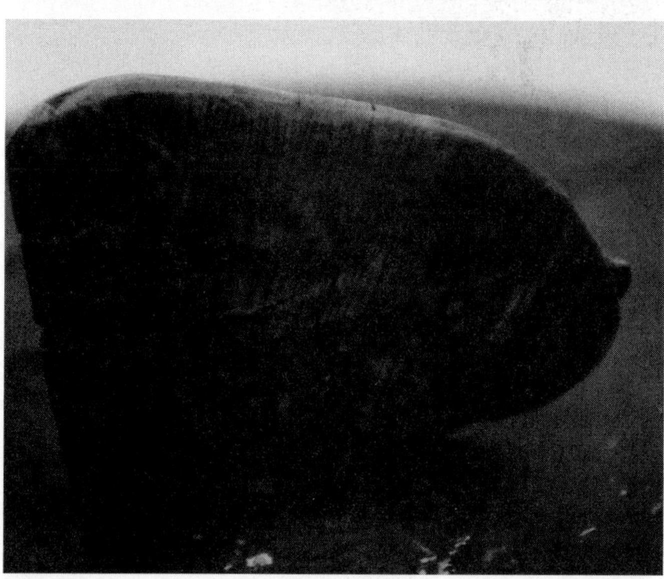

Four views of burl carving in the form of a turtle on a log in which is embedded a Civil War bullet, dated 1898 and marked "Lookout Mt.," end carved with a flaming heart and a heart in hand, which extends onto the bottom of the piece, possibly from a GAR reunion, minor handling wear, 6 in. by 4 in. by 4 in.
$800-$1,000

Wedding spoon, circa 1880, pine, with geometric pattern carved on ringed handle, light varnished finish, probably Norwegian-American, 8 in. by 2 in.
$70-$80

Five carved wedding spoons, circa 1880, all with scratch-carved decoration, Norwegian-American, two with birds on branches, two with floral motifs, and the center spoon with the images of a Victorian lady in long dress and holding a parasol, all decorated on reverse of bowls, maximum dimensions 7 in. by 2 1/4 in. **$80-$150 (lady spoon)**

Carved and painted whimsy with matching paint on small box, circa 1930s, in stylized floral decoration in dusty blue, red, orange, and white, purely decorative since carving won't fit inside box, carving is 6 in. by 2 in. by 2 in., box is 5 1/2 in. by 2 1/2 in. by 3 in. **$110/pair**

Where can I find them?

Blondell Antiques
1406 2nd St. SW
Rochester, MN 55902
(507) 282-1872
Fax: (507) 282-8683
www.blondell.com
antiques@blondell.com

Country Comfort Antiques
Third and Main Streets
Winona, MN 55987
(507) 452-7044

Mark F. Moran Antiques
5887 Meadow Drive SE
Rochester, MN 55904
(507) 288-8006
mfmoran@charter.net

Wrought Iron

The term "wrought" is applied to metals beaten or shaped with a hammer or other tool. At very high temperatures, wrought iron is extremely malleable and can be rolled or hammered into virtually any shape.

Bar, possibly for utensils, two hooks, three brass knobs with escutcheons, iron has primitively engraved tulips, some wear, 21 3/4 in. long.................................... **$575**

Bird spit and broiler, penny feet, adjustable rack in base, six prongs, pull handle, 19 3/4 in. tall by 11 in. wide by 11 3/4 in. deep........... **$225**

Bird roaster, tripod base, penny feet, tapered column, turned finial, adjustable bell-shaped bracket, 23 1/2 in. tall................................ **$450**

Broiler, rotary, medallion finial on handle, worn penny feet, 24 1/4 in. long. **$250**

Broiler, rotary, twisted detail and wavy lines, circular top, 12 in. diameter, 27 in. long. **$175**

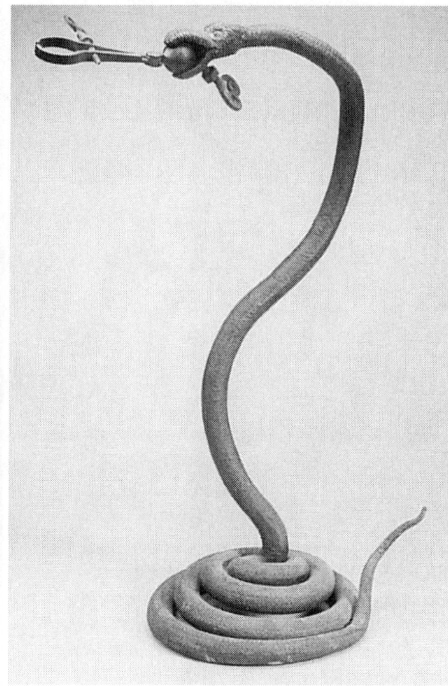

Iron holder, hand-wrought, figural, a tall upright snake with a coiled lower body, holding in its open mouth a ball joint with caliper-form clamp, 19th century, 20 1/4 in. tall. **$2,500-$3,000**

Broiler, stationary, platform with 15 scrolled sections that join at turned handle, three short feet, pitting, 31 in. long by 19 in. wide. **$575**

Calipers (double), ring finial, marked "J.R.," pitted, 17 1/2 in. long. ... **$120**

Candle stand, tripod base, penny feet, square column with chamfered corners, adjustable cross bracket, two sockets with small scrolled hooks on the bottom, 21 7/8 in. tall........................... **$700**

Door handle, thumb latch, serpentine or vining ends, with mismatched bar, 13 1/2 in. long. **$600**

Figure, patriot on horse, 12 in. tall by 12 in. long. **$575**

Fire carrier, scrolled finial at end of handle, rectangular tray for coals with sliding cover, scrolled finger loop, 24 1/4 in. long................ **$600**

Fire-starting strikes, some tooling, group of six. **$325**

Flesh fork, two tines, incised lines, large hook with scrolled tip, 17 3/8 in. long..................................... **$50**

Flesh fork, two tines, tapered flattened handle with rounded end, marked "W. Priar," 17 1/4 in. long. **$85**

Frying pan, "W. Foster," round pan, flared sides, tapered iron handle ending in large loop, late 19th century, pitting and rust, 1 1/2 in. tall by 8 3/8 in. diameter by 19 in. long. **$150**

Frying pan, "Whitfield," No. 5, flaring sides, long flattened diagonal handle with beveled edges ending in a loop, substantial pitting, significant rust, 2 in. tall by 11 in. diameter, 24 5/8 in. long. **$130**

Frying pan, unmarked, flaring sides, flattened handle with beveled edges ending in large loop, black paint, late 19th century, minor rust, 2 1/4 in. tall by 10 7/8 in. diameter by 40 1/2 in. long. **$185**

Kettle shelf, three penny feet, twisted iron cross-member, ring top with smaller inner ring, 12 in. tall.... **$225**

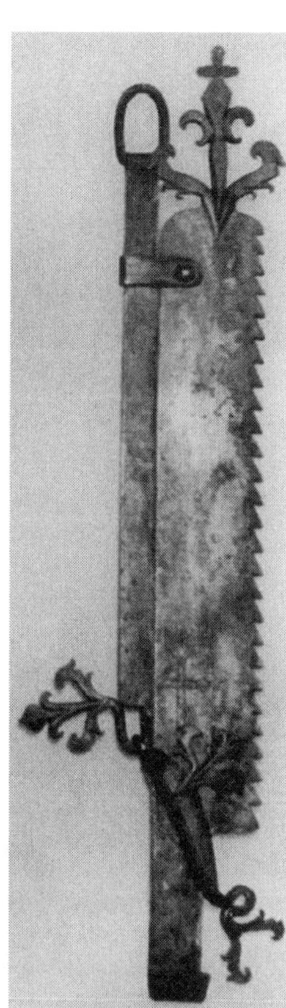

Trammel, hand-wrought, scalloped and scrolled finials on top, side bar and catch, engraved detail with a cross and "1809," adjusts from 43 in. to 60 in. **$500-$600**

Lark spit, hanging, four cast lead faces around top, five hooks for birds, incomplete brass wire wrap, 17 1/4 in. tall........................... **$335**

Peel, 45 1/2 in. long. **$75**

Peel, ram's head finial, 41 in. long, pair. **$225**

Peel, ram's-horn finial, tapered square-to-round handle, 36 1/2 in. long. **$180**

Scraper, wide oblong blade with rounded top, long round handle with flattened end having scrolled heart motif, 19th century, 6 1/4 in. wide, 45 1/4 in. long............... **$425**

Shutter dogs, square mounting plates, square shaft extending out from center, large diamond-shaped end with pod-shaped top and scrolled bottoms, painted gray, late 18th or early 19th century, 5 1/2 in. tall by 3 7/8 in. long by 1 3/4 in. wide... **$55**

Skewer pins (four) and hanger... **$250**

Sickle, tapered crescent-shaped blade, turned wooden handle, illegible mark, 18 1/2 in. wide by 21 in. long..................................... **$30**

Spatulas, one marked Krider, one with heart handle, 12 3/4 in. long, group of three. **$240**

Spatula, wrought iron and brass, 12 in. to 18 in. long, group of four.**$225**

Trivet, heart motif, footed, round outer shelf, inner heart shelf, tapered handle with hole at center, pointed end, pitted. **$170**

Utensils, four tasters (three with brass bowls, one with copper bowl) and skimmer with brass bowl, three marked "T. Loose" (20th century Pennsylvania metal smith), group of five. **$285**

Wafer iron, oblong irons with incised shield surmounted by crown with bird and "1773," flanked by floral designs, tapered square handles with one ending in loop, minor rust, 9 1/8 in. by 5 1/8 in. by 42 in. long. **$550**

Utensil rack, hand-wrought, a flattened bar with double scrolls at each end, an upright center flat bar with pairs of small scrolls below the large forked curled-under top scrolls, 28 in. long, 14 1/2 in. tall. **$2,000-$2,500**

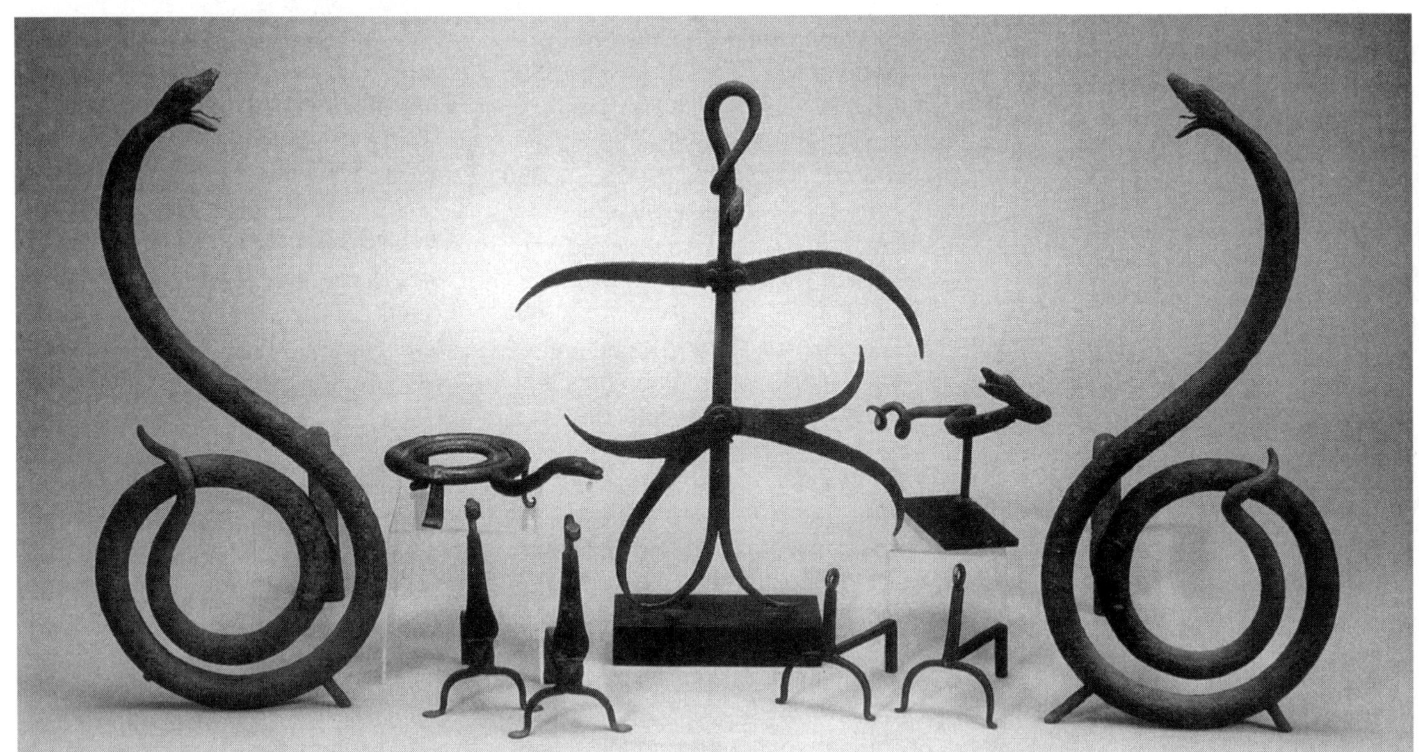

Far left and right: Hand-wrought iron andirons, modeled as upright coiled serpents, the head with an open mouth and projecting tongue, S-form body ending in a coiled tail, bolted to a log support, found in New York state, surface rust, 19th century, 19 3/4 in. tall, **$5,500/pair**. *Back row, left: Hand-wrought iron trivet, model of a coiled snake, incised underside, on three short scroll legs, found in Pennsylvania, minor surface corrosion, 19th century, 4 3/4 in. by 10 1/2 in. by 3 1/4 in. tall,* **$1,000**. *Back row, center: Hand-wrought iron calipers, the handle in the form of a coiled snake continuing to a shaft with four bifurcating riveted arms, with stand, possibly Boston Foundry, late 18th century, surface corrosion, 12 3/4 in. wide by 17 in. tall,* **$2,900**. *Back row, right: Hand-wrought iron door handle, modeled as a snake, the head with an open mouth and teeth, curving body and coiled tail, with stand, late 19th/early 20th century, surface corrosion, 12 1/4 in. long by 3 1/2 in. tall,* **$1,150**. *Front row, left: Hand-wrought iron miniature andirons, knife blade-style, polyhedron finial on shaft, arched legs to penny feet, American, late 18th/early 19th century, worn black paint, 4 in. wide by 6 3/4 in. tall,* **$70/pair**. *Front row, right: Hand-wrought iron miniature andirons, gilded forward looped finial on a simple square shaft above curved front legs with penny feet, American, early 19th century, 3 1/2 in. wide by 5 in. tall,* **$460/pair**

Miscellaneous

Items in this section do not easily fit into other categories, and include fraternal pieces, plaster castings, feather trees, quack medical devices, musical instruments, and even collages.

Framed Masonic certificate of the Third Degree, framed, circa 1830, showing three pillars and the all-seeing eye, minor fading and fold marks, 17 in. by 13 in. ....**$200-$250**

Miniature carved axes set in a birch wood base, circa 1920s, axes with carved and varnished handles, the wood heads painted black and silver, probably from a Modern Woodmen of America lodge, minor handing wear, 8 1/2 in. by 6 3/4 in. by 2 1/2 in. **$80**

Miniature castle, tin, circa 1900, possibly a 10th wedding anniversary gift, cutout windows, and soldered turrets, battlements, and roofs, near mint condition, 10 in. by 10 in. by 8 in. **$350-$450**

Cast plaster figure of a little girl seated on a wall, holding a bouquet, circa 1920s (?), with twigs embedded in back to act as reinforcement, moderate flaking to soft plaster, 8 1/4 in. by 5 1/2 in. by 1 3/4 in. **$85**

Figures of an Amish boy and girl, signed "Ewertz," by Henry or Maxime Ewertz, circa 1949; terra cotta, made in Hatfield, Pa. The couple created a series of figures showing the Amish in various activities in the 1940s and 1950s. Good condition with significant paint flaking, boy stands 19 in. tall. **$2,000-$3,000/pair**

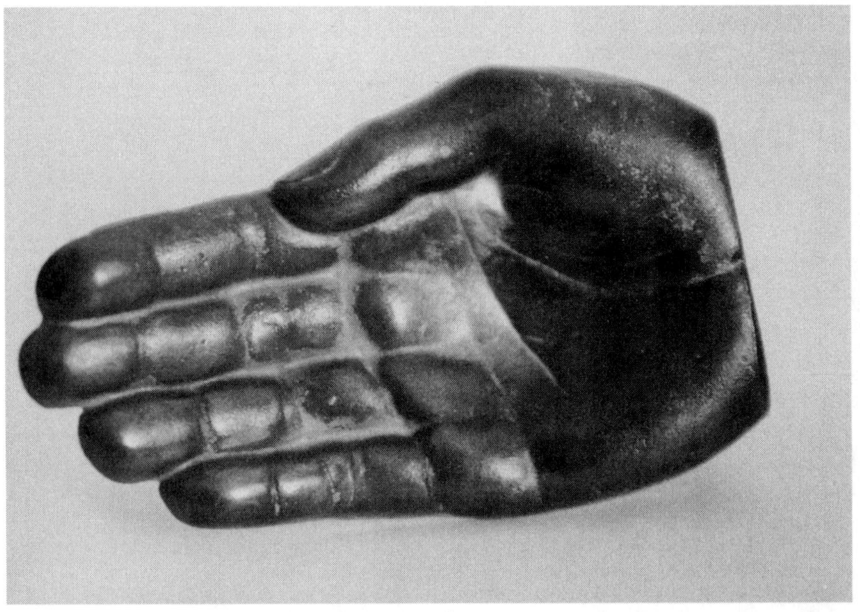

Cast iron life-size human hand with hinged back, exact use unknown but may be a lodge piece or even a door knocker, marked twice on reverse with style numbers Y1657 and Y1658, 7 in. by 4 3/8 in. by 1 1/2 in. **$850**

Cello, circa 1915, made out of a pitchfork on which is mounted a wooden box with a round hole; one string was stretched from the top of the handle across the box and secured at the fork; part of a collection of odd musical instruments played by a traveling evangelist named Orben Sime (1903-1975), who supposedly made this cello when he was 12 years old; significant handling wear, overall good condition, 65 in. by 12 in. by 4 in. **$300-$400**

Christmas trees made from artificial materials, especially goose feathers, were popular in the late 19th century. Many were made in Germany to resemble white pines and were designed to sit on a table. The feathers, usually dyed green or white, were wrapped around wire branches, and these were then attached to a wooden rod, which served as the truck of the tree. The trunk was inserted in a base, usually a turned wood cylinder. Prices for vintage feather trees in good condition range from about **$300** *for a small example to nearly* **$1,000** *for large and elaborate ones with full branches, large bases, and original fencing around the bottom. These trees are being widely reproduced today, so check closely for signs of handling, and for old painted bases and fences.*

Fiddle, circa 1890, crudely handmade, painted yellow and brown, decorated with brass tacks, untouched original surface, 15 in. by 7 in. by 3 in. **$300-$400**

Two views of flag stand, cast iron, from a Grand Army of the Republic post in rural Michigan, dated 1883, 4 in. by 8 in. square. **$80-$100**

Lodge initiation device, circa 1890, from an Improved Order of Red Men lodge in Elgin, Minn., cast iron and painted three-wheel base topped by log covered in wool fleece with goat's head attached, significant handling wear, 56 in. by 46 in. by 38 in. Prospective lodge members rode this contraption while being rolled up and down the street (or lodge hall) in an initiation ritual. Such lodge goat rides could be ordered in various models and were used by many fraternal organizations in the late 19th and early 20th centuries. **$400-$500**

Mailbox figure, and detail, circa 1970s, welded iron pipe painted red, black, and blue, in the form of a waving man wearing a hat; the man's face has metal washers for eyes, wrought iron handlebar mustache, and the initials "DWB" on the front of his hat (for the maker, Daniel W. Bannitt, Goodhue, Minn.); weathered surface, overall excellent condition, 68 in. by 32 in. by 32 in. **$600-$800**

Oversized wooden mallet from an Odd Fellows lodge, circa 1950s, marked in ink with the number 1, with applied decal showing the all-seeing eye, heart in hand, sword and scales, three interlocking links containing the letters "F L T," which stand for friendship, love, and truth, and the initials "I.O.O.F" for the International Order of Odd Fellows, minor handling wear, 14 in. by 10 in. by 5 in. **$60-$80**

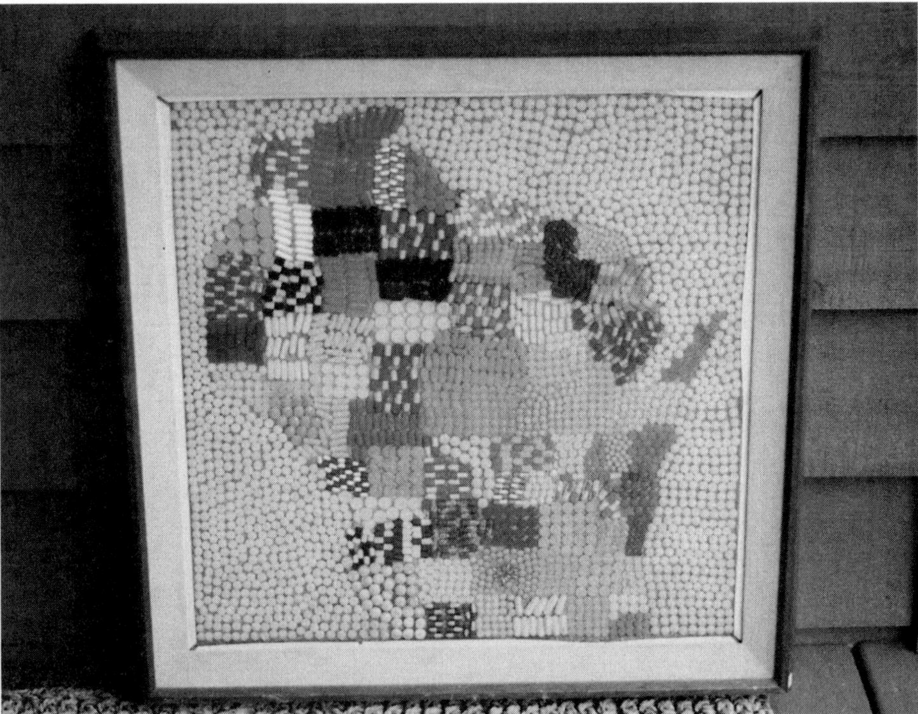

Collage map of Wisconsin, circa 1950s, with each county done in multicolored prescription pills, framed under glass, from a defunct museum of medical advertising and oddities, overall size 22 in. by 20 in. **$400-$500**

Quack medical device, circa 1930s, made by the Spectro-Chrome Institute, Malaga New Jersey, cast aluminum with box containing a large electric light and sliding colored glass panels. Light was projected onto the "patient" and "cures" performed using a combination of colors; the most common paint finish on these devices is blue. Minor wear with light and electric cord intact, 40 in. by 16 in. by 14 in. (For a detailed history of the inventor, Dinshah P. Ghadiali, and the rise of Spectro-Chrome Therapy, visit the Web site: http://www.mtn.org/quack/amquacks/ghadiali.htm.) Though hardly limited to country folk, the Spectro-Chrome device, and other quack medical remedies, had a large following in rural America early in the late 19th and early 20th century. **$250-$350**

Wood blocks, early 20th century (?), into which have been pounded metal rods that form the letters "R" and "B," and corresponding letters written faintly in ink on other sides, exact use and origin unknown, 4 in. by 4 in. by 3 1/2 in. **$80/pair**

Three views of shoeshine box, scrap wood, sheet metal and wire, painted black and red, made in 1908 by James Horkau, Eau Claire, Wisconsin (?), with arching metal footrest (?), twisted wire handle and small upper compartment (lined with cut paper images) decorated with stylized horseshoes on sides, main section with applied wood panels on all four sides attached with pegs, each decorated with bent wire, also bent wire decoration on the corners, inside of main lid has a photograph of a public gathering and a label on which is written in ink, "James Horkau Maker Nov. 10, 1908"; inside lined with cut paper images from popular magazines, original untouched surface, excellent condition, 13 1/2 in. by 13 3/4 in. by 11 3/4 in. **$1,500-$2,000**

Shooting Gallery Figures

Background: Many a person has been coaxed to "step right up" and test his skill by shooting at arcade targets. Popular at fairs and carnivals during the 19th century, most shooting galleries featured cast iron figures that are now eagerly sought by collectors.

Note: All figures are cast iron unless otherwise noted.

Bird, 2 1/2 in. high, set of three **$165**

Bird in flight and donkey, bird 4 1/2 in. high on steel base, donkey 6 in. high excluding wooden base. **$143/pair**

Birds and stars, bar with alternating pattern, eight targets, 4 1/4 in. high by 26 in. wide. **$429**

Rooster shooting gallery figures, mounted together. **$275/pair**

Squirrel and duck, cast iron squirrel with traces of red paint, 7 3/4 in. long, heavy sheet-steel duck, pitted from use, 6 1/2 in. long, no bases. **$154/pair**

Shooting gallery figures, circa 1910, painted sheet iron, in the form of Uncle Sam, Columbia ("Lady Liberty"), the Spirit of '76 fife and drum soldiers (three figures secured with screws), a Revolutionary War-era soldier blowing a trumpet, a spread-wing eagle, plus two clowns painted in a commedia del arte style, and a windmill with spinning blades; these were not targets, but were designed to become animated when certain targets were hit: Uncle Sam and Columbia each wave an arm (Sam also nods his head), the drummers have carved and painted wooden hands holding drumsticks to play drums (missing), and the bugler raised and lowered his instrument; some surface rust and bullet impact marks, with some paint loss, overall very good condition; Sam is 71 in. tall, Columbia is 64 in. tall, as is the tallest of the marchers; the eagle is 48 in. wide, and the clowns are 20 in. tall. **$75,000+/set**

Country Antiques Resources

Americana, Art, Canes/Walking Sticks, Folk Art

Mark F. Moran Antiques
5887 Meadow Dr. SE
Rochester, MN 55904
(507) 288-8006
mfmoran@charter.net

Architectural Items

Architectural Artifacts, Inc.
4325 N. Ravenswood
Chicago, IL 60613-1111
(773) 348-0622
http://www.architecturalartifacts.com
sales@architecturalartifacts.com

Architectural Emporium
207 Adams Ave.
Canonsburg, PA 15317
(724) 746-4301
http://www.architectural-emporium.com/
sales@architectural-emporium.com

Baskets, Coverlets, Folk Art, Furniture

Wayne Mattox Antiques
82 Main St. N
Woodbury, CT 06798
(203) 263-2431
www.antiquetalk.com
tiquetalk@aol.com

Clothing

Cynthia's Antique & Vintage Linens
PO Box 586
Farmington, CT 06034-0586
(860) 677-5423
www.antique-linens.com/index.html
cynthia@antique-linens.com

Country Store, Household, Mechanical, Patent, Sewing, Tools

Larry and Carole Meeker
Purveyors of American Patented & Mechanical Antiques
5702 Vacation Blvd.
Somerset, CA 95684
(530) 620-7019
Sales: (888) 607-6090
Fax: (530) 620-7020
www.patented-antiques.com
clm@patented-antiques.com

Folk Art, Furniture, Quilts, Rugs, Signs

Country Comfort Antiques
Third and Main Streets
Winona, MN 55987
(507) 452-7044

Furniture (Norwegian And American), Art, Folk Art

Blondell Antiques
1406 2nd St. SW
Rochester, MN 55902
(507) 282-1872
Fax: (507) 282-8683
www.blondell.com/
antiques@blondell.com

General Line

Antique Manor
Highway 63 North
Stewartville, MN 55976
(507) 533-9300

Mary Lou Beidler
Early American Antiques
2736 Pecan Rd.
Tallahassee, FL 32303
850-385-2981
http://www.antiquearts.com/stores/beidler/
beidler@AntiqueArts.com

Freward & Alk Antiques
414 Lazarre Ave.
Green Bay, WI 54301
(800) 488-0321
(920) 435-7343
www.the-antique-shop.com
leesa@the-antique-shop.com

Graniteware

National Graniteware Society
PO Box 9248
Cedar Rapids, IA 52409-9248
http://www.graniteware.org/
info@graniteware.org

Hunting, Fishing

Tom Bachler
www.oldfishdecoys.com

Drexel Grapevine Antiques
2784 US 70 E
Valdese, NC 28690
(828) 437-5938
www.drexelantiques.com
info@drexelantiques.com

Fritz Antiques
PO Box 575
Zephyr Hills, FL 33539
(813) 788-2312
www.fritzantiques.com
fritzantiques@earthlink.net

Dave Harmon
7445 Trailwood Dr.
Minocqua, WI 54548
(715) 358-3501
djharm@newnorth.net

Hawks Nest Antiques and Decoys
154 Mallard Pond Rd.
Hinesburg, VT 05461
(802) 482-2076
thegreatest35@gmavt.net

Michael R. Higgins
14485 117 St. S
Hastings, MN 55033
(651) 437-2980

Steven Michaan
www.fishdecoy.com
(914) 763-5022
smichaan@ix.netcom.com

W.L. "Ole" Olsen
15 Doe Lane, Antelope Acres
Townsend, MT 59644
wlmolsen@aol.com

Sportsman's Antiques
1967 Court
Memphis, TN 38104
(901) 726-5810
tbruehl@aol.com

Lighting

Darrell Kleckner
http://www.aladdincollector.com/

Aladdin Knights
http://www.aladdinknights.org/

John Kruesel's General Merchandise
22 Third St. SW
Rochester, MN 55902
(507) 289-8049
www.kruesel.com

Quilts, Rugs

The Antique Quilt Source
3064 Bricker Rd.
Manheim, PA 17545-9644
(717) 492-9876
http://www.antiquequiltsource.com/
strongg@paonline.com

Marie Miller Antique Quilts
1489 Route 30
PO Box 983
Dorset, VT 05251
(802) 867-5969
http://www.antiquequilts.com
larry@antiquequilts.com

Sharon's Antiques and Vintage Quilts
(610) 756-6048
http://www.rickrack.com
quilts@rickrack.com

Carol Telfer Antiques
312 Cobourg St.
Stratford, Ontario
Canada N5A 3G5
(519) 271-0941
http://www.caroltelferantiques.on.ca/index.php
ctelfer@caroltelferantiques.on.ca

Betsey Telford Antique Quilts
dba Rocky Mountain Quilts
130 York St.
York Village, ME 03909
(800) 762-5940
(207) 363-6800
http://www.rockymountainquilts.com/
quilts@rockymountainquilts.com

Mary Ann Walters
Log Cabin Antiques
4200 Peggy Ln.
Plano, TX 75074
(972) 881-2818
www.quiltsquilts.com
logcabin@flash.net

Samplers

www.madelenaantiques.com/

Needlework Antiques
524 N. Oklahoma Ave.
Morton, IL 61550
(309) 263-7766
Fax: (309) 263-4304
www.needleworkantiques.com
Dawn@NeedleworkAntiques.com

Sewing Items

Anne Powell Ltd.
PO Box 3060
Stuart, FL 34995-3060
(561) 287-3007
For Orders Only: (800) 622-2646
Fax: (561) 287-3007
www.annepowellltd.com/index.htm
info@annepowellltd.com

Stoneware

Adamstown Antique Gallery
2000 North Reading Rd.
Denver, PA 17517
(717) 335-3435
http://www.aagal.com/Antiquetobacciana.htm
adamsgal@dejazzd.com

Country Side Antique Mall
31752 65th Ave.
Cannon Falls, MN 55009
(507) 263-0352
www.csamantiques.com

Tools

The Tinker
John W. and Mary Lou Hunziker
2828 Mayowood Common St. SW
Rohester, MN 55902
(507) 288-4898

Wagons, Carriages, Sleighs (Cutters), Tack

Colonial Carriage Works
N5109 Hwy 151
Columbus WI 53925
(920) 623-1998
http://www.colonialcarriage.com/
cw@powerweb.net

First Shot Carriage
PO Box 282
Gonzales, TX 78629
(830) 857-6521
www.firstshotphoto.com
Hugh@firstshotphoto.com

Chats Tractors
Bob Chatterton
1550 Tower Rd.
Macomb, IL 61455
(309) 833-5697

Dick Chatterton
5117 E Co. 17
Avon, IL 61415
(309) 465-3364
http://www.chatstractors.com/
ron@chatstractors.com